1001 ESCAPES
TO EXPERIENCE BEFORE YOU DIE

drifting down the Nile, to chug gently on a train through the Australian outback or to punt slowly through the flood plains of the Okavango in a dug-out canoe or mekoro allows you space and time to really get under the skin of a place and a culture. The only thing to happen swiftly is the metamorphosis from stressed out to blissed out.

But whether your notion of escape embraces a reconnection with your inner self or a total departure from it, this book also celebrates the vital element of fantasy, which sets so many of these journeys, hotels, and retreats apart. I am as inspired by the excessive flights of fancy that go into creating the architectural folly that is the gilded Burj Al Arab in Dubai, as I am by the driftwood creativity of an Evason Hideaway or the fairy tale allure of sleeping in a yurt. They are all escapes that awaken the senses, kick-start the jaded palate, and represent the antithesis of home.

The temptations are all here in the pages of this book. We have long moved on from the notion that "getting away from it all" means a piña colada, a beach, and a T-shirt to prove you were there, but with time being an increasingly precious commodity, it is more important now than ever to make those breaks resonate and ring true.

This collection of toothsome images and descriptions of undulating dunes, rippling shorelines, and flirting palms is certainly nectar for the soul, but on a lighter note is also a diverting indulgence which is perfect to dip into at bedtime or bath time, or as a distraction on the commuter train. We all need to dream. So even if you never make it to the mythical portals of the Gazelle D'Or, or fail to embark on that hike you promised yourself up the Vikos Gorge, sometimes just knowing that places like this still exist in the world is reassurance and wish-fulfilment enough.

Catherine Fairweather

Catherine Fairweather, London

Introduction

By Helen Arnold, General Editor

The dizzying pace of twenty-first-century life and state-of-the-art technology means that you are never more than a phone call or email away from the office, making it increasingly difficult to escape from the pressures of the modern world. However hard you try to get away, your cell phone rings and everyone wants a piece of your time. It's hardly surprising, then, that sometimes we just want to escape from it all.

In this book we've decided to focus on the decidedly relaxing. From a yogi retreat in the Himalayas to a remote Scottish hideaway, a tranquil garden in the middle of a bustling city to the cool and calm of a church in the heat of summer, we've concentrated on escapes that are contemplative, tranquil, relaxing, meditative, or spiritual. We've left out the adrenaline-busting, nerve-shredding, thrill-a-minute type of escapes for another time. However, that's not to say that the escapes we've included in this book are dull and pedestrian—far from it. There is plenty of variety in these escapes to provide a calming respite from reality. What could be more chilled out than snorkeling in the crystalline waters off the balmy coast of Belize, among the manta rays and marine turtles, or ambling on horseback through the perfumed orange and lemon groves in Andalucia?

Thirty or forty years ago it would have been financially impossible for the average person to visit remote destinations such as Bhutan or Bengal. However, the growth of discount airlines and the increased number of routes have opened up parts of the world that were formerly the preserve of the very rich or those with plenty of time on their hands—or both.

All the escapes selected for this book offer a chance to get away from the mundane, the everyday, and the routine, and provide an opportunity to relax and recharge your batteries in beautiful, unfamiliar surroundings and return home relaxed, rested, and with renewed vim and vigor.

Looking around the world, there's a huge variety of relaxing places to stay. Canada, for example, has some wonderfully remote lighthouses where you can hole up far away from the crowds. Check into Quirpon Lighthouse Inn on Quirpon Island, a tiny speck of land to the north of Newfoundland, which is completely deserted save for the two fully and lovingly restored lightkeeper residences. There are also some amazing hotels included in the book, from world class hotels with Michelin-starred restaurants such as Le Manoir in the depths of the English countryside, or the iconic Peninsula Hotel in Hong Kong, to simpler properties such as the homely Sonderho Kro in Denmark converted from former fishermen's cottages. We've also included rather less conventional accommodations, such as the stunning

Ice Hotel in Sweden, sculpted entirely out of ice, and a tree house at the appropriately named Tranquil Resort in Kerala, India. While they offer varying levels of comfort and luxury, rest assured they are all laid back and lovely and you simply won't want to leave.

France has an amazing selection of former chateaux that have been converted into hotels, enabling you to live out your Louis XIV fantasies to the fullest, from the imposing eighteenth-century Chateau Lasalle deep in rural Gascony to Chateau de Montriou in the Loire Valley, while Portugal has an equally impressive collection of *paradors*—former castles, palaces, fortresses, and monasteries now converted into stunning accommodations. The U.K. is bursting at the seams with ancient country-house hotels filled with faded chintz, labradors snoozing in front of crackling log fires, and butlers bearing the perfect gin and tonic. Marrakech in Morrocco is renowned for its beautiful *riads*, converted townhouses that provide a welcome oasis from the surrounding alleyways. Riad El Fenn is one of the most sumptuous, but there are hundreds of others to suit all budgets.

An increasing health-conscious world population and the growing recognition of the link between mind and body means that spa breaks have never been so popular. No longer the preserve of pampered princesses and bored housewives, spas are now attracting greater numbers than ever before. Few new hotels open nowadays without the requisite spa. But the health retreats described in this book are more than simply a whirlpool tub and a dingy treatment room tacked on to a new-build as an afterthought. These are sublime, relaxing refuges where you can succumb to the ministrations of experienced therapists and drift off into a state of blissful relaxation, or experience healing and invigorating treatments that target specific problem areas. For the ultimate in pampering, head for Chiva Som in Thailand, or Ananda in the foothills of the Himalayas. Those who prefer something a bit more puritanical to kick-start a healthy lifestyle might want to check into the Spartan, but brutally effective, Mayr & Mohr spa in Austria.

For the ecology-conscious there are also some great eco-lodges and environmentally friendly retreats to visit. Central America in particular seems to be blazing a trail in this area, offering a wide selection of eco-lodges. From Nitun Reserve, deep in the heart of the Guatamalan rain forest where you can take fascinating wildlife treks, to Morgan's Rock Hacienda and Eco-lodge in Nicaragua where you can saddle up one of the horses and ride along the Pacific, you're spoiled for choice. Costa Rica has countless eco-lodges, but those listed in this book are something special.

El Silencio, for example, boasts not only impeccable green credentials, but is also utterly luxurious, while La Cusinga Lodge doesn't simply pay lip service to environmental concerns; all of the lodge's cabins and furniture have been made using wood grown on site in a sustainable plantation.

However, not all of our escapes are sedentary. One of the best ways to get to know a place is by walking. While some of the stunning routes we've included are more taxing than others, there's no reason why you can't pick up a route midway, or pick and choose how much of a walk you do. From the famed pilgrims' route to Santiago Compostela in northern Spain, where you will be following in the well-trodden footsteps of pilgrims from centuries ago, to the wild and beautiful but decidedly unromantically named GR20 walk in Corsica, where you're unlikely to bump into another soul for days, a walk is the perfect way to clear your mind of worries and sink exhausted but happy into bed for a dreamless sleep. In fact, the great outdoors and nature offer a wide variety of different terrains and climates where you can escape from it all. Go camel riding in the shifting sands of the Dubai desert, snorkeling in the azure Caribbean Sea off Peter Island, or bicycling down Haleaka volcano in Hawaii; admire the surreal, stunning Perito Moreno Glacier in Argentina; gaze wonderingly at the dancing Northern Lights; or simply enjoy flopping, Robinson Crusoe-style, on a deserted beach on Bora Bora.

Africa is the place to head to if you like your wildlife raw and untamed. And banish any thoughts of camping boy-scout style. While you can choose to rough it, there is now a great selection of luxury camps where you can enjoy getting back to nature without having to sacrifice your creature comforts. Some of the best include the Selous Project in Tanzania, where you can escape the hordes of tourist-packed jeep convoys in a private nature reserve, or Singita Faru Faru Lodge in the heart of the Serengeti, a perfect location to view the epic annual migration of more than a million wildebeest. Chiawa in Zambia is an award-winning retreat that oozes luxury yet still manages to meld beautifully into the landscape, and it is particularly known for its canoeing safaris.

There's something undeniably soothing about the sound of water, be it the crashing of the waves on a beach or the gentle plop of an oar as you paddle your way along a waterway. Try out a floating hotel in Sweden, go canoeing along the Ardeche in France, go kayaking on the Yukon in Canada, or visit an underwater hotel in Florida where you need to don a scuba-diving kit to reach your room. Alternatively, enjoy the waters in Evian in France, renowned for their health-giving properties, or in Bath in England, where for centuries aristocrats descended upon this beautiful town to benefit from the health-giving waters. Or, you can soak in one of Iceland's geothermal hot springs, where the warm water works wonders on aching muscles.

If you want to sit back and relax as the world passes effortlessly before your eyes, we've also included some of the world's most spectacular train rides, from the epic Trans-Siberian route in Russia to the Kuranda Railway in tropical Queensland, Australia. For a different perspective, try gently drifting over the rugged landscape of Cappadoccia in central Turkey in a hot-air balloon, seeing the Egyptian sights from the luxury of a Nile cruise, or take a leisurely drive through California's scenic Big Sur.

Whether you eat to live or live to eat, for many people eating and drinking is one of the central pleasures of visiting new places. France is still renowned as one of the world's gastronomic centers, which is why some of the French escapes focus on food and drink. Go wine tasting in the Loire, sample Armagnac in Gascony, sip champagne in the musty vaults at Reims, or enjoy a Michelin-starred dinner at the Oustau de Baumaniere in Provence. Gastronomes and vinophiles will find themselves transported to food heaven. But France is not the only country to offer food-related escapes. You can taste Madeira on the eponymous island where it is made; eat delicious organic food at Petersham Nurseries, a Bohemian garden center in London; and enjoy Michelin-starred cuisine at Le Quartier Français in the heart of South Africa's winelands.

If it's a temporary refuge from the hustle and bustle of city life you're looking for, where better to head than a leafy, verdant garden? The Jardin Majorelle in the heart of dusty Marrakech is an oasis of green, while the Plantem um Blumen garden in Hamburg, Germany, is a botanical bolthole, the perfect place to take some time out on a sunny day.

However, the ultimate escape has to be to outer space. Inhospitable, barren, and (as far as we know) uninhabited, it has to represent the absolute pinnacle in getting away from it all. Currently in its infancy, commercial space travel offers a very real escape from the world, for the brave—and for those with exceptionally deep pockets. With the price busting budgets of $200,000, who knows what will happen. Perhaps, in a few years' time, it may be as affordable as today's budget airlines.

I hope that this book manages to entertain, inspire, and encourage you to break away from the workday and the routine, and start planning your very own escape. Bon Voyage!

Index of Escapes

Canoe the Yukon River

Location Yukon, Canada **Website** www.touryukon.com;
www.naturetoursyukon.com **Price** 💲💲

You have just left the city of Whitehorse, but already you have the teal-green waters of the Yukon River to yourself. Above soars a pair of white-headed bald eagles. The only sound is the slosh and drip of your paddle as you glide along. You may even find yourself alone when you reach your campsite—save for the black and grizzly bears that inhabit the surrounding woods. Even in peak season, the Yukon River is a sparsely populated place.

It was not always so. As you pitch your tent, you will notice rusting artifacts from the Yukon's gold rush days, for this is Klondike country. The story goes that in the summer of 1896, a rich seam of gold was struck in the creeks of the Klondike River. The United States was in the grips of depression, and when miners carrying boxes of nuggets reached the outside world, they elicited a frenzied reaction. "GOLD! GOLD! GOLD! GOLD!" hollered the *Seattle Post Intelligencer* on July 17, 1897. "Sixty-eight Rich Men on the steamer Portland. Stacks of yellow metal." Around 100,000 dreamers headed north to seek their fortune. Many climbed over the Chilkoot Pass and White Pass, then built boats to paddle along these same waters, which bustled with stern-wheelers and wood camps until the 1950s, when the Klondike Highway was built. Today, you can still see the dilapidated ruins of one or two of those mighty boats, laid up on the shore.

As the world's cities have become ever more packed, this tiny corner of the globe has settled ever more blissfully into tranquility, a remote retreat ruled not by humans but by moose, wolves, and bears. **PE**

← *The fast-moving Yukon makes canoeing a joy. If you are feeling indolent, the river will do most of the work.*

Explore Dawson City

Location Yukon, Canada **Website** www.dawsoncity.ca
Price 🟠

Dawson is the town that sprang up in response to the Klondike gold rush of the late nineteenth century, and to this day it maintains an eccentric, Wild West vibe.

Hordes of hopefuls, including a young Jack London, abandoned the city slog and set off for the Klondike. Hardly any of them found their fortunes. Within a couple of years, the rush had moved on and Dawson's population began to decline. Nearly 40,000 people lived in Dawson in 1898; now there is a population of just 2,000. Somehow, though, it has retained its charm.

The buildings are in traditional style; raised wooden boardwalks line the roads. Tourists can hike and paddle the river, pan for gold in the creeks, or try their

> *"You can drink it fast, you can drink it slow. But the lips have gotta touch the toe."*

Sourtoe Cocktail Club rule

luck at the casino, Diamond Tooth Gertie's. They tour the town, listening to its extraordinary stories, and chat with the colorful local characters. Brave souls can visit the Sourdough Saloon in the Downtown Hotel and order a "sourtoe cocktail"—a shot of whiskey garnished with a severed human toe (from a supply that have been dehydrated and preserved in salt). The first toe—the frostbitten digit of a man who smuggled bootleg booze over the border to Alaska during Prohibition—is sadly no longer. It had to be replaced after one over-enthusiastic drinker downed ten cocktails, fell backward off his bar stool, bumped his head, and swallowed the toe. **PE**

Stay at Inn on the Lake

Location Marsh Lake, Yukon, Canada　**Website** www.exceptionalplaces.com　**Price** 💲💲

On the shores of Marsh Lake, a little more than half an hour's drive from the Yukon's capital—Whitehorse—sits the log cabin retreat of Inn on the Lake. It's one of those places where your every whim seems to have been catered to before you'd even dreamed of it, and from the moment you step out onto the lodge's spacious deck (a glass of wine or a cold beer has already been pressed into your hand), you feel yourself sink into a deep relaxation.

Stretch out and soak up spectacular views over the snowcapped mountains, pristine forest, and crystal-clear lake, which freezes over in winter. If this seems insufficiently arduous, why not grab the binoculars and birding field guide that live on the windowsill and spot a loon or two while you sip a sundowner? In the evening, there is a four-course dinner, which guests eat together at a long table. During the summer there's fishing, kayaking, and canoeing on the lake, or hiking and mountain biking in the surrounding wilderness. Passes to the nearby golf course are included in the package. In winter, the Yukon days are crisp and skies are often blue. Guests can ski (cross-country, backcountry, and downhill are all on the menu), drive snowmobiles or dog teams, try their feet at snowshoeing—or their hands at ice fishing—and at night lie back in the hot tub and watch the northern lights dance green and red against black starry skies.

The lodge is open year-round, and accommodation is available both in the main house and in independent cabins. The biggest of the cabins comes complete with its own deck and hot tub, both of which face north, to guarantee the best views of the Aurora Borealis. Steal a few nights here during winter, and you can curl up for a romantic evening in the steamy waters while the northern lights fill the sky. **PE**

⬆ *A major attraction for visitors to the Inn on the Lake is the opportunity to see the magical northern lights.*

Dogsled Across the Yukon Territory

Location Yukon, Canada **Website** www.muktuk.com; www.uncommonyukon.com; www.bluekennels.de **Price** 🌓🌓

It is silent out there, except for the rhythmic patter of husky paws on snow and the gentle creaking of the sled. Occasionally the dogs' heads pivot in unison to left or right—perhaps they have scented a flock of pure-white ptarmigan or a snowshoe hare amid the surrounding spruce trees. You may be able to spot a line of tiny wells in the powder, indicating that a wolf has walked this way before you. For you are traveling through one of the last remaining great wildernesses in the world. It is a territory larger than the state of California, yet one that only 31,000 humans call home. There are, however, 70,000 moose for company, along with considerable numbers of grizzly and black bears, caribou, wolverines, and Dall sheep.

You leave the forest trail and mush along the surface of a river. Evening is falling and a full moon rises high in the sky, casting a silvery light across this remote, bitterly beautiful land. Later, perhaps, the northern lights will dance across the starry night sky for you.

Afterward, you may find yourself under "The Spell of the Yukon," along with poet Robert Service: "Some say God was tired when He made it / Some say it's a fine land to shun; / Maybe; but there's some as would trade it / For no land on earth—And I'm one."

Visitors to the Yukon Territory can try their hand at dogsledding for anything from half a day to a week—or more. They can base themselves in comfortable accommodation at a kennel or can opt to camp with dogs along the extensive trails of the north. They can even, if they wish, watch how the experts do it and follow the course of the Yukon Quest, billed as "the toughest dogsledding race in the world." Inaugurated in 1984, it runs each February, when conditions are often at their harshest, for 1,000 miles (1,600 km) between Fairbanks, Alaska, and Whitehorse. **PE**

⤒ *Journey to the pristine heart of the Yukon wilderness with a loyal team of canine companions.*

Drive the Ice Road from Inuvik to Tuk

Location Northwest Territories, Canada   **Website** www.tuk.ca; www.inuvik.ca; www.explorenwt.com   **Price** 💲💲

Slowly, cautiously, you inch out of Inuvik and onto the winter road that is carved for 120 miles (193 km) into the ice of the Mackenzie River and then across the Beaufort Sea. It leads to the Inuvialuit settlement of Tuktoyaktuk, usually referred to simply as Tuk, which sits on the shores of the Arctic Ocean, at the most northerly limits of Canada.

The road is wide and smooth, like a skating rink. Contrary to your expectations, your surroundings are not all white. The sun reflects primrose yellow from the sheer ice. The snow, banked up to the sides, casts shadows of purplish blue. At first, weak little trees grow on the river's banks. Then they disappear and the landscape grows wide and flat.

In places, pingos push up from the earth. A little like giant molehills that stretch to more than 150 feet (45 m) in height, these formations were created when underground water was trapped, then frozen and subsequently expanded under the permafrost.

Finally, the river ends and you strike out across the ocean. Tiny spots of buildings appear in the distance. On and on you drive, through this vast expanse of frozen silence where perspective is thrown from all known proportions. You arrive on the main street of the village, where a schooner lies grounded—this boat once took local children to residential church schools. Farther along, the village cemetery's archway is inscribed, "Eternal rest grant to them, O Lord, and let perpetual light shine upon them." (Ironically, perpetual light at times shines on the living here, too, courtesy of the Midnight Sun, a feature of northernmost latitudes.) The light shines over a hodgepodge of crosses that looks across the muted pinks and purples of the Beaufort Sea. If one must perish, you consider, there can be few better spots to be buried than this. **PE**

⤒ *Plan your trip around the seasons: In summer, the road turns to river and there is no land access to Tuk at all.*

Unwind at King Pacific Lodge

Location Princess Royal Island, British Columbia, Canada   **Website** www.kingpacificlodge.com   **Price** ⊖⊖⊖

Canada's Great Bear Rainforest sweeps along British Columbia's Inside Passage and is more than twice the size of Yellowstone National Park. In the midst of all this unbroken, pristine wilderness, more than 150 miles (240 km) from the nearest paved road, is the King Pacific Lodge, a floating fishing lodge moored on the serene waters of Princess Royal Island's Barnard Harbor, home to black wolves, grizzlies, black bears, and a maximum of thirty pampered guests.

The flight there takes you over nothing but trees, lakes, and rivers, the lodge's isolation is genuine enough to lure A-listers such as actor Kevin Costner, who is a longtime devotee. Every spring this unique hotel is towed 100 miles (160 km) to the north, moved from its winter home in the coastal town of Prince Rupert to its summer surrounds on Princess Royal Island, where the lodge's seventeen rooms offer either wilderness or ocean views and access to everything that true wilderness is meant to be.

Humpback whales have been known to breach in the waters of Barnard Harbor just a few feet away from the lodge. Guests can kayak to uninhabited islands or take guided hikes to as-yet-unnamed peaks. If you're lucky, you may even be fortunate enough to see the rare Kermode "spirit bear"—a black bear with a recessive gene that gives it a white coat.

King Pacific Lodge sits on an old navy barge and was designed by a team of marine architects. A Toronto-based firm was responsible for the hotel's interior, which features furniture made from driftwood and unadorned wooden railings and overhead beams above Inuit tapestries hanging alongside paintings by local artists. Its hull contains freezers and coolers to store meat and fish, and vegetables are flown in weekly with the hotel's guests. **BS**

⊡ *The Great Bear rain forest behind King Pacific Lodge is a huge tract of undisturbed temperate wilderness.*

Relax at Knight Inlet Lodge

Location Glendale Cove, British Columbia, Canada
Website www.knightinletlodge.com   **Price** 💲💲

Tucked away in picturesque Glendale Cove, 36 miles (60 km) from the mouth of Knight Inlet and accessible only by seaplane or boat, is Knight Inlet Lodge, a floating eco-lodge anchored beneath the glacier-fed waterfalls and temperate rain forests of the Coast Range, amid the largest concentration of grizzly bears in British Columbia. The lodge's twelve rooms are simple yet spacious and spread across a collection of buildings on the water's edge. They date from the 1940s; most rooms have either a king- or queen-size bed and a single bed, and all have private bathrooms. Meals in the large communal dining hall are first-rate and include Dungeness crab, salmon, and prime rib.

This is the place serious bear watchers come to see grizzlies and their newborn cubs in their natural habitats. Every April, the bears descend from their mountain dens into the streams and estuaries that empty into Knight Inlet to graze on the area's abundant berry crops and natural grasses. Viewing the bears takes different forms and varies from season to season, from standing offshore in lodge boats to venturing on land and using specially built tree stands; Knight Inlet Lodge works with hunters and the local community to restrict the practice of legal trophy hunting. The grizzly population depends on the yearly migration of Pacific salmon through the rivers, and the lodge also actively supports methods of sustaining the salmon population in the region's rivers.

The area is home to timber wolves, sea lions, otters, and bald eagles. Whale-watching tours featuring orcas, humpbacks, and minkes complete a smorgasbord of wildlife viewing that would satisfy the palate of even the most discriminating outdoor enthusiast. **BS**

Stay at Clayoquot Wilderness Resort

Location Vancouver Island, British Columbia, Canada
Website www.wildretreat.com   **Price** 💲💲💲💲

Horseback riding, bear- and whale-watching trips, kayaking, trekking—these are just some of the activities available at Clayoquot Wilderness Resort, possibly North America's only luxury safari-style resort. This tented camp is surrounded by verdant rain forest; in 2000, the area, near British Columbia's Tofino, was designated by UNESCO as a Biosphere Reserve.

The twenty tents (twelve doubles and eight family-sized) offer lots of space and homey features, such as remote-controlled propane woodstoves, Adirondack furnishings, and an abundance of candles and kerosene lamps that muster up a wonderfully rustic

> *"Clayoquot Sound is a place of wonder, one whose beauty takes the breath away."*
>
> **Jean Chrétien, former Canadian prime minister**

atmosphere at night. The ranch cookhouse has a huge stone fireplace and an open kitchen where up to six diners can watch culinary maestros prepare the resort's famed delicacies. An area called The Healing Grounds boasts three cedarwood hot tubs, seawater baths, and four massage and treatment tents, plus a new spa building with two indoor treatment rooms for water therapies. Add in the exotic, untamed surroundings and wealth of wildlife and it's safe to say today's urban explorers have never had it so good. **PS**

➡ *Inspired by the late-nineteenth-century Great Camps, Clayoquot offers sophisticated comfort in the wild.*

Canoe at Poets Cove

Location Vancouver Island, British Columbia, Canada   **Website** www.poetscove.com   **Price** 🌖

The romantically named Poets Cove, southwest of Pender Island, is shielded from the ocean's swell by Canada's Vancouver Island, creating a calm and quiet inlet where time seems to stands still. With forty-six quaint yet modern vacation cottages, most of which feature hot tubs on the deck, it is an ideal place to get away from it all and breathe in nature. And as the majority of the local population is in North Pender, the southern part is almost uninhabited.

Take a ferry from the mainland across the Strait of Georgia—or even better, take a propeller seaplane. With around a hundred mooring rings, the marina at Bedwell Harbor has become famous among the wealthy Seattle-based yachting crowd. A hot destination for fishing, boating, and scuba diving, it is at its best in low season, when taking a canoe to the waters effectively means having the bay to yourself. Wrap up warmly in waterproof gear before venturing straight from the deck onto the bay, out onto the glimmering water, lying as still and flat as an oil slick. The first paddle strokes send ripples out as far as the eye can see. It is so silent, it is almost eerie. Gathering speed very quickly, without having to struggle against any waves, it is difficult to believe you are on the Pacific. But you are, so be sure to keep an eye out for killer whales twice the size of your canoe.

Follow the coastline, gliding gracefully, and take in the panorama with its stunning wooden log cabins and giant designer houses. Carry on north toward the Pender Island Bridge, passing below to get to Mortimer Spit, a steep hill covered in dense forest. Paddling alone on the incredibly blue waters, moving past remote deserted beaches, and being utterly at one with nature offers a serene and almost magical way to see the really great outdoors. **RCA**

⬆ *Two canoeists glide gently into the twilight, the bay to themselves, on the calm waters of Poets Cove.*

Drive the Icefields Parkway

Location British Columbia, Canada **Website** www.icefieldsparkway.ca **Price** 💲

Nestled in the majestic Canadian Rocky Mountains, the south-to-north highway route linking Jasper to Lake Louise near Banff is an area of outstanding natural beauty. Dubbed the Icefields Parkway, it is just that: a route through the frozen landscape. Following the Continental Divide, it crosses the rugged landscape of the National Parks of Jasper and Banff and stretches 143 miles (230 km), offering an unbroken supply of breathtaking vistas.

Leaving the small ski town of Jasper behind, it soon becomes apparent that a four-by-four vehicle is crucial. With temperatures hovering around the -10°F (-25°C) mark, everything is covered in a blanket of fresh snow with a deliciously crisp and crunchy cool layer of ice. Said to be one of the world's most spectacular mountain highways, the Icefields Parkway was completed in 1940 and is open year-round, although in winter the few buildings along the route, including the solitary gas station, are shut.

Although the speed limit appears a little slow at 55 miles per hour (90 kph), the road is fraught with danger. Roads are snow-packed, covered in slush, and sometimes patched with ice, making for treacherous conditions. Prepare wisely before setting out: Fill up with gas, take supplies, get a national parks permit, and wear cozy thermal underwear.

Follow the Sunwapta and Athabasca rivers up to Tangle Ridge via the Montane Forest. Keep an eye out for bighorn sheep, elk, caribou, moose, or even grizzly and black bears that roam freely through the park's trees and dense snow. The all-white scenery is overwhelming, and the Columbia Icefields, Bow and Crowfoot glaciers, Athabasca Falls, and Peyto Lake are awesome. Locals boast about the 33 feet (10 m) of snowfall every season, and it is easy to believe. **RCA**

⊞ *The Icefields Parkway is your passport to a humbling world of breathtaking, sparkling landscapes.*

Visit Eagle's Eye Suites

Location Kicking Horse Mountain, British Columbia, Canada
Website www.kickinghorseresort.com **Price** 🌓🌓

The champagne powders of Kicking Horse Mountain in British Columbia cover more than 2,700 skiable acres (1,090 ha), with over one hundred ski runs and seventy inbound chutes. Presiding over it all at an altitude of 7,700 feet (2,345 m) above the town of Golden at the confluence of the Rocky, Purcell, and Selkirk mountains are the aptly named Eagle's Eye Suites. Winner of Ski Canada's Best Private Mountain Chalet award and Best On-Mountain dining in Canada's highest restaurant, Eagle's Eye is complemented by an oversized log fire, floor-to-ceiling windows, and a 360-degree view of the surrounding mountain peaks.

From Kicking Horse Resort a leather-lined VIP gondola complete with surround sound and a glass of wine will keep you warm as you ascend to your boutique hideaway. Exclusivity is the key ingredient at Eagle's Eye Suites. You are greeted by attentive hotel staff who will wrap you in fleecy blankets as they lead you to one of only two suites, aptly named Sunrise and Sunset, which beckon you with soaker tubs, private balconies, heated bathroom floors, and an around-the-clock personal valet service.

Waking up on the summit guarantees you can be the first to descend mountain slopes every bit as steep as those in Jackson Hole and Whistler, with endless route options once the sole preserve of heli-skiers. If you are not the skiing type, visit in the summer months and see the nearby Kicking Horse Mountain Grizzly Bear Refuge—the world's largest enclosed habitat. Hiking is popular, too, from twenty-minute jaunts to the six-hour haul via Dogtooth Ridge to the Gorman Lake area. **BS**

↩ *Be the first to welcome the sunrise—while relaxing in the lap of luxury—in mountaintop Eagle's Eye Suites.*

Go Ice Walking in Jasper

Location Jasper National Park, Alberta, Canada
Website www.pc.gc.ca/pn-np/ab/jasper **Price** 🌓

In summer, the canyons of the Rocky Mountains are filled with foaming, rushing rivers that are deathly in their speed. However, in winter, these waters stop still. Waterfalls no longer tumble, but turn to white ice that drips like a vast candle frozen in time. Visitors can easily explore this winter wonderland on an ice walk.

Various companies offer guided ice walks within Jasper National Park; they provide rubber boots and ice cleats. One of the most popular treks is through Maligne Canyon. Here, the canyon's walls soar almost a hundred feet (30 m) above the floor and torrents of solid ice, created by an underground water system that seeps through the limestone walls of the canyon

---

"Each footstep can send sounds of crushing ice softly echoing off the walls above the group."

John Korobank, journalist

---

and freezes, plunging from rocky outcrops like enormous stalactites. Beneath them, rippling statues have formed in otherworldly shapes. Intricate alabaster curtains cover solitary grottoes; gleaming ice walls hide caverns and crannies. It is not all white: In places, the ice is turquoise, blue, or the palest jade green, and always, from hour to hour, it is changing.

The routes on ice walks tend to be around 2 miles (3.2 km) long and are even suitable for children, who particularly enjoy slithering down natural ice slides. Most operators require that participants be at least six or seven years old; some also offer evening tours where you walk by the light of a headlamp. **PE**

Visit Cape D'Or Lighthouse

Location Cape D'Or, Nova Scotia, Canada
Website www.capedor.ca   **Price** ⊖

The view from the restaurant of Cape D'Or Lighthouse is, by any definition, a memorable one. Fifteen large glass windowpanes covering three walls of the restaurant look directly out over the Bay of Fundy, Cape Split, and Ile Haut with its 300-foot (90-m) cliffs, all the while watching the world's highest tides rise and fall and peregrine falcons in flight while dining on the freshest of fresh local seafood.

The first lighthouse on Cape D'Or was built in 1922, although the current concrete tower dates back to 1965. When the light was automated in 1989, the lightkeeper residence was converted into a bed-and-breakfast, which offers visitors the choice of staying in individual rooms or the option to take over the whole property.

The tower, lightkeeper residence, restaurant, and interpretive center preside over an ocean seemingly at war with itself. The rising and lowering of the tides here represents a movement of water comparable to the flow of all of Earth's rivers. To witness it is to see standing waves up to 10 feet (3 m) high churning in a frenzied tempest that has, over the eons, sculpted myriad rock shapes such as Hopewell Rocks in New Brunswick and the jagged beauty of Cape Split. Away from the coastline, soil rich in organic silt laid down by the formation of vast tidal flats is home to vineyards and apple orchards.

Talk to the locals and they will tell you it is the sunsets that gave this place its name. In French, Cape D'Or means "Cape of Gold," and every night as you gaze westward out across the frigid waters of the Bay of Fundy and run your eye across the peculiar hues the setting sun creates here, concerns evaporate, worry lines fade, and tranquility reigns. **BS**

Visit West Point Lighthouse

Location Prince Edward Island, Canada
Website www.westpointlighthouse.com   **Price** ⊖⊖

West Point Lighthouse on the North Cape Coastal Drive, in the extreme southwestern tip of Prince Edward Island, was built in 1875 and is the tallest square lighthouse on the island. Designed in the style of the square, tapered, timber lighthouses that became popular along Canada's eastern seaboard in the late nineteenth century, it boasts distinctive broad, black striping and a gabled roof. It received a detailed and meticulous restoration by volunteers and began to offer overnight accommodation In 1984. Eight rooms, all with private baths, are now available in the old lightkeeper's inn, although the most popular room by far is on the second level of the lighthouse itself

> *"The lighthouse combines distinctive architecture, folklore, shipwrecks, and dramatic scenery."*

Proprietors, West Point Lighthouse

with its high ceilings and windows that afford, as one would expect, unobstructed ocean views across the western entrance to Northumberland Strait.

A flight of stairs ascending the east wall allows visitors to climb to the top, where the distinctive red light continues to burn twenty-four hours a day. The Lighthouse Craft Guild next door operates a small gift shop and there is an on-site museum. On the third weekend of July each year, West Point Lighthouse hosts a lively lighthouse festival. **BS**

➜ *Originally built in 1875, an automated electric light was installed at West Point Lighthouse in 1963.*

Stay at Amangani

Location Jackson Hole, Wyoming, U.S.A.
Website www.amanresorts.com **Price** ⊜⊜

High in the Rockies, on the doorstep of Yellowstone National Park, the jagged peaks of Wyoming's Teton range rise abruptly out of the valley. This is the bucolic idyll of Westerns. In winter, the valley is peppered with thousands of elk, which share their refuge with free-roaming bison, wolves, grizzlies, and mountain lions.

The inhabitants of Jackson Hole are pathologically outdoorsy. Winter's deep snows mean that if residents are not skiing or snowboarding, they are snowshoeing, mushing a dogsled, or ice skating. In summer, they join the hikers, bikers, kayakers, and fishers at nearby Yellowstone. Jackson Hole Mountain Resort has a cult skiing image, famed for its pristine conditions.

> *"For the mountain men, a 'hole' indicated a high valley that was surrounded by mountains."*

Jackson Hole Chamber of Commerce

Amangani is the best place to savor this landscape. The view from here is so untouched it feels polar. In the early evening, the white world turns bluey-pink and the stark mountain peaks pierce the sunset; the perfect place to watch is in the chic lounge, or from the heated outdoor pool. The hotel is built from cedar and is designed to blend into its setting. High redwood ceilings are supported by vast Oklahoma sandstone columns that dip down to a lounge where skiers gather in the evening by the roaring fire. Each suite has views of snowy landscapes from a sunken bath. The 1970s retro minimalism of Amangani adds to the magic of this hidden valley. **LB**

Unwind at Home Ranch

Location Elk River Valley, Colorado, U.S.A.
Website www.homeranch.com **Price** ⊜⊜⊜

Home Ranch is a passport back to the time of the American Wild West. Guests stay here to experience the traditional ranch vacation—no cell phones, no television, just pure 360-degree views of nature. The ranch is set in one of the United States' last alpine ranching valleys, the Elk River Valley, with 580 acres (235 ha) of aspen and evergreen forest, silver birch trees, wild deer, and soaring eagles, plus the wild Elk River running through it.

The luxury accommodation at the ranch consists of six comfortable rooms within the main house and eight private cabins, all of which have a hot tub in which to soothe your saddle-sore behind. Each day includes a variety of rides—some up into the wooded hillside for lunch, others working cattle in the pastures—as well as training in horsemanship and plenty of time to experience both the ranch and the natural delights of the Elk River Valley. As the sun sets, the campfire is stoked and cowboy nightlife is laid on for you. Afterward, you can curl up under your down comforter while the wood-burning stove rushes and keeps you warm all night.

Two things in particular make this place really special: the natural surroundings and the absolute lack of contact with the outside world. Simple pleasures, but oddly hard to come by today. It really does feel as though you have stepped back in time, into an era when being this close to Mother Nature was normal, and the modern scourges of cell phones and television were unknown and undreamed of. As you sit and watch the fire crackle in the evening, the sparks rise up to the starry sky just as they did a hundred years ago; when you sleep at night, all you will hear is the silence. Nature in the raw is a beautiful thing. **LD**

Stay at Sundance

Location Near Provo, Utah, U.S.A.
Website www.sundanceresort.com   **Price** ⑤⑤

A regular on "world's best hotel" lists, Robert Redford's rustic Sundance resort is unique. It sits in 6,000 acres (2,425 ha) of wilderness on the slopes of the 12,000-foot (3,660-m) Mount Timpanogos. Rivers burble and birds sing in summer; in winter, mugs of hot chocolate steam beside a crackling fire waiting for skiers to return. The cozy rooms feature American quilts and Native American wall hangings, and the food is superb, whether in The Foundry, praised by Zagat's for its luxury brunch, or the five-star restaurant.

Winter sports remain the key draw in this area. In January, you might find yourself sharing the slopes with luminaries of independent cinema, many of

---

"Our commitment to Sundance has always been to develop very little and preserve a great deal."

Robert Redford, actor and director

---

whom stay here during the annual Sundance Film Festival. Out of season, the lush pastures are great for hiking, mountain biking, and riding. A luxury spa draws on the Sioux idea of Hocoka, a sacred place in which body and spirit can be revived.

Long before eco was chic, Sundance was making a stand. And a passion for the environment is carried through from the Aveda products in the bathroom to the hybrid cars and regeneration projects the resort carries out on the surrounding hillsides. **LD**

← *Sundance offers a cozy, relaxing gourmand's paradise for the environmentally aware.*

Enjoy Circle S Ranch

Location Lawrence, Kansas, U.S.A.
Website www.circlesranch.com   **Price** 💲💲

When visitors ask Jack Cronemeyer, proprietor of the Circle S Ranch, what there is to do around here, he replies, in a relaxed Kansas drawl, "Absolutely nothing." That is the joy of it.

There are things to do, of course, if you must. You can stroll along the Hawks Nest Trail, or laze on the hill under the apricot tree (planted by Mary Cronemeyer's grandmother) and dig into a picnic. You can hike through the tall-grass prairie, visit the bison, longhorns, Herefords, and Angus cattle, and then soak it all away in the eight-person hot tub. Or you can spend a carefree hour with the ranch's licensed massage therapists. Alternatively you could just plant yourself in a rocking chair on the porch and rock there for a good while.

The ranch has been in Mary's family for five generations; three of those were educated in the schoolhouse, which still stands. Her uncle Millard's sweat-stained cowboy hat decorates the lodge's Great Room. The lodge itself is new, though. Jack, a fifth-generation Kansas carpenter, built this 11,000-square-foot (1,022-sq-m) inn using many traditional building techniques, and the pair have fitted it out with every luxury. There are touches of the prairie—original western paintings by regional artist Ernst Ulmer, for example—alongside comforts such as thick bath towels, luxurious meals, and an ample bar.

Each of the twelve guest rooms has a unique decor. The cowboy room, for instance, features horns over the queen-size bed and a corrugated tin shower with a bucket for a shower head. If you really want to take it easy, many of the rooms also feature claw-foot baths, from which bathers can admire views over the ranch. And it's blissfully quiet. **PE**

Stay at The Point

Location Upper Saranac Lake, New York State, U.S.A.
Website www.thepointresort.com   **Price** 💲💲💲💲

Often rated the number-one resort hotel in the United States, The Point is one of the nation's most exclusive hideaways. Built in the early 1930s in the style of the Great Camp Movement, and once home to William Avery Rockefeller, The Point is a pristine retreat spread over 10 acres (4 ha) along a small peninsula on the shores of Upper Saranac Lake, surrounded by the forests of the Adirondack Mountains.

Adirondack-style furniture adorns the eleven rooms, and cathedral ceilings combine with huge room sizes to give the impression of a grand lakeside home. There are four rooms in the Main Lodge, one of which, the Algonquin, was the property's original library. Eagles

> *"The Point [has a] unique combination of warm hospitality, grace, and rustic elegance."*
>
> **Proprietors, The Point**

Nest has three rooms, as does the Guest House, and there is one room in the converted boathouse over the water, which offers a large canopied bed and stunning panoramic views across the lake to the wilderness beyond.

Dinner is taken in the Main Hall or can be brought to your room. The menu changes every week and is fastidiously prepared by The Point's chefs and kitchen staff, who have been trained by renowned London-based, three Michelin–starred chef Albert Roux. **BS**

➔ *As might be expected of a former Rockefeller residence, The Point is the last word in rural luxury.*

See Saugerties Lighthouse

Location Esopus Creek, New York, U.S.A.
Website www.saugertieslighthouse.com   **Price** $$

At one time there were sixteen lighthouses guiding ships along the commercially important Hudson River, but of the handful that survive today, only one invites visitors to stay the night. The beautifully restored Saugerties Lighthouse, built in 1869, sits in splendid isolation as a landmark beacon on the river, and its operational light tower offers panoramic views of the Hudson River with the Catskill Mountains to the west and Magdalen and Cruger islands to the south.

The lighthouse can be reached either by boat or by a half-mile walk through a nature trail. Breakfast is provided for overnight guests, and for dinner you can either dine at a local restaurant or carry food to the lighthouse and cook for yourself, either in the kitchen or on the outdoor barbecue; public tours and special events are also available.

Furnished as it may have looked in the early twentieth century, the building also contains a small museum, gift shop, parlor, kitchen, keeper's quarters, two guest bedrooms, and a shared first-floor bathroom. The toilet operates on a composting system because the lighthouse is too far to be linked up to the municipal sewage system, and instructions for its use are provided on arrival.

Saugerties Lighthouse is open year-round, though weekends are reserved well in advance and weekday stays are very popular between April and October. Once booked in, however, you are guaranteed one of the most relaxing couple of days possible this close to New York, with the sights and sounds of the Hudson River Valley literally all around you. The lighthouse is the perfect place to kick back and relax, although canoeing, kayaking, fishing, wading, and swimming are all there to be enjoyed as well. **HA**

Stay at 60 Thompson

Location New York, New York, U.S.A.
Website www.thompsonhotels.com   **Price** $$

There is hip, there is achingly hip, and there is New York's 60 Thompson. This Soho hotel is fairly small but features one hundred rooms, each decorated in deep, beautiful hardwood. The interior offers a Zen-like calm that spreads like a massage from the lobby into the rooms, all of which are typical New York size (cozy rather than generous) and brim with aesthetic thrills. Walls are adorned with modern photos from a series of contemporary artists, including Laura Resen. The beds are sheer luxury, bedecked with superb coverings courtesy of Sferra. Bathrooms are marble-clad and feature glass shower-closets; minibars are stocked with exclusive drinks and snacks.

"A magnet for downtown celebs, 60 Thompson provides excellent people-watching opportunities."

New York Times

The dreamy sumptuousness of 60 Thompson is perhaps the reason why the hotel attracts such high-caliber guests: Gwyneth Paltrow, Jennifer Aniston, and Russell Crowe are just some of the celebrities who have called the hotel home, doubtless taking advantage of the larger suites, with designated living and working areas.

The hotel has some of the city's slickest amenities. In the restaurant, Kittichai, chef Ian Kittichai serves traditional Thai cuisine with an exciting contemporary twist; the Thom Bar is the place for quiet drinks. In the summer, 60 Thompson's A60 bar gives an unparalleled 360-degree view of the downtown area. **PS**

Unwind at The Mercer

Location New York, New York, U.S.A.
Website www.mercerhotel.com **Price** 💲💲💲

Situated in a stylish neighborhood on one of the ultra-cool corners of retail heaven Soho, The Mercer's Romanesque revival style and location puts it high on the list for visiting movers and shakers. It also has the unique accolade of being New York's first-ever loft hotel, a phenomenon that was pioneered here in the sixties by artists who took one look at the multitude of abandoned warehouses and transformed the tumbledown ruins of a long-gone industry into havens of creativity and style.

The elegance of this seventy-five-room boutique hotel, spread over six floors, is manifested through the coolly exposed brickwork, huge windows, and iron column work, which give a sense both of space and permanence. The rooms themselves are large—huge by Manhattan standards, in fact—and feature high ceilings, walk-in closets, and furnishings designed by Christian Liagre, mostly in dark, African woods. Admire the pastel upholstery as you lie back on your generously proportioned bed and flick on your flat-screen television. You can also check out the comprehensive entertainment system, or slip from between your cozy Frette linens and cross the hardwood floors. Romantics may wish to inquire about the rooms with working fireplaces, leather banquettes, and marble tubs big enough for two.

World-class chef Jean-George Vongerichten is in charge of the delightful kitchen, and he also designed the exquisite twenty-four-hour room service menu. Greenwich Village is just around the corner; Times Square and Central Park are fifteen minutes away. In terms of both location and style, The Mercer does it better than most—which is doubtless why *Vogue* dubbed it "the hottest hotel in New York." **PS**

Stay at The Library Hotel

Location New York, New York, U.S.A.
Website www.libraryhotel.com **Price** 💲💲

For aspiring authors and would-be poets, New York's Library Hotel is the place to stay. As the name suggests, it is the perfect refuge for bibliophiles worldwide. Tucked away in a classic early-twentieth-century brownstone just around the corner from Grand Central Station, this classy and cultured boutique hotel mixes a love of all things bookish with a passion for contemporary design. The library theme is no gimmick, however: Each of the ten floors is dedicated to one of the ten major categories of the Dewey decimal system, and each of the sixty rooms is appointed with books and art that explore a topic within their floor category. The Library contains more

> *"A refuge of calm … from the glut of other boutique hotels that think they're nightclubs."*
>
> *Independent*

than 6,000 carefully selected volumes—and if that is not enough, the New York Public Library and the Pierpont Morgan Library are a short stroll away.

Guests can request a room based on their personal interests, ranging from poetry and the classics to fairy tales and erotic literature. Although small, the rooms are comfortable, stylish, and come fully equipped. The three public lounges have the feel of a private members club, and there is also the Writers Den—a mahogany-paneled room with open fireplace—and the Poetry Garden, a lovely greenhouse. And when you have had enough of using your head, you will find New York literally at your feet. **PS**

Explore Wave Hill Gardens

Location New York, New York, U.S.A. **Website** www.wavehill.org **Price** $

For a bucolic escape from the hustle and bustle of New York City, the Bronx might not be the first place that springs to mind. However, hidden away in this less than salubrious part of town is Wave Hill, 28 gorgeous acres (11 ha) of lush greenery that was bequeathed to the city for use as a public garden and cultural center, and is one of the most beautiful spots in New York.

Formerly a private estate, Wave Hill has at various times in its past been home to a British ambassador as well as to Theodore Roosevelt and Mark Twain. Nowadays, it is one of the city's best-kept secrets, a carefully cultivated oasis that offers spectacular views over the Hudson River and the Palisades below. For the very best views, head to the Pergola Overlook and the Elliptical Garden, where you can sit in quiet contemplation on a bench and enjoy the vista. They are particularly beautiful at sunset in the autumn.

Each season a riot of colorful plants transforms the pergola. Stroll along the wooded paths and visit the wild garden, where, as the name suggests, flowers and plants are allowed to grow freely; gaze at the limpid garden pool overgrown with water lilies and sprawling vines; and do not miss the Alpine Green House that houses high-altitude plants and flowers. These tiny, gemlike flowers are at their best in late winter and early spring. Hardy alpines planted within the cracks of a rustic stone wall create a vertical eye-level garden of flowers and foliage.

Breathe in the heady scents from the herb garden, where mint, rosemary, thyme, laurel, and a host of other plants that are grown for both medicinal and culinary purposes flourish. In the hot summer months, seek respite from the sun in the shade of an elm, beech, maple, or redwood tree. Wave Hill Gardens is horticultural heaven, indeed. **HA**

⊡ *The Flower Garden at Wave Hill uses both vintage and modern plants to create year-round color.*

Relax at Gramercy Park Hotel

Location New York, New York, U.S.A. **Website** www.gramercyparkhotel.com **Price** ⑤⑤⑤

Gramercy Park Hotel is the latest notch in the boutique bedpost of Ian Schrager—the entrepreneur best known for setting up Morgans (the hotel that more or less invented the concept of the "design hotel"), Mondrian, Royalton, Paramount, and St. Martin's Lane in London, among others.

Like most of Schrager's other spots, the Gramercy puts an emphasis on the unique, the surprising, and the romantic. The lobby and public areas are particularly vivid, containing haphazard combinations of contemporary artworks, wild furnishings, and antiques that create a wholly memorable entrance.

The 185 guest rooms and luxury suites are equally idiosyncratic. Some are reminiscent of the Renaissance, with the requisite collections of furniture and objets d'art. Yet this kind of detailing might be balanced with photographs drawn from the hallowed Magnum photos archive—classic images by photographers such as Henri Cartier-Bresson, Robert Capa, Weegee,

and a host of other famous names—or with hand-woven rugs or contemporary mahogany furniture. The hotel's bars and restaurant are talking points of the town. The Wakiya, the Rose Bar, and the Jade Bar, plus the Private Roof Club & Garden, provide plenty of opportunities to unwind and enjoy terrific food and beverages amid the assortment of custom-designed furniture and twentieth-century art by artists including the likes of Andy Warhol, Cy Twombly, Julian Schnabel, and Damien Hirst. Music in the bars comes courtesy of playlists—not just any old playlists, of course, but custom-made lists from world-renowned DJs. You can find a state-of-the-art gym (Aerospace) on the second floor, and a spa (Aerospa) offers a vast array of treatments. Gramercy Park is simply a one-stop shop for all things in New York. **PS**

⬆ *Surreal interior design touches and a wealth of original art make the Gramercy a visual feast.*

Stay at East Brother

Location San Francisco, California, U.S.A.
Website www.ebls.org **Price** 💲💲

East Brother Light Station is an impeccably restored Victorian lighthouse perched atop a tiny island in San Francisco Bay. You can stay and share the island with the seals, but beware: This is no ordinary luxury escape.

Although only a few minutes' boat ride from downtown San Francisco, arrival is an adventure. Guests are warned they will need: "The physical strength to climb from a bobbing boat up a vertical ladder 4–12 feet (1.2–3.6 m) in height, depending on tides." If in one of the five charming period rooms, you cannot use the shower unless staying for more than one night. (There is no freshwater other than what can be collected in the original rainwater cistern.)

"One of the most peaceful bed and breakfast getaways on the West Coast."

San Francisco Chronicle

So why escape there? Firstly, the light station is a unique experience, offering marvelous views of Mount Tamalpais, the San Francisco skyline, and the Marin coast. Moreover, although it is a nonprofit-making operation, you'll find your stay surprisingly indulgent: You are served champagne and hors d'oeuvres upon arrival, a multicourse dinner with wine in the evening, and a gourmet breakfast the next day. The most popular room is in the wood-paneled foghorn building, nestled close to the water's edge. **SH**

⬅ *East Brother has been safeguarding shipping for more than 133 years and is still in operation today.*

Enjoy Yoga at Sivananda

Location Grass Valley, California, U.S.A.
Website www.yogafarm.org **Price** 💲

Party seekers beware: Tucked away in northern California's Sierra foothills, this ashram is a haven for those seeking a healthy break with a spiritual dimension. The Yoga Farm, as it is known, runs a year-round schedule of retreats for those in search of disciplined relaxation. You will be turfed out of bed at 5:30 A.M., to the sound of a chiming bell, for morning satsang—meditation, chanting, and a talk—and the days end at 10 P.M. In between, you will eat two generous, hearty vegetarian meals, outside in the lovely grounds, weather permitting, and have two yoga classes and some time off to sink into the beautiful setting and calming vibes.

The Sivananda yoga movement owns retreat centers worldwide, where both experienced yogis and beginners immerse themselves in the restful yoga lifestyle. This ashram sits in the foothills of the magnificent Sierra mountain range, among ancient oak trees. There is also a lake, where guests can swim in the long, hot summer months, or just sit, chill out, and reflect.

Wondrously, there is no cell phone reception, although there is a satellite wireless Internet connection, and the focus is on leaving busy lives far behind. Organized, themed retreats (a children's yoga camp and an ayurveda rejuvenation weekend, for example) run throughout the year, but guests can stay on an individual basis for as long as they desire to. Accommodation is in attractive, well-maintained cabins above the lake in the grounds, or in dormitories in the main building. Ashram living is not about luxury. It is about a nurturing, wholesome, and hugely rewarding experience for those with a passing interest (or more) in yoga and its accompanying lifestyle. **LC**

Bask in the Natural Spa at Calistoga Ranch

Location Napa Valley, California, U.S.A.   **Website** www.calistogaranch.com   **Price** ⊖⊖⊖

The first thing you notice when you hit Calistoga Ranch—situated just two hours from San Francisco—is just how incredibly big it all is. The size of the site is 157 acres (64 ha), but it is within a region so large you are guaranteed some extra visitors. Everything from deer to rattlesnakes can be spotted within the grounds, although the latter are thankfully confined to the farthest reaches of the region.

The forty-six rooms at the ranch nestle in Californian pines and boast peerless views of the surrounding terrain. The smallest dwellings offer some 6,460 square feet (600 sq m) of space and include outdoor showers, although the largest of them all is the Estate Lodge—a whopping 25,830 square feet (2,400 sq m) right on the gorgeous banks of Lake Lommel, with the forest at the rear. The Estate Lodge, with its two private bedrooms, indoor and outdoor living room, two half baths, two fireplaces, and an outdoor hot tub, is a natural choice for honeymooners.

There is a guests-only dining room, where chef Eric Webster impresses with simple, high-quality American cuisine. Wine buffs will also love it. Not only is nearby Napa Valley renowned for its wines (Calistoga's Old and New World vintages are exceptional), but the resort also has its own vineyard and offers wine-tasting classes and tours of the wine caves and vineyard.

Cars are not allowed on Calistoga Ranch, so transportation comes in the shape of golf carts. There is no chance of being disturbed by traffic noise when you are relaxing in the Bathhouse, Calistoga's natural spa, which draws water from local hot springs and promotes a variety of boutique treatments. The yoga deck and pool offer views onto the vineyard; both are wonderful ways to either start or end a day at one of the United States's classiest ranches. **PS**

⊼ *If you're traveling in Napa Valley, the richly appointed Calistoga Ranch is worth branching off for.*

Unwind at Spa Vitale

Location San Francisco, California, U.S.A. **Website** www.hotelvitale.com/spavitale **Price** Ⓢ

Wallowing naked in an outside tub in the bustling heart of San Francisco may sound like a fairly far-out activity. It's true there are not many places in the world where you can de-stress in this way in such an urban environment without the fear of Peeping Toms. Rest assured, though: There is no need to worry about such matters here. Hotel Vitale has created a wonderful bamboo roof garden to preserve your modesty. The tall, willowy trees provide a perfect barrier from prying eyes in nearby skyscrapers, and the city itself seems curiously removed from this small oasis.

Spa Vitale is the spa within Hotel Vitale and is in the penthouse. Offering three treatment rooms, it is small and intimate rather than flashy and commercialized like so many spas; the comparative intimacy ensures a friendly, attentive approach. The spa's most unique attraction is the rooftop bathing ritual, and it is a simple but striking concept. Two deep, set-apart bathing tubs nestle beneath a willowy line of bamboo

trees. An extra layer of trees divides each of the two tubs, so two friends can enjoy the ritual together while retaining their privacy. Other than this, only one tub is in use at a time—so on those occasions, you have the whole rooftop to yourself.

You will be handed a fluffy white bathrobe and towels and led to an invitingly full bath infused with seasonal bath products made exclusively for Spa Vitale by SumBody. An herbal drink and tray of bath products are placed by the tub, together with an exquisitely arranged plate of fresh fruit—and yet more fluffy white towels. There is nothing left to do but de-robe and climb in, placing the cucumber slices on your eyes as you sink back into the steam. Let the city sounds wash over you as you enjoy what has to be a truly unique urban experience. **LC**

⬆ *Bliss in the heart of the city: Spa Vitale's rooftop tubs offer a luxurious outdoor bathing experience.*

Drive Through Big Sur

Location Big Sur, California, U.S.A.
Website www.montereyinfo.org **Price** ⊝

Big Sur Coast Highway is a stretch of Route 1 between Los Angeles and San Francisco where nature remains untouched. Some 200 miles (320 km) north of Los Angeles along Route 1 (the Pacific Coast Highway), the town of San Luis Obispo and the small fishing village of Morro Bay are the two alternative starting points of the Big Sur drive. This 144 miles (230 km) of highway is almost deserted, featuring just a handful of small towns and a couple of hotels, including the Post Ranch Inn, where celebrities like to take time out.

The wildlife protection area has recently seen California condors reintroduced. They swoop high over the precipices while, down below, local residents

> *"It was always a wild rocky coast, desolate and forbidding to the man of the pavements."*
>
> Henry Miller, writer

include sea otters and sea lions with the occasional migrating whale. Deer and foxes are often sighted, and the shy and elusive cougar is also at home here.

The narrow two-lane road snakes its way along the jagged cliff hugging the mountainside. Soak up the scenery as the road weaves along the sheer drops past Point Sur lighthouse before ending at picturesque Carmel, the heart of the West Coast's idyllic coastal country, best known for its fine beaches and movie-star resident (and onetime mayor) Clint Eastwood. **RCA**

➡ *After 1932, the remote coastal towns of Big Sur were finally connected by this striking coastal highway.*

Drive Through Death Valley

Location California/Nevada, U.S.A.
Website www.nps.gov/deva   **Price** ◑

Like the moon's surface, the parched salt flats of Death Valley are devoid of human life, yet hauntingly beautiful. The national park that straddles California and Nevada across 140 miles (225 km) is one of Earth's least hospitable places: 3 million acres (1.2 million ha) of arid desert. It was given its name by a group of lost pioneers in the winter of 1849. Other spots in the vicinity share in the fatalism of that title, from Last Chance Canyon to Badwater and the Devil's Golf Course (an expanse of uneven, sharp clumps of rock salt said to be so jagged that "only the devil could play golf on such rough links").

Death Valley was born millions of years ago when an inland sea evaporated, leaving just salt behind. With most of the desert under sea level, it has record temperatures of 130°F (55°C). Amazingly, life does go on: More than 1,000 species of plants thrive here, including 50 species indigenous to the area and found nowhere else in the world. The animal kingdom, too, is alive and well with coyotes, rattlesnakes, scorpions, kangaroo rats (who can survive without water), black widow spiders, and even pupfish in Salt Creek.

Drive across the barren landscape and stop for a photo in the salt flats or take the 9-mile (14-km) loop around the volcanic hills dubbed "artist drive" because of their multicolored rocks. There is only one place to stay in Death Valley: Furnace Creek, home to the Inn and the Ranch motel. The motel is itself rather basic, but the Inn, dating back to 1927, is a historic landmark. With hostile terrain comes solitude, and Death Valley delivers plenty of that. **RCA**

◀ *A warm welcome to Death Valley—the hottest, driest, and lowest desert in the United States.*

See Zion National Park

Location Zion National Park, Utah, U.S.A.
Website www.zionmountainresort.com   **Price** ◐◐

The oldest of Utah's parks, Zion was first brought to wider national attention by pioneering Mormon settlers in the 1860s who spoke of its glory; one of them, Isaac Behunin, gave the canyon its biblical name.

The walls of red-and-white Navajo sandstone that project parallel up to 2,000 feet (600 m) were carved by the relentless Virgin River, though this may seem quite unlikely today as the river meanders serenely along the canyon bed, creating an oasis of waterfalls and wild meadows. If you have the time, the park's 229 square miles (593 sq km) can cater for a wide range of engaging sports, including hiking, bicycling, riding, rock climbing, and rappelling.

"While it sits in the middle of nature, guests need only to step inside their cabin to feel pampered."

nationalparkreservations.com

The ideal base from which to launch into such a throng of activity—or simple meditation, if you wish—is a mere three-minute drive from the park's eastern entrance at the suitably rustic Zion Mountain Resort. Accommodation can be found in cozy wooden cabins for couples and spacious lodges for families and larger groups, all with glorious views across the mountains. Nearby are grazing buffalo, casually roaming the open plain as guests relax on private patios or unwind in a hot tub after the exertions of the day. The resort is also within comfortable driving distance of several other parks and monuments—notably Bryce Canyon and the north rim of the awe-inspiring Grand Canyon. **SG**

Stay at the Four Seasons

Location Las Vegas, Nevada, U.S.A.
Website www.fourseasons.com   **Price** 💲💲

The infamous "City of Sin" in the Nevada Desert is just the way it looks on television: totally over the top. A jungle of casinos, neon, and hordes of people looking for a good time, the legendary Las Vegas Boulevard, better known as "The Strip," is where it all happens.

The only hotel "on Strip," as the locals say, without a hectic casino floor is the Four Seasons. Luxurious and exclusive, it takes up the top floors of the Mandalay Bay building and is the Strip's smallest hotel, with "only" 400 rooms. Curl up in a plush Strip-view suite to watch the Vegas craziness from above via the floor-to-ceiling windows. The glamorous rooms come with a 42-inch plasma screen, DVD player, and marble bathroom.

> *"There is only one true luxury resort … in town, located on the top five floors of Mandalay Bay."*
>
> *New York Times*

Guests can enjoy an alfresco breakfast at the Verandah restaurant. For dinner, the restaurant goes Italian with beef carpaccio and truffle gnocchi on the menu, or you can opt for surf 'n' turf at Charlie Palmer's. Here you'll find an elegant bar where the ambience is more low-volume jazz than the usual raucous Vegas pop. At the spa, try the very Vegas champagne mud wrap or the golden body treatment with passionflower oil. With pristine service and a wonderfully secluded pool the hotel is a real treat, despite the steep price tag. Meg Ryan, Reese Witherspoon, and even Michael Jackson have all found sanctuary in this relaxing refuge from the ultimate twenty-four-hour city. **RCA**

See the Grand Canyon

Location Arizona/Nevada, U.S.A.
Website www.nps.gov/grca   **Price** 💲

It is more than a great chasm, more than the result of millennia of erosion, and more than one of the world's greatest views. The Grand Canyon is an experience that humbles every visitor. Whether you are driving, hiking, bicycling, riding, or white-water rafting, this is nature at its most raw and beautiful. It feels so huge and timeless that humans and their problems seem insignificant in comparison.

The sheer size of it is worth stressing: The canyon is 277 miles (445 km) long, 1 mile (1.6 km) deep, and up to 18 miles (29 km) wide. It was carved by the Colorado River and is mostly contained within Grand Canyon National Park—one of the first areas to be designated national park in the United States. It attracts five million visitors a year and has become one of the world's most popular natural attractions.

People come to stare at this gorge's intricate and colorful landscape of spires, rims, and cliffs. They watch the changing light and shadows on the rocks. (Sunrise and sunset are almost spiritual events here.) There is plenty of accommodation inside and outside Grand Canyon National Park and an array of activities to engage in. Some visitors wander along trails, watching ravens soaring above the rim and listening for the roar of the rapids far below. Others can ride mules. Perhaps the most memorable canyon experience is the glass-bottomed Skywalk, run by the Hualapai Indian tribe on their reservation. This horseshoe-shaped steel frame, with a glass floor and sides, projects 70 feet (21 m) into thin air from the canyon rim. It is not for the fainthearted. **SH**

➡ *The timeless grandeur of the Grand Canyon offers visitors a welcome tonic to the stresses of modern life.*

Explore Monument Valley

Location Utah/Arizona, U.S.A.
Website www.navajonationparks.org **Price** 🌓

This mesmerizing corner of the Arizona desert will be familiar to anyone who has ever watched a cowboy film, seen the surreal fantasies of painter Max Ernst, or read Paul Auster's 1989 novel *Moon Palace*. Like neon motel signs and roadside diners, we feel we have been there even before we see it for the first time. In the evocative Goulding's Lodge hotel—where director John Ford stayed—this is particularly so. Turn on the television and watch a film—Ford's *Stagecoach* (1939), perhaps, or *The Searchers* (1956)—from the hotel's extensive collection of Westerns. Let your eyes skip between the valley on the screen and the sun setting on the real thing beyond.

"If ever a place cast a spell, rooted you to the ground and refused to let you leave, this is it."

Los Angeles Times

It's worth taking time (perhaps in winter, after the main tourist season) to study the distinct forms: the much-filmed twin Mittens, the lofty Totem Pole, the arch of the Ear of the Wind. The buttes are stratified, their distinct rocks marking out the eons; the steeples and slender towers look fragile and weather worn.

Part of the Colorado plateau, Monument Valley acquires its deep sunset reds from the iron oxide in the Cutler Red siltstone, whereas manganese oxide shows up as blues, greens, and grays in the strata. The Grand Canyon is nearby and the Navajo Nation spreads all around—Monument Valley is a natural, and spiritual, magnet for any experience of the American West. **CM**

Discover Lake Powell

Location Utah/Arizona, U.S.A.
Website www.lakepowell.com **Price** 🌓

There was much hostility from environmentalists and anthropologists in the 1960s toward the controversial scheme to dam the Colorado River and flood Glen Canyon, creating Lake Powell—comparable to filling the Grand Canyon with water. Yet few could deny that the resulting artificial landscape is a staggering sight.

Crystal-clear turquoise waters reflect the towering rich-red canyon walls that ascend from the water, interspersed by wondrous arches, magnificent spires, and sandstone buttes, as well as countless inlets, and sandy beaches. The lake stretches for 186 miles (300 km) across southern Utah and northern Arizona, and comprises 2,000 miles (3,220 km) of coastline and ninety-six water-filled side canyons, many of which are accessible only by boat.

In fact, there is no finer way to appreciate what delights the lake has to offer than by houseboat. Rentals are available at Wahweap, Bullfrog, and Antelope Point marinas, and only a houseboat allows you the freedom to search out remote corners in which to dock. Boats range from the luxurious, complete with hot tub and wet bar for up to fourteen people, to those that feature only basic comforts. Water sports dominate the baking summer, though fishing is best enjoyed in the cooler months: April through June and October to November. The most popular mooring point lies near the spectacular Rainbow Bridge National Monument. At 290 feet (88 m) high and 275 feet (84 m) across, this breathtaking geological formation and deeply spiritual place is the world's largest natural bridge. **SG**

➔ *Named for explorer John Wesley Powell, Lake Powell has more coastline than the entire U.S. west coast.*

Stay at Dunton Hot Springs

Location San Juan Mountains, Colorado, U.S.A.
Website www.duntonhotsprings.com **Price** $ $

Tucked away in the San Juan Mountains, this romantic old mining town turned resort offers a refreshingly new tourist experience. Although the town where Butch Cassidy and the Sundance Kid are rumored to have hidden after robbing a bank in Telluride in 1889 may appear sleepy, nothing could be further from the truth. There is an abundance of activities to satisfy even the most hyper vacationer: Take a horse into the terrain to discover thunderous waterfalls and silent lakes, go desert hiking, heli-skiing, or snowmobiling in virgin powder, get your adrenaline pumping with river rafting, or enjoy a gentle afternoon's fly fishing on the Wet Dolores. Stay in finely

> *"Dunton Hot Springs ranks in our Top 10 favorite places on earth— a romantic, magical experience."*
>
> LuxuryTravelMagazine.com

furnished hand-hewn log cabins, dine on delicious local organic cuisine in an old saloon, enjoy reviving holistic Elemis treatments in a tepee. Plus, of course, you can soak in the town's natural, therapeutic hot springs, as the Ute Indians did thousands of years ago.

An array of fascinating sites lies just a short distance away, including haunting Monument Valley and Canyon de Chelly in the Navajo Reservation, and the town's own vineyard in McElmo Canyon. And how about having the whole town to yourself? Dunton Hot Springs can be reserved exclusively for private use for up to forty-two people, making it ideal for weddings and family celebrations. **LP**

Relax at Mii Amo

Location Sedona, Arizona, U.S.A.
Website www.miiamo.com **Price** $ $

Sedona is known throughout the United States for being the seat of strong spiritual energy, partly because of its powerful color combination of red-orange rocks, cornflower-blue sky, and evergreen vegetation. This part of Arizona is famed for its new-age spirituality, and there is definitely something special about these parts.

Super spa Mii amo is set within Boynton Canyon, overlooked by a wind-carved rock formation called Kachina Woman. It was voted the world's best spa in 2007 by *Travel + Leisure* magazine, and the staff, location, treatments, and facilities all score a perfect ten. There are sixteen casitas and suites on-site—the largest being the Mii amo suite—all with private courtyards and views of the Boynton Canyon. If you feel the need to take your soul on a journey, this is the place to do it. Create a link with your inner self in a soul-seeker session, restore your energy in the Crystal Grotto at the heart of the spa, or have a Mii amo signature massage with mineral crystals from Sedona. This is a place where magic happens.

The name *Mii amo* comes from the Native American word for "journey," and the spa offers a variety of ways to take your body and soul to a new level, whether by spending the day experiencing treatments from a traditional facial to an aura reading, or staying here for a three-, four-, or seven-day break. You can sign up for a straightforward spa package, a fitness package that includes hiking around Sedona, a new-age, Native American–influenced package, complete with sweat-lodge-style sessions, or a combination of all three. **LD**

➡ *The architectural style of Mii amo blends in almost seamlessly with the striking Arizona red-rock.*

Stay at Rancho de la Osa

Location Sonora Desert, Arizona, U.S.A. **Website** www.ranchodelaosa.com **Price** 💲💲

Set in a traditional hacienda dating back to 1885, the Rancho de la Osa is just a mile away from Arizona's border with Mexico in the arid Sonora Desert. Miles away from U.S.-style civilization, its closest neighbor is the one-shop town of Sasabe.

Hip yet mellow, this is the ideal place to don a pair of cowboy boots and an old Stetson and head out on a ride across the dried-out riverbeds. It is the perfect place to indulge your inner cowboy. The electric pinks, yellows, and blues give the adobe-style buildings and Adirondack chairs a distinct modern Mexican vibe. In the cool cantina, with its giant sombreros and decorative piñatas, western-style saddle bar stools await, inviting. After a ride in the dusty heat through Geronimo's old stomping ground, ordering a fresh Corona (like John Wayne must have done when he stayed) is pure bliss. Aching and parched, it is the bona fide way of propping up the bar, listening to the lady wranglers' chat, the ranch hands' tall tales, and the

compulsory country soundtrack. For lazy days, there is the pool, the in-room massages, and the deliciously unavoidable siesta. For a little more action, try hiking, biking, and bird-watching, or possibly even watching a ranch hand hunt for rattlesnakes.

Meals are served in the hacienda or alfresco, with everyone tucking into gorgeous balsamic-glazed salmon or cookout-style steak at the grill. There is a real flavor of cowboy camping days—without any compromise on comfort.

At night, before retiring to the simple, uniquely styled rooms, there is an inescapable dreamer's ritual to attend to. The clear desert skies put on their nightly show, and it is impossible not to spend a while staring at the star-filled sky. Without a doubt, this is one of the most amazing views anywhere. **RCA**

⬆ *One of the last great haciendas, Rancho de la Osa is also rumored to be the oldest building in Arizona.*

Stay at The Sanctuary

Location Miami, Florida, U.S.A.
Website www.sanctuarysobe.com **Price** 💲💲

Miami's South Beach is known for many things, but tranquility has not traditionally been one of them. That was until the Sanctuary Hotel arrived: an ultra-luxury modern boutique hotel exuding Zen cool and a quietly Scandinavian designer edge that allows one to wallow in an exclusive milieu for a fraction of the price.

The hotel is centered around an open-air inner courtyard that comprises a multitude of small fountains wrapped in bamboo. The thirty-one rooms are modern but have a soothing ambience, and feature state-of-the-art Italian kitchens, flat-screen plasma televisions, and wireless Internet access, as well as whirlpool tubs, fully stocked in-room fridges, and—in

> *"Almost too cool for words … we think this hotel should be renamed the Swanktuary."*
>
> *New York Times*

selected rooms—steam showers. This being Miami, there is, of course, a modicum of hedonism. In the Sanctuary's case, this means a small roof bar that happens to be fairly lively at weekends and an infinity pool, which makes for a great hanging-out spot.

The hotel's Italian restaurant, Sugo, is a well-known local hot spot and sits in the middle of the stylish lobby. The Sanctuary Spa and Salon is the perfect place to give your body some deluxe attention. Guests can also avail themselves of various concierge services, including being picked up in a Bentley, procuring a jogging companion, and a G4 private aircraft for charter. Intimacy and indulgence, South Beach–style. **PS**

Relax at The Standard

Location Miami, Florida, U.S.A.
Website www.standardhotels.com **Price** 💲💲

There's one thing that you can guarantee from André Balazs's Standard hotels: a unique experience. Miami's version is in a surprisingly quiet neighborhood, the residential Belle Isle. The Scandinavian-style spa/hotel has tranquility as a byword. Music is banned from the pool—surely a first for a Miami Beach hotel.

As a place to unwind, it is both ultra-relaxing and unconventional, with a hydrotherapy area taking pride of place. There's a plunge pool, hot tub, and 12-foot-tall (3.6-m), three-inch-wide (7.6-cm) column of falling water to relax in; DJ-spun music plays through underwater speakers in the chlorine-free Sound Pool. There's also the hammam, Aroma Steam Room, Cedar Sauna, Roman Waterfall Hot Tub, and Mud Lounge—staying dry seems to be one of the biggest challenges here. Still a little tense? Then book a session with acupuncturist Lori Alexandra Bell.

Food is high on The Standard's menu, too. The Lido restaurant offers a fresh-fruit-and-organic-farm-egg breakfast; the Bayside grill aims for a healthful Mediterranean-inspired spread; another in-house eatery serves fish-based dishes dressed with home-grown herbs—all under the watchful eye of superchef Eric Ripert. Balazs's vision is everywhere: He's added his own touch to the existing white marble, terrazzo floors, and steel elevators with some seriously stylish touches such as Hans Wegner rocking chairs, vintage furniture from Denmark, Anne Jacobsen sconces, and Aalto tea trolleys. The rooms themselves are suitably hip and minimal, with light wood, crisp whites, sandy tones, and up-to-the-minute facilities.

The result is both delightful and dotty: wellness culture combined with left-field comfort—and all delivered with a raised eyebrow. **PS**

Discover Venetian Pool

Location Miami, Florida, U.S.A.
Website www.venetianpool.com **Price** 💲

The Venetian Pool is an incredible piece of living history (hence its place on the U.S. National Registry of Historic Places) and a beautiful escape in the heart of Miami. Step through the original wrought-iron gates and into another era—a time of whimsical architecture and romantic visions of how cities should be.

This was the quarry for the coral used in the model suburb of Coral Gables in the 1920s. Then, marvelously-named architect Phineas Paist and artistic adviser Denman Fink used it to create a pool inspired by the lagoons of Venice. With 820,000 gallons (3.1 million l) of spring water—and vivid imaginations—they created a Mediterranean-style oasis of tranquility.

> *"For a swimming hole like no other, don't miss the Venetian Pool in Coral Gables."*

South Florida Sun-Sentinel

The swimming pool is surrounded by Spanish buildings, a tropical garden, and a grotto carved from the coral. There is a cave, a veranda full of parlor palms, and a rock diving platform. Wander among birds-of-paradise, fuchsias, and bougainvilleas; cross a Venetian-style bridge to discover the artificial island and its swaying coconut palms. Everywhere there are Latin arches and fountains amid ferns and flowers. After dark, the Venetian lanterns and underwater lights illuminate the scene in a flickering, romantic glow.

After a multimillion-dollar restoration program in 1989, visitors are now able to enjoy this Floridian fantasy world as it was originally intended. **SH**

Unwind at Little Palm

Location Little Torch, Florida, U.S.A.
Website www.littlepalmisland.com **Price** 💲💲

Florida has so much to offer, from the perpetual good weather that earned it that Sunshine State moniker to the beautiful Caribbean-style keys. For a really private hideaway, however, check into the ultra-exclusive Little Palm Island Resort in Little Torch. A million miles away from the rest of the world, the resort—accessible only by boat or seaplane—is a tranquil spot where elegance and casual cool rule. Even the staff look like they have stepped out of a fashion magazine.

The thatched cottage suites on stilts have a colonial feel, with their mosquito-netted beds, rich animal-print fabrics, and luxurious bathrooms. There is even an exterior shower for a spot of alfresco cleansing.

The vibe here is more Bali than Florida. Spend the day by the pool, on the palm-fringed beach, or swinging in a hammock. It may seem quiet, but there is plenty to do: You could try snorkeling, kayaking among the mangroves, or even taking out one of the hotel's Boston Whaler boats for a spin to explore neighboring islands.

It is all about romance at Little Palm. Take the welcome champagne hamper to the dock for the show: impossibly electric-pink sunsets followed by a candlelit dinner on the beach under the warm glow of the tiki torches. Delicious dishes include tuna tartare, rosemary lamb chops, and shrimp risotto. Breakfast is even better, with eggs Benedict, lobster, smoked salmon, and incredible pastries.

And if that is not enough to have you totally smitten, make sure you meet the miniature key deer. They amble through the property freely and, at night, even come to steal bread off your table. With their big eyes and wet noses, they are so lovely it is hard to resist the temptation to take one home. **RCA**

Visit Jules' Undersea Lodge

Location Key Largo, Florida, U.S.A.
Website www.jul.com **Price** 💲💲

Just think of it as a goldfish bowl in reverse. Here, you sit inside the world's only underwater hotel and look out as the fish swim by. Jules' Undersea Lodge was originally a research laboratory, created so that scientists could study the continental shelf off the Puerto Rican coast. Ocean experts Ian Koblick and Neil Monney decided to develop the facility—which sits at the bottom of the Emerald Lagoon in Florida's Key Largo Undersea Park—into a lodge. They named the venture after Jules Verne, author of *Twenty Thousand Leagues Under the Sea*—and managed to fit it out with hot showers, a DVD player, a microwave, and a fridge.

The lodge usually accommodates two couples, although six can stay here at a squeeze. The journey is not exactly straightforward. To reach the lodge, you must scuba dive down 21 feet (6 m), although you do not have to be a qualified diver to do this: In three hours, the Jules' staff can teach you all you need to know. Couples can even get married here—the notary public dives down for the service.

The bedding, admittedly, is not all that romantic. The duvets and pillowcases all have an underwater theme; cuddly fishes are available for those who left their teddy bears at home. Still, this underwater escape has attracted its fair share of notable guests, including former Canadian prime minister Pierre Trudeau, rock star Steve Tyler of Aerosmith, and Jon Fishman of the rather-too-aptly-named Phish.

The big attraction is the real fish, though. Wake up in the morning and you will see angelfish, parrotfish, barracuda, and snappers peering in at you through the windows. Are you watching them? Or are they, perhaps, making their own observations on the behavior of the strange humans inside? **PE**

Explore Islamorada

Location Islamorada, Florida Keys, U.S.A.
Website www.casamorada.com **Price** 💲💲

Pass the first of the Florida Keys—Key Largo, of Bogie and Bacall fame—and stop at Islamorada, the quiet and unpretentious "purple isle." Its most stylish hideout, Casa Morada, was set up by businessmen who decided to escape to the picturesque keys and create a boutique escape with a cool Caribbean feel. With reggae in the air, unfussy white decor, and tall palm trees, it is totally tropical. The bedroom is simple sophistication: an elegant wrought-iron bed swathed in white linens, a single dazzling orchid, and—of course—views over the intense blue waters. The hotel's tiny man-made island, covered in white sand, is home to a glorious pool and a cozy bar where guests gather

> ## "Radiates serenity and style in an area where serenity is aplenty but style elusive."
>
> *New York Times*

at night. At breakfast, fresh muffins, bagels, cake, and fruit make for a tasty start to the day before lying in a hammock, going bonefishing, or heading offshore for wahoo, tuna, or sailfish. After all, Islamorada is the "sport fishing capital of the world."

Another option might be to explore the reef that runs along the keys' entire 110 miles (177 km) or take a drive along the scenic road to Key West, the road itself a masterpiece of early 1900s construction with 43 bridges, including one 7 miles (11 km) long. **RCA**

➡ *The perfect end to a perfect day at Islamorada—enjoy the sunset with a cocktail in your hand.*

Discover Haleakala Volcano

Location Maui, Hawaii, U.S.A. **Website** www.nps.gov/hale
Price 💲

Maui needs no introduction. Synonymous with surfing paradise, this idyllic Hawaiian island has far more to offer—from helicopter tours to horseback riding or diving with turtles and sharks, to biking down a 10,000-foot-high (3,050-m) volcano. The Haleakala volcano, in a 28,655-acre (11,595-ha) park of the same name, earned its name from early Hawaiians who called the summit "house of the sun," believing it rose from behind the volcano's peak. For the best view, get up to the summit to take in the 2-mile- (3.2-km-) wide, nearly 2,600-foot- (800-m-) deep crater coated with fluffy white clouds. Some people cycle up the volcano (the record stands at less than three hours), but the fun

"Visually expansive, the summit eludes any attempt to understand its scale or dimensions."

U.S. National Park Service

part is bicycling the 28-mile (45-km) winding asphalt road down again. Early birds can join a sunrise expedition up to the top, definitely worth it if you can bear the early start around 2:30 A.M. To guarantee a little solitude at the top, you might try going alone on a Sunday—when tour companies are shut—and avoid the "honeymoon season" throughout spring and fall. After watching the stunning sunrise, it's time to whiz down, catching the incredible coastline views on the way: liberating and thrilling. **RCA**

➦ *Maui's terrain is otherworldly—astronauts practiced moon walks here before the 1969 moon landing.*

Unwind at Hana

Location Maui, Hawaii, U.S.A.   **Website** www.slh.com/hanamaui   **Price** 💲💲

Surfing aside, the island of Maui has a wealth of attractions to offer. Part laid-back cool, part glamorous, part outdoorsy, there is something for everyone in this most famous of Hawaiian islands. To really escape from the crowds, however, head east to quiet, unspoiled Hana.

Hit the notorious 52-mile (84-km) "Road to Hana," twisting and turning along the cliff edge. With 600 curves and fifty-four bridges, the narrow route is not for the fainthearted. It is more than just scenic: Dramatic cliffs, lush tropical flowers, and aromas make for an exhilarating drive. The reward is Hana, a very, very quiet spot. It feels a million miles away from Maui's busier commercial side. Indeed, there is little here, aside from a few private villas, said to belong to the likes of Woody Harrelson and Oprah Winfrey, and the Hana-Maui resort, which is actually in the heart of the town, alongside the school, church, and library. Daytimes are spent surfing, swimming, and trekking through the dense tropical forest. At night, the bar and restaurant at the hotel are the only places to meet. Quaint Hawaiian cottages overlooking the wild Pacific coastline blend in with nature, making the most of the trade winds for natural air-conditioning. Rest assured, all other modern conveniences—including a luxurious sunken bathtub, a well-stocked minibar, delicious locally grown coffee, and cookies—are available. The resort has everything you could wish for to relax in style: from a luxurious heated wellness pool, to a fitness room with incomparable Pacific views, an outdoor lava-rock whirlpool, and the Honua Spa. The spa's philosophy is that true balance and health come from the gifts of the earth and nature—a perfect match for Hana, a place of nurturing and well-being among Hawaiian people. **RCA**

⬆ *Find true peace in the Pacific: Hana-Maui offers a wealth of wonders to soothe today's troubled brows.*

Enjoy Esperanza Resort

Location Los Cabos, Mexico   **Website** www.esperanzaresort.com   **Price** 💲💲

You know you have come to the right place when the hotel manager offers a complimentary head and neck massage as soon as you have checked in. Overlooking the glimmering Sea of Cortez and the Pacific Ocean in a breathtakingly natural setting, the Esperanza resort has fifty casitas (small villas) and six luxury suites spread across 17 acres (7 ha) of land.

From the outside, the resort resembles a Mexican village, with casitas connected to the resort's facilities via traditional stone footpaths. The interiors are decidedly elegant, decorated with original Mexican artworks, handcrafted furnishings, and fine Italian linens. Many have large outdoor terraces with views of the ocean, and the in-room amenities include fully stocked minibars and entertainment centers, plus roomy bathrooms with gorgeous complimentary products. The six luxury villas, some of which are situated on a secluded beach, boast larger dimensions as well as private pools and butler service.

You can dine alfresco at the Mediterranean-inspired restaurant at Esperanza, which is carved into the bluffs overlooking the Sea of Cortez and offers 180-degree views from each table. The bar serves appetizers and snacks together with an extensive tequila and cigar menu. With more than one hundred different kinds of tequila to choose from, a visit to the bar can be a little dangerous, although the abundance of activities on offer will soon cure any morning-after fatigue.

You can go whale watching and take a sea trip on a glass-bottom boat as well as fish, surf, dive, and windsurf. Not a water fan? Take a guided tour through the desert and along empty beaches, have a game of tennis, play golf, or ride a horse. Or there are always more of those luxurious massages available in the wonderful all-natural spa. **PS**

⬆ *For those in need of pampering, the idyllic spa offers therapeutic massages and revitalizing treatments.*

Stay at Las Ventanas Al Paraiso

Location Los Cabos, Mexico   **Website** www.lasventanas.com   **Price** 💲💲💲

A camera phone is recommended for a stay at Las Ventanas because no one back home will believe you when you reel off your "spotted" list. The air corridor from Los Angeles to Las Ventanas to Baja California's tip is thick with rock stars, fashion designers, and ex-presidents. Although privacy goes with the territory (there is no sign outside, so taxi drivers and chauffeurs must know where it is), there is no stopping the gushing from the celebs themselves. Jennifer Lopez told *Harper's Bazaar* that her favorite indulgence is "the Spa at Las Ventanas," whereas Jessica Simpson told *Rolling Stone* that the infinity pool is the best in the world. Why do they come? Well, 365 days of sunshine help, but with a fleet of Porsche Boxters for rent, twenty-four-hour butlers, and a palatial pool villa, Las Ventanas deals in only one currency—*la buena vida*.

Xeriscaping (the art of desert landscaping) finds a natural home in this exclusive corner of Mexico, where an eighteen-hole Robert Trent Jones II golf course winds its way around the resort and up the hilly desert landscape. The cacti-studded desert tableau is offset by a series of stunning infinity pools that lick the jewel-blue Sea of Cortez, and the resort's low-slung, whitewashed adobe villas straddle a generous swath of the Los Cabos coast. From the high-precision binoculars that thoughtfully dangle from the sea wall for use during the annual whale parade to the "hot type" unpublished novels that are made available to guests, they have thought of everything here. Romantics can even ride a white stallion for that ultimate beach proposal. Now, that is service.

Oh, and nobody really cares whether or not you have got a Lear jet parked nearby, which is just how it should be. What is good enough for Jennifer Lopez is good enough for the likes of us all. **TM**

⬆ *The Mexican-Mediterranean style of architecture reflects the desert location of this exceptional hotel.*

Hike the Copper Canyon

Location Chihuahua, Mexico
Website www.coppercanyonguide.com **Price** ●❶

Mexico's Copper Canyon, in the Sierra Madre in the state of Chihuahua, is the largest canyon system in the world. Its maze of gorges comprises six interconnecting canyons that are even larger and deeper than the Grand Canyon; they provide awe-inspiring scenery of sheer rock walls, waterfalls, caves, and prime hiking territory. The name of the canyon comes from the copper-colored moss that grows around the canyon.

The canyon is home to the Tarahumara Indians, a seminomadic group who retreated there after the arrival of Spanish explorers in the sixteenth century. Over the years, Jesuit missionaries have also made the canyon their home, and Mennonites too have several settlements in the area. There are also more typical Mexican towns, some of which have a distinctive frontier feel to them, with plenty of cowboys.

To get to the start of your hike, take a train ride on one of the world's most exciting train tracks. From *El Fuerte*, the views are astounding as you pass over thirty-seven bridges, past towering canyon walls and cliffs, and then through eighty-six tunnels in total. There are many day hikes to take in the area, either around the rim of the canyon or down at the bottom, and plenty of guides willing to take you on week-long tours or longer. The rugged trails take you deep into the gorge, and, because many guides are well-acquainted with the local Tarahumara Indians, you might even get an insight into their lives. The hikes offer a chance to glimpse unspoiled wilderness and to enjoy the vast views of the huge canyon. **LD**

➡ *Mexico's Copper Canyon affords ample hiking and walking opportunities for all skill levels.*

Stay at One&Only Palmilla

Location Los Cabos, Mexico
Website www.oneandonlyresorts.com   **Price** 🅢🅢🅢

There are not many places on the planet where you can wriggle your toes in powder-soft sand as you sip a perfect margarita, watching whales glide by in the distance from an infinity pool. One&Only Palmilla, sandwiched between San Jose del Cabo and Cabo San Lucas on the southernmost tip of the Baja Peninsula, is the quintessential chic beach resort—and much more besides. It is the hotel's stunning location, where the Pacific Ocean merges with the Sea of Cortez in the Los Cabos Corridor, that makes it utterly unique.

The ambience of the resort is conducive to serious relaxation. Surrounded by exotic blooms, rooms have terraces or balconies with daybeds overlooking the

> *"[One] of the region's most upscale resorts . . . complete with acres of vanishing pools."*
>
> *New York Times*

dramatic surf—ideal for siestas. You are also provided with a telescope for whale watching or stargazing. The Palmilla first opened in 1956 as a small, exclusive fishing lodge, popular with the likes of John Wayne and Bing Crosby. These days you are more likely to bump into Demi Moore or John Travolta. It is now a luxury beachside oasis complete with first-rate spa, beautifully manicured grounds, and a golf course, and there is still ample opportunity for world-class fishing. We are sure Bing would have approved. **LP**

← *Palmilla's stone fountains, whitewashed walls, and wrought-iron doors hark back to old-world Mexico.*

Enjoy Hotelito Desconocido

Location Jalisco, Mexico
Website www.hotelito.com   **Price** 🅢🅢🅢

If you are looking for the ultimate in eco-friendliness, this has to be it. The Hotelito Desconocido is a haven for nature lovers in the midst of a huge bird and turtle reserve in the wetlands, between the Sierra Madre Mountains and the Pacific Ocean. There is a touch of magic in the air as guests are rowed from the main hotel's lodge across the estuary to their beachside huts, where cacti poke out of the sand.

The colorful rooms are basic yet perfectly charming. Without electricity, the only amenities are a shower, sink, and toilet, as well as a mosquito-netted bed. You can lounge sleepily in shaded hammocks or on the pristine 40-mile (65-km) beach where, at dusk, turtle hatchlings dive into the sea under the gaze of a handful of relaxed guests. The food on offer here is fittingly simple, healthful, and delicious: calamari salad, seviche, and coconut cake.

After dark, signaling with a flashlight summons the boat for a pickup on the room side of the estuary to take you to the extraordinarily decorated El Cantarito restaurant for a candlelit evening meal. Sip a cold beer or a margarita and chat at the bar, or share a game of pool in the bar's dim twilight. Turn-down service involves dozens of tea lights twinkling in the dark, and in lieu of room service, you can hoist a flag up outside your window to indicate you would like a delivery of fresh Mexican coffee and cookies before breakfast. It is definitely different and really rather romantic.

It is quite impossible to remain in touch with the rest of the world here, but that is the entire point. With the closest village a few miles away, Hotelito makes sure you are in a world of your own: the sweetest seclusion. No wonder Madonna, Mick Jagger, and Quentin Tarantino have all hidden out here. **RCA**

Rent a Villa at Cuixmala

Location Jalisco, Mexico   **Website** www.cuixmala.com
Price 💲💲

Modern-day fairy tales do not come much better than this. Cuixmala is a hot resort where luxurious villas are tucked away in a vast 25,000-acre (10,117-ha) ecological reserve fringed by golden beaches. This is a private sanctuary in more ways than one. Come here to rest your head, laze on deserted beaches, and get close to nature. Then discover the birds and animals that have made their home in this eco-reserve—from jaguars and sea turtles to exotic zebras and antelopes.

The top house is Casa La Loma with its distinctive blue and yellow striped dome. It looks like a castle and has a view out across the empty beach of Costa Alegre to the rolling Pacific surf. There are four other villas, fully staffed and decorated in sumptuous Mexican and European designs, as well as nine comfortable casitas (small villas) with a shared pool, clubhouse, and restaurant. Make yourself at home, then explore the organic farm on horseback, past mango and papaya trees, citrus orchards, and all those beaches. Some are perfect for snorkeling and kayaking; others have hammocks strung between coconut palms to escape the sun. Enjoy a picnic on a stretch of unspoiled beach, followed by a boat trip across the lagoon where you can watch the sunset as well as spot dolphins and whales. Finish the day with a cold margarita.

Celebrities adore this super-hip eco-resort. Food served in the gourmet dining room has been grown organically at the ranch or highland farm, and the two-tiered seating in the screening room has Indian pillow-topped settees the size of double beds. Perfect for weary A-listers. **AD**

➡ *The magnificent Casa La Loma was once the tropical hideaway of the late industrialist Sir James Goldsmith.*

Discover Isla Contoy National Park

Location Isla Contoy, Mexico   **Website** www.cancundays.com/islacontoy.php   **Price** 💲

Located at the confluence of the Caribbean Sea and the Gulf of Mexico, Isla Contoy is the most important nesting place for seabirds in all of the Mexican Caribbean. This little island, just 5 miles (8.5 km) long, is a protected nature reserve and a well-known spot for an eco-adventure.

Just 200 visitors are allowed on its silky-sand shores every day, arriving in boats that run from Isla Mujeres or Cancun (approximately a two-hour trip). Here you can sit on the beach and watch the brown pelicans and double-crested cormorants on the water, or head inland to the Puerto Viejo lagoon, an important nesting site. The island is uninhabited, and a trip here is like being a castaway for the day. Climbing up the observation tower provides you with a great view of the whole island.

It is not just the birds that love to nest here. Isla Contoy is an important nesting site for four types of sea turtle, with secluded palm-fringed, white-sand beaches giving them the chance to bury their eggs undisturbed. The water around the island is crystal clear, so you can see from your boat what is going on under the sea: great manta rays swooping around and plenty of tropical fish against a backdrop of coral.

Boat trips to the island typically stop at the Ixlache reef so that visitors can go snorkeling. Giant stingray, primary-colored parrot fish, clown fish, barracuda, and angel fish are just some of the species you might see—not to mention the turtles. Every summer, visitors have the chance to see the world's largest living fish (the whale shark) pass by Cancun—a viewing trip may be incorporated on your watery safari. A trip to the island is certainly an adventurous addition to any journey to this part of the Mexican coast and is not to be missed. **LD**

⬆ *The uninhabited Isla Contoy provides an important habitat for birds and sea creatures in the Caribbean.*

Enjoy the Spa at Esencia

Location Yucatan Peninsula, Mexico
Website www.hotelesencia.com   **Price** ⊖⊖⊖

Along a 2-mile (3.2-km) empty stretch of one of
Mexico's best beaches, you will find Esencia—a quiet,
understated seaside escape on the Mayan Riviera.
The hotel stands in a 50-acre (20-ha) private estate,
with two swimming pools, a day spa, a gourmet
restaurant, and a beguiling beachfront.

From the paths snaking through the lush gardens to
the thatched cabins to shade guests lounging on the
beach, this estate has a simple, relaxed style. The
modern property and many of the buildings once
served as the exclusive winter retreat of an Italian
duchess. Esencia still benefits from her sense of taste.
The hotel itself is a whitewashed low-rise stucco
building with dark-wood shutters, terra-cotta-tiled
roofs, and verandas. In front are lawns, decks, and sofas
leading down to the white sands.

Esencia's circular spa is set in a quiet corner of the
estate. It offers an array of treatments using indigenous
fruits, plants, and herbs, many of which are grown in
the garden. There are five treatment rooms, four
whirlpool tubs, and two Mayan-style domed steam
rooms. Treatments include massage, herbal saunas,
and facials, all performed with traditional organic
methods. Yoga and meditation classes are also available.

Bedrooms are simple and elegant, featuring native
hardwood furnishings, white walls and floors, high
ceilings, louvered doors, and windows with sea and
garden views. A private chef is available, but most
meals are eaten at the Sal Y Fuego Restaurant, which
offers rustic Mexican cuisine, including fresh local
ingredients and indigenous cooking methods. **SH**

⊡ *The cool modern architectural style of the Esencia
displays elegance, luxury, and impeccable taste.*

Relax at Chimino

Location Laguna Petexbatún, Guatemala
Website www.chiminosisland.com **Price** $

The sudden screech of a rogue howler monkey may wake you in the middle of the night or you may be startled by a crocodile swimming past the window of your room, but that is all part of the appeal of staying at one of the world's top eco-archaeology escapes.

Chimino is a fortified island set in a huge lagoon deep in the Guatemalan jungle. Guests stay in one of five modern rustic houses built from local mahogany trees that had already fallen. Their roofs are draped with shaggy palm thatch. These houses, which sleep up to five, stand hundreds of feet from one another, overlooking the lagoon. Colorful toucans and parrots perch on branches outside, staring in, as interested in you as you are in them. The houses may look primitive, but inside they are equipped with simple beds, hot water, and bathrooms. You may feel up close and intimate with the jungle, but the owners assure guests that the bungalows are insect- and animal-proof.

A similar central building has a bar, restaurant, terrace, and hammocks. Down on the water, there is a floating wooden deck for sunbathing, swimming, canoeing, or fishing. The lodge cook prepares fresh fish from the lagoon for a traditional regional dinner.

The teeming wildlife is just part of the island's appeal. Many visitors come to see the overgrown tumbling stone ruins. Easy paths from the bungalows lead to the remains of an impressive Mayan citadel, including its defensive walls, ceremonial pyramids, and palaces. It is believed it was home to a branch of the Mayan royal family between 600 and 900 C.E., who barricaded themselves here as their civilization mysteriously declined. Even they found it a good place to relax: Deep in the jungle, archaeologists have unearthed a court for playing ball games. **SH**

Stay at La Lancha

Location Near Tikal, Guatemala
Website www.blancaneaux.com **Price** $

Francis Ford Coppola's latest exotic jungle lodge recalls scenes from his epic *Apocalypse Now*. The movie mogul opened La Lancha on the shores of Lake Petén Itzá deep in the Guatemalan rain forest. However, you will not find Marlon Brando muttering "the horror, the horror" here. Coppola has created a desirable escape perched on a steep jungle hillside, with a two-tier swimming pool with its own waterfall, an open-sided restaurant overlooking the lake, and beautifully decorated Mayan-style casitas (small villas) to stay in.

The casitas have basic wooden decks and balconies with views through the trees and across the lake. Inside are simple whitewashed walls, tiled floors, high

> *"I loved the unspoiled area with howler monkeys living just outside the deck of my room."*
>
> Francis Ford Coppola, director

wooden ceilings, and marble bathrooms. Color comes from Mayan wall hangings, rugs, cushions, and sofas. There is a restaurant, relaxed all-day bar, sun terrace with sofas and a fountain, and a small beach area on the lake. Guests can relax, take boat trips, go kayaking, fishing, or horseback riding, or take Spanish lessons. Farther afield, there are splendid Mayan ruins. The hotel arranges excursions to all of them, plus early morning bird-watching trips—watch out for toucans, parrots, kingfishers, hummingbirds, and vultures. **SH**

➡ *La Lancha has a thatched-roof restaurant open to the forest where local and Italian food is served.*

Unwind at Nitun Reserve

Location San Andrés, Guatemala   **Website** www.nitun.com
Price $$

Although not the most luxurious of escapes, there is something uniquely peaceful about curling up in a hammock at Nitun and watching the hummingbirds hover above you. Special feeders are hung around this eco-lodge so guests can see six different species of these tiny colorful birds perform their acrobatics.

Nitun was set up by a former coffee plantation owner in the rain forest alongside Lake Petén Itzá. It is an exciting place, with palm-thatched buildings built from rock and wood among the trees along the shoreline. The interior is as different from a corporate hotel as you can get—with rough stone and log floors and simple furniture. Nitun does not feel like a

> *"Once ensconced in this verdant beauty ... the temptation is to find a hammock and never leave."*
>
> Lucas Vidgen, journalist

luxury intrusion into the forest, but a cozy part of the environment. However, there are still fans, fly screens, and private bathrooms with plenty of hot water.

The central lodge is a two-story house containing a restaurant, bar, and lounge. The food prepared in the open-plan kitchen has been acclaimed as some of the best in the country. Days are spent exploring the forest on wildlife treks and boat trips around the lake. The site is surrounded by a nature reserve, and the owners run things on strict ecological lines. **SH**

← *The lodgings at Nitun Reserve are welcoming yet rustic, in keeping with its jungle surroundings.*

Enjoy Villa Sumaya

Location Lake Atitlan, Guatemala   **Website** www.villasumaya.com
Price $$

There is more to Guatemala than dense jungle, as this atmospheric retreat demonstrates perfectly. Villa Sumaya sits high in the mountains at 4,500 feet (1,370 m), on the shore of a beautiful lake, in lush orchid gardens facing the peaks of three conical volcanoes. The stunning landscape is at the heart of the Guatemalan highlands, and this picturesque and unpretentious hotel is a great place to stay to explore the surroundings.

Villa Sumaya stands on the edge of Lake Atitlan and was once the vacation home of a wealthy Guatemalan family. It has been converted into a hotel that is so peaceful and inspiring it has become renowned as a center for yoga and meditation breaks. Amid all this natural beauty, the hotel buildings have traditional thatched roofs and open sides to reveal the stunning panorama. There are stone paths winding through the terraces, where you will find sun loungers, a hot tub, saunas, and pergolas.

The cabanas are simple but comfortable. The color scheme is muted earthy brown and ocher, with handmade tiled floors, wicker chairs, candles, and hammocks. The decor consists of Mayan textiles and local folk art. You will spend most time on the spacious veranda, though, gazing at the view across the lake.

At the lakeside is the Blue Tiger Temple, the venue for all sorts of events and classes: yoga, dance, meditation, massage, aromatherapy, tai chi, Reiki, shamanistic ceremonies, impromptu drama, and family reunions. The pretty restaurant stands next to a fountain and serves a healthful blend of international and local food. The specialty is fresh fish from the lake, and it is hard to resist the smell of homemade bread and tortillas that drifts across the gardens daily. **SH**

Enjoy Parrot Nest Lodge

Location Cayo, Belize   **Website** www.parrot-nest.com
Price $

If your idea of a tropical getaway is spending a night in a thatched tree house at the top of a 100-foot (30-m) guanacaste tree in the depths of the Belize rain forest, then you need look no further than the splendid isolation of Parrot Nest Lodge.

Just a short drive from the tourist town of San Ignacio and enclosed on three sides by the Mopan River, Parrot Nest Lodge is an eclectic world of rustic yet comfortable living set amid lush, landscaped gardens. It provides an ideal base for exploring the many natural wonders of the surrounding Cayo district. The lodge offers full- and half-day trips that will take you into the depths of Belize's forests. A full-day excursion to the Rio Frio cave followed by a swim in the temperate waters of the cave's nearby rock pools is a must, as is a visit to Big Rock Falls and the recently discovered Mayan ruins at Caracol.

Half-day trips, for example, include horseback riding and dropping into a local Mennonite community at Barton Creek outpost. You can take a canoe through the Barton Creek caves with experienced guides from Parrot Nest Lodge, who will explain the formation of the cave and navigate its labyrinth of passages. Or why not just float downstream on the Mopan River on one of the lodge's giant inner tubes that will leisurely transport you past the spectacular Bullet Tree Falls. Along the way you can be guaranteed a sighting of the river's resident iguanas, and maybe even catch a glimpse of one of its giant otters.

The crystal clear waters of the Mopan River make it ideal for a long refreshing swim, and treks from the lodge that head along a series of so-called "medicinal trails" will take in some of the numerous examples of the region's rich medicinal flora. **BS**

Stay at Blancaneaux

Location San Ignacio, Belize   **Website** www.blancaneaux.com
Price $ $

Nestled in the Mountain Pine Ridge Forest Reserve, close to the Maya Mountains, Blancaneaux was once a lodge for jaguar hunting. When film director Francis Ford Coppola fell for the area sometime after Belize's independence in 1981, he snapped up this property as a retreat for family and friends; after extensive renovations he opened Blancaneaux Lodge in 1993.

Today Blancaneaux boasts cabanas and villas overseeing the river, all with screened porches, showers, and Japanese baths. Luxury cabanas add a walled garden with outdoor shower to the equation, and the Enchanted Cottage also has a fireplace in the bathroom and a steam room. There are seven family-

---

"Beautifully decorated, the staff are terrific, the food is good, and the sense of escape complete."

Daily Telegraph

---

sized villas; you can even rent out Coppola's own, complete with art and personal memorabilia. One of the two restaurants, Montagna, reflects Coppola's love of southern Italian dishes, and you can sip fine wines from his own Californian estates in Napa and Sonoma.

As Blancaneaux boasts its own stables, horse treks into the forest are a must. There are a multitude of Mayan ruins in the reserve nearby; after a day of sightseeing, guests can unwind with a Thai massage in the spa—all this and not a jaguar in sight. **PS**

➡ *Subtle nighttime lighting at one of Blancaneaux's two swimming pools adds to the exotic atmosphere.*

Snorkel at Hol Chan Reserve

Location Hol Chan Reserve, Belize
Website www.holchanbelize.org **Price** $

Just off the balmy tropical coast of Belize lies one of the world's greatest natural wonders—a 180-mile- (290-km-) long coral reef second only in extent to Australia's Great Barrier Reef. Although it may be smaller, Belize boasts one significant advantage over its antipodean rival: ease of access.

In places, the reef sits less than 1,000 feet (300 m) from the shore in calm, shallow, almost crystal-clear waters that make snorkeling the reef about as easy and laid-back an experience as you could wish for. The reef is a biologically intense environment, providing homes to a vast assortment of creatures—from brightly colored, almost fluorescent fish to giant manta rays and marine turtles—who weave in and out of the strange, undulating coral structures.

Renting a kayak and snorkeling gear to undertake your own coral exploration will set you back just a few Belizean dollars. For other rewarding wildlife-watching opportunities, take an organized tour, which will take you to some of the reef's more hard-to-reach spots. The most renowned is probably the Hol Chan Reserve, named after a narrow gap in the reef cut hundreds of years ago by local Maya tribes as an access passage for their boats. Today it acts as a bottleneck for marine animals traveling between the waters inside the reef and the open seas beyond. It is a particularly good place for spotting large fish, such as sharks, groupers, and barracuda, great numbers of which assemble both here and at the evocatively named Shark Ray Alley, where guides are allowed to bribe the fish with food to make an appearance. **JF**

→ *The shallow, turquoise waters of the seas around Belize provide endless opportunity for snorkeling.*

Stay at Sabalos Jungle Lodge

Location Los Guatuzos Nature Reserve, Nicaragua
Website www.sabaloslodge.com   **Price** ⓢ

From the frontier town of San Carlos, a two-hour panga ride on the coffee-colored waters of Nicaragua's Rio San Juan will bring you to the riverbank huts of Sabalos Lodge. Partially hidden by the dense greenery of Los Guatuzos Wildlife Refuge, the seven cabins offer wilderness accommodation at its most adventurous. Yaró Choiseul-Praslin owns the lodge, a silver-haired Sandinista who led the agricultural reforms of the 1980s. His tales of revolution regale the multinational visitors who venture into the jungle. Wooden walkways lead to an open-sided dining room and to the huts scattered among the jungle foliage. Sparse

---

"[I dined] to a background of oscillating crickets and the chirpy banter of frogs."

Joe Cawley, *Guardian*

---

on refinements, the huts offer soft mattresses, mosquito nets, private bathrooms with water, and electricity—at least until 9 P.M., when the generator is switched off and the lodge is plunged into darkness.

Lying in bed, listening to the soundtrack of jungle life, it is easy to imagine that this is virgin territory, uncharted by all but the most daring, but for centuries, pirates and buccaneers navigated this river. Downstream is El Castillo, a fortress laying testimony to those trying to thwart such attacks. Local excursions include wildlife walks and kayaking, although the true beauty of a stay at Sabalos Lodge need not extend far beyond the gentle sway of a hammock. **JC**

Relax at Morgan's Rock Hacienda and Eco-lodge

Location San Juan del Sur, Nicaragua
Website www.morgansrock.com   **Price** ⓢⓢ

It is said that good things come to those who wait. In the case of Morgan's Rock in Nicaragua it could not be more true. After an exciting journey in a tiny propeller plane to Granada's landing strip, there is a two-hour drive on bumpy roads. Past Lake Nicaragua, past scrawny dogs and barefoot children, past overcrowded buses and horse-drawn carts, it is a long way to the dirt track leading to this exclusive eco-resort hidden deep in the rain forest.

Arriving at the lodge is like stepping into the Garden of Eden: Giant butterflies flutter in the lush forest. The tempting pool enhances the picture-perfect view of the dazzling ocean below. With just fourteen cottages, the lodge offers high-end tourism with a taste of nature. Big on reforestation and sustainable development, as well as guest pampering, Morgan's Rock Lodge aims to become entirely self-sufficient.

Reaching the eco-designer cabins requires a mini Indiana Jones adventure: walking the solid hanging bridge suspended 72 feet (22 m) over the canopy. The cabins blend in perfectly with the environment: emerald tones, netting for walls, eucalyptus pillars, and decadent hanging daybeds.

The noise of the Pacific and its sonorous waves crashing onto the beach below is overwhelming, and the sounds of nature are all around. The 6 A.M. coffee delivery is surprisingly welcome, signaling time to join the turtle hatchlings fleeing into the surf. There is so much to do: surfing, kayaking, fishing, or even riding with Jesus, the weathered animal whisperer. **RCA**

➡ *Morgan's Rock has its own stables so that guests can ride through the ecosystems, ending up on the beach.*

Stay at El Silencio

Location Bajos del Toro, Costa Rica
Website www.elsilenciolodge.com **Price** 🟢🟢🟢

Steeped in its own cloud forest reserve, El Silencio is a sophisticated retreat of just sixteen elegant villas. Each is poised on the jungle-clad hillside so that there are perfect views of mountain and forest through huge windows. The design is simple, using natural materials, and yet is utterly luxurious: Expanses of polished wood and woven bamboo sit well with bathrooms of polished stone with rain-head showers. Step out onto the private balcony and there is an open hot tub. Surely this is damaging the fragile ecosystem? Not a bit—the retreat is entirely carbon neutral. El Silencio is silent, too. Whereas Costa Rica's most famous cloud forest at Monteverde attracts hordes of visitors, El

> "In the country that invented eco-tourism, El Silencio sets a new standard for responsible luxury."

concierge.com

Silencio offers the same breathtakingly diverse wildlife, but without the crowds. Your dedicated eco-concierge will accompany you up magical trails through dense forest to three lovely waterfalls.

You could use El Silencio as a base to go rafting, visit coffee plantations, or see Poás volcano, with its steaming turquoise crater. But the magic of El Silencio lies in doing nothing—other than eating exquisite organic food created by chef Marco González, and yielding to pampering in the spa. **CD**

⬅ *The simple wood and bamboo design of the villas works in harmony with the natural surroundings.*

Stay at La Cusinga Lodge

Location Parque Nacional Marino Ballena, Costa Rica
Website www.lacusingalodge.com **Price** 🟢🟢

There are countless eco-lodges in Costa Rica. Few, however, live up to their environmental credentials as well as La Cusinga on the country's Pacific Coast. All of the lodge's cabins and furniture have been made using wood grown on-site in a sustainable plantation, electricity is provided by hydro and solar power, and the food served here is harvested locally or caught fresh from the ocean. Never fear, this is no Spartan back-to-basics hideaway. It may preach a green message, but it also offers a supreme level of comfort and cooking, allowing you to relax in a glorious natural setting without feeling too guilty about the environmental impact of your actions.

The lodge's greatest asset is its location, perched on a hill overlooking a bay where every year thousands of humpback whales arrive to breed. All around grows thick, lush rain forest where dazzling tropical birds (including the toucan, after which the lodge is named) feed on fruits, and white-faced capuchin monkeys scamper excitedly in the treetops.

The luxuries here are all organic. There are no hot tubs, but in the jungle you will find a crystal-clear pool where you can swim alongside iridescent fish. Sun loungers have no place on this beach, a stretch of chocolate-colored sand backed by a swaying border of palm trees, and entertainment comes courtesy of the startling sunsets, the rhythmic pulsing drone of a million cicadas, and the roars of howler monkeys.

The lodge is also well positioned for exploring some of Costa Rica's natural wonders. To the north is Cerro Chirripó, the country's tallest mountain, and to the south is the ecologically stunning Parque Nacional Corcovado, one of the largest swaths of virgin rain forest outside of the Amazon Basin. **JF**

Raft the Pacuare River

Location Pacuare River, Costa Rica   **Website** www.ticotravel.com
Price $

The Pacuare River stretches 18 miles (29 km) from San Martín to Siquirres and there are fifty-two rapids along the way, including those of the 5-mile (8-km) Pacuare River Gorge, which is considered to have some of the most exciting white water in South America. If you cannot imagine what battling white water in an inflatable raft might feel like, one of the gorge's rapids is named the "pinball." Yet the river, whose rapids range from class two to class four, is suitable for novices with a guide—just don't expect to stay dry.

There are peaceful stretches, too. After the adrenalin-pumping gorge, where you paddle for all you are worth across foaming eddies and through bottlenecks strewn with boulders, you will arrive at the tranquil Valle del Pacuare where the teal-green waters run smooth. The river borders the Talamanca mountain range, renowned for its wealth of wildlife, and here you will have the chance to catch your breath and admire the untouched wilderness through which you are floating. You will pass through virgin rain forest where vertiginous gorges are spotted with glittering waterfalls. Toucans and parrots soar above the canopy, watching monkeys who leap from branch to branch. You may also see ocelots and sloths while over the water and through the trees dancing morpho butterflies flash their vivid, metallic-blue wings.

Several guides offer the Pacuare River rafting trip; most work out of the town of Turrialba in Cartago province. The 18 miles (29 km) are usually completed in four hours, but some visitors opt to extend their rafting journey to two days. **PE**

➔ *A trip in a raft down the Pacuare River is a great way to immerse yourself in Costa Rica's stunning nature.*

Unwind at Pacuare Lodge

Location Siquirres, Costa Rica
Website www.junglelodgecostarica.com   **Price** 💲💲

As the raft enters the rapid and starts spinning, buffeted by an unseen force of water, there is no time to feel exhilaration or panic. Your guide is instructing you to paddle madly, and in another moment the raft goes soaring up, only to deliver you with one rushing surge, breathless and drenched, on the calm river again. Soon, this experience becomes nearly pleasurable.

Pausing at a waterfall to wallow in warm shallows, the surroundings are idyllic: Dense virgin rain forest rises up from the river, and tall trees sprouting orchids send long lianas trailing down into the flowing water. After another bout of rapids, it is a relief when the rafts come ashore at a clearing in the jungle. Here, as if miraculously, you'll see a beautiful wooden palenque and staff emerging with goblets of cold lemonade. This is Pacuare Lodge, hidden on a bend in the river in 25,000 acres (10,115 ha) of deep, protected forest. Accessed only by raft (although children may come by jeep and cross the river in a basket), the Pacuare experience starts with adventure, but ends with a deep sense of peace. Hundreds of species of birds can be seen in the beautiful gardens, and you will wake to the sound of howler monkeys calling through the forest.

Garden-view rooms are simple wooden palm-thatched cabins, open on all sides to the exotic gardens, but choose the much grander river-view cabins for their extensive space, verandas with hammocks, and stylish outdoor showers. As night falls, candles are lit, and guests gather in the palenque to sip caipirinhas before a superb three-course meal—carpaccio of fresh tuna, filet mignon, seared tilapia—served by local staff who are genuinely delighted to welcome you to their paradise. There can be no more romantic place to be marooned. **CD**

Relax at La Paloma Lodge

Location Drake Bay, Costa Rica
Website www.lapalomalodge.com   **Price** 💲💲

Many hotels in Costa Rica call themselves remote, but not all require a two-hour boat trip through mangrove swamps and out into the Pacific Ocean. Hidden high up in the jungle overlooking the beauty of Drake Bay (Sir Francis clearly enjoyed the view, too), on the southern tip of Costa Rica, La Paloma Lodge attracts mainly nature lovers who have come to discover the Parque National Corcovado and is both luxurious and designed in aesthetic harmony with the environment.

A twenty-minute boat ride takes visitors to the park office, from where multilingual guides lead parties into more than 100,000 acres (40,470 ha) of virgin and secondary rain forest. Other tours include kayaking,

> ## "Corcovado—the most biologically intense place on earth."
>
> *National Geographic*

horseback riding, bird-watching, and a particularly unforgettable and fascinating night-bug tour—not one for arachnophobes, certainly. Caño Island, 12 nautical miles (22.2 km) off the Osa Peninsula, as the whole area is known, is an archaeologist's dream. Perfectly round spheres, varying in size from a soccer ball to some 6.5 feet (2 m) high, were brought to the island by pre-Columbian indigenous groups. It still remains a historic puzzle.

For those who want more privacy, there are seven deluxe "Sunset Ranchos," two-story cabins perched on a cliff top, with only the melody of the jungle and the crashing of the Pacific to disturb the silence. **DN**

Enjoy Lapa Rios Eco-lodge

Location Osa Peninsula, Costa Rica
Website www.laparios.com **Price** 💲💲

Lapa Rios is tucked away in the Osa peninsula, one of the most biologically diverse regions in the world. Some 375,000 acres (152,000 ha) make it one of the largest existing wet forests on the Pacific Coast of Mesoamerica. It boasts the "who's who of endangered species," from puma to ocelot and tapir, and the rain forest is teeming with wildlife.

Set in 1,000 acres (405 ha) of private rain forest, the fourteen-bungalow lodge is all about sustainable development, supporting the environment and the local community—built to prove that "a forest left standing is worth more than one cut down." The main wooden lodge is thatched and furnished with wicker. Atop a wooden spiral staircase some 33 feet (10 m) above the dining room, the observation deck offers views from tropical rain forest to the Pacific coastline.

The local food is a revelation. Red snapper, burritos, or fajitas are served up in banana leaves. The smiling staff are jovial and eager to perfect their English. The fish seviche is tangy and fresh, tender pieces of fish blended with exotic fruit and lime juice, as well as sweet peppers and cilantro. Grilled jumbo shrimps taste surprisingly sweet on their olive linguine followed by sweet homemade brownies with macadamia nuts accompanied by glorious local coffee.

The bungalows are stunning, with wooden flooring, white and dark green linens, and romantic mosquito nets over the bed. Luxuries are kept to a bare minimum—with no televisions or phones, of course. Nip into the outside shower to hear the symphony from the jungle, or head to the cliff-top pool. Toucans, parrots, and scarlet macaws sit patiently while howler monkeys growl in the distance. The total immersion in nature is both invigorating and beguiling. **RCA**

Stay at Cambridge Beaches

Location Somerset, Bermuda
Website www.cambridgebeaches.com **Price** 💲💲

One look at Bermuda's famous pink-sand beaches and it is easy to see why Catherine Zeta-Jones and Michael Douglas call this subtropical paradise "home." Given their warm blush tones by particles of crushed coral, the pastel-colored sands literally glow alongside the clear turquoise waters.

Everywhere you turn in Bermuda, you see color. The azure waters of the ocean mirror the deep-blue sky. Wedged in between are candy-colored houses, in shades of green, pink, and yellow, nestled in lush green subtropical foliage. At the stunning Cambridge Beaches in Somerset, guests stay in luxury cottages painted in pastel pink. With four sandy beaches and

> *"For snob appeal, Cambridge Beaches is numero uno in Bermuda."*
>
> *New York Times*

coves lined with palm trees, it is a water lover's paradise. Dipping below the surface, snorkelers can admire the brightly colored tropical fish and exquisite coral sculptures. Divers can explore the skeletons of wrecked ships that rest on the sandy seabed. At night, guests fill the waterside alfresco restaurant Breezes.

Candlelit tables are set up on the powdery sand, and the Atlantic Ocean laps just a few feet away. For the ultimate romantic dining experience, staff will arrange dinner on a private island. Diners are escorted by speedboat to a sandy key, where a candlelit table awaits. After the meal, guests are returned to the resort, and the rising tides reclaim the island again. **JP**

Rent a Villa on Salt Cay

Location Salt Cay, Turks and Caicos
Website www.saltcay.org **Price** $

Salt Cay calls itself "the island that time forgot," because since the salt trade dried up, it has stood still. All around it, Caribbean islands have soaked up the tourist traffic and grown luxury hotels; 2-mile-long (3.2-km) Salt Cay, however, has planted its feet in the past. Here, you can rent a villa that has no key—because you do not need one. Roosters wake you in the morning; there are few cars; cell phones have no reception.

The island is not just for those who wish to switch off and enjoy rum punch, sunsets, and grilled fish. Divers admire the pristine reefs, especially the 7,000-foot (2,134-m) Columbus Passage, a top drift-diving destination. Between 3,000 and 5,000 North Atlantic

> *"Buoyed by margaritas and somewhat sunburned, we ended the day very happy campers."*
>
> *Guardian*

humpback whales migrate around these islands every year, from December to mid-April, making it the world's largest humpback whale breeding grounds.

Only around eighty people live on Salt Cay. Tourism is still small scale, and you might find yourself one of the only non-natives here. You certainly will have a large part of the island's white-sand beaches to yourself for romantic strolls, beachcombing, and whatever it is we did with our time before technology and the modern world cluttered it up. **LD**

← *If you have ever thought, "Stop the world, I wanna get off," head back in time to Salt Cay.*

Discover Cayo Levisa

Location Archipiélago de los Colorados, Cuba
Website www.cubahotelbookings.com **Price** ◐

A two-hour road trip from Havana gets you to Palma Rubia, a one-horse town and jumping-off point for the Archipiélago de los Colorados, a cluster of tiny islands facing the Florida straits, enveloped by thick jungles of tropical mangrove and bordered by sugar-white, soft-sand beaches. Most idyllic among these is Cayo Levisa, where the virgin sands look across to the nearby black-coral reef and the daily grind has never been invented. There's nowhere to stay except twenty little bungalows, dotted among the pine trees, simply and rustically put together with local materials, and right on the beach.

The outdoor bar is the focal point in the evenings, and the friendly barmen keep the cocktails and the Cuban music flowing. Other than the bar and grill, there is one restaurant, and that is it. The only thing that could disturb you are the day-trippers who arrive mid-morning and leave late afternoon. There is abundant marine life, with snorkeling and diving on tap—this region is home to one of the largest coral reefs in the world, and there are about twenty-three identified dive sites within a forty-five-minute boat ride.

The joy of Cayo Levisa is that it is completely different from other Cuban resorts, which are, with the exception of a few places, almost all soulless all-inclusive vast "party" venues block-booked by cheap package vacation companies. This, by contrast, is practically your own private island; just 1.8 miles (3 km) of fabulous white sand washed by a warm clear aquamarine sea. The island is just several hundred yards wide at most points. The archipelago includes Cayo Paraíso, an even smaller little island reputed to be a favorite fishing haunt of Ernest Hemingway. All in all, a dreamy Caribbean paradise. **LB**

Explore the Viñales Valley

Location Pinar del Rio, Cuba
Website www.cubahotelbookings.com **Price** ❶

If you want to see a valley so magnificent that it gets you thinking about what the Garden of Eden might have looked like, travel to Cuba. Richly fertile, with endless tobacco, sugarcane, and coffee plantations, the western province of Pinar del Rio is blessed with a lush greenness, beautiful rivers, and natural springs. The pretty village of Viñales is tucked into the breathtaking Sierra de los Organos mountains, and the Viñales Valley is UNESCO-protected. A glance from the road down to the town will tell you why: Nothing can prepare you for your first view of the mogotes—tree-covered limestone knolls, molded by underground rivers, rising dramatically out of green landscape.

"We are only 150 kilometers from Havana, but millions of years away."

Reina María Rodríguez, Cuban poet and novelist

The eerily quiet, humid, countryside can be explored on foot, bike, or horse. The sleepy village of Viñales itself is a classic small Cuban country town, with a strip of colonial-style bungalows painted in various pastel shades overlooked by pines. Most of the houses are a good deal smarter and the owners more house proud than the average Cuban campesino. This is the best place to sample rural Cuban hospitality, too: The people are friendly, sweet, courteous, and helpful, more so than any streetwise Habanero. **LB**

➔ *With its distinctive round-topped hills, the valley is an outstanding example of natural beauty.*

Relax at Saba Rock Bar

Location Virgin Gorda, British Virgin Islands
Website www.sabarock.com **Price** 💲💲

"Remote" and "idyllic" are words that spring to mind when you come across the tiny island turned watering hole for passing yachts. Accessible by boat or seaplane, Saba Rock benefits from that "end of the world" feeling, probably because it appears to have been carelessly dropped into the Caribbean Sea. In the North Sound of Virgin Gorda in the British Virgin Islands, Saba Rock is wedged right between the Bitter End Yacht Club and the uninhabited national park of Prickly Pear Island. Just a stone's throw from the island is the renowned Eustatia Reef, a snorkeling heaven and home to yellow-head jaw fish, sail-fin blennies, angelfish, and sea horses, among others.

"By far the Caribbean's least spoiled inhabited island, Saba is spectacular."

Condé Nast Traveler

With a colorful history rich in pirate tales featuring everyone from Bluebeard to Captain Kidd, the rock is still one of the yachting crowd's favorite stops. Its relaxed Caribbean vibe is enhanced by the dark wooden decks, palm trees, crystal-clear waters, and local air-conditioning: overhead ceiling fans gently whirring with the sweetly scented trade winds.

Watch the world go by with a cool drink, or hit the hammock. At night, the bar and restaurant come alive with steel bands. If you don't want to get back below deck, check into one of their nine rooms and suites. There's no doubt that Saba Rock is one of the coolest bars on Earth—or rather, on sea. **RCA**

Visit Biras Creek

Location Virgin Gorda, British Virgin Islands
Website www.biras.com **Price** 💲💲💲

The archipelago of the British Virgin Islands includes some sixty volcanic isles surging out of the sea with a jagged, rough coastline dotted with pristine white-sand beaches. None is more idyllic than Biras Creek, a low-key hideaway on the northeastern tip of Virgin Gorda. The island, first named the "Pregnant Virgin" by Christopher Columbus because of its rotund shape, was rechristened the "Fat Virgin" when the technical impossibility of its original name dawned on him.

Biras Creek, accessible only by boat, is in a unique setting, wedged between the peaceful Caribbean Sea and the Atlantic Ocean. The journey over the tempting waters is full of promises. From the arrival at the jetty, with its aquamarine waters amid the mangroves, to the smiling faces all around, guests and staff alike, the ambience is utterly enchanting. No matter which way you turn, you are surrounded by tones of brilliant blue.

Each view is reminiscent of glossy brochures selling paradise. They say that there are three different paces here: slow, slower, and full stop. Borrow a bike to explore, or a Boston Whaler dinghy to visit the nearby deserted beaches of Prickly Pear Island or watch the wildlife go by: Geckos and the grumpy iguanas wander around oblivious to their human neighbors. Spend a lazy day on the beach interrupted only by the tasty lunchtime grill, snorkel in the limpid sea, hit the gym or even the spa.

With recently revamped suites, an affiliation to the Relais & Chateaux group (synonymous with gourmet cuisine and top-end service), the 140-acre (57-ha) estate feels like a private tropical sanctuary. **RCA**

➡ *The view over the creek itself is always idyllic, whether in bright sunshine or the fading light of the evening.*

Enjoy Virgin Gorda's Baths

Location Virgin Gorda, British Virgin Islands
Website www.bvi.com **Price** $

There is more to be seen in the Virgin Islands than deserted beaches lined with swaying palm trees tucked away among the many tiny coves and inlets.

On Virgin Gorda, the third-largest island, one of the hottest attractions is the natural miracle dubbed "The Baths." They are exotic pools and grottos formed by giant granite boulders that appeared approximately 70 million years ago when molten rock merged into the layers of lava on the Caribbean seabed. The magma slowly formed enormous pieces of granite made of feldspar and quartz. Some 50 million years later, a shift in the continental plates lifted the seabed and the granite was exposed.

"A bed of sand with massive granite boulders . . . strewn in irregular piles along the coast"

Condé Nast Traveler

Arrive early to have the place to yourself, pay the $3 fee, and walk into the grottoes, a magical place where it is easy to lose your bearings. Hidden rooms with shafts of light and transparent shallow waters are almost surreal. Some pools are deep enough for snorkeling, but be careful of the north swell. Follow the trail to the white-sand beach, where boulders are scattered. One of the beaches below the Baths, the Crawl, even has its own lagoon, protected by the rocks with a reef busy with turtles, rays, and sea horses. **RCA**

← *Unspoiled and lush, the exotic British Virgin Islands offer a wealth of sea, sun, sand, and solitude.*

Snorkel at Peter Island

Location Peter Island, British Virgin Islands
Website www.peterisland.com **Price** $

After a long flight, followed by a transfer on a tiny eight-seater propeller plane, hopping on board the launch to get to the private shores of Peter Island is a real thrill. On arrival in the all-inclusive tropical haven, a golf cart whizzes you to your plush room, where the Caribbean views stretch all around.

Although the resort has the requisite trimmings, from a huge spa to live music and luxurious rooms, the real attraction is in the crystal-clear waters. Head to Deadman's Beach, named after Blackbeard left fifteen pirates stranded across the water on Dead Chest with just one bottle of rum. One escaped and made it to the shore. The rest, as they say, is history.

Within yards of the sand, you will be immersed in snorkeling heaven, swimming among a rainbow of blue tangs, orange and yellow long-snout butterfly fish, and shimmering purple-hued Creole wrasses. Farther afield, toward the waters known as the "Indians," there is more prime underwater viewing with moray eel, sea turtles, trumpet fish, and bar jacks weaving through the brain corals. The area is dotted with protected dive sites such as Salt Island's 310-foot- (95-m-) deep wreck, which is recognized as one of the world's best. Hop onto the ferry to Jost Van Dyke Island, an unspoiled oasis with just 150 inhabitants. Explore the picture-postcard waters off Diamond Cay or the atoll of Sandy Spit, a tiny, pristine, palm-fringed islet and snorkeling favorite.

At the end of the day, reward yourself with a rum and coconut "Painkiller" cocktail at the Soggy Dollar Bar, which was once accessible only by swimming to shore, or join the yachting crowd at Foxy's, the beach shack where Foxy himself tells his dubious jokes between Calypso renditions. **RCA**

Go Diving in Little Cayman

Location Little Cayman, Cayman Islands
Website www.paradise-divers.com   **Price** 🌔

Little Cayman is said to be tiny—just 10 miles (16 km) long by 1 mile (1.6 km) wide, with a handful of permanent residents—but that only counts the part above water. The Cayman Islands make up an underwater mountain range whose peaks just poke their tips beyond the surface. Underneath, there are cliffs and drop-offs that create some of the most renowned diving sites in the world. Most famous are Bloody Bay and Jackson Blight, two distinct walls that both fall within Little Cayman's Bloody Bay Marine Park.

Bloody Bay's wall starts at just 20 feet (6 m) below the water's surface but it drops to 1,000 feet (305 m) or more—some claim the wall plunges a staggering 6,000 feet (1,829 m). The wall is covered in sponges and corals in extraordinary shades of red and yellow. Starfish undulate infinitely slowly, while moray eels dart their toothy heads in and out of the crevices. Gaudy angelfish, butterfly fish, and parrot fish show off their vibrant hues as they scoot alongside elongated trumpet fish with tubular snouts. Eagle rays and stingrays, sharks, barracudas, and groupers swim nearby, as do the turtles for whom the Cayman Islands were originally named—when Christopher Columbus arrived here in 1503 he named the islands "Las Tortugas." All this is set against the incredible azure waters of the Caribbean Sea.

Above the water, Little Cayman is a peaceful place. There is not a great deal to do other than dive, snorkel, and watch the wildlife. A small number of hotels and resorts invite you to lie back beneath the warm Caribbean sun and do nothing much at all. **PE**

→ *A diver hovers above the colorful reef of Little Cayman, which offers some of the world's best diving.*

Stay at Eden Rock

Location St. Barthélemy, French West Indies
Website www.edenrockhotel.com **Price** 💲💲💲

Once upon a time, Eden Rock was a private house owned by Rémy de Haenen, the first mayor of the Island of St. Barts and friend of Greta Garbo, Howard Hughes, and Robert Mitchum. Today it is no less than the Caribbean's glitziest institution, a family-owned hotel that has been the height of glamor and sophistication for decades.

We are talking full-blown glamor here, from the thirty-four exquisite suites and villas, including Villa Rockstar, a 16,000-square-foot (1,485-sq-m) party pad complete with golf putting green and cinema, to the resort's 65-foot (20-m), fully crewed *Princess* yacht, which has a personal watercraft in the hull. An island

"Discover private moments of contact with the natural magnificence of the Caribbean."

L.A. Confidential

tour on the yacht may be pricey, but at least any passing boats (containing the likes of P. Diddy) should approve of your suitably swish mode of transport.

The chic island boasts pretty coves, rugged beaches, and marine reserves teeming with a rainbow of underwater life. Back on dry land, the sights are equally impressive—as previous guests Mick Jagger and Mariah Carey can attest. Romantics will love the Garbo Suite, oozing 1930s Hollywood charm, with a wood and white-leather bed and a Philippe Starck bathroom. James Bond wannabes might be seduced by the James Suite, sitting at the water's edge with a private pool, deck, and hot tub. **LP**

Unwind at La Samanna

Location St. Martin, French West Indies
Website www.lasamanna.com **Price** 💲💲

St. Martin is a unique island split between two nationalities: French and Dutch. A fascinating mix of cultures, its dual personality means food is a priority on the French side—excellent patisseries and restaurants abound; the Dutch half has casinos and a busy nightlife. Thankfully, there is more to it. Visit the two capital cities—Marigot and Philipsburg—with their distinctive charm and architecture, the 7-acre (3-ha) Eden Park, and the 1,400-foot (426-m) Paradise Peak for stunning island views, or disappear to La Samanna, a classy and elegant resort with an air of quiet grace.

This glamorous retreat is the epitome of Caribbean chic. The upper rooms have very private rooftop terraces where whitewashed walls sparkle against azure blue cushions, while below hammocks hang lazily in the gardens beyond the atmospheric terraces, pleasantly shielded by palm trees.

The resort's bijou Elysée spa, named after the "abode for the blessed" in Greek mythology, has eight soothing massage rooms and more space to relax in. The choice of treatments is extensive, with everything from shiatsu to reflexology, Thai massages, and hot stone therapy, as well as Pilates and yoga; there is even a personal trainer on hand for one-to-one training.

At sunset, the pool area comes alive with burning torches and live music for cocktail hour. The hotel's restaurant on the hillside has fantastic views over the Baie Longue, and offers a fusion menu blending European and Caribbean dishes. Lobster ravioli and delicious confit duck come with a flabbergasting wine list. It is an epicurean's dream come true. **RCA**

➡ *The unobstructed views from the beach at La Samanna are among the best in the Caribbean.*

Stay at Zandoli Inn

Location Near Fond St. Jean, Dominica
Website www.zandoli.com   **Price** 💲💲

Like the small native lizard it is named after, Zandoli Inn bathes in the sun by the rocks on the southeast coast of Dominica. It is a small hotel, rather like a villa, with five rooms and a plunge pool, surrounded by 6 acres (2.4 ha) of rain forest and whispers of the sea. As the sun goes down, the heavy scent of ylang-ylang wafts in through the gauzy curtains hanging between your open veranda and the simple yet stylish bedroom, and the scene is set for total relaxation.

The most rugged and mountainous of the Lesser Antilles, Dominica is sandwiched between Guadeloupe and Martinique, and its topography means that getting around is no easy feat. Zandoli Inn is just 13 miles (21 km) from Roseau on the island's southeast coast, but feels farther. With wonderful hiking trails in its grounds and beyond, it is easy to lose yourself in the forest among date palms, vanilla vines, nutmeg, and avocado trees, while watching tropical birds flit overhead, seeking hummingbird nests, or just enjoying the huge, brightly colored indigenous flowers. With only five rooms in the hotel, staying here is an intimate experience. The boulder shoreline is a popular meditation spot, and Zandoli is a popular honeymoon spot, too. Importantly, there are no televisions, radios, or telephones in the whole place.

Being green is another theme. There is a freshwater plunge pool to help you cool off, which is treated with chemicals that are kind to the environment (you can also snorkel off the boulders near the hotel), and water for the showers is heated by the sun. You can enjoy fresh local fruit as well as plenty of local specials in the evening, when a communal meal is served; cocktail hour heralds rum punch and Kubuli beer as the perfect accompaniment to the sunset. **LD**

Visit Carlisle Bay Resort

Location Carlisle Bay, Antigua
Website www.carlisle-bay.com   **Price** 💲💲💲

Antigua has a beach for every day of the year; the island's 365 beaches and tempting waters are some of the Caribbean's finest. A hub in the Leeward Islands, Antigua has a real celebrity following: Oprah Winfrey, Denzel Washington, Morgan Freeman, and Eric Clapton all own villas here. For holidaying celebs such as Donatella Versace, the place to be is Carlisle Bay, a swish, luxurious haven to the south of the island.

Far from having the usual rough-around-the-edges Caribbean decor, the Carlisle has managed to blend regional style with urban, contemporary cool. The hotel's interior is sumptuous: an entrance pavilion with plantation-style shutters, oversized exotic floral

> *"This is a place that feels like a sanctuary, the perfect retreat in which to wind down."*
>
> *Daily Telegraph*

arrangements, and sleek dark furniture covered in crisp white fabrics. The elegant rooms decorated in subtle grays and lavenders have rich Jim Thompson raw-silk curtains, decadent daybeds, and enormous oval bathtubs for two. Gadgets include a snazzy espresso machine and fiber-optic bedside reading lights. Choose from two gourmet restaurants on the spot: Indigo On The Beach or the Asian fusion East.

Plus, there is the stunning swimming pool, slick spa, ultra-hip library, forty-five-seater, blue-leather screening room, and a poolside bar for sipping refreshing vodka, coconut rum, and pineapple Indigo Coolers. You simply will not want to leave. **RCA**

Enjoy Hermitage Bay

Location Hermitage Bay, Antigua
Website www.hermitagebay.com **Price** 💲💲💲

Set high above a hidden bay that has been in private hands for more than a century and only a twenty-minute drive away from the capital, St. John's, the twenty-five Balinese-themed wooden cottages of Hermitage Bay tumble down a secluded hillside overlooking the azure waters of the Caribbean. Antigua has reserved one of its finest beaches for this exclusive hideaway, a world of mahogany floors, infinity plunge pools, and impeccable service.

Roomy cottages are adorned with the finest of linens, massive flat-screen televisions, iPod docking stations, and wireless broadband Internet connectivity. It could, therefore, be some time before you get

> *"The views from the hillside cottages are worth staying for alone."*
>
> *Daily Telegraph*

around to venturing beyond your wall of solid timber, bifolding doors onto the wraparound veranda, and the panoramic views to the bay and ocean beyond.

To emphasize Hermitage Bay's commitment to relaxation and well-being, motorized water sports are banned in favor of less intrusive, more leisurely pursuits such as sailing and windsurfing. If you would rather have a massage over the water on the end of a wooden pier beneath a purpose-built thatched roof than in the in-house spa, then that is what you can have. And the most noise you are likely to deal with once the sun goes down on this 10-acre (4-ha), all-suite resort is the lapping of the waves. **BS**

Stay at Jumby Bay Resort

Location Jumby Bay, Antigua
Website www.jumbybayresort.com **Price** 💲💲💲💲

Jumby Bay Resort, a 3,000-acre (1,215-ha) private island, has recently undergone a multimillion-dollar renovation that has freshened up the resort to high standards. The calming beige and cream color schemes of the rooms are astutely matched to British colonial furnishings, which include ample beds and ultra-roomy bathrooms (indoor soaking tub included). Nearly all Jumby Bay suites feature their own entrance and courtyard, large terraces with teak furnishings, and private plunge pools. There are bookable in-room treatments: The Beach Pavilion's massage therapists are adept in Eastern and Western techniques.

For naturalists, Jumby Bay is as exciting as it is relaxing, with wildlife such as White Egret and Blue Pelican (and sheep) roaming around. The crowning glory is Pasture Bay Beach, a protected nesting site for the endangered hawksbill turtle. Guests can sign up for the turtle-watch scheme and play an active role in helping out. For outdoors types, various water sports are available, including snorkeling (lessons can be arranged), sailing, windsurfing, kayaking, waterskiing, diving, boat rentals, and deep-sea fishing. Three tennis courts, bike tours, trail walking, and croquet are also all available. And let's not forget deluxe retail therapy at The Beach Pavilion, which also features a fitness center should you want a workout.

For sustenance, The Veranda is beautiful, breezy, and open for breakfast, lunch, and light dinner, whereas the Estate House, a 230-year-old colonial manor house, provides a more upmarket experience—just the thing after a hard day's sunbathing. **PS**

➡ *Jumby Bay is home to the endangered hawksbill turtle, which lays its eggs on Pasture Bay Beach.*

Relax at Rock Cottage Villa

Location Blue Waters, Antigua **Website** www.bluewaters.net
Price 💲💲💲

Perched on a rocky outcrop in the Caribbean, Rock Cottage is the kind of place where you can stay holed up for days and—happily—not see another soul. Located in Soldiers Bay on Antigua's north coast, this private property allegedly has ocean views of 270 degrees. Whether that figure is accurate or not, few can argue that this hideaway has a panoramic and spectacular vista over the vast, twinkling ocean.

A fusion of whitewashed walls, marble tiles, and wooden shutters set against the rich-blue sea and emerald-green foliage, Rock Cottage is everything the Caribbean should be. Along with a choice of sundecks and dining areas to suit the position of the sun, it also

> ## "This was about as close to perfection as a Caribbean holiday could possibly get."
>
> *The Mail on Sunday*

has a private whirlpool tub and five huge, airy bedrooms housing vast beds. Perhaps the pièce de résistance is the upstairs "his and hers" bathroom with its twin sinks set before shuttered windows, fringed by swaying palms, that open over the deep-blue water. Guests may be able to tear themselves away from those bathroom views, but there really is no need to leave the cottage, let alone the island—unless you want to play at being James Bond for a day and make use of the private motorboat moored below. **NS**

➡ *If you feel like losing track of time, in a beautiful and genuinely unusual location, Rock Cottage is for you.*

Visit Palm Island

Location Palm Island, St. Vincent and the Grenadines **Website** www.palmislandresortgrenadines.com **Price** 🚫🚫🚫

Imagine having a Caribbean island as your plaything. Walk around the coast barefoot, paddling your way along the white-sand shoreline, or explore all 135 acres (55 ha), puttering along paths between palm trees and exotic shrubs, looking out for wildlife.

Palm Island is situated near the southern tip of St. Vincent and the Grenadines, an idyllic archipelago of thirty-two islands and cays known for its natural beauty and clear waters. The island resort has been kept carefully low-key. All forty-two low-rise guest lodgings blend with the vegetation on the shoreline— and provide a total break from the life you have left behind. There are no televisions or phones in the rooms, just great views of the beach and other islands.

Rooms have custom-made bamboo furniture, ceiling fans, woven rattan ceilings, exposed beams, and rich fabrics. You will also find the normal mainland hotel luxuries of marble bathrooms, air-conditioning, cotton bathrobes, mini-fridges, safes, hair dryers, and coffeemakers. Stays here are all-inclusive and guests are welcome to enjoy three fine meals a day in the two restaurants, plus afternoon tea, cocktails, and beach barbecues. It is all so very romantic: You can have lunch privately anywhere on the island and dine by lamplight at the water's edge. For those seeking activity beyond lounging on beach hammocks, the resort offers tennis, mini-golf, bike trails, and non-motorized water sports like windsurfing, snorkeling, kayaking, and catamarans. For quieter days, there is a spa, salon, swimming pool, gym, and library.

It is easy to explore beyond Palm Island with scuba-diving and excursions to nearby islands. Yet perhaps the most luxurious trip of all is an evening cruise aboard the resort's private boat *The Pink Lady*, sipping champagne as the sun sets over the Caribbean. **SH**

⤴ *Indulge your Robinson Crusoe fantasies to the hilt on your own private Caribbean resort—Palm Island.*

Rent L'Anse aux Epines

Location Prickley Bay, Grenada   **Website** www.lanceauxepineshouse.com   **Price** 💲💲

From the sea, this small round tower looks like an old lighthouse or castle turret. As you land on the Caribbean island, though, you will find it is really an old stone sugar mill tower. The tower has been converted into a vacation home for those who need a very special escape indeed: a memorable hideaway for those who demand the very best. The location could not be bettered: on the side of a hill on the shores of Prickley Bay, Grenada, with wonderful views over the Atlantic Ocean and the Caribbean Sea.

The sugar mill tower belongs to the old nineteenth-century colonial estate house L'Anse aux Epines, which can be rented along with the tower to create a property for up to fourteen guests. The tower can be rented alone and sleeps up to four. You will find the sugar mill right on the water's edge in a private part of the lush 2-acre (0.8-ha) gardens of the main house. Inside the conical building are two bedrooms, a kitchen/bar and covered verandas, a small plunge pool, and access to a long, private swimming dock (shared only with the main house). The bedrooms have four-poster beds, flat-screen satellite televisions with DVD players, telephones, and Internet access. The gardens have private walkways, hideaways, and a 20-foot (6-m) waterfall. They lead down to the private beach and deepwater private dock. The infinity pool is 65 feet long (20 m): the biggest private pool in the Grenadines. There is also an "aqua gym" pool and a whirlpool hot tub.

Guests have the services of a staff of five: a cook/housekeeper, two domestic staff, and two groundsmen. A massage therapist and gourmet chef are available at extra cost and a sailing yacht is available for guests. If that is not enough, visitors can also use the property's powerboat, which comes with its own captain. **SH**

⬆ *A luxurious Caribbean retreat with a difference: a converted sugar mill complete with tower.*

Explore Carriacou Island

Location Carriacou, Grenada
Website www.carriacoupetitemartinique.com **Price** 🍶

Dotted with half a dozen swaying palms, Sandy Island is a mere 300 feet (90 m) long. Spread a towel, catch the sun, savor a picnic, or snorkel in some of the Caribbean's clearest, most fish-thronged waters—and you will likely have the place to yourself. When the sun starts to sink, meander the mile back to mainland Carriacou, the largest of the Grenadines, a necklace of island gems scattered between Grenada and St. Vincent, and discover a lively nightlife scene.

"Largest" is, of course, a relative term. Carriacou is 7 miles (11 km) long, by an average of 2 miles (3 km) wide, rising to a 956-foot (291-m) peak. Volcanic in origin, it was once covered in sugarcane and cotton fields, but tourism is now the key industry. Not that it has in any way damaged the laid-back ambience here. Yes, you can send e-mails to the outside world, but it is more important to relax over a thirst-quenching rum punch.

The only energetic pursuit for the locals seems to be boatbuilding, using skills bequeathed by the Scottish ancestors who gave so many of the islanders their surnames, after liaisons with West African slaves. Lively little Hillsborough is the island capital, where the high-speed ferry from the much larger sister island of Grenada docks. There is also a tiny landing strip, whose operation involves using part of the road and holding up the traffic so that the planes can land.

At the end of May, Belair Park hosts the Maroon Festival, whose high spot is the sprinkling of rum and water onto the ground as a blessing before the music and dance spectacle kicks off. If you are really lucky, you might stumble on to a local maroon celebration, where the community pools resources so that everyone can eat, drink, and have fun for free. **RsP**

Stay at Maca Bana Villas

Location St. George's, Grenada
Website www.macabana.com **Price** 💲

A tiny Grenadian boutique resort in junglelike surroundings on a hillside above the idyllic Magazine Beach, Maca Bana is the ultimate place to play pampered Tarzan and Jane. Visitors stay in seven artistically designed "banas" dotted among tropical landscaped gardens, with an infinity pool overlooking the beach and a central waterfall feature.

It is a peaceful haven among coconut trees with strong eco credentials, and solar panels and water heaters supply energy. The intimate resort boasts an organic nursery, fruit tree orchard, and herb garden that supplement the local produce used in the Aquarium restaurant and the bar that sits right on

"Decorated by the artist owner, the villas are well equipped with … hot tubs and staggering views."

Observer

the beach. Each charming villa, set among babbling streams and ponds of koi, has a sleek, fully fitted kitchen, and guests can make their own meals or take advantage of the personal chef in the privacy of their sundeck.

Spa treatments can be arranged in the comfort of the villas or in the gentle breeze outside, and private yoga, tai chi, and meditation lessons add to the deep sense of soulful relaxation, as do the various art and cooking lessons on offer. The banas have outdoor hot tubs, spacious decks, and balconies, with plenty of loungers and love seats to make the most of the Caribbean vistas and dreamy sunsets. **LP**

Relax at Estate House

Location Mount Hartman Bay, Grenada
Website www.mounthartmanbay.com **Price** 💲💲💲

Mount Hartman Bay Estate, on a private peninsula on Grenada, is fit for the likes of James Bond. The Estate House, carved into the hillside with a grass and cactus roof and internal waterfalls, is spectacular. Locals call it the "Cave House" because when arriving from the private jetty or helipad, guests enter through a large door in the cliff.

Once inside, the fixtures and fittings are world class, recalling Le Corbusier and Gaudí. White columns drape to the floor, the polished wood bar is backed by a mossy waterfall, and an oversized dining table invites you to sit and enjoy the exclusive view. The thatched Beach House at the back of the property has a patio opening onto a secluded beach sheltered by coral reefs, and the library inside the house is stocked with must-read books: The owners ask guests to bring a copy of their favorite book to leave here.

Grenada was renowned as an island that sailors could smell before they could see it—the Spice Island's air is heavy with ginger, nutmeg, cloves, cinnamon, and cacao—and the estate's chef knows how to make the most of it. Roger Williams is an award-winning Grenadian chef and creates culinary heaven with the local ingredients.

If you are looking for the ultimate party house, for a maximum of twenty-four extremely well-heeled visitors, this is the place. Your every whim will be catered to—with everything from a 40-foot (12-m) yacht and its captain, to sea scooters and Mitsubishi Shoguns at your disposal. You can choose to picnic on a quiet, forgotten cay for lunch, snorkel on the coral reef in the afternoon, or explore the tropical rain forest all day with a guide. Or simply relax on the beach and let the world revolve around you. **LD**

Enjoy Mount Plaisir

Location Mount Plaisir, Trinidad
Website www.mtplaisir.com **Price** 💲

Mount Plaisir stands right alongside the largest nesting site for leatherback turtles in the western hemisphere. Every year these rare, endangered giant leatherbacks navigate the globe and return to this beach in their thousands. During the summer nesting season, these huge creatures lay their eggs in the sand in the night just outside the hotel rooms. Thousands of hatchlings complete the cycle by pushing out of the sand and rushing back into the sea.

The thirteen suites face the Caribbean Sea with the rain forest rising up the spectacular Mount Ju behind. The simple rooms are decorated with work by local craftspeople. There is a candlelit restaurant, and much

> *"Go on foot to the rain forest, where you'll see the pawi, a bird that lives here and nowhere else."*
>
> *Harper's Bazaar*

of the produce used in the kitchen is grown on the organic estate or caught off the beach. The sweetbreads, cakes, and coconut bread are renowned across the island.

Mount Plaisir is a relaxed base for wildlife trips into the forest, canoe trips along the Grande Riviere, or long beach walks. Trips into the forests with guides can end with a night spent sleeping high in a tree or climbing a hill to watch the sunset over neighboring Tobago. The local birdlife is particularly abundant, and some rare species live only in this area. Guests watch for the extraordinary daily return to their nests of the beautiful yellowtails in huge flocks. **SH**

Stay at Hotel Passion

Location Cartagena, Colombia
Website www.lapassionhotel.com **Price** 💲💲

In the heart of the old walled city of Cartagena is La Passion—a small hotel created with all the emotion and romance that its name implies. Overlooking the Caribbean Sea, Cartagena de Indias is one of South America's most beautiful and vibrant cities, and this boutique hotel captures much of the Colombian city's spirit with its beguiling shabby-chic grandeur.

La Passion is too small to be a retreat for the glitterati. The ancient granite staircase rises to just eight high-ceilinged bedrooms. These traditional spaces combine eclectic antiques, ethnic fabrics, and modern conveniences. Expect to find murals, ancient floor-to-ceiling windows, wicker chests, old carved-

---

"The city, his city, stood unchanging on the edge of time."

Gabriel García Márquez, *Love in the Time of Cholera*

---

wood headboards, Persian and Colombian rugs, Moroccan ashtrays, and lamps from Seville. You may get a vast concrete bathtub, fashionably flaking plaster, or grand distressed French furniture. Amid all this period style there are still state-of-the-art features such as air-conditioning and plasma televisions.

La Passion is more than just style. There is substance, too, especially in the rooftop pool that is subtly lit at night and gives striking views of the city's monuments and the sea beyond. The hotel has its own speedboat that can whisk guests to nearby islands. There is even a small wooden fishing boat hung from the ceiling for guests to use as a swinging sofa. **SH**

Trek to Ciudad Perdida

Location Sierra Nevada, Colombia
Website www.hosteltrail.com/turcol **Price** 💲

Colombia's steamy, jungle-rich Caribbean coast is shrouded in mystery and intrigue, a landscape where guerrilla tribes roam and coca plantations thrive. It is also home to Ciudad Perdida, a stunning ancient city dating back to 800 A.D. Suitably remote, it takes three days of hard trekking to reach the foot of the mountain that marks the entrance to the archaeological site. Here 1,200 small, slippery, uneven steps rise up out of a river. Not as well-trampled as Machu Picchu and nowhere near as touristy, the city was discovered only in 1972 by treasure looters.

On reaching the top of the steps at the mountain's summit, the remains of the old city are spread out. Over a hundred stone terraces that once provided the base for huts are linked by a labyrinth of winding paths and steps. There is an eerily quiet feel to the place, especially when you think of how many thousands of people lived up here until it was abandoned during the Spanish Conquest. As so few tourists visit, it is easy to wander alone and feel like you are the first person to come and explore the weed-covered and palm-fringed ancient terraces studded with wildflowers. The place has the feel of discovering a secret garden.

The site's lofty position offers sweeping views of the lush jungle-covered mountains as well as revealing a sky rich with exotic birds and brightly colored butterflies. Local tribes, descendants of the Lost City inhabitants, live up here in thatched huts. The natives say they knew about the city for years before it was found in the 1970s, but unsurprisingly they wanted to keep this peaceful retreat to themselves. **JK**

➡ *A seemingly never-ending series of moss-covered steps, flanked by dense jungle, leads to the Lost City.*

Walk Along Tayrona Beach

Location Near Santa Marta, Colombia
Website wikitravel.org/en/El_Parque_Tayrona **Price** ◖

On the northern tip of Colombia's coast is Tayrona National Park, an area of 58 square miles (150 sq km) that is said to harbor some of the best beaches in South America. Here the foothills of the Sierra Nevada de Santa Marta—one of the highest coastal mountain ranges in the world—plummet toward stretches of powder-fine white sand and the lapping waves of the turquoise Caribbean Sea.

These beaches are not easy to get to, though. The nearest town is Santa Marta, from where most people take a bus or a taxi to the gates of the park at El Zaino. From there, a van can transport you to the beginning of the walking trails. Most people hike the rest of the way, although the footsore can rent a mule.

The beach at Arrecifes is about a forty-minute walk away. It is a wild and untamed spot where waves lash sea-sculpted boulders and swimming is off the menu due to dangerous riptides. However, a rocky path leads to the beaches at La Piscina or El Cabo where the waters are kinder. Hike for an hour or so up a steep trail from El Cabo and you will come to El Pueblito, an abandoned village from pre-conquest days. You may spot titi monkeys as you climb; you will certainly see some of the park's 200 bird species. Somewhere deep in the jungle, jaguars roam.

You can spend the night in an "ecohab"—a round, thatched cottage invoking the style of traditional Kogui homes—set into the cliffs at Cañaveral, a forty-five-minute walk from Arrecifes. Otherwise, just rent a hammock, hang it between two trees, and let the sounds of the Caribbean Sea lull you to sleep. **PE**

➔ *The lush rain forest of Colombia's Tayrona National Park grows almost to the sea.*

Cruise the Galapagos

Location Galapagos, Ecuador **Website** www.celebrityxpeditions.com **Price** 💲💲💲💲

> "Met an immense turpin: took little notice of me. They well match the rugged lava."

Charles Darwin, *Galapagos Notebook*

⬆ *The Santa Fe land iguana is one of the unique species native to the Galapagos Islands.*

➡ *Kicker Rock, the remains of a lava cone eroded by the sea, is a popular sight for cruise visitors to the islands.*

A trip to the Galapagos, nineteen small, rather scrubby islands 600 miles (965 km) off the coast of Ecuador in South America, is like a dream come true. It is a chance to get up close and personal to exotic creatures such as dancing booby birds, lumbering sea lions, and giant iguanas that have no fear of humans—a truly awesome and thrilling experience.

There are a couple of hotels on Santa Cruz, the island capital, but it is infinitely preferable to take a cruise, visiting two or more islands a day, to observe the animals that inspired Darwin's theory of evolution. As this is such a special place, it is worth paying for the best—and that means Celebrity Xpeditions' ninety-eight-passenger yacht. There are no casinos and no lavish evening production shows, but there are spacious cabins, great menus, and a cold towel and fruit juice to welcome you back on board after a few hours' trekking through the scrub.

As human visitors pose a genuine threat to the fearless animals, visitors to the Galapagos are kept on a tight rein. You can land only with a guide registered with the National Park, and once ashore (transfers are by inflatable boats), you must not stray from the beaten track. None of this is a great hardship though, because you learn so much: that the frigate birds have bloated red chests to attract passing females and that the booby dance is a mating ritual, for example. And did you know that marine iguanas in the Galapagos are black, except on Española, where they are red and green during the mating season? Guides will also find giant boulderlike tortoises in the highlands of Santa Cruz, creatures that were nearly driven to extinction by whalers in the nineteenth century. Alternatively, you may take a trip to the cliff from which, in summer, albatrosses launch themselves into the air. **JA**

Relax at Hotel Monasterio

Location Cusco, Peru
Website www.monasterio.orient-express.com **Price** 🟢🟢

Gisele Bündchen and Leonardo DiCaprio have laid their A-list heads on the soft linen pillows. Jane Fonda, Ben Kingsley, and Goldie Hawn have all sampled the famous house cocktail, the pisco sour, at the chichi bar, and Colombian pop pixie Shakira has had her morning coffee in the shady courtyard. Where are we? Cusco's Hotel Monasterio, one of the luxury properties at the vanguard of South America's style revolution.

Converted from a sixteenth-century monastery and built around a cloistered courtyard, the Monasterio has an ambience of calm efficiency. Gregorian chants accompany the serene breakfast buffet, a private chapel is at your disposal, and the bath butler service offers a

> ## "The five-star Hotel Monasterio is one of the grandest establishments in South America."
>
> *Independent*

soak fit for an Andean princess. The heart of the hotel is a central courtyard with soft fountain and 300-year-old cedar tree surrounded by gardens and cloisters.

The hotel takes a very modern approach to the issue of altitude sickness (the thin air at high altitude deprives the body of up to 30 percent of usual oxygen levels). Fifty bedrooms here are enriched with oxygen gently pumped through filters to reduce atmospheric pressure and aid gentle slumbers. It is all part of life enjoying Cusco's finer side. **DA**

→ *The chapel is adorned with seventeenth-century paintings—one of the delights at Monasterio.*

Enjoy Reserva Amazonica Lodge

Location Near Puerto Maldonado, Peru
Website www.inkaterra.com   **Price** 💲💲

Gazing down on the Peruvian Amazon region with the aid of a satellite image, the town of Puerto Maldonado appears as a series of rough gray smudges in unending green, and a tawny river winds away through thick rain forest. Unlikely as it seems, an hour down the river and a short scramble up a rough clay riverbank is one of Peru's most enchanting and exciting hotels.

Inkaterra's Reserva Amazonica Lodge is part of a private 30,000-acre (12,140-ha) nature reserve. It is a haven of peace and quiet luxury in a wild natural setting: from screeching macaws in vivid primary colors to delicate pygmy marmosets; from single-minded columns of leafcutter ants to elaborate heliconia blossoms, spectacular in crimson. All of this is before you have even made it to your room.

Traditional constructions updated by the addition of tight-fitting mesh screens, the thirty chic cabanas are open to the elements so that on the hottest of nights, a faint breeze might float up from the river. A heavenly lack of phones, Internet, and even electricity (which is rationed) is complemented by thoughtful, luxurious touches and by discreet staff who know when to offer a cocktail, hand you an ice-cold washcloth, or light you to bed with glowing kerosene lamps.

If you are lucky enough to be in one of the two "suites Tambopata," their private plunge pools and terraces are the ideal spot to relax and cool down after an excursion into the jungle. Activities include trekking through the trees in thrall to one of the Reserva's knowledgeable guides; spotting the sentinel, flash-lit eyes of caimans on the riverbanks on a nighttime boat trip; or an electrifying canopy walk 100 feet (30 m) above the ground through whispering treetops. **CR**

Visit Machu Picchu Sanctuary Lodge

Location Cusco, Peru
Website www.machupicchu.orient-express.com   **Price** 💲💲💲

Despite increasing limits on the number of people trekking the Inca Trail to Machu Picchu, the iconic fifteenth-century Inca citadel, voted one of the new Seven Wonders of the World in July 2007, remains one of the world's most popular tourist attractions.

Machu Picchu attracts up to 700,000 visitors each year. In high season, you can see nothing but waterproof jackets clambering over the Sun Gate at dawn. The Machu Picchu Sanctuary Lodge is the ideal place to escape the hordes and get a feel for the spirituality of this UNESCO World Heritage site; the only hotel within the grounds, it has two suites and twenty-nine rooms.

> *"You can't help but think of the mysterious mountain gods whom the Andean people still venerate."*
>
> *Independent*

The views, obviously, are spectacular. It is well worth splashing out for a Mountain View room, or better still a Panoramic Room, which comes with its own balcony overlooking the ancient site. Equally impressive is the Tampu Restaurant Bar, where the gourmet dinner is served with views across the ancient ruins.

The hotel will arrange guided visits of the site with knowledgeable guides, but most of all this is a place to escape into another world and be alone. Get up early and walk around the citadel in the morning half-light to really appreciate the unique atmosphere. The crowds are already approaching the Sun Gate, but for a few precious moments you can enjoy perfect peace. **DA**

Walk Through the Andes on the "Other" Inca Trail

Location Ollantaytambo to Machu Picchu, via Choquequirao, Peru
Website www.peru.info; www.aito.co.uk **Price** ❶

As wear and tear have impacted the traditional "Capaq Ñan" Inca Trail from Ollantaytambo to Machu Picchu, walkers have sought alternative ways of reaching the unmissable UNESCO World Heritage site. The 75-mile (120-km) route from Cachora is, if anything, more impressive—and more demanding—than the more established trail, and passes through the great, rarely visited citadel of Choquequirao, meaning "Cradle of Gold." You ford teeming rivers and hundreds of streams and pass through high Andean hamlets, swaths of sun-dappled forest, and idyllic wide-open valleys en route. The six- to eight-day walk involves Inca staircases that attack the slopes frontally, and less aggressive zigzags designed for mules, goats, and llamas. You are in one of Peru's most inaccessible corners—little wonder the Incas retreated up these valleys in the 1560s, after Spain took Cusco.

Orchids are as good a reason as any to stop and catch your breath, as are the perfumed scents of peppermint and *muña*, a wild oregano that keeps flies away. Peaches, Cape gooseberries, prickly pears, and blackcurrants can all be picked freely.

Choquequirao comes like a dream vision, sitting in a saddle at a natural high pass between two peaks. When the sun begins to set, you can grasp why the ancient tribes wanted to have their homes above the clouds—the cradle of gray ashlar stone glows gold. From here it is another three days to Machu Picchu. But you arrive knowing you have seen a far less famous but larger and probably more important Inca city. **CM**

↗ *A Choquequirao jaunt will take in irrigation channels, ruins, ceremonial chambers—and magical sunsets.*

"Choquequirao truly is the lost city of the Incas ... [it] does not appear in any of the chronicles of the age."

New York Times

Stay at Hacienda de Cayara

Location Near Potosí, Bolivia
Website www.cayara.com.bo   **Price** 💲

The pièce de résistance of Bolivia's heritage of colonial haciendas, Cayara is a gem. Set 15 miles (25 km) outside of Potosí in a rural village idyll, it remains one of the very few working haciendas still in Bolivia today.

The property, originally built in 1557 and home to Spanish nobility, has a living-museum feel, with cobweb-strewn passages leading to secret, hidden nooks and crannies. The 247-acre (100-ha) grounds are home to a working dairy farm, which makes about 75 gallons (350 l) of milk daily, used to make the delicious Cayara-brand dairy products served at meals. Although with private bathrooms, the twenty rooms are fairly basic, and when the mercury plunges at night, the lack of

> "One of Bolivia's most endearing and eccentric hotels, Hacienda de Cayara."

Michael Jacobs, *Independent*

heating will certainly be character building. But it is worth it. By day, guests can explore the portrait-adorned dining hall or blow dust from the covers of ancient tomes in the library to really get the feel of stepping back in history. Then, how about a sunny stroll through the fields of the estate and a homemade Cayara ice cream? (The vanilla flavor is particularly good.)

Most of all, the quintessential Cayara experience is all about taking a post-lunch siesta in the sunny plant room, or curling up by the open fire after a hearty, three-course dinner with a drink and chewing the fat with your fellow guests. This place is living history at its most evocative. Do not miss. **DA**

Enjoy Chalalan Eco-lodge

Location Near Rurrenabaque, Bolivia
Website www.chalalan.com   **Price** 💲💲

Deep in the remote Madidi National Park, in the Bolivian Amazon, a dream has become reality. In 1992, the community of San Jose de Uchupiamonas needed to create an economic alternative to cash crops and stop the migration of their children to big cities in search of work. With the help of a government grant, seventy local families began construction of Chalalan Eco-lodge, accessible only via a five-and-a-half-hour canoe trip along the Beni and Tuichi rivers. The lodge is hidden from the prying eyes of the twenty-first century in a lost world of chinchillas, monkeys, tapirs, alligators, and more than 350 species of bird.

The lodge sits on the shoreline of Chalalan Lagoon, a pristine body of water that doubles as Chalalan's private swimming pool. The twenty-eight traditionally styled cabanas share four standalone bathrooms, and running water is supplied via a solar-powered system. There are more than 15 miles (25 km) of hiking trails along which local guides point out the forest's fauna and its rich tapestry of medicinal and endemic plant life. Night hikes with headlamps are available to observe the surreal nocturnal habits of the Madidi's frogs, birds, black caimans, and other night dwellers. San Jose residents also hold informal cultural evenings in which they share their traditional stories on the origin of the forest and its many inhabitants with guests.

Known as one of the world's biodiversity hot spots, this pristine rain forest has more than 45,000 species of plants and, despite the difficulty in getting here, still provides indelible memories to more than 1,000 intrepid tourists a year, who come to learn about the fragility of the forest, and who in turn help the people of San Jose preserve this unique wilderness for the enjoyment of future generations. **BS**

Unwind at Hotel Rosario

Location La Paz, Bolivia
Website www.hotelrosario.com **Price** 💲

La Paz can get to be a bit much. The sprawling market district behind San Francisco Cathedral is exhilarating but exhausting, so this charming little colonial-style hotel at the heart of the market provides a rare oasis of tranquility, with surprisingly high standards of accommodation in a budget category.

Adapted from a nineteenth-century hacienda and built in a typical Spanish style around a sunny courtyard, this is a really pleasant, airy place in which to escape the bustle of the nearby market, with plenty of quiet corners of the plant-dotted terrace to sit, read a book, and soak up the atmosphere of quiet refinement at your leisure. The rooms manage to be both comfortable and stylish, with ethnic woven blankets and bedspreads adding a homey feel to the decor. Many of these are available to buy downstairs in Anyi, a community arts shop that sells handicrafts created by a local artisan project.

The final touch to foster the boutique-hotel-meets-Andean-tradition ambience is the on-site Tambo Colonial restaurant, which serves up a huge mix of international favorite dishes in a buffet style. At weekends, the restaurant comes alive to the sound of panpipes and charangos, a traditional ukulele-style instrument, with live folk tunes supplied by poncho-wearing local musicians.

In the reception area downstairs there is a help-yourself supply of free *maté* (a coca-leaf tea good for altitude sickness), and snacks are also served here throughout the day, making this a perfect community area to swap experiences with other travelers. On the same level, the in-house agency, Turisbus, can arrange excursions to Lake Titicaca and onward transfers across the border into Peru. **DA**

Visit Hostal de Su Merced

Location Sucre, Bolivia
Website www.desumerced.com **Price** 💲

Set in a beautifully restored colonial hacienda dating from the eighteenth century and boasting a fantastic panoramic view across Bolivia's so-called "White City" from its roof terrace, Hostal de Su Merced is a real find, offering a welcome retreat from the busy streets.

Opened as a hotel in 1997 for a major political summit, this place stands out both for its tasteful decor and for the fact that, unlike many other hotels in Sucre, it benefits from plenty of light and air, lending a sunny feel to the property. Whereas the rooftop is a haven for sun worshippers, the downstairs patio is cooler, splashed by a mosaic-decorated fountain, and a great place to read while sipping a cool drink.

> *"You can have a breathking view of the city, breathe the purest air, and enjoy the sun."*

Proprietors, Hostal de Su Merced

The standard of the facilities makes this the natural choice for a place to stay in Sucre—the twenty-one rooms are spacious, with tasteful period fittings, and there is a good buffet breakfast (lots of muesli and yogurt) and free Internet access in the computer room. More crucially, however, Merced captures a step-back-in-time ambience that recalls the finesse of a former age. Meals are served in a genteel dining room, all starched tablecloths and immaculate service; it feels like stepping onto a film set as an extra. A pre-dinner drink in the bar epitomizes the colonial age with faded works of art on the wall, battered leather seats, and the delicate chink of ice in crystal glasses. **DA**

Explore Laguna Verde

Location Salar de Uyuni, Bolivia
Website www.enjoybolivia.com **Price** ◑

The Salar de Uyuni, the sprawling salt flats in Bolivia's remote southwest, nudging the Chilean border, is the country's greatest natural wonder. With a spectacular, snow-blind landscape and an array of exotic flora and fauna, the area is flatter than Holland and whiter than Mont Blanc, with temperatures that fluctuate from -22°F (-30°C) at night to 86°F (30°C) by day.

Local tour operators can arrange a three-day tour of the region by jeep. Starting out from the train hub at Uyuni, one of the highlights of this tour is a chance to visit Laguna Verde (green lake), which is set some 14,435 feet (4,400 m) above sea level. The water's elaborate colors reflect the high mineral content of the region: magnesium, calcium, lead, and arsenic. The lake sits at the foot of Volcan Licancabur, a towering volcano astride the Bolivia-Chile border. Laguna Verde and its sister lake, Laguna Colorada (colored lake), form part of a protected area: the "Eduardo Avaroa" National Andean Fauna Reserve. The surface of the landscape around the lakes is pure crystalized salt and masks a vast expanse of subterranean lakes, the water from which rises to the surface during the rainy season (December to March).

The lagunas perfectly encapsulate the serene natural beauty of the Salar. They also provide a harsh but evocative habitat for indigenous species. Andean flamingos are abundant and take on a delicate pink glow caused by the pink algae that is their main source of food. The animal population includes Andean foxes and rabbitlike viscacha, whereas the flora includes quinoa plants and the kenua bush. **DA**

⮕ *The thermal waters of Laguna Verde are set in one of the world's last great wildernesses.*

Relax at La Posada del Inca

Location Lake Titicaca, Bolivia   **Website** www.titicaca.com   **Price** ⊖⊖

A visit to Lake Titicaca, a sacred place of worship and mysticism straddling the Peruvian–Bolivian border at an altitude of 12,530 feet (3,820 m) above sea level, is a true escape. The Isla del Sol, where La Posada del Inca nestles among rural villages, is—according to legend—the birthplace of the Inca civilization.

With that kind of pedigree, La Posada has a lot to live up to, which it does magnificently. This seventeen-room, terra-cotta-tiled, converted hacienda, built around a series of small, sunny courtyards in private grounds, feels perfectly in keeping with the mystical ambience of the Isla del Sol. The hacienda offers a very peaceful away-from-it-all experience of serene island life with great views across to both the Isla de la Luna and the spectacular mountains of the Andean Cordillera Real range.

Condors soar overhead, and the waters of the lake lap gently around you. The sense of perfect calm is everywhere. The accommodation has a comfortable yet rustic feel: Bedrooms are furnished with chunky wooden beds and handcrafted knickknacks. All rooms have private bathrooms, with solar-powered showers providing dribbles of hot water. As the late afternoon sun sets over the island, the guests gather on the sun loungers in the garden to chat, read, and soak up the prevailing chilled-out atmosphere.

After the sun goes down, meals are served in a modern, communal dining hall that feels a little like a school cafeteria. The food is generous (try the fresh trout, straight from the lake) but a little on the pricey side. Crillon Tours, a La Paz–based tour agency, which also runs a hydrofoil service across the lake, exclusively manages the property and offers packages only on a full-board and transport basis. So splash out: True hideaways like this are few and far between. **DA**

⬆ *The perfect chill-out retreat: Isla de Sol, in Lake Titicaca—there are few places more peaceful.*

Stay in a Treehouse at Ariau

Location Near Manaus, Brazil **Website** www.amazontowers.com **Price** 🄢🄢

Deep in the Amazon rain forest sits the Ariau Amazon Towers—the only hotel that is situated amid the forest canopy and also the largest treetop hotel in the world. It consists of seven accommodation towers and ten gravity-defying tree houses, and includes what must surely be one of the most extraordinary honeymoon suites ever built, at the apex of a 110-foot (30-m) mahogany tree.

Tower Five has rooms with 360-degree panoramic views of the surrounding forest and its resident fauna, which include red macaws, sloths, and spider monkeys among others. A restaurant in Tower Four cooks regional specialties such as freshwater pirarucu, and the restaurant walls proudly display the signatures of its ever-growing list of famous guests, whose number includes Kevin Costner, Jennifer Lopez, and former U.S. president Jimmy Carter. Do not be surprised if the place looks more than a little familiar either. Cinema and television have both employed the startling resort as a backdrop. It was used in the Hollywood movie *Anaconda*, and also served as the setting for the reality television show *Survivor*.

This vast assemblage of towers and tree houses, which was the brainchild of the famous French naturalist Jacques Cousteau, is interconnected by 5 miles (8 km) of catwalks and represents the gateway to one of the wildest and most biologically diverse regions on Earth. It is just downstream from the Anavilhanas archipelago, the largest concentration of freshwater islands on Earth and home to the rare pink dolphin; day trips can include piranha fishing on the hotel's private boat. If that seems too much of a risky pastime, take a refreshing swim at canopy level in the hotel pool and admire the unique perspectives afforded by this one-of-a-kind hotel. **BS**

⬆ *For a bird's-eye view of the rain forest, check yourself in at the Ariau Amazon Tower Hotel.*

Bird-watch at Fazenda Barranco Alto

Location Matto Grosso do Sul, Brazil
Website www.fazendabarrancoalto.com.br   **Price** 🟢🟢

"The remoteness of the location and the limited number of rooms make for an intimate experience."

Tribes Travel

With room for a mere nine guests and accessible only by private plane, the Fazenda Barranco Alto is hidden away in a remote paradise and enjoyed by the privileged few. Set in the grassy savannas, forests, and lagoons of this vast Brazilian wilderness, this is a nature reserve like no other. It is an area that hums and moves with the incessant activity of the wildlife all around.

There are more than 450 species of birds that fly in after the rains stop in April. Jabiru, hyacinth macaw, and hummingbirds are as common as sparrows are in the United Kingdom, and in the morning you will be thrilled to see swirling flocks of waking birds. Guests soon become used to regular visits from howler monkeys, giant otters, and crab foxes, too, but it is the rare sighting of the jaguar that is most coveted. Patient devotees observe this majestic creature as it patrols its territory, and its paw prints pepper the clay of the marshlands just in case you miss the animal itself.

Guests can go on an open-vehicle Land Rover safari with the very knowledgeable owner, Lucas Leuzinger. Touring the grasslands and marshes, you will see herds of white-lipped peccaries and caimans basking in the sunshine on the shores of the Rio Grande. Or spend your days in the saddle, trailing a giant anteater or splashing through a flooded water meadow, and you will feel truly in the Pantanal habitat. Go canoeing or fishing, or take part in the cattle mustering: Barranco Alto is still a working ranch, so you can join in with the cowboys. At the end of the day, a delicious home-cooked meal, a campfire, and the brightest Milky Way you have ever seen will be all yours. **SWi**

◄ *The green-winged macaw (Ara chloroptera) is one of the many exotic birds to be seen in the Pantanal.*

Stay at Pousada Maravilha

Location Fernando de Noronha, Brazil
Website www.pousadamaravilha.com.br **Price** 💲💲💲

Fernando de Noronha is one of Earth's peerless places. It was a stop on Charles Darwin's famous 1839 *Beagle* expedition, became a UNESCO World Heritage site in 2001 (with nearby Rocas Atoll), and is one of Brazil's top scuba-diving spots, with spectacular flora and fauna. Its environmental fragility means it is monitored by Brazil's Environmental Protection Agency; visitors are limited to 700 a day, and Fernando de Noronha's sixteen beaches are kept immaculate, with clear waters giving visibility of up to 165 feet (50 m).

Pousada Maravilha has only eight exclusive rooms (five bungalows and three deluxe apartments), with huge beds, outdoor showers (and bamboo hammocks),

> *"Heaven is one word that immediately comes to mind ..."*
>
> *Travel+Leisure* magazine

Japanese hot tubs, and furniture from top Brazilian designers Artefacto. Floor-to-ceiling windows help make the most of the spectacular bay views. The infinity pool is one of the few places you might actually see a fellow guest before having a dinner that has been lovingly prepared by chef Adriana Sala. You can also dine at the Brazilian/Italian restaurant bathed in a mixture of candlelight and the pool's luminescent glow. Organized activities include guided island tours, scuba diving, surfing, and the magical experience of watching baby Green Sea turtles hatch on the beach in the middle of a velvet night—just as Darwin did almost two hundred years before. **PS**

Unwind at Anima Hotel

Location Tinharé Island, Brazil
Website www.animahotel.com **Price** 💲💲

Set in 15 acres (6 ha) of private rain forest on the island of Tinharé on Brazil's beautiful Bahia coast, Anima Hotel is a group of nine exquisite bungalows, just 8 miles (15 km) south of the town of Morro de San Paulo, and set on the pristine Encanto beach.

The bungalows are spread among the hotel's luxurious foliage; high ceilings, bamboo partitions, and private decks provide an overwhelming sense of privacy. Anima Hotel's restaurant serves a mix of local and international cuisine, and though the menu changes with the seasons, year-round favorites may include delicacies such as shrimp in fruit sauce with sweet chilies and banana flambé with rum, spices, and coconut sorbet served with wines from Anima Hotel's private cellar. Alternatively, if you happen to snare an octopus from the rock pools next to the hotel, the chef will happily cook it for you. Breakfasts are entirely homemade and include pastries, preserves, fresh breads, and local favorites such as tapioca crepes.

The atmosphere here is completely laid-back. Hammocks are slung above wooden balconies where you can laze away your time reading a book from the hotel's multilingual library. An outdoor lounge is set on a raised wooden platform open on all sides to permit cooling ocean breezes free rein; it also doubles as a conference center and exhibition space for the display of local arts and crafts as well as programs designed to make guests more aware of local customs, history, and traditions. Here you can also find binoculars for viewing the area's abundant birdlife, and board games to while away the hours.

You can reach Tinharé Island by boat from the historic town of Salvador in two hours, or via a twenty-minute flight from Salvador International Airport. **BS**

Relax at Etnia Pousada

Location Trancoso, Brazil **Website** www.etniabrasil.com.br
Price 💲💲

Etnia Pousada is in Trancoso, the hippest and most cosmopolitan village in Bahia, which in turn is the coolest part of Brazil. It is an area of beautiful unspoiled beaches, rural charm, and a relaxed, bohemian way of life. You cannot help feeling like a model here, even if you are in a scruffy T-shirt and flip-flops. Etnia is a deliciously stylish boutique hotel, often used for photo shoots by fashion magazines.

You will find the hotel's eight eclectic rooms among the trees. Each has a different ethnic theme: There is an African bungalow with leopard-skin upholstery and tribal wood carvings, a Moroccan suite with Arabic arches and whitewashed stone steps, and a minimalist Japanese one, too. Others showcase Roma, rural, Mediterranean, Indian, or Brazilian styles.

Most rooms have elegant, modern four-poster beds with fine Italian linen and are draped with mosquito nets. The rooms also have polished concrete floors, walk-in showers, private verandas, and gardens. It is no surprise when you learn that the owners are from the world of Italian fashion.

The public rooms feature open-sided walls with pure white drapes fluttering in the breeze, matching white cushions on rattan armchairs, and low-level lighting after dark. There is a large open-air pool, small spa center for massages and yoga, and hammocks dotted around the palm, banana, and mango trees.

It is only a short stroll to Trancoso's grassy and traffic-free square, lined with impressive boutiques selling the latest hot fashion labels and handmade jewelry; the white colonial church and several laid-back restaurants are just around the corner. In the daytime, many hotel guests head to the nearby beaches—they are some of the best in Brazil. **SH**

Stay at Fazenda da Lagoa

Location Ilhéus, Brazil **Website** www.fazendadalagoa.com.br
Price 💲💲💲

Forget the throngs and thongs at Copacabana beach, Bahia is Brazil's new hot spot, and there is nowhere hotter than Fazenda da Lagoa. The owners fell in love with it at first sight, and it is easy to see why. It stands on a virgin white-sand beach, with rain forest and mangroves to the rear and a saltwater lagoon close by. The husband and wife team describe the place as a *planetinha* (little planet).

Each of the spacious fourteen bungalows has a deck, outdoor shower, television, CD and DVD players, hammocks, air-conditioning, and gauze-netted beds. The interior design is enough to put a smile on your face: pop-art style, bright and bold, designed by

> *"If you're not a morning person, you'll relish the breakfast protocol at this hotel."*
>
> i-escape.com

architect Lia Siqueria and decorated by Carioca artist Mucka Skrowronski. However, this is not just a luxury wilderness retreat because it is also an eco-hotel. You will find biodegradable toiletries in the shower, and there are plenty of outdoor activities to enjoy, such as kayaking, surfing, and river trekking.

Location aside, it is the little unexpected things that make Fazenda da Lagoa so special. Sure, the infinity pool is impressive and very stylish, as is the spa, but better still is the fact that when you are ready for breakfast, you simply raise a flag outside your bungalow, and the kitchen is alerted to deliver your food basket to your private terrace. **LD**

Enjoy Corumbau

Location Corumbau, Brazil **Website** www.corumbau.com.br
Price 🏵🏵🏵

In the language of the indigenous Pataxos people, *Corumbau* means "distant place." So when you wake up in Corumbau that first morning after arriving at Fazenda São Francisco and decide it would be nice to walk the length of the private beach, you better make sure you take some water with you because this is no ordinary resort beach. It stretches for more than a mile along the Bahia coastline with another 5 miles (8 km) of uninhabited beaches on either side. There is a coral reef breaking just offshore, and you can dive its aquamarine waters and come face-to-face with a myriad of tropical fish and plant life.

Brazil's Bahia coast—also known as the "coconut" coast—is a 124-mile (200-km) stretch of beautiful beaches and coconut groves, and the *fazenda* (ranch) sits within one of these groves. Its six spacious bungalows are elegantly furnished in dark Brazilian timbers, and all have private terraces. There are also two suites in the main house, and both offer dramatic ocean views. Traditional, gourmet seafood dishes are included in the room rate and are prepared fresh each day.

A large outdoor pool is surrounded by a deck that leads to a square, sunken outdoor lounge area with stylistic references to the architecture of ancient Mayan temples. After your swim, take a stroll through the surrounding virgin mangrove swamp to a nearby Pataxos Indian village. The Pataxos people were the first South American tribe to make contact with Europeans when the Portuguese explorer Pedro Cabral sailed into Porto Seguro in 1500, and today you can buy handicrafts and works of art from their descendants.

You can get to Fazenda São Francisco from all major Brazilian cities via Porto Seguro and from there by seaplane, boat, schooner, car, or helicopter. **BS**

Unwind at Tauana

Location Corumbau, Brazil **Website** www.tauana.com
Price 🏵🏵🏵

There is an air of intimate luxury at Tauana, a new hotel on an unspoiled Bahia beachfront. Here you can relax listening to the slight noise of wind rustling leaves and the gentle lap of the waves, but otherwise it is silent.

Portuguese architect-owner Ana Catarina Ferreira da Silva designed everything herself in an ultra-cool blend of Brazilian and Danish design, with a hint of 1960s modernism. It conforms to many of her eco-principles, too. There are just nine bungalows, but she planted 30,000 trees on the huge estate. Building wood is from sustainable sources, and traditional Indian building methods were used. The gourmet restaurant uses ingredients from the hotel's own

> *"Brazil is to cool what China is to commerce. And Bahia is the country's beachside boom state."*
>
> New York Times

organic garden, and visitors move around at night with lanterns, keeping light pollution to a minimum.

The huge bungalows are so shaggily thatched that they look like something from a Gauguin painting; inside they are as minimalist as a modern art gallery. Wood floors are highly polished, flimsy white drapes flutter in the breeze, and slumped amid candles and low sofas, you stare through walls of glass at the beach beyond. It might feel like you are part of something from the pages of a glossy magazine. However, do not worry that you will look out of place in such a manicured photo set—spending time at Tauana will soon make you feel like one of the beautiful people. **SH**

Visit Convento do Carmo

Location Salvador do Bahia, Brazil
Website www.conventodocarmo.com.br   **Price** 💲💲

Located in the picturesque district of Pelourinho in pretty Salvador (in Brazil's Nordeste region), the Pestana Convento do Carmo Hotel is designated by UNESCO as a Cultural Patrimony of Mankind. The building itself dates from 1586, having been commissioned by the First Order of Carmelite Friars to be used by the Sisters of Carmelita. Over the years it has played a part in a host of historic acts, from the Dutch invasion to Bahia's independence. Today it is one of the most luxurious hotels in the country. The seventy-nine beautifully appointed rooms and suites come equipped with LCD television sets, a pillow menu, and luxurious Egyptian cotton linens. There is a

"Pestana Convento do Carmo is one of the best new hotels in the world."

Travel+Leisure magazine

spa, whirlpool tub, sauna, and pool to relax in; you can, of course, also spend time reading in the library or any of the public salons. History lovers will delight not only in the convent's past, but also in the museum next door, which houses more than 1,500 exhibits.

Right outside this peaceful paradise is Salvador, founded in 1549 and itself a UNESCO World Heritage site. Famous for its fabulous carnival and generally colorful, festive atmosphere, the city was Brazil's capital for two centuries, and remains a meeting point for African, Portuguese, and indigenous cultures. With its great architecture and quaint cobbled streets, it is a wonderful place to discover, too. **PS**

Relax at Txai Resort

Location Itacare, Brazil
Website www.txai.com.br   **Price** 💲💲

On an undeveloped stretch of Brazil's famous Cacoa Coast, set among 247 acres (100 ha) of rare Atlantic coastal rain forest, Txai Resort is a secluded enclave of guest rooms sprinkled throughout the grounds of a privately owned coconut plantation.

Ocean views are unavoidable in this eco-friendly hideaway with natural springs and waterfalls aplenty in the surrounding verdant hills. There are forty rooms, all with king-sized beds, mosquito nets, and wraparound sofas, including twenty-six bungalows with thatch and wood ceilings, color-washed exteriors, and private spa baths. Two even have their own private plunge pools. Most bungalows are found on the resort's lower levels within easy walking distance of the palatial swimming pool, but others are scattered along the hillside and offer a mix of floor plans that can cater to every need. One bungalow has a mezzanine, making it ideal for a family of four, whereas others can be booked to sleep up to eight people.

With breakfast, lunch, and dinner included in the room rate, most meals tend to be eaten in the resort's Bahian-style restaurant. Menus are changed daily and follow a largely Brazilian theme, ranging from traditional fish stews and shrimps served with black beans and manioc through to the humble pizza.

The resort's hilltop spa offers hydro-massage, hot stone treatments, yoga, and a range of facials and manicure treatments that may well be a requirement rather than just an excuse to relax after a heady day of exercise. Activities include kayaking or sailing in a traditional Bahian boat along the Rio de Contas, riding horses through the rain forest trails, or hiking the beach trail to the Camboinha outlook to gaze over the beaches of this unspoiled corner of Brazil. **BS**

Enjoy Villas de Trancoso

Location Trancoso, Brazil
Website www.mybrazilianbeach.com   **Price** 💲💲

The Trancoso Villa complex is a timber and thatch, five-star enclave, nestled amid palm and acacia trees. It consists of five villas designed by the noted architect Ricardo Salem, with interiors by the São Paulo–based Sig Bergamen, and represents the epitome of privacy and luxury. Its pure tranquility is able to attract the most discerning of travelers.

The one- and two-bedroom Trancoso Villas have all been constructed using rare Brazilian timbers and are filled with native furnishings, mosquito nets, and hand-painted cushions. They are superbly located on a landscaped and terraced beach just 1 mile (1.6 km) south of the historic village of Trancoso, founded in 1586 and spread along a cliff top with views over miles of pure white-sand beaches. Over the past seven years, this sleepy fishing village has been reinvented as one of the most trendy destinations in South America and boasts such regular visitors as actor Leonardo DiCaprio, model Naomi Campbell, and the former vice president of the United States Al Gore.

The villas all come with an English-speaking staff of cleaners, cooks, and a concierge, and there are hammocks, a cabana, white marbled infinity pool and swim-up pool bar, and indulgent waterfall showers that will leave you feeling pampered and refreshed. Dinners can be eaten by torchlight under the stars and range from the exotic to a simple burger and fries.

The experience can also include horseback riding along pristine beaches, kayaking, and off-road bicycling, or you can play at Trancoso's Villa Golf, the newest addition to the Trancoso Villa complex. **BS**

⬈   *Many of the villas have an open-plan design that accentuates the quality of the craftmanship.*

"It was wonderful in all respects . . . a very precious thing in such beautiful surroundings."

John Danilovich, U.S. Ambassador to Brazil

Relax at Sitio do Lobo

Location Ilha Grande, Brazil
Website www.sitiodolobo.com.br   **Price** $\textcircled{S}\textcircled{S}$

Lying in a hammock at Sitio do Lobo clutching a cocktail, gazing across the clear blue water to the mountains in the distance, it can feel as if you are miles away from civilization. And, in this case, you really are. The hotel is hidden among the scented tangerine trees and exotic flowers of an almost deserted island, two hours south of Rio de Janeiro.

This is definitely an escape from normal modern life. Ilha Grande is 25 miles (40 km) wide, yet has no roads. The nearest village is almost an hour away—by kayak. Sitio is a slightly ramshackle, back-to-nature sort of place, with just nine rooms blended into the jungle along the shore. It stands on the Bay of the Stars, the site of a nineteenth-century coffee plantation. Nestled among its acres of lush vegetation, the Sitio was a wealthy Brazilian family's Costa Verde retreat for twenty years. Many rich and famous friends visited, including soccer star Ronaldo and Prince Rainier of Monaco. Only recently has the luxury retreat been opened up to paying guests. And that makes for a comfortable, lived-in feeling.

This is definitely no chain hotel. Sofas are built into giant granite boulders; there are thatched massage huts and wooden verandas overlooking the sea. Bamboo furniture is embedded with tiny seashells, and exposed granite is incorporated into the walls. There are eccentric ornaments everywhere, from model boats to handmade wooden frogs. Food is simple and fresh, with plenty of seafood and local fruit. There is also a heliport, and the hotel's speedboat whisks guests around the bay. However, guests are encouraged to travel by kayak instead, to explore the surrounding national park or visit empty sandy beaches—the island has 102 of them. **SH**

Stay at Solar da Ponte

Location Tiradentes, Brazil
Website www.solardaponte.com.br   **Price** $\textcircled{S}\textcircled{S}$

Standing grandly beside the beautiful main square and ancient stone bridge in one of Brazil's most historic villages, it looks like a stately official building or wonderful mansion. Yet Solar da Ponte is actually an elegant period hotel, with eighteen spacious rooms opening onto verandas, gardens, a pool, and a sauna.

The derelict building was bought by an English naturalist and his Brazilian wife in the 1970s. They have been exquisitely restoring it for thirty years, and it is now something of a monument in its own right. Solar da Ponte is regularly judged as one of the country's finest hotels. It is in the center of the colonial gold-mining town of Tiradentes, in the state of Minas Gerais.

"One of the best hotels in Brazil . . . a wonderfully civilized base for exploring."

Tatler Travel Guide

The eighteenth-century gold boom helped pay for the architecture; guests can stroll along the cobbled streets and leafy squares lined with lavish historic buildings, with the brooding São Jose mountains in the background. It is a favorite weekend retreat for wealthy families from Rio.

Inside, Solar da Ponte is comfortably full of antique furnishings, fresh flowers, and local art. There are reclaimed wooden floors, traditional wooden beds, and full-length windows that look out over the peaceful gardens, where colorful orchids bloom and exotic birds sing in the trees. Watch out for the marmoset monkeys frolicking on the lawn, too. **SH**

Enjoy Ponta dos Ganchos

Location Santa Catarina, Brazil
Website www.pontadosganchos.com.br **Price** ⦵⦵⦵

Set amid lush tropical rain forest on a privately owned lagoon dotted with tiny islands, Ponta dos Ganchos is the ultimate paradise hideaway. The luxury resort, in the southern state of Santa Catarina on Brazil's "Emerald Coast," contains just twenty rustic-chic cabanas, some with a sauna, whirlpool tub, and infinity pool. No under-eighteens are allowed, which means that peace and quiet is a given, making the resort a hit with honeymooners and couples. With more than three staff per bungalow, the service aims to please.

There is plenty here to keep you busy. Activities range from tennis and volleyball to deep-sea fishing, canoeing, and diving. The Arvoredo Biological Marine Reserve, which has some of the best diving sites in Brazil, is less than an hour away by boat. There is also a fitness center and cinema. One of the biggest draws in the resort is the luxurious Christian Dior spa, the only one in the Americas, as well as open-air shiatsu and ayurvedic treatments. Nearby, the Island of Anhatomirim has one of the oldest forts in Brazil, and there is a pretty little fishing village just down the lane.

Menus change daily and there are no time restrictions, meaning that you can eat breakfast at midnight if you wish. For romantic dining, you can book a private gazebo on one of the islands, perhaps ordering a plateful of Santa Catarina's famous oysters and mussels, considered by many to be the best in the world. For all its opulence, much has been done to run the resort along environmentally friendly lines, with electric cars available for rent and a natural waste treatment system in the offing. **TW**

↪ *Each of the resort's bungalows has a private veranda with hammocks, sun beds, and a superb sea view.*

Discover Iguazú Falls

Location Paranà, Brazil; Misiones Province, Argentina
Website www.iguazuargentina.com **Price** ◑

It is strange, perhaps, to think of these mighty waterfalls as an escape, unless you are planning to go over them in a canoe, in which case your mad dash might be only briefly pleasurable. But to stand at the edge of the "Garganta del Diablo" (Devil's Throat) and look down into the vast horseshoe-shaped chasm, where unimaginable quantities of water are tumbling into piling clouds of steam and great dusky swifts dart and weave through hovering rainbows, is to enter a dreamlike world of fairy-tale proportions.

The grandest falls in South America drop 242 feet (74 m) through subtropical rain forest, extending nearly 1.8 miles (3 km) in width, and encompassing 272 different waterfalls. However, size is not the issue here. The magic of Iguazú lies in being able to immerse yourself in this watery paradise, gazing at the incredible torrents from so many different angles. The Brazilian side offers a complete, far-off panorama, but for a real escape you have to enter the Argentine Iguazú National Park, take the eco-train into the forest, and prepare to explore.

The path to the Garganta del Diablo runs over the wide Iguazú River, where it flows smooth and quiet. Mounting columns of mist and a deafening roar herald the drama to come, and once you reach the falls themselves, it is impossible not to stand mesmerized by the sheer volume of cascading water. Take a boat dashing straight into the drenching spray, or hike the Macuco trail to spot abundant birdlife. Iguazú is an utterly exhilarating experience and one to which you will escape, endlessly, in your memories. **CD**

← *Water cascades spectacularly down a cliff face on the Argentinian side of Iguazú Falls.*

Stay at Cabo Polonio

Location Cabo Polonio, Uruguay
Website www.discoveruruguay.com **Price** ⊖⊖

Could Cabo Polonio be the hippie ideal? Spanning miles of the rugged coastline for which Uruguay is justly renowned, this protected nature sanctuary is one of the best-kept secrets in South America: a haven for in-the-know locals looking for tranquility and unspoiled beauty amid sea lion colonies and rolling sand dunes. It is far removed from the glitz and the bustle of nearby Puntas del Este and Diablo.

With just two hotels in the vicinity (development ceased when the land was designated as protected in the mid-1900s), most visitors sleep in the rustic beach *posadas* (lodges) or rainbow-colored shacks dotting the grassy knolls behind the dunes. There are no cars

"Being in Cabo Polonio was like being in a galaxy far, far away."

Kelly Westhoff, Go-Nomad.com

here (there is also no electricity for that matter), other than the odd four-by-four shepherding visitors between the dunes; at other times a neigh announces the arrival of a horse-drawn buggy into the area's epicenter, el Cabo. It is the town that time forgot, where the most notable citizens are the sea lions from the colony lying some 100 feet (30 m) into the sea, presided over by the lighthouse guarding the bay.

Gentle breezes envelop as cares are washed away with the sound of the lapping ocean; hampers are unpacked on the white sand and friendships are forged over campfires. This is the ultimate beachside idyll—protected by man and gifted by nature. **VG**

Explore the Atacama Desert

Location Atacama Desert, Chile **Website** www.awasi.cl
Price 🌏🌏

It is hard to imagine anywhere more remote than the Atacama Desert. Stretching for nearly 1,000 miles (1,600 km) along the Chilean side of the Andes, where volcanoes are still smoking, this is the driest place on Earth. Here the skies are so clear that astronomers can see light from the earliest galaxies in the universe. Yet at its heart, there are vivid blue salt lakes where bright pink flamingos seem to hover in a perpetual haze. The silence is so profound that you can hear them sipping.

Geysers spout great columns of steam into a cobalt-blue sky, over rivers of red-hot algae. Moon Valley boasts vast dunes: the Earth twisted and eroded into such fantastic shapes it could easily pass as another planet. Particularly stunning are the sunsets over Atacama, when Licancabur volcano turns purple in the setting sun and there is a real sense of isolation. Darkness descends, the sky fills with stars—and fortunately, at this point, your dedicated guide takes you back to your sumptuous oasis, Awasi.

A world away from busy San Pedro de Atacama, Awasi is beautiful, calm, and very exclusive. A series of airy spaces, open to the sky, leads to the restaurant, offering sublime modern dishes. Traditional textiles and adobe architecture are subtly combined with contemporary furnishings, giving the local aesthetic some five-star style. The rooms are exquisite: some circular, with high thatched roofs and sunken baths. Best of all, Awasi is the only hotel in Atacama where each guest has their own dedicated guide. They find parts of the Moon Valley where no one goes, and visit the Tatio Geysers after the crowds have left. **CD**

➡ *The Atacama Desert, with its mighty volcanoes and lunar landscape, has an eerie beauty all its own.*

Stargaze at Elqui Domos

Location Paihuano, Chile
Website www.elquidomos.cl **Price** $

In 1982 when scientists first measured Earth's magnetic field by satellite, they found our planet's center to be in central Chile's dry Elqui Valley. So it should come as no surprise that in 2005 the clear skies of this supposed magnetic epicenter were chosen to be the site for the construction of one of only seven astronomic hotels worldwide and the only lodge of its kind in the southern hemisphere.

Huddled together, the accommodation resembles some sort of futuristic, Arthur C. Clarke–style attempt at survival in a post-apocalyptic world. In reality, it represents a bold new approach to environmentally sensitive tourism. Elqui Domos is a collection of seven geodesic domes, each possessing two levels. The living area and bathroom are below, whereas the bedroom above has a removable window in the ceiling to allow unfettered observation of the night sky. A telescope is provided in each dome, just to ensure you never lose sight of the reason for coming here. Each dome has its own terrace with views of a more terrestrial nature.

Hotel staff can organize activities such as horseback riding and mountain biking, or a visit to a vineyard or the home of Nobel Prize winner Gabriela Mistral to fill up the daylight hours until the sun goes down and the exciting stuff begins. Astronomy courses and an abundance of astronomic literature are available, as are hammocks and outdoor wooden bathtubs in which to read. A number of international observatories are in the area, including the Mamalluca amateur observatory, which welcomes visitors. **BS**

◀ *Each dome at Elqui Domos comes equipped with a terrace and telescope from which to view the sky.*

Stay at Hotel el Pangal

Location Robinson Crusoe Island, Chile
Website www.enjoy-chile.org **Price** $$

Named after the novel based on Scottish sailor Alexander Selkirk, who was marooned here between 1704 and 1709, Robinson Crusoe Island is a lonely place, ringed mostly by precipitous sea cliffs. Populated mainly by vagabonds and marooned sailors until the early nineteenth century, it is now home to the town of San Juan Bautista (population 600) and the isolated and unique Hotel el Pangal.

You can either walk to the Hotel el Pangal or arrive via an inflatable boat that will ferry you across the bay from San Juan Bautista. The hotel has a restaurant and a tea salon and is surrounded by lovely terraced gardens, but you do not come here to experience the

> ## "[Robinson Crusoe Island] is the ultimate escape, an unvanquished Pacific island. . . ."
>
> Diana Souhami, *Guardian*

hotel's fine cuisine and stunning ocean views. Robinson Crusoe Island is the Hotel el Pangal's backyard, and what a backyard it is.

Almost two-thirds of the island's vascular plants are endemic, including two species of bromeliad found nowhere else. Much of the island's original forest has been overtaken by invasive plants from South America and New Zealand, although large stands of native forest can still be found at higher altitudes. The primeval *Lactoris fernandeziana*, considered to be a living fossil, is also found nowhere else in the world, all of which helps make Hotel el Pangal much more than just a place to lay one's weary head. **BS**

Unwind at the Secret Ranchito

Location Patagonia, Chile **Website** www.i-escape.com **Price** ⑤⑤

The rustic delights and spectacular Andean vistas that encircle the Secret Ranchito in southern Chile will, happily, never be disturbed or eroded by the encroachment of mass tourism, its grand isolation guaranteeing to preserve it for only the most determined of souls. Getting here is an adventure in itself. An early morning flight from the Chilean capital Santiago to Puerto Montt is followed by a private charter flight to the town of Chaiten. A representative from Expediciones Chile will then take you on a four-hour shuttle into the Andes to a nondescript village called Futaleufu for the final twenty-minute walk to your accommodation. And not a moment too soon!

If you like absolute isolation totally removed from any vestiges of civilization, this is the place to come. Your luggage is brought in on top of an old ox cart, and a four-by-four vehicle is parked for your sole use fifteen minutes' walk from your lodging at the other end of a timber and rope suspension bridge strung across a small but spectacular river gorge. Fly fishing enthusiasts will delight at the abundance of brown and rainbow trout to be found in the cold, clear waters of the nearby Azul and Futaleufu rivers. Explore the river all the way to the Argentine border by kayak or by raft, or just recline on the hammock strung over the white sands of your private riverside beach.

Accommodation is a one-room timber dwelling divided into a kitchen and bedroom with wool rugs and simply furnished, with another adjacent cabin, both of which enjoy magnificent views across to the granite face of Tres Monjas. Hot showers, a telephone, radio, and CD player mean you do not have to leave all the comforts of home behind, but this is as close as you are ever likely to get to a memorably primitive sojourn surrounded by nature at its grandest. **BS**

⬆ *High up in an Andean valley, the Secret Ranchito can be reached only by foot, horse, water, or helicopter.*

Cruise the Chilean Fjords

Location Southern Chile　**Website** www.explore.co.uk; www.lata.org　**Price** 🟢🟢

At the southern tip of Chile, islands and icebergs feather around the tip of the mainland, and channels and straits carve routes from the Pacific to the Atlantic. Here at the ends of the earth, you will find the ultimate escape.

Along Chile's west or Pacific coast, the fjords are as deep and dramatic as their northern counterparts, but with the addition of near total isolation, ice-blue icebergs, and only a handful of native people. Cruises generally travel along the fjords from Puerto Montt, reachable by air from Santiago, to Puerto Natales, which you cannot reach by road, giving you the only access route to this part of the country. Inlets around here were navigated by Magellan in 1520 and again by Darwin in the early nineteenth century, en route to the Galapagos.

The spectacularly remote area holds beinlets, snowcapped mountains, pristine wilderness, and breaching whales, and it is not difficult to see what makes a trip here so special. In our busy world, where everything is only a click of a mouse away, just getting here is an organizational feat. The 685 miles (1,100 km) take around four days to travel at a leisurely pace, allowing you to stop and notice the smallest details, like dolphins following in the wake of the boat and seals playing along the shore, for example.

Albatross, giant petrel, and Magellan penguins are just three of the delights for bird-watchers. As the cruise ship anchors, you can take a canoe to explore the islands and inlets nearby. It is an enchanting area teeming with wildlife and very few visitors. Just a handful of fishing villages and cattle ranches stud the coastline, and penguin colonies number more than people in many areas. As night falls, the Milky Way stands out brightly in the pitch-black sky. **LD**

⬆ *A boat enters the icy waters of the Amalia Fjord in Southern Patagonia, Chile.*

Stay at Puyuhuapi Lodge

Location Chiloé Island, Chile
Website www.patagonia-connection.com   **Price** 💲💲

It is hard to imagine a more romantic arrival. After rumbling over gravel roads between fairy-tale forests along Chile's remote but spectacular Carretera Austral, you come, at last, to a tranquil little hamlet on the edge of a fjord: Puyuhuapi. The last stretch of your journey must be done by boat, crossing the glassy waters to find a cathedral-like wooden building poised right on the water against a backdrop of virgin forest. It seems an unlikely place for a luxurious spa, and yet inside this beautiful structure there are immaculate pools, fed by three kinds of natural waters. This is Puyuhuapi's secret: There is not only clear seawater from the fjord and a spring of crystalline snowmelt, but healing, mineral-rich hot springs, too. From this rare combination, Puyuhuapi's owners have created a superb range of treatments and brought in gifted specialists to transform guests' well-being with a whole range of therapies.

Friendly, attentive staff give Puyuhuapi its warm, relaxed atmosphere. Although the accommodation is simple rather than chic, the comfortable rooms are designed with natural materials and huge windows to make the most of tranquil views onto the fjord. Fine cuisine completes the luxurious treatment, which feels particularly miraculous at this remote extreme of Patagonia. Guests can conclude their trip here with an unforgettable voyage to see the mighty glacier at Laguna San Rafael.

It is Puyuhuapi's complete contact with nature that is so special: Take a kayak out onto the water to explore, or hike to the awe-inspiring hanging glacier on the other side of the fjord. After a day of exertion, there is no better therapy than to bask in hot pools under a flawless sky and watch the heavens fill with stars. **CD**

Visit Clos Apalta Winery

Location Santa Cruz, Chile
Website www.closapalta.cl   **Price** 💲💲

Clos Apalta is an oenophile's paradise: a tranquil retreat where visitors can live and breathe wine. Cocooned into a forested hillside of Chile's Colchagua Valley, the winery and lodge was founded by the Marnier-Lapostolle family (the producers of Grand Marnier) in 1994, but it already has the reputation of being one of the country's leading wine producers. The winery itself is beautiful; of its five storeys, three are dug into the granite hillside, providing a cool environment for the wine to age. At the heart of the building is a dramatic spiral staircase that resembles wine being poured into a glass. Visitors can watch how the wines are created as well as taste some of them.

> *"Each casita has been named for one of the primary red grape varieties planted at the vineyard."*
>
> Manos Angelakis, LuxuryWeb.com

Four luxury casitas are within staggering distance of the winery, each with its own hot tub, fireplace, king-sized bed, and terrace. These plush pads are equipped with fully stocked fridges and iPod sound systems. The food here is taken as seriously as the wine, with a local chef preparing gourmet meals, washed down with glasses of the vineyard's finest wines, plus Pisco Sours flavored with a nip of Grand Marnier. The 450-acre (182-ha) vineyard can be explored on horseback, or admired from the comfort of the infinity pool. **JK**

➡ *The striking über-modern architecture of the Clos Apalta winery stands out against the lush hillside.*

Relax at Indigo

Location Puerto Natales, Patagonia, Chile
Website www.indigopatagonia.com **Price** $$

Arriving in Puerto Natales, with its weather-beaten tin houses and solitary air, feels a bit like winding up at the end of the world. There is good reason for this: This waterside town is just 100 miles (160 km) from the southern tip of the Americas in Patagonia—in short, the last place you would expect to find one of the country's most original design hotels.

Located on the shores of the romantically named Sound of Last Hope, Indigo works a fresh, Nordic-chic aesthetic (blond woods, whiter-than-white sheets), complementing the contemporary architecture by leading Chilean architect Sebastián Iriarrázaval. Instead of baths the rooms have rain-forest showers. There are,

---

"By far the best feature of Puerto Natales is the view from Hotel Indigo."

Christabelle Dilks, *Guardian*

---

however, three huge rooftop hot tubs, affording direct views of the indigo-colored fjord, the constantly changing hues of the vast sky, and the peaks of Torres del Paine far in the distance. Whatever the weather (most of the year quite chilly), it will not touch you in the steamy waters.

Most visitors use Puerto Natales as a base for a trip to Torres del Paine 50 miles (80 km) to the north, a national park with some of the world's most beautiful trekking circuits, taking you past glaciers, peppermint-hued lakes, and thrusting pink granite peaks. What makes Indigo stand out is its well-executed brand of laid-back luxe, ideal for post-trek pampering. **IA**

Enjoy El Manantial

Location Purmamarca, Argentina
Website www.hotelmanantial.com.ar **Price** $$

The "wellspring of silence" is a bold claim for a hotel, and it is not made lightly here. El Manantial del Silencio is a truly peaceful retreat in the ancient village of Purmamarca, tucked away from the famous Quebrada de Humahuaca. Tourism has really boomed in this magnificent gorge of colored rock since UNESCO declared it a World Heritage site in 2002. Fortunately, most visitors charge up the center of the valley, leaving charming Purmamarca less visited. Yet here is one of Argentina's most famous views: the Cerro de Siete Colores, which boasts at least seven colors among its vivid stripes. The mountain gives a dramatic backdrop to the tiny town's popular market and traditional adobe church, which contains a series of beautiful paintings under a cactus-wood roof. Day visitors might mill around in the morning, but after noon, Purmamarca recovers its deep feeling of tranquility.

El Manantial's magic lies in its design. Inspired by early colonial architecture, its comfortable rooms echo the simple local way of life; there is an almost monastic purity to the white walls and linens and bottle-green shutters. Traditional textiles and paintings bring a welcome dash of color, but everything sits in harmony with the view of the mountain from the window. Before dining on a carpaccio of guanaco, or ravioli stuffed with handmade goat cheese made by the prizewinning chef, recline before a crackling fire with a gin and tonic. Attentive staff will arrange all your adventures in the Quebrada and beyond.

Indelibly printed on most guests' memory is the vision of the salt flats above El Manantial at sunset: A shimmering sea of white, fringed by copper-tinged clouds suspended above imposing, distant mountains, and—naturally—perfect silence. **CD**

Unwind at Estancia Colomé

Location Calchaquí Valley, Argentina
Website www.estanciacolome.com   **Price** 🌓🌓

The journey to Colomé is part of its magic. From the crumbling colonial splendor of Salta city, the road snakes up through the dramatic Cuesta del Obispo, a deep gorge cut into green velvety mountains, then streaks straight across a red plateau filled with cactus. Nothing else seems to grow here at the 26,900-foot (8,200-m) altitude. But, descend through canyons of terra-cotta rock into a remote valley of stark and spectacular beauty, and suddenly you come to a stretch of emerald green, perfectly ordered, rows of vines. Here owner Donald Hess is miraculously producing award-winning Malbecs. In the heart of the vines, surrounded by fragrant lavender, and perfectly poised for wide-open views, is another miracle: one of Argentina's most stunning hotels.

Just nine enormous, luxurious rooms, meticulously designed and decorated in deep earth tones, lead off from a central open courtyard where a Zen-like fountain murmurs. The entire estate is biodynamic, a system that sees the land and every creature on it as part of the same organism, and so owner Hess cares for the 400 Andean people living on his 96,000 acres (38,850 ha) as part of his family. Thus Colomé is utterly harmonious with its surroundings.

Whether climbing up the paths into ancient mountains, riding horses with the horse whisperer, or simply lounging around by the pool and soaking up the views, a deep sense of peace descends. As night falls, roll an inky Amalaya around your glass, sip the intense wine made from these beautiful landscapes, and blissfully unwind. **CD**

↗ *Estancia Colomé has the highest-altitude vineyards in the world, which produce award-winning wines.*

"Life is too short to look at bad art, drink bad wine, or stay in bad hotels."

Proprietor, Estancia Colomé

Explore Tierra del Fuego National Park

Location Tierra del Fuego, Argentina
Website www.parquesnacionales.gov.ar   **Price** 💲

Close to the Chilean border, the spectacular Tierra del Fuego National Park protects 155,000 acres (63,000 ha) of the southern tip of the Andes, from north of Lake Kami to the coast of the Beagle Channel.

Miles of deserted hiking trails cross the main island of the archipelago past waterfalls, through forests, and across peat bogs to reach viewpoints looking across the panoramic scenery of rugged coastline and snowcapped mountains. On the way, it is possible to catch a glimpse of condors, albatross, cormorants, and orange-billed steamer ducks. There is color in the park throughout the year, especially from the glaciers, but autumn provides the real spectacle when the forest-clad hillsides bloom in a sea of red foliage.

Argentina's only coastal national park, Tierra del Fuego's mountains are divided by deep glacial valleys, where lakes and rivers flow. This proximity to the sea, along with dominant westerly winds, means low, moderate temperatures year-round. Even in summer, the mercury rarely goes above 50°F (10°C). These conditions mean that unique flora grows here, such as Sea Pink and Diddledee, rare lichens, and mosses.

The region's original inhabitants were the Yamana, a tribe who lived on the shores of the Beagle Channel and Lake Roca. Living off what they could harvest from the sea, they moved around in bark canoes, hunting sea lions and fishing. Ruins still remain of a settlement at Lapataia Bay. Today visitors can camp within the park to make the most of the setting, or stay at nearby Ushuaia, the southernmost city in the world. **AD**

➡ *The rugged natural beauty of Tierra del Fuego offers a fantastic landscape for hikers and eco-tourists.*

Stay at House of Jasmines

Location Salta, Argentina **Website** www.houseofjasmines.com
Price 💲💲

Hollywood actor Robert Duvall and his Argentinian wife, Luciana, originally bought this secluded 120-year-old colonial estate as their personal retreat. Now it has been sold to a local family who has opened it as an exclusive rustic boutique hotel. The House of Jasmines is in the northwestern Argentinian province of Salta, where the subtropical forest meets the canyons and foothills at the edge of the Andes. Guests arrive at this quiet spot down a long avenue of eucalyptus trees. At the end is the old whitewashed and jasmine-covered estate house with terra-cotta-tiled roof and verandas.

It feels intimate and personal, with just seven suites. The hotel manages to retain the feeling that this is still

"On foot or horseback guests are free to roam the Edenic grounds."

Travel+Leisure magazine

a private home. The decorative style is gently luxurious with a rustic flavor: beamed ceilings, wrought-iron chandeliers, local antique chairs and lamps, four-poster beds, and rush-matting floors. Some suites have roof terraces; all have memorable views across the garden, estate, and mountains.

The spa has masseurs, steam rooms, and saunas. There is a pool in the beautiful gardens. White wooden chairs are dotted around the lawns and under the overhanging plants for shade—perfect for relaxing with a glass of the local Torrontes wine. The hotel's land stretches along the Arenales River, and is rampant with orchids, roses, and yet more wild jasmine. **SH**

Discover Iruya Village

Location Salta, Argentina **Website** www.enjoy-argentina.org
Price 💲

The drive alone is unforgettable. Head north through the vast Quebrada de Humahuaca gorge, which was declared a UNESCO World Heritage site for the savage beauty of its stratified orange-ocher rock, and then strike off across wildly beautiful landscape on a rocky road that crosses several rivers before climbing to a mountain pass, the Abra del Condór, at a breathless 13,120 feet (4,000 m). From here, the track slaloms down vast slabs of mountainside. It seems incredible that anyone lives here, but finally, at the end of the road, perched on a precipitous slope above you: Iruya.

Andean village life is being changed forever by the arrival of television, modern influences, and, of course, tourism. But Iruya somehow retains its identity. With one main street giving access to provisions stores, a tiny post office, and one intermittently functioning phone center, Iruya is cut off from the world. Watch villagers driving goats into the mountains or striding out along paths threading into remote valleys, and you will want to follow. The idyllic hamlet of San Isidro is three hours' walk away. At Easter the houses are strewn with flowers, and in summer, roofs are covered with tiny peaches drying in the sun. From Iruya, there are blissful walks all around, but the real pleasure of arriving here is that you will not want to leave.

Bring a book, allow at least five days, and prepare to slow down. Stay in villagers' houses, snuggling under heavy llama blankets in winter, or in a comfortable room at Hostería Iruya. Gaze out from the terrace over the valley below; look up to a night sky filled with stars, and listen to the exquisite silence. **CD**

➡ *The mountain village of Iruya offers a rare glimpse of a vanishing way of life for Andean people.*

Relax at Estancia El Colibrí

Location Córdoba, Argentina
Website www.estanciaelcolibri.com   **Price** 💲💲

Blending together effortlessly the ambience and tradition of an old Argentine estancia with the style and luxury of a contemporary five-star hotel, El Colibrí is a working cattle ranch that shrugs off rustic chic for modern elegance. Set in 420 acres (170 ha) of land, it is part private garden and part national park, and the views are endless.

Its nine rooms are divided into three suites and six junior suites and deluxe rooms, all with personal details, including a roaring open fire to welcome you. Beyond the rooms, the hotel extends: The summerhouse has a relaxing bar and living room, with an Andalucian arch, tiled floors, chandeliers hanging from the high-beamed ceiling, and acid-colored, elegant furniture. No wonder *Harpers* staged a fabulous fashion shoot here; *Vogue* and *Tatler* have also tipped it as a hot retreat.

The beauty is not just skin deep: Guests say that the service and attention to detail they have experienced stay with them, whether that is wine tasting with their host in the extensive cellar, learning to play polo or dance the tango, or the superb bush barbecue out on the ranch, with grilled llama, pork ribs, and lamb.

You can look out to the Córdoba Mountains from the swimming pool, or indulge in a Finnish sauna, Turkish bath, or hot tub to soothe your aching muscles after a long jaunt on horseback, where you can learn the art of cattle rustling or sheepherding. Special indulgence is reserved for the final night, when guests are treated to a personally prepared dinner for two in the privacy of their own balcony. **LD**

◄ *The charming colonial-style ranch house is set in the middle of the beautiful Argentine campo.*

Ride Horses at Los Potreros

Location Córdoba, Argentina
Website www.ride-americas.com   **Price** $

There is something strange going on at Los Potreros, a 6,000-acre (2,428-ha) cattle ranch high in the hills of the Sierras Chicas. Everyone, from the gauchos to the kitchen girls to the guests, seems to be perpetually smiling. Maybe it is something they put in the maté.

Los Potreros has belonged to the Begg family for generations. They breed cattle, as they have for hundreds of years, but nowadays Robin and Kevin Begg run a tourist operation, too, offering luxurious horse-riding vacations. Born in Argentina but educated in the United Kingdom, Robin and Kevin appear to be quintessentially English. The farmhouse dining room blends Sheffield silverware with battered

---

"If Michelin did a Riding Tour Guide, Los Potreros would come out top."

Lord Patrick Beresford, *Ultimate Travel*

British tomes: Winston Churchill's *The Second World War,* and *Lady Chatterley's Lover.* There is homemade marmalade for breakfast. Step outside, however, and it is glorious Argentina, complete with bickering parakeets and beret-bedecked gauchos. The horses—criollos and *paso peruanos*—are well mannered and soft mouthed. Visitors can embark on multiday trail rides, play polo, or merely amble for a couple of hours in the estancia's swaying, pale-gold tussock. On your return, you will be greeted with tea, homemade cake, or perhaps even a glass of Los Potreros's own label wine to whet your appetite before dinner. Really, this is not a difficult riding vacation at all. **PE**

Stay at Alvear Palace Hotel

Location Buenos Aires, Argentina
Website www.alvearpalace.com   **Price** $$

This grand old hotel, with its stately feel and chic location in the Recoleta region, is a genuine Buenos Aires institution. Indeed, this is the very place where Evita Peron—the erstwhile first lady of Argentina and a national heroine—enjoyed having afternoon tea. Today, it is still where the beautiful people hang out to enjoy the hotel's signature afternoon tea service, served in the elegant Winter Garden lounge from 4 P.M. every day. Little has changed since Eva's day, but the rhubarb pie is fresher than ever.

The hotel itself oozes with period charm: Think a decor straight from Versailles at the time of Louis XVI with historic artworks adorning the walls and Renaissance furnishings gracing the elegant suites. The in-house restaurant, L'Orangerie, also has a decidedly European feel, and the spa offers a comprehensive range of treatments. The main selling point, however, remains the hotel's Evita-rich heritage. It is just a short hop from the hotel's front door to the Recoleta Cemetery, where her body was laid to rest under cover of darkness in 1974, and a quick taxi ride across town brings you to the presidential offices of La Casa Rosada, where she delivered her most memorable and moving speeches, her fist raised and her hair scraped back in a severe bun.

Today the Alvear Palace is far more closely associated with the Hollywood A-list than with any heads of state: Actors Antonio Banderas, Catherine Deneuve, and Salma Hayek are among many of the big-name celebrities who are known to soak up the hotel's refined ambience. For Evita purists, however, the hotel will forever be her domain, and the legions of ladies of a certain age returning each afternoon to have tea are testimony to her enduring legacy. **DA**

Enjoy La Corona Sanctuary

Location Buenos Aires Province, Argentina
Website www.lacoronasanctuary.com **Price** 💲💲

Just a four-hour drive southwest of Buenos Aires, among the open horizons of the pampas, La Corona Sanctuary is both a luxurious home and a working farm, owned by the same family since 1875. It also offers a complete program of yoga and holistic spa treatments, including shiatsu and Reiki healing.

La Corona's emphasis is squarely on relaxation and indulgence. There are just six rooms here: two in the pool house affording privacy away from the main residence, with French doors opening onto manicured lawns, and four rooms in the main house, including one large double room overlooking the veranda. Attentive staff are on hand to cook you breakfast,

> "It does not take long to attune to the rhythm of this boutique resort."

travelintelligence.com

clean your room, make you tea, and launder your clothes, leaving you free to begin your day with an hour of yoga before heading out to the bird sanctuary or taking a leisurely ride in La Corona's horse and buggy. For those after more sedentary pursuits, there are hammocks sprinkled throughout the home's lush gardens and a billiards table, and for lunch you can indulge in an *asado*, a traditional Argentine barbecue.

It is the spa that this hotel has built its reputation around. Guests are encouraged to stay a week or more so they can take advantage of the many treatments at their disposal, including asanas programs that focus on the regeneration of the whole body. **BS**

Visit Dos Talas

Location Buenos Aires Province, Argentina
Website www.dostalas.com.ar **Price** 💲💲💲💲

Just two hours' drive from the frenzy of Buenos Aires across the flat pampas where vast fields are dotted with cattle, a long track leads between silvery elms into a plantation of soaring monkey puzzle trees and to a clearing of pristine green lawns. There sits a grand French-style chateau dating from 1893 that has sweeping staircases, balconies, and yellow awnings. Under the tall eucalyptus trees, a long table is laid for lunch and your hosts are waiting to welcome you, grilling huge, succulent home-reared steaks on a traditional Argentine *asado*. Sip a glass of Malbec, bite into a spicy empanada, and relax. You are home.

No trip to Argentina is complete without staying at an estancia, the cattle farms that made Argentina wealthy. Dos Talas is both the most romantic and the most authentic example. Here, you are a guest of the owners, descendants of the founder Pedro Luro. They will show you the park, filled with avenues of towering trees, created by Argentina's leading landscape architect, Charles Thays; they will invite you to make yourself at home in the gracious interiors, which thronged with the life of literary salons when Gatsby-style parties spilled from the high-ceilinged rooms onto the elegant terraces. The history is palpable: in the extensive library and in the evocative photographs that cover the antique tables. Guests sleep in carved mahogany beds on crisp white linen and wake to fling the French doors open onto a private balcony. Spend the morning strolling around the grounds and the afternoon sitting by the pool, gazing out over the apparently limitless plains. As the sun sinks on the curving horizon, set out with the resident gaucho to ride a horse into the sunset. Filled with peace, you will return to dine in style and sleep deeply. **CD**

Enjoy Faena Hotel

Location Buenos Aires, Argentina
Website www.faenahotelanduniverse.com   **Price** 🌑🌑

Arriving at night at this decadent Buenos Aires beauty is perhaps the best way to appreciate its sumptuous decor and sophisticated brand of chic. It is certainly the best way to savor the Faena's electrifying Philippe Starck design, from the red-lit walkway into a towering, spice-scented hall, and from the wild whimsy of its Bistro restaurant to the cool splendor of one of 110 bedrooms in signature white, red, and gold.

Playing up the drama of the hotel concept at every turn, the Faena deftly marries audacious fantasy with the decadence and drama of the belle epoque. And it is appropriate, too, because the hotel is housed in what was once a grain storehouse from where Argentina's agricultural riches were exported to the world in its turn-of-the-century heyday. After a cozy aperitif to the strains of a grand piano in the rich wood and leather library, modeled on the old-fashioned luxury of a 1900s ranch, it is a deliciously shocking thrill to move on to the Bistro for dinner. There the menu treads a sure-footed line between timeless excellence and the stylishly modern. A dinner here studded with airs, foams, spherifications, and deconstructions of classic dishes is de rigueur for lovers of both fine cuisine and haute design. If you get the timing right, you can then move on into the snug cabaret theater, where one of the city's finest tango shows comes complete with an orchestra, free-flowing wine and champagne, and wonderfully saucy dancers. There, huddled at a tiny, intimate, candlelit table, the theatricality of the entire place crystallizes into a sensual, melancholy pageant of tango. **CR**

→ *Wall-mounted unicorn heads gaze across the opulent, theatrical decor of the Bistro restaurant.*

Stay at La Pascuala

Location Tigre River Delta, Argentina
Website www.lapascuala.com   **Price** ⬡⬡

Just an hour from Buenos Aires, there is a wild, romantic, natural paradise only *porteños* (inhabitants of the Argentine capital) know about. Viewed from above, the Tigre River Delta is an ornate lacework of rivers strewn with hundreds of islands.

As your kayak slips away from the small town of Tigre, with its century-old rowing clubs in palatial buildings, there is a blissful sense of escaping to the jungle. The river narrows to a tunnel between tall trees and lush vegetation, with shafts of sunlight streaming through to illuminate pleasure boats cruising gently by. The banks are lined with quaint wooden houses on stilts, and families drinking maté on rickety old jetties wave as you row past. Later on, once you have crossed the Paraná River to enter the remote second section of the delta, there are few houses. The rivers are quieter here, the vegetation more wild, the domain of herons and garzas. Then, deep in the jungle, a series of tall stilts rises up from the river and, amid the trees, you glimpse the elegant buildings of La Pascuala. Concierges meet the boat and carry your bags to your room while you slip into the tub. You have arrived.

La Pascuala is a haven of good taste and luxury in the depths of beautiful wilderness. Each suite is an individual lodge on stilts, secluded by greenery, and with its own veranda where you can stretch out on loungers in perfect privacy. The bedroom is immense; the bathroom is almost equally expansive, and even the bathtub has a view. Drink gin on the terrace before slipping into the intimate dining room for a superb dinner. The service is discreet and top-notch. There is no more romantic retreat from the city. And you do not have to row: A fast motor launch whisks you here from Tigre's train station in an hour. **CD**

Enjoy Estancia Peuma Hue

Location Bariloche, Patagonia, Argentina
Website www.peuma-hue.com   **Price** ⬡⬡⬡⬡

Open the curtains and there is the lake, stretching out before you, ultramarine blue and glistening. To your side, a great wall of mountain, snowcapped and thickly forested, descends to the water. Explore trails to waterfalls through a cathedral of coihue forest—spotting the scarlet-headed Magellanic woodpecker among innumerable other birds. Take a kayak out on the water or ride with the horse whisperer to remoter lakes not reached by road: You will have it all to yourself. Argentina's Lake District is unmatched for natural adventures within a spectacular setting: dramatic mountains and lakes of all hues immersed in virgin forest. But, uniquely, Peuma Hue has its own

> *"Our first goal was to preserve Peuma Hue's pristine forests, waters, and fauna."*

Proprietors, Estancia Peuma Hue

private stretch of lakeshore and a vast swath of mountainside, so guests can explore this natural splendor alone. No wonder that Peuma Hue means "place of dreams" in the native Mapuche language.

The estancia is the creation of owner Evelyn Hoter, whose aim is to offer complete contact with nature. She and her staff welcome guests by the fire each evening with a glass of wine before a delicious dinner, and make expert guides on hikes and adventures. Four beautiful cabins scattered in the grounds offer a spectrum from a luxurious suite with a grand bed and double whirlpool tub to the perfectly secluded mountain cabin, perfect for a romantic retreat. **CD**

Spend an Afternoon at Las Balsas

Location Villa La Angostura, Patagonia, Argentina
Website www.lasbalsas.com.ar   **Price** 🌎

Villa La Angostura in Argentina's Patagonia is a quaint village with a friendly atmosphere. Despite being in South America, it has a slightly Swiss feel to it, which could be down to the very tempting chocolate shops on every corner, or perhaps the chalet-style homes. Set aside from the small town, Las Balsas is a hideaway in a league of its own. Hidden far down a small dirt track, within the Nahuel Huapi National Park—one of the most beautiful spots in Patagonia—this certainly is not a place you will stumble across by chance.

With just twelve rooms and three suites, it is guaranteed to be intimate. Each room has its own style, from the all dusty-pink room with its stunning views framed by the Andes to the elegant red-striped scheme. There is even a sophisticated, simple beige suite transformed with original varnished canoes cut in half and upturned in lieu of side tables. In addition to the interior and exterior pool, there is a stone spa with an incredible array of treatments: everything from a "golden face mask," with gold acting as an anti-inflammatory and antioxidant, to a full-body "chocotherapy," using chocolate as a base element.

The hotel's star attraction is definitely the restaurant and the charming wine-tasting lounge built from cypress and stone. Nibble on trout seviche, king crab with coconut milk, or venison with a blackcurrant and chocolate sauce before trying the Argentine's favorite dessert: *dulce de leche* served with red fruit sherbet and coconut cookie by chef Pablo Campoy. Las Balsas might be in the middle of nowhere, but that does not mean you have to compromise on comfort. **RCA**

↗ *The distinctive blue clapboard hotel is a luxurious paradise off the beaten track.*

"Each room or suite has its own style and a privileged view of Nahuel Huapi Lake."

Road & Travel magazine

Explore Seven Lakes Route

Location Patagonia, Argentina
Website www.patagonia-argentina.com **Price** ❶

Some say that getting to your chosen destination is as much of an adventure as the time spent there. This is certainly the case when traveling from the tiny town of San Martin de Los Andes in Patagonia to Villa La Angostura along the "Ruta de los Siete Lagos"—the Seven Lakes route.

The road, part of National Route 234, winds its way across 67 miles (107 km) of the Neuquén Province's two national parks: Nahuel Huapi and Lanin, with about 25 miles (40 km) of dirt tracks. Be warned about the lack of asphalt; the dust and gravel roads are more suitable for rally driving. The charming ski resort of San Martin is all wood and stone cabins, stores crammed with ski gear, alpaca sweaters, and scarves. Tranquil, it is the last sign of civilization until Villa La Angostura.

The scenery is so extreme that it causes visitors to catch their breath in surprise. Without veering off route, all seven lakes are visible across the flawless mountainous landscapes against the backdrop of the Andes. Machónico, Escondido, Correntoso, Espejo, Lácar, Falkner, and Villarino are each as beautiful as the last.

This is not the Patagonia of flat pampas, but rather a South American equivalent of the Alps, and magnified. You would expect bears and mountain lions to roam the hills, but instead only horses and fuzzy-headed cows wander across the road to graze where the grass is greener. Visit in the spring when melting ice and heavy waterfalls have new life sprouting vivid red and orange blooms to coat the already striking scenery. It is also the end of the ski season, which means everyone else has gone home. **RCA**

➦ *Every turn in the road uncovers a picturesque panorama of lake, mountains, and dense forest.*

Stay at Estancia Cristina

Location Patagonia, Argentina
Website www.estanciacristina.com **Price** 🜲🜲

As the boat leaves civilization behind and enters the more remote reaches of turquoise Lago Argentino, slipping between icebergs the size of houses, it is reasonable to wonder where you are going to end up. The three-hour journey takes visitors to the mighty Upsala glacier, past sheer walls of ice rising to a staggering 230 feet (70 m) above you, then suddenly calving off with a roar into the water beneath. As the boat approaches the end of the lake's northernmost arm, four tiny buildings can be seen, isolated on the wild shore, against a backdrop of magnificent mountains: This is Estancia Cristina.

This remote Patagonian farm, founded by a hardy English family a century ago, now welcomes visitors to stay in plush new cabins, where they can lounge by a picture window to survey the fabulous views with a fine glass of wine before dinner. Spare a thought for the original inhabitants, though, who raise sheep here through the austere winter, while you ponder whether to eat the seared salmon or the Patagonian lamb, cooked slowly over an open fire. Walking back in the chilly starlit night toward the cozy guest cabins offers just enough austerity to make you appreciate your warm room and comfortable bed.

The really unforgettable experience of Cristina, however, is to travel with your guide up to a mountain ridge where long stretches of vermilion rock, polished smooth by ancient glaciers, lead to a spectacular vista. Far below, stretching out to the distant horizon, lies Upsala glacier: silent, unfathomable, and awe-inspiring. Hike down a stunning canyon to find fossilized ammonites and mollusks, but no mark of man anywhere. Just herds of guanacos, wild horses, and rivers filled with Chinook salmon. **CD**

Relax at Design Suites

Location El Calafate, Patagonia, Argentina
Website www.designsuites.com **Price** 🜲🜲

Designed by world-renowned architect Carlos Ott, the five-star Design Suites hotel is a masterpiece of environmental architecture. Using only local materials, this luxury hotel encompasses an art gallery, a design shop, and a gourmet restaurant with views over Lago Argentino that defy belief. Although it is an impressive edifice, the real attraction lies in its details; a Patagonian design collective was commissioned for the furniture and interiors. Each of the sixty suites has floor-to-ceiling windows that frame a vista of the beautifully barren Patagonia, with mountainous peaks in the distance and a mirrored lake at the fore. An indoor-and-outdoor heated pool, spa, sauna, health

> ## *"The Design Suites cater to the design-conscious visitor. It's an impressive destination hotel."*
>
> *Wallpaper*

club, and wine bar complete a stay at what must be one of the most impressive hotels in South America. No one visits Patagonia for a hotel alone. If visitors can be dragged out of the hotel, they will walk out into El Calafate: the gateway to the famous Perito Moreno glacier. As its crumbling face crashes into the lake with clockwork regularity, visitors are all but dumbstruck at this unique sight. Beyond El Calafate are lakes and mountains perfect for skiing in winter and hiking in summer. But these are only two of a host of activities the hotel can organize. Soar over the glacier in a hot-air balloon or travel by horse up into the forests and deep into the national parks. **DN**

View the Patagonian Wilderness from Eolo

Location Near El Calafate, Patagonia, Argentina
Website www.eolo.com.ar **Price** 🌀🌀🌀

Few places inspire a greater sense of solitude than the wild panoramas of Patagonia, near the southern tip of South America, where the treeless, uninhabitable steppes roll out interminably, and the silence is broken only by the wind. For visitors preferring white cotton and soft blankets to chilly nights under canvas, there is no finer perch from which to contemplate the Patagonian wilderness than Eolo. Its seventeen suites all have vast picture windows framing unimaginable views across the empty plains and boundless skies, punctuated only by lakes, mountains, and—on a clear day—the pointy peaks of Torres del Paine straddling the border with Chile.

This luxury lodge, on a 4,000-acre (1,618-ha) cattle ranch, sets the benchmark for indulgent Patagonian retreats. The rooms are the height of comfort (king-sized beds, fluffy towels, generously upholstered armchairs), the decor is impeccably stylish yet always discreet (rightly leaving the big statements to nature), and the helpful staff and all-inclusive rates eliminate the merest hint of hassle. Staff will even prepare you a gourmet lunch box.

Eolo redefines the vacation cliché "getting away from it all." Understandably, the owners have refrained from installing televisions in the bedrooms—the view offers something considerably more engaging. Borrow binoculars or use the huge telescope in the lounge to zoom in on the hawks, eagles, and Patagonia hares that populate the plain. Do not miss the creaking mass that is the Perito Moreno glacier, the world's largest advancing glacier, just a half-hour drive away. **IA**

↗ *The Eolo building itself sits at the top of a treeless hill, with a spectacular view of the plains below.*

"This hushed valley hideaway lies nestled in a serene landscape blanketed in tall tufts of coirón."

preferredboutique.com

See Perito Moreno Glacier

Location Santa Cruz Province, Argentina
Website www.parquesnacionales.gov.ar   **Price ()**

Patagonia tempts us with its absolutes: the dry desert, the frozen seas, the dead-straight highways. But it is also a region of awesome juxtapositions. Head west across the arid steppe at the fiftieth parallel in Argentina and you arrive at the Perito Moreno glacier, cradled by ancient beech forests and framed by the jagged peaks of the Andes. The centerpiece of the stunning Parque Nacional Los Glaciares, the Moreno is surreally beautiful and beguiling. Almost discovered by FitzRoy and Darwin on their landmark voyage of 1831 to 1836, the glacier was finally sighted by its namesake, Francisco Pascasio Moreno, in 1877.

Today, visitors can choose how they want to experience this vast, creaking, ever-expanding tongue of ice. Some like to trek across the cakelike surface, others go ice climbing, or hover just below the cigar-shaped clouds in microlight aircraft. Idlers can simply take a seat and gawp from the comfort of the platform on Península Magallanes or ride in one of the numerous catamarans and cruisers that pass close to the continually collapsing—technically speaking, calving—wall. This wall reaches heights of 200 feet (60 m), whereas the glacier itself spreads over some 160 square miles (414 sq km), making it as big as the city of Buenos Aires. Impressed? Then consider that the Southern Ice Field, for which the Moreno is an outlet glacier, is the same size as Israel. The Perito Moreno ruptures every four to five years when the water flowing through the Brazo Rico undermines its east-facing central wall, causing a spectacle that brings in visitors from all over the world. **CM**

➡ *The awe-inspiring Perito Moreno is one of only three Patagonian glaciers that are not retreating.*

Europe offers an enviable variety of places to stay that suit every taste and budget. Choose between a French converted windmill, a Scottish castle, a Greek island, or an Italian medieval fortress. If you want more action, try a horseback ride through the hills of southern Spain, a canal trip through Burgundy, or a train journey through Germany. The choice is yours.

← **Castello Di Vicarello, Italy**

EUROPE

Explore St. Helena

Location St. Helena, South Atlantic
Website www.sthelena.se   **Price** 🚫🚫

It is not surprising that the British chose remote St. Helena as the final place of exile for Emperor Napoleon, because this tiny speck in the South Atlantic is more than 750 miles (1,207 km) from the nearest dry land. Funding is in place for the construction of an airport that is set to commence operations in 2010, but for now the only regular scheduled way to get to the island is aboard the mail ship RMS *St. Helena*. This rugged little workhorse is the island's lifeline, bringing in some 1,500 tons of supplies and up to 170 passengers on each voyage. Visitors board in Cape Town, spend two days and nights sailing up to Namibia's wild Skeleton Coast, then head off toward the

> *"Desolate and lush by turns, it has a landscape that seems to offer the whole planet in miniature."*

Jenny Diski, *Observer*

sunset into the vastness of the Atlantic Ocean for five days out at sea, to arrive in a time warp of Englishness.

A starkly barren, red volcanic rock coastline gives way to a lushly green, subtropical interior that is dizzyingly hilly. Those who have a head for heights can climb the 750 steps of the Jacob's Ladder staircase, that soars up the cliff from the friendly little capital town of Jamestown. Others might prefer to while away the afternoon watching fishermen tend their lobster pots. It is all remote but surprisingly civilized.

Returning to Europe entails another two days by sea to the even less populated Ascension Island, followed by a military flight to Brize Norton, England. **RsP**

Dogsled in Greenland

Location Kangerlussuaq, Greenland
Website www.greenland.com   **Price** 🚫🚫

In the snow and ice-bound wonderland that is Greenland you can witness nature at its most raw, go whale-watching, or kayak the icy waters. Most of all, though, you'll want to dogsled and, after a few days' tuition, you can even drive the dogs yourself.

Hurtling through a whiter-than-white wilderness behind a howling pack of eager husky dogs is an almost otherworldly experience. Pull on a pair of snug musk ox–fur boots and a cozy sealskin coat and liberally apply sunblock against a sun that glares fiercely from an impossibly blue sky, even with the temperature at -30°F (-34°C). Then sit yourself on a reindeer-skin-clad sled as your Inuit driver urges dogs on: Here they run side by side, six abreast, rather than in the more familiar setup of pairs in a line.

Fly into Kangerlussuaq airport, a gateway that, amazingly, cancels fewer flights because of bad weather than almost any other airport on Earth. This is the land of the midnight sun and the incredible natural light show afforded by the northern lights. The unforgiving savageness of the environment is never more than a few steps away. And, in any case, the road runs out just a few miles beyond city limits.

For 10,000 years a unique partnership between humans and their dogs has helped make this place inhabitable, and sledding with them gives a fascinating insight into this relationship. With luck you might get to have lunch in a freshly built igloo and finish your day with a glass of 30-year-old whiskey chilled by ice lumps hewn that afternoon from the 15-million-year-old polar ice cap. **RsP**

⇨ *Beautiful sunsets light up the ice and cast a wonderful sheen over the frozen landcapes you sled across.*

See the Northern Lights

Location Iceland **Website** www.icelandtotal.com
Price ◑

In ancient Iceland, citizens believed that if a pregnant woman looked at the northern lights, her child would be born cross-eyed. Native Americans imagined they could conjure up ghosts and spirits if they whistled to the lights. Today astronomers' explanations are more prosaic. Through explosions and flares, the sun emits particles that travel toward Earth and penetrate its upper atmosphere at the polar regions. Molecules and atoms in Earth's atmosphere collide with the sun's particles, absorbing some of their energy. In order to return to their nonenergized state, they emit light as photons—which we see as the northern lights.

The northern lights are best seen beneath the "auroral oval," which lies around Earth's magnetic poles. Iceland sits right in the middle and, as long as the sky is clear and dark, it is one of the top places in the world to see the aurora, especially between September and March. Tour operators take guests away from the interference of the city lights, and usually provide warm shelter.

A good display can last just minutes, but is so striking that you will remember it forever. Green and red ribbons weave across black starry skies, then tumble into three-dimensional tepees before twirling heavenward like a green genie. They seem to die away, but then, just as you think the show is over, pale fingers of jade creep up from the horizon, and then grow stronger into spikes, and finally streaks that hurtle across the heavens. Now you feel that you have not only escaped the hubbub of the modern world, but reached a new universe altogether. **PE**

◁ *The northern lights dance in green ribbons and swirls across the night sky above Iceland.*

Visit Snæfellsjökull Glacier

Location Snæfellness Peninsula, Iceland
Website english.ust.is/Snaefellsjokullnationalpark   **Price** ❶

There are so many stories about this area of Iceland that it is hard to know where to begin. New agers claim it as a seat of mystical energy, the country's Nobel Prize–winning author Halldór Laxness came here for inspiration, and Jules Verne chose it as the doorway to the heart of the world in *Journey to the Center of the Earth*. Mysterious lights seen here at night suggest visits by otherworldly visitors—it is nature, but not quite as you know it.

The peninsula can be seen on a clear day from Reykjavik across Faxaflói Bay, capped with the precious white peak of its cone-shaped glacier. The area around the glacier is a national park and includes winding single-track roads, cliffs full of nesting seabirds, lava-strewn pastures, and the kind of peace and quiet that you can find only up here at the end of the world.

Beaches around the peninsula show glimpses of another world; pods of orca prowl, and twisted pieces of rusty metal are all that is left of boats run ashore on the black sand in years gone by. In Djupalonssandir, great round rocks, once used by the Vikings in tests of strength, sit to the left of the path on the way to the beach. Some of Iceland's best-loved sagas took place here, and Christopher Columbus allegedly spent a winter in the region. There are not many places left in the world that can genuinely lay claim to the adjective "unspoiled," but this is one of them. Breathe in the air fresh from the glacier and feel blessed to be alive as you watch the hardy Icelandic ponies canter in deep pasture, pale manes flying out behind them. **LD**

← *This isolated church with its typically Icelandic red roof sits in the lap of Snæfellsjökull Glacier.*

Relax at Landmannalaugar Hot Springs

Location Near Reykjavik, Iceland
Website www.landmannalaugar.info   **Price** ❶

The hot springs at Landmannalaugar have long been a popular destination for visitors seeking relief from a number of ailments. Whether you suffer from chronic arthritis, head-splitting migraines, depression, or simply stress, the hot springs are renowned for their healing and therapeutic powers.

Lying 1,970 feet (600 m) above sea level, and comprising one of the largest geothermal fields in the country, Landmannalaugar (which means "hot springs of the people" in Icelandic) is surrounded by volcanic peaks and black lava fields. This part of Iceland in the southern highlands is rich in geothermal activity—

> *"[It is] a stream that mixes with a hot spring into a shallow pool, surrounded by wildflowers."*
>
> *Observer*

numerous hot and cold springs run down from the lava field and converge in vast open-air hot baths that are popular for swimming and bathing. It is reasonably accessible in summer, although the road is a bit rough and makes for a bumpy journey.

Once you have overcome the initial heart-stopping shock of getting undressed in such a chilly climate, it is sheer bliss to plunge into the steaming hot, mineral-rich water. Aches and pains simply ebb away as the soothing heat works its magic. To make the most of the spring, ensure that you move around in order to experience the rejuvenating contrast between the hot and the icy water swirling around. **HA**

Unwind at the Blue Lagoon

Location Grindavik, Iceland **Website** www.bluelagoon.com
Price $

The Blue Lagoon may be a man-made attraction, but it seems to meld into Iceland's unearthly lunar landscape. Located about 24 miles (39 km) outside Reykjavik and about 8 miles (13 km) from Keflavik International Airport, the Blue Lagoon is (deservedly) one of the country's top attractions.

Measuring a massive 53,800 square feet (5,000 sq m), the giant outdoor geothermal baths are rich in natural mineral salts and algae, said to have a curative effect on the skin, especially for those suffering from psoriasis. Clouds of steam float above the milky blue waters, which top a toasty 104°F (40°C), making it hard to drag yourself out—especially when wearing a bikini and the air temperature is below freezing. In winter, the lagoon is often surrounded by snow, and it is then that the contrast between the icy-cold air and the cozy warmth of the water is irresistible. In fact, Icelanders believe the ideal outdoor temperature to make the most of the lagoon is a teeth-chattering 14°F (-10°C). Slather on silica mud, available in boxes around the pool, to cleanse and exfoliate, and if you get bored with bathing, head to the sauna and steam room. For a rejuvenating back massage, stand underneath the lagoon's small waterfall, which pounds away aches and pains.

The surrounding scenery is strange yet dramatic. The lagoon is nestled in among black lava rocks, there are mountains in the distance, and a power station nearby pumps the geothermally heated water from a mile belowground. Stay in until your skin is as wrinkled as a prune—it will do you the power of good. **JK**

← *Clouds of steam hang above the Blue Lagoon,
where the waters are much warmer than the air.*

Explore the Faroe Islands

Location North Atlantic, Faroe Islands
Website www.visit-faroeislands.com   **Price** $

The Faroe Islands are a daunting panorama of jagged volcanic mountains, immense sheer-sided cliffs, long dark fjords, and bleak windswept moorland. North Atlantic waves crash against black rock pillars standing alone in the sea, and basalt peaks loom through dark clouds. It looks like a scene from *The Lord of the Rings*.

The eighteen Faroe Islands are a self-governing part of Denmark, located between Scotland and Iceland. They offer one of the most authentic escapes available anywhere in Europe. Although much of the land is dramatically steep and wild, cut by deep fjords, the capital, Tórshavn, is surprisingly cosmopolitan and there are good galleries, museums, restaurants,

> *" . . . a remote land where the sheep are fearless, the birds are shrewd, and the weather is a state of mind."*
>
> Sarah Crown, *Guardian*

and bars. The hotels are products of the 1970s, with lots of mirrors and an enthusiastic use of the color orange. Stay in a bed-and-breakfast or rent a traditional wooden house with the old, dark wooden upper floor, balcony, and living grass–covered roof.

Relax and enjoy the unspoiled green countryside with stunning seascapes around every corner and the freshest air in Europe. The maritime climate means it is rarely freezing, but changeable between wet and misty, clear and sunny. Take a memorable trip by boat or subsidized inter-island helicopter to gaze at cliffs and rocks overflowing with seabirds. Whales are common offshore—and on restaurant menus. **SH**

Enjoy Storfjord Hotel

Location Sunnmøre, Norway
Website www.storfjordhotel.com   **Price** $$

Small is definitely beautiful when it comes to the chic Storfjord Hotel. It is handcrafted using *lafta* (cross logging with whole timbers) and has just six rooms, exquisitely designed to ensure guests are never far from nature. Set in 6 acres (2.4 ha) of private grounds amid thousands of acres of protected forest in western Norway, the hotel lies between three mountains and a lake and overlooks the stunning Sunnmøre Alps.

A fusion of modern style and authentic tradition, each room has a luxurious bathroom and a large balcony to take in the panoramic views—some even have four-poster beds. Rooms also come equipped with a television, DVD player, and wireless broadband Internet access to keep in touch with the outside world. Spend the day kayaking in the Glomset Bay or hiking to the summit of nearby Hautua Mountain for magnificent views across the village to Storfjorden, Skodje, and the surrounding lakes and fjords. The more adventurous can take the ferry to the rugged mountains of the Sunnmøre Alps for high-altitude walking. Return to the hotel for dinner in the timbered hall in front of a roaring open fire and a nightcap on the gallery landing overlooking Glomset Bay and the snowcapped mountains in the distance.

Many guests use the hotel as a base to explore Norway's stunning west coast, with Ålesund and the islands to the west and the dramatic fjords and mountains to the east. Sitting at the gateway to the Golden Route, from here take in some of the world's most breathtaking scenery, including Geirangerfjord, a UNESCO World Heritage site. A drive through the valleys, high mountains, and deep fjords offers views of tumbling waterfalls and majestic mountains. Mother Nature has never looked so good. **AD**

Discover the Lofoten Islands

Location Lofoten Islands, Norway
Website www.lofoten.info   **Price** ◑

They look like sheer walls of mountains rising dramatically from the sea. Venture closer to the Lofoten Islands, though, and you will find sandy coves, spectacular moors, and lonesome marshes. Simple wooden buildings, often painted deep rust red, lie scattered amid the green.

The Lofoten Islands lie north of the Arctic Circle, but their climate is surprisingly mild. They have been inhabited for 6,000 years, although the fishing village of Henningsvær, the largest community in the Lofotens, has a population of only 500. It was not connected to the other islands by bridges until the early 1980s.

Alongside its fishing interests, this is an artistic community, with art displays and a glassblowing studio. Killer-whale safaris depart from here in winter—the whales follow migrating herring up the Tysfjord and Vestfjord—and there are trips to spot sea eagles in the summer months. Some of these birds have wingspans of 6.5 feet (2 m). Røst and Værøy have eider ducks, puffins, and majestic white-tailed and sea eagles. Outdoor sports enthusiasts can hike, bike, climb, and kayak in the summer months and enjoy the midnight sun. From mid-February to April, the Lofoten Islands buzz with life as fishermen from across Norway's coast stream here for the cod that swim in their millions to spawning grounds nearby.

To really experience a new way of life, try staying in a fisherman's cabin, or *rorbu*, many of which have been converted to provide accommodation ranging from rustic to luxury. Some wharf buildings, or *sjøhus*, have also been converted into guesthouses. **PE**

↗ *A small village on Moskenes Island—one of the Lofoten Islands—in winter.*

"[The Lofoten Islands] have a mystical presence in the collective psyche of [the Norwegians]."

Independent

Enjoy a Snowmobile Safari

Location Luosto, Finnish Lapland
Website www.snowgames.fi **Price** 🌀🌀

The northern lights, the natural phenomenon caused when electrons from outer space collide with Earth's atmosphere, light up the skies of the Arctic Circle with streaks of red, pink, and green. The native Sami people nicknamed the lights "the foxfires," believing them to be sparks brushed into the night sky by the tail of the Arctic fox. The farther north you travel, the more likely you are to see this stunning natural spectacle. It appears year-round, but is more obvious during the winter months, when the long, dark nights provide the perfect backdrop for this celestial light show.

There are many ways to enjoy the lights, from midnight snowshoe treks to husky-drawn sled rides. One of the most exhilarating options is to join a snowmobile safari. Against an inky-black night sky, the winter landscape is bathed in a soft, blue glow of reflected moonlight and the absolute silence is broken only by the nasal hum of the snowmobiles as they wind through the powdery trails. The freezing temperatures are cold enough to turn the tears on your eyelashes into icicles, but the snowmobiles' seats and handles are heated, keeping you toasty and warm inside your thick Arctic snowsuit. Cups of hot, tangy lingonberry juice help to warm you from the inside.

The sky above is painted with fiery streaks of color that dance across the heavens, shifting and shimmering like a heavenly fireworks display. The pine trees are heavy with snow, their branches buckled under the weight like bizarre sculptures. Lit up by the headlights of the snowmobiles, snow crystals make everything look like it has been dusted with glitter. **JP**

⬅ *Snowmobiling across frozen Lapland is an exciting way to experience the splendor of the northern lights.*

Stay at Utter Inn

Location Lake Mälaren, Västerås, Sweden
Website www.vasterasmalarstaden.se **Price** 🌀🌀

The Utter Inn (Otter Inn in English) is one of the strangest places to sleep in the world. First, you board a rubber dinghy in the port of Västerås and are taken out 0.6 miles (1 km) on Lake Mälaren. Your destination appears to be a small shed floating on a diving platform. The small red hut contains a bathroom and a hatch in the floor. Open the hatch and descend a metal ladder to find your bedroom—in a watertight chamber suspended in the water beneath the hut.

Is the Utter Inn an escape? Some find it more like solitary confinement from which they want to escape. Others enjoy the isolation, the peace, and the slight sense of danger. You are not only literally sleeping with

> *"[It] includes a sense of risk taking and adventure that tends to expand the sensory input."*
>
> unusualhotelsoftheworld.com

the fishes, but can watch them, too. Or rather, be watched by them, in a bizarre reversal of a goldfish bowl. The lake's pike and perch gather at the room's windows, peering in at their unusual visitors.

The Utter Inn is the brainchild of Mikael Genberg, a local artist. His previous work was The Woodpecker, a treehouse hotel where food was hoisted up by rope. At Utter, dinner can be delivered by boat in the evening, or else guests can paddle to shore in an inflatable canoe. A picnic breakfast is also provided. Guests can sunbathe on the floating platform and, as far as leisure facilities go, the hotel is unique in that it floats within its own swimming pool. **SH**

Relax at the Icehotel

Location Jukkasjärvi, Sweden **Website** www.icehotel.com **Price** $ $

> "[T]he ice itself is completely transparent ... which makes it look otherworldly."

Juliet Eilperin, *Washington Post*

⬆ *A woman lies on a bed covered in reindeer skins at the Icehotel in Lapland, Sweden.*

➡ *A room inside the Icehotel—the hotel changes each year as old sculptures melt and new ones are carved.*

Back in the late 1980s, a Swede named Yngve Bergqvist had a vision. In Swedish Lapland, 125 miles (200 km) north of the Arctic Circle, he would build a hotel made entirely from ice. Funding did not come easily and so the Icehotel started small. As the years passed, Bergqvist was proved right, and visitor numbers rocketed.

Now the building is an ice sculpture gallery as much as a hotel. Step through the main doors into a hallway filled with decoratively carved columns and elegant figurines of glistening beauty. Corridors to the side branch off to the ice suites, where sculptors from across the globe create their own personal visions in ice. Each winter the artworks are different: Although the hotel stores some of the larger ice blocks through the summer months, come spring the sculptures melt and slide gracefully back into the Torne River from where their material came.

Whatever the outside weather, temperatures inside the Icehotel hover around 23°F (-5°C) and guests staying the night in the cold rooms are provided with puffy purple sleeping bags, cold-weather suits, and boots. (For those a bit less bold, there are warm rooms, too, in another building.) The bed frames are made from ice, but their bases are of slatted wood, with mattresses and cozy—if slightly smelly—reindeer skins on top.

Down another passage, the ice bar serves vodka cocktails in shot glasses made from ice. The hotel uses more than half a million of these glasses each year but, on the bright side, nobody fights over who will do the dishes. Visitors must wear gloves to hold the glasses; otherwise they will slip right out of their hands. As they drink, the heat from their lips molds the cups exactly to the contours of their own mouths. **PE**

Experience the Nordic Light Hotel

Location Stockholm, Sweden   **Website** www.nordiclighthotel.se
Price 🌀🌀

> "[T]he best thing ... is the choice of rooms. It's like choosing clothes, [including] S, M, L, and XL."

Jeanette Hyde, *Observer*

The Nordic Light Hotel, as the name suggests, is all about light. The responsive sound and movement systems in the lobby and multiple light settings in the rooms are intended to re-create the ever-changing patterns of the northern lights, as well as provide light therapy for the hotel guests.

The hotel has become a hip place to be, and not only for those interested in the interplay of light and color. It is the official hotel for Stockholm Design Week, alternative fashion fair +46, and Future Design Days, so Nordic Light tends to draw in a design crowd. They come to enjoy a stay in one of the 175 comfortable rooms, which offer a Scandinavian mix of minimalist white, wall projections instead of art, and light beds where guests can choose their own color, mood, and speed. Visitors can sip cocktails in the lounge (which hosts a few club nights during the week) and generally hang out and look good against some of the best designer surfaces Sweden has to offer.

You cannot get away from the light though. As well as the in-room settings, room service offers light therapy administered by professional light therapists and masseurs. This is no novelty: Not only has it been proven to help combat jet lag, but infrared light also allegedly increases blood circulation, detoxifies, and reduces swelling, as well as reducing cellulite buildup and improving the body's elimination systems. Laser acupuncture is also available, which can minimize pain and provide cures for myriad ailments—and with no side effects. If you are unsure, however, you can always book a normal massage at the same time. **PS**

🔲 *The lobby of Stockholm's ultra-hip Nordic Light Hotel, complete with moving light projections.*

Stay at the Grand Hotel

Location Stockholm, Sweden **Website** www.grandhotel.se
Price 🌑🌑🌑🌑

Whether it is beneath the chandeliers and painted ceilings of the opulent hall of mirrors, in the candlelit intimacy of the wood-paneled French dining room, or lounging on plush sofas between gilded pillars of the vast lobby, the Grand Hotel in Stockholm has been grand for more than 130 years. This glorious Scandinavian institution is one of the few surviving classic city hotels of Europe and is proud of its status as a Swedish national monument.

The Grand stands in the heart of Stockholm, right on the harborside opposite the Royal Palace. It is part of Swedish tradition to eat a herring smörgåsbord in the Grand's veranda restaurant overlooking the

> *"The signatures in the guest book read like an almanac of twentieth century life."*
>
> Tim Ecott, *Guardian*

paddle steamers that dock outside. Many rooms have the sense of being part of a stately home, but best of all is the four-room penthouse, which overlooks the busy waterfront. This is the Nobel Suite, where for more than a hundred years the winners of the Nobel Prize have stayed. You may even find yourself sitting in the same armchair that Albert Einstein once enjoyed.

Nobel Prize winners are just the tip of the celebrity iceberg, though. Frank Sinatra once got so drunk in the bar that a doctor had to be called, and Greta Garbo once hid in the bathrooms to avoid the staff. The Grand exudes a sense of glamour so palpable that it rubs off, making all guests feel special. **SH**

Relax at Smådalarö Gard

Location Stockholm, Sweden **Website** www.smadalarogard.se
Price 🌑🌑

There are few more life-affirming experiences on the planet than taking a plunge in an ice-cold pool after a wood-fired sauna, and here at Smådalarö you can set your senses to "stunned" by doing just that. With your skin dancing with pleasure at the juxtaposition of wood-smoked prickly heat and icy water, or a dip in the heated hotel pool, you will be primed and ready to enjoy a host of activities in this wonderfully calm manor house, located some forty-five minutes from Stockholm's busy city center.

Built in 1810, the fully refurbished, four-star hotel has sixty-two state-of-the-art rooms and is renowned as a top-class conference center. The open fireplaces and snug rooms add to the romantic atmosphere no matter what the Swedish weather is doing outside, with Gökboet (the Cuckoo's Nest) a favorite with honeymooners. Weather permitting, a row on the lake, a round on the nine-hole golf course, boat trips in the hotel's own yacht, rowing, fishing, walking, or a swift game of *boules* or tennis can help you meet future sauna mates; alternatively, you can stay in and relax with a game of billiards or darts, or work on your winter tan in the solarium. The Hemviken waters of this wonderful archipelago present the seasons in their myriad colors—fall has never looked as beautiful as in Scandinavia—and Dalaröhas has long been a meeting place for seafarers and trading travelers, so you are in good company historically.

The restaurant and Nämdö dining room provide haute cuisine Swedish style, with the best of the archipelago's fish and shellfish sparkling next to all kinds of local game and poultry on the menu. Plunging into Smådalarö's atmosphere is guaranteed to revitalize even the most weary of souls. **PS**

Enjoy Villa Källhagen

Location Stockholm, Sweden **Website** www.kallhagen.se
Price 💲💲

Villa Källhagen is a small, intimate hotel situated in Stockholm's Royal Djurgården Park—a famous part of the cityscape that has been popular with visitors for a good 200 years. As is typical in Northern European countries with long hours of daylight in the summer, Villa Källhagen's alluring architecture features a great deal of glass to enable the building—and its guests—to make the most of the light.

The twenty park-facing bedrooms have huge windows that look out onto the park and the pretty Djurgården canal, and skylights let light into the bathrooms. Rooms are spacious, a feeling enhanced by the natural light, pale woods, and pleasingly

> "...a warm, welcoming setting in harmony with the natural surroundings of Djurgården."

countrysidehotels.se

colored fabrics. All rooms have balconies or terraces, too, so you can get the most of the fresh Scandinavian air. Lovers of Swedish cuisine (especially fish) will appreciate the hotel's gourmet restaurant, which specializes in traditional dishes like fried Baltic herring.

The hotel makes for a superb spring or summer escape, but the interior is remarkably cozy in winter, too, especially when the large open fire is lit, the bar is open, and the night winds howl outside. A sauna and relaxation room are also on-site, and you can rent bicycles to get out into the countryside. The villa is ten minutes from the heart of the city, making it a perfect base for those wishing to explore Stockholm. **PS**

Stay at Långholmen Hotel

Location Stockholm, Sweden **Website** www.langholmen.com
Price 💲💲

A book of escapes is incomplete without at least one prison: Långholmen was once Sweden's biggest jail. The grand nineteenth-century buildings on a leafy island near the city center have been converted into a hotel, with the former cells as bedrooms. The old Crown Prison was used for the capital's most notorious prisoners until 1975 and still has its original stairwell in the middle of all the old cells. It now forms an airy atrium between the bedrooms.

The cells themselves still have small windows, without the iron bars, and the old high-security doors have been retained. Inside, they each now have a shower, toilet, telephone, free wireless Internet access, radio, and cable television. Walls are decorated with newspaper clippings detailing prisoners' crimes and trials. Guests even get a copy of a former inmate's daily routine, which shows reveille at 5:45 A.M. and bedtime at 7:45 P.M., but don't worry, it is just to emphasize how things have changed.

The vast jail now has 102 bedrooms, as well as a separate youth hostel, conference center, museum, and four restaurants, including one in the basement where female prisoners were forced to spend their days at spinning wheels. Fortunately, the menus offer more than just bread and water. On top of all that, there is even a patio café where you can play *boules* in the old exercise yard.

The island itself is one of the largest among hundreds that form the Swedish capital, and its history means that it has remained an almost undeveloped piece of countryside only a fifteen-minute walk from the Royal Palace and the old city. There is even a small beach just outside the old prison walls that has become popular with summer bathers. **SH**

Recharge at Yasuragi

Location Hasseludden, Sweden   **Website** www.yasuragi.se
Price 🟢🟢

Yasuragi means "inner peace and harmony," and that is what you get. A tranquil, spacious retreat twenty minutes from Stockholm, it never feels crowded, even when all 166 rooms are occupied. The Buddhist aesthetics of simple, pared-down elegance create a sense of calm, combining natural light with the soft glow of lanterns, rush matting, and untreated pale-wood walls hung with spectacular kimonos.

Once inside, a kimono, slippers, swimsuit, and towel are all you need—and they are provided. Inner peace begins with water and the indulgence of the Japanese bathing ritual. With guidance from a bath hostess, you choose a washing station in the dimly lit wet area of the beautiful washrooms and begin this slow, meditative process, alternating hot and cold water with meticulous cleansing. Afterward, time in the stone spa pool or sauna and then a few lengths of the enormous pool are the perfect precursor to a soak in the hot springs outside, surrounded by trees.

From Zen meditation classes and blissful shiatsu massage to flotation tanks and Seitai, a form of yoga, you cannot help feeling healthy—and the food helps. Breakfast takes attention to detail to new heights: eggs boiled for three, five, or ten minutes; five different types of milk; a huge variety of teas; and meat, cheese, and breads to fill you up until evening. Then, you have two restaurants to choose from. Teppanyaki has twelve grilling points, each with its own chef who explains the culinary traditions of the simple menu as they prepare and cook it over high flames—a virtuoso performance with delicious results. **OM**

↗ *Yasuragi's teahouse by the enormous pool is a fusion of Buddhist and Scandinavian aesthetics.*

"Simplicity has become a rare luxury, and this is what gives Yasuragi that sense of exclusivity."

Proprietors, Yasuragi

Relax at Park Hotel Kenmare

Location County Kerry, Ireland **Website** www.parkkenmare.com
Price 💲💲

The Park Hotel overlooks a sweep of Kenmare Bay, with grand vistas out to the Caha mountains. It is an exceptionally tranquil place to stay, yet it is just a few minutes' walk from Kenmare—an attractive town unspoiled by tourism, with an enticing set of shops, decent restaurants, and venues for Irish music. An imposing, gray-stone building surrounded by pretty gardens and lawns, the hotel has an eighteen-hole golf course on its doorstep and there are spectacular walks in the Kerry countryside a short drive away.

Unusually, its spa, SÁMAS, is open only to hotel residents, so it is an exclusive, unhurried place to escape to without the babble of day guests. There is no risk of having your stay disturbed by weddings or conferences either, because this family-owned and family-run hotel has chosen not to host them. Interiors are decked out with traditional furnishings, original oil paintings, and antique furniture, although the forty-six bedrooms also offer a flat-screen TV, DVD, CD, and MP3 player, as well as a selection of movies and music CDs. The deluxe rooms are more spacious and have sitting areas with views out to the water. The SÁMAS spa offers an indulgent set of treatments. The thermal suites share an open-air vitality pool overlooking shrubs and flowers, with the bay in the distance. If you have the energy, you can do lengths in a gleaming 82-foot (25-m) lap pool. Feast in the Park's elegant dining room, or head into town, where Mulcahy's and Packies are both chef-owned restaurants that come highly recommended. Each evening, classic films are shown in the hotel's private cinema. **CSJ**

← *Spa treatments at Park Hotel Kenmare finish with relaxation in a light-filled room with glorious views.*

Unwind at Temple Country Retreat and Spa

Location County Westmeath, Ireland
Website www.templespa.ie   **Price** 💲💲

> *"A sense of calm and tranquility seemed to permeate throughout the bright, airy two-story [spa]."*

Grace Heneghan, *Holistic Health*

In a 250-year-old farmhouse on the site of an ancient monastery, this adult-only destination health spa is the perfect place to escape the daily grind. Pamper your troubles away with luxury treatments in the tranquil surroundings of the rolling Westmeath countryside.

There might be an old-world charm to the location, but there is nothing dated about this contemporary spa, just ninety minutes from Dublin. An oasis of wellness, its natural light floods in to illuminate the high-ceilinged rooms that house the vitality suite, a pool with hydro-jets, the sauna, and steam room. Luxuriate in a marine body wrap, indulge in a vinotherapy facial, or unwind with a full-body massage.

The idea behind this family-run retreat is to replace what everyday life takes out of you, focusing firmly on relaxation and well-being. Choose from eighty different holistic, healing treatments in the spa, then go walking and bicycling in the 100 acres (40 ha) of parkland. Best of all, guests are actively encouraged to do absolutely nothing. It is a blissful chill-out experience that will stay with you long after you leave.

Inspired by the site's previous incarnation as a monastery, the twenty-three rooms in the cloistered spa building overlook the internal gardens. For a real treat, there are suites with whirlpool tubs and balconies. Food is healthy with an emphasis on great flavor. Only the best local ingredients make it to the table.

A cross between a bed-and-breakfast where staff offer a warm welcome and a modern spa, the Temple offers a real escape in an idyllic pastoral setting. **AD**

🔽 *The Temple's twelve-seat vitality pool with therapeutic water jets is ideal for unwinding.*

Relax at Delphi Mountain

Location County Galway, Ireland
Website www.delphimountainresort.com   **Price** 🌑🌑

A lavish hideaway on the wild, west coast of Ireland, Delphi Mountain Resort is the place to go in search of some serious pampering. Rooms look out over the mountains, and plush split-level suites have a cozy living room and mezzanine bed area.

The big draw, of course, is the spa. You can choose from massages and treatments (shiatsu, aromatherapy, Reiki), a myriad of scrubs and wraps, facials, and seaweed or detox baths. Or for something different, you can try cryotherapy: an algae wrap for the legs that is great for getting rid of puffiness. There is also a sumptuous health suite with a luxurious whirlpool tub, sauna, and dry-stone wall steam room, as well as a

> *"The thermal suite and relaxation rooms have one of the best views in Ireland."*
>
> Fionnula Quinlan, *Irish Examiner*

hydro-pool complete with star-lit canopy. The relaxed atmosphere and friendly staff make this a haven of peace and tranquility.

This is a wilderness retreat in more ways than one, though, and there is much to indulge in outdoors—from sea kayaking and bicycling to hiking. Explore sea caves, surf, and ride horses at the beach; canoe and water-ski in the nearby loch; or abseil and trek through the breathtaking countryside. The Peregrine restaurant features superb fresh local seafood, ranging from Killary mussels to scallops and sea bass; vegetables come from the resort's own organic gardens. Body and soul have never been so in tune. **AD**

Stay at Bellinter House

Location County Meath, Ireland
Website www.bellinterhouse.com   **Price** 🌑🌑

What do you get when you take a beautiful Georgian country house set in 12 acres (5 ha) of gorgeous Irish parkland and wave a contemporary wand over it? With Bellinter House, the result is an outstanding blend of elegant stateliness and the feel of a deluxe hotel with all modern conveniences. Ireland, as the locals will tell you, is a bit like that itself, with a head set firmly on the future and a heart full of tales of wondrous myth and lush green natural beauty.

The interior of Bellinter House has been lovingly preserved, from the drawing room's plasterwork to the sash windows and floorboards. The view over the river makes the hour's drive from Dublin more than worthwhile—and that is before you take in the thirty-four rooms, individually appointed with vintage furnishings and equipped with custom-built plasma screens and an entertainment system that will keep you fully absorbed as you recline on your luxurious bed. There is also an elegant drawing room with large sash windows and wonderful views, a well-stocked library and games room, and two excellent bars. The Bellinter Bar provides a rustic warm-up for the delights of the more sophisticated basement wine bar, which hosts a superb, naturally lit restaurant (aptly named Eden) with plenty of space to enjoy the locally sourced, fresh, and imaginative menu. Try out the many fine wines or, if you prefer, pair Guinness with steak—an equally sublime combination.

Bellinter's terraces and lawns are ideal for alfresco dining, and the nearby Boyne is perfect for a spot of fishing, a relaxing way to while away the afternoon before coming home to a dip in the outdoor hot tub or perhaps another Guinness in front of a roaring open fire. Rural hospitality at its best. **PS**

Experience Ashford Castle

Location County Mayo, Ireland   **Website** www.ashford.ie
Price 🅢🅢

This is a true castle, with turrets and ramparts, armor, and oak paneling. Its first stones were laid in 1228 by the de Burgo family, and for eight centuries its inhabitants have gazed out upon the blue waters of Lough Corrib, Ireland's second-largest lake. There have been various owners, who have added a French-style chateau and, later, Victorian extensions. From the seventeenth century, the Guinness family used the castle as a hunting and fishing lodge until they sold it in 1939 and it was transformed into a hotel.

The turrets and ramparts have seen a range of high-ranking guests. The Prince of Wales, who later became King George V, visited in 1903; the billiards room was

> *"The guardian mountains which arise are as still and calm as the visions of an Icelandic god . . ."*

George Moore, novelist-guest in the 1880s

built especially for his visit and the restaurant is named for him. U.S. president Ronald Reagan also stayed at Ashford; for his visit they commissioned a special bed.

Today, Ashford Castle has eighty-three bedrooms and a spa offering treatments using Ya Kon products. Outside are 350 acres (141 ha) of wooded parkland. Guests can play a round on the golf course or take a lesson in the art of falconry. There is also archery, clay-pigeon shooting, and cross-country riding. The lake is known for its stocks of wild brown trout and salmon. Alternatively, you can join the castle's resident historian for a trip to Inchagoill Island to see St. Patrick's church, built by St. Patrick in 450 C.E. **PE**

Stay at Ice House Hotel

Location County Mayo, Ireland   **Website** www.icehousehotel.ie
Price 🅢🅢

The Ice House Hotel, situated on the beautiful and tidal River Moy estuary, is a renovated ice house, dating back 150 years, where ice was stored to pack the river's famous salmon. Today, it is a great place to chill, rather than be chilled, with a luxury spa and exciting architecture that led *Condé Nast Traveler* to describe it as one of Ireland's most stylish and innovative new hotels, and a funky base from which to explore Ireland's wild, west coast.

The modern architecture is dazzling: The carefully restored white house is joined by a contemporary slate wall stylishly crisscrossed with orange lines. Inside the hotel, the thirty-two rooms and suites are divided between the iconic nineteenth-century building, complete with period furniture and sash windows, and the new wing with minimalist rooms and floor-to-ceiling windows with views of the River Moy. Bathrooms have underfloor heating, soft towels, and L'Occitane products; bedrooms are spacious with modern art on the walls and plasma televisions.

Down in the Pier restaurant, the very best local and fresh food is served up in the original vaulted ice store, with Connemara lamb, Irish beef, roast pigeon, and rabbit loin on the menu. The luxurious spa is outstanding, too, and well worth a long visit. It comprises five treatment rooms named after ships wrecked on the Moy in times gone by, plus outdoor hot tubs overlooking the river. Some of the signature spa treatments include prescription facials and body massages with warm pebbles of Inniscrone.

The hotel is also a perfect base for the west coast's many festivals, as well as hikes or salmon fishing on the Moy. It might have been cold inside once upon a time, but now this hotel exudes warmth. **LD**

Enjoy Yoga on Clare Island

Location County Mayo, Ireland **Website** www.yogaretreats.ie
Price ⊖

With mountain views on one side and Atlantic rollers on the other, this rural retreat is about as far away as you can get from the rest of the world. Although the dramatic landscapes are a big draw, the center offers yoga fans, from beginners to keen enthusiasts, a place to practice away from the pressures of daily life.

The traditional island cottage, which provides accommodation, has been renovated using eco-friendly materials, including solar panels and wood-burning stoves for heating. Wood, hemp, terra-cotta, and natural slate all add to the cozy feel. The new timber yoga studio has stunning views over Clew Bay and Croagh Patrick.

The center is a haven of serenity set in 240 acres (97 ha) of land grazed by sheep and horses. Organic gardens supply fruit and vegetables for the table, and there are acres of native woodland to explore after yoga classes. More than 90 percent of the fresh produce on the vegetarian menu is locally sourced, organic, or homegrown, from farmhouse cheeses and butter to freshly baked bread and homemade soy milk. Even the drinking water comes from a spring near the house.

Clare Island itself provides a unique setting for exploration and introspection—an island off an island, off an island, on the edge of Europe, this is about as remote as yoga retreats get. It is the ideal base to practice mindfulness before applying it to daily life. This is no ashram, however, and there is a relaxed and fun approach. When no courses are running, it is possible to rent out one of the houses. **AD**

↗ *Remote, peaceful, and with scenic sea views, the Clare Island retreat is the ideal place to practice yoga.*

"The dramatic scenery and invigorating sea air make a retreat on Clare Island . . . unforgettable."

i-escape.com

De-stress at Ard Nahoo

Location County Leitrim, Ireland   **Website** www.ardnahoo.com   **Price** 🌀

Ard Nahoo is a peaceful eco-retreat set along a single-track road amid the lush beauty of the North Leitrim Glens. Such a magical location as this deserves to be preserved and protected, and it is with this in mind that Ard Nahoo has been created. The three cabins that make up the charming accommodation have been built using environmentally friendly practices.

This simple health farm has built its entire ethos around the mantra of integrity. Choose from a range of holistic treatments tailored to the individual and designed to restore, rebalance, and calm the body and soul. As well as offering a variety of enticing massages and facials, there is an innovative "Detox Box," which claims to soothe muscles, clarify the skin, and burn away a fat-busting 900 to 2,400 calories a session. The Ard Nahoo yoga philosophy, with its emphasis on balance and harmony, draws on the serenity of the environment. Classes are held in the tranquil studio overlooking the grounds.

In between treatments and yoga sessions guests have plenty of time to explore the extensive grounds and the beautiful hills of Leitrim. Take part in one of the guided walks that highlight the native plants and trees, as well as explaining their connections with Irish folklore. The scenery, in the heart of Yeats country is at once uplifting and soothing. By day, there are the forty fabled greens of the Irish countryside; by night, the stars shine in the endless sky.

You could, with the simple facilities provided, cater for yourself. Much nicer, though, to order from a range of tasty vegetarian dishes prepared by local chef Maria and delivered to your cabin. Indulge yourself with delicious local food and ravishing surroundings, and let the magic of Ard Nahoo wash over you. The focus here is firmly on relaxation. **SWi**

⬆ *Ard Nahoo provides an ethical break in the middle of breathtaking natural surroundings.*

Relax at O'Fabulous

Location County Donegal, Ireland   **Website** www.ofabulous.com   **Price** 💲💲

Small but perfectly formed, the glamorous retreat O'Fabulous more than lives up to its name. All glittering golds and shimmering glass, this boutique hotel in the heritage coastal town of Ardara has been beautifully styled. The late nineteenth-century building has five eclectic rooms to choose from, with beautifully soft cloud beds (an ingenious design of three layers) to sink into at night. The bathrooms come equipped with roll-top baths, heavenly Jo Malone toiletries, rainfall showers, and thick, soft robes to wrap up in. The furnishings are equally opulent and luxurious, featuring billowing layers of rich velvet, Irish linen, and cool satin and silk.

If you can tear yourself away to step outside, there are glorious windswept walks with stunning mountain views from the Glengesh Pass, as well as heather-clad moors to roam. Go to Loughros Point for views out across the Atlantic, then take in lungfuls of fresh air exploring Glenveagh national park—a nature reserve

with Glenveagh Castle, a Victorian folly, set amid scenic lakes and woodland. This is the perfect setting for a dramatic and romantic getaway.

In fact, it is worth staying at O'Fabulous for the Irish breakfast alone—thick slabs of homemade bread, porridge with Irish whiskey, fresh-laid eggs with succulent sausages and bacon. The passion for food carries on throughout the day, with afternoon tea served by the fire. In the evening, the menu offers Donegal crab and creamy champ (mashed potato) together with a first-class wine list. Then retire to the retro cocktail bar to kick back with a Bellini in hand.

Far away from the tourist hordes, it is everything that a boutique hotel should be. Oozing sophisticated personality and luxury, O'Fabulous always makes for an indulgent, relaxing retreat. **AD**

⬆ *O'Fabulous is a feast for the eyes—ornate mirrors, elegant wall coverings, and chandeliers.*

Explore Lusty Beg Island

Location Fermanagh Lakes, Northern Ireland
Website www.lustybegisland.com   **Price** 💲💲

Derived from the Gaelic word *Lusteabeg* meaning "small and fertile," Lusty Beg Island is a tranquil Irish idyll located in the northern tip of Fermanagh's Lower Lough Erne, 22 miles (35 km) from Enniskillen.

Once a penitential retreat for monks, the 75-acre (30-ha) island changed hands between various owners through the centuries, including a Canadian aristocrat, and a captain from the British army (who built the first chalet for rent in the 1950s), before it was passed back into the hands of a local couple. The island is now a protected bird sanctuary and isolated getaway for those looking for a quiet life.

Lusty Beg is accessible only by boat or ferry, the latter of which can carry just two cars at a time and crosses the lake on an archaic rope pulley system. Once on the island, there are no roads; one nature trail circumnavigates the shore, providing countless opportunities to spot local birdlife, including a colony of breeding sandwich terns, unique to the island. Kayaks are available for those who prefer to investigate the island from the water; other facilities include a games room, tennis courts, and an indoor pool.

Accommodation is varied, with a choice of bed-and-breakfast rooms or five-star self-catering chalets with private balconies overlooking the lakes. A short stroll from the living quarters is Island Lodge, housing the one bar on the island, which regularly entertains guests with traditional Irish music, and two excellent restaurants famed for their fresh fish.

Sailors and water sports enthusiasts will love Lusty Beg and might even be seduced by the secluded setting and quiet charm of the island, a place where time seems to stand still, making it difficult to do anything but stop, relax, and enjoy. **LM**

Stay at Belle Isle Castle

Location County Fermanagh, Northern Ireland
Website www.belleislecastle.com   **Price** 💲

It is easy to be king of the castle—you simply have to rent your own. This seventeenth-century castle is one of Ireland's most luxurious vacation homes. It stands on the 470-acre (190-ha) Belle Isle Estate in County Fermanagh, close to the lough water's edge amid a landscape of lakes, islands, hills, and woods.

Guests can rent cottages and apartments, but the most memorable option is to have exclusive use of a wing of the castle. The eight bedrooms are a blend of original features with antiques and modern facilities. This means beautiful old furniture, working fireplaces, and gilt-framed paintings and mirrors. Guests have use of a kitchen and seven bathrooms, too.

"Nestling close to the water's edge and set within a landscape of lakes and islands of gently rolling hills."

discovernorthernireland.com

You can opt for self-catering, bring your own chef, or take advantage of the full catering service available. With an award-winning cooking school and working farm on the estate, quality is unlikely to be an issue. Guests also have use of a banqueting room for up to thirty diners with its own minstrels' gallery. The castle also offers an all-weather tennis court, game shooting, and pike fishing. Guests have access to a wooden cruiser that can carry sixteen people around the picturesque inlets and islands of Lough Erne. **SH**

➡ *Renovated in 1993, the seventeenth-century castle has a relaxed, country-house style throughout.*

Discover Tory Island

Location Donegal, Ireland
Website www.oileanthorai.com **Price** ⊖

"[It is] a place of bewitching beauty ... which has also beguiled generations of artists."

Kevin Connolly, BBC journalist

It is not often that visitors are greeted personally by the king upon arrival, nor is it customary to meet him in the local pub for a drink, but this is often the case on the windswept island of Tory, 9 miles (14 km) off the coast of Donegal. Despite its relative remoteness in the harsh Atlantic Ocean, Tory has a die-hard population of fewer than 180 people, all of whom proudly speak Irish as their first language. The island's history can be traced back 4,000 years to Neolithic times and counts Colmcille, or St. Columba, as one of its more famous sons. He built a monastery here in the sixth century, which dominated island life until it was destroyed by invading English troops in 1595; now only the bell tower remains standing.

Accessing the island can sometimes be a challenge, because high winds and furious seas dictate ferry times more than the timetable, but once on the rugged rock, it is easy to feel comfortable because everyone is inviting, warm, and courteous. There are a few places to stay, including the hotel near the port and a hostel, which are by no means luxurious, but you do not visit Tory to wallow in luxury, you visit for the *craic* (good times). Listen to Patsy-Dan Rodgers, the king of Tory, a fine accordion player and artist, regale you with tales of the island in the Club Soisialta (social club); sing and dance with the locals at a ceilidh or explore the nooks and crannies of the island that hold secrets of the past.

However you choose to spend time on Tory, a visit to this weather-beaten and seemingly little island teetering on the edge of civilization is sure to be relaxing, enjoyable, and invigorating. **LM**

◰ *The jagged rocks known as Balor's Teeth are named for an evil Formorian king who lived on the island.*

Stay at Scarista House

Location Isle of Harris, Hebrides, Scotland
Website www.scaristahouse.com **Price** ⊖⊖

Walk across the huge empty sands at Scarista Bay on the Isle of Harris in the Outer Hebrides, then look back to the shore beyond the grassy dunes where hardy sheep graze in the salty spray. Alone in the center of the bay, with heather-covered mountains rising behind, is a whitewashed Georgian manse.

This little hotel is in one of the most beautiful and remote places in the United Kingdom. Scarista House is like a cozy, miniature country-house hotel, with open fires in antique fireplaces, big, comfy sofas, and old books, antiques, and framed prints everywhere. There is even a cuddly cat called Max. Guests hardly notice the absence of television.

> ## "We walked for forty minutes on the beach . . . and met precisely four people."
>
> Caroline Boucher, *Observer*

Instead they lounge around the house eating and drinking or take walks across the spectacular 3-mile (5-km) beach strewn with shells trying to find otter footprints. Days are filled with boat trips around Harris or as far as the deserted island of St. Kilda. Guests can visit local artists, discover the standing stones at Callanaish, or simply tour the island in their car.

Scarista is highly acclaimed for its food. Many of the staples are made in the kitchen, such as bread, yogurt, cakes, muesli, marmalade, and ice cream. There is ample use of local ingredients: Scallops and lobsters are served fresh from the bay, and the Highland lamb once roamed the surrounding hills. **SH**

Unwind at Pool House

Location Ross-shire, Scotland
Website www.poolhousehotel.com **Price** ⊖⊖

Nestling beneath tranquil mountains at the head of scenic Loch Ewe in Wester Ross in the northwest Scottish Highlands, Pool House is a lavishly romantic hideaway that wins awards for environmental friendliness as well as luxurious pampering. This 300-year-old house was once the home of Osgood Mackenzie, founder of the famous nearby Inverewe Garden. Since acquiring the hotel in 1991, Peter and Margaret Harrison and their daughters Liz and Mhairi have transformed it into a graceful haven of elegant Victoriana, crammed with antiques, paintings, porcelain, and curiosities.

Pool House oozes country elegance. Open log fires warm the wood-paneled rooms, including an opulent library with inviting sofas—the perfect setting for a lazy afternoon tea. The cozy bar boasts a huge selection of single-malt whiskies. The suites are enormous, sumptuously furnished, and individually styled. The huge beds, some of them four-posters, and spacious Victorian bathrooms create the air of a stately home. Although most suites maintain the Victorian theme, the Nairana suite reflects the grand palaces of Rajasthan, whereas Bramble is decorated with French antiques.

Fine dining overlooking the panoramic loch, beneath a ceiling shimmering with thousands of hand-painted stars, is a memorable experience, although exquisite sunsets and occasional otter sightings can cause guests to abandon their award-winning seven courses for the photo of a lifetime. Pool House is run almost entirely by the charming owners, and without a hint of ostentation. In so many ways, Pool House comes as close as any hotel to capturing the magic of the Scottish Highlands. **ML**

Explore Uig Sands

Location Isle of Lewis, Scotland
Website www.bailenacille.com **Price** ⑤⑤

At Baile na Cille there are always more beaches than guests. The tiny hotel stands next to Uig Sands, one of Britain's most remote but beautiful bays, and there are twenty-four other beaches within walking distance. Not bad for a hotel with a maximum of sixteen guests.

This is a chance to escape to your own beach; however, rather than sunbathing and swimming in the waves, you will be walking, picnicking, spotting birds and wildflowers, fishing, photographing, exploring, and just breathing the fresh air straight off the Atlantic. When it is time to go back inside again, there is the cozy old manse waiting for you.

The house's claim to historic fame is that this was where the Lewis chessmen were first brought on their discovery in the dunes in 1831. The chessmen turned out to be early Viking examples of the game. The hotel has been created from the former big old house plus its stables and outbuildings. There are three sitting rooms: one with TV, one with a stereo, and one with billiards and foosball. If the weather is wild outside, there are board games, jigsaw puzzles, and books, but if the sun is shining, there is a garden to sit in and a croquet lawn and grass tennis court.

Meals are hearty communal gatherings with fine dishes using plenty of local produce. There are enormous Scottish breakfasts on offer, including porridge if you want. Dinner is a five-course, no-menu feast, and the bedrooms are warm, cozy, and unpretentious. At Baile na Cille a sense of remote escape pervades everything, and you will definitely not get your cell phone to work here. **SH**

➔ *The garden of the hotel overlooks the beautiful 2-mile (3.2-km) golden stretch of Uig Sands.*

Discover Balfour Castle

Location Orkney Islands, Scotland
Website www.balfourcastle.co.uk **Price** 💲💲

This is the most northerly castle-hotel in the world. It was the summer home of the Balfour family from the mid-nineteenth century until 1960, when the last of its heirs died. The castle was bought by Polish cavalry officer Captain Tadeusz Zawadzki and is now run by his Scottish wife and two of her daughters.

Despite the change of hands, the castle still oozes heritage. Log fires roar amid Victorian antiques. Stags' heads adorn the walls; gas used to be pumped through their antlers to illuminate lamps upon the tips. In the library, false bookshelves give onto a secret passage through which, legend has it, the Balfour family used to scurry when unwanted guests rang at their door. The laird's bedroom features a magnificent four-poster bed into which is carved the Balfour family's coat of arms. Another of the bedrooms adjoins a turret in which a shower room is housed.

The dining room serves local meat and game, fish caught in the surrounding Atlantic and North Sea waters, and fruit and vegetables grown in the castle's own kitchen garden. Guests who wish to catch their own dinner can help the hotel staff to haul in the lobster pots. The romantically inclined can wed in the castle's tiny chapel, which holds just twenty people.

History buffs can visit the 5,500-year-old village at Skara Brae, and for bird-watchers the Orkney Islands are paradise. Puffins nest here from May to July, and visitors commonly see razorbills, guillemots, fulmars, skuas, eider ducks, and Arctic terns. For those who want to get up close to the wildlife, it is said that the local seals swim toward those who whistle. **PE**

↩ *You would not think that just beyond the castle walls are uninhabited islands and sea caves to be explored.*

Stay at Lighthouse Cottage

Location Orkney Islands, Scotland
Website www.orkneylighthouse.com **Price** 💲💲💲

There cannot be many places more remote than a lighthouse keeper's cottage in Orkney, off the most northern tip of the Scottish mainland. Rugged, raw, and utterly beautiful, it is the place to see porpoises, seals, and whales, as well as an abundance of seabirds.

Choose between two cottages, both designed and built by Thomas Stevenson (father of Robert Louis) and his brother David in the 1850s. Enough original features remain to let your imagination run wild and dream of stormy days when the headland was battered by fierce winds. The cottages are private and secluded, enclosed within walled grounds, 1 mile (1.6 km) from the nearest neighbor.

"When the lights come out, I am proud to think they burn more brightly for the genius of my father."

Robert Louis Stevenson, Scottish novelist

The island is a place of historic interest. Delve into local archaeological finds, including the Dwarfie Stane, thought to be Britain's only example of a rock-cut chamber tomb dating from the Neolithic period or early Bronze Age. There is good sea fishing from the cliffs around the lighthouse and trout fishing at nearby Heldale Water. The most well-known landmark is the Old Man of Hoy, a sea stack of rocks rising 450 feet (137 m) out of the Atlantic, which makes a challenging climb for even the most experienced rock climbers. Visit in autumn and winter and you might be treated to the greatest light show on Earth—the aurora borealis—with a free front-row seat. **AD**

Explore Armadale Castle Gardens

Location Isle of Skye, Scotland **Website** www.clandonald.com
Price ⑤

Find inner peace while strolling quietly through this unexpectedly tropical garden, in the midst of the rugged and green Isle of Skye. Exotic flowers and trees thrive in this 40-acre (16-ha) woodland garden thanks to the Gulf Stream that treats this part of Scotland to a warm and frost-free climate.

Surrounding the ruins of Armadale Castle, the gardens are part of a sprawling 40,000-acre (16,185-ha) highland estate that was once in the hands of Clan Donald, one of Scotland's largest clans. The Clan Donald Lands Trust took over the estate in 1971, transforming the neglected grounds into the pristine gardens seen today. Groves of 200-year-old lime trees line the castle's main driveway, as well as more recently planted thuja and monkey puzzle trees. Keen gardeners will love the attention to detail: the herbaceous borders, the ponds dotted with water plants from around the world, and the wide variety of shrubs and trees. Beneath the trees are smatterings of bluebells, orchids, and wild meadow flowers. An oasis of tranquility, this glorious location is ideal for outdoor weddings, with both religious and civil ceremonies taking place in the grounds.

Leading off the gardens are a number of nature trails that offer uninterrupted views over the lovely Sound of Sleat, the body of water that separates the Isle of Skye from the Scottish mainland. The trails provide the best vantage points to see the wealth of wildlife in the area: Keep your eyes peeled for roe deer, red deer, otters, birds, and, if you are lucky, a golden eagle. The cost of this back-to-nature experience? A small entrance fee gains you access to the castle, the gardens, a museum, and the nature trails. **JK**

Walk to the Falls of Glomach

Location Lochalsh, Scotland **Website** www.lochalsh.co.uk
Price ❶❶

Brave the wilds of the West Highland mountains to reach one of Britain's highest waterfalls. You will need to pull on walking boots, though, because it takes a good five to seven hours to trek the challenging yet rewarding 5 miles (8 km) to the tumultuous Falls of Glomach, accessible only on foot.

East of Duich on the Scottish mainland, the falls are most dramatic after a bout of heavy rain, although bad weather can lead to poor visibility so it is best to hire a guide to avoid getting lost. Begin the hike at the National Trust for Scotland's countryside center in the hamlet town of Morvich. While walking through the

> ## "Often the mountain gives itself most completely when I have no destination."
>
> Nan Shepherd, Scottish poet

open hill country, you may be fortunate enough to spot rarely seen majestic red deer and golden eagles. The path to the waterfall may be well trodden, but it still feels gloriously secluded. Walkers can feel the waterfall's vibrations before they see it. "Glomach" means "gloomy," and you will understand why if you visit the falls in bad weather. When the temperature drops, the falls are framed by striking ice sculptures. Although there is not as much water during the summer months, the views are unparalleled. **JK**

→ *Set in a steep gorge, the spectacular Falls of Glomach tumble 375 feet (114 m) down into a dark abyss.*

Recharge at the Witchery

Location Edinburgh, Scotland   **Website** www.thewitchery.com
Price 🟢🟢

With its lavishly indulgent, antiques-filled suites hidden within atmospheric sixteenth-century buildings at the gates of the historic castle, The Witchery offers the most romantic accommodation in Edinburgh. Centered around a merchant's house dating back to 1595, the cluster of suites is a fantasy of gothic indulgence, verging on decadence. Each suite is filled with antiques and opulent period textiles. Walls are oak paneled and hung with tapestries, mirrors, and carvings; ceilings are ornately painted and gilded.

The original Witchery suite, the Inner Sanctum, sets the standard with its antique four-poster bed, dramatic red and gold walls, separate library–sitting room, and raised breakfast area overlooking the Royal Mile. The red lacquer bathroom contains an antique roll-top bathtub big enough for two. The baroque Old Rectory suite has oak paneling and red fabric walls and a lavish bed crafted from an antique pulpit. Tall gilded bookcases flank the marble fireplace, and a separate dressing room leads to the chapel-like bathroom with a painted vaulted ceiling and mirrored and gilded walls. The bathroom of the Library suite is a book-lined hideaway reached by a secret door, and also features a bathtub big enough for two.

The downside of such a perfect lust-den is that, with just seven suites, The Witchery is often booked months in advance, often by Hollywood stars such as Jack Nicholson and Michael Douglas. If you cannot get a room, book a table in the candlelit restaurant. It serves an award-winning modern Scottish menu and boasts sensational decor and opulent upholstery. **ML**

← *The Old Rectory bathroom is romantically styled and features mirrors on every wall.*

Unwind at Fenton Tower

Location East Lothian, Scotland
Website www.fentontower.co.uk **Price** $ $

In 1591, James VI of Scotland, son of Mary, Queen of Scots, found himself surrounded by a rebel army in Fife. Luckily the townspeople helped him to escape, and he took a ferry over the Firth of Forth to North Berwick, where he sought refuge at Fenton Tower. If the tower is fit for a king on the run, it is surely good enough for your average twenty-first-century urbanite looking for an escape from the madding crowds.

This magnificent fortified sixteenth-century tower, which stands proud over the fertile farmland of East Lothian, offers stunning views over the Firth of Forth and is just 20 miles (32 km) east of Edinburgh. For centuries it stood in ruins after being ransacked by English invaders, but in 1998 a meticulous restoration project was undertaken, and it now provides luxury accommodation for up to twelve people, combining modern facilities with the informality of a private home. Guests can enjoy impeccable service and outstanding cuisine in a secluded environment.

The warm pink harling on the exterior matches the original and was created by combining local soil with crushed seashells. With narrow defensive windows on the ground floor, you could be forgiven for thinking that the tower would be a gloomy place inside. The unusually large windows on the upper levels flood the rooms with natural light—some have a double or triple aspect, perfect for admiring the views.

Fenton Tower is surrounded by many excellent golf courses, including the world-famous Muirfield. There is also shooting and fly fishing aplenty. If you would prefer to make the most of being the king of your own castle, the tower has 20 acres (8 ha) of private land around which you can stroll, or simply daydream by the delightful *laich* (small Scottish lake). **HA**

Discover Y Goeden Eirin

Location Near Caernarfon, Wales
Website www.ygoedeneirin.co.uk **Price** $ $

A weekend at this homey bed-and-breakfast in a tranquil North Wales village offers much more than just a rural escape. Named after a collection of short stories written in Welsh by the dramatist John Gwilym Jones, it is less a guesthouse and more a center of learning about Welsh culture and arts—with rooms.

The co-owners, John and Eluned Rowlands, are former academics, and the house is lined with bookcases groaning under the weight of literary tomes. Original works by Welsh artists adorn the walls, attracting a steady flow of literary societies for dinners and academics for research trips. Welsh is the first language spoken around the house, and if you are

> *"An education in Welsh culture, and a stylish spot from which to explore the country."*

Alastair Sawday, travel writer

interested to learn more about the local culture, John leads regular study evenings. Guests can also explore the area with its walking trails and historic castles.

The guesthouse itself is cozy and relaxed with accommodation for up to six people. A home-cooked dinner, prepared on the warming stove, is served in the dining room, furnished with a traditional Welsh dresser, of course. Evenings are focused around the lounge with a carafe of sherry and a good book. Most striking of all, however, is the little boy's room, where pieces of the Berlin Wall are displayed in a glass case, and a slab of Welsh slate, engrained with political slogans, stands guard over the washbasin. **DA**

Explore the Anglesey Coast

Location Anglesey, Wales
Website www.angleseycoastalpath.co.uk **Price ❶❶**

Anglesey, the rural island in North Wales, is a pretty sleepy place, but the inauguration of the Isle of Anglesey Coastal Path is enticing visitors to explore the superb scenery of the North Wales coastline. The 125-mile (200-km) walking path, marked with distinctive yellow signs featuring the Arctic tern, passes through twenty towns and villages, where good facilities to eat, drink, and stay overnight can all be found within easy walking distance.

The full twelve-stage trail, along terrain that is gently undulating and suitable for all abilities, passes through a picture-postcard landscape of farmland, coastal heath, salt marsh, dramatic cliffs, and pristine beaches. Equip yourself with a copy of the O. S. Explorer maps 262 (west coast) and 263 (east coast) before setting out, and allow 2 weeks to cover the whole path, walking a daily average of around 7 miles (11 km). The path has its official start and end point at St. Cybi's Church in Holyhead, but each of the twelve stages can be tackled as an individual day hike, ranging from 7 to 13 miles (11 to 21 km) per day. Some of the sections, particularly the far northern trails from Cemaes to Church Bay, make for bracing strolls against a dramatic backdrop of wild, windswept scenery.

The most popular leg starts in Beaumaris and continues via Penmon Point, with great views across to Puffin Island, toward Llanddona, a pristine beach for swimming. This 6-mile (10-km) stretch on the eastern side of the island offers a good taster for the trail. The final stretch is a tiring 2 miles (3.2 km) along the shoreline, but well worth the effort. **DA**

↗ *The lighthouse on Llanddwyn Island remains attached to the mainland on all but the highest tides.*

"Cemaes . . . is flanked by exceptionally attractive stretches of rugged coastline."

Isle of Anglesey County Council

Stay at St. Curig's Chapel

Location Snowdonia, Wales
Website www.stcurigschurch.com   **Price** 💲💲

There is a wonderfully aristocratic and bohemian air to this hidden little bed-and-breakfast. The atmosphere owes something to a brazen, open-plan conversion of a nineteenth-century stone chapel and plenty to the exuberant personality of the owner.

Enjoy sumptuous distractions while you have breakfast sitting at a long wooden table, gazing out across the open space of the former apse. Around you are the chapel's original, elegant arched windows, marble pillars, stained glass, and, towering above everything, a stunning gilded mosaic domed ceiling. The dome was commissioned by William Sackville-West, a lieutenant-colonel in Her Majesty's Regiment of Grenadier Guards and local estate manager, in memory of his wife, Georgina.

St. Curig's was taken over by Lady Alice Douglas and her huge but docile dog Brecon in 1998. The renovation project was arduous, but the result is a unique and somewhat eccentric place to stay. The bedrooms are luxurious, with hand-carved four-poster beds and heated slate floors. One room still houses a stone pulpit.

There is nothing retiring about the bubbling hot tub in the corner of the former churchyard. It looks right up into the heart of the Snowdon horseshoe— the curve of peaks with Wales's highest mountain at its heart. Pen-y-Pas, the starting point of most paths up Snowdon, is a few minutes away by car. If you have just walked Snowdon, or any of the surrounding peaks, this is the perfect place to relax. Rest assured that less arduous forest paths lead right from the chapel door. Some even lead straight to a nearby pub. **SH**

▣ *St. Curig's was first opened in 1883; the B&B retains all the charm of the original chapel.*

Relax at an Eco Retreat

Location Powys, Wales
Website www.ecoretreats.co.uk   **Price** 😐😐

There is something stirring in the Dyfi Forest. As dawn breaks over Wales, the sun picks out an unusual array of shapes: four, 21-foot-diameter (6-m), North American Indian tepees and one 18-foot (5-m) Mongolian-style yurt in the middle of the forest. The encampment is an undeniably low-tech experience, with private compost toilets and solar showerbags to provide you with warm water, although some creature comforts can be found in the form of organic bed linen, china, and glassware.

The owners have leased the land from a local organic farm and only use fair-trade and locally-supplied goods in the welcome hampers. All the waste products go back to nourish the earth, and everything is recycled to keep the green credentials in impeccable order.

Eco Retreat is more of an experience than a mere place to stay: an escape from the trappings of modern life. There is no electricity, no running water, and, crucially, no reception for your cell phone. Cook at dusk and bed down on a plump mattress by candlelight. This is a place to let the mind wander, emerging cleaner, greener, and refreshed from the forest. Guests are invited to join a communal meditation session on their second night in camp, and a reiki/spiritual healing session is included as part of the deal. A free ticket for the nearby Center for Alternative Technology is also included. Most of all, however, this place is the ultimate chill-out zone with plenty of space, and you are guaranteed not to see a single soul from the door of your tepee as you look out over the silent forest. **DA**

← *The Eco Retreat is an award-winning tourism project and offers a true get-away-from-it-all experience.*

Rent Trehilyn Isaf Cottage

Location Pembrokeshire, Wales
Website www.underthethatch.co.uk   **Price** 😐😐

As one of the best-preserved Pembrokeshire cottages, Trehilyn Isaf enjoys a wonderful coastal location on the Strumble Head peninsula, a landscape that is all black crags and megaliths, hills swathed in mist, and tall cliffs. If the cottage seems vaguely familiar, that might be because its restoration was filmed for the BBC television series *A Pembrokeshire Farm*. Local architectural historian Dr. Greg Stevenson advised on the program and calls the house "a complete gem."

The cottage, which is the greenest of the properties let by Welsh social enterprise company Under the Thatch, has been fully restored using authentic sustainable methods such as low-toxin paints, sheep

> *"The house feels alive—not in an Amityville way—and organically a part of the landscape."*

Niall Griffiths, *Guardian*

wool for insulation, lime for rendering the cottage, and carbon-neutral central heating. Although the beautifully renovated old farmhouse may be environmentally friendly, this is not at the expense of modern creature comforts. Inside, the cottage is the perfect fusion of traditional features, such as a huge inglenook fireplace, and sleek minimalism. It is the kind of place you walk into and feel instantly calm.

If you can tear yourself away from your snug little sanctuary, make sure you enjoy the spectacular walk to Aber Mawr Bay, surrounded by rugged cliffs a couple of miles away, and check out the stunning views at nearby Strumble Lighthouse. **HA**

Unwind at Seaham Hall

Location County Durham, England
Website www.seaham-hall.co.uk   **Price** ⊖⊖

Seaham Hall & Serenity Spa has a great history. In the late eighteenth century, it was constructed as a vast stately home. It later became famous as the place where Lord Byron married Annabella Milbanke in 1815. Throughout World War I, the hall was used variously as a military hospital, tuberculosis sanatorium, pioneering cardiac treatment center, and nursing home until—finally—in 2002, the building was restored to its former glory and redeveloped by Tom and Jocelyn Maxfield as a world-class luxury hotel and spa.

One of the most notable things about the newly reincarnated Seaham Hall is the impressive plethora of contemporary art. Stained-glass artist Bridget Jones has created a ceiling in the lobby atrium based on Byron's poetry. The work of painters Dale Atkinson and Paul Gallagher adorns the walls, and sculptural works by Nicolaus Widerberg, Andrew Burton, and William Pye can also be found throughout the hotel. The nineteen suites are reliably modern, with "intelligent" lighting and adjustable air-conditioning. Some have two-person baths. The drawing room (where Byron married Milbanke) is still licensed for civil weddings, whereas the White Room restaurant serves up delicious, simple food at wooden tables.

Yet the hotel is only half of the story. Follow an underground tunnel to discover the Serenity Spa: Asian in design and offering more than forty-five treatments for soul, body, and mind. Amid the revitalizing scent of jasmine and the sound of flowing water, you will find a lovely 65-foot (20-m) swimming pool, black granite steam room, plunge pools, ice fountain, and traditional Turkish hammam. Not only a pretty face, Seaham Hall also delivers some quite serious inner healing, too. **PS**

Relax at Swinton Park

Location North Yorkshire, England
Website www.swintonpark.co.uk   **Price** ⊖⊖

If you like your English grandeur, then Swinton Park makes the perfect escape. This thirty-bedroom luxury castle-hotel comes complete with its own turrets, long echoing corridors, and enormous staircases leading up to what are huge, individually decorated and designed bedrooms.

Swinton Park makes an ideal retreat for anyone looking to explore the surrounding Yorkshire Dales, but with 200 acres (80 ha) of its own lakes, gardens, and parkland, there is little reason to venture farther afield. If you are feeling adventurous, you can have a go at a bit of falconry, fishing, or off-road driving. The restaurant at Swinton Park is worth a visit, too. With

> *"The view of deer, daffodils, and emerald parkland forced us into our wellies for a blustery walk."*
>
> Jill Hartley, *Guardian*

much of the produce grown in the 4-acre (1.6-ha) walled garden, the biggest of its kind in the United Kingdom, the emphasis is on delicate seasonal cuisine. The hotel is well established as a haven for culinary fans because it also has its own cooking school, run by celebrity chef Rosemary Shrager.

When you have finished your day's activities, why not retire to the games room for a frame of snooker or treat yourself to a massage in the spa and whirlpool tub? This is English country living at its finest. **RS**

➡ *Swinton Park is the kind of place where you expect to bump into Jeeves and Wooster.*

Walk the Wolds Way

Location Yorkshire, England **Website** www.nationaltrail.co.uk
Price ❶

To the inhabitants of Yorkshire, this region is "God's own county," and it is not difficult to see why. Wild, expansive, tranquil, at times even awesome, the breathtaking scenery seems to go on forever. Hidden away in this landscape is Britain's most peaceful national trail, which was created twenty-five years ago by a group of rambling enthusiasts.

The 79-mile (127-km) Yorkshire Wolds Way remains the least visited of England's national trails. For many, that is a blessing: There is an overwhelming sense of freedom, and it is not unheard of to wander alone for days without chancing upon another soul. Walkers are more likely to catch a glimpse of some unexpected wildlife—an occasional deer grazing on a slope or a kestrel soaring high overhead.

The views are astonishing: from sweeping vistas south across the Humber to the towers of Lincoln Cathedral at the start of the walk, or north to the dramatic outcrop of Filey Brigg at its finish. You will pass by England's famous deserted medieval village at Wharram Percy, abandoned at the time of the Black Death in the fourteenth century, and the many Bronze Age burial mounds that decorate the Wold tops. The villages along the way can make visitors feel like they are stepping back in time. You do not need to arrive on horseback to call in at the Ferry Inn at Brough, although it is the place where the highwayman Dick Turpin was arrested. After a reputed 200-mile (322-km) dash from London on his trusty mare Black Bess, the long arm of the law finally caught up with Turpin in 1739, and he was hanged soon afterward at York. **SWi**

← *The Yorkshire Wolds Way wends through dramatic open field tops, chalk valleys, and pretty villages.*

Relax at The Samling

Location Lake District, England **Website** www.thesamling.com
Price ❷ ❸

Think of The Samling as a home away from home, albeit a particularly luxurious one with beautifully rugged views of Lake Windermere, a bubbling outdoor hot tub, and a well-stocked wine cellar. From the moment they arrive, guests are made to feel that this is their domain, a place where formalities should be left at the door. It is hard not to unwind as the pretty, eighteenth-century, gabled house works its charms in minutes and cocoons you in warmth.

Clusters of colorful clematis and Virginia creeper give The Samling its lived-in appearance. There are just thirteen individual suites—many with gorgeous lake views—and each room has a unique character

> "... nowhere in so narrow a compass with such a variety of the sublime and beautiful."

William Wordsworth, on the Lake District

and features. For example, Methera, decorated in cool blues and greens, has a separate sitting area with fireplace and is bathed in sunlight for much of the day, whereas The Bothy is a cottage close to the main house with a Victorian bath and rain shower, and a sitting room set into a conservatory.

The decor combines traditional character with contemporary comfort, so there are lots of open fires, candles, and two-person bathtubs. The Samling is a place where visitors relish being holed up, although with 67 acres (27 ha) of land and, of course, the stunning Lake District scenery on the doorstep, there is much to experience outside, too. **LP**

Explore the Leeds and Liverpool Canal

Location Leeds to Liverpool, England
Website www.penninewaterways.co.uk/ll   **Price** 💲

There are few more relaxing ways to travel than by narrow boat. Once you have mastered the rudder system of steering—push left to go right, right to go left—off you go, at a pace slightly faster than walking.

The Leeds and Liverpool canal has 150 years of history rising up along its banks and the story of the Industrial Revolution unfolds before your eyes. Shipley, Saltaire, and Skipton may not have quite the same ring as Hamburg or Florence, but you will marvel at the grand architecture of the former millhouses and candy factories, designed and built with the care previously reserved for cathedrals. Step ashore and wander

---

"Vessels 60 feet long, 14 feet wide, and 3.5 feet deep can pass through its ninety-two locks."

Leeds and Liverpool Canal Society

---

around the remarkable "model" village of Saltaire, created by the impressively named Titus Salt for his workers. The harmonious design of the houses is matched by the solid beauty of the library, gymnasium, concert hall, and factories with their majestic chimney towers, modeled on Tuscan campaniles.

Titus Salt ensured there were no pubs in Saltaire, but the Leeds and Liverpool canal has got some wonderful places to drink beer. One of the greatest pleasures during a narrow boat vacation, next to firing up the engine on a misty morning after a hearty breakfast, is mooring up at a riverside pub as the sun goes down and strolling up to the bar for a pint. **SWi**

Visit Kielder Water and Forest Park

Location Northumberland, England
Website www.visitkielder.com   **Price** ❶

If it is peace and tranquility you are after, look no further than Kielder Water and Forest Park. It is famed for having the darkest night skies in England, thanks to minimal light pollution, and also happens to be situated in Northumberland, which was recently voted the most tranquil spot in the country by the Campaign to Protect Rural England.

The park is home to northern Europe's largest man-made lake and England's largest forest. With more than 232 square miles (600 sq km) to explore by bike, on horseback, or on foot, the park is so large that there is room to get away from it all and not bump into another soul for hours. For leisurely strolls or rides, there is a multitude of forest trails to choose from, including the lakeside way, which hugs the 27-mile (43-km) Kielder Water shoreline. In this haven for wildlife, expect to see deer, otters, badgers, bats, and rare species of birds. The park is also home to around 60 percent of England's native red squirrel population, the last remaining stronghold in the country.

Thanks to its inky black skies, Kielder Water and Forest Park and the Kielder Observatory are perfect for stargazing; you can learn more about astronomy in the observatory, which is open most days and occasionally in the evenings. There is also an abundance of contemporary art and architecture in this striking rural setting. With plenty of picnic spots and places to eat throughout the park, visitors are spoiled for choice when it comes to spending a day or weekend in this most peaceful area of England. **HA**

➡ *Its pure air and wilderness make Kielder Water and Forest Park stunning to walk around and explore.*

Punt on the Cherwell

Location Oxford, Oxfordshire, England
Website www.cherwellboathouse.co.uk   **Price** ⑤

When it comes to boating vessels, there can be nothing more peculiarly English than the punt, a flat-bottomed boat with a square-cut bow, designed for use on small rivers. The punter propels the boat along with a long pole by pushing it against the riverbed. Sometimes he falls in, or gets stuck in low-hanging branches, and everything goes wrong.

For those in search of a rural idyll in the heart of a bustling university town, punting in Oxford makes for a blissed-out experience. It mostly takes place on the River Cherwell, which flows through Oxford's green belt of fields and woods, before joining the Thames near bucolic Christ Church Meadow. There are various

---

"Spend the day [passing] historic Oxford colleges, botanical gardens, and tranquil English countryside."

oxfordpunting.co.uk

---

places to get on a punt, but Madgalen Bridge is too crowded and Folly Bridge is a hazard, with many long rowboats and motorized boats flying around. The pastures of Port Meadow offer good shallows for punting, but the best jumping-off point is the Cherwell Boat House. On the banks of the Cherwell, this idyllic boathouse is a restaurant, café, and punt station extraordinaire. *Brideshead Revisited* fans will be in their element, but cream flannels, Champagne, blazers, and strawberries are optional these days. **LB**

↩ *A few lazy hours on the river in a handcrafted punt is a highly civilized way to spend a summer's day.*

Experience Malmaison

Location Oxford, Oxfordshire, England
Website www.malmaison-oxford.com   **Price** ⑤⑤

On the whole you would not consider a prison to be the kind of place you might want to escape to. The former Oxford castle, which recently became the United Kingdom's first prison to be converted into a boutique hotel, offers the kind of luxurious living that former convicts could only have imagined.

Originally constructed by William the Conqueror in 1071 and later extended, the castle sits in a 5-acre (2-ha) site. On passing through a restored courtyard, visitors enter the imposing frontage of the hotel, complete with flag-adorned turrets and cruciform arrow slits. In more recent decades, the building was better known as H. M. Prison Oxford, and *The Italian Job* starring Michael Caine was filmed on location here.

Now, with ninety-four sleek and chic bedrooms, a buzzy bar, and a brasserie, Malmaison Oxford is a place where you would be more than happy to serve a lengthy sentence. On entering, the first area you encounter is the most memorable: A Wing is a vast, glass-roofed atrium with galleried landings lining the walls above. Linked by iron staircases, the whitewashed walls of these floors are studded with tiny red doors—the original cells. Three cells have been knocked together to form each guest room, and inside the arched windows remind guests they are also in a castle.

Present-day inmates are spoiled in a way that former prisoners could only dream of: extra-comfy beds, crisp white sheets, power showers, minibars, and mood lighting all conspire to make you feel utterly indulged. Little touches like the toiletries you are encouraged to take away, DVDs in every room, and a CD library all help to make Malmaison a place where you would be delighted to spend a stretch of time. **HA**

Relax at The Victoria

Location Norfolk, England   **Website** www.holkham.co.uk
Price $

Situated opposite the pine-tree-studded, sandy path that leads down to the beautiful Holkham beach, The Victoria has become the place to stay for many visitors looking to explore the north Norfolk coastline. Combining a relaxed, family atmosphere with enough edge and chic to keep the hordes of weekenders happy, The Victoria has the feel of a popular pub, mixed with the exclusiveness of a boutique hideaway.

Food at The Victoria is designed to suit the everyday palate, but the use of seasonal local produce means the menu is always changing and is full of Norfolk delights, such as crab from nearby Cromer or venison and game from the Earl of Leicester's adjoining estate. Guests quickly feel at home, be it lolling around in a compact, individually designed bedroom, or grabbing a latte in one of the quiet, cozy lounges.

The beach is the big draw here, though. It is ideal for taking long, windswept walks surrounded by blue sea and dramatic skies, or building sand castles with the kids. If Holkham looks familiar, that could be because it was immortalized in the closing scenes of the Hollywood movie *Shakespeare in Love*, when Gwyneth Paltrow got sand between her toes. After a day on the beach, head back to the hotel, where traditional English style meets the days of the Raj in the form of the claw-footed bath in your room, or the Adnams ale on tap at the bar, and the imported Rajasthani furniture and other colonial artifacts that add to the bohemian charm. If you really want to hide away, you can stay in one of the three lodges within the earl's estate that have been restored recently. **RS**

→ *Holkham Estate provides a rich and varied habitat for wildlife, including several endangered species.*

Visit Chelsea Physic Garden

Location Chelsea, London, England
Website www.chelseaphysicgarden.co.uk **Price** $

An oasis of calm, this "secret" walled garden in the heart of London's fashionable Chelsea offers visitors a tranquil retreat from the metropolis. This lovely 4-acre (1.6-ha) garden was founded in 1673 by the Worshipful Society of Apothecaries to enable apprentices to identify different plants. Its location, on the bank of the Thames, was chosen for its proximity to the river and also because it created a warmer microclimate, allowing non-native plants, including olive and pineapple trees, the chance to survive.

Today, the garden continues to research the properties, origins, and conservation of more than 5,000 plants, and visitors are given audio guides that give an interesting commentary about the garden's history. The pharmaceutical garden offers a fascinating insight into those plants that have proven value in medicine: varieties such as Madagascan periwinkle, which is used in anticancer drugs; woolly foxglove, used to combat abnormal heart rhythms; and meadowsweet, from which aspirin was first derived. In the garden of world medicine, visitors can inspect plants used across the world, including those used by Maoris in New Zealand and Aborigines in Australia.

The perfumery and aromatics garden is a delight and contains a vast collection of scented plants and flowers, including lavender, rosemary, geraniums, and lime verbena. Along the west side of the garden is the historical walk, which shows the work of some of the characters associated with the garden's history. The café offers delicious light food, and in good weather you can sit outside and breathe in the scented air. **HA**

→ *Steeped in botanical history, the garden is the ideal place for a pleasant stroll away from the city bustle.*

Stay at Barnsley House

Location Gloucestershire, England
Website www.barnsleyhouse.com **Price** ⊖⊖⊖

In recent years the Cotswolds has become something of a Mecca for urban sophisticates in search of rural bliss. They flock to these parts to play lord and lady of the manor in one of the new breed of rural-glam country-house hotels. Barnsley House is one of the trailblazers of this chic country set.

This super-stylish historic manor house is set in 11 acres (4.5 ha) of gorgeous gardens designed by the former owner and legendary gardener Rosemary Verey. Visitors used to come here to admire the verdant surroundings, but nowadays that is a luxury reserved for the well-heeled hotel guests. Stroll around the sunny terraces, the ancient meadows, and the ornate formal lawns, or relax by the temple and pool garden.

The garden is not the only draw to Barnsley House. Prepare to swoon at the stunning spa; built within a sunken garden, it has floor-to-ceiling windows letting daylight flood in and a sauna, steam room, and relaxation room. Outside there is a warm hydrotherapy pool complete with back-massaging showers. Spa aficionados will be delighted with the myriad of treatments on offer.

With only nine rooms, all individually designed, Barnsley manages to retain an intimate feel, although not at the expense of comfort. Beds are huge, pillows are plump, freshly cut flowers from the garden perfume the air, and the bathrooms are decadently luxurious. Think walk-through showers, double-ended roll-top bathtubs, and funky lighting, not forgetting plasma screen televisions. Just across the road, and under the same ownership as Barnsley House, is the cozy village pub. Nip over for a drink before dinner and rub shoulders with the locals—Kate Moss and Liz Hurley are said to be regulars. **HA**

Relax at Lucknam Park

Location Wiltshire, England
Website www.lucknampark.co.uk **Price** ⊖⊖⊖

Turn off the leafy country road, through the old stone gate, and enter a mile-long avenue of lime and beech trees, three deep and almost 200 years old. Eventually this tunnel of trees opens out to reveal a perfect lawn in front of Lucknam, often called the quintessential English country-house hotel. In its 500 acres (200 ha) of parkland on the rolling hills outside of Bath it has a Michelin-starred restaurant, award-winning spa and indoor pool, exquisite garden dating back hundreds of years, and even an equestrian center with thirty horses, which guests may use to explore the estate.

The building dates back to a wealthy seventeenth-century merchant who earned a fortune importing

> *"Lucknam Park is the sort of hotel in which to entertain the fantasy of never having to leave."*
>
> Kate Kellaway, *Observer*

tobacco from Virginia, then built the central part of the property. It was enlarged by successive owners and now has become a world-class hotel with an opulent traditional atmosphere.

The best bedrooms, at the front of the house, have four-poster beds, dining tables, sitting rooms, marble bathrooms, and inspiring views across the parkland. Among the antiques, ornaments, and lush fabrics, the modern touches are discreet. Downstairs, head chef Hywel Jones has been voted the best hotel chef in Britain. His menus mix traditional and modern cuisine and make ample use of the area's finest suppliers, plus Lucknam's own herb garden. **SH**

Visit Royal Crescent Hotel

Location Bath, Somerset, England
Website www.royalcrescent.co.uk **Price** ⊖

Jane Austen fantasies come alive at this elegant hotel ideally situated in the middle of Bath's architecturally renowned Royal Crescent. The Royal Crescent Hotel occupies two historic buildings virtually unchanged since the eighteenth-century when the aristocrats of the day would visit Bath during the "season" for the water's health-giving properties.

The exterior of the hotel looks much as it did 250 years ago, while inside huge vases of scented lilies perfume the air, a fire crackles in the drawing room, and discreet staff appear as if from nowhere exactly when you need them. The bedrooms have been lovingly restored to ensure they are just as they were in the eighteenth century. Carpets, color schemes, and furniture have all been carefully chosen to ensure authenticity, but not at the expense of comfort.

For a spa, head to the Bath House, which offers a range of treatments including a warm relaxation pool where gothic windows allow natural light to flood in. After a few languorous lengths, soak in one of the toasty hot tubs before steeling yourself for an invigorating plunge in one of the icy tubs of cold water, a practice said to do wonders for the circulation.

Of course you do not need to stay for long to enjoy the best of the hotel: Do not miss out on eating at the Royal Crescent's restaurant, the Dower House, which overlooks the garden. Or on a sunny day, find yourself a seat under a flower-adorned magnolia tree in the tranquil and secluded garden, listen to the birdsong, and enjoy an indulgent afternoon tea just like those elite Georgians did back in Bath's heyday. **HA**

← *The Royal Crescent Hotel is situated in the middle of Bath's beautiful eighteenth-century Royal Crescent.*

Enjoy Thermae Bath Spa

Location Bath, Somerset, England
Website www.thermaebathspa.com **Price** ⊖

As the sun sets across the Georgian rooftops of Bath, there is no finer place to be than wallowing in the steamy warmth of the rooftop pool at Thermae Bath Spa. It is the only spot in Britain where visitors can escape into spring water that is naturally heated. Hotel spas, even in Bath, make do with warmed tap water. Thermae uses mineral-rich spring water bubbling up from the limestone at 113°F (45°C)—just like the Romans who built the elaborate bathing complex that still stands a few hundred yards away.

There is a contemporary sense of luxury within the modern construction. More than 140 architects competed to win the contract. Nicholas Grimshaw's

> *"[The rooftop is] best enjoyed at night, when the skyline is floodlit … and the water begins to steam."*

Vincent Crump, *The Times*

winning design uses traditional Bath stone, like the Georgian buildings surrounding the spa, plus giant swaths of glass and quirky round portholes.

The usual treatments are available, as well as private escapes to the restored Georgian Hot Bath and the secluded Cross Bath, a stand-alone bathhouse across the street built above the site of the original Roman cistern. At the main three-story spa, there is everything a latter-day Roman bather could want: aromatic steam saunas in circular glass pods, an indoor pool with gently flowing currents, bubbling foot baths, a huge shower big enough to soak a dozen people at once, and the highlight, a rooftop pool. **SH**

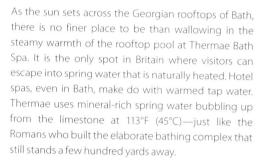

Stay at Babington House

Location Somerset, England
Website www.babingtonhouse.co.uk   **Price** 💲💲

Babington House is a deliberate attempt to establish a retreat for media types and stylish urbanites looking for a country break. It is both a private members' club and a luxury hotel and restaurant, part of a small chain of boutique premises owned by British entrepreneur Nick Smith. He chose the basics well: Babington is an old, honey-colored stone mansion that dates back to 1370. Deep in rural Somerset, in England's West Country, the building stands amid 18 acres (7 ha), down a long avenue of trees.

The secret of Babington's success is the mix of classic style and contemporary cool. Everything centers on the main house, with its library, bar, and

---

" . . . material girls can check out Room Six, which Madonna loves for its bath on the balcony."

Susan D'Arcy, *The Times*

---

pool room. You eat at the informal "House Kitchen," the more secluded "Log Room," or out on the terrace if the Somerset weather allows. Across the garden the Cowshed Spa offers indoor and outdoor pools, a gym, steam room, sauna, aroma rooms, and a movie theater. In the gardens there are also grass and hard tennis courts, a cricket pitch, croquet lawn, lake (with resident swans), and a period walled garden. Bedrooms are situated either up the grand mahogany staircase in the main house or across the crunchy gravel in the converted gate lodge, coach house, and stable block. One room has a freestanding bathtub next to the bed; another has a whirlpool tub on a private terrace. **SH**

Explore Lundy Island

Location Bristol Channel, England
Website www.lundyisland.co.uk   **Price** 💲

The tiny island of Lundy, 3.5 miles (5.5 km) by 0.5 miles (0.8 km), is a well-kept secret. After a two-hour ferry trip from the North Devon port of Ilfracombe, arriving on the island feels like you are stepping back in time to the 1950s. The island's craggy shoreline has been ravaged by the waves and the winds, not to mention the Vikings, pirates, and smugglers over the years, but Lundy remains blissfully untouched by the modern world. There are no cars, just a handful of people, one pub, and fields stretching to the puffin-packed cliffs full of lambs, deer, and feral goats.

Accommodation ranges from a sheltered campsite to a thirteenth-century castle, a Georgian villa, a fisherman's chalet, and a lighthouse. There are twenty-three iconic places to stay, each furnished with care and with special touches like naval charts and paintings of shipwrecks on the wall, open fires, and bookcases full of wildlife books and board games. The attention to detail makes a stay all the more special.

For such a small place, there is plenty to do. Wardens organize walks, snorkeling safaris, and boat trips around the island, during which you can hear the breeding colony of gray seals singing before you see them. Divers love the island for its pristine waters, and it is becoming one of the most lusted-after rock-climbing locations in the United Kingdom. Lundy has a timeless, wholesome feel to it, where the simple things in life take center stage, such as swimming in the sea or enjoying a pint in the Marisco Tavern. From the southern tip of the west coast of the island, there is nothing but sea between here and the United States. **LD**

▸ *The lighthouse on Lundy is one of the historic buildings preserved by the Landmark Trust.*

Experience Bryher Island

Location Isles of Scilly, England
Website www.tresco.co.uk/stay/hell-bay   **Price** 💲💲

The boat from the biggest island, St. Mary's, meanders between rocks to a stone jet on Bryher. An old four-by-four vehicle bumps along rutted tracks to the hotel. Bryher, just half a mile wide, is the smallest of the inhabited Scilly Isles. Seventy inhabitants look across to the island of Tresco, considering it rather brash because it has a concrete road. St. Mary's, at 2.5 miles (4 km) wide, with an airport, seems like downtown New York from Bryher's bracken-covered hillocks.

Bryher is also the most westward isle; its most famous landmark is its only hotel, Hell Bay. The hotel has a friendly, down-to-earth vibe: Hot flasks are offered to guests going for a walk, and after dark you

> *"Outside, there is wilderness; inside, you retreat to designer plumbing and three-course dinners."*
>
> Richard Woods, *The Times*

can borrow a flashlight. The low-rise complex of whitewashed buildings stands a few yards from a pretty sandy cove. Pray for a storm. Gales smash spray against the windows while diners feast on Bryher crab and lobster served with vegetables grown on the island.

Inside, the hotel is like a Cape Cod boathouse, with wicker chairs, wooden floors, and pastel paintwork. There is modern art everywhere, including a Barbara Hepworth, but the images commanding most attention are the views from the big picture windows. **SH**

← *The coast of Bryher faces the full fury of Atlantic storms—hence the name of the hotel.*

Stay at Fort Clonque

Location Alderney, Channel Islands
Website www.landmarktrust.org.uk   **Price** 💲💲

Military history fans will be in their element at Fort Clonque, which was held by the Germans during their occupation of the Channel Islands in World War II. Perched perilously on an exposed rocky promontory that can be reached only by a causeway that is cut off from the mainland at high tide, latter-day guests can sleep inside this cavernous gun emplacement, which was built on the specific orders of the German High Command. Despite the 19-foot (5.8-m) thick walls, you will still be lulled to sleep by the incessant crashing of waves onto the granite rocks around you.

Fort Clonque, firmly ensconced on the steep southwest coast of the island of Alderney, at the end of a long causeway just 5 miles (8 km) from mainland France, is built into and follows the natural contours of its undulating, isolated promontory rather than being constructed on top of it all. The result is a picturesque ensemble of towers, gun emplacements, and ramparts spread over several levels.

The first defensive works here were begun in 1847, although its significance as a military outpost was not realized until the German occupation, which added many of the officer's quarters and casements still in place today. Fort Clonque offers accommodation for up to thirteen people throughout the officers' and soldiers' quarters, the gatehouse, the upper magazine, and the German bunker. There is a modern kitchen, and food and supplies can be garnered from nearby St. Anne. Care should be taken not to linger in case the tide prevents you from getting home. Alternatively, the housekeeper can do the shopping for you in advance, if you ask nicely. A log fire and upright piano help soften the harshness of the environment and create an air of romance and informality. **BS**

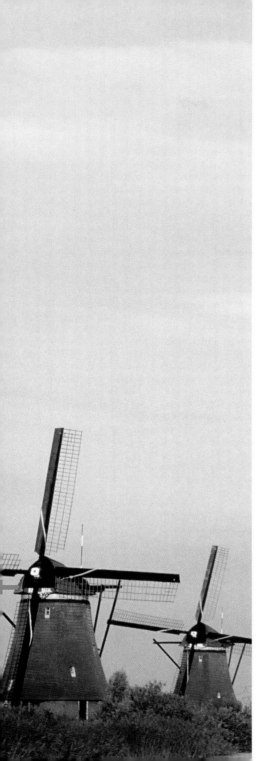

Discover Kinderdijk Park

Location Near Rotterdam, Holland   **Website** www.kinderdijk.com
Price ❶

For a classic Dutch landscape that looks like an Old Master's canvas, look no further than Kinderdjik Park. Here, on the watery banks of the canal and only 10 miles (16 km) from Rotterdam, there are nineteen traditional windmills that date back to the mid-1700s. It is the largest concentration of old windmills in the Netherlands and used to perform an extremely useful function: With much of the Netherlands at or below sea level, flooding has always been a serious issue, and for more than 200 years the windmills drained the Alblasserwaard polders of excess water ensuring the surrounding land did not flood.

If you come in the second week of September, the windmills are floodlit at night, providing an unforgettable spectacle. Otherwise, come on a Saturday in either July or August when all nineteen of the mills are fully operational. Most of these beautifully preserved windmills are now occupied, although one is open to visitors. For a small entrance fee you can clamber up the steep and narrow stairs to each floor and poke around the cramped living quarters of the original miller and his family. Do not worry—even though the sails of the windmill give the distinct impression they are going to knock your head off on entering and leaving the building, their clever design means any unfortunate decapitations are avoided.

You can ride a bike along the banks of the canal, or even skate on the canal in winter if it is cold enough. If that sounds too energetic, take a boat ride along the glassy waters or simply stroll along the paths and enjoy the tranquility of this serene area. **HA**

◄ *The haunting beauty of the Kinderdijk windmills are a designated UNESCO World Heritage site.*

Dine at Posthoorn

Location Monnickendam, Holland
Website www.posthoorn.eu **Price** 🅢🅢

The ornate, seventeenth-century coach house stands among humble fishing cottages in a bohemian harbor-side village just twenty minutes' drive from the center of Amsterdam. Throughout history, horse-drawn stages used to stop here, and the Posthoorn was always a well-known meeting place for dignitaries traveling along the coast road. Three years ago, the new owners restored and converted the buildings to what they call a stylish "suite hotel and restaurant." This elegant new restaurant with rooms has become a well-known meeting place for dignitaries of a different sort: contemporary Dutch TV, film, and arts celebrities.

Style and design is everything here, with dramatic antique chandeliers carefully placed together with modern, dark-wood furniture and old china vases alongside sleek, polished floors. The wood-paneled bar has an open fire and a cigar menu. There are just five luxury rooms above the gourmet dining room, and they are decorated with astonishing finesse. The bedrooms are unashamedly romantic, with candles and roses everywhere. Each suite is named and styled after a famous visitor to the Posthoorn. The Napoleon Bonaparte Suite has classic, patterned linen wallpaper and rich chocolate colors, and the Persijnen Kamer (after the Persijn family, who founded Amsterdam) is a cozy attic with exposed beams and fluffy cushions.

Downstairs, the restaurant serves modern French-Mediterranean cuisine with regional Dutch ingredients in a simple, uncluttered environment. You will sit in comfy upholstered armchairs on a polished wooden floor with modern art on the wall. There are classic, high, monumental ceilings hung with enormous modern lightbulbs. Or you can eat under the canopies of the brick-paved courtyard outside. **SH**

Stay at Hotel Julien

Location Antwerp, Belgium
Website www.hotel-julien.com **Price** 🅢🅢

With a tram line rumbling by outside in the narrow bustling streets of the old city of Antwerp, Hotel Julien may not initially seem particularly enticing. However, on opening the huge, wooden doors of this charming pair of sixteenth-century merchants' houses joined by a tranquil courtyard, any concerns soon melt away.

Check in at a limed-oak reception desk with a glass wall that allows you to see into the light-flooded outdoor courtyard and exquisite dining room and lounge. Ornate doors and heavy paneling provide the perfect backdrop for an eclectic mix of contemporary and antique furniture. Flop down on one of the gorgeous cowhide Eames chairs close by or slip into

> *"The . . . townhouse has been spruced up . . . to create a hotel that looks like a magazine shoot."*
>
> Katie Bowman, *The Times*

the gilt-ceilinged library and enjoy, by the fire, the freshly brewed coffee and Belgian chocolates that are available around the clock, before climbing the blond-wood staircase to one of eleven stylish bedrooms.

Upstairs, the color palette is soft and neutral, with restrained shades of crisp whites, soft grays, creams, and blues. Choose a room with cathedral views and exposed timber A-frames in the attics, or a loftier-ceilinged room with a terrace and an altogether grander and more elegant feel. For breakfast, sit in the sun-dappled dining room at the communal antique Flemish table and feast on homemade breads, jam, cheese, salmon, eggs, yogurt, and fresh fruit salad. **SWi**

Unwind at Pand Hotel

Location Bruges, Belgium
Website www.pandhotel.com   **Price** ⊖⊖

Situated in the heart of Bruges, just a short stroll away from the canals, the enchanting Pand Hotel is run by the Vanhaecke family, who have converted this eighteenth-century house into a wonderful boutique hotel. Their quest has been aided by the convenient fact that the Vanhaeckes are also established antique dealers—so all of the wonderful pictures and furniture you see in the hotel are not only unique, but have been carefully handpicked by resident experts.

It would be easy to get the impression from this description that the Pand Hotel is somewhat old-fashioned. In truth, it blends its passion for antiques with sophisticated modern touches and even the odd funky furnishing, lending the place broader appeal. There are twenty-six bedrooms in all, which have been individually appointed. Air-conditioning and wireless Internet access are housed in refined spaces fitted with antiques and Ralph Lauren fabrics, and marble bathrooms are stocked with Annick Goutal body care products. Junior suites include a whirlpool tub and flat-screen televisions, and there are also two guesthouses—one above the canal in a sixteenth-century gabled house, the other in a manor house of the same period.

You would expect a hotel like this to have a library, and the Pand's is beautifully intimate and comes complete with an open fire, Louis Vuitton suitcases, and wooden collectibles. Equally cozy is the candlelit bar, which boasts a leather Chesterfield, mahogany furniture, and an incredibly snug ambience. A clapboard breakfast room leads onto a small courtyard, and there is even a sauna downstairs. All the services of an international deluxe hotel, in other words, with the care and intimacy of a private mansion. **PS**

Enjoy the Duke's Palace

Location Bruges, Belgium
Website www.kempinski-bruges.com   **Price** ⊖⊖

Amid the cobblestone alleyways and canals of the Belgian town of Bruges, the Kempinski Hotel Duke's Palace, built for Duke Philip III in 1429, has undergone an extensive restoration and is now one of the finest palace hotels in Europe.

Just a short walk from Bruges's colorful market square, it is part hotel, part art gallery. Its rooms are decorated with period ornaments and meticulously restored fifteenth-century artwork. Many historic features have been retained, including the grand ballroom and a heritage-listed chapel, with its expanses of original stained glass still intact and its walls adorned with centuries-old frescoes.

"[W]ith its soaring turrets and tranquil gardens, [it is] a perfect base from which to explore."

Suzanne Cadisch, *Independent*

The hotel's gourmet restaurant serves Belgian specialties, and the bar is home to the most extensive selection of wines and beers in Bruges. Once a month, the large, landscaped garden is transformed into an outdoor exhibition area where guests may buy work from local and regional artists. Handmade chocolates are available in the lounge and are best consumed in front of the fifteenth-century fireplace and its roaring fire on a cold winter's night.

There are also three treatment rooms offering a range of massage and facial therapies, surrounded by stylishly appointed hammams and a sauna, gymnasium, and indoor swimming pool. **BS**

Visit the Royal Greenhouses in Laeken

Location Brussels, Belgium
Website www.monarchie.be/en/visit   **Price** 〇

Brussels's surreal side emerges in the mysterious paintings of Magritte—and in the clash of the magical and the mundane seen in the Royal Greenhouses in Laeken. Set on the edge of the city, these palatial greenhouses are where the heady scents of the colonial Congo are transported to everyday Brussels. Entranced visitors drift past orchids, azaleas, and camellias, breathing in the steamy fragrances of bitter oranges and damp ferns. The sinuous art nouveau lines reveal shifting perspectives and sudden glimpses of green canopies, cupolas, turrets, and vaulted tunnels of glass.

The city's tropical greenhouses began as a royal whim, a work of self-glorification spearheaded by King Leopold II (1835–1909). Leopold never deigned to visit the Belgian Congo, but, as a passionate plant man, he expected the Congo to be shipped to him at regular intervals. The challenge was to create "an everlasting springtime in a perfect palace of glass," teasing a tropical garden to grow in northern climes.

Leopold's architects and gardeners fulfilled his every wish, but credit must also be given to the king, whose passion for building was matched by his fascination with exotic plants and palms: from rubber plants and weeping figs to pineapples and dwarf bananas. In these winter gardens, Leopold entertained his friends, swam in his glass-canopied pool, and paraded on an African elephant. Do contact the greenhouses before you travel however, as they can only be visited in a limited summer period. **LGS**

← *This path runs through the center of Palm House in the Royal Greenhouses in Laeken in Brussels.*

Explore the Halligen Islands Archipelago

Location Schleswig-Holstein, Germany
Website www.wattenmeer-nationalpark.de/flag/engl.pdf   **Price** 〇

They are less an archipelago, more small banks of land barely rising above sea level. The Halligen Islands have always been at the mercy of the North Sea—a storm or a high tide can swamp much of the land. If both arrive together, parts of an island can be lost forever. So it is a precarious place to live—houses are built on man-made mounds of earth at least 3 feet (1 m) high to protect against flooding. Yet there is a distinctive beauty to these ten slivers of land. The skies are open and the panoramas wide. Flocks of birds wheel over thatched cottages, redbrick farmsteads, dikes, and fragile causeways. The straight lines of the horizon are

"[The] salt marshes and tidal flats of the Wattenmeer are places of constant flux."

Alan Harper, *Guardian*

punctuated only by the occasional, lone wooden windmill or sturdy stone lighthouse. It is peaceful, rural, and seems a long way from the stresses of a city.

The sea has claimed many of the Halligen over the centuries. Sometimes islands are joined to the mainland by silted causeways and then separated by tidal erosion. There is more legal protection for this watery landscape than physical protection. It is part of Wattenmeer National Park, and visitors come to take guided walks on the tidal flats and to look at migrating birds and distinctive plants. Others just enjoy the ferry trips or the ride on the distinctive narrow railways that link some islands, almost through the waves. **SH**

Visit the Island of Rügen

Location Rügen, Germany **Website** www.ruegen.de
Price 🌓

Imagine a quiet island with dazzling white chalk cliffs and long sandy beaches backed by calm expanses of beech woods. Dotted among the rolling hills are pretty cottages, biking and walking trails, medieval churches, stately homes, and castles. Rügen may be Germany's largest island, but it is little known elsewhere. It lies in the Baltic Sea in the northeast of the country, yet benefits from an unusually mild climate.

The island rose to fame in Germany when it was featured in the landscapes of the nineteenth-century romantic painter Casper David Friedrich, and today it is one of the country's most popular vacation destinations. Rügen is easy to reach: A road and railway bridge connects the island with the mainland and there are many ferry connections.

The resorts on the long coastline have sandy beaches and piers, and boat trips are available to Denmark, Sweden, Poland, and neighboring German islands. Visitors simply go to the beach or explore the countryside and coastline—the island contains two national parks and a nature reserve. The spectacular wooded cliffs offer panoramic views of the Baltic Sea and Germany's coastline, and inland the landscapes range from heather-clad hills to reed beds, from woods full of wildflowers to lush, flat farmland.

Much of the architecture dates back to the spa boom of the nineteenth century, and many of the little towns and villages are linked by a historic narrow-gauge steam railway. You may not escape other tourists on Rügen, but you may feel as if you have escaped from the twenty-first century. **SH**

→ *The pier in the resort of Sellin on the Island of Rügen has retained its traditional architecture.*

Stay at Kempinski Grand Hotel

Location Mecklenburg-Vorpommern, Germany
Website www.kempinski-heiligendamm.com **Price** 💲💲

Looking like a huge, resplendent wedding cake, the Kempinski Grand Hotel Heiligendamm glitters a brilliant white in the sharp midday sun, contrasting beautifully with the azure of the sky and the pale turquoise Baltic Sea. Known as the White Town by the Sea, Heiligendamm is Germany's oldest seaside spa, a dazzling collection of six neoclassical buildings, founded in 1793 by the Grand Duke of Mecklenburg Friedrich Franz I, who came here to take in the clean salty air, lush beech forests, and tideless waters.

The building was briefly used as a sanatorium and hospital in the 1930s but, after a lavish restoration project in 2003, there is little reminder of its recent past, except perhaps for the well-heeled guests trotting to and from the super-deluxe spa in fluffy white slippers and soft, commodious dressing gowns. Tony Blair, Vladimir Putin, and Nicholas Sarkozy descended on the resort for the thirty-third G8 summit, and outside of the political arena Bono and Sir Bob Geldof, among others, have also paid visits.

Dining is taken very seriously. There is an Asian restaurant, a sushi bar, and a number of other upmarket eateries, not to mention the Friedrich Franz gourmet restaurant, one of only a handful in Germany to have a Michelin star. For the fresh-air enthusiast, many sports are available, including horseback riding and sailing. A thirty-minute bicycle ride to the pretty village of Kühlungsborn makes for an ideal day out, as does a trip on the narrow-gauge steam railway, still chugging away after more than 140 years in service. **TW**

← *The Kempinski Grand Hotel Heiligendamm is right on the shore of the Baltic Sea and has lovely views.*

Escape the Crowds at Bürgerpark

Location Bremen, Germany
Website www.buergerpark.de/en **Price** 💲

Right in the center of one of Germany's biggest cities, Bürgerpark has densely wooded surroundings that are more readily associated with rural areas than major conurbations. Unlike the gardens and parks in most cities, though, it was not devised as a playground for the ruling classes but instead developed for, and by, the Bürger—that is, the ordinary citizens.

In the 1860s, the people of Bremen formed the Committee for the Afforestation of Bürgerweide, and since then they have preserved the park through personal initiatives and donations. Apart from the forestlike terrain and the large meadows, there are also

"Bürgerpark is . . . reckoned to be one of the best landscaped parks in Germany."

Independent

landscaped park areas and an animal enclosure. One of the aims of the park is to provide a nature reserve for city dwellers—in particular children—who are unable to travel into rural areas, and the nature and adventure trail within the park provides information about plants and animals as well as their habitats.

The emphasis on furnishing a well-balanced outdoor experience is exemplified by the Finnbahn, a running track devised with a medical institution to reduce stress on the joints. In addition, several venues on the grounds stage cultural events, and the revenue from the concerts and theater performances contributes directly to the maintenance of the park. **DaH**

Enjoy Bühlerhöhe

Location Baden-Baden, Germany
Website www.buehlerhoehe.de   **Price** ⊖⊖⊖

Situated high up in the Black Forest and surrounded by 44 acres (18 ha) of wooded parkland, Schlosshotel Bühlerhöhe provides the ideal sanctuary from the pressures of modern life. Yet despite its seclusion, it is only 9 miles (14 km) to the elegant spa resort of Baden-Baden, the summer stomping ground of the European aristocracy in days gone by and whose old town and famous casino are still popular attractions.

The hotel's five-star attention to detail is evident in the decor, facilities, and service that maintains elements of privacy and restfulness. All seventy-seven bedrooms and thirteen suites have been lavishly redecorated and furnished with high-quality, king-size

> "[It is] situated at one of the most breathtaking panoramic viewing points of the Black Forest."

luxurytravelmagazine.com

beds and luxurious mattresses. The spa and health clinic equal that of the hotel rooms for decadence, and pampering and relaxation are the order of the day. Within the wellness area of the hotel, beauty and spa treatments are offered to guests in thoughtfully decorated rooms, the subtle lighting adding to the style and ambience.

Fitness training is also available for those who desire a more active retreat, and a sumptuous swimming pool filled with the hotel's own supply of fresh springwater waits to be dived into. The surrounding woods also provide the perfect backdrop for a gentle afternoon stroll. This is luxury at its best. **TW**

Visit Planten un Blomen

Location Hamburg, Germany
Website www.plantenunblomen.hamburg.de   **Price** ❶

The German city of Hamburg is most famous for its pretty canals and waterways, its red-light district, and its vast harbor that houses some truly enormous ships. Yet it is possible to escape all the bustle in what is in fact a very green city and home to a number of parks. The most tranquil of these gardens is the Planten un Blomen (plants and flowers) park.

The public park was built on the site of the former Zoologischer Garten zoo and surrounding cemeteries in 1930 for a large flower exhibition. The expansive area remained as parkland and was redesigned in 1953, 1963, and 1973 to house various international horticultural exhibitions. The result is an oasis of green and calm in the heart of the city.

The park's extensive square of greenery reaches from the Dammtor railway station almost to the city's St. Pauli neighborhood. Visitors stroll along its pathways admiring the picturesque displays of plants and flowers or popping into various cafés for a glass of wine or a chilled beer. Tropical greenhouses packed with beautiful orchids are situated on the eastern side of the park and were once part of the Alter Botanischer Garten (Old Botanical Garden).

In the height of summer there are jazz concerts at the music pavilion, and light shows are held over the lake nightly at 9 P.M. accompanied by classical music. In winter, the park becomes home to Germany's best and biggest open-air ice-skating rink. Particularly noteworthy is the Japanischer Garten (Japanese Garden), which has a lake at its center, with an authentic Japanese teahouse on its banks. **CK**

➡ *Tulip heads in the botanical garden of Planten un Blomen park provide a diversion from the skyline.*

Rejuvenate at Parkschlösschen

Location Bad Wildstein, Germany
Website www.parkschloesschen.de   **Price** 💲💲

Parkschlösschen is not the place to rekindle a flagging love life: Guests at this charming old hotel in the rolling hills and vineyards of the Moselle Valley in western Germany are advised to remain celibate during their stay. It is not because the proprietors are particularly prudish; the sex ban is all in the name of health.

This rambling and peaceful retreat hidden among tall trees offers an escape into a world of alternative therapies and is a leading proponent of ayurveda, a 5,000-year-old Eastern healing art using detoxification, herbal preparations, nutrition, and massages. The entire 11-acre (4-ha) park and art nouveau castle are run on the ayurveda theory of "health deriving from harmony with yourself and nature." The hotel was completely renovated with natural materials like wool, wood, slate, and marble, and the water is supplied from a nearby thermal spring. All rooms have been systematically purged of the "harmful influences" of electric cables (now fitted with double insulation), and water pipes (covered with a marble shield) are decorated in gentle pastel colors.

Parkschlösschen's team of ayurveda doctors (with conventional medical backgrounds) monitor guests to ensure they get the maximum benefit from their stay. It has become a haven for stressed executives, those recuperating from illness or surgery, and health-conscious visitors. Guests swim, play tennis, or hike in the woods, and there are saunas, massages, yoga, meditation, and alternative treatments. The hotel has a no-children policy, and cell phones are actively discouraged. The gourmet meals are vegetarian and dairy-free and no alcohol, coffee, or tea is served. Instead, guests are encouraged to drink warm water. **SH**

Explore Kellerwald National Park

Location Kassel, Germany
Website www.nationalpark-kellerwald-edersee.de   **Price** ◖

What a forest! Kellerwald National Park covers the hills and valleys disappearing to the horizon, wrapping around lakes, and encasing rivers. You can walk all day and not reach the end of it. This pristine wooded wilderness is the biggest deciduous forest you will find in central Europe, flowing over hills and mountains for approximately 14,000 acres (5,665 ha). Carved by the Eder River into canyons, hills, and valleys, it makes a perfect escape from the urban world.

The sea of red beech trees here is extraordinarily old. More than a third were planted more than 120 years ago and many started growing in the

> *"The ancient trees with their countless hollows . . . are already home to a number of rare species."*
>
> germany-tourism.de

seventeenth century. Kellerwald National Park is also home to rare species including the black stork, eagle owl, raven, wildcat, red kite, stag beetle, and fire salamander. You may spot a red deer, hear woodpeckers, and see bats swooping around as night falls. More than 400 springs originate in the park, uniting to form forest creeks with the highest biological water quality—perfect for brown trout.

This is such a total escape that there is not even a human safety policy in place. Old trees in danger of falling or breaking are not removed and visitors are told to proceed at their own risk, particularly after storms, and the forest is all the better for it. **SH**

Follow the German Wine Route to the Pfälzer Wald

Location Rhineland-Palatinate, Germany
Website www.germany-tourism.de **Price** 🌡️

Leaving the autobahn far behind, follow the roads through the beautiful open countryside around Kandel, Minfeld, Winden, and Bad Bergzabern and explore the quiet lanes by car, bike, or on foot. Here, orchards of apples and pumpkins provide autumn color, and small fields of corn mingle with vineyards that supply new wine sold locally from the roadside.

The *Deutsche Weinstraße* (German wine route) passes through many beautifully preserved, half-timbered villages where vines twist their way up houses and bunches of grapes hang in the sunshine; look for the signs with a wine jug indicating a place to taste the wine. The Mediterranean-like climate allows apricots, sweet chestnuts, figs, and lemons to thrive, and these too are sold in baskets at the end of driveways.

Despite the route being marked as a tourist trail, the roads are quiet in the nearby sleepy villages and not marked on the tourist maps. They become ever more remote as you climb up into Pfälzer Wald Natural Park, the woods and twisting roads hiding any habitation. The evergreen, sweet chestnut, and oak trees give way every now and again to rich glades dappled with sunshine; the river valleys of the Saarbach and Speyerbach twist below the roads in mirror image, and the hilltops provide striking views over the *wald*. Forest villages punctuate the routes, providing welcome bakeries with wafting smells of fresh-baked bread and roadside restaurants serving rustic local fare. The residents may be there, but it gets increasingly hard to spot a tourist. **CM**

⬈ *These scenic autumnal vineyards line the route as you wind your way into Pfälzer Wald Natural Park.*

"Here the climate is mild, the scenery like Tuscany's, and people are warm and friendly too."

germany-tourism.de

Relax at Bareiss Hotel

Location Black Forest, Germany
Website www.bareiss.com   **Price** ⊖⊖

It is well worth taking the scenic route to the Bareiss Hotel and Spa, lost in the depths of the Black Forest near Baiersbronn-Mitteltal, in southwest Germany. The winding roads snake through dark, enchanted forests, taking you deep into the Hansel and Gretel landscape.

The beauty of Bareiss is that it can be anything you want it to be: a gourmet's dream, a place of pampering, or simply somewhere to enjoy nature. With five pools, three saunas, and whirlpools, Bareiss is renowned for its state-of-the art spa. Offering everything from ayurveda to osteopathy means that whether you want to indulge in some marine-inspired Thalgo body treatments or go for an exotic Tibetan back massage,

> *"A meal at Bareiss is an assault on all the senses. Expect extraordinary, multilayered tastes."*
>
> Sue Style, *Financial Times*

it is all possible. Guests can also enjoy golf, fishing, or hiking, and can even take painting or cooking lessons. Among the restaurants at Bareiss is one with three Michelin stars and an 18,000-bottle wine cellar run by Claus-Peter Lumpp, who trained with Alain Ducasse. There is also a Mediterranean restaurant with light Italian meals on the menu, as well as an authentic historic Tyrolean parlor, the Dorfstuben. A rustic, wood-paneled bistro, it has an impressive collection of traditional wall-mounted clocks, and smiling waitresses in traditional garb dish up Black Forest specialties like bacon pancakes, sausage salad, and freshly smoked trout, with cool draft pilsner. **RCA**

Camp at Hopfensee

Location Bavaria, Germany
Website www.camping-hopfensee.de   **Price** ⊖

A campsite unlike any other, this vast yet peaceful complex sits next to the beautiful Lake Hopfen, the verdant pastures of the King's Nook, and the Bavarian Alps juxtaposed side by side. The lake is considered one of the warmest in the Bavarian Allgäu region and is ideal for swimming, fishing, and nonmotorized water sports. The picturesque town of Füssen is 3 miles (5 km) away, and a little farther on sits one of the busiest tourist destinations in the region, King Ludwig II's fairy-tale Neuschwanstein castle. You can see the plains from the grounds of the castle, and the temptation to dodge the crowds to reach the green fields below is compelling.

In the exclusive grounds of the five-star campsite, you can escape the throng, whiling away your time in the spa—a place that "patients" visit to be "cured" of their ailments; the pure air and the relaxation alone are often enough. Based upon holistic medicine therapies developed by Kneipp, a native of the area, the registered physiotherapy practice on the campsite offers a selection of treatments for many common ailments. These must be booked in advance—up to three months for summer visits. However, for guests who simply need relaxation, the spa, situated in the center of the campsite, also offers massages, bath and beauty treatments, a sauna, and a solarium.

The campsite, with its heated indoor swimming pool, is open all year, and in winter it includes a 38-mile (61-km) cross-country skiing trail direct from the site, with skis, toboggans, and bicycles for rent. The spacious campsite spots are for trailers or motor homes (tents are not allowed—despite the name). If you do not wish to self-cater, there is an airy glass-roofed restaurant that serves superb food. **CFM**

Discover Berchtesgaden

Location Bavaria, Germany
Website www.kehlsteinhaus.de/en/index.php   **Price** 🌀

Seventy-five miles (120 km) southeast of Munich, near the Austrian border, the breathtaking winding roads of the German Alps lead up to a mountain retreat that has been a popular vacation destination since the days when the concept of pleasure trips was still completely alien to ordinary people. Members of the Bavarian nobility first appropriated Berchtesgaden for themselves, as did the Nazis later on, before the area finally became a getaway to be enjoyed by everyone.

Within the national park itself, the snowcapped twin peaks of the Watzmann mountain loom over Berchtesgaden's picturesque church spires and the deep glacial Lake Königssee. The surrounding alpine

> ## "Dramatic mountain scenery in the area offers some of the best views in the Alps."
>
> William Cook, *Guardian*

meadows are populated with cattle, and ancient traditions that appear quaint to urban visitors are still upheld in Berchtesgaden. Mountain hiking and boating on Lake Königssee are among the most popular activities, with the awe-inspiring scenery inducing a sense of peace. For those who are more inclined towards physical exertion skiing is an option in winter, while the Watzmann Ostwand cliff provides a challenge for rock climbers. Meanwhile, Adolf Hitler's former residence, the Eagle's Nest, is a reminder of Berchtesgaden's links with the Nazis. Despite these links, the area's indisputable beauty and its slow pace of life make for a perfectly relaxing stay. **DaH**

Stay at Schloss Elmau

Location Bavaria, Germany
Website www.schloss-elmau.de   **Price** 🌀🌀

"A place of healing for healthy people who feel burdened" was how Johannes Müller, philosopher and founder of Schloss Elmau, described the castle in 1914 when it first opened. It instantly became a magnet for artists, bohemians, and aesthetes of all kinds looking for a cultural hideaway to rejuvenate their tired minds and bodies. It is still run along the same lines, and visitors come as much for its cultural leanings (there are around one hundred events throughout the year, including a literature week, jazz festival, dance and poetry workshops, and political debates) as for the scenery and pampering.

A fire in 2005 destroyed much of the building but a complete restoration has returned it to its former glory, and more besides. Set in a valley all on its own and framed by the Wetterstein, a near-vertical rock face, the scenery is truly deserving of the much-touted epithet "breathtaking." If you have ever wondered what it must be like to find yourself in the movie *The Sound of Music*, this must surely come close: soaring mountains, wildflower-strewn hillsides, crystal-clear lakes, the tinkling of cowbells, and more than 70 miles (112 km) of hiking and mountain-bike trails to explore. The famous picture-book hunting lodge of King Ludwig II is a three-hour hike away.

Each of the elegant 140 rooms and suites in the Elmau, some with walk-in closets, comes with a Bose sound system, silk-covered walls, and gleaming floors made of polished oak or teak. There are two luxury spas, concert halls, three libraries, a bookstore, an upmarket shopping arcade, and six wonderful gourmet restaurants. Once a year, usually in November, chefs from around the world come to take part in the hotel's international gourmet festival. **TW**

Discover Ushant

Location Finistère, France **Website** www.ouessant.fr
Price ❶❶

In French the name is "Ouessant," in English "Ushant." It is a wild, rocky place 10 miles (16 km) outside of Brest and surrounded by ferocious cliffs and dangerous seas, tides, and currents. Amid the Atlantic waves, France's most westerly point seems a vulnerable little dot. It is just 4 by 2 miles (6 by 3 km) but has become world famous because of its location, its devastating winter storms, and a history of sea battles between the French and the English in times gone by. Ushant is also a regular on radio shipping forecasts, standing guard at the entrance to the busiest shipping channel in the world with its ring of lighthouses.

You arrive via a potentially choppy ferry journey from Brest or the Breton fishing village of Le Conquet. The boat docks at Stiff Bay, and it is best to travel around the island on a rental bike or minibus. To some, the treeless sheep pastures are bleak; to others the rocks, grass, and thick-walled white houses crouched against the elements are beautiful.

On the other side of the island, the one village is called Lampaul. In it you will find a couple of bars, a restaurant and bakery, two small hotels, some bed-and-breakfast accommodation, and a few *gîtes* (small vacation homes). In the summer, hydrangeas and fuchsias drape against whitewashed stone walls. In winter, you realize why windows are set 3 feet (1 m) deep into the walls for protection.

Visitors wander around breathing the bracing clean sea air deeply. You may spot seals and seabirds, or you may choose to spend your time taking photographs, painting, walking, or bicycling. **SH**

← *The Créac'h lighthouse on the island of Ushant rises high above the rocky coast that surrounds it.*

Relax on the Île de Batz

Location Finistère, France   **Website** www.iledebatz.com   **Price** ❶❶

At just 2 miles (3.2 km) long by 1 mile (1.6 km) wide, Île de Batz is only a speck on the map just off Roscoff in northern Brittany. But it is a big step back in time to the romantic France of horse-drawn plows, old men in berets, and bicycling housewives wobbling on their way home. On the island, the sand is white, rocks are sculptures of rounded granite, and cottages shelter beneath pines and palms. The only traffic is tractors. There is not a single amusement arcade, nightclub, or noisy road in sight—just lovingly tended fields of organic vegetables, eighteen beaches, and 10 miles (16 km) of jagged coastline.

Batz is adored by Parisian high-fliers, politicians, and celebrities, who change into baggy shorts and flip-flops to taste the simple life among rugged seascapes and hedgerows teeming with fuchsias, nasturtiums, and hydrangeas. They sit at harborside cafés eating crêpes and sipping Breton cider; they stroll around the island's lighthouse, duck ponds, and overgrown forts.

The small exotic garden of tropical flowers was created by a rich Parisian in 1897 when he discovered the average temperature on the island varies by only a few degrees throughout the whole year. Frost is extremely rare thanks to the sheltered location and warm sea currents. One of the best-loved sights here is the ancient French captain who sits in the harbor every day looking out to sea cuddling his equally ancient pet tortoise.

There are two old-fashioned hotels, forty *gîtes* (small vacation homes), and a few guesthouses, but hardly any non-French speakers. Making it more difficult for outsiders is the use of the ancient Breton tongue for many signs, place and house names, and even items on restaurant menus. One of the best places to stay is a stylish bed-and-breakfast called Ti Va Zadou. **SH**

⬆ *Many small boats dot the shore of the tiny island of Batz off the coast of northern Brittany.*

Explore the Fjords of Finistère

Location Finistère, France   **Website** www.finisteretourisme.com   **Price** 🌓

The most westerly *département* in France, Finistère derives its name from the Latin for "the ends of the Earth." In the native Breton tongue, still spoken in these parts, its name *Penn ar bed* means "the beginning of the world." Whichever way you look at it, the area is renowned for its dramatic coastline and sense of isolation from the rest of the world—whether it is at the start or the end of it. Like its counterpart Land's End in England, the rough, rugged coastline is endowed with romantic tales, shipwrecks, smugglers, and myths and legends.

The wild coastline here looks out to the English Channel along the north coast of the département and is known for its *abers*, or fjords. There are three of them along the north coast: L'Aber Ildut, L'Aber Wrac'h, and L'Aber Benoît, funnel-shaped fjords that give a dramatic shape to the coast. L'Aber Ildut is the smallest and divides the Atlantic Ocean and the English Channel; L'Aber Benoît is 5 miles (8 km) long and has

eight villages along it; and L'Aber Wrac'h is the most celebrated. It holds five islands within it, including Vierge Island, which has the tallest lighthouse in Europe, a popular yachting harbor, and many pretty stone villages.

Perhaps the best way to explore Finistère is by foot. It is known as the coast of legends for good reason—fairy stories abound, linking tales of King Arthur and Celtic travelers with Cornwall, and there are megaliths, Celtic sites, and holy springs to visit. You can follow *le sentier des lutins* (the pixie footpath) along the most exposed and westerly headland, La Pointe du Raz, which takes you between the moorland and the sea. The Path of Lighthouses takes you on a 62-mile (100-km) trek from Portsall to Brest, taking in 23 of Finistère's 111 lighthouses on the way. **LD**

⬆ *A wooden staircase leads down to the waters of Aber Wrac'h fjord on Finistère.*

Discover Paimpont Forest

Location Ille-et-Vilaine, France
Website www.bretagne35.com   **Price** ❶

Paimpont Forest sits in the municipality of Paimpont, a land of high moorlands, deep valleys, and dense sun-dappled woodlands. Known in mythology as Brocéliande, the brooding forest is haunted by the spirits of King Arthur and his queen Guinevere, the fabled knights of the Round Table, the wizard Merlin, and the fairies Viviane and Morgane. In fact, dozens of legends of that far-off Celtic age of courtly romance and chivalry are set in the region. Here it is easy to imagine Morgane leaning out over the Étang des Forges lake to be entranced by the Fountain of Youth or to shed a tear at Merlin's Tomb—especially if you have imbibed a little of the local cider.

> *"Whoso pulleth out this sword of this stone and anvil, is . . . king born of all England."*
>
> Thomas Malory, *Le Mort D'Arthur*

Age-old Megalithic sites pay testament to the area's rich and mysterious history, whereas the wild valleys of the Aff and Serein rivers pay testament to the power of nature. There is a wealth of marked walking, bicycling, and horseback-riding trails.

The award-winning Brocéliande Gardens at Bréal-sous-Montfort must not be missed, nor should ancient Rennes, the capital of Brittany, which today proudly flies the black-and-white Breton flag over its cobbled medieval streets. Other nearby attractions to visit include the book-lover's town of Becherel, the flour mill museum at Médréac, the park at Treffendel, and the museum at Saint Meen le Grand. **RsP**

Visit Mont St. Michel

Location Manche, France
Website www.ot-montsaintmichel.com/accueil_gb.htm   **Price** ❶

The sight of Mont St. Michel nestling in a huge bay like a medieval monastic pyramid attracts four million visitors a year. They converge on the gothic spires, tumbling gardens, and unbroken fortifications perched dramatically on an isolated mound of rock a mile offshore.

Few people know the best way to savor this amazing place, though. Simply wait until the buses and visitors leave in the late afternoon—then you have the fairy-tale island to yourself until mid-morning the next day. Better still, the cheap souvenir stalls shut as visitors leave, so the main street suddenly slips 600 years backward through time.

Stay at the fifteenth-century, half-timbered inn overhanging the ancient cobbled street leading up to the abbey. It is actually built into the island's fortifications at the back. It may be a cheap, friendly auberge, but St. Pierre's is a listed French historic monument in its own right. Inside is a creaking labyrinth of old beams, wood paneling, tapestries, leaded windows, winding staircases, ancient wooden shutters, and exposed stone walls. The restaurant is a classic Gallic affair with an open fire and red checkered tablecloths, serving dishes like shellfish from the bay and roast lamb from inland farms.

It is cozy rather than luxurious, but what five-star hotel has a door from its landing onto the ramparts of a World Heritage site? Using their hotel key, guests can pop out in the middle of the night in their pajamas to stand on the battlements and watch the tide rushing in across the vast mudflats. **SH**

➡ *The isolated, fortified island of Mont St. Michel rises high above the mudflats like a fairy-tale castle.*

Enjoy Abbaye de la Bussière

Location Côte-d'Or, France
Website www.abbaye-dela-bussiere.com   **Price** 💲💲

The monks may have long since departed, but there is still an air of tranquility surrounding Abbaye de la Bussière, set deep in the heart of the Burgundy countryside. This former monastery, which dates back to the twelfth century, is situated in 15 acres (6 ha) of beautiful parkland in a lush valley between Beaune and Dijon. It is studded with fifty-one species of tree, with a small river, the Arvot, flowing through the grounds and feeding the large ornamental lake. The building has been transformed into a luxury country house hotel by English owners, the Cummings family, who are also proprietors of the renowned Amberley Castle Hotel in Sussex, England.

The grand interiors have been sympathetically refurbished and include dramatic vaulted ceilings, 20-foot (6-meter) high stained-glass windows, stone balustrades, and a romantic sweeping staircase. Although the Abbaye is unmistakably ecclesiastical in appearance, there is nothing remotely monastic about the eleven rooms: Toile de Jouy fabrics, chaise longues, and enormous beds (some four-poster) piled high with plump cushions make the rooms a far cry from their simpler origins. The bathrooms are decidedly twenty-first century, with power showers, whirlpool tubs, and Bulgari toiletries.

Although the interiors owe more than a passing nod to English country house style, the food here is undoubtedly Gallic. In a region known for its cuisine and wine, the Abbaye can hold its head high. Chef Olivier Elzer already has one Michelin star to his name, and conjures up imaginative dishes for his guests such as snails and scallops or beef and pigeon, relying heavily on local produce. Naturally, each dish is paired with fine wines from the best regional producers. **HA**

Cruise the Burgundy Canal

Location Côte-d'Or to Nièvre, France
Website www.burgundy-canal.com   **Price** 💲

Cruising on the Burgundy Canal is the perfect way to discover this attractive corner of France, renowned for its wine and culture. The quiet waterway retains an old-fashioned charm with beautifully converted barges gliding past vineyards and sunflower fields, rolling farmland, and forested hills at their most glorious in autumn colors.

Itineraries vary, but a typical cruise would take a week to sail the 31 miles (50 km) from Dijon to Vandenesse, traveling by day at a leisurely pace and allowing ample time to appreciate the scenery. Pampered by captain and crew, all you have to do is relax. Deluxe barges have spacious decks with alfresco

---

"Said to be the most beautiful canal in France, it [winds] through glorious countryside."

Liz Myers, *Guardian*

---

dining and often a whirlpool tub; belowdecks, soothing decor greets guests in the lounge and dining areas, bar, library, and bright double or twin cabins.

For those who want a little more, almost anything can be arranged, from hot-air ballooning to horseback riding or golf. Passengers may hop off the boat to bike or walk along the banks and rejoin at the next lock. Predinner drinks are served on deck as the sun sets over the water and every meal is a gourmet treat, to be enjoyed with fine local wine. **SoH**

➡ *The medieval village of Châteauneuf overlooks the Auxois plains and the Burgundy Canal.*

Stay on *Bateau Simpatico*

Location Paris, France **Website** www.quai48parisvacation.com
Price 💲💲

In the world's most romantic city, what could be more romantic than staying on a boat on the River Seine, just at the foot of the Eiffel Tower? The idea is simple: *Bateau Simpatico* is a converted Dutch cargo barge moored on the Left Bank. It has been painstakingly restored and is now full of the polished brass and varnished wood that conjures up the image of classic wooden sailing ships. Now the owner rents the boat out to visitors as a floating vacation home.

You reach the *Simpatico* via a tree-lined street leading down to a cobbled riverside dock. It was once a busy working quay for the builders of the Eiffel Tower; now it is the peaceful mooring for a community of houseboats. For tourists, this is a fabulous location—within walking distance of the cafés, restaurants, shops, museums, and monuments of central Paris. Catch the waterbus nearby for trips upriver to the Louvre Museum or Notre Dame Cathedral or use the two free bicycles provided.

The old sailing barge is almost one hundred years old and surprisingly spacious. Inside there is a king-size bedroom, full-sized and well-equipped kitchen, bathroom with shower, and huge living room. The boat can sleep up to four. Amid the wood-paneled interior, you will find a leather sofa and armchairs, dining table and chairs, library of maps and books about Paris, plus assorted nautical knickknacks like an old sea chest and a pair of binoculars. The huge open deck above is a memorable spot to relax under a parasol with coffee and croissants in the morning or cocktails in the evening. **SH**

⬅ *The* Simpatico *(center) is moored on the doorstep of the Eiffel Tower, on the banks of the River Seine.*

Explore the Marais

Location Paris, France **Website** www.parismarais.com
Price 🚻

The Marais, a neighborhood located in Paris's third and fourth arrondissements, offers ample opportunity to discover the heart of the city. Originally marshland (*marais* means "swamp"), the neighborhood was occupied by Parisian nobility in the seventeenth and eighteenth centuries and later by workers and artisans. In the early twentieth century, a thriving Jewish quarter grew up in the Marais, and it now has a large Chinese community and a vibrant gay scene.

At the heart of the Marais is the signature Paris square Place des Vosges, built by King Henry IV of France in 1605 and considered one of the most beautiful public squares in the world. Built with a small

> *"There is one thing stronger than all the armies in the world, and that is an idea whose time has come."*
>
> Victor Hugo, French writer, lived in Place des Vosges

public park in the center, the square is fronted on four sides by harmonious redbrick and stone facades; restaurants, galleries, and boutique stores line the arcades that run along the square. Stop for an aperitif at one of the many cafés or have an impromptu picnic in the park with a baguette, cheese, and other treats purchased from the local shops. (For a quintessential Parisian baguette, try the Levain du Marais on Rue de Turenne, one block east of Place des Vosges.)

The Marais is one of two protected areas in Paris, with strict zoning and preservation laws. Its narrow streets lined with independent cafés, stores, and galleries provide an intimate window into the past. **BS**

Discover Montmartre

Location Paris, France
Website www.parisdigest.com/promenade/montmartre   **Price** ◑

Often regarded as the last Parisian village because of its original rural setting, the French capital's highest point is famous for its bohemian past. Named after the 425-foot (130-m) hill Montmartre, nowadays the area is a major tourist hot spot; its connection with the likes of van Gogh and Toulouse-Lautrec is thoroughly exploited on Place du Tertre, where aspiring painters sketch tourists who are willing to part with a few euros. However, once you venture beyond the various souvenir shops, the alleyways surrounding the stunning nineteenth-century Romano-Byzantine-style basilica Sacré-Coeur are a throwback to the quarter's days as a village, and offer refuge from the hustle and bustle of the metropolis below.

Another church in the area, St. Jean l'Evangéliste de Montmartre, is far less frequented by tourists yet equally intriguing. Located near Montmartre's seedy Pigalle area, the church combines Moorish influences with art nouveau to create a unique atmosphere. Not far from here, the Chapelle des Martyrs—named in honor of St. Denis, who was allegedly beheaded on the site—is another quiet spot to escape the crowds.

A short walk south, the intimate garden café at the Musée de la Vie Romantique makes for a perfect break before heading back toward Sacré-Coeur and the most surprising sight in the entire city: Les Vignes de Montmartre. The vineyard—now owned by the city of Paris—was initially created in 1930 in order to prevent investors from building new houses. These days it is the pride of the locals, and the bucolic setting makes you feel as though you are anywhere but in a city. **DaH**

→ *Night or day, Montmartre bustles with activity— there is plenty to explore just off the beaten path.*

Discover Île de Ré

Location Charente-Maritime, France
Website www.hotel-de-toiras.com **Price** ❶

La Rochelle is one of the most perfectly preserved medieval port towns in France, thanks to its fastidious council, but its best-kept secret is the Île de Ré, joined to the mainland by a great curving bridge. This is a flat, narrow, and sandy isle dotted with a collection of small, exquisitely tasteful towns and villages. Every building is required to have whitewashed walls, curled orange tiles, and green-painted shutters, creating a beautiful, rustic symmetry.

This tiny Atlantic island is a place for wealthy but discreet Parisians who come here year after year. In the small, honey-colored harbor of Martin de Ré, bohemian and faintly aristocratic artists rub shoulders in charming bistros, watching the oyster trawlers come and go. To get in the thick of it, choose a spacious, opulent, ornate, French-style suite at Hotel de Toiras—perhaps the Marechal, with its splendid views of the harbor. The hotel adjoins La Table d'Olivia, a bijou restaurant. Everything in Saint Martin is about seafood, especially mussels and oysters; the northeast of the island is fringed with oyster beds.

Wandering the streets you will find local markets selling glossy fruit and vegetables, stores selling wares for the home, clothing boutiques, and plenty of well-dressed Parisians. Walk the fortifications, or rent a bicycle and head to the sandy, southern beaches. When autumn is edging in and the seasonal visitors have beaten their retreat, there is an alluring slowness to life here. The focus reverts to everything to do with oysters and mussels, and a delicious silence descends in Saint Martin's misty streets. **LB**

⬅ *Building codes enforced by the local government ensure that Île de Ré remains a picturesque village.*

Stay at Le Moulin du Port

Location Charente-Maritime, France
Website www.bookcottages.com **Price** ❷❷

Nestled in the small village of Cravans, midway between Bordeaux and the coastal town of La Rochelle, the disarmingly charming and rustic nature of Le Moulin du Port is a delight. A meticulously restored old windmill converted into a contemporary bed-and-breakfast that can accommodate up to six people, it overflows with character and history, and makes an ideal escape if all you want to do is fade into anonymity and become part of the daily ebb and flow of a typical French village.

Le Moulin is set alongside an adjoining house under which flows a small, pretty stream that can be seen through specially installed glass panels in the floor.

> *"Just a short drive away are the beaches and caves of Meschers [and] the sandy beaches of Royan."*

Proprietors, Le Moulin du Port

The interior of the mill is spread over two levels, ensconced within textured walls of hewn stone and exposed wooded trusses overhead. On the ground floor, the centerpiece is a magnificent grand piano set alongside an open fireplace with a steep, open-tread staircase leading up to a mezzanine level containing two small bedrooms.

The house itself has a compact and functional kitchenette, a living and dining area, and a quaint, lovingly manicured garden that is beautifully framed through a set of double French doors. The bathroom is located outdoors and there is also an outdoor swimming pool and covered terrace. **BS**

Relax at Château Bauduc

Location Gironde, France **Website** www.bauduc.com
Price Ⓢ

If the wine from Château Bauduc is good enough for Michelin-starred chef Gordon Ramsay, then it should surely satisfy the palate of the most discerning wine drinkers. The Bordeaux Blanc is a house wine in all of Mr. Ramsay's European restaurants, and not only can you stock up on the vintage, but you can also stay in the beautiful eighteenth-century farmhouse set in the grounds of the 250-acre (101-ha) estate. A stay at La Lisière des Vignes (The Edge of the Vines), which sleeps eight people comfortably in the heart of the vineyards, is not just about relaxation—although there is plenty of opportunity for that (the owner's château is the only neighbor). It is also a chance to witness the wine-making process firsthand and to sample some of the fine vintages to boot.

The farmhouse is only 15 miles (24 km) from Bordeaux and St. Emilion, and within half an hour's drive of the international airport, not to mention the long sandy beaches of the Atlantic coast just an hour away. It is ideally situated for exploring southwest France and the châteaux of Bordeaux. That is if you can drag yourself out of the swimming pool that accompanies the farmhouse or get up from the table that sits underneath the shady vine-covered pergola in the south-facing garden.

The interior of the house is exquisitely decorated with every attention to detail considered. It has been completely renovated in recent years, using only the finest furnishings and materials. With the owner's château as the only neighbor, it is perfectly possible to feel that you have truly escaped the trappings of modern life. Rented on a weekly basis, the house sees some guests returning year after year, such is the marvelous allure of the place. **CFM**

Visit Les Sources de Caudalie

Location Gironde, France **Website** www.sourcesdecaudalie.com
Price ⓈⓈ

To visit Les Sources de Caudalie is to not only treat yourself to one of Bordeaux's most luxurious spas, but also to immerse your spirit and soul in the traditions of French viticulture in a wine-growing community that can trace its beginnings to the fourteenth century.

Today the 138-acre (56-ha) vineyard of Les Sources de Caudalie includes the eighteenth-century main house Château Smith-Haut-Lafitte as well as various outbuildings reconstructed around four abandoned barns. Rooms vary in size from "comfort rooms" with king-size beds and terraces to a choice of spacious suites with terraces and fireplaces.

The hotel's heart and soul, however, is to be found in its wine. Its 15,000-bottle wine cellar, hewn out of solid rock by the hotel's owners, is the repository of generations of viticulture. Its vines have an average age of thirty years and a planting density of close to 10,000 vines per hectare. Merlots and cabernet sauvignons dominate, and the hotel also has its own on-site wine cooperative. The hotel's restaurant, La Grand Vigne, modeled after the style of eighteenth-century greenhouses, overlooks one of the property's many ponds, offering delicacies such as Arcachon Bay oysters and stuffed squid sewn with carrot.

The phrase "vinotherapie spa" was invented here after a hot spring with unusually high concentrations of minerals was found running 1,600 feet (500 m) below the château's foundations. Today various vinotherapie packages are made available: therapeutic treatments that use grape seed polyphenols to help arrest the skin's natural aging process. **BS**

⮕ *You can choose to stay right by the water, in the lovely, private Île aux Oiseaux accommodation.*

Explore the Dune du Pilat

Location Gironde, France
Website www.littoral33.com/gb/dune_pilat **Price** ❶

This mammoth sand dune is the highest of its kind in Europe, measuring a staggering 328 feet (100 m) high and 1,640 feet (500 m) wide. Snaking its way for 1.8 miles (3 km) along France's southwest coast in the Arcachon Bay area, the dune is a tremendous sight and can be found just 37 miles (60 km) outside Bordeaux. It is carved by the wind and is constantly growing and changing. With no vegetation, this desertlike landscape is magical in appearance; the constantly blowing winds create many curvy patterns and sandy ripples.

For imaginative visitors, the dune offers unparalleled adventure opportunities. Climb to the top via one of two staircases and then take an exhilaratingly sandy slide down to the sea. Fly a kite or simply take a stroll and breathe in the salty air, letting the wind whip your hair while enjoying the sweeping views of the deep-blue Atlantic on one side and the lush green of the pines on the other. Serious thrill seekers can go hang-gliding or paragliding to appreciate the sheer scale of the dune from a bird's-eye view.

At the foot of the dune is a dense forest of pine trees, beyond which lies a labyrinth of creeks and lagoons. At sunset the dune takes on an atmospheric pinkish glow, making it a popular time to visit for photographers. At this time of the day, it is also worth viewing the dune by taking a boat ride on the Bay of Biscay. When you are done with the dune, head to Arcachon for dinner. It's home to 2,500 oyster farmers, and every restaurant serves up fresh oysters with a bottle of the finest local wine. **JK**

⬅ *The vast Dune du Pilat is the tallest sand dune in Europe, and is a constantly shifting desert landscape.*

Experience Camp Biche

Location Tarn-et-Garonne, France
Website www.campbiche.com **Price** ❸❸❸

High on a hill in the medieval town of Lauzerte in southern France, Camp Biche is a fitness camp with a difference. When former options trader Libby Pratt and her husband, Craig, moved here from the United States, they noticed that the French lived life a little differently. So, in 2001, Libby decided to create a luxurious hideaway where people could come to enjoy a time-tested approach to health and fitness. Camp Biche emphasizes the simpler aspects of the good life: delicious local organic food, invigorating exercise, and stunning natural surroundings. A week at the camp can undoubtedly get you in shape, but it might mark a more profound change, too.

> *"The traditional formula of rigorous exercise and calorie deprivation [gets] a five-star French polish."*

Ian Belcher, *The Times*

The day starts at 7 A.M. with an abdominals and weights session, complete with mantras to help you feel more positive about your figure; a light breakfast follows, and then participants walk out of the door of the medieval mansion across the fields on a four or five-hour hike. Hiking is at the heart of the Camp Biche exercise program, and each walk starts with an hour of silent meditation to instill calm into your thoughts.

Lunch is back at the house, and the afternoon is filled with more glorious exercise: hatha yoga, weights, or Pilates. After a soothing hour-long massage, it is time to relax in the hot tub before a gourmet dinner with wonderful French wine. **LD**

Explore the Canal du Midi

Location Southwestern France **Website** www.midicanal.fr
Price ⑤⑤

You proceed at a leisurely speed of 4 miles per hour (6.4 kph) yet life never gets boring. World War III could break out and you would not notice. Welcome to France's wonderful Canal du Midi. There is a towpath alongside the entire 150 miles (240 km) that link the Étang de Thau and the town of Sète, on the Mediterranean, with bustling Toulouse and the River Garonne (which eventually becomes the Gironde), above Bordeaux, before spilling out into the Atlantic.

Bicycle riding or rambling by the waterway is part of the fun, but the real pleasure comes when you climb aboard your rental craft. You will soon get the knack of steering the boat (available for parties of two to

> *"Light filtered through delicate foliage, at times making rainbows of color on the water."*
>
> Sarah Poyntz, *Guardian*

twelve) and negotiating the many locks—there are ninety-one in all, but you will be averaging only 10 miles (16 km) or so each day, so you are unlikely to face them all. There is usually someone there to lend a hand, and the lock-keeper will happily sell you eggs, wine, or other fresh local produce, and exchange a yarn or two. If you do not want to cook, there are plenty of enticing restaurants and cafés en route.

Try to schedule in the spectacular walled city of Carcassonne and the eight-lock staircase at Fonséranes, on the outskirts of Béziers; another thrill is negotiating the dank and dark 570-foot (173-m) tunnel at Enserune by the beam of your navigation light. **RsP**

Go Armagnac Tasting

Location Gers, France **Website** www.buscamaniban.com
Price ⑤

Gascony, deep in rural southwest France, is renowned for its food and drink. The gently rolling landscape is dominated by hilltop castles that command stunning views over fields full of huge dazzling sunflowers. The region is also the home of foie gras, cassoulet, and most famously, Armagnac. Armagnac is the oldest brandy in France, predating cognac by a couple of centuries, and in the Middle Ages it was known for its therapeutic properties. It became very popular in the sixteenth century and went on to become a truly commercial product. Charles de Batz (better known as D'Artagnan of *The Three Musketeers*) was probably the first person to export Armagnac.

No visit to Gascony would be complete without sampling some of this local spirit, and where better to do it than straight from the producer? The biggest producer in the region is Château Laubade, but one of the most beautiful estates is that of the family-owned Château de Busca-Maniban in the Ténarèze area, where most Armagnac production is now based. Classed as an ancient monument, the château dominates 494 acres (200 ha) of vines, mainly planted in Ugni Blanc, the grape type most associated with Armagnac. This is a proper seventeenth-century château with a proper chatelaine, and, if you are in luck, Madame Flirane de Ferrone will personally show you around the salons before letting you loose on a fantastic range of traditional Armagnacs, distilled only once for an extra full body and intense golden fruit flavor. The brandies have all been aged in local oak, and the 1976 vintage is a particular treat. After a few glasses of this heady drink, it is likely you will need a lie down in order to gather your wits, so find a shady spot under a tree and snooze in the Gascon sunshine. **HA**

Walk the Pilgrim Route from France to Spain

Location From Lourdes, Hautes-Pyrénées, France to Santiago de Compostela, A Coruña, Spain **Website** www.worldwalks.com
Price $

For more than a thousand years all roads in Northern Spain have led to Santiago de Compostela, the site of the cathedral where, according to legend, the remains of St. James the Apostle lie. It has been the site of many pilgrimages since medieval times. These days, on the walk from Lourdes to Compostela, you'll still see plenty of pilgrims, though nowadays there are fewer bare feet and many of your fellow travelers will be on bikes or in cars—but where's the satisfaction in that? Religious devotion doesn't motivate all of the thousands who converge each year on these much trammeled routes but if you are on a verified foot pilgrimage (get a Pilgrim's Passport at the start of your journey in Abbey Roncevalles) you can stay in one of the almost free roadside hostels.

Starting on the edge of the Pyrenees, the distance of the trip is 470 miles (750 km). You'll wander through spectacular mountain scenery, ancient hamlets, and wooded trails. Crumbling chapels pepper the way and you'll come across the ancient cities of Burgos and Leon too with their vast gothic Cathedrals, to give you a taste of where you're really heading.

Many aim to arrive in Santiago on July 25 for the three day festival of Sant Iago. As well as the street parties and general merry-making, the fiesta features the spectacle of the swinging of the cathedral's mighty incense holder, which traditionally carries people's prayers up to God (and was used to mask the stench of unwashed pilgrims). Whether you are spurred on by religion or emotion, there's something life-changing about a voyage as epic as this. **SWi**

↗ *The entire walk can take up to 31 days, but is easily broken into smaller sections for a more relaxing time.*

"I was suddenly transported back to the Middle Ages, when millions of pilgrims came [for] absolution."

Derek Bishton, *Daily Telegraph*

Explore Mont Perdu

Location Hautes-Pyrénées, France
Website www.worldheritagesite.org   **Price** 🌓

The "lost mountain" of the Pyrénées (called Monte Perdido in Spanish), Mont Perdu is the heart of the mountain chain and the dramatic natural border between France and Spain. Standing 10,997 feet (3,352 m) high, it is the Pyrénées' third-highest peak and the centerpiece of the Ordesa y Monte Perdido National Park, and is inscribed on the UNESCO World Heritage List for its classical geological landforms. What is more, it remains a European "lost world" where pastoral ways of life have been preserved.

The diversity of animal and plant life here is staggering. There are 1,500 species of flower alone, as well as mammals like the Spanish ibex, whose steady feet help it climb the precarious cliffs and crags, and wild boar, commonly hunted in the region. Eagles soar around the peaks and, if you are lucky, you might see a fabled Lammergeier, the bearded vulture native to the region, which has a wingspan of 10 feet (3 m).

Walking in the Pyrénées certainly takes your breath away—not only because of the steep climbs, but also the astounding valleys, high mountain waterfalls, and deep-blue lakes. The snow-tipped range is tackled by walkers year-round, who choose either to camp or to sleep in the small mountain huts or rustic bed-and-breakfasts along the way.

Once here, it is hard to imagine that life is going on in busy cities elsewhere. This region remains undeveloped and is home to a few scattered villages where life continues as it always has. The nature of the terrain means that things here are unlikely to change, which is reassuring to know. **LD**

← *The Arrazas River runs through the Tozal del Mallo Mountains in Ordesa y Monte Perdido National Park.*

Do Yoga in the Pyrénées

Location Ariège, France
Website www.yogafrance.com   **Price** 🌓🌓

This small, elegant country château is more than 200 years old and stands in a quiet valley through the Pyrénées, among flower meadows, wooded hills, and a tree-shaded brook. In front of the house is a clear lake where the dragonflies hover and deer drink—it is also perfect for a cooling dip.

Domaine de la Grausse is a tranquil spot for a vacation, but add in the benefits of the yoga sessions here and it becomes a perfect way to escape the pressures of modern life. The special yoga breaks in this remote spot run between May and October. Guests stay in beautifully converted farm buildings on a self-catering basis. There are double and single

> *"Breathe in the pure, invigorating mountain air, a gift and joy for Pranayama yogic breathing."*

Proprietors, Domaine de la Grausse

rooms, kitchens, and shaded dining patios. Visitors can buy fresh produce at the village market nearby or eat at the local cafés and restaurants.

The experienced resident yoga teacher, Dagmar, conducts sessions in the morning and evening. She combines the best of various schools of yoga and adapts to her pupils' needs. The sessions are suitable for all skill levels and are held either on the top floor of the château, with French windows overlooking the lake, or, on the hottest days, in a renovated stone barn built into a dramatic rock face. Guests can also unwind with guided meditation sessions and holistic therapies, including Reiki, massage, and reflexology. **SH**

Rent Moulin de Perle

Location Pyrénées-Orientales, France
Website www.pyreneesgites.com **Price** 🌀🌀

The Moulin is an ancient water mill in a picturesque valley in the spectacular lower Fenouilledes foothills of the French Pyrénées. The owners have restored the mill and its old outbuildings to create three self-contained *gîtes* (small vacation homes), which sleep three, five, or six people. It is possible to arrange for bed-and-breakfast accommodation, and regular painting vacations are available with expert tuition. The views of vineyards, forests, rivers, and stunning gorges with historic Cathar castles perched on rocky outcrops ensure that there is plenty of inspiration for artists. Back at the gîtes themselves, visitors can expect

> *"Laze in the sun or potter around discovering the outstanding scenery and pretty villages."*

Proprietors, Moulin de Perle

exposed beams, wood-burning stoves, views of the nearby stream, charming patios, and pretty gardens. The rugged, bare stone walls, terra-cotta roofs, and sky-blue paintwork are complemented by lush, flowering creepers, potted plants, and overhanging trees. The site is surrounded by 4 acres (1.6 ha) of wild meadows where orchids flower alongside the old mill stream, which is ideal to paddle in on a hot day.

The Moulin is situated midway between two small villages, making it a very peaceful spot and a perfect base for touring the region. The local village swimming pool and tennis court are also easily accessible, only a five-minute walk away. **SH**

Explore the Black Mountains

Location Black Mountains (Tarn, Hérault, and Aude), France
Website www.blackmountainholidays.com **Price** 🌀

The Black Mountains get their rather forbidding name from the densely forested slopes that make them seem dark from afar. Get closer, however, and you will realize why the French value this area so much. The highly protected countryside is perfect for walking, fishing, horseback riding, and exploring. It is dotted with historic castles from Cathar times, including the World Heritage site of the Citadel of Carcassonne and the stronghold of Hautpoul, Châteaux de Lastours, and Château de Saissac.

The Black Mountains form part of Languedoc National Park and join onto the southwestern end of the Massif Central in the border area of the Tarn, Hérault, and Aude *départements*. The pinnacle of the range is the Pic de Nore, a serious 4,000-foot (1,219-m) mountain that towers over Carcassonne's plain. From here the Pyrénées shimmer on the western horizon. On the hills themselves, the vegetation changes dramatically, depending on if the weather is coming from the Mediterranean or the Atlantic. In the Orb Valley, for example, you will see mimosa, olives, and cherries, but just a few miles west the prevailing winds are from the Atlantic and the fruit and flowers give way to beech trees.

The highlight of any escape here is swimming in the cool, clean mountain lakes. Several are so popular with locals they are like small seaside resorts. Lac du Pradelle and Lac du Montagne have their own lifeguards, pedal boats, tennis, mini golf, walking trails, and even a choice of restaurants. **SH**

➔ *The Rigole canal flows through the Black Mountains before feeding the Canal du Midi.*

Stay at Les Fermes de Marie

Location Haute-Savoie, France
Website www.fermesdemarie.com   **Price** 🟢🟢

Many travelers have dreamed of staying in one of those lovely old wooden farm huts you see scattered high up on Alpine slopes. French couple Jocelyne and Jean-Louis Sibuet did more than dream: They found and bought more than twenty wobbly old wooden chalets, farms, and sheds, brought them down the mountain timber by timber, and reassembled them as a sort of makeshift village on the edge of the upmarket resort of Megève.

Inside, the old rooms have been filled, not with animals and piles of hay, but with old Savoie shepherd's furniture and folk art, whereas modern features like satellite TV, sumptuous beds, and opulent marble bathrooms have been discreetly added. The extraordinary rustic feel has been retained thanks to the weathered wood everywhere and the homey details. It must have seemed risky at the time, but the plan worked incredibly well—the Sibuets have managed to create a unique luxury hotel with the feel of a group of romantic old barns in the hills.

This eccentric escape works equally well throughout the year. In winter it is a ski center with shuttle buses that whisk you to ski lifts. In summer, you can walk in the mountains, go mountain biking, play tennis, or simply relax and enjoy the hotel's facilities and Megève's shops, cafés, and bars. The hotel's well-equipped spa, gym, and pool and the renowned gourmet restaurant entice guests at any time of year. The sixteen-room spa even uses its own specially developed products created from mountain plants like horsetail and arnica. **SH**

➜ *It's almost impossible to find somewhere more quintessentially alpine than Les Fermes de Marie.*

Balloon over Puy-de-Dôme

Location Puy-de-Dôme, France
Website www.france-balloons.com **Price** 🟢🟢

If you were to draw a picture of a volcano, it would probably look like one of these perfect lava cones. In the volcanic Auvergne region of central France, the Chaîne des Puys are one of the country's most popular attractions—more than 80 mountains lined up north to south with clear volcanic origins. Something about the way the craters rise up green from the plain makes them seem more than the result of a tectonic collision, more mythical, and certainly photogenic. And the view from above, drifting with the wind at sunrise or sunset in a hot air balloon, can't be beaten.

From this vantage point, the Chaîne des Puys betray nothing of their belligerent, violent beginnings forged over 3,000 years ago. You can see the Massif central, the Cantal mountains, and as far as Mont Blanc to the east on a good day. Puy-de-Dôme is the tallest of the 80 mountains in the chain, reaching 4,800 feet (1,463 m) high, while the smooth grassy crater of Puy de Pariou rises to 3,970 feet (1,210 m), with a walking track leading to its center.

This region brings in half a million visitors a year, many of whom walk up the Sentier des Muletiers, the old Roman way, to the top of Puy-de-Dôme and the old Roman temple to Mercury that stands there. Other temples have stood here at the top of the mountain since pre-Christian times, such is the mountain's pull. Others choose to paraglide or hang glide from the top, for different aerial views of the region. The volcanos have given their minerals to Volvic water, produced here, as well as their lava to the farmhouse roof tiles, tennis courts and roads that you'll see from above. **LD**

◄ The craters of Puy-de-Dôme seem very green and soft, and show no signs of volcanic activity.

Canoe the Ardèche

Location Ardèche, France
Website www.france-voyage.com/en **Price** 🟢

The 20-mile (32-km) stretch of the Ardèche River between Vallon Pont d'Arc and Saint Martin d'Ardèche is not reserved for white-water daredevils. The only real requirement is that paddlers be over the age of seven and able to swim—there is always the risk that the stunning scenery might distract you so much that you end up taking an unintended dip.

The route runs through a chalk and limestone canyon that has been carved out through the millennia; it is the highlight of Ardèche National Park, and its starting point, the Pont d'Arc, is a natural stone bridge that soars an impressive 197 feet (60 m) above the teal-blue waters. At places, the cliffs tower an

---

"Despite terrifying names like Dente Noir (Black Teeth), the rapids are easily negotiated."

Gordon Lethbridge, *Independent*

---

incredible 1,000 feet (305 m) above you. Many companies rent out canoes and kayaks for anything from a couple of hours to two days. For the latter, there are campsites en route at Gaud and Gournier—they are equipped with showers, barbecues, and drinking water, but do need to be booked in advance.

The more adventurous might want to visit early in the season. In April and May the water is high and fast, and you can extend the trip to take in longer sections of the river. In late summer, the ride is more leisurely, with lazy sections for gentle floating mixed with faster, fun-packed rapids. And when you want a break from the water, you can stop at the beaches on the way. **PE**

Explore Tarn Gorge

Location Cévennes (Gard, Lozère, Ardèche, and Haute-Loire), France
Website www.mairie-albi.fr/eng/tourism/tarn.html **Price ❶**

If France ever had a Wild West, this must be it. In the remote Cévennes region, the shallow River Tarn carves a course through an extraordinarily deep and long limestone gorge to make one of the great natural wonders of Europe. Drivers heading down the A75 *autoroute* across the austere, lonely plateau of the Grands Causses Regional Natural Park gain a tantalizingly brief peep over it from the elegant 1,125-foot (343-m) high Millau Viaduct—a road bridge that broke world records for its height, which often stands literally above the clouds.

The gorge really deserves more than a brief peep, though. There is a magnificent walk above the point where the gorges of the Tarn and Jonte meet near Le Rozier, passing a succession of jaw-dropping viewpoints and ledges with plummeting sides that are no treat for vertigo sufferers.

You can also explore the gorge from the water, at your own pace in a two-person canoe, which you can rent at the village of La Malène. The sturdy plastic craft require no expertise whatsoever—if you have rowed a boat in the local park, you can canoe on this docile stretch of the Tarn. The amiable current takes you at sufficient speed for paddling to be reduced to occasional steering around a tree trunk or tiny rapid. Here the cliffs rise sheer and blot out half the sky beneath the aptly named heights of Point Sublime. As the tourist boats chug past self-importantly, you can feel smug at taking the ultraslow, nonmechanized option and pull up at will on the shore or on a tiny gravel islet and picnic or swim the afternoon away in this wonderfully secretive place. Farther down a flag shows you where to beach your boat, and a bus will take you back to the village where you started. **TL**

De-stress at La Chaldette

Location Aubrac (Cantal, Aveyron, and Lozère), France
Website www.lachaldette.com **Price ❸**

The healing and calming effects of the Aubrac's thermal springs have been enjoyed since the Middle Ages. Located almost 4,265 feet (1,300 m) above sea level in central southern France, La Chaldette is a state-of-the-art health resort in the tranquil village of Brion. The modernist architect Jean-Michel Wilmotte has installed stylish floor-to-ceiling windows to allow mood-enhancing sunlight inside, and a minimalist streamlined interior to clear the mind of clutter.

Stressed-out urbanites can surrender to a rainwater shower massage or a hydromassage bath with flowers and oils, then languish on an outdoor recliner, serenaded by cicadas, an occasional cow horn, and

> *"La Chaldette benefits from a healthy climate and has particularly pure air."*
>
> Proprietors, La Chaldette

soothing springwater trickling under foot. The hotel's convivial owners have combined rustic charm with contemporary chic in their apartment-styled rooms, built around a central staircase.

The chef's *cuisine de terroir* (a modern twist on locally sourced, traditional cuisine) includes gourmet plates of duck à l'orange and crème brûlée with blueberries. Gastronomy coupled with a glass of the local Coteaux du Languedoc in the wood-fired lounge and a restful sleep swathed in crisp white cotton works wonders on the mind and body, whereas the fresh, pure air, views of unending green valleys, and cascading water restore a sense of inner peace. **SD**

Stay at Jardins Secrets

Location Gard, France
Website www.jardinssecrets.net   **Price** 💲💲

Arriving at Jardins Secrets, you would be forgiven for wondering whether you had come to the right address. The unprepossessing side street and nondescript door in the wall do not begin to hint at the oasis within. Walk over the threshold and you step into an enchanted garden; orange and lemon trees grow profusely, a banana plant flourishes in a corner, and bougainvillea tumbles down a wall.

Jardins Secrets, a seventeenth-century villa situated on the edge of the ancient town center of Nîmes, is more like a private house than a hotel. This impression is amplified by the lack of a reception area; on arrival visitors are ushered straight to their rooms with none of the tedious form filling that too many hotels require.

The four guest rooms are large and opulent, and stuffed full of beautiful objets d'art, paintings, thick silk curtains, and freshly cut flowers. Some rooms have four-poster beds, made up with beautiful crisp linen, and all have double doors that open directly onto the garden while green-painted shutters keep the morning light at bay. Gilt-framed mirrors and twinkling eighteenth-century chandeliers adorn the bathrooms, which are dominated by vast claw-foot bathtubs.

A baby grand piano adds a touch of class to the salon, whereas in other areas you will see piles of books and photographs, instruments, and even aviaries of tiny song birds. However, as the hotel name suggests, the garden is really the highlight, offering a wonderfully relaxing and verdant hideaway from the heat and bustle of the city. After walking around the ancient Roman remains of Nîmes, return to the Jardins Secrets for a leisurely siesta on one of the loungers in a shady spot, take a dip in the cool saltwater pool, or simply breathe in the heady perfume of the roses. **HA**

Visit Sénanque Abbey

Location Vaucluse, France
Website www.senanque.fr   **Price** 💲

Home to a community of Cistercian monks, the mellowed stone walls and mottled roof tiles of the twelfth-century working monastery are soothing to the eye; it is difficult not to fall in love with the architecture and the silence. Surrounded by wooded hills, guests are invited to stay for a spiritual retreat for a maximum of eight days.

Temporary residents are allowed regardless of gender or faith but are expected to partake in the life of prayer and silence; indeed silence is expected at all times, including during meals, with an exception of fifteen minutes a day. The resident monks have a structured routine beginning at 4 A.M. that includes

> *"The Sénanque abbey is one of the purest examples of early Cistercian architecture."*

www.senanque.fr

five orders, such as Vespers and Mass, and those on retreat are invited to attend these services. The rest of the day is taken up with reading, meditation, and working in the gardens; the surrounding fields in summer are filled with a purple hue, the uniform lines of lavender providing an amazing display of color. The monks cultivate the lavender, as they have done for centuries, producing honey (from the abbey bees) and distilling essence.

Those staying for a retreat may leave the abbey grounds, and the terrain provides some spectacular walking territory, especially for guests who feel the need to operate their vocal cords. **CFM**

Unwind at La Mirande

Location Vaucluse, France
Website www.la-mirande.fr **Price** 💲💲

In the shadows of the medieval splendor of Avignon's historic Papal Palace, the opulent La Mirande, adorned with Belgian tapestries and wallpapers printed from age-old woodcuts, is this ancient city's most desirable address and one of Europe's finest hotels.

Part of a historic complex of buildings that can trace their beginnings to the establishment of the papacy here in 1306, La Mirande first became a hotel in 1796 and for more than two centuries was known as the Hotel Pamard. Throughout its twenty guest rooms and its public spaces, attention to detail is evident, from the silk-lined curtains and antique glass windows that frame the daily life of the city to the oak parquet

> "The culinary art of La Mirande tends to prefer the . . . harmony of unexpected combinations."

Claude Eveno, *La Mirande*

on its floors, the Carrara marble in its bathrooms, and the master paintings on its walls. Meals in La Mirande's elegant Michelin-starred restaurant are served over a floor of needlepoint carpet and beneath a magnificent renaissance double caisson ceiling, and presided over by the hotel's head chef, Julien Allano. If you would like to have dinner in a more select environment, the guest table in the hotel's nineteenth-century kitchen can be made available on Tuesdays and Wednesdays.

This is reminiscent of the great aristocratic homes of France, and it is often whispered that if the pope had been given a taste of life at La Mirande, he may not have been in such a rush to return to Rome. **BS**

See Le Grand Blanc

Location Vaucluse, France
Website www.provenceweb.fr **Price** 💲

Lying to the east of the Provençal village of Apt, just beyond the reach of the Luberon Valley, the mountains and surrounding valleys of the Grand Luberon embody all the stereotypes of what constitutes simple, rural French living.

The 3,690-foot (1,124-m) Mourre Negre is its highest point, dwarfing the lesser summits of the nearby Petite Luberon range and towering over the flat, desolate plain of the Plateau des Claparèdes, which bursts to life in a sea of lavender fields stretching for miles all the way to the village of Bonnieux. The landscape is full of ancient hilltop villages, and everywhere you look there are reminders of a simpler time, such as the ever-present dry-stone *bories*, igloo-shaped huts of stone dating back as far as the thirteenth century and constructed for no other reason than to clear the surrounding fields of rocks to make them ready for plowing. The towering presence of Le Grand Blanc, with its vast forests of oak and cedar and limestone outcrops, is a beacon to travelers and locals alike.

A thin covering of generally poor soil is characteristic here and has prevented large-scale agriculture, allowing the many hamlets and villages of the region to maintain their traditional ways of life. Once refuges for the Waldenes religious sect in the fifteenth century, medieval towns such as Gordes and Roussillon now attract celebrities, expatriates, and sun-seeking tourists all eager to experience a region that has altered little since the creation of the Parc Regional du Luberon in 1977, which encircles the area and ensures this tiny corner of rural France will retain its charm. **BS**

➡ *Gordes is typical of the traditional medieval villages on the hillsides of the Luberon Valley.*

Visit Parc Ornithologique

Location Bouches-du-Rhône, France
Website www.beyond.fr/sites/camargue.html   **Price** 🌓

The Camargue is known for its wild horses and for its greater flamingos—and it is the latter that you will see at the Parc Ornithologique du Pont de Gau. These striking pink birds with their long, gangly legs are in residence all year, but their gatherings are most spectacular during the winter months: their mating season. From December to March, as many as 20,000 flamingos gather in the Parc Ornithologique to select a mate, and each day visitors can see them dance through their synchronized courtship movements. With their graceful necks stretched taut and their beaks held high, they strut together in formation, turning their heads to the left and the right. If you are lucky, you will see them take flight together, soaring high into the sky in a great mass of pink feathers.

The park covers 150 acres (60 ha) of wetland and invites visitors to stroll around its 5 miles (8 km) of paths that weave through the marshes and lagoons where local and migrating birds—including herons, storks, egrets, teals, geese, and swans—feed. Tuck yourself into one of the specially constructed hides en route and you will be able to observe the park's feathered residents wading, fishing, and flying as if you were not there. Venture a little farther and you will find the aviaries, which house injured birds that the park staff are nursing back to health. Information boards along the pathways help visitors identify the birds and understand their habits, and guided tours offer more in-depth information. There are also eagles, hawks, harriers, buzzards, and vultures in the park, so keep one eye on the sky as you are strolling. **PE**

➡ *Flamingos stand at sunset in the shallow water of the Parc Ornithologique in the Camargue.*

Stay at Abbaye de Sainte Croix

Location Bouches-du-Rhône, France
Website www.hotels-provence.com   **Price** $\bullet\bullet$

"Twenty thousand years ago, the Salounet plateau on the Abbey estate was home to the Salians."

Relais & Châteaux guide

This magnificent twelfth-century monastery, set amid perfumed gardens of lavender and rosemary, has been restored and converted into a luxury hotel. It is situated on one of the last strongholds of the Alpilles hills, and the Romanesque abbey, with arched vaulting and small windows, has been beautifully conserved.

The monks' formerly Spartan cells have been converted into twenty-one comfortable rooms and four apartments, which vary from the simple to the grand. Heavy stone walls provide respite from the blazing Provençal sun, keeping the whitewashed rooms cool in the hottest of summers—although there is also air-conditioning just in case. Vaulted ceilings, baronial fireplaces, and heavy beams all add to the rustic Provençal charm, as do the terra-cotta floor tiles scattered with handmade colorful rugs. Some rooms have views over the romantic gardens, whereas others look out over the valley. Dine on the restaurant's panoramic terrace and savor excellent local cuisine and wine while surveying the stunning landscape all around, including the nearby medieval town of Salon de Provence.

In the summer, the public sitting areas flow out onto vine-covered terraces. Rustic furnishings complement handpicked objets d'art. There is also a pool to cool down in and a tennis club next door for the energetic, but it is best just to soak up the sun with a glass of rosé in one hand and a good book in the other while reclining on the terrace listening to the chirp of the cicadas and the tolling of a distant church bell. *La vie en rose* indeed. **HA**

◪ *The Abbaye de Sainte Croix provides a luxury retreat into Provence in a setting brimming with history.*

See the Calanques

Location Bouches-du-Rhône, France
Website www.francethisway.com **Price** ❶

A few minutes' drive out of the busy town of Marseille a piece of nature survives untouched. Amid the beautiful *calanques*, pine trees, rocky cliffs, and turquoise waters, you feel as if you have stumbled upon the Caribbean. Derived from the Corsican word *calanca* meaning "inlet," the *calanques* were once ancient river mouths. They puncture the shore as far as 2.5 miles (4 kilometers) inland. These areas of outstanding natural beauty are now protected and have been left wild and unspoiled.

Some have a few small, shedlike homes dubbed *cabanons* at the edge of the water with tiny restaurants nearby. In Sormiou, Le Lunch restaurant offers plastic furniture and rather overpriced fresh fish, but it has a unique selling point: The Mediterranean gently laps at its feet while all around, the views offer only blue sea and impressive limestone cliffs. As for the others: Queyron, Podestat, En Vau, Port Pin, and Port Miou, they are all just beach, rocks, and pine forests at the edge of the translucent aquamarine water.

With access closed to traffic in the summer in order to preserve the area during the busy tourist season and prevent forest fires, getting to the beach means a long walk, sometimes up to 2 miles (3 km). Port Pin and En Vau are fantastic sights, though, well worth the hour-and-a-half trek through the Gardiole forest and down the steep hill. Although the calanques are a popular escape, thankfully, most people are put off by the robust hike.

Another option is to arrive by boat and head to the dive sites, like the grottos of "des Trémies," "des Capélans," or Castelvieil. For the lazy visitor, a drive up to the Corniche des Crêtes and Cap Canaille will give a glimpse of the paradise below. **RCA**

Enjoy Mas de la Fouque

Location Bouches-du-Rhône, France
Website www.masdelafouque.com **Price** ❸❸

Beyond the city of Arles and on the western borders of Provence—where the Rhône delta plunges into the Mediterranean—lie the wetlands of the Camargue. Glittering waters stretching as far as the eye can see and vast marshlands where wild white horses and ebony bulls still roam, there is a touch of magic in the air. With the accent on the conservation of nature and a way of life heavy with tradition, the 45,000 acres (18,000 ha) of swamps, lakes, and rice paddies are alive with folklore and legends.

Retreat to the Mas de La Fouque, a hip hideaway in the natural park overlooking the sparkling wilderness. Dreamy, chic, and full of character, it has strong

> *"All around are sea, beaches, and a wealth of wildlife (birds, flamingos, Camargue horses, wild bulls)."*
>
> Caroline Raphael, *Observer*

Moorish influences. The ultra-romantic rooms are decorated with spectacular antiques, linens, driftwood and wrought-iron four-poster beds swathed in long mosquito netting. One of the rooms is even a gypsy caravan on the edge of the lake.

Get into the spirit of things and go riding with the local cowboys through the rushes. Find out about all the Camargue's deepest secrets and see up close the glorious pink flamingos that dot the landscape, or simply while away the day by the glorious pool. The Mas has its own powerboat to cruise down the Rhône River for a private beach picnic. It brings together a relaxed vibe with rustic style naturally. **RCA**

Enjoy Le Prince Noir

Location Bouches-du-Rhône, France
Website www.leprincenoir.com **Price** ⑤⑤

Classified as "one of the most beautiful villages in France," Les Baux de Provence cascades over 17 terraced acres (7 ha) of what was once a fortified Roman plateau. Today it is home to twenty-two historic monuments, including churches and chapels, and hewn straight out of its limestone rock face is the unique Le Prince Noir bed-and-breakfast.

Offering just three rooms, this charming, history-laden hideaway is an artist's house and the highest residence in the village. Ensconced in the center of one of the most popular tourist destinations in Provence, it makes a perfect base from which to explore the surrounding Alpilles mountains and nearby towns such as Arles and St. Rémy de Provence. The exposed rock walls of Le Prince Noir's rooms provide a natural barrier to blistering Provençal summers. There is one double bedroom, a suite with two rooms and private terrace, and an apartment with a kitchen, a master bedroom, separate living area, and two generously apportioned private terraces with panoramic views over Les Baux and the surrounding countryside and beyond to the Mediterranean. The breakfasts at Le Prince Noir are divine, but Les Baux has a small population of around 500, so you have to drive elsewhere to find one of the area's many fine restaurants for dinner.

A night at Le Prince Noir affords the opportunity to see Les Baux in much the same way as its residents do: quietly. Spend your day touring and return to Les Baux in the late afternoon when you can share this classic caricature of Provence with only the village cats. **BS**

← *The picturesque medieval village of Les Baux de Provence (population 500) at sunset.*

Eat at Baumanière

Location Bouches-du-Rhône, France
Website www.oustaudebaumaniere.com **Price** 💲💲

Provence is justly famed for its exceptional cuisine, and it comes to the peak of perfection in Oustau de Baumanière. This seventeenth-century farmhouse has delighted the palates of its guests since Raymond Thullier first opened it in 1945.

Now run by his grandson, the world-class master chef Jean-André Charial, the Baumanière restaurant is the proud owner of two Michelin stars for its haute cuisine and its wonderful specialties that take Provençal cooking and contemporary techniques to a sublime standard. The signature *gigot d'agneau en croûte* (leg of lamb in pastry) alone draws gastronomes from far and wide to sample its delights.

> *"L'Oustau is a secret . . . born from the encounter between a place and a man. . . ."*
>
> Frédéric Dard, writer

Although the restaurant itself is reason enough to visit, the boutique hotel is also guaranteed to melt hearts. Comprising three vine-clad stone houses sitting astride classical gardens, Oustau de Baumanière even has a moat and drawbridge. The rooms are of the highest quality, furnished with antiques, four-poster beds, and marble baths. The sitting rooms are covered with early frescoes. Outside there is a large swimming pool and landscaped terraces that have played host to the likes of Winston Churchill, Elizabeth Taylor, and Pablo Picasso. Oustau de Baumanière also happens to be situated in Les Baux de Provence, named one of the most beautiful villages in the world. **PS**

Relax at Couleurs Jardin

Location Var, France
Website www.gigarobeach.com **Price** 💲

Celebrities and mere mortals have been flocking to St. Tropez since the early 1950s, but the resort became world famous thanks to Brigitte Bardot's cult film *And God Created Woman*. Today everyone from P. Diddy to Hugh Grant vacations here, and during the summer season, people-watching is a bona fide sport. Luckily it is possible to escape the ostentation just a few miles away on the other side of the peninsula in the small village of La Croix Valmer.

Unpretentious, La Croix Valmer has its own beautiful beaches and unspoiled pine forests stretching from Gigaro to the natural preserve of the Cap Lardier, covered in what locals call maquis, or low-lying, fragrant Mediterranean brush. The rough, jagged rocks contrast against the azure Mediterranean Sea along Gigaro beach. Houses are well hidden among the eucalyptus, cactus, and pine trees. The village is probably the French Riviera's best-kept secret, with just a handful of restaurants set alongside the white-sand beach, some established for more than twenty years serving yearly regulars.

The best time to visit is undoubtedly in the low season, just after Easter but before July, when the crowds arrive in the area. As the sun sets, set up camp at Couleurs Jardin, a beautifully laid-out little beach house decorated in driftwood, with the odd exotic plant, and a few splashes of bright color. The sea breeze, grayed wooden tables, frilly place mats, and candlesticks give the place a laid-back but stylish feeling. In the middle of the terrace, a pine tree grows low between the tables and the bamboo roofing. Order yourself a bottle of fresh rosé—it will come served with a smile and a clear ice bucket, a bowl of strong garlic olives, and a peerless view. **RCA**

Visit the Gardens of Rayol

Location Var, France
Website www.domainedurayol.org   **Price** ●

Only an hour's drive from the mayhem of St. Tropez, at the foot of the steep Maures massif, sits a tranquil house and garden overlooking the sea. The original owner of Le Rayol-Canadel-sur-Mer built a vast garden in the grounds of his domain on a wild promontory of land overlooking the Bay of Fig Trees in 1910. However, over the years, the house and garden fell into disrepair until it was acquired by the Coast Conservancy in 1989. The conservancy ensured its precious flora and fauna and unspoiled oceanfront cliffs would be preserved.

The gardens have since been transformed into a collection of gardens representing the regions of the world that enjoy a Mediterranean climate, so you can take a tour of the world's huge variety of botanical species all in one place. Wander around the Canary Islands garden, then admire the Joshua trees, cacti, and yucca from Baja, California. Pungent eucalyptus trees and cacti from Australia vie in the New Zealand garden, whereas the Mediterranean landscape is bursting with olive, pine, and palm trees. Also represented are gardens from Chile, Mexico, and South Africa. Unlike many formal gardens, the plants and trees in Domaine de Rayol are not labeled, so you will need to take a book if you want to identify them.

You cannot fail to be impressed by this beautiful garden on the headland, encircled by a verdant amphitheater of trees, and its jaw-dropping setting overlooking the Mediterranean. In the summer months, walk down the steep steps to the beach, take an invigorating dip in the clear blue water, and discover the local marine life. **HA**

⬈ *The beautiful cacti on show here are from the dry, desert gardens of Baja, California.*

"An extraordinary garden nestles at the foot of the Maures massif at Le Rayol-Canadel-sur-Mer."

frenchgardening.com

Relax at Le Couvent des Minimes Spa

Location Alpes-de-Haute-Provence, France
Website www.couventdesminimes-hotelspa.com **Price** 💲💲

When Provence-based cosmetic and perfume company L'Occitane decided to open their first spa in France, they stumbled upon an ancient empty convent in the foothills of the Alps not far from their headquarters. The 300-year-old white stone walls and bell tower of Des Minimes overlook lavender fields, olive groves, and blossoming almond trees. Old wooden shutters, balustraded terraces, fountains, and terra-cotta tiles give it the perfect character for a Provençal showpiece.

After a lavish refurbishment by a specialist architect and local craftspeople, Des Minimes opened in 2008 as a small forty-six-room hotel and spa, with a fine restaurant. Any monastic hardships are certainly long gone. Rooms and suites are modern and well equipped, designed with simple pale colors and ample use of wood, stone, and fine fabrics.

Guests may lounge on private terraces admiring the views toward the mountains or cool off in the hotel's vaulted cellars tasting vintage wines. There is floodlit tennis and a heated outdoor pool, plus golf nearby. Or visitors may wander the extensive grounds discovering cloisters, the original chapel, ancient carvings, or the remains of terraced gardens that once gave the monastery a national reputation for botanical excellence. Both the restaurant and the spa use ingredients grown on-site or sourced in the immediate area: Asparagus and truffles may appear on the restaurant's menu, and local honey, lemon, olive oil, and lavender are prime ingredients in the spa. **SH**

⬅ *L'Occitane's modernization of the 300-year-old convent preserved the building's original style.*

Explore Mercantour National Park on Horseback

Location Alpes-Maritimes, France
Website www.horseandventure.com   **Price** ❺❺❺❺

> *"This is the genuine ancient trail used for the transhumance of all livestock."*

Horse and Venture wesbite

For centuries, shepherds and farmers have moved their livestock between their winter and summer grazing grounds in a tradition known as the transhumance. Today, native Californian Denis Longfellow, resident of rural France for thirty years, guides his troupe of Merens horses between Sainte-Agnès, just a couple of miles inland from the Mediterranean coast north of Nice, to his ranch in the mountains using the same trails that this land's inhabitants have used since ancient times. And he takes visitors along for the ride.

It is a three- to five-day journey (accommodation is in comfortable *gîtes*) down to the coast in the autumn and back up to his ranch at Le Boréon, on the edge of Mercantour National Park, in the spring. Virtually uninhabited, Mercantour National Park, known as Little Switzerland for its Alpine-style landscape, boasts 10,000-foot (3,048-m) peaks, but it also has olive groves and fields of lavender. There are some 2,000 species of plant here; many of them are rare, including edelweiss and the martagon lily, saxifrage, and gentian. The park's resident animals include several thousand chamois, marmots (visitors often hear them whistle), wild boar, and a few recently reintroduced wolves.

Visitors can ride in the park even if they do not want to embark on the transhumance because Longfellow offers half-day and day rides here in the summer and from the village on the coast in the winter. He is in Sainte-Agnès from October to mid-June, and in Le Boréon the rest of the year. The transhumance takes place at the end of September and in mid-June. **PE**

↖ *Discovering Mercantour National Park on horseback will transport you to a bygone age of cowboys.*

Discover Piana

Location Corsica, France **Website** www.sipiana.com/en/index
Price ◑

Situated on the jagged west coast of Corsica, the Calanques are bizarrely shaped red rock pinnacles that provide a stunning backdrop for Piana, officially recognized as one of "the most beautiful towns in France." There is a wild savagery about the location that lends it a haunting atmosphere, which is quite appropriate: In 1489, there was a ruthless massacre by the Genoese overlords, which left just women and children alive. Blood once streamed down the narrow alleyways that today give the village much of its charm, but the mood now is of sublime tranquility.

Set on a narrow plateau some 1,437 feet (438 m) above the dazzling blue Mediterranean, Piana overlooks the Gulf of Porto and the Scandola and Senino peninsulas. Its exquisite pink-washed houses cluster around the picturesque oversize church of Sainte Marie, built with public funds between 1765 and 1795 to serve a population of only 735. From the church, a steep and narrow lane runs down precipitously to the little fishing boat haven of Ficaghjola and on through the hamlet of Vistale to the sheltered little beach at Arone, where it is safe to swim.

After witnessing a dazzling island sunset, it is hard to resist the temptation to stay, so head for the Hôtel des Roches Rouges, one of several establishments that capture Corsica's true spirit of appealingly faded-at-the-edges elegance. This one has been newly restored and now has light-filled rooms and elegant antique furnishings. Gastronomic dinner menus are dominated by the freshest of fish and seafood, caught by local fishermen and brought straight to the table. **RsP**

◩ *The pink rocks of the Calanques of Piana provide a rugged backdrop to a Mediterranean escape.*

Walk in Corsica

Location Corsica, France **Website** corsica.forhikers.com/gr20
Price ◑

The unromantically named GR20—part of the Grande Randonnée (big excursion) network in Europe and sometimes called *Fra li monti* (across the mountains)—runs diagonally from north to south across the island of Corsica. It offers visitors the chance to walk into the hills of Corsica on one of Europe's finest but most demanding trails.

This 112-mile (180-km) hike reaches heights of more than 6,561 feet (2,000 m) but you do not need to be a climber to make the journey, just confident about walking on rugged terrain. Simply follow the red and white rectangles painted on rocks and trees; it takes around fifteen days to complete. Naturally, you can

> *"Corsica [is] a sort of paradise, the kind of place we all dream of finding before everybody else."*
>
> Craig R. Whitney, *New York Times*

tackle as much or as little of the route as you like. The northern section is the most mountainous and difficult, but also the most beautiful. The northern starting point is near Calvi, and the trail ends near Porto Vecchio in the south, but there are plenty of points where you can join or leave the trail.

Between November and May, the trail is dangerous because of snow, and in the height of summer it can get too hot; June and September are therefore the best times to go. Highlights include hanging suspension bridges and climbing chains bolted into rocks at difficult spots. Along the way you will see magnificent views of nature in all her glory. **SH**

Stay at Palais Schwarzenberg

Location Vienna, Austria
Website www.palais-schwarzenberg.com **Price** 💲💲

There cannot be many hotels in the world like the Palais Schwarzenberg. It sits in its own 20-acre (8-ha) park in the center of the city of Vienna, making a night here a bit like staying at Buckingham Palace in London. One notable difference, though, is that the Palais Schwarzenberg is open to all—if you have the money.

It was back in 1962 that the owners, the princes Schwarzenberg, took the unusual decision to turn a wing of their palace into a hotel. (The hotel now takes up the whole central part of the building.) The present appearance of the palace dates from 1716 when the Schwarzenbergs first acquired it and had it altered by the best architect of the time, Johann Bernhard Fischer von Erlach. The building was situated in an area of the city that was rapidly filling up with impressive noble palaces. Higher up the hill, Prince Eugene of Savoy built the Belvedere Palace, which now houses Austria's national collection of paintings.

The central dome of the Palais Schwarzenberg was destroyed by a bomb during World War II, but otherwise the building remains much as it was. There is a sumptuous marble parlor and a dining room stuffed with fine art treasures, including Rubens paintings, Meissen porcelain, and Gobelins tapestries. There are now thirty-eight traditionally furnished rooms and suites in this five-star hotel, the best of which have beautiful views looking out over the formal gardens behind. There is a lovely terrace where you can eat outside in the summer months, oblivious to the traffic on the busy Schwarzenberg Platz. The hotel has always prided itself on a French style of cooking as distinct from the more homey Viennese cuisine encountered elsewhere in the city. **GMD**

Recharge at Palais Coburg

Location Vienna, Austria
Website www.relaischateaux.com/coburg **Price** 💲💲

Housed in the former town palace of the dukes of Coburg, the Biedermeyer Palais Coburg hotel opened in 2003 as Vienna's latest five-star hotel. Each of the thirty-five suites has been individually designed and the whole mass slotted into the original framework of the palace. There is even a roomy, indoor swimming pool: a rare luxury in Vienna.

Nothing of importance from the old palace appears to have been lost, and the "family parlor" is a treat. It contains portraits of all the Coburgs at the time of building and illustrates the singular success of the small dukedom that provided monarchs for half of Europe.

"Surrounded by tropical plants, the spa offers the ideal setting for relaxation . . . after tiring days."

Proprietors, Palais Coburg

With chef Christian Petz at the helm, the Palais Coburg boasts one of the finest restaurants in Vienna. It also possesses one of the very best wine cellars in the world with vintages going back to the eighteenth century, some of which may be enjoyed in the hotel's wine bar and parlors.

The Palais Coburg was built on the site of one of the bastions of the old city wall and looks out toward the famous Ring and the City Park beyond. The strong, military vaults have been exposed to make a striking lobby. The deep cellars of the bastion, where the soldiers would have slept, are still there and have been incorporated into the impressive hotel fabric. **GMD**

Relax at Hotel Schloss Fuschl

Location Salzburg, Austria
Website www.schlossfuschlresort.at **Price** 💲💲💲

Since 1450, this fairy-tale former hunting lodge and castle has presided grandly over its tiny peninsula overlooking Austria's Lake Fuschl. A secluded, palatial world of tranquility, this classically styled hotel has been voted one of Europe's top twenty-five resorts by *Condé Nast Traveler*.

Most of the opulent rooms are within the castle proper, although six rooms in the classic Salzkammer style are available in the Jaegerhaus hunting lodge, which is set within the shadows of the castle walls. There are also six lakeside cottages that come complete with their own private terraces and replete with all the facilities one would expect of a grand hotel. More than 150 works of art, known as the Schloss Fuschl Collection of old masters, adorn the castle's extensive public spaces.

Dining at the Hotel Schloss Fuschl will be a fondly remembered highlight of any visit, with vast breakfasts served on the hotel's lakeside terrace. Lunch and dinner menus include delicacies such as smoked trout caught fresh daily from the hotel's own private fishery, complementing traditional Austrian fare in the award-winning Imperial Restaurant. Whatever else you do, be sure not to leave without having tasted the famous Schloss Fuschl tart.

If you would like to learn more of the castle's colorful history, there is an exhibition hall on-site that will take you on a journey back through the centuries. There is a library in the castle's tower, and a castle boat is available for trips across Lake Fuschl. There is also a nine-hole golf course, and the hotel's unique collection of vintage cars can be made available to guests for romantic excursions. **BS**

Visit Archbishop Dietrich Mausoleum

Location Salzburg, Austria
Website www.salzburg.info **Price** 💶

Located on the right bank of the River Salzach, the Linzergasse is one of Salzburg's main shopping streets and has always been an important thoroughfare in the history of the town. But sneak through the ornamental iron gates off the busy pedestrian street and you enter into the silent world that is the cemetery of St. Sebastian's Church. Occasionally the copper bells of the baroque church will break the silence, but their resonant tones tend to enhance a visit to the cemetery rather than encroach upon peaceful contemplation. Commissioned by Prince-Archbishop Wolf Dietrich in 1595, the cemetery is designed in an Italian style,

> *"Wolf Dietrich von Raitenau . . . brought Italian Renaissance architecture and styles to the city."*
>
> *Encyclopedia Britannica*

bordered by cloisters. In the middle stands Gabrielskapelle (St. Gabriel's Chapel). It was built from 1597 to 1603 as a mausoleum for the famous archbishop who ruled Salzburg for much of the baroque period. Inside you sit in virtual darkness, except for the light that comes in through the circular rooftop windows and plays games on the ornately colored ceramic walls. The chapel provides a welcome, cooling retreat from the heat of summer and offers brief respite when snow covers the graves. The cemetery ceased to be a burial ground in 1888, so you will not be intruding on a family's immediate grief during your period of quiet contemplation. **CFM**

Unwind at Mavida Balance Hotel and Spa

Location Near Salzburg, Austria **Website** www.mavida.at
Price 💲💲

Situated overlooking the shimmering freshwater lake Zeller See and surrounded by the Austrian Alps, this ultra-modern hotel is the last word in cutting-edge chic. It is a member of the award-winning Design Hotels Group, and the interior of this smart wellness retreat is the work of the German-born designer Niki Szilagyi.

For those keen to detox, Mavida's spa offers traditional Finnish saunas, as well as unique treatments such as the Mavida Crystal Spa that uses precious stones and rare oils to help you achieve inner—and outer—tranquility. Guests who want to achieve Zen-like calm in a hurry should try the floatarium; a couple

> "The minimalist decor confirms its status as a rival to the most sophisticated of urban retreats."

Independent

of sessions promises to offer the same relaxing benefits as a week's vacation. Outdoor enthusiasts may take the hotel's bikes on a pleasant ten-minute ride to the southern shoreline of the Zeller See and the hotel's own private beach. The lake is surrounded by more than thirty 9,840-foot (3,000-m) peaks. The historic town of Zell am See is only a short drive away, and the hotel is adjacent to the Alpine meadows and mountain streams of the beautiful Hohe Tauern National Park. Back at the hotel, the gourmet cuisine, prepared in the exhibition kitchen, reflects traditional Austrian and Mediterranean delights and is enhanced with fresh food from the hotel garden. **BS**

Take the Cog Train to Schafbergspitze

Location Upper Austria **Website** www.schafberg.net
Price 💲

There are two ways to reach the Schafbergspitze Hotel, the only residence perched on the top of the highest mountain in the Salzkammergut region: walk, or take the traditional, steam, cog mountain railway. Whichever method you choose, on a clear day the journey offers stunning views. A series of seven blue glacial lakes appears far below, and snowcapped Alpine mountain ranges spread for miles across the valley. When the day-trippers depart, Schafberg Mountain is yours for the night, and you will be staying at the summit, 6,000 feet (1,780 m) above sea level.

The cog railway, the oldest in Austria, has been running from the small lakeside village of St. Wolfgang since 1893, and the journey takes about forty-five minutes, with uplifting views at every turn. The 150-year-old hotel has been run by the Pasch family since the 1960s and is open from the beginning of May to the end of October. It has twenty-five double rooms with five family rooms, all with private bathrooms, and some with south-facing balconies offering views of the Wolfgangsee (Lake Wolfgang). Simply but tastefully furnished in classic Austrian style with pine furniture, the rooms are light and airy. Wholesome and traditional Austrian food is served from the kitchen in a selection of dining rooms that includes an open summer terrace providing a birds-eye view of the region; good food is, naturally, an important aspect of the hotel given its location. Packages that include the cost of a return train fare on the cog railway are available. **CFM**

➡ *The steam train chugs up slopes studded with wildflowers, traveling high up into the clouds.*

Enjoy Schloss Dürnstein

Location Lower Austria
Website www.relaischateaux.com/durnstein   **Price** ⊕⊕

The baroque Schloss is the centerpiece of the quiet hamlet of Dürnstein, a picture-postcard village in the Wachau wine region which became a World Heritage site in 2000. The main street contains a number of cute cafés and bars, and the baker Schmidl, whose *Laberl*, or rolls, are famous throughout central Europe. He also makes one of the best wines in the village.

The Austrian emperor Leopold was staying in the Schloss in 1683 when he learned that the Turks had been repelled from the gates of Vienna, and the hotel is still frequented by princes and kings today. Members of the British, Japanese, and Spanish royal families have been recent guests. The building was acquired

> ## "[The hotel's] decor evokes the styles of baroque, biedermeier and empire."

Proprietors, Schloss Dürnstein

by Raimund Thiery in 1937, and his family, still the owners, have turned it into an elegant five-star hotel stuffed with fabulous antiques.

In recent years, the kitchens have improved beyond measure, and it is now a delight to eat in the main dining room, or in summer to sit on the terrace overlooking the Danube. Naturally, the collection of Wachau wines is second to none. There is a warren of gorgeous vaulted rooms on the ground floor, and many of the bedrooms contain priceless furniture. On the terrace is the lovely swimming pool. The view of the Schloss from the south side of the Danube is said to be one of the most romantic in Austria. **GMD**

Discover Mayr & Mohr Spa

Location Kärnten, Austria
Website www.mayrandmore.at   **Price** ⊕

Forget scented candles, aromatherapy oils, and frangipani blossoms: This former hospital turned Austrian health spa has a very strict results-focused approach and is not your typical indulgent spa. Think formidable matrons in crisp white uniforms, early morning starts, and a frugal diet—the staff aim to provide a life-changing experience.

The concept is based on the Mayr method, which believes that the digestive system is the key to good health. You will have a strange diet, herbal tea, medical examinations, detox massages, and urine analysis as part of your weeklong treatment. Good health is at the heart of everything—which is why there is no elevator in the hotel—and the fresh air and Alpine scenery does wonders for your well-being, too. The hotel occupies an enviable spot on the edge of Lake Worth, so you can enjoy boating on the lake, not to mention golf nearby. All the rooms in the four-star hotel have views of the gardens or the lake.

The award-winning Mayr & Mohr Health Spa might not be a chic tropical retreat or a massage heaven, but a week here can be enough to change your body and mind, providing you with something more than mere therapy. Stress therapies, burn-out solutions, and numerous other cures for hectic, unhealthy lifestyles are on offer, and because every program is tailored to suit the needs of the individual, the prescription is different every time.

Your skin will be brighter, you will sleep better, and you will be more energetic as a result of the Mayr treatments. The experience could even give you the building blocks to create a new start, leaving behind old habits and stepping forward into a new awareness and a new way of living your life. **LD**

Cross-country Ski at Ramsau

Location Tyrol, Austria
Website www.tirolarena.com   **Price** 💲💲

Imagine taking giant steps and gliding with effortless ease through a snowy mountain landscape of spiky peaks and silent forests that looks like something out of C. S. Lewis's Narnia books. This is one way of envisaging cross-country skiing in the Tyrolean Alps. The rhythmic swooshing of your skis as they press down against the sparkling snow and a friendly *Grüss Gott* greeting from a passing skier make this a bewitching mode of travel.

Cross-country skiing can be as energetic or as leisurely as you like. At its extreme, it can be a complete workout for arms, legs, and just about everything else. At its most docile, it can be an amiable shuffle at walking speed from a coffee and apple strudel indulgence at one mountain café to a beer at the next watering hole.

Leutasch, not far from Innsbruck, is the king of all Austrian cross-country ski areas, with an admirable snow record and well over 125 miles (200 km) of prepared tracks beneath the pyramidal 8,730-foot (2,661-m) peak of Hohe Munde. Between the low-key villages dotted in the main valley, the track rises very, very gently, and here a procession of skiers of all ages and fitness levels makes its way along.

Farther up, the terrain becomes distinctly hillier as you head into the trees; the crowds thin out dramatically, only to reappear at the next refreshment hut. With typical Austrian precision, each route is color coded for difficulty and equipped with diagrams showing the rises, falls, and overall distance. Getting lost is never a concern. **TL**

↗ *A cross-country skier glides through a smooth patch of snow in the beautiful Tyrolean Alps.*

"How liberating to replace plastic boots with delicate skis, gliding through a silent landscape."

Stephen Venables, *Guardian*

Relax at the Posthotel

Location Tyrol, Austria   **Website** www.posthotel.at
Price ⊜⊝

At the Posthotel Achenkirch, the management and staff do not much care for the term "wellness." Recognized as having one of the leading spa and treatment centers in Austria, the Posthotel was practicing the concept of wellness to a grateful clientele twenty years before the word became commonplace in the hotel industry's lexicon.

The Posthotel's approach to the well-being of its guests now borders on the legendary, offering everything from body peels, anticellulite treatments, and oxygen therapy through to the application of various Asian disciplines such as tai chi. Anything is possible here, from a simple Shaolin massage to floating on a waterbed in a body pack while gazing through the spa's glass atrium at twinkling stars in the Tyrolean night. The Posthotel's facilities are staffed by trained therapists who continue to set the trends in holistic approaches to health and inner well-being.

The hotel's forty-three rooms are furnished in a country-house style with natural wood floors and Japanese tub-style baths filled to overflowing with scented water. Bay windows and private terraces are standard, as are the little things like complimentary fruit baskets and in-room high-speed Internet access.

The Posthotel's kitchen serves seasonal, locally sourced meals and is a regular recipient of the prestigious Gault Millau toque for fine cuisine. Tennis, squash, sailing on the beautiful Lake Achensee, or horseback riding against the backdrop of the magnificent Karwendelgebirge Mountains should leave you feeling refreshed indeed. **BS**

→ *Guests will find a five-star welcome nestled deep in the woodlands of the idyllic Tyrolean Achental valley.*

Stay at Riffelalp Resort 2,222m

Location Valais, Switzerland **Website** www.riffelalp.com
Price Ⓢ

Standing on your balcony, gazing out toward the majestic Matterhorn, it is impossible not to be awestruck. The Riffelalp Resort 2,222m, looming at 1,975 feet (602 m) above the hustle and bustle of Zermatt below, is blessed with stunning vistas toward the huge beast of a mountain. The view is especially enchanting in the orange glow of early morning.

In a lovely setting among Alpine forests, accessed only via hiking paths, ski trails, or the nearby Gornergrat cog railway, the large hotel provides a civilized base for a ski vacation or a summer break, when the meadows are carpeted with flowers.

Its rooms have all the contemporary touches one could wish for—whirlpool tubs, DVD players, Bose sound systems—as well as a sense of style and character that rarely comes as standard. The spacious Matterhorn and Monte Rosa suites are ideal for families and there is plenty on-site to keep visitors occupied, from a converted chapel for concerts and a home cinema, to heated indoor and outdoor swimming pools (with superb views of that famous peak), a state-of-the-art spa, and two bowling alleys.

A wine-tasting session in the cellar is a perfect way to begin an evening, followed by local specialties in one of the three restaurants—be sure to sample a cheesy raclette. Round off the evening with a digestif as the pianist tinkles away in the cozy bar. Perhaps the best feature offered by the resort however is the ski in/ski out piste access, which means that a good day's skiing starts right outside the front door. **LP**

◄ *The resort is blessed with stunning vistas toward the iconic and colossal Matterhorn.*

Camp at Whitepod

Location Berne, Switzerland
Website www.whitepod.com **Price** $

What appears at first glance to be a collection of giant white golf balls set around an Alpine chalet is actually a series of dome-shaped tents, or "pods." Perched at 5,577 feet (1,700 m) above the village of Les Cerniers, these pods make up one of the hippest eco-retreats.

The brainchild of Swiss entrepreneur Sofia de Meyer, the Whitepod experience was born from a desire to create a mini-resort that made the most of its surroundings yet did nothing to harm their beauty. Raised on wooden platforms and designed like traditional igloos, the pods are waterproof and UV resistant, flame-retardant, and insulated with fabrics that are also used by NASA. Heating comes courtesy

> *"You are gifted grand cru air quality, gob-smacking views, and a real sense of being among nature."*
>
> Simon Mills, *Guardian*

of tiny woodstoves, and each room has a comfy bed bedecked with industrial-strength comforters and pillows, organic bedding, and sheepskin. Panoramic windows offer views of Les Diablerets Massif, an Alpine chalet that dates back to 1820. It is where you will find the dining room serving up the resort's delicious cooking, all locally procured and/or organic.

Once here, guests can enjoy snowshoeing, ice climbing, backcountry skiing, horseback riding, and even dogsledding. After you have expended all your energy, you can take advantage of the camp's on-site therapists, who offer a range of treatments from hour-long massages to reflexology and osteopathy. **PS**

Stay at Beau-Rivage

Location Vaud, Switzerland
Website www.lhw.com/beaurivage **Price** $$$

Tourists have been dropping into Lausanne ever since Lord Byron arrived with the Shelleys in 1817, and Mary sat down to write *Frankenstein*. The Hôtel d'Angleterre where they stayed is still standing, and has recently been incorporated into a snazzy new extension of the venerable Beau-Rivage.

The Beau-Rivage was not around in the days of Byron and the Shelleys. It was built in 1861, marking the height of British interest in Lake Geneva. Summers in Switzerland offered the chance to enjoy the lake and the fresh air of the mountains. Every commune had its "grand hotel," but the grandest of the grand was the Beau-Rivage. Success meant that an entire new wing had to be tacked on by the turn of the century, linked to the old building by an exquisite art-nouveau ballroom.

There are glorious rooms throughout, but possibly the nicest are in the art-nouveau wing. They look out over the great expanse of the placid lake to the mountains on the French side, illuminated by the setting sun at gloaming. There is a formal garden, swimming pool, and spa. The clientele is not always the youngest; many come to service their bank accounts. Politicians are commonplace here; they are best spotted in the dreamy dining room with its encrustations of stucco and magnificent paintings. There is a choice of fine restaurants in which you may dine, but make sure you try the fish from the lake: pollen, char, and perch fillets, drunk with the marvelous limpid wines of the Vaud, from vineyards just a mile or two to the east. There is plenty to do, but a most pleasant way to relax is to take one of the turn-of-the-century paddle steamers down to the Château de Chillon, immortalized by Byron. **GMD**

Relax at La Réserve

Location Geneva, Switzerland
Website www.lareserve.ch **Price** ⊙⊙⊙

Fresh, revitalizing mountain air, a wonderful lakeside setting, and a unique sense of style combine to make La Réserve a literal breath of fresh air. Unpretentious yet thoroughly cool, the Swiss retreat straddles the shore of Lake Geneva and sits in a landscaped park, ensuring privacy and plenty of space for relaxation. Do not get too relaxed, though, because La Réserve has a definite party edge to it: Every night cocktails flow in the bar as a DJ plays until the early hours, and the Chinese and French restaurants are buzzing with the young and beautiful people of Geneva society.

By day, hangover shaken off, the cosmopolitan city of Geneva is just a complimentary boat hop away. La Réserve's Venetian-style, elegant wooden *motoscaffo* whisks you there in minutes. Or guests can just enjoy the hotel's vibe or indulge in a range of activities, including wakeboarding on the lake.

The building may look underwhelming from the outside, but inside rooms are beautifully designed with oiled wooden floors, decadent colors, rich velvet bedspreads, and granite bathrooms. Many rooms have lake views or vistas toward the Alps, and some have generous terraces. Good looks aside, it is worth visiting La Réserve for the award-winning spa alone. In its own wing, it has seventeen treatment rooms and a varied menu of therapies, as well as indoor and outdoor pools, sauna, and hammam. Personalized programs are offered, incorporating water therapies and jasmine flower baths. But the outdoor pool is the best place to be on a sunny day, sipping a glass of crisp wine and knowing you are part of something rather special. **LP**

↗ *The sleek and, at times, daring decor is the work of hot interior designer Jacques Garcia.*

"The style is loosely inspired by African lodges, with animal-print carpets and a tented restaurant."

Condé Nast Traveler

See Piedmont by Bicycle

Location Piedmont, Italy **Website** www.piemontefeel.org
Price 💲

The region of Piedmont is in the northwest tip of Italy, bordered by Switzerland to the north and France to the west. Renowned for its white truffles and outstanding cuisine, Piedmont is also recognized as one of Italy's greatest wine regions.

This agricultural paradise provides the perfect backdrop for a bicycle safari. Gentle slopes give way to orchards and fields of sunflowers. Winding roads unfold to reveal tiny hamlets and picturesque medieval villages. The views are never ending: from undulating vineyards to the bordering Alpine mountain ranges. On a clear summer's day, you can even see across to the majestic peak of Mont Blanc.

The capital of Piedmont, Turin, is the ideal starting point for a two-wheeled tour. There is a network of bicycle paths crisscrossing the medieval city, which allows you to view the myriad castles, cathedrals, and museums. Travel on through towns such as Bra, known as the capital of gourmet, and Alba, the home of white truffles. However, perhaps the real magic is found when bicycling between the towns, where the air is scented with wildflowers and filled with birdsong.

Quiet country roads lead you through groves of chestnut trees, alongside rushing rivers, and through lush pine forests. Recharge in the little villages along the way, stopping for lunch at one of the many gastronomical restaurants. Try to time your tour to coincide with one of the many food festivals held during the year, including those dedicated solely to truffles, snails, and cheese. After settling in each night, enjoy a glass of the region's world-famous Barolo. **JP**

➡ *Ride the gentle slopes of Piedmont to work up an appetite for the culinary delights the region offers.*

Experience L'Albereta

Location Lombardy, Italy
Website www.relaischateaux.com/albereta **Price** ⊖⊖⊖

Set in the hills of Franciacorta, L'Albereta offers a perfect getaway for foodies and sybarites. It has been stylishly turned into a chic country house hotel, which is home to a world-class, two-Michelin-starred restaurant, presided over by Italy's most feted chef Gualtiero Marchesi, and an equally impressive spa.

Marchesi trained with the Troisgros brothers in Roanne and was the first Italian to gain three Michelin rosettes. In recent years he has been designated a national treasure and has his own "national" cooking school. At L'Albereta he interprets Italy's grandest traditions in a French way: Risotto is made with the finest chicken stock, saffron, and a little cheese, with a

---

"Marchesi's cooking is influenced by his love of art, most obviously in dishes inspired by paintings."

theworlds50best.com

---

perfect square of gold leaf in the middle. Another item on the menu to try is his version of the classic "tournedos Rossini." Marchesi uses veal rather than beef fillet, rendering the meat all the more succulent.

The hotel boasts every comfort, including elegant drawing rooms, an indoor swimming pool, and a helipad. One room even has a retractable glass roof. L'Albereta's location is perfect for excursions to this little-known corner of Lombardy. A must-see is the city of Bergamo, for its churches and art collections. **GMD**

⬅ *The rambling nineteenth-century villa seems to rise organically from the surrounding vineyards.*

Ride Through the Tyrol

Location South Tyrol, Italy   **Website** www.theridingcompany.com
Price ⊖⊖

You may wake up and wonder where you are: Although South Tyrol is in Italy, the majority of its inhabitants speak German as their mother tongue. Nestled right on the Austrian border, it is a land of chocolate-box mountains and verdant valleys, of orderly apple orchards and sweetly clanging cowbells. It is also home to the Haflinger horse—a small, chestnut-colored breed with a striking white mane and rhythmic gait that was first developed in this part of the Dolomites in the late 1800s.

Head to the riding stables at Tolderhof and you will be able to saddle up a Haflinger and take half-day or full-day rides into the surrounding Alpine scenery. There is also an indoor riding school where dressage and jumping are taught, and anyone wishing to build up their confidence before braving the outdoors can do so. Riding is certainly not an indoor occupation, nor is it just a summer occupation here: In winter, you can canter through the white, virgin snow. You can even try your hand at ski jeering, in which a skier is harnessed to a horse and travels behind it like a water-skier on snow. You will need to be able ski, but previous riding experience will not be necessary.

Accommodation is available in the four-star Hotel Post, which comes complete with a spa offering massages and aromatherapy soaks for those with sore muscles. The hotel also features a gourmet restaurant that serves up five-course dinners—plenty of food to keep you going on your rides. Alternatively you can stay in an apartment next door to the riding stables, where you will still have access to the hotel's facilities. There is also an art-nouveau villa, Villa Prugger, which can accommodate up to thirteen people and has its own large garden. **PE**

Enjoy Vigilius

Location South Tyrol, Italy   **Website** www.vigilius.it
Price $\ominus$$\ominus$

Accessible only by cable car, the remarkable Vigilius Mountain Resort sits 4,920 feet (1,500 m) above everyday life and has jaw-dropping views of the dramatic Dolomites. Come here to escape the pollution and stress of the city—larch wood scents the pure, clean air, and the resort is shrouded in serenity.

This modern lodge is a bold departure from traditional Tyrolean chalets. The ultimate in eco-chic, star architect Matteo Thun has used glass and local wood to skillfully integrate the low-lying building into its natural setting. His inspiration was a wind-fallen tree, and guests will find the reception in the upturned root and bedrooms in the trunk. The grass-covered roof helps energy conservation, whereas inside, open-plan rooms are styled with minimalist furniture and are cleverly divided with internally heated clay walls. Furnished in the main with exposed timber, all rooms have balconies or terraces to take in the views.

The sophisticated spa has a range of treatments and massages, along with a steam room, sauna, and yoga classes. Try the signature hay bath for a circulation-boosting treat. Hearty Tyrolean cooking, from stews to strudels, features on the menu at the Parlour Ida restaurant, whereas the vegetarian 1500 serves Mediterranean-inspired dishes. End the night with a drink by the log fire in the lounge or step outside to the terrace to enjoy the celestial views. In winter, when the mountain is blanketed in snow, go tobogganing, skiing, and snowshoeing. Alternatively, in summer, walk some of the 31 miles (50 km) of hiking trails, or try Nordic walking, paragliding, and archery. **AD**

→ Go for a dip in the infinity pool for the sensation of swimming into the mountains.

Stay at Bauer Palladio

Location Venice, Veneto, Italy   **Website** www.bauerhotels.com
Price 💲💲

Arriving in Venice feels much like walking onto a movie set, so incredible are the vistas. While you are visiting the city, you might as well go the whole way and stay at the exclusive Bauer Palladio Hotel on the secluded island of Giudecca. This landmark of Venetian history is situated just yards from the world-famous Hotel Cipriani and is a must for those who like to brush shoulders with celebrities yet keep one foot firmly in the past. The hotel is just the other side of the Grand Canal but feels like a million miles away from the hordes of tourists at St. Mark's Square.

The building is a converted convent, originally designed in renaissance style by Andrea Palladio, and combines an imposing exterior with a somewhat austere interior. However, its cavernous sitting and dining rooms are beautifully decorated to give a surprising sense of intimacy. At the hotel, the thirty-seven rooms and thirteen suites are subtly designed with antiques, tapestries, and handcrafted touches, with either a garden or lagoon view. Great pains have been taken to keep many of the Renaissance features.

The hotel's spa offers postcardlike views of the Venice lagoon, and there you can enjoy a range of treatments. However, the highlight of any stay here has to be the private solar-powered shuttle that ferries guests from the hotel across to Bauer's sister hotel, Il Palazzo, just yards from all the Venice landmarks. Hot and tired from a day of shopping and exploring, simply walk down to the jetty, skip onto your private boat, and be whisked over the glittering lagoon to the tranquility of your hotel just five minutes away. **RS**

◁ *The elegant hotel has been carefully restored and is located on the waterfront, providing wonderful views.*

Visit Cinque Terre

Location Liguria, Italy
Website www.lecinqueterre.org/eng **Price** 🌓

"Each town is a unique destination carved rather amazingly into the steep terraced-vineyard coastline."

Ariel Foxman, *New York Times*

Cinque Terre (five lands) is a UNESCO World Heritage site made up of five small villages, linked by a picturesque walking trail. Each village can be reached by train or boat, but the only way to explore the rugged coastline is by foot.

The southernmost village, Riomaggiore, was established many centuries ago as the perfect location to plant olive trees and grapevines. The pretty stone houses are built vertically, like multilevel towers, to accommodate the steep terrain. Vertiginous staircases allow access between the homes and buildings. Here you will find the start of the famous Via dell'Amore, or Lover's Walk. This 0.6-mile (1-km) paved pathway links Riomaggiore with its closest neighbor, Manarola. Cut into the rock face, it takes just twenty minutes to walk and allows visitors spectacular views back over the village and out across the Mediterranean.

The route from Manarola to Corniglia takes around an hour. The middle of the five villages is surrounded on three sides by ancient stone terraces and lush green grapevines. Vernazza is a traditional fishing town with a natural harbor. It is accessible only by foot because the locals decided long ago not to build road access, in order to retain the character and quiet pace of life. The final leg of the Cinque Terre walk stretches to Monterosso and takes around ninety minutes. This is the steepest and most demanding part of the walk, but also one of the most beautiful. The hike will lead you through winding olive orchards and verdant vineyards, and will reward you with dramatic ocean views you will not want to leave. **JP**

◤ *The small town of Manarola is the second-smallest of the Cinque Terre, perched on rocks above the sea.*

Discover Emilia-Romagna

Location Emilia-Romagna, Italy
Website www.emiliaromagnaturismo.it **Price** $

From the spectacular scenery to the frantic bustle of the cities, there is no doubt that driving through Emilia-Romagna is an experience in itself. The Italians drive like they live: with passion and excitement. You either keep up—or get left behind.

Emilia-Romagna is renowned for its beautiful landscapes and outstanding food. It is the perfect location for a driving tour that takes in all the wonderful scenery and all the culinary delights. Fly in to Parma, nestled in the lush valley of the Po River. The city is famous for its cured ham, prosciutto di Parma. From there it is a laid-back drive to Reggio-Emilia, where you may sample another local gastronomic favorite: Parmigiano-Reggiano cheese. Drive east and you will hit Modena, the home of the eponymous balsamic vinegar. Production of this sweet-and-sour ingredient can be traced as far back as the eleventh century. While in Modena, there is no more fitting stop than Maranello—also known as the city of the Ferrari. The town has been home to the famous sports car since the early 1940s. Creator Enzo Ferrari moved to Maranello after bombs destroyed his original factory in Modena during World War II.

After admiring the finest in Italian automotive engineering, continue the drive through green countryside, along the foothills of the Apennine mountains to the capital of Bologna, known with good reason as the gastronomic capital of Italy. Sample the famous meat-based pasta sauce that the locals refer to as *ragù* but the rest of the world knows as Bolognese. The hills behind Bologna are dotted with rustic Italian villages and towns to explore. From here it is an easy journey to Ravenna, where you can marvel at the ornate Byzantine architecture. **JP**

Stay at Casa Argento

Location Tuscany, Italy
Website www.invitationtotuscany.com **Price** $$

The views from this stylish mountain retreat are so spectacular that you can see all the way to Corsica. Perched high in the Apuan Alps, above Camaiore and Pietrasanta, this is the place to come if you want to leave the stress of city life far behind.

The restored house was once part of the nearby medieval silver mines. Guests may rent the whole house, sleeping up to six, or just the upper section, for three people. Either way, absolute privacy is promised because no one else shares the property with you.

Head for the hills and spend your days following paths snaking around the mountains and surrounding valleys. Then come back to cool off with an outdoor

> *"If Tuscany had only Florence it would still be a region to love. But it lays claim to several more gems."*
>
> Sir Arnold Wesker, British playwright

shower in a cave carved out of the rock and soak in the open-air whirlpool tub. Placed on the terrace looking out across the Mediterranean, it is the perfect spot to unwind with a glass of wine in hand.

There is much to do in the surrounding area. In summer, spend the day at the beach, just twenty-five minutes away, or take a drive to find cozy restaurants with traditional menus in local villages. Combine a visit to the quarries, where the white marble came from for Michelangelo's *David*, with a trip to nearby Pietrasanta, a center for local sculptors who exhibit their work there throughout the year. There is also sightseeing aplenty in the cities of Lucca and Pisa. **AD**

Relax at Grotta Giusti

Location Tuscany, Italy
Website www.grottagiustispa.com   **Price** 🅢🅢

Grotta Giusti Spa's claim to fame is its natural grotto turned sauna. The amusingly named Hell, Purgatory, and Paradise "rooms" have 100 percent humidity and increases in temperature. However, the resort is not all about the bat cave. The nineteenth-century edifice is a graceful villa full of antiques and paintings with classic old-world charm. Plush velvets, grand lounges, but, most of all, marble features add an air of grandeur.

The real attraction is the natural thermal water, rich in bicarbonate, sulfate, chloride, magnesium, and calcium. It was discovered in 1849 and has had crowds flocking to it ever since. At an admirable 93°F (34°C), it is recommended for everything from muscular to

---

"Verdi called the Grotta the 'eighth wonder of the world' . . . That said, it's not for claustrophobics."

The Times

---

cardiovascular problems. What is more, the waters even gush out of the taps in the marble bathrooms. In the modern well-being center there is an Asian area, a gym, an open-air thermal pool with a waterfall and underwater hydro-massage, and even a medical aesthetic center offering both ancient and cutting-edge techniques. The treatment menu includes mud therapy, Swedish massage, and Namikoshi shiatsu massage, for example, and the aromas of dog rose, liquorice, sea tangle, and olives hang in the air. Grotta Giusti is a lot more than a thermal spa; it is now a fully fledged resort with pools, tennis courts, and a gourmet restaurant. Nothing like purgatory. **RCA**

Explore Boboli Gardens

Location Florence, Tuscany, Italy
Website www.firenzemusei.it   **Price** 🅢

Florence's—indeed Italy's—most famous garden may be listed in every guidebook, but climb the calf-crushing steps to leave the Pitti Palace behind and you can soon find yourself "lost" in areas of garden that barely see visitors. As a whole, the garden's 111 acres (45 ha) are a great place to escape the rigors of sightseeing in Florence; however, some areas are less frequented than others, so if you crave total peace (and respite from the Tuscan sun), avoid the amphitheater directly behind the Pitti Palace leading up toward Neptune's Fountain. Here the garden consists of symmetrical lines and patterns made from neatly clipped box hedges around formal pools with gruesome stone statues.

Elsewhere, particularly to the west of the palace (with the palace behind you and turning right), the secret, winding paths are your solace, and the hazel bushes, tall pines, and cypress trees your cover, protecting you from the heat of summer days—and the visitors thin out. The hedge-lined, soft-grass plots, small groves, and meadows are perfect for afternoon siestas and for wearing out young children safely, away from the busy city streets. There are good views of Florence from the eastern side of the garden, where a small café also serves refreshments.

Most visitors enter the gardens via the Pitti Palace at the Piazza dei Pitti, but there is a much quieter entrance/exit through the Forte di Belvedere that leads out onto a quiet, suburban street with open fields. Be warned however that the gardens are closed on the first and last Monday of each month. **CFM**

➔ *There are some quiet, shady spots in addition to the manicured gardens and formal pools by the palace.*

Stay at Castello di Vicarello

Location Tuscany, Italy   **Website** www.vicarello.it
Price 💲💲

A secluded estate in the Grosseto area surrounded by the rolling Tuscan greenery of olive groves and vineyards, Castello di Vicarello sits perched on top of a hill like a fairy-tale castle. The exquisite eleventh-century *castello* blends historic atmosphere with modern luxury to create an intimate rustic hideaway. There are four suites and one villa to choose from, filled with antiques and elegant furniture in a seamless blend of Italian and Asian styles.

Two infinity pools set among olive trees, a cobbled courtyard, and lush grounds with plenty of shady corners in which to curl up with a book or eat an intimate lunch tick all the boxes when it comes to romantic surroundings. There are terraces to relax on, honey-colored gravel paths to wander, and comfortable rattan chairs to ease into and enjoy a drink in as the sun goes down. A small spa offers soothing treatments and yoga sessions. Suites looking out over the panoramic views have low-beamed ceilings, large windows, and thick stone walls.

Traditional Tuscan and Mediterranean cuisine, using homegrown ingredients, is the highlight of the kitchen. Think pan-fried pigeon with bacon, sage, and white grapes, washed down with a glass of Castello di Vicarello, a blend of cabernet sauvignon and cabernet franc from the estate's own vineyard.

It takes no time at all to adapt to the deliciously slow rhythm of life and be seduced by the evocative scenery. Take a walk around the gardens, among roses, trailing jasmine, lavender, and mulberry trees. On clear days, the fresh salty sea breeze blows inland and the shimmering water can be seen in the distance. Siena is an hour's drive away, or you can explore Uccellina National Park and the springs at Saturnia. **AD**

Unwind at L'Andana Hotel

Location Tuscany, Italy   **Website** www.andana.it
Price 💲💲

L'Andana was once the hunting lodge of the Grand Duke of Tuscany, Leopold II. It is situated in a secluded spot, nestled amid centuries-old olive groves and vineyards in the Maremma, with nothing to disturb the tranquility except the background hum of cicadas and the cooing of doves.

The property has since been converted into a luxury hotel by world-famous restaurateur Alain Ducasse in partnership with spa innovators Espa to cook up L'Andana, a thirty-three-room gastronomic retreat and spa. The rooms are elegant and stylish, with beautiful silk curtains, Italian fabrics, Tuscan antiques, and sumptuous, richly colored bedspreads. However, it is

> *"L'Andana is a reflection of the Maremma ... unique, authentic, generous."*
>
> Alain Ducasse, cofounder

the bathrooms that really impress; they are wall-to-wall marble, some with vast bathtubs that are big enough for an entire football team.

For the ultimate in pampering, be sure to try the deeply relaxing holistic back, face, and scalp massage with hot stones. Surrender to the skilled ministrations of the therapist and drift off into a heavenly half slumber. Afterward, take a dip in the vitality pool, or be tempted by a range of mouthwatering snacks from the gourmet spa menu. To work off all that overindulgence, take a stroll around the lovely gardens. There is also a three-hole golf course and a tennis court if you are feeling energetic. **HA**

Experience Ripa d'Orcia

Location Tuscany, Italy **Website** www.castelloripadorcia.com
Price $

The walls, battlements, and towers of Ripa d'Orcia Castle still stand on an isolated hilltop in Tuscany, as they have done for centuries. You reach the castle by traveling along a gravel track winding up through the woods along the Orcia Valley. At the hilltop, enter the fortifications through a gatehouse. There is no drawbridge these days, but you still feel like you are intruding into the medieval world. Inside is a hamlet and church, plus a maze of stone stairways, paths, gardens, outbuildings, and turrets. It feels like a museum village—still with its bakery, carpentry workshop, blacksmith's forge, olive mill, and granaries.

The castle has long been the home of an aristocratic Sienese family who painstakingly maintain it. They still live in the main castle but have opened hotel rooms and vacation apartments in many of the other houses inside the ramparts. Inside, you will find nothing has been spoiled. Rooms are simple and rustic, with wooden Tuscan furniture, exposed beams, terra-cotta tiled floors, and heavy window shutters. Some have open fireplaces and private terraces, and all offer terrific views. Rooms have no televisions or telephones but there are modern bathrooms. The only concession to modernity is that on a terrace with panoramic views they have built a fabulous open-air swimming pool.

The communal dining room serves hearty dishes using fresh produce from the castle gardens, and guests can use a reading room in an old converted granary that has a big open fireplace. The castle still has an 800-acre (324-ha) estate and makes olive oil and vinegar as well as red, white, and sweet wine. The ancient wine cellar has been converted into a beautiful tasting room for the estate's wines and extra-virgin olive oil that can be bought on-site. **SH**

Relax at Terme di Saturnia

Location Tuscany, Italy **Website** www.termedisaturnia.it
Price $

Natural springwaters have been flowing into a volcanic crater in front of what is now the Terme di Saturnia Spa and Golf Resort for more than 3,000 years. The chic, minimalist hotel set at the foot of the ancient village of Saturnia in the Maremma region has one of the most famous spas in the world, renowned for its medical care as much as for its conventional beauty treatments, which take place in any one of fifty treatment rooms.

The water follows a subterranean route that filters slowly through micro-fissures in the rock, absorbing salts and minerals on a journey that takes more than forty years to reach the hotel's thermal pool, which

> *"The pool is a crater of an extinct volcano filled with rainwater filtered through the ground."*
>
> Denis Campbell, *Observer*

bubbles night and day. There are 140 rooms, one indoor and six outdoor pools, two restaurants, a fitness center, tennis courts, and a replica of a traditional Roman bathhouse, as well as a championship eighteen-hole golf course.

The Tuscan landscape, with its ocher-brown hills and lush vineyards, hilltop villages, and medieval castles, has been seducing visitors for centuries; in the Maremma, cowboys still ranch cattle the old-fashioned way and Etruscan ruins dot the landscape. The nearby medieval town of Montemerano and the magical town of Pitigliano are well worth dragging yourself away from the hotel for a day. **TW**

Stay at Borgo Santo Pietro

Location Tuscany, Italy
Website www.borgosantopietro.com **Price** 💲

Around 700 years ago, Borgo Santo Pietro was a resting place for pilgrims from all over Europe on their way to Rome. The tiny settlement dates back to the thirteenth century and stands on a rise among cherry orchards and ornamental gardens. The pretty village of Palazzetto is a five-minute stroll down the old Pilgrim's Way. Siena and the Tuscan coast are both half an hour away.

The old villa and its outbuildings have only recently been lavishly converted into a boutique hideaway. The Borgo has become all you would expect from a luxury Italian escape, with state-of-the-art spa treatments in the old bakery, fresh-off-the-vine food from the

> *"Cortona was the first town we ever stayed in and we always came back to it."*
>
> Frances Mayes, *Under the Tuscan Sun*

organic garden, and a chemical-free, freshwater infinity pool surrounded by immaculate flower gardens. Yet it is intimate, too, with only eight bedrooms. They are packed with period style; you will find details like ornate plasterwork, gilt-framed mirrors, tapestries, beamed ceilings, freestanding bathtubs, and open fires. The enormous beds have special handmade mattresses from Denmark.

Guests can eat in the villa's ornate candlelit dining room, outside by the colonnaded terrace, or in the garden beside the pool. Expect menus of the finest Italian dishes, using produce from the hotel's garden or local farms wherever possible. **SH**

Explore Monte Amiata

Location Tuscany, Italy
Website www.sienaonline.com **Price** 🚻

In the distance the peak rises majestically, dominating the Tuscan skyline. Monte Amiata is the second-highest volcano in Italy, after Mount Etna. Reaching 5,680 feet (1,731 m) high, it is the northernmost peak of the Tuscan anti-Apennines, a string of volcanoes dotted along southern Tuscany.

Although it last erupted 180,000 years ago, the superheated core still fuels the hot-water springs found at its base. For centuries, Italians and other visitors have flocked to these hot-water springs. The mineral-rich waters are considered to have relaxing, healing properties. There are many health centers in the vicinity, most offering year-round bathing in the heated waters. Some have built spa complexes around the springs; others are untouched pools, carved by nature into the surrounding landscape.

However, soaking in the geothermal hot springs is just one of the many ways to enjoy Monte Amiata. Marked walking paths crisscross the dormant volcano, making it a popular destination for hikers. The upper slopes are covered with thick forests of beech, fir, and chestnut trees, whereas lower down you will find olive trees and strangely shaped volcanic boulders. From December to March these trails are blanketed with fresh snow. Skiers can opt to go cross-country through the forests or to visit one of the mountain's ski fields.

There are hundreds of different walks that take in the fascinating and diverse sights of the mountain, from freshwater springs to the tiny villages and towns that coexist on the slopes of the volcano. One of the most famous is the town of Abbadia San Salvatore. Built around one of Tuscany's oldest Benedictine monasteries, the town is a perfectly preserved example of eleventh-century architecture. **JP**

Discover the Maremma

Location Tuscany/Lazio, Italy
Website www.lamaremmafabene.it   **Price** ◑

If you think Tuscany has become too tame and touristy, think again. The Maremma, a spectacular area of coast, forest, and mountain that straddles southwest Tuscany and northern Lazio, still clings to its wild side. It is famous, in particular, for its 100 miles (160 km) of rocky coastline scattered with fishing villages and pretty bays that are perfect for swimming.

Those who like their wilderness amply peppered with eateries should head to the Gulf of Follonica, whose beaches at Cala Martina, Cala Violina, and Castiglione della Pescaia always provide plenty of opportunities for feasting between sunbathing stints. Try the local pecorino cheese, washed down with a glass or two of Morellino di Scansano. Alternatively, the islands of Giglio and Giannutri feature cliffs that plummet into the jade Mediterranean Sea, or visit the promontory of Monte Argentario, which is known for its scuba diving.

The pine forests that border the beaches are spotted with lagoons teeming with waterfowl and other birdlife; this whole area was marshland until Mussolini had it drained. Bird-watchers should head to L'Oasi della Laguna, a bird sanctuary open to visitors from September to April, or to Lago di Burano, which is the most important birding site in Italy: More than half the species that live or migrate in the country can be seen here.

If you visit during one of the festivals, keep your eyes peeled for the *butteri*, or cowboys, who saddle up for special events and ensure that, still today, the Maremma delights in its wild side. **PE**

↗ *Its marshes drained less than a century ago, the Maremma remains relatively undiscovered.*

"Landscapes are the equal of anything in Tuscany, especially the Argentario."

Tim Jepson, *Daily Telegraph*

Explore Perugia

Location Umbria, Italy **Website** www.comune.perugia.it;
http://tourism.comune.perugia.it **Price** 🏛

Perugia is a fascinating fortress town of massive stone walls and red-tiled roofs, ancient gates and archways, sun-drenched, classical frescoes, and panoramic views. It is the quintessential Italy portrayed in early renaissance art. If you look out from the Duomo at the city's highest point, you'll see the endless lines of hills, with their willowy cypresses and steep terraces of olives and vine, stretch away into the distance. But with so much of interest within the ancient ramparts, it's the perfect place to engage in that most Italian of pastimes—the *passeggiata*, or "stroll"—and take in all the cultural delights while you're at it.

The many styles of Perugia's architecture offer a portal into its remarkable past. The massive Etruscan city walls and Arch d'Agusto were built in the 4th century B.C.E. (a reminder of the existing civilizations that the Roman bully-boys hijacked) while the more recently built medieval Priors' Palace, with its delicate patterning of white and pink stone, houses the National Gallery of Umbria. Next to it, in the Cathedral square, extraordinary 13th century sculptures decorate the Fontana Maggiore, and the sound of modern life chimes in with the tolls of the bells in the background.

To get a taste of Perugia's more bloody past go down into the bowels of time. An escalator will take you to the Rocca Paolina—once the headquarters of the Baglioni family. This bloodthirsty clan once dominated the city until the equally unpleasant Pope Paul III murdered the lot and buried their remains under the rock of their fortress—along with their palaces, seven churches, and 138 houses. **SWi**

➜ *The medieval Fontana Maggiore, sculpted by Nicola and Giovanni Pisano, was designed by Fra Bevignate.*

Relax at Todi Castle

Location Umbria, Italy   **Website** www.todicastle.com
Price 💲💲💲

This imposing family-owned medieval fortress stands amid the rolling green hills of Umbria in central Italy and offers you the chance to escape to your own Italian castle. Although Todi Castle may be a perfect mix of relaxed self-catering and luxury service now, this was once the real thing: a fortified stronghold with a long history of conflict. In the Middle Ages, vats of boiling oil were thrown from the battlements, and the remains of many dead soldiers have been found around the site. The high stone walls, tower, arrow slits, and secret underground escape passages remain, as does a sense of history in everything you touch.

Your rental includes having breakfast prepared, rooms cleaned, and quality linen and towels provided. After that, the castle owners provide as little or as much service as you want—you can use the well-equipped kitchen yourself, or have lunches and dinners prepared for you.

There are four bedrooms in the main castle, plus a separate wing that sleeps three more, and three other villas on the estate that are available to rent. Outside is a garden with a swimming pool, terraces with panoramic views, and sloping green lawns leading to olive groves, vineyards, and a fenced deer park, all bordered by rows of cypresses. Apart from that, there is plenty to do in this remote spot. The owners provide private tours, mountain bikes, treks, visiting massage, personal trainers, food tasting, and cooking demonstrations—including a course in making your own pasta. They will even take you on a tour of the local wine cellars, farms, and olive oil mills. **SH**

← *The west view of Todi Castle in Umbria, with its sloping green lawns and orchards.*

Visit Italy's "Other" Lakes

Location Lazio, Italy   **Website** www.lagodibolsena.org/en
Price 💲

Forget Garda, Como, Lugano, and Maggiore and try this trio of volcanic lakes in Lazio, north of Rome. Lake Bracciano might be better known for its lakeside castle, the setting for Tom Cruise and Katie Holmes's wedding in 2006, than for its lake, but that is definitely a good thing. Undiscovered by mass tourism, the lake provides respite from Rome's hot summers, with plenty of water sports, including sailing and waterskiing, all surrounded by forests, olive groves, and gardens. The castle itself can be visited, and you can discover the legends of loves lost, death, secret passageways, and medieval mischief, as well as walk around its candlelit ramparts.

> *"There is no heavy industry in this area, which means the waters are mercifully clear of pollution."*

Stephen Pritchard, *Observer*

Lake Bolsena is the largest volcanic lake in Italy, a circular 71-mile (115-km) lake with two small islands in the center. Surrounded by low, vine-covered hills, it has some great swimming beaches and is one of Europe's cleanest lakes. On the uninhabited side of the lake, there are small secluded beaches, and the lake is popular with sailors and snorkelers, too.

Lake Vico is the smallest lake, still stretching to over 7 miles (11 sq km), and is a volcanic crater surrounded by nature reserves and overlooked by Mount Venere; according to legend, it owes its origins to Hercules. He defied local orders to pick up his club and, when he did so, a river appeared and created the lake. **LD**

Stay at Sunflower Retreats

Location Lazio, Italy
Website www.sunflowerretreats.com **Price** ⊖⊖

When Rome fell, Casperia was born—a fortified hilltop haven that protected the natives from any invading barbarians. Just forty-five minutes from Rome, the sun-baked medieval village now provides an atmospheric setting for Sunflower Retreats yoga vacations. From the mysterious Forani Palace within the village itself to the nearby caves where St. Francis of Assisi lived and taught, there is a spiritual dimension that lends itself perfectly to the more contemporary pursuit of well-being.

Yoga is central to the Sunflower Retreats experience. In a converted barn there is a studio with a freshwater spring bubbling away beneath the floor. Daily classes

> *"Enjoy an authentic Italian village lifestyle and benefit from a truly holistic and spiritual experience."*
>
> *The Italian Magazine*

as well as massage, Reiki, and beauty treatments help to banish any work-related weariness. You can also while away the hours with a little wine tasting or Italian cooking classes. The inviting lounge café is shared by guests and locals and has organic breakfast buffets, snacks, drinks, and evening entertainment.

With olive groves, shady woodland, and mountains to explore, as well as neighboring villages, this is a place to be active, even if the pace stays slow. Sunflower Retreats creates a companionable group vacation for single travelers, but it works just as well for friends and couples with a fondness for yoga and passing time in the idyllic countryside. **OM**

Enjoy La Posta Vecchia

Location Rome, Lazio, Italy
Website www.relaischateaux.com/posta **Price** ⊖⊖⊖

It is a setting reminiscent of a painting by the French seventeenth-century master Claude Lorraine. La Posta Vecchia sits next to a gothic castle, the foundations of which appear to go down into the water itself. Despite the feeling of being transported back in time, it is only a short taxi journey from the center of Rome, and at night you can see the twinkling lights of the Lido di Faro, close to the city's main airport.

La Posta Vecchia was originally a guesthouse for Prince Odescalchi, who owned the castle next door; then it was a posthouse (hence the name) before being left derelict for a century. The American millionaire John Paul Getty bought it in 1965 and called in archaeologists who discovered the house was built on the site of a Roman villa. The finds they made are housed in the basement of the hotel.

The place is still filled with some of Getty's collection of antiques: A magnificent tripod table and Marie de Medici's dowry chest are just two such objects. Some of the treasures are in the bedrooms, including a seventeenth-century bed that formerly belonged to the Prince Colonna in one of the suites.

La Posta Vecchia opened as a hotel in the early 1990s, and a dining room and a swimming pool now fill the previously open arcades at either end of the building. Most of the wine is of the standard luxury Brunello and Barolo types, but there are local wines, including some top Frascatis that make you want to revise your opinion of this oft-derided grape. In the summer, you dine on the terrace, just above the lapping waves of the Mediterranean. **GMD**

▢ *The front of luxury retreat La Posta Vecchia, formerly the guesthouse of Prince Odescalchi.*

Visit the Sabine Hills

Location Lazio, Italy   **Website** www.sabina.it/index-i.html
Price ◑

Less than an hour from Rome, the Sabina landscape is a mass of rolling hills dotted with medieval villages draped on their peaks. One such tiny village is Roccantica, with its maze of cobbled streets overlooked by a medieval fortress. Every August, Roccantica hosts a four-day festival that includes falconry displays, flamethrowers, and banquets of wild boar, culminating in a colorful medieval pageant for the Procession of the Assunta. If ambling around this charming village is not energetic enough, take a full-day trek to Monte Pizzuto, which at nearly 4,265 feet (1,300 m) is the region's highest peak. Its summit rewards you with spectacular views of Monte Terminillo covered in winter snow, the Tiber River cutting through the valleys below, and—on a clear day—the Tyrrhenian Sea beyond Rome.

However, you do not need to go this high for magical views and peaceful, unspoiled hikes. Casperia, another hilltop village of honey-colored stone, towers, and turrets, is the starting point for several more gentle walks along old mule tracks and wooded trails, through forests of green oak alongside silvery olive groves and vineyards. If you prefer ambling around ancient historic buildings, be sure to stop at the abbey in Farfa or the Church of Santa Maria in Vescovio, a former cathedral whose beauty lies in its simplicity, much like Sabina itself.

Finally, before heading back to the city, treat yourself to a glass of wine in the piazzas of Poggio Mirteto or Casperia and sample the delicious local extra-virgin olive oil, another of Sabina's great secrets. **SWa**

⤷ *The village of Toffia (population 850) rests*
   on top of the Sabine hills to the north of Rome.

Enjoy Villa Dragonetti

Location Abruzzo, Italy   **Website** www.villadragonetti.it
Price 💲💲

The Hotel Villa Dragonetti is a masterpiece of Italian art. Originally built as a summer residence for the Dragonetti de Torres family, this sixteenth-century property has been carefully restored to its glorious former status. Hidden away in the small, largely undeveloped village of Paganica at the foot of Abruzzo's soaring Gran Sasso mountain range, the villa is immediately striking from the outside, with its spacious, verdant grounds, garden maze, and pool.

The architecture of the villa dates back to the sixteenth century, but the interior was redecorated in the eighteenth century by specially commissioned French artists; their dramatic frescoes of flora and fauna cover the interior of Villa Dragonetti from top to bottom, lending the place an ornate and sophisticated time-warp feel. There are just four double rooms and three junior suites available. The limited occupancy creates an authentically intimate atmosphere. Rooms are reasonably spacious, decorated with frescoes or wall paintings, and also come furnished with authentic period antiques like big dressing tables, armoires, and heavy curtains. The bathrooms are equally flamboyant and distinctive, and there are three more rooms in the guesthouse in addition to a small patio.

Villa Dragonetti's restaurant is very well known in the local area, chiefly for the regional dishes that are its specialty, although guests will also appreciate the delicious homemade breakfasts that greet them every morning. The gardens are lush enough to be used for weddings, and there is an outdoor swimming pool where guests can enjoy an aperitif before their evening meal or a dip before lunch. Dragonetti makes a beautifully refined base for skiers, hikers, or just admirers of cultured accommodation. **PS**

Stay at Sextantio

Location Abruzzo, Italy   **Website** www.sextantio.it
Price 💲💲

Sextantio Albergo Diffuso, set in a timeless medieval Italian town known as Santo Stefano Di Sessanio, is not so much a hotel as an ambitious cultural project. Just a few years ago, this tiny hamlet was all but a ghost town. Daniele Kihlgren, a Milanese entrepreneur, fell in love with the place while passing by on his motorcycle and decided to launch a rejuvenation project. His aim was to boost tourism in the area while preserving centuries-old culture and folklore.

Kihlgren and a carefully selected team of specialist archaeologists and researchers have crafted a hotel that is as close to the Middle Ages as possible. This means the rooms, hewed naturally from rock and

---

"With its architectural beauty and hilltop setting, Santo Stefano gives a real sense of going back in time."

Marc Zakian, *Town & Country* magazine

---

stone, are cavelike and come with immense, wooden doors (with long iron keys) and natural fireplaces. The bed linens are woven by hand in a local workshop, and food is cultivated locally, too. Touches like designer bathrooms, heated floors, and remote-controlled lighting have also been added to ensure comfort.

The hotel has functioning medieval-style workshops, a Middle Ages–style restaurant, and exhibition spaces. Outside the Sextantio complex, life goes on in the village much as it has done for all those centuries. **PS**

➡ *Sextantio has been sensitively restored to resemble how it would have looked not 50, but 500 years ago.*

Unwind at La Masseria San Domenico

Location Puglia, Italy **Website** www.masseriasandomenico.com
Price 🌜🌛

"You're slathered in mud and placed in a plastic pod. Warm jets of water help detoxify your skin."

Tatler

Indulge in luxurious seclusion at this lavishly styled five-star resort on the Puglian coast, deep in Italy's heel. The dazzling white, fifteenth-century *masseria* is a restored farmhouse with an ancient watchtower where the Knights of Malta once defended themselves against Ottoman attack.

There is a magical Moorish feel to it all. The thirty-two rooms and sixteen suites have wrought-iron beds and luxurious soft furnishings. French doors open straight onto the olive groves, and mesmerizing views look out across the lush estate to the dazzling Adriatic. In the center of the manicured grounds, surrounded by olive trees, sits a magnificent free-form saltwater swimming pool fringed with rocks. Fifteen minutes away is a stretch of private beach with chic cabanas—just a short hop on the free golf cart shuttle.

The spa offers thalassotherapy to detoxify and cleanse the body and soul, using seawater and mineral-packed seaweed from the Adriatic. There are tennis courts, a water gym, and an eighteen-hole golf course as well as windsurfing and diving. Meanwhile, around Puglia there are caves, stalactites, and rock formations at Castellana Grotte, near Bari, to explore. The baroque town of Lecce is the nearest big city and has plenty of buzz, whereas the nearby hilltop towns of Ostuni and Martina Franca offer a wealth of historic churches, cafés, and art galleries.

Dress up for dinner at the San Domenico restaurant, with its dramatic columns and arched stone ceiling. Once used as an olive press, the dining room now serves ingredients straight from the resort's farm. **AD**

🔲 *The gleaming white stone of the restored farmhouse keeps the* masseria *cool even in the hot summers.*

Discover Puglia by Car

Location Puglia, Italy   **Website** www.viaggiareinpuglia.it/hp/en
Price $

Puglia is Italy's heel. Surrounded by ocean—this is where the Adriatic and Ionian Seas meet—it is a land of whitewashed houses perched on spectacular cliffs, of olive groves and vineyards, of monumental cathedrals, and quaint, cobbled lanes. Mass tourism has never made it here (do not forget your phrasebook) and, with its panoramic views and regular points of interest—from historic shipyards to white-sand beaches and family-owned eateries serving handmade pasta—this is the perfect place for a road trip away from the crowds.

There are many routes to choose between, but those with a penchant for sea views may like to take a coastal drive starting in Margherita di Savoia, known for its salt mines and salt mine museum. Admire views over the Strait of Otranto as you continue to Trani, a historic fishing port: Visit the dramatic cathedral before heading to the harbor for some freshly caught fish. Next stop is Molfetta where the lively beaches attract the surfers. Monopoli is another attractive old town a little farther southwest.

Make time to stroll around Brindisi, which bristles with ancient brickwork, before admiring the prehistoric cave paintings near Otranto, Italy's most easterly town. (Gothic novel enthusiasts should pack Horace Walpole's *The Castle of Otranto* as their vacation reading.) Around the cusp of Italy's heel you reach Gallipoli—not to be confused with the World War I battleground. This Gallipoli sits on a breathtaking stretch of beach, and its old quarter perches on a limestone island linked to the mainland by a sixteenth-century bridge. Finally, drive up the Ionian coast, whose beaches have crystal-clear water. The villages around Ginosa are particularly picturesque. **PE**

Stay at Parco del Vaglio

Location Puglia, Italy   **Website** www.cvtravel.co.uk
Price $$$

Puglia's landscape is distinctively hot and arid, with plains covered with lines of olive groves. Its distinctive architectural feature is the "trulli" house. These dwellings are mysterious, whitewashed, circular stone buildings with conical black slate roofs, like windmills without sails. Most date from the fifteenth century, and they are believed to have been a popular way of avoiding taxes. Trulli houses were constructed without concrete and could be dismantled to evade housing tax inspectors, then rebuilt when the coast was clear.

Despite these humble origins, thousands of the hobbitlike dwellings have survived. The best collection of trulli can be found in the World Heritage–listed

> *"[Alberobello] is of outstanding universal value . . . an exceptional example of a form of building."*
>
> **UNESCO World Heritage Committee**

town of Alberobello, where there are more than 1,500 examples, many still inhabited. Tourists flock there making it very busy, especially in summer; a trullo in the countryside provides a more authentic escape.

Parco del Vaglio is one of the very best—a gorgeous group of carefully restored trulli that have been combined to form one big self-catering vacation house that sleeps up to eight. Or it can be partitioned to form smaller units. Within the traditional thick stone walls, the single-story house stays cool in summer without air-conditioning. There are original stone floors and high vaulted ceilings, too, plus modern luxuries and en suite showers. **SH**

Relax at La Sommità

Location Puglia, Italy   **Website** www.lasommita.it
Price 💲💲

Hidden away in a maze of tiny alleyways at the top of whitewashed Ostuni is the luxe design den La Sommità. The historic palazzo looks out across olive groves and down to the glittering blue Adriatic Sea. It might be the ultimate in Italian chic, but it has still held on to sixteenth-century features such as cool vaults, twisting staircases, stone walls, and sculpted columns.

Guests are cocooned in rooms with cream-colored walls and fabulous furniture—the minimalist interiors are from Milanese boutique Culti, which has a stake in the hotel. If you like what you see, you can buy it and have it shipped home. Bag a room with a terrace and views out to sea for a private breakfast or evening

> "Ostuni is a circular town built around a hill and La Sommità is right at the top."

Condé Nast Traveler

aperitif. There is a winter sunroom to relax in when the temperature is not soaring outside and a subterranean spa in the old wine cellars, which offers bespoke treatments to ease away the aches and pains of traveling. Best of all is the dining room serving authentic Puglian cuisine. The locally caught fish is cooked to perfection, and wines and pastas are second to none. Grab a table outside in the Spanish garden, among orange blossom and olive trees.

La Sommità does not have a pool, but guests instead have access to a private strip of beach. Horseback riding and biking are available, and Italian cooking classes can also be arranged. **AD**

Stay at Torre Camigliati

Location Calabria, Italy   **Website** www.torrecamigliati.it
Price 💲

Although many of Calabria's old baronial buildings now lie in ruins, Torre Camigliati, an eighteenth-century hunting lodge set in the heart of the Sila Grande region, has been lovingly restored to its former splendor. Part hotel, part cultural center, and part literary park, the lodge principally celebrates the life and work of British author Norman Douglas, who wrote the nineteenth-century Grand Tour travelogue *Old Calabria*. Surrounded by a 200-acre (80-ha) private estate, there is a fantastic sense of intimacy and tranquility about the place.

On the first floor are several reception rooms resplendent with nineteenth-century furniture. Twelve guest rooms have been similarly refurbished in period style, with iron beds, antique wardrobes, and views onto the park outside conjuring up a timeless ambience. More modern are the six mini-apartments nearby, which have been converted from workers' cottages and offer self-contained accommodation for couples and families. The public areas continue the lodge's grand theme, with large living rooms and fireplaces, an attractive breakfast room, and a spacious hall that is occasionally used for concerts and exhibitions. On the ground floor lies the visitor center: a vast selection of books on the Grand Tour, exhibitions by photographers such as Mimmo Jodice, and a shop selling Calabrian crafts.

The immediate surroundings are perfect for contemplative hikes and quiet strolls; press a little farther and you will discover a network of medieval villages, Byzantine churches, seductive countryside, ancient Albanian communities, and even evidence of Grecian settlements. Guided walks and excursions to nearby places of interest are happily arranged. **PS**

Explore the Aeolian Islands

Location Sicily, Italy   **Website** www.italiantourism.com/island6a.html
Price ●●

Smoldering volcanoes, bubbling mud baths, and steaming fumaroles—this has always been a volatile part of the world. These islands are seven volcanic sisters—Lipari, Vulcano, Salina, Panarea, Stromboli, Filicudi, and Alicudi—that lie off the coast of Sicily, and they are hot in the literal sense of the word.

Stromboli and Vulcano are active volcanoes, and volcanic activity is everywhere on this archipelago, but each island has its own character. On some, volcanoes with smoldering craters are staggered by canyons. Some have black-sand beaches, whereas others are sugar-white; some are barren, others verdant. There are splintered coasts that fall sheer to the sea with rocks that nature has modeled into strange shapes next to the deep, impossibly blue sea.

In addition to varying terrain, each island has a different vibe. The jet set favors glamorous Panarea, rammed with super-yachts in summer, whereas Alicudi is a rustic island of donkeys, where the eighty or so permanent residents are said to detest the sight of one another. Salina is the most verdant, and stunning Stromboli has little coves of black sand tucked into lava crags. Unpretentious Lipari, a place of rustic restaurants and flower-strung gullies, has a year-round population and a sizable town. There, you can eat dishes with delicious local ingredients such as wild fennel, cherry tomatoes, and endless varieties of local fish in its cobbled streets. If you can stand the sulfuric stench in Vulcano, you must wallow with all the visiting Italians in the baths said to cure joint diseases and neuralgia and do wonders for the skin. **LB**

↗ *The island of Lipari, the largest of the Aeolian Islands, located off the coast of Sicily.*

"They are a mixed bag of rough and sparkling jewels that attract an equally mixed crowd."

Condé Nast Traveler

Explore Las Islas Cíes

Location Galicia, Spain   **Website** www.turgalicia.es
Price 🕙

The wild and stunning Atlantic coastline of Spain surely has to be the ultimate place to go for dramatic stretches of unspoiled beaches. Just north of Portugal, the Galicia region is where you will find Las Islas Cíes. An archipelago off the northwest coast by the city of Vigo, it was once a pirate haunt and nowadays is an uninhabited and pristine national park area that is open to the public only in the summer months.

Take the ferry from Baiona to spend some long, lazy summer days on the Praia das Rodas, a perfect crescent of soft, pale sand backed by small dunes sheltering a calm lagoon of crystal-clear sea. It is the closest you will find to a Caribbean idyll this side of the Atlantic, with turquoise water, white sand, and shady pine trees lining the shore. A campsite has views out to sea, but it is not all Robinson Crusoe fare. There is a good restaurant with fantastic seafood in this tranquil setting, although you will have to carry your bags and camping gear more than half a mile (1 km) from the ferry to the campsite.

On the western side, towering granite cliffs take the full force of the pounding Atlantic, surrounded by numerous caves. Three main islands—with two linked by a sandbar—are fringed by smaller islets and rocky outcrops. Although a big draw here is the quiet beach, the wildlife also attracts a fair share of visitors. Inland, the islands are covered with pine and eucalyptus trees, dotted with purple foxgloves and white asphodels.

Spend the day wandering marked trails and looking for wildlife, then laze on the beach. There is even a designated nudist beach for those so inclined. **AD**

← *Las Islas Cíes archipelago forms part of a protected nature reserve that is home to colonies of seabirds.*

Stay at Hostal dos Reis Católicos

Location Galicia, Spain
Website www.parador.es/en **Price** 😊😊

The Hostal dos Reis Católicos is the king of all Spain's paradors. These eighty-five state-funded hotels and hostels are housed in some of the country's most important historic buildings. The Católicos sits on the Plazo do Obradoiro, flanked by the equally spectacular Romanesque cathedral and military college.

Said to be the oldest hotel in the world, it began life in 1499 as a hospital for the thousands of pilgrims who converged on the holy city of Santiago de Compostela (now a UNESCO World Heritage site). In keeping with 1,000 years of tradition, modern pilgrims are still given free food and lodging if they complete the Way of

> *"Even if I were not able to find my sword, the pilgrimage . . . was going to help me to find myself."*
>
> Paulo Coelho, *The Pilgrimage*

St. James (whose remains are said to lie beneath the cathedral). Today, apart from modern bathrooms and some luxuries, the building looks much as it must have done originally. Delicious food is served in the atmospheric restaurant that was once a stable. Looking at its cloisters, manicured herb gardens, and four-poster beds, you could be forgiven for thinking you had stepped back 500 years. If further evidence were needed of the hotel's grand status, kings, queens, and presidents have all graced its hallowed halls. **TW**

⬅ *The 500-year-old courtyard of the Hostal dos Reis Católicos in Santiago de Compostela.*

Relax at Hotel Posada del Valle

Location Asturias, Spain
Website www.posadadelvalle.com **Price** 😊😊

Luxury and pampering are resolutely not the name of the game at this characterful farmhouse nestling at the foot of the Picos Mountains in northern Spain. But if stunning countryside, strong environmental values, extensive walking, and homegrown food are high on your list, Hotel Posada del Valle will fit the bill.

Owners Nigel and Joann Burch converted this stone-and-wood farmhouse to a traditional twelve-bedroom hotel in the mid-1990s. He is a renowned horticulturist and she a chef—a winning combination for a hotel operation dedicated to serving fine, locally grown food. The house sits in its own EEC-registered, 18-acre (7-ha) organic farm, complete with goats, a breed of rare Xaldas sheep, free-running chickens, and two Asturian ponies. The farm also has traditional hay and wildflower meadows, and produces cider.

Early in 2008, the business won the Spanish Organic Food and Biodiversity award for its restaurant, which serves delicious meals sourced, where possible, from ingredients grown on the farm. Guests are treated to fresh apple juice and homemade bread at breakfast time. The hotel is tucked away in rolling, dazzlingly green countryside and the nearest town with restaurants is a forty-five-minute hike, but guests are well catered for by the imaginative evening menu.

It is entirely possible to enjoy a wonderfully peaceful vacation here without a car—Nigel and Joann have compiled at least a week's worth of walks starting from the hotel, and taxis are available for those wanting to stray farther afield. Within a twenty-minute drive, the magnificent, unsung beaches of northern Asturias are there for the taking, and the lovely city of Oviedo is ninety minutes away by FEVE train. **LC**

Stay at Marqués de Riscal

Location Basque Country, Spain
Website www.starwoodhotels.com   **Price** 💲💲

Love it or hate it, Frank Ghery's makeover of the Spanish Marqués de Riscal winery has dragged the tiny village of Elciego into the future. There is a feeling of exclusivity as you walk the hotel's red carpet toward the sleek rooms, where pale maple wood, leather touches, and dark marble bathrooms ooze luxury. The bedrooms are definitely twenty-first century, complete with sleek Bang and Olufsen flat-screen televisions. Ghery's personal touch is everywhere. He handpicked the interiors: everything from the Alvar Aalto inspired furniture and the bright red Ligne Roset "pop" chairs.

Take a tour of the ancient winery, dating back to 1858, and do not miss the extraordinary "cathedral of wine." Slightly spooky, the "crypt" contains around 16,000 bottles from every single year since its first vintage. Bottles lie covered in dust, like forgotten treasures. To sample the wine while taking in the view, head to the hotel's fabulous rooftop lounge. Overlooking Elciego's medieval cathedral, it is the perfect spot to try one of the 1,000 bottles from the Vinoteca bar, a gigantic library of Riojas, Rosados, and white Ruedas. For dinner, try the impeccable gourmet restaurant. Simple, yet sophisticated, it has won several awards for its croquettes, and the meatballs with truffle are a must.

After that you can relax at the Caudalie Vinotherapy spa, with its beautiful pool and serene lounge. Soak in a giant barrel-shaped whirlpool tub filled with a potent mix of crushed grape seed while sipping a restorative grape infusion, of course. Who knew that there were so many ways one could enjoy vino? **RCA**

← *Slightly surreal, Ghery's distinctive titanium wave-roof stands out proudly amid the Riojan vineyards.*

Unwind at Mas de Torrent Hotel and Spa

Location Catalonia, Spain   **Website** www.mastorrent.com   **Price** ⊖⊖

This former *masia* or farmhouse is the kind of place where you can hide away for days. Sitting deep in the Catalonian countryside between Barcelona and Girona, the hotel has managed to retain enough of its original characteristics to enable you to imagine the sprawling eighteenth-century rural home it must have been. An olive press still stands in what is now the games room, whereas each of the ten self-contained bungalows has antique furnishings that add to the charm.

The hotel spills out into the expansive grounds, where orange trees line paths leading to each of the bungalows. They have everything you need to feel perfectly at home, including two bathrooms, an enormous bedroom, and a separate living room. Seven of these bungalows, the luxury suites, also have a private pool. The hotel even provides a thoughtful selection of books for guests to dip into while they lounge in the sunshine, and the array of toiletries in the bathrooms are ideal for pampering. If your tension is more deeply rooted, visit the Mas Spa or arrange for a masseuse to come to your room and treat you to a thorough full-body massage.

So much relaxation can build up an appetite, so order room service or venture over to the gastronomic restaurant, where you can indulge in the extraordinary "tasting" menu, sampling an aperitif, four starters, a fish dish, meat dish, predessert, and dessert, all created using the wealth of fresh seasonal produce available in the region. The hotel also has its own herb and vegetable gardens.

After so much feasting, you may feel that some exercise is in order the next day, so head to the hotel's vast outdoor pool for a few lengths, play tennis, or borrow a bike from the hotel and head out to explore the surrounding countryside. **JED**

⬆ *The yellow-stone hotel maintains the look and feel of the eighteenth-century farmhouse it once was.*

Stay at Hostal Sa Rascassa

Location Catalonia, Spain   **Website** www.hostalsarascassa.com   **Price** 🟢🟢

Hostal Sa Rascassa counters all the preconceptions that great escapes should be expensive and luxurious. A wonderful getaway, Sa Rascassa has only five simple rooms, and none of them have telephones. Spread out under a canopy of pines, the hotel was built in 1916, but has the feel of an ancient landmark. It's just 130 feet (40 m) from the seashore at Cala d'Aiguafreda, and guests come here to soak up the stunning scenery, from the Pyrénées all the way down to the empty beaches. There are no bars or discos for miles around; this is blissful seclusion at its very best.

Decorated in Mediterranean colors with traditional oak furniture, rooms are cozy and have heating for cooler autumn months. The restaurant offers a fine selection of Spanish cuisine with distinctly local touches, from Iberian pork and grilled cockles to freshly caught sardines, sea bass, and monkfish. Eat inside or take a table out in the courtyard, sitting under twinkling lights strung between the pine trees.

Find a quiet corner looking out across the cove and take in the views with a glass of Rioja and a bowl of olives. It is a tranquil delight.

At the end of a narrow road in an idyllic bay, just a few miles from Begur, Hostal Sa Rascassa is the perfect base from which to explore the coastline. Follow walking trails around the rocks, go swimming in the sea in warmer summer months, and explore the local region. This is the real Spain, a million miles away from packed beaches and rowdy bars. It is actually where Barcelonans come for weekends. Visitors can wander the cobbled streets of Begur shopping for antiques or browse the work of local artists at the weekly craft market. Drive on to find the charming medieval towns of Pals and Peratallada and Salvador Dalí's museum at Figueres. It is like taking a step back in time. **AD**

⬆ *The hostal's restaurant opens onto a charming courtyard that is illuminated with lanterns.*

Enjoy Parador Castillo de Santa Catalina

Location Andalucía, Spain
Website www.paradores.es   **Price** $$

> *"You half expect Charlton Heston as El Cid to come riding out of legend for a beer at the pool bar."*

David Clement-Davies, *Guardian*

Overlooking the Andalucían city of Jaen, this parador is a hotel with atmosphere. Its public rooms have vaulted ceilings and arches that stretch to more than 65 feet (20 m) high. Many of its forty-five bedrooms harbor four-poster canopied beds, are hung with tapestries, and feature balconies with extraordinary views out across the olive groves and rocky mountains of the Sierra Morena and Sierra Nevada. The dimly lit dining room keeps the Arabic architectural theme, and serves up local specialties such as *ajo blanco* (cold garlic soup); *ensalada de perdiz* (partridge salad); *pipirrana* (mixed salad); and *morcilla en caldera* (stewed black pudding). If you need a little exercise to work all that off, there is also an outdoor swimming pool.

The hotel is not as old as it seems. Although it butts up against the ancient *castillo*, the hostelry dates back only to the 1960s. The castle was built during Moorish rule, but fell into Christian hands when Ferdinand III's troops stormed it in 1246. For the next two centuries, the Moors continued to attack, but the Christians held firm, building their own fortress and chapel on the site. The Christian monarchs, Ferdinand and Isabel, finally threw the Moors out of Spain in 1492, but this did not mean that peace would reign over Jaen. Napoleon invaded in 1810, and threats during the Carlist wars of the late nineteenth century inspired more fortifications.

It is all quiet now, though. Indeed, the buildings and their lush surrounding gardens exude an ambience of such peace and serenity that General de Gaulle chose this escape in which to write his memoirs. **PE**

⬑ *The parador is on the site of a thirteenth-century Arabic fortress, high on Santa Catalina hill.*

Stay at Hospes Palacio del Bailio Spa

Location Córdoba, Andalucía, Spain
Website www.hospes.es   **Price** 💲💲

Understated luxury is the order of the day at Hospes Palacio del Bailio. Hidden among the narrow backstreets of the ancient city of Córdoba, this beautiful hotel is housed in a sixteenth-century mansion that, by turns, has also served as a military headquarters and a stables.

Like many Andalucían buildings, it is set around a central courtyard in the Moorish style, this one filled with the tangy scent of citrus from the immaculately pruned orange and lemon trees and the soothing trickle of an eighteenth-century stone fountain. As well as being stunning, the hotel conceals a rare treasure: the remains of a Roman house, discovered by

> *"This hotel is . . . 'the evolutionary surprise that allows you to express your inner self.'"*
>
> *Condé Nast Traveler*

chance by a previous owner. Today the remains lie underneath the five-star restaurant's glass floor and are lit up to spectacular effect at night.

A dip in the infinity pool is the perfect antidote to the effects of the hot southern European sun. The Bodyna spa is a major feature of the hotel, part of it situated in a courtyard flanked by stone columns, with a further three spas on the lower ground floor built around original Roman thermal baths. Just a fifteen-minute walk away you will find the wondrous Córdoba *mezquita*, the most magnificent mosque built by the Moors and rightly deserving of its designation as a UNESCO World Heritage site. **TW**

Visit Coto Doñana

Location Andalucía, Spain
Website spainforvisitors.com/sections/donana.htm   **Price** 💲

Wildlife-watching can be frustrating at times. No matter how meticulous your preparations, you can never guarantee that the animals are going to put in an appearance. What makes a trip to the Parque Nacional del Coto Doñana such a rewarding and ultimately stress-free experience is that the sheer abundance of wildlife here means the odds of spotting something of interest are very much in your favor. With the park home to more than 300,000 birds, you would be unlucky not to see anything noteworthy.

The park's name derives from the famously antisocial Duchess Doña Ana de Silva y Mendoza, who built a residence for herself here, as far from civilization as possible. Doñana encompasses more than 500 square miles (1,300 sq km) of coastal territory, made up mostly of sand dunes, marshland, and lakes that provide perfect living and breeding conditions for around 125 bird species—among them some of the few surviving pairs of the rare Iberian eagle. Another 125 species, including red kites, bee eaters, hoopoes, and golden orioles, are migratory visitors, not to mention tasty treats for one of the park's other celebrated residents, the pardel lynx, for whom Doñana is one of its last remaining refuges.

You can tour parts of the park on foot, along trails that link the main visitor centers—where there are exhibitions on the local wildlife—and take you past marshes and lakes where hides have been set up for observing the wildlife. For an in-depth exploration of the park, however, your best bet is to prebook a four-wheel-drive tour with a guide, who will be able to take you into some of the park's more inaccessible areas to the very best wildlife-watching vantage points. **JF**

Explore Zuheros

Location Andalucía, Spain   **Website** www.zuheros.com.es
Price ❶❷

It is a vision of Spain that you will remember for years to come: one of Andalucía's most celebrated *pueblos blancos* (white villages) nestled in the rocky mountains, with blue sky above and olive groves leading to it. Zuheros, in the center of the Cordoba/Malaga/ Granada triangle, is one of the best examples of the country's Moorish villages, with narrow streets and a history dating back to pre-Roman smugglers.

The town has fewer than 1,000 residents and only a handful of inns and hotels, but that has not stopped it from attracting tourists of all stripes. Little local restaurant Los Palancos, Llana 43, serves hearty, rustic dishes—including young goat, rabbit, and suckling pig—and attracts those looking for tranquility and a hideaway in the Andalucían mountains. Hard to believe, really, that it is only an hour and a half from the fleshpots of Malaga and Marbella.

Zuheros is on the fringes of the Sierra Subbetica natural park, which has great walking potential, and the old railroad running through the village has been transformed into a walking and bicycling route. Just 2.5 miles (4 km) uphill from the village, the big must-see is Las Cuevas de las Murcielagos (cave of bats), which is full of stalactites and stalagmites as well as its famous mammals. There is plenty of evidence of Neolithic life in the caves of the region, too, including cave paintings. Las Balanchares goat cheese factory in the center of the village is internationally known, and the cheese is very popular grilled as a tapa dish in the area and beyond. Bring some home, with a bottle of local olive oil, to prolong that vacation feeling. **LD**

➡ *The village of Zuheros in the mountains of Andalucía is one of the best examples of a* pueblo blanco.

Unwind at Trasierra

Location Seville, Andalucía, Spain
Website www.trasierra.co.uk **Price** 🌓🌓🌓

If the prospect of your average health retreat conjures up images of sadistic boot camps and cold showers, then think again. Trasierra is a sixteenth-century, family-run hotel that has been designed for people who appreciate beauty, comfort, good food, and peace. You can also come here to kick start a new healthy lifestyle, as twice a year Trasierra is taken over by In:Spa, experts in residential health retreats

The sun-scorched Sierra Morena mountains form a wild, romantic landscape of olive and chestnut trees where wild boar roam and bulls shade themselves beneath branches. In a remote valley lies Trasierra, amid 3,000 acres (1,210 ha) of olive and orange groves

---

"There is nothing ordinary to be found at Trasierra; this is a place that nurtures dreams."

Independent

---

and consisting of a collection of whitewashed buildings linked by terra-cotta walkways. Archways lead to carefully tended aromatic gardens, and inky water shimmers in a deep pool with red-earth vistas beyond. Inside, the rooms are decorated in a blend of English country house and traditional Spanish style.

The day starts early with a poolside yoga class as the sun rises behind the mountains. At breakfast time, feast on delicious fruit salad, porridge, thick smoothies, and freshly squeezed juices. Then a morning of hiking in the wild mountains will set you up just in time for a light, detoxifying lunch. Afternoons are spent having massages, reflexology, or simply lazing by the pool. **HA**

Stay at Hotel Cortijo Fain

Location Andalucía, Spain
Website www.arcosgardens.com **Price** 🌓🌓

This boutique hotel may be compact, but the bedrooms themselves are as spacious as some city-center apartments. Even the smallest rooms have sitting areas that open onto immense bathrooms with deep bath and separate wet rooms. Shutters mean you can leave the windows open all night and enjoy the scent of air softly scented by eucalyptus trees. However, this will mean you are likely to be woken by birdsong, before rolling over and giving in to a few more hours' sleep in the extremely comfortable beds.

The setting exudes romance, with each room in the *cortijo* (farmhouse) named after one of the many poets inspired by nearby Arcos de la Frontera, the prettiest of Andalucía's *pueblos blancos* (white villages). The hotel is based around a 300-year-old central courtyard, complete with a fountain and bright bougainvillea. Many of the hotel rooms have windows on two sides, enhancing their natural lightness and allowing guests to take in views of the courtyard as well as gardens planted with hundreds of ancient olive trees. These trees shade the pool so that while you swim you may hear the occasional plink of an olive dropping onto the surrounding flagstones.

The design is quintessentially Andalucían, with the *cortijo*'s original architecture preserved as much as possible, and the original stables converted to a charming tapas bar. Further accommodation is available in the town-house hotel suites, which can be found between the first and ninth holes of the eighteen-hole golf course. The course itself offers outstanding views of Arcos de la Frontera. Prime time for this is in the late evening, when you can borrow a golf cart and drive out as the sun sets, watching rabbits and grouse scattering across the greens. **JED**

Relax at Escondrijo

Location Andalucía, Spain
Website www.escondrijo.com   **Price** 🅢🅢

Vejer de la Frontera is a whitewashed Spanish *pueblo* (house) that seems to have stood still in time. Tucked into the village's maze of cobbled lanes sits Escondrijo, a boutique hotel with just five elegantly appointed suites. The house has been built from the remains of the ruined Vera Cruz Chapel, and some parts of the house date back to Moorish days, as can be seen from the galleried interior courtyard and twelfth-century well.

The rooms are both comfortable and contemporary, and each one is decorated with its own particular style. The high ceiling creates a sensation of great space in one open-plan room; another room has a more sultry feel with shuttered windows and walls

> *"[Escondrijo] is not just some self-catering duplex . . . it is a dream of the Spanish Golden Age."*
>
> Juliet Kinsman, *Observer*

and drapes in gloriously wanton red. The upper-floors have private terraces with spectacular mile-long views.

Away from the house, guests can drive to the dune-backed beaches of the Costa de la Luz in minutes. Activities include windsurfing and kite surfing, scuba diving, and whale- and dolphin-watching. You can walk through the pine trees that perch on the cliffs above the crashing waves, or ride horses through the surf. You can also hire mountain bikes, play a round of golf, or indulge in a spot of bird-watching. For the best of Spanish culture, Cadiz, Jerez, and Seville are all just a day trip away, so guests can tour the sights and still be safely back on the Escondrijo terrace for sundown. **PE**

Enjoy Casita La Laguna

Location Andalucía, Spain
Website www.vivatarifa.com/laguna   **Price** 🅢🅢

This secret hideaway for two is in a truly beautiful location. Looking out across the straits to Morocco, there is just your loved one and the sea for company. The tiny *casita*, south of Tarifa, is hidden among the sand dunes and pine trees at the end of a narrow track, and romantic seclusion is what it is all about. Cuddle up and enjoy the views across to North Africa and the lights of Tangiers glittering in the distance.

Inside, the interior is cool and uncluttered, decorated with Moroccan-style lanterns and ceramics. High windows let light flood in, and a wood-burning stove offers heat on cooler nights. The *casita* is also eco-friendly, with electricity from wind and solar energy and water from the nearby spring. Outside there is a wonderful terrace where you can sit to watch the blistering sunset, and the sheltered garden leads to the deserted beach for sunbathing and feasting on picnic lunches far away from the crowds. If you hanker to do more, the *casita* is attached to a farm, where you can hire horses and ride through the pine forest and along the beach to the fishing village of Bolonia.

From the *casita* it is a fifteen-minute drive to Tarifa, where it is easy to spend a pleasant day wandering the winding streets, stopping to sample traditional tapas, before exploring the castle and harbor. Alternatively, take a day trip across the water to Morocco, only forty-five minutes by hydrofoil. At night, wander down the road to the local fish restaurant or cook dinner for two and eat outside on the terrace under a star-studded sky. The local market in Tarifa is a great place to stock up on supplies, from freshly caught fish to locally grown herbs and vegetables. Then fall asleep to the sound of Atlantic rollers pounding on the beach. This *casita* has to be the very definition of tranquility. **AD**

Stay at Hoopoe Yurt Hotel

Location Andalucía, Spain **Website** www.yurthotel.com/about.html
Price ⊙⊙

"Life in a yurt is as romantic as you imagine it to be, but that doesn't make it easy."

Tiffanie Darke, *The Sunday Times*

"Getting back to nature couldn't be easier at this solar-powered retreat," enthused a journalist for the United Kingdom's *Independent* newspaper. Tucked away in a spectacular corner of Andalucía, the yurts bask in 7 acres (3 ha) of olive groves and cork oak trees, nestled twenty minutes' walk away from the picturesque village of Cortes de la Frontera.

Private views of the mountains are part of the deal for guests staying here. Each yurt—and there are now five—boasts spectacular views of the blue-hazed Grazalema Mountains, plus its own private meadow, equipped with hammock, outdoor furniture, and private bathroom. Anyone deterred by the thought of alfresco showering and trips to the outside compost toilet could do well to suspend judgment. Your flower-strewn meadow really is private.

The Hoopoe Yurt Hotel is for anyone who relishes spending time outside, far away from modern trappings yet within walking distance of bars and shops. It is difficult to imagine a more restorative sanctuary. You will wake to the sounds of goat bells plus an army of resident birds: sparrow hawks, turtle doves, and honey buzzards. It may all be wonderfully "back to nature," and impressively environmentally friendly, but the yurts are large and comfortable, with indoor furniture in case the weather falters.

Foodies will rejoice. Young British owners Ed and Henrietta organize a three-course, locally sourced, mostly organic meal with wine four days a week. Dinner is enjoyed under a pergola, lit by Chinese lanterns, perched by the swimming pool. **LC**

⬉ *Comfort is a big part of any stay here. The yurts all have double beds and private bathrooms.*

Experience Los Castaños

Location Andalucía, Spain   **Website** www.loscastanos.com
Price 🌓🌓

Los Castaños is a five-bedroom hotel in Cartajima, one of the *pueblos blancos* (white villages) behind Marbella and Ronda. Here the hills wind steep and scenic. Vertiginous gorges and stomach-lurching switchbacks vie for your attention with mind-boggling views. The mountain roads here were once famous for their bandits.

Survive the road and it is relaxation all the way. The mother and daughter owners aimed to create a laid-back, rural idyll, and they have succeeded. The rooftop terrace with its plunge pool, the plush sofas and open fire, and the massage room all ensure that your stress levels plummet. Should guests insist that they achieve something during their sojourn here, there are sketch

---

"… you begin to appreciate the harmony of an older, slower, and more peaceful way of life."

Scotsman

---

pads in each room. If the environs inspire you, Los Castaños hosts painting vacations, with tuition from a local artist. There are writing courses, too. Alternatively, a local ornithologist will take you on a bird-watching walk—four species of eagle inhabit this area. Energetic guests can hike the walking paths that link the seven villages of the Alto Genal; trails run through chestnut groves and over limestone crags. Or why not swim in the river, or ride horses in Ronda? The brave can try out caving or rock-climbing in the Los Riscos. At the end of the day, guests return to the hotel to eat a candlelit dinner and compare stories as they dig into Andalucían and African flavors. **PE**

Relax at La Cazalla

Location Andalucía, Spain   **Website** www.lacazalladeronda.com
Price 🌓🌓

Ronda is a much-visited beautiful town in Spain's Andalucía region. Its whitewashed old quarter stands along the precipice of a dramatically deep gorge crossed by an eighteenth-century stone bridge. Just ten minutes from the bridge, down a rough track, you will find the most secluded place to stay—a tiny and romantic six-room hotel in an undisturbed valley surrounded by mountains and oak forests.

Owner Maria Ruiz looked long and hard for a site to build her hotel, and she has used the secret spot to create a charming rustic hideaway that feels more like a wonderful private house than a hotel. It is certainly a total escape. You can either relax, slumped among the cushions, drapes, Moorish tiles, and antiques, or wander the hills all around. Some guests play boules in the garden; others simply sit in the quiet and read.

The hotel is quirkily luxurious, with arabesque arches, whitewashed walls, old paintings and books, fans, and mosquito nets. There is a hidden outdoor swimming pool but no televisions, cell phone reception, or air-conditioning. It is like staying with a lovely old aunt. You will find a bowl of walnuts by the fireplace, a sprig of scented rosemary on your pillow. A well-stocked fridge in your room includes cold meat, cheese, wine, and beer. Whichever way you look, there are great rural vistas, and there are also binoculars in each room, for gazing at the view and spotting the beautiful local birdlife.

La Cazalla has no menus, but the fine dinners are cooked with the very best ingredients that the kitchen staff can find in the local markets, plus their own award-winning homegrown herbs, vegetables, and fruit. It is most enjoyable to eat outside savoring the silence by flickering candlelight. **SH**

Visit the Generalife Gardens of Alhambra

Location Granada, Andalucía, Spain   **Website** www.alhambra.org
Price 💲

"A pearl set in emeralds" is how one Moorish poet described the ancient Alhambra complex in Granada, Spain. Once the lavish home of the Nasrid sultans in the thirteenth century, this walled complex includes a stunning former palace and the Alcazaba Fortress. Surrounding it are some of the world's most beautiful, traditional Islamic gardens.

Gardens are considered a vital element to the Islamic way of life. They are seen as an escape from the baking heat of the desert, and water plays a vital part in their design. Flowing water not only soothes the soul, but also cools the stone buildings. The gardens of Alhambra are known as *Generalife*, which translates to "garden of paradise," "orchard," or "garden of feasts."

Built in the fourteenth century, the Patio de la Acequia lies at the heart of the gardens, a long, thin irrigation trough decorated along one side with more than a dozen fountains, each sending a thin stream of water arcing through the air. Continue through the northern portico to the Patio de los Cipreses. Here you will find a rectangular pool framed by a low, neatly manicured hedge. In the center sits a second, smaller pond, with a stone fountain trickling in the middle. The design is unexpected and perfectly symmetrical.

Most of the gardens follow this same ordered, geometric feel. You will find box hedges sculpted into exotic shapes, from turrets to triangles to perfectly formed stars. Every corner reveals another beautiful view; every courtyard holds another stunning example of Arabic art and architecture. **JP**

← *These fountains line the beautiful Moorish Patio de la Acequia in the gardens of Alhambra.*

Stay at the Parador de Granada

Location Granada, Andalucía, Spain
Website www.parador.es   **Price** 💲💲

Few hotels in the world can rival the magnificent surroundings of the Parador de Granada. This popular, state-run hotel chain has successfully converted close to one hundred historic buildings into grandiose places to stay for tourists, yet all are surpassed by the beauty and wealth of history that exists at Granada.

The building resides in the heart of the majestic Alhambra, the vast fortress complex that stands imperiously against the backdrop of the Sierra Nevada. Built in the fourteenth century, it formed part of a palace and mosque at a time when Granada was one of the most flourishing and envied cities in the Islamic

> ## "It fulfils one of the romantic traveler's greatest dreams: to sleep inside the walls of the Alhambra."
>
> *Condé Nast Traveler*

world. With the Christian reconquest of the city in 1492, the building was converted into a Franciscan monastery and chapel. Subsequent years saw the building slide into dilapidation, leaving scant trace of the original features, yet the appearance today is one of Moorish-inspired architectural touches, soothing fountains, and gardens flourishing with wisteria. Numerous works of art and classical furniture line the cloister and interior rooms, from which all windows offer breathtaking views, especially those above the Albaicin. **SG**

⬅ *The monastery was the first holy place built in Granada on the orders of the Catholic monarchy.*

Discover the Cuevas Pedro Antonio de Alarcón

Location Andalucía, Spain
Website www.andalucia.com/cavehotel   **Price** 💲

You do not need to be a caveman to live in a cave, the residents of Guadix, near Granada, are keen to point out. More than half the population of this town is troglodyte (this is the largest concentration of inhabited caves in Europe), and their dwellings boast all modern conveniences—Internet, electricity, running water, and the rest. In the Cuevas Pedro Antonio de Alarcón, the "cave hotel" that lies a little way out of town, there is even one suite with a whirlpool tub.

People in this part of the world have been living in caves since the eighth century. Some stories relate that the caves became better developed when the Moors, escaping the Christian reconquest, fled to the hills and burrowed beneath the ground. Whatever the reason for their existence, caves have their advantages. Their temperature is constant year-round, with the mercury hovering at about 66°F (19°C). Log fires warm the caves when necessary, with smoke puffing up through whitewashed chimneys that poke skyward from the rich, brown soil of the hills. Some people report improved sleeping patterns—something to do with a connection to the earth, apparently—whereas others cite the individuality of their dwellings as the main attraction. After all, no two caves are alike.

The Cuevas Pedro Antonio de Alarcón complex has twenty-three apartments, each with views over Guadix and the Sierra Nevada. There is central heating, hot water, TV, telephone, bathroom, kitchen, and a private barbecue for each. There is also a restaurant and swimming pool. Nearby attractions include horseback riding and climbing in the surrounding hills, and the Roman thermal baths in Guadix. Wearing skins and clubbing down your dinner are not encouraged. **PE**

Enjoy Los Jardines de Palerm

Location Ibiza, Spain
Website www.jardinsdepalerm.com   **Price** 🇸🇸

Ibiza may be known for its clubbing scene, but there is one tiny corner where visitors can reach absolute relaxation. Los Jardines de Palerm is a bijou hotel (there are only nine rooms) created from a converted seventeenth-century finca. Overlooking the bay of San Antonio, it is a haven of peace and quiet, yet near to the beaches and the nightlife if you want them.

Most guests remark on the tranquility of the exotic water gardens and infinity pools. Terraces with loungers are scattered through the landscaped grounds, so guests have no trouble finding a peaceful corner to call their own. Minimalist, white rooms decorated with pretty Chinese ceramics and antique

---

"[It] allows total privacy in grounds punctuated with water gardens and two stylish infinity pools."

Harpers Bazaar

---

manuscripts inspire further serenity. There is no restaurant, but breakfast is served, and kindly staff even rustle up food for those who partied into the small hours and missed the official meal. The chef will also conjure up a sandwich or salad for those who cannot tear themselves away from their lounger at lunchtime, and there is an honesty bar so people can help themselves to drinks.

The atmospheric town of San José is just minutes away by foot, with its whitewashed buildings, palm trees, and pottery shops. Sit quietly and enjoy the view from a tiled bench in the main square but not for too long; Los Jardines de Palerm is calling. **PE**

Explore Formentera

Location Formentera, Spain
Website www.turismoformentera.com   **Price** 🇸🇸

Although Formentera lies just a few miles to the south of Ibiza, it seems a world away from its nearest neighbor. If Ibiza is Spain's party island—filled with pumping nightclubs, heaving bars, and hordes of sweaty revelers—then Formentera is very much the chill-out alternative. Situated off the east coast of Spain, and accessible only via ferry (one hour) or hydrofoil (twenty-five minutes) from Ibiza, the island has yet to succumb to the ravages of mass tourism.

Those few tourists who do make it here, most of whom are day-trippers, will find a tiny place—its 32 square miles (83 sq km) make it the smallest of the inhabited Balearics—of great bucolic charm. Rolling hillsides blanketed in olive trees and dotted with small stone villages lead down to beaches that are among the most pristine to be found anywhere in Spain. The clean white sand and clear blue waters give the coast an almost Caribbean appearance.

Windsurfing is popular, and snorkeling and diving equipment can be rented by those who want to get in among the colorful fish that inhabit the coastal waters. A network of bicycle tracks allows for easy, relaxed exploration of the island, taking you past the beaches and up into the wild, windswept countryside at the center of Formentera.

The nightlife is as relaxed as the gentle lapping waters of the Mediterranean, with the island home to a fine collection of small, cozy restaurants, many boasting idyllic beachfront locations. Those on the northern shore, facing Ibiza, provide picture-perfect sunset-watching opportunities. **JF**

➡ *The sunsets are spectacular from any angle as the color of the rocks is gently transformed before you.*

Enjoy Finca Las Longueras

Location Gran Canaria, Canary Islands
Website www.laslongueras.com   **Price**

Built in 1895, this large rural mansion on the island of Gran Canaria is situated in the middle of an agriculture plantation growing bananas, oranges, avocados, and papayas, intoxicating the visitors who stumble across it with its heady, tropical perfume. Even those who discover this place of wonder—situated at the end of a winding gravel road high up in the hills—can easily find themselves lost again, adrift in the maze of paths meandering through the plantation.

This luxury rural hotel, also known as the Red House (La Casa Roja), is inspired by colonial style with its white, decorative arched porch and high ceilings, and was formerly home to an aristocratic local family.

"Contemplate romantic sunsets amid tropical surroundings, perfumed by orange blossom."

Proprietors, Finca Las Longueras

The sense of grandeur lives on, from its ornate brass bedsteads and long corridors to its huge arched windows and vast antiques collection.

Finca Las Longueras has nine double bedrooms, but you need never see another soul in these sprawling 427 acres (173 ha) perched on the edge of the Atlantic Ocean. Sit amid the orchards with a glass of wine and watch the fireball of a sun sink behind the mountains, or start the day with an orgy of fruit, fresh from the trees that surround you. If the scent of orange blossom becomes too overwhelming or the sense of pure isolation becomes too much, this gem is just 20 miles (32 km) from the hubbub of Las Palmas. **NS**

Stay at Finca Malvasia

Location Lanzarote, Canary Islands
Website www.fincamalvasia.com   **Price**

In the 1700s, looming volcanic cones sprayed Lanzarote with molten lava, redefining the vista into a surreal, jagged environment. To some, bedding down in a valley between two volcanic cones may not sound like a sleep-inducing experience, but British owners Tarnya and Richard Norse-Evans have created a tranquil hideaway here on the island.

Four retro-rustic cottages form an L-shape around a carved swimming pool, an oasis of gleaming white and tropical flora amid a landscape of ash-black lava. Bougainvillea clambers over the ocher rooftops, and palm trees shade the private gardens. The cottage interiors pair old with new: high-tech entertainment systems housed on bare stone shelves; terra-cotta floor tiles splashed with bright rugs; and stylish bathrooms dominated by indoor foliage. At night, the silence is overwhelming. With near-zero light pollution, the razor-sharp sky feels only a stretch away.

The hotel's relative isolation certainly does not mean there is nothing to do. Spa treatments and massages are on offer in a stone yoga yurt, sandy beaches are less than 6 miles (10 km) away, and a network of trekking trails for the more adventurous crisscrosses the region. Creative writing, cooking, and painting classes are also arranged on request. Although self-catering, organic breakfasts featuring homegrown fruits are delivered to the secluded terraces. For stocking up the fridge, a local farmers' market sells cheese, fruit, vegetables, and fresh bread every weekend. For stressed-out suits in need of some "away-from-it-all" time, couples seeking the perfect anti-resort, or artists searching for an inspirational retreat, the volcanic cones of Lanzarote's interior are the ideal subtropical escape. **JC**

Unwind at Aquapura

Location Douro Valley, Bragança to Oporto, Portugal
Website www.aquapurahotels.com **Price** 💲💲💲

The Douro River winds between the green hills of northeast Portugal. The slopes above the river are still covered with terraced vineyards as they have been for hundreds of years. This unspoiled historic valley is a World Heritage site and is famous for its port wine.

Aquapura is a luxury hotel and spa, based around a striking terra-cotta-colored mansion on the south bank of the river, facing the historic town of Peso da Régua. A chic modern glass extension holds a huge spa center. Its Asian-themed interior mixes flickering candles with dark-wood surfaces. The treatment rooms use local natural products and have huge picture windows overlooking the Douro Valley.

"[A] long tradition of viticulture has produced a cultural landscape of outstanding beauty."

UNESCO World Heritage Site Committee

In the hotel restaurant, expect to find Portuguese regional specialties reinvented by a French chef. He uses local olive oils and ports for many of the sauces. Eat outside under wicker umbrellas on the patio or inside in the modern formal restaurant.

The Aquapura holds nothing back in the quest for luxury and style. The elegant and spacious bedrooms have a relaxed minimalist theme and offer twenty-four-hour, decadent in-room dining, luxurious double bathrooms, four-poster king-size beds with crisp cotton linen, and in-room spa treatments. Some have balconies overlooking the historic cloisters and, of course, the River Douro below. **SH**

Relax at Flor Da Rosa

Location Portalegre, Portugal
Website www.pousadasofportugal.com **Price** 💲💲

If you want turrets, then look no further. Although it began life as a monastery, this building seems more like a castle than a religious establishment. It was built in 1356 for the knights of the Order of Malta and was audaciously—and highly successfully—renovated by Portuguese architect Carrilho da Graca. The building is steeped in history and has magnificent vaulted ceilings and medieval cloisters.

One of the most dramatic rooms is the bar. Once the monastery's refectory, it keeps its vaulted ceilings, arched windows, and stone pillars and blends these with sleek, geometric sofas in brown leather and lime-green linen. In the bedrooms, crisp white linen-covered armchairs sit before eons-old stone walls. There are just twenty-four rooms—and most guests concur that the three in the tower are the best.

The pousada sits in a sleepy little Alentejo village, not far from Crato, which is famous for its pottery, still made in the traditional way. Also nearby is the picturesque walled town of Portalegre.

Flor Da Rosa also has a pool, on whose blue waters the imposing turrets reflect strikingly. For those who want peace and quiet, this is the perfect spot to stay and be still, to lounge by the pool in the daytime, eat in the pousada's restaurant—which serves up excellent local fare and offers wonderful views from stunningly modern panorama windows—and perhaps sip a little *vinho do porto* on a super-chic sofa before sinking into bed. For those wanting a bit more action, there is a golf course, tennis court, horseback riding, fishing, shooting, and bird watching nearby. Oh yes, and there is cable TV, wireless Internet, air-conditioning, and the rest—but then, what else would you expect from a fourteenth-century monastery? **PE**

Explore the Serra de Estrela

Location Serra de Estrela, Portugal
Website www.quintadoriodao.com/eng/out/estrela.html **Price** ◖

Soaring to a lofty 6,541 feet (1,993 m), the appropriately titled Mountains of the Stars—the tallest peaks in mainland Portugal—really do reach for the heavens. Unusually, you can get to the top quite easily because there is a paved road up to the summit plateau and the point known as the Torre (tower). Views look out as far as the sea, about 100 miles (160 km) away.

A massive granite ridge stretching for more than 60 miles (100 km) and with more than half its area set at over 2,300 feet (700 m), this is a truly awesome showcase of what nature can accomplish. Strangely shaped crags, deep gorges, rushing mountain streams, and placid lakes pepper the unique landscape.

> *"Near [its] top there was said to be a lake in which the wrecks of ships floated up to the surface."*
>
> Herman Melville, *Moby Dick*

The Mondego—the longest river flowing entirely within Portuguese territory—has its headwaters here, as do the Alva and the Zêzere. A protected nature park, the range has a thriving ski resort at Lorigã and gives its name to a hardy breed of dog, a type of smoked sausage, and a tasty hard cheese.

There is abundant wildlife and a wonderland of waterfalls, woods, and mysterious caves. The bears are gone, and wolves are now extremely rare, but you will likely meet otters, water voles, and many rare birds. **RsP**

⤷ *The small and picturesque village of Belver sits on the Tagus river in the Serra de Estrela.*

Unwind at Penha Longa

Location Near Lisbon, Portugal
Website www.penhalonga.com **Price** $$

> *"The building is a graceful palazzo-style structure set among rolling hills, clear lakes, and lush gardens."*

New York Times

Only a short drive from Lisbon, this hotel feels like it is in a different world. Your first glimpse is likely to be the Penha Longa itself, the long rock that inspired monks to build a monastery here in the belief it was a holy site. Today the place still exudes much of the peace from its secular days, and the fourteenth-century monastery still stands—you can even arrange to get married in the small chapel there.

Close to this ancient building, and before the modern hotel, you will find the Asian-inspired spa where guests are served fruit teas and may lounge beside water features inside or out while waiting for or recovering from a treatment such as the seaweed wrap. If you can tear yourself away from here, there is a fabulous pool to wallow in, overlooking the expansive greenery of the Atlantic golf course. Then there is the elegant 194-room hotel. It currently has four different restaurants, including Serra, by the pool, and Midori, offering Japanese cuisine. The newest addition is Arola, where chef Julio Pereira creates Portuguese cuisine with a contemporary twist. Breakfast is served in Assa Massa or the club lounge, with an array of fresh fruit, muesli, breads, and a fantastic selection of homemade preserves to choose from, reminiscent of the best kind of delicatessen.

The broad balcony of the club lounge is situated in the perfect spot to offer the best view of the sun rising over the surrounding hills, so sit back, dig in, and watch the holy Penha Longa rock slowly illuminate with the early rays of the sun. **JED**

◸ *The blue agapanthus, or Lily of the Nile, planted in front of Penha Longa give off a wonderful scent.*

Experience
Lapa Palace

Location Lisbon, Portugal
Website www.lapapalace.com   **Price** ⑤⑤⑤

Lapa Palace was originally built in 1870 for the Count of Valenças. Its elegant pink facade and inner combinations of marble stucco, carved wood, and beautiful azulejos tiles have been lovingly cared for over its years of private ownership. Since opening as a hotel in 1992, Lapa Palace has won accolades galore, and it is not difficult to see why.

The hotel's central Lisbon location amid beatific gardens, streams, and ornamental fountains is on a hill that allows both easy access to the city center and exceptional views of the Tagus river. Some 109 rooms are available, with even the most standard enjoying terraces or balconies, reproductions of French and English furniture, marble bathrooms (some with bas-relief and whirlpool tub), and classic eighteenth-century design. Twenty-two individually decorated palace rooms and suites feature restored antiques from the original palace, and the fourteen Italianate villa rooms situated in the former stables have their own private gardens—perfect for whiling away the southern European warm evening sunshine.

The hotel has attracted its fair share of high-profile guests, most of whom are drawn to the Royal Suite, with its pastel rococo styling, or the honeymooners' favorite, the Tower Room, which has an Elvis-style pop-up TV at the end of the bed, a two-person whirlpool tub, and a private turret to dine in. After a workout in the wellness center or the heated pool, have one of the fifty varieties of tea in the Rio Tejo bar. The in-house restaurant Cipriani is regarded as one of the best restaurants in Lisbon and has an excellent reputation for its contemporary cuisine. All in all, it is aristocratic quality you can count on. **PS**

Recharge at
Palácio Belmonte

Location Lisbon, Portugal
Website www.palaciobelmonte.com   **Price** ⑤⑤

When Maria and Frédéric Coustols bought Palácio Belmonte, it was a crumbling building in need of restoration. Several years and millions of euros later, it is now a ten-suite hotel and a classified National Monument, mere cobblestones away from São Jorge Castle in the old Jewish medieval quarter of Alfama.

Although the owners have introduced some modern touches, perfectly preserved nineteenth-century bathtubs and original blue and white tiles are just some of the older features. The suites, all named after prominent Portuguese individuals (ecologists, writers, inventors, and so on) are appointed with genuine

> *"Made from the shell of a former count's palácio, the Belmonte is still fit for nobility."*
>
> *Condé Nast Traveler*

eighteenth-century furnishings: mirrors, armoires, canvases, and drawings. Romantics may want to request the Bartolomeu de Gusmão Suite, on top of one of the Moorish towers with its own terrace overlooking Alfama and the Tagus river.

The garden completes the hotel's charm—an Eden of whitewashed walls, fruit trees, and bougainvillea. The black marble swimming pool is another talking point, as is the library, which holds more than 4,000 books and publications in a variety of languages. The Belmonte even has its own chapel. An all-around cultural experience as well as a chic luxury destination, Palácio Belmonte is a once in a lifetime indulgence. **PS**

Stay at the Ritz

Location Lisbon, Portugal
Website www.fourseasons.com/lisbon **Price** 💲💲

If it is luxury with a capital "L" you are after, it does not get much better than Lisbon's Ritz. At first glance the hotel may seem like one of Lisbon's many period buildings, but it is its interior details that stand out.

The hotel is built on one of Lisbon's seven hills, and the views across many of the city's well-known landmarks (including Edward VII Park, St. George's Castle, and the Tagus river) are immensely impressive. Once inside, the public areas do not fail to seduce: a riot of tapestries, paintings, and antique reproductions, including pieces commissioned by Portuguese artists of the period. The accommodation features suites that are enormous and beautifully furnished with marble

> *"[The] suites boast the finest decoration you'll see in any major Portuguese hotel."*
>
> *New York Times*

bathrooms, large mahogany canopied beds, antique satinwood dressing tables, and very plush carpeting.

The hotel restaurant, Varanda, is one of Lisbon's top dining spots and consequently manages to attract the city's glitterati. The lounge bar has a great terrace that overlooks the park. On the subject of fantastic views, even ardent relaxation aficionados might want to take a peek at the rooftop gym, which boasts a running track with wonderful 360-degree views of the city, before popping back down to the in-house spa, a Zen-inspired creation with great steam baths, foot massages, blissful treatments, and changing rooms with heated limestone floors. **PS**

See Jerónimos Monastery

Location Lisbon, Portugal
Website www.mosteirojeronimos.pt **Price** 💲

For a sense of peace close to some of Lisbon's most popular tourist attractions, the sixteenth-century Jerónimos Monastery in the Belém quarter is unbeatable. Although most tourists flock to the nearby Antiga Confeitaria de Belém to feast on pastries, or head to the riverside to explore dramatic edifices such as the Monument of the Discoveries, the monastery is large enough to swallow up crowds of curious tourists without losing any of its overwhelming serenity.

Corridors spiral around each other, unfolding into rooms where you will find the tombs of poet Fernando Pessoa and historian Alexandre Herculano, along with those of hundreds of Jerome monks. Other paths lead into the central apex where the only roof is the sky, seemingly held up by pinnacled towers. Every surface is pure white stone embellished by the imaginations of sailors who paused here to pray before setting out on endless voyages. Those who returned gave thanks in the form of fantastical depictions of their travels: the things they saw or dreamed up while overseas.

The monastery captures the state of mind of these brave adventurers, and among their fairy tales you will find scenes from the Bible. Noah's ark is a particularly fine example, with hordes of animals spilling over the bows of an archaic ship, not unlike the flimsy vessels in which the sailors searched for new worlds.

The church here still hosts Mass, and sitting in the rear of the church listening to the murmuring Portuguese is sure to lull you. Just be careful not to fall asleep. Who knows what kind of dreams you might have in this magical place? **JED**

➔ *The structure seems strangely organic, as though the place has grown from the earth rather than been built.*

Visit Nossa Senhora Do Monte

Location Lisbon, Portugal   **Website** www.golisbon.com
Price 🌓

Lisbon is built on seven hills. On the brow of the highest stands Nossa Senhora do Monte, Our Lady of the Hill. Dressed in white, with one hand slightly raised in benediction, she gazes upon the red rooftops of the city and the waters of the Tagus river beyond. Behind her stands her chapel, which was originally built in 1243. It is on the site where the first bishop of Lisbon, São Gens, was martyred in the fourth century c.ε.

Around the chapel, a viewpoint (Miradouro) has been thoughtfully landscaped. There are pretty, tiled, terraced areas and benches beneath the trees. Shift your gaze to the left and you will see the fabulous crenellations of the Castelo de São Jorge. The castle is just a short walk from the Miradouro and well worth a visit, too. Here you can climb the towers and walk along the ramparts. Grab a coffee and sit at one of the restaurant's outside tables and you will be rewarded with yet more incredible views across the city.

If you cannot bear to climb up here (it is about a thirty-minute hike from the city center), take the number 28 tram. Lisbon's trams are famous for their retro design, and the number 28 route, which tours the city's hills, is one of the highlights of any trip.

Locals say that the best time of day to come up to the Miradouro is at sunset. In good weather, the sky turns deep blue, then melds into a dusky pink where it meets the dark, inky waters of the Tagus. Our Lady of the Hill shines brightly, illuminated in her own glass sanctuary, while far below the lights of the city twinkle yellow and orange in the warm Lisbon twilight. **PE**

➜ *Nossa Senhora do Monte sits atop Portugal's highest hill—it's a steep walk to get there, but well worth it.*

Swim with Dolphins

Location Pico, Azores
Website www.dolphinconnectionexperience.com **Price** $

On the volcanic island of Pico in the Portuguese Azores, you can be inches away from dolphins and whales feeding in the warm and unpolluted currents of the Gulf Stream each summer. Pico is one of the most naturally beautiful places on the planet, attracting scientists, divers, and photographers to marvel at the resplendent green landscape, clear blue sulfur volcanic rock, and fascinating marine life.

A former world-famous whale-hunting location, the tranquil fishing village of Lajes do Pico is now a dolphin and whale hot spot. When whale hunting was banned in the 1980s, islanders began taking tourists out on boats from the Espaço Talassa (whale-watching center). By adopting the honed skill of the "Vigia" (the original whale hunters), along with modern sonar, the guides can track down schools of up to 200 dolphins.

The Dolphin Connection is an environmentally conscious company offering swimming-with-dolphin vacations to rebalance, rejuvenate, and change your life forever. Don your wetsuit and speed out to sea on a hard-hulled boat to spot calm, peaceful Rissos and Sperm Whales. Slip into crystal clear water to lie on the surface while Bottlenose dolphins dance beneath you, or splash about with Spotted dolphins as they cut through waves at extraordinary speed, and get high on hormones released by the brain after the exciting dolphin encounter. When you are not in the water cavorting with cetaceans, wander around Pico, where baroque churches, tiny squares, cobbled streets, and quaint buildings reveal a land and lifestyle that is untouched, unhurried, and calm. **SD**

← *Encountering a school of dolphins in the wild is one of the highlights of a trip to Pico.*

Discover Casa Dos Barcos

Location San Miguel, Azores
Website www.casadosbarcos.com **Price** $$

Fly to the middle of the Atlantic, land on a small volcanic island, and head into the forested hills. On the lush southern shores of a lake, formed by the crater of an extinct volcano, stands an elegant historic boathouse, available to rent by the night.

Casa dos Barcos stands beside Lagoa das Furnas, the most beautiful natural sight on San Miguel island. It is about an hour's drive from Ponta Delgada, the island's main town, and 3 miles (5 km) from the village of Furnas, famed for its hot springs, "caldeiras" (geysers), thermal baths, natural warm-water swimming pool, and stately parks and gardens. The Casa is part of a nineteenth-century estate created by

"Furnas is a picturesque village inside a huge crater . . . [with] lush vegetation and thermal springs."

Cathy Packe, *Independent*

José do Canto, a local aristocrat, who employed leading botanical, landscape, and architectural firms from London and Paris. Behind the Flemish-style boathouse are landscaped gardens with paths, streams, and exotic plants. It has become famed for the walks through old camellia trees that flower spectacularly between December and March. Just along the sandy shoreline is the estate's gothic chapel.

Guests at the Casa can use free canoes and bicycles, and there are stables close by. Other highlights include the man-made, hot-water swimming pool in the Parque Terra Nostra in Furnas and the steaming caldeiras on the opposite shore of the lake. **SH**

Hike Through Vikos Gorge

Location Vikos-Aoos National Park, Greece
Website www.meteo.noa.gr/Primavera/index.htm **Price** ❶❶

There is a lot more to Greece than sun-drenched islands and ancient ruins. The Vikos-Aoos National Park in northern Greece includes the extraordinary Vikos Gorge: one of the natural wonders of the world. It is 7 miles (12 km) long and is officially categorized as the deepest gorge in the world, with limestone walls more than a mile high. It runs along the Voidomatis River and you can hike right through it.

The ancient trails of mule caravans and nomadic shepherds will take you along the gorge, climbing steep paths to villages and chapels along the way. Sometimes the path follows a ledge winding up through broad-leaved forests; other times a cobbled trail will cling to the banks of the river. The park is an unspoiled 49 square miles (126 sq km) of forests, mountains, and remote villages. Hikers will discover springs, gorges, pine forests, rocky pinnacles, river pools, wildflowers, lakes, and ancient stone bridges. If you are lucky, you may spot bears, boars, foxes, trout, and deer. In spring, you may find yourself tramping through huge swaths of wild-growing crocuses.

There are serious peaks in the park, such as Gamila at 8,192 feet (2,497 m). Trek up here to find Drakolimni —the Dragon Lake—and breathtaking views. Farther into the Pindos Mountains are monasteries perched on impossibly steep pinnacles. Despite the old stone paths, hiking is challenging and strenuous. Respite is provided by gentle Alpine-style pastures and tiny traditional villages of slate houses and farms. Visitors can stay in small family hotels or village pensions. Rooms are clean, comfortable, and very cheap. **SH**

→ *The Vikos-Aoos National Park offers some of the most dramatic and rewarding hiking in Europe.*

Discover Meteora

Location Thessaly, Greece **Website** http://odysseus.culture.gr
Price ❶

As you pass the village of Kalambaka, prepare for an unexpected sight. Rising out of the ground like a series of giant stalagmites are towering rock formations, framing the horizon with their unearthly presence.

As if this natural wonder were not enough, you soon discover that their peaks house a cluster of settlements, an architectural miracle in itself. Their history dates back to ascetics of the eleventh century who first dwelled in caves and huts. Yet food, supplies, and even people were eventually ferried up there using a system of ropes, ladders, and pulleys.

Scientists believe that the rock towers were once part of a vast inland sea, later shaped and formed by earthquakes and the elements. Poets, thinkers, and travelers have all come here to reflect both on the spirituality of this area and the sanctity of the monasteries. Today, the six buildings that are still functioning contain beautiful religious art, frescoes, mosaics, and paintings, which show the dedication of the monks and nuns to their way of life. Although access to some places, like the Great Meteoron and Agia Triada, requires myriad steep steps, others like Varlaam and Roussanou can be accessed by bridge. This has prompted plenty of tour buses and souvenir stalls, but most monks are happy to have a chat with visitors, and the nuns sometimes offer sweets as you relax in the shady courtyard. When you have visited the museums inside, outside the views of the green hillsides and snowcapped mountains in the distance make this a place in which to reflect on the ways of the modern world—and take a glimpse into the past. **JW**

⬅ *It remains a mystery how the Byzantine monks built the monasteries in this seemingly inaccessible spot.*

Discover Argentikon

Location Chios, Greece **Website** www.argentikon.gr
Price ❸❸❸

This site has been dedicated to luxury for hundreds of years. Behind its high stone walls and heavy bronze-studded gates, Argentikon was the summer residence of the Argenti, a wealthy Genoese family who came to administer this distant Mediterranean island colony in the Middle Ages. The green valley of Kambos was the prettiest, most sheltered part of the island—now known for its walled orchards—and the Genoese aristocrats built their villas there. Chios has long since returned to the ownership of Greece, but Argentikon still stands as a monument to a wealthy colonial past.

Among the period buildings, there are now just eight suites. Guests will find exposed beams, frescoed

> *"Chios is so unique, so genuinely odd, that at times you don't feel like you are in Greece at all."*
>
> Jonathan Futrell, *Guardian*

ceilings, and Venetian furnishings inside. The rooms are more like museums than hotel accommodation. The bedrooms have fireplaces, marble bathrooms, and balconies. There is a spa, sauna, massage room (in the old chicken house), outdoor swimming pool, and gardens lush with palm trees, roses, and citrus groves and dotted with carved marble. The fertile estate is useful in other ways, too. The kitchen uses plenty of the fresh vegetables and fruit for its menus, complementing the fish bought straight from the quaysides of Chios. You can also drink wine that has come from the estate's own vineyards, and even eat marmalade made from its own orange groves. **SH**

Explore Hydra

Location Hydra, Greece **Website** www.hydra.com.gr
Price ◖◗

Only 38 miles (70 km) from the busy port of Piraeus, this gorgeous island has a pretty port town crammed with donkeys and cafés. It has always been a place of maritime success. At its zenith, during the eighteenth and nineteenth centuries, Hydra had the most successful commercial fleet in Greece; it even ran the blockade during the Napoleonic Wars. When Greece rose up against the Turks in 1821, the wealthy maritime merchants—responsible for building all the wonderful mansions, or *arondika*, of Hydra town—rose up, too, converting their merchant ships into battleships.

Later, in the 1950s, the writers and artists started coming—and have never stopped. Many, such as Leonard Cohen, have become semipermanent fixtures, lavishing money and loving care in the restoration of the old sea merchants' homes, or in the creation of galleries, museums, and shops.

One of the many simple joys of Hydra is the fact that all motorized vehicles are banned. Water taxis are available to whisk you off to various beaches and tavernas dotted around the coast, or you can simply use your legs or rent a bike.

Hydra is wonderful for walking. Start with a climb up to the Mansion of Lazaros Koundouriotis, once the home of a wealthy merchant, now the home of the Historical and Folk Museum and the public art gallery. A strenuous walk to the Profitis Ilias monastery and Agias Evpraxias nunnery will reward you with views of the Peloponnesus. Boundouri is a path that leaves the port toward the fishing village of Kamini; it is magical at night, with its own small, delightful harbor. **LB**

⤷ *Hydra rises amphitheatrically above its harbor like a romantic whitewashed stage set.*

Explore Lycabettus Hill

Location Athens, Greece   **Website** www.tourtripgreece.gr
Price ◑

Athens is the ultimate city of contrasts in its relentless concrete sprawl, traffic chaos, ancient monuments of soaring beauty, and wonderfully atmospheric streets. Every day, hordes of tourists make the trek up Acropolis Hill, as much to look out over the metropolis as to enjoy the Parthenon. If you can linger a little longer, consider Lycabettus Hill, a patch of pine-studded wilderness in the dusty city which, at 909 feet (277 m), offers a wonderful panorama of the Acropolis, most of Athens, and across to Piraeus and the Saronic Gulf.

Ancient mythology says that Athena created Lycabettus when she hurled a missile at the daughters of King Cecrops in a fit of pique, but missed, and created the hill instead. Although most tourists access Acropolis Hill from the chaotic streets of Monastiraki or Plaka, Lycabettus is in the middle of Kolonaki, whose broader and wealthier streets offer a calmer vibe. It is possible to drive to the summit, but better to take the funicular railway, which departs every half an hour from the corner of Aristippou and Ploutarchou Streets in Kolonaki. Alternatively, there are three options for actually walking up the hill: the gentle circular route (Sarantapichou), the steep Ploutarchou, or the even steeper woodland paths that snake to the top.

At the top, you will find the eighteenth-century Agios Georgios, a modest church. At midnight on Good Friday, Athenians appear in large numbers to watch the procession of the Easter flame from here. On the way, you will also see a beautiful open-air amphitheater that overlooks the city. After a sunset drink at Orizondes, the restaurant at the peak, or Prasini Tenta, the informal café halfway down, make your descent through the shade of the pines, back into a land of sirens, horns, and frenetic activity. **LB**

Stay at Porto Zante

Location Zakynthos, Greece   **Website** www.portozante.com
Price ⑤⑤

A hidden treasure lies on the unspoiled island of Zakynthos, just west of Greece's mainland. Tucked away in a secluded bay, Porto Zante De Luxe Villas occupy a sandy slice of private beach in the area of Tragaki, on the island nicknamed Flower of the East by the Venetians who ruled it during the Middle Ages.

The boutique-style, all-villa hotel makes the most of the natural beauty of its surroundings, decorated thoughtfully with luxurious furnishings and paintings by prominent Greek artists. There are several types of villa, the most indulgent being the four-bedroom Imperial Spa Villa with a heated pool and in-room spa. Many of the villas have private pools and gardens and

> *"Even just arriving here is luxurious, with limousine transfer included to and from the airport."*
>
> *Condé Nast Traveler*

occupy heavenly spots on the seafront; each is finished with luxurious touches such as sumptuous bedding, Bulgari toiletries, and Valentino bathrobes.

There is just enough here to keep guests quietly occupied: The Club House restaurant whips up tasty Greek specialties with a modern slant, there are thalasso therapy treatments in the spa fit for island beauties, or you can devour a book while swaying peacefully in your poolside hammock. The more adventurous visitors can also charter a yacht. **LP**

➡ *With a view like this to sit at all day long at Smugglers' Cove by Porto Zante Villas, why go anywhere else?*

Experience Pelion

Location Pelion, Greece   **Website** www.pelion.gr   **Price** 🔴

Some call the Pelion region of Greece "The Mountain of Four Seasons," and it is not hard to see why. Situated west of Skiathos, Pelion is a mountainous peninsula flanked by the Pagasetic Gulf to the east and the warm waters of the Aegean Sea to the west. In an area of just 78 acres (31 ha), the landscape switches from coastal villages to dense forest, to a peak of 5,000 feet (1,500 m). In summer, there are myriad trails and nature walks through thick glades of beech, oak, maple, and chestnut trees. In winter, you can ski while looking out over the spectacular sea views.

Traditional Pelion architecture is unique and striking. Stone is used for the ground and middle floors, whereas the upper levels are constructed from a mix of stone and timber. You will not find this style anywhere else in Greece. The villages that line the west coast are undeniably Greek, with gently sloping hills blanketed in olive groves and eucalyptus trees. On the southern tip, and stretching around to the eastern coast, the scenery seems to take on a more Tuscan look, with snaking lines of Mediterranean cypress and poplar trees. The northeastern corner is arguably the jewel in the crown of this lovely landscape.

Four hours' drive from Thessaloniki, you will find the charming seaside village of Damouhari. This close-knit Greek village, situated on the mainland in the Pelion peninsula, has a beautiful backdrop of olive groves and a tiny pebble-beach harbor overlooking the blue-green Aegean Sea. It provided the beautiful backdrop for several key scenes from the smash-hit musical-turned-movie *Mamma Mia*. This unspoiled chunk of Pelion has long been a favorite hideaway for Greek vacationers, but is for the moment still largely unknown to foreigners. We hope the success of the *Mamma Mia* movie does little to change that. **JP**

⬆ *There are many hidden bays such as this in Pelion, with lush vegetation and pebble beaches.*

Relax at Elixir Spa

Location Attica, Greece **Website** www.grecotel.com **Price** ❸❸❸

Wallowing between mock-classical pillars in the bubbling spa pool, you can gaze through a glass wall to the Temple of Poseidon on the southernmost point of the European mainland. Surely, this fabulous octagonal spa was inspired by the Greek gods? Well, no, actually, say the owners, it was inspired by the James Bond film *Dr. No.* You can easily see the 007 influences: It is part of a money-is-no-object lavish modern resort in a fantastic Mediterranean landscape, but there is no evil genius at work here. In fact, it is a luxurious paradise that even the heroes of Greek mythology would have enjoyed.

You enter the spa through a huge round bronze door, a bit like stepping through a porthole. Private treatment rooms have an intimate atmosphere with scented candles and soothing music. Therapies include shiatsu, aromatherapy, reflexology, and hot stone therapy. The local specialty pays proper homage to the sea god—the "Poseidon Elixir" is inspired by grooming rituals of the classical era. Finely ground olive seeds, natural sea salt, and rich clay are applied in successive scrubs and rubs, combined with sessions in the sauna, to remove toxins. The sequence culminates in a theraputic, forty-five-minute, four-hand massage with a natural deep-penetrating cream of dandelion and pear extracts that is guaranteed to leave the skin silky smooth and glowing.

The spa is part of the Grecotel Cape Sounio resort: a five-star collection of 124 luxury bungalows covering 75 acres (30 ha) in an amphitheater landscape facing the brilliant blue sea. Many of the fabulous terra-cotta bungalows have their own private pools and gardens, balconies, and amazing views. The resort boasts five restaurants, three pools, a private beach, and its own yacht. Dr. No would have been impressed. **SH**

⬆ *The spa rooms are eight-sided, and glass exterior walls showcase memorable sea views.*

Relax at Grand Resort

Location Attica, Greece **Website** www.grandresort.gr
Price 💲💲

Here is the ultimate in sun and sea hotels. The Grand Resort occupies a peninsular 22 miles (35 km) south of the Greek capital, Athens, and is one of the most luxurious hotels you can find, not just on the Athenian Riviera, but anywhere on the Mediterranean.

The Grand Resort lives up to its name: It offers every conceivable extra from personal trainers to electric shuttles that trundle around the 72-acre (29-ha) site. If your idea of luxury means not moving from your room at all, you will appreciate the in-room dining (with a personal chef), in-room tailors, pianists, hairdressers, and spa therapies. Facilities that other hotels would boast about, such as the beachside spa, gym, and

> *"The resort is stunning architecturally, quietly joyous in a pre-Zorba the Greek way."*
>
> Helena Smith, *Guardian*

waterfront ballroom, are hardly worth mentioning among jet-set glamor like this. The quality of the resort's helicopter services, yacht rental, and private chauffeurs are more important to guests.

As for the rooms and villas, rest assured there is a comprehensive range, starting from palatial and reaching right up to extraordinary. Many of the villas are on the water's edge, and have private infinity pools, marble bathrooms, heated floors, and a choice of pillows. More highlights of the resort include sixteen private sandy beaches, ten restaurants, an Olympic-sized seawater pool, and facilities for just about any sport you could wish to try on vacation. **SH**

Visit Amorgos Island

Location Amorgos, Greece **Website** www.amorgos.net
Price ❶

Glistening in the sunlight, the whitewashed facade of the Byzantine monastery of Panagia Hozoviotissa juts out of the cliffs toward the Aegean Sea, affording an azure vista far out into the horizon. It was this mixture of drama and solitude that drew French director Luc Besson to Amorgos to film his 1988 classic *The Big Blue*. Today, the island continues to beckon the faithful back every year, to revel in its rugged natural beauty.

The north-to-south coastal road winds its way through the mountains, with a sheer drop giving way to deep, crystal-clear waters and hidden coves. It is a long, lonely drive, except for a few stray goats, and the undulating road gives the feeling of flying as it takes you between the island's three towns. Even in the main "resort" of Aegali, the pace is always slow. Priests play backgammon in the tavernas, shading themselves from the afternoon sun. If the slightly larger crowd in mid-August is too much for you, take a small boat from the harbor to your own secluded (possibly nudist) stretch of beach, or out to one of the mysterious, uninhabited islands. Alternatively, arm yourself with a map and clamber over the scrub and barren paths to your own spot beyond the bay—be it shallow and sandy, or just rocky with a leap into the big blue itself.

Many of the island's 1,900-strong population reside in the capital, Chora, one of the best-preserved towns in the Cyclades. Pause for a while among the houses of blue and white, and look up toward the Venetian castle on the hill. Pirates, Roman exiles, and Minoans have all walked here, and the island's history dates back to 4,000 B.C.E.—at times lawless, always atmospheric. **JW**

➡ *As you climb the myriad dusty steps leading to Panagia Hozoviotissa, time appears to stand still.*

Experience Skyros Island

Location Skyros, Greece   **Website** www.skyros.co.uk
Price ⑤

Visitors are encouraged to come to Skyros island with an open mind. Stay here to chill out, be creative, learn a new skill, or socialize, and, if you need to, find the inspiration to change your life.

Courses led by experts cover everything from qigong, yoga, and massage to filmmaking, art, and singing. Workshops take place at the Skyros Center, tucked away in the cobblestone town, where you can stay in one of the modern rooms with private bathrooms. For a more authentic slice of Greek island life, you can book into a traditional house run by a local landlord. Atsitsa is a more basic, bohemian course center, set by the sea and surrounded by pine forests. Here there is a greater emphasis on physical activities such as sailing and windsurfing. Up to ninety people can be accommodated in this spacious stone villa, sleeping five to a room, or in very rustic, two-person bamboo cabins under the trees. This is the place to get back to nature, with open-air showers and meals eaten outside, but if you want a tad more luxury, upgrade to the nearby Atsitsa Taverna.

Each day after breakfast, there is an hour for the communal *Demos*, or people's assembly, when facilitators outline the day's schedule and guests offer feedback. Most guests are in their mid-thirties and upward, but age becomes rather irrelevant. Whoever you meet and whichever course you choose, you will have plenty of free time for the beach, massages, suppers out, moonlit walks, midnight skinny-dipping, cheesy disco dancing, philosophical debate, group hugs—whatever floats your boat. **CSJ**

← *The island is dedicated to holistic well-being and is home to a magical community.*

Stay at Nafplia Palace

Location Nafplion, Greece   **Website** www.nafpliapalace.gr
Price ⑤⑤

Sometimes all you need is a drink, somewhere to sit, and a great view. The Nafplia Palace was built on that simple principle. The architects sited it within the Bronze Age fortress of Akronafplia, on the rocks above the old town of Nafplion, the first capital city of Greece.

The views from here are stupendous: right across the tiled rooftops of the city, along the coast past sandy beaches and plunging cliffs, across the crescent of the Bay of Argolis to the misty mountain peaks in the distance. By day you can admire the bougainvillea trailing across the walls of the town below; by night guests can sit and watch the lights twinkling right around the bay, looking up to the stars if they wish.

> *"[Greece's] only hotel in a historic monument.... There are grandiose sea views from the elegant rooms."*

Dana Facaros, *The Sunday Times*

A view this good influences the whole hotel experience. All the newly renovated modern rooms and villas face out across the bay, whereas the two bars and three restaurants are perched on the cliff to take advantage of a panorama that can distract even the hungriest diner. Many of the villas have private infinity pools and outdoor whirlpool tubs facing the sea. Others boast exclusive terraces—for soaking up that memorable vista. There is a deliberate attempt to create a luxurious atmosphere. The view is so important that the best rooms offer guests remote control mattresses so they can prop themselves up and simply stare at the vision out of the window. **SH**

Explore Kastellorizo Island

Location Kastellorizo, Greece   **Website** www.kastellorizo.de
Price

"The famous aqua-colored cave of Kastellorizo is one of the rarest geological phenomena."

Kastellorizo municipality website

Greece's remotest island is a hidden gem. It is only a stone's throw from the Turkish coast, but visitors normally reach the island by taking a flight, ferry, or catamaran from Rhodes, 60 miles (96 km) away.

Kastellorizo has retained its underground status by staying out of the travel brochures and off the tourist trail. With a surface area of only 3.5 square miles (9 sq km), it is virtually impossible to get lost on this tiny island, which has just 250 inhabitants, most of whom are fishermen. At the beginning of the last century, the island had 15,000 inhabitants, but the majority of them emigrated to Australia when Greece was bombed during World War II, and the population has remained small ever since, lending the island an air of tranquility.

Kastellorizo's attractive horseshoe-shaped port is dotted with vibrantly colored, neoclassical houses that date back to the Byzantine period when the color of the homes reflected the social status of the residents. Behind the port are crumbling and abandoned homes that line the backstreets like an atmospheric ghost town, with history oozing from every brick. Beyond the island's only settlement are rocky cliffs, and at their peak are the ruins of a fourteenth-century castle, Castello Rosso, after which the island is named. There are no roads and few guesthouses, but a raft of charming portside tavernas and top-notch restaurants, serving up grilled fish and home-cooked Greek fare, provide a place for visitors to while away the evenings. The island is traffic-free, but it is easy to get around on foot—there is no need to rush, because there is a real feeling that time has long forgotten this spot. **JK**

⬉ *Kastellorizo may not have any beaches, but its clear waters are awash with dolphins, turtles, and seals.*

Unwind at Perivolas

Location Santorini, Greece **Website** www.perivolas.gr
Price 🄢🄢

If the Perivolas infinity pool looks familiar, you have almost certainly seen it before, gracing the front cover of every quality travel magazine worth its high-gloss pages. After seeing it, it will be no surprise that this stunning hotel is consistently voted among the best in the world because romantic hideaways do not come much better than this.

Just a short walk away, the town of Oia pulses with the constant flow of tourists flocking to see the awe-inspiring volcanic geology of the Santorini caldera, but at tranquil Perivolas a peaceful atmosphere prevails. Faithful to Santorini's unique traditional architecture, Perivolas is fashioned from a series of 300-year-old

---

"The stunning infinity pool overlooks Santorini's famous flooded volcano."

Condé Nast Traveler

---

caves, previously the homes of local fishermen and farmers. The original shape of the caves has been preserved in each of the seventeen private houses' uniquely structured, sloping whitewashed walls, but the cave comparisons end there. Each house is kitted out in modern, understated style and comes complete with a private stone terrace with stunning views.

For something special, check in to the Perivolas suite. A central sitting area leads onto the bedroom, a spa facility with steam bath and massage pool, and a private pool with views of the Aegean. As the sun sets over the caldera, guests can finish the day in the candlelit bar, which opens onto the pool terrace. **HO**

Stay at Santorini Grace

Location Santorini, Greece   **Website** http://santorinigrace.com
Price 🄢🄢

Location, location, location is what makes Santorini Grace such a winner. Situated in the beautiful village of Imerovigli on the northwest of the volcanic island of Santorini, and high above the caldera—a deep basin formed by the volcano sinking into the sea—the newest hotel from the award-winning Grace Hotels stable offers the perfect vantage point from which to admire the famous Santorini sunsets over the Aegean.

You realize you are somewhere special as soon as you arrive. A welcoming glass of champagne is proffered, as well as an iced towel to cool you down. This stylish, chic property comes with nine individually styled rooms decorated in pale calming shades, and will appeal to those seeking a relaxing and romantic escape. It combines first-class service and the finest food and drink with a real sense of privacy and serenity. From deluxe rooms with plunge pools, to superior suites facing the sea, junior suites with jaw-dropping views, and the ultimate in exclusive accommodation (the honeymoon suite and the Grace suite), whichever room you find yourself in, king-size beds, luxurious bed linen, and a pillow menu all guarantee a good night's sleep. There are Korres toiletries with which to pamper yourself and satellite TV, DVDs, wireless Internet, and iPod speakers for your entertainment.

The hotel also has an intimate restaurant serving up Mediterranean fusion cuisine. It has a beautiful domed ceiling, but best to dine alfresco under the starlit sky to make the most of the stunning panoramas. If you get carried away by the sheer romance of the Grace, then you can tie the knot in the tiny church of Agios Ioannis Katifois nearby, which dates back to the fifteenth century. A more idyllic setting for a wedding would be difficult to imagine. **HA**

Stay at
Elounda Peninsula

Location Crete, Greece   **Website** www.eloundapeninsula.com
Price $ $ $

"It enjoys unparalleled views and a tranquil setting. . . . The view is blue as far as the eye can see."

greekhoneymoon.com

If only life were always like this: straightforward, with no decisions to make except which treatment to have in the spa, whether to play golf or take out a yacht for the day, or where to enjoy a predinner cocktail. Fortunately, life can be like this some of the time; at least it can at Elounda Peninsula in Crete. While hordes of tourists noisily congregate around busy corners of the island in their organized groups, the prevailing ambience here is one of tranquility.

Stretched out on a peninsula overlooking the Bay of Elounda, Mirabello Bay, and the glittering Aegean Sea, the hip hotel, which has no guest rooms, only suites, is permanently bathed in a swath of blue. Luxurious marble bathrooms offer spectacular vistas toward mountains and the ocean, so that you can even admire the view while you are splashing about in the bathtub. For those with serious cash to flash, there is the once-in-a-lifetime experience of staying in the Peninsula Palace. Located directly on the water's edge, it is exquisitely furnished and comes with immaculately manicured gardens and staff quarters, as well as a stylish private sailing boat.

To top it all, the hotel complex has a first-class Six Senses Spa offering a full range of holistic treatments and an authentic Turkish hammam. Have your body and feet polished with Cretan olive stones after a day spent exploring the island—if you can drag yourself away from the beach, that is. It promises to appeal to the five senses and awaken the sixth. An escape truly fit for Greek gods and goddesses. **LP**

◤ *The jetty bar offers a wonderful setting to enjoy drinks, with views through the floor to the sea below.*

Unwind at
Blue Palace Resort

Location Crete, Greece   **Website** www.bluepalace.gr
Price ⬧⬧

The Blue Palace Resort and Spa is made for romance. Highly popular for weddings and honeymoons, it even has its own romance department. The dedicated staff are highly attentive, and the Greek tradition of *philoxenia*—love of the stranger—is here in full swing.

The resort lies just outside the village of Elounda and close to the fishing village of Plaka, hugging a steep hill on Crete's northern coast. Facing the picturesque isle of Spinalonga, a former leper colony, the hotel is blessed with natural beauty but has also been cleverly designed to reflect its heritage. Upon entering the barrel-vaulted lobby, one is immediately

> *"This peaceful resort is set on a beautiful and otherwise undeveloped stretch of coast."*

Lynne Truss, *The Times*

transported to a bygone era, because the building has been carefully modeled on the sixteenth-century Venetian arsenals of Heraklion, Crete's capital. The original design of the 36-foot (11-m) high columns has been imitated, and they are spectacularly lit up at night. Five tempting restaurants, where dishes are concocted from the very best local produce, mean that there is never a lack of choice when it comes to dining, but it is the hotel's hedonistic spa that particularly stands out. Thalasso treatment pools are filled daily with fresh, heated seawater drawn from the Cretan Pelagos, and Cretan herbs are used in the hydromassage bath for the ultimate in relaxation. **LP**

Visit the Restored
Settlement of Milia

Location Crete, Greece   **Website** www.milia.gr
Price ⬧⬧

"Don't imagine we're some group of extremists living off spring onions and wearing potato sacks," say the owners of Milia village. In fact they simply own houses and land in the same area and are united by a passion for all things natural and traditional. Their little Cretan mountain village has become a world-renowned haven of tranquility, recycling, and sustainability.

The stone houses have been immaculately restored and stand on fertile slopes above a stream, amid olives, pears, herbs, and flowering shrubs. Visitors stay in one of thirteen rooms in the old village houses. Do not expect the Ritz Carlton; they are simple homes, but prettily furnished with reclaimed furniture and colorful textiles. Some houses are built right into the rocky slopes, so huge boulders appear along the side of rooms. Solar energy provides electric power, although guests are encouraged to use candles. Comforts are basic, but rooms have private bathrooms and fireplaces for heat during the winter. They all have a balcony, small terrace, or garden where guests linger to admire the views across the valley.

The atmosphere is friendly and relaxed. You will sit at chunky monastic tables in the communal dining room to sample delicacies made from produce cultivated organically on the village farm. Meals include rabbit with mizithra goat cheese; potato, chestnut, and onion stew; pork with orange cooked in the woodstove; and *kalitsounia* (small cheese pies). Days are spent exploring footpaths into the hills or using the village's mountain bikes. There are lessons in traditional Cretan cooking and wine tasting, and some guests enter into the spirit of Milia so enthusiastically that they spend their vacations helping with jobs around the village. **SH**

See Valley of the Butterflies

Location Rhodes, Greece
Website www.rodosisland.gr **Price** ❶

Every year, a gorge in Rhodes becomes a temporary home to millions of delicate Jersey tiger moths. Despite this misnomer, Valley of the Butterflies attracts half a million tourists annually. You can get here by catching a bus from Rhodes town or you can drive, but if you are staying in one of the resorts on the north coast, such as Tholos, you might like to try the hour-long walk to reach the natural park. Your efforts will make the lush greenery of the Petaloudes Valley all the more refreshing. Waterfalls gush and leafy trees cast deep pools of shade where log bridges stretch over the River Pelekanos.

At the beginning of June, the first few moths flutter into the valley, and the best time to soak up the true tranquility of this place is with these early arrivals. Although the highest numbers of moths are here in July and August, this period is also when most tourists visit, transforming the valley paths into thoroughfares. However, in June, you may have the valley to yourself, apart from the occasional moth wafting by, to feed on the pine resin that fills the valley with its heady scent, and giving you the chance to admire its flashing red, black, and brown wings. After a couple of months of replenishing their strength, the moths go into a gentle frenzy of reproduction in August, before drifting away from the valley in September.

There is also a museum here with displays on the valley's plants and animals. Even when the moths are not here, this is a wonderful place to meander in the dappled sunlight and enjoy the cool air, dampened by spray from the waterfalls. **JED**

↩ *Arriving at the Petaloudes Valley is like coming across an oasis in a desert, quite unlike the Rhodes terrain.*

Stay at the Anassa

Location Latchi, Cyprus
Website www.anassa.com.cy **Price** ❺❺

Sleep with the balcony doors open and wake to cream drapes swaying in a warm Aegean breeze. Walk outside and gaze at the long, long beach, hazily disappearing toward the hills of the Akamas National Park and the Baths of Aphrodite in the distance. The Anassa's dreamy atmosphere is helped by its peaceful location, alone on one of Cyprus's best beaches and backed by pine-forested mountains. Guests stay in a cluster of whitewashed villas under terra-cotta roofs surrounding the grand neoclassical palazzo of spas, restaurants, and cool, airy public rooms. Tall windows and balconies overlook paths winding through landscaped gardens to a quiet seashore.

"The 'It Girl' of the Mediterranean hotel scene; glamorous, fashionable and dripping in style."

Food and Travel magazine

The Anassa may feel like a five-star ancient monastery but is really a late-twentieth-century construction. Everything you touch is either marble, polished wood, fine linen, wrought iron, clean stone, or lush cream fabric. The hushed indulgence reaches its epiphany at the Romanesque spa and in the arched stone cellar where the finest of the four restaurants is housed. It serves a nine-course gourmet menu. But reverential tranquility is not compulsory—you can eat barbecued fish on the beach serenaded by bouzouki players. There are water sports, diving, and tennis on tap, and the best view of the rugged Akamas peninsula comes from the deck of the Anassa's private yacht. **SH**

Stay at Hotel Vila Bled

Location Upper Carniola, Slovenia
Website www.relaischateaux.com   **Price** 🔇🔇

Taking in the glorious view across sparkling Lake Bled to the soaring peaks of the Julian Alps, you would be forgiven for thinking you had landed in an alpine paradise. St. Mary's Church sits atop a huge rock on a tiny island before you, and all is still, except perhaps for a few people canoeing or jogging around the lake.

The snapshot is from Vila Bled, once the private residence of the leader of the former Yugoslavia, Marshal Tito. It is clear to see why it was here that Tito set up home, as did princes from imperial Austria and Yugoslav royals before him. There are rowboats, tennis courts, and swimming from a private lido, perfect for entertaining visiting statesmen and -women, and

> "[It has] breathtaking views of the lake … and many of its original fifties socialist-chic furnishings."

Robert Boynton, *Travel+Leisure* magazine

ample opportunities for horseback riding, fishing, and hunting. The estate, set among 12 acres (5 ha) of colorful flowers and greenery, also offers a spa, sauna, and hammam, but it is the picturesque lakeside setting that makes it extra special.

Inside, there are austere marble staircases and wooden floors, an atmospheric piano bar, and some enormous suites. There are also features reminiscent of its fascinating communist past, such as the ballroom covered in Tito's prized murals depicting the victories of the People's Red Army. Beyond the estate are dense wild forests, and Slovenia's capital, Ljubljana, is 31 miles (50 km) south. **LP**

Relax at Kendov Dvorec

Location Goriška, Slovenia
Website www.kendov-dvorec.com   **Price** 🔇🔇

Escape the hustle and bustle of city life by going back in time to an era when life moved at a far slower pace. Nestled in among the Slovenian mountains an hour's drive from the lively capital, Ljubljana, Kendov Dvorec (meaning "Kenda Manor") dates back to 1377, a time when Kenda landowners farmed the Idrija Valley. The area is still as richly green and full of fresh air as it was all those years ago.

Now a calm retreat that oozes class, Kendov Dvorec's eleven plush guest rooms are all named after former members of the Kenda family and are individually decorated, decked out with nineteenth-century antique furniture. Think hand-carved beds and oversized wardrobes. Pretend you are the lord of the manor by staying in his former room, a spacious affair beautifully decorated in a baroque style and enjoying stunning panoramic views over the old city center and church, backed by wooded peaks. It might have once been home to the region's most powerful men and women, but this five-star bed-and-breakfast has a very homey feel, with local handmade lace decorating the tablecloths, curtains, and bedcovers, plus a fabulous garden cloaked with flowers and hundred-year-old apple trees.

The house restaurant serves up Slovene cuisine with a modern twist, using only the best ingredients. There is no menu, so the chef will explain the dishes on offer, normally local specialties washed down with wine from nearby vineyards. Do like the locals and swim or fish for marble trout in the Idrijca River; bike or hike to alpine lakes and waterfalls, or go rafting or kayaking. Most important, take every opportunity you can to inhale deeply, filling your lungs with the crisp, pure alpine air. **JK**

Enjoy Nebesa

Location Goriška, Slovenia
Website www.nebesa.si/ang/nebesa.html   **Price** ⬤⬤

These four Alpine cottages for two sit 2,950 feet (900 m) up the slopes of Mount Kuk. Perched so high that you are even above the cloud level, there are staggering views across snowcapped mountains and green valleys. The wooden and stone chalets are simple but stylish, with a full glass wall looking out to the meadows and woodland rolling down the steep hillside, dotted with roaming wild deer.

A large sitting room downstairs leads to a kitchen and bathroom. Upstairs, the attic bedroom has low eaved ceilings and a comfy double bed. It is minimalist without being too fashionable, with contemporary chrome lights and coffee-colored wool sofas to add

> *"Glass-walled fronts mean views are ever present and wild red deer wander through the meadows."*

i-escape.com

warmth. Nebesa offers guests only bed-and-breakfast, though there is a kitchen. Help yourself during the day to drinks and snacks, from local wine to cheese and cold meats, all of which are included in the price. Breakfast is put in your fridge to eat at your leisure.

The nearest town is a fifteen-minute drive away, so you will need a car to get around. That just adds to the magical sense of isolation. If you can pull yourself away from the views and the fantastic wellness center—complete with sauna, whirlpool tub, and heated pool—go hiking for panoramic views from Slovenia all the way to Italy. Alternatively, drive to Kobarid for walks around the Soča River. In winter there is great skiing. **AD**

Dine at Hiša Franko

Location Goriška, Slovenia
Website www.hisafranko.com   **Price** ⬤⬤

Located in the Soča Valley in the far west of Slovenia, near the border with Italy, Hiša Franko is a small boutique hotel that has been making waves far and wide. Deep in the least developed region of Slovenia, the restaurant alone is worth the trip.

Run by husband and wife team Valter and Ana, the menu is eclectic—expect nettle risotto alongside scallops, bitter cacao noodles, mountain lamb, rabbit, and Mediterranean tuna. Desserts like fruit sorbet and Cuban chocolate soufflé finish the meal with a flourish. All the food is organic and local. It is served in a relaxing red room with starched white tablecloths and dark-wood furniture and matched with Italian or Slovenian wine: Valter is an expert sommelier and is happy to lend his expertise to interested parties. Five and eight-course tasting menus are also roundly celebrated for their inventiveness and exquisite presentation. Although there is accommodation at Hiša Franco, guests visit for the food experience: It is an inspiring place for those who know their cuisine. In the summer, dining takes place in a glass-walled room, and there is also a private dining room for special occasions. Such is Valter's enthusiasm for Slovenian wine that you will inevitably join him in the cellar for a tasting session and take home a few bottles of your favorite wine at cost price.

Rooms at the restaurant exhibit a similar attention to detail, with plenty of creative touches. Rooms 9 and 10 both have a separate enclosed terrace, and all are individually decorated in a modern, sleek style. The surrounding countryside is fantastic to explore, either by foot, bike, or by heading down one of the rivers on a kayak or white-water raft, and Ana can provide luxury packed lunches for all excursions. **LD**

Explore Slovenia by Bicycle

Location Slovenia **Website** www.slovenia.info
Price 💲💲

Its glorious countryside crisscrossed by an extensive network of bicycle paths, Slovenia has in recent years become one of Europe's best destinations for biking vacations. It may be small, but Slovenia manages to pack meandering rivers, snowcapped mountains, craggy caves, ancient villages, primeval forest, and rolling farmland into its compact dimensions.

There are several options for those who like their biking to be freewheeling and easy. The region to the southwest of the capital, Ljubljana, which heads down toward the Italian border and Adriatic coast, is filled with quiet, idyllic country lanes. For a bit of pampering, visitors could try the northwest, around Maribor, a wine-growing region famous for its spa towns and vineyards. After a hard day in the saddle, riders can fortify themselves with a dip in the healing, thermal waters of the local hotels and a glass of regional wine.

To appreciate the best views the country has to offer will require a little more exertion. Narrow paths lead up into the Slovenian Alps, winding past verdant peaks, pine-clad slopes, and crystal-clear glacial lakes. One of the most popular rides is to Lake Bled, whose tranquil waters have been guarded by the famous Castle Bled, which has perched upon a 425-foot (130-m) cliff for more than a thousand years.

If you do not feel up to mountain riding, you could always head in the opposite direction. Peca Mountain offers a very unusual bicycling experience. Instead of making a lung-bursting trip to the top, cyclists put on headlamps to guide themselves along a 3-mile (5-km) subterranean path through a disued mine. **JF**

➡ *A cyclist rides through the valley of Voje above Bohinj in the Julian Alps, Slovenia.*

Discover Pristava Lepena

Location Goriška, Slovenia **Website** www.pristava-lepena.com **Price** ⊜

Gazing across the churning jade waters of the Soča River, it is easy to see why this magical corner of Slovenia was chosen as the background for the Chronicles of Narnia film *Prince Caspian*. Luckily you do not have to travel to another world to enjoy this unspoiled alpine wilderness.

The Soča River flows through the Triglav National Park, where the fresh Alpine air collides with the balmy Adriatic breezes from neighboring Italy. Over thousands of years, the icy, clear waters of the river carved out the Trenta Valley. Today it is lush with green meadows and brightly colored wildflowers. Tucked in the fertile valley, overlooked by the majestic limestone peaks of the Julian Alps, is Pristava Lepena.

Owners Milan and Silvia Dolenc have created the perfect getaway for outdoor enthusiasts. A cluster of eight traditional wooden and stone chalets, Pristava Lepena both blends in with and takes full advantage of its magnificent natural surroundings. Guests can choose from a myriad of activities. Horse lovers relish the opportunity to trek through forests and mountain ridges on one of the village's purebred Lipizzaner horses. Alternatively there are walking or mountain biking trails, tennis courts, and a swimming pool. The river hosts a range of water sports, including rafting, kayaking, and canyoneering. But it is the top-notch fly-fishing that attracts keen anglers from all over the world. Marble, rainbow, and brown trout can all be caught in the cool, clear waters.

The restaurant offers locally sourced, traditional cuisine, such as fresh lamb on a spit and grilled trout. Braver souls might even attempt the homemade spirits. Afterward, you can warm yourself by the open fire or sit out on your private terrace and soak in the surrounding Alps. It is a truly unforgettable view. **JP**

⊡ *Pristava Lepena's location in a secluded valley high in the Julian Alps is perfect for enjoying the mountains.*

Stay at the Pucić Palace

Location Dubrovnik, Croatia **Website** www.thepucicpalace.com **Price** 💲💲

Amid all the hustle and bustle that is Dubrovnik on a typical summer day, the five-star Pucić Palace Hotel is a romantic haven. Though right in the center of the Old Town, it is a million miles from the camera-toting tourists who pack the city's narrow streets.

Across from the Gundulić Square, named after a seventeenth-century Dubrovnik-born dramatist and poet, the Pucić Palace was once one of the finest noble homes of its time. It was converted into a hotel at the end of the nineteenth century. Originally a three-star hotel, it was renovated and reopened in 2002 with just nineteen rooms, each named after a writer or artist from the city's past.

There are two suites and one single room, but mainly deluxe and executive rooms—the latter with better views than the deluxe rooms—all exquisitely finished with high-beamed ceilings and dark-oak floors. They are furnished with antiques but feature every modern convenience a twenty-first-century traveler could possibly want. A notebook, printer, scanner, and fax can even be provided on request. Bathrooms are equally luxurious, with freestanding tubs, soft cotton bathrobes, and Bulgari products.

The rooms are superb, but the pièce de résistance has to be Defne, the rooftop restaurant, where you can feast on Eastern Mediterranean cuisine to the gentle sounds floating up from the street below. The Café Royal brasserie on the ground floor has seating inside and out, in Gundulić Square, during the summer. Do not miss the stone soup, literally flavored with minerals from pebbles taken from the Adriatic Sea. Razonoda wine bar is a great place to hang out in the early evening with a glass of your favorite tipple, served with traditional, local nibbles such as Dalmatian smoked ham and homemade cheese. **JA**

⬆ *The Pucić Palace offers an intimate luxury experience in the heart of Dubrovnik's Old Town.*

Unwind at Villa Dubrovnik

Location Dubrovnik, Croatia **Website** www.villa-dubrovnik.hr
Price 😊😊😊

"Watch the sun go down over the Adriatic from one of three vine and flower-covered terraces."

Liz Bird, *Guardian*

Built as a resting place for Tito's officials in the 1950s, this intimate and upmarket pad has a colorful past. Communism may be long gone—along with the officials—but Villa Dubrovnik remains a relaxing haven for those in need of indulgence.

Clinging onto a cliff's edge, its low-rise terraces spectacularly draped over the Adriatic Sea, this charming hotel affords fantastic views of ultra-chic Dubrovnik. More than sixty steep, cypress tree–lined steps lead down from the road to the creamy-colored villa's main entrance. Once inside, the style is completely minimalist, with sleek white walls and simple furnishings lending the place a light, airy feel.

Rooms are also simple but clean, all with French doors opening out onto balconies offering stunning panoramic views of the sea, the island of Lokrum, and the ancient city walls in the near distance. All communal areas have generously sized terraces with plenty of loungers, shaded by vines and umbrellas, and every meal is served up on a different level. An à la carte restaurant cooks up divine food, and a bistro offers snacks. There is also a well-equipped fitness studio for those who fear overindulging.

Wander down to the water's edge via the hotel's verdant gardens (or by taking the elevator), where there is a small and secluded private pebble beach for sun worshippers and swimmers. You can reach the shops, bars, and restaurants of Dubrovnik's Old Town by taking a leisurely twenty-minute stroll or, better still, by using the hotel's private boat service. **JK**

↖ *All rooms in the glamorous Villa Dubrovnik have terraces with views of the sea and the Old Town.*

Visit Mljet and St. Mary's Church and Monastery

Location Mljet, Croatia   **Website** www.visitcroatia.com
Price ⊖

With an almost otherworldly beauty permeating Mljet, it is no wonder that the tiny island is a treasured national park. It is liberally sprinkled with hallmarks of the Croatian countryside—emerald green valleys, bristling conifers, and fascinating stone architecture—from the man-made gothic turrets of the villages to the natural wonders of its karst cliffs.

With salt lakes, pine forests, sleepy villages, and a unique ecosystem, Mljet is an island whose lore precedes it. Its roots stem from the Illyrians; its history, like its country's, is peppered with occupations, settlers, invaders, reclamation, and myth. Such is its legacy that this little island, seemingly lost in the sea, is even said to be the place where Calypso ensnared Odysseus, keeping the mighty warrior captive in a cave for seven years.

Then there are the sunken lakes that, like the snakes eaten up by the illustrious mongeese still flocking over the island, the elusive seals, and the bura winds that clip the island's hinterland and shores, appear and vanish like its legends. These lakes, great and small, have been providing an attraction to visitors from nearby Dubrovnik and beyond for eons.

A boat carries visitors from the shore to the tiny islet in the center of the Great Lake. Stretched across its curious surface are the Benedictine Monastery and enchanting Church of St. Mary, remnants from the years when Mljet was under the jurisdiction of Benedictine Monks. The charming stone monastery has been an epicenter of culture and spirituality throughout the ages, hosting famous poets as its abbots, such as Ignjat Đurđević, and drawing Benedictines from across the neighboring lands. **VG**

Recharge on Palmižana Island

Location Near Hvar, Croatia   **Website** www.palmizana.hr
Price ⊖

Set in 740 acres (300 ha) of unspoiled and uninhabited wilderness on a tiny island in the Adriatic, Palmižana resort is a ten-minute boat ride from Hvar. The air is rich with the scent of exotic flowers, pines, and wild herbs, and tropical vegetation, such as cacti and eucalyptus, flourishes.

Under the shade of the century-old pine forest are stone bungalows that can accommodate sixty guests; all are individually decorated and brightly colored with highly patterned bedspreads and modern Croatian artwork. Run by members of the Meneghello family, who have managed the estate for over a hundred

> *"My kids were wild about the Palmižana beach, which is sandy and shallow and lined with caves."*
>
> Josip Novakovich, *New York Times*

years, the two restaurants, Toto's and Palmižana Meneghello, are renowned for their fish dishes. Guests may even accompany the chef on his purchasing trips to vineyards and the fish market.

A short walk across the pine forest leads to the beach, studded with secluded coves and hidden bays where you can strip off and bare all if you feel like it: Palmižana has a long tradition of nudity, and skinny-dipping is commonplace. Warm temperatures last from April to November, and the island is famed for its high number of sunshine hours. The waters surrounding the island are a haven for divers, awash with shipwrecks and tropical fish. **JK**

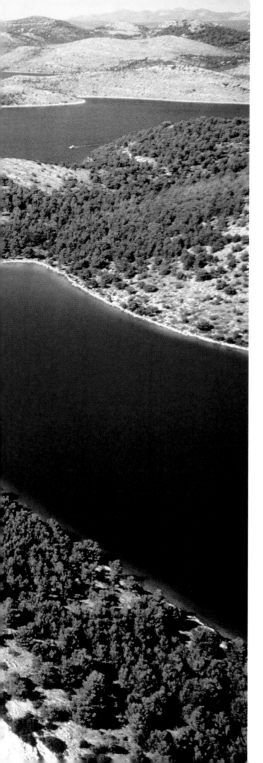

Visit the Kornati Islands

Location Kornati, Croatia **Website** www.kornati.hr
Price $

When George Bernard Shaw traveled around the Adriatic, he stopped on the coast of what is now Croatia and fell in love with the archipelago of the Kornati Islands. They are still as beautiful today as they were all those years ago.

The 140 islands cover an area of 124 square miles (320 sq km), much of it protected by a national park. Within it are crystal-clear waters, hidden coves, underwater reefs, ancient archaeological remains, and the famous crowns (sheer rocks soaring out of the sea). These fascinating steep cliffs are the sides of a large tectonic rift that stretches from Istria and ends in Middle Dalmatia, caused by the northern motion of Africa and its collision with Europe.

There are no permanent residents on the islands, and most of the region belongs to the people of Murter Island, who come to tend the olive groves, the vineyards, and orchards. They stay in cottages when there is work to be done, and rent the accommodation out to vacationers when the farming is finished. With no electricity or running water, these traditional retreats are as far removed from the outside world as you can get. Alternatively, you can take a day trip from Zadar, Sibenik, or Split.

Some of the most beautiful islets to explore by boat are Koromacna, Opat, Stiniva, Striznja, Sipnata, and Lopatica. You can stop at one of the many piers dotted around the islands for a delicious lunch at a seafood taverna. There is good diving and snorkeling in the surrounding waters, or you can hike across the desertlike landscape for panoramic views. **AD**

← *The islands of the Kornati archipelago provide an echo of the untouched, rugged Mediterranean.*

Sail Croatia's Coast

Location Croatia   **Website** www.dalmatiancoast.com
Price 💲💲

There are more than a thousand islands scattered off Croatia's Adriatic coast, creating between them a coastline that stretches to 3,600 miles (5,794 km) in length. For nautical enthusiasts, this archipelago is heaven-sent. There are numerous yacht-charter companies along the coast that rent out vessels, whether you are after a bareboat charter or a luxury yacht with skipper and crew. The waters are blue, the weather is gentle, and the islands, of which about fifty are inhabited, are close enough to reach with the tiniest of hops.

Above all, though, it is the diversity that keeps the sailors happy. Some islands are long established on the tourist trail. Take Rab, for example, which was declared a health resort by the local council as far back as 1889. More than half a century later, Britain's Duke of Windsor (formerly King Edward VIII) came to the island with his wife (Wallis Simpson); it is said that he was the first to swim here without clothes and thus started the island's tradition of nudism. You might stop in Silba, which has restaurants and stores but no roads, ensuring back-to-nature tranquility, or Pasman, whose many white-sand coves attract those in need of a rest.

Many like to visit the Kornati Islands, an archipelago of 147 different islands, islets, and reefs that together make up a national park. Here you will find traditional fishing villages and quiet bays. Between the islands winds a labyrinth of marine passages: Local legend has it that the islands were created when God had finished making the world and, finding he had some materials left over, simply threw them into the sea. **PE**

⬅ *The warm, limpid waters off of Croatia's coast are perfect for exploring by boat.*

Stay at Zabola

Location Transylvania, Romania   **Website** www.zabola.com
Price 💲💲

Zabola, the estate of the Count Mikes family, dates back to around 1400 and was at one time a fortified building with a tower and ceilings intricately painted with frescoes. The grand house sits at the end of a tree-lined estate with a stunning lake in 84 acres (34 ha) of parkland at the foot of the Carpathian Mountains. Six airy guest rooms are housed within the Machine House, which once held generators for the hospital set up here under communist rule.

Today, open fires roar a warm welcome and the red room, with blood-red walls, is the closest thing you will find to a spooky Dracula encounter. Soak in the freestanding bathtub surrounded by antler-clad walls

> *"[U]pmarket accommodation that conveys both colonial-era India and old school Transylvania."*
>
> Andrew Eames, *CNN Traveler* magazine

for a real-life gothic experience. Then enjoy the fruits of the chef's labors in the kitchen, from venison and beautifully cooked wild mushrooms to homemade dips and jams, all made using local produce.

There is much to explore in the surrounding area, although hunting has now been replaced with more nature-friendly bear-watching trips. Take a guided trek through fairy-tale woodlands, or take the estate's horse and trap on a tour of carefully preserved local villages. Farther afield is the medieval settlement of Sighisoara, the birthplace of the infamous Vlad the Impaler, who skewered his enemies on wooden poles and inspired Bram Stoker's Count Dracula. **AD**

Explore the Danube Delta by Boat

Location Danube Delta, Romania
Website www.deltadunarii.ro/?lg=en   **Price** 💲

Dubbed Europe's avian Serengeti due to the 300 species of bird that live here, the Danube Delta is one of the last surviving great wildernesses on the continent. After a 1,700 mile (2,735 km) journey winding across Europe, the Danube finally reaches the Black Sea, where it splits into many channels. Vast expanses of swamps, forests, and lakes, surrounded by thick reed beds, provide a sanctuary for the vast diversity of wildlife, plants, and trees. Herons, pelicans, red breasted geese, pygmy cormorants, and a fantastic collection of mammals including otters, mink, muskrat, and wild boar reside here. It was named Landscape of the Year 2007-2009, and UNESCO has given the status of Biosphere Reserve to large swathes of it.

One of the best ways to explore this watery wilderness is to take a boat trip deep inside the delta for bird-watching and fishing, or simply relaxing. To really immerse yourself in the Delta, however, spend a few days on a houseboat, or floating hotel as they are known locally. Explore wooded islets, marshes, sand dunes, and villages before mooring in a convenient spot. Smaller boats enable you to navigate some of the narrower channels and backwaters.

But if you'd rather keep your feet on dry land, the luxurious Delta Nature Resort is the place to stay. It offers comfortable villas with large terraces that provide sweeping vistas over the Delta. Facilities include a gloriously well-positioned pool, and an observation tower to give you a bird's-eye view of the wonderful natural spectacle. **HA**

➡ *The scenic Danube is home to 160 varieties of fish, and 1,200 species of plant.*

Enjoy Aquacity

Location Poprad, Slovakia **Website** www.aquacity.sk
Price ⊖

Chill down to minus 186°F (-121°C) in the world's coldest place, all in the name of a health kick. It might sound like the stuff of science fiction, but it is considered a wonder treatment for top athletes and is available for everyone at Aquacity, a water park and spa center in Slovakia, situated at the foot of the snow-peaked High Tatras Mountains. Exposing bodies to temperatures this low is part of a process known as cryotherapy.

The treatment is carried out under strict medical supervision, and patrons wear insulated shoes, socks, ear protectors, gloves, and a paper mask to cover the nose and mouth, plus shorts and a T-shirt. The experience begins in the antechamber, chilled to a mere minus 76°F (-60°C), where people undergoing the treatment stamp their feet and huddle together for up to a minute to eliminate moisture from the surface of the body.

Next up is the mother of all freezers, the cryo-chamber itself, chilled to an inconceivable minus 186°F (-121°C)—that is colder than the Antarctic, where the coldest temperature ever recorded was only minus 128°F (-89°C). The temperature is so extreme that people feel nothing but a tingling sensation, but you can leave the chamber at any time if the cold becomes unbearable.

After treatment, users undertake a supervised low-impact gym workout to get the blood flowing to the muscles and joints. Patients report a reduction in pain thanks to an increase in blood flow. It is also said to help conditions such as arthritis, lower-back disorders, and osteoporosis. The release of endorphins during the treatment is also considred to be helpful for people suffering from depression. **JK**

Discover Spiš on Foot

Location Spiš, Slovakia **Website** www.slovakia.travel
Price ⊕

In a country blessed with a multitude of beautiful landscapes, Spiš is considered a little bit special, even by the Slovaks. Interestingly, the region has no official status within Slovakia. It is not an administrative area, but rather a place defined by its shared culture, dialect, and dress. For the Slovakians its influence is profound—everyone can tell you how to get there—yet its name appears on no maps.

Its borders are generally defined as being the Tatras Mountains to the north (known as the "miniature Alps"), the Lovoca Mountains to the east, and the Slovenské Rudohorie Mountains to the south. It is a rolling, hilly place filled with beautiful walking routes

> *"Summers in mountainous Spiš are lazy and relaxed, and the fields and forests fill with hikers."*
>
> Jaime Gill, *Guardian*

that take you along steep, forest-clad canyons, dotted with waterfalls and fast-flowing streams, and past great, snowcapped peaks. In the summer people come to hike the trails and soak in thermal spas, and in winter they come to ski.

Spiš's attractions are historic as well as natural. Its major landmark is the majestic Spiš Castle—one of Europe's largest fortresses—which looms on perilous cliffs 2,080 feet (634 m) above sea level and provides towering views of the surrounding landscape. **JF**

⮕ *The World Heritage site of Spiš Castle, the largest ruined castle in the country.*

See Slowinski National Park

Location Middle Pomerania, Poland
Website www.mos.gov.pl   **Price** ◑

Hauntingly beautiful sand dunes are a unique feature of Poland's coastline. Set in Slowinski National Park between the pretty towns of Rowy and Leba, these giant, desertlike dunes can rise up to a colossal 138 feet (42 m) above sea level. Shifting up to 32 feet (10 m) per year, the dunes leave behind dead tree stumps, evidence of a deeply buried ancient forest. This stark sight adds to the mysterious and desolate beauty of this vast open space that stretches for miles.

Perfect for those people who like to explore and really get back to nature, the dunes are rich in flora and fauna. Heathers, crowberrys, orchids, and pines dot the otherwise barren landscape. A designated UNESCO Biosphere Reserve, the rolling dunes are home to 250 species of resting and migratory birds, including rarely spotted varieties such as the white-tailed eagle and the black stork.

Cars and buses are banned from the pristine white sands, helping to maintain its peaceful charm. Walk through the park to reach the dunes and make the return trip to Leba by walking 5 miles (8 km) along the beach, or even by swimming back.

During the balmy summer months, the sun beats down on the dunes, but the relentless sea breezes that whip up the sand and keep it on the move ensure the temperature remains pleasant. Alongside the dunes are several clear lagoons, where deer and boar often gather on the shores. Beyond this is a dense pine forest where elk, raccoons, and badgers roam. Spend the night in the nearby tranquil town of Leba, surrounded by pine forest, and enjoy the wildlife. **JK**

⬅ *Huge sand dunes stretch to the horizon in Poland's Slowinski National Park.*

Explore Białowieża Forest

Location Podlaskie Voivodeship, Poland
Website www.whc.unesco.org   **Price** ◑

Białowieża Forest is as wild and magical today as it was 500 years ago when the Polish royal family banned logging and settling to safeguard it as a hunting ground. A model of tranquility and nature, it remains unspoiled and undeveloped by man. Sprawling across Poland's border with Belarus, this peaceful region clings to the past, with farmers still tending to their land with horse-drawn plows.

One of Europe's last remaining primeval forests, which once spanned the entire continent's lowlands thousands of years ago, this is the landscape of fairy tales. A dense and beautiful network of oak, spruce, and hornbeam trees is mixed together with marshes,

> *"[T]his immense forest range . . . is home to some remarkable animal life."*
>
> **UNESCO World Heritage Committee**

peat bogs, and streams. The numerous decaying trees add to the serene yet eerie atmosphere. Rich in wildlife, Białowieża throbs quietly to the sound of woodpeckers and the song of the 228 bird species that make the forest their home. The world's last remaining herds of bison, the largest land mammal in Europe, are kept in a reserve here. Watching these huge, slow-moving animals trudging through the snow in winter is a moving experience.

Trails for walkers, bikers, and horse riders mean it is possible to visit the forest without a guide, giving visitors the chance to soak up the fresh pine-scented air and enjoy the beauty of the area at a relaxed pace. **JK**

Visit Kazimierz Dolny

Location Lublin Voivodeship, Poland
Website www.kazimierz-news.com.pl   **Price** ◑

Landscape artists flock to Kazimierz Dolny because it is thought to be blessed with an effervescent light. The appeal of the tiny, sleepy town has not been lost on film directors, either, who have often used its atmospheric streets as a setting for romances and historical thrillers. Sitting proudly on the banks of the Vistula River, Kazimierz Dolny in eastern Poland is flush with peaceful cobbled streets lined with historical buildings. A laid-back retreat for stressed-out city dwellers who swarm here during the summer months from the nearby cities of Warsaw and Lublin, Kazimierz Dolny's large population of artists and writers helps maintain its bohemian ambience.

The town was founded in the fourteenth century by the much-loved King Kazimierz the Great as a community for the Jewish population, and he built a castle here as his summer residence. The gothic castle was destroyed by the Swedes in the 1650s, but its ruins are still open to the public today and offer sweeping views of the city and the River Vistula from its hilltop vantage point. Both World Wars shattered much of the town, with the second wiping out almost its entire Jewish population, but authorities worked wonders to restore the medieval houses to their former splendor, and every corner of the town tells a historic tale.

Rynek, the market square, is the prettiest part of town, with a well marking its center. It is here you will find several opulent houses, dating back to 1615. All town houses have roofs covered with wooden tiles, and in the balmy summer heat there is a faint yet pleasant smell of pine in the air. **JK**

⇨ *A view of the traditional town center of Kazimierz Dolny from the "Hill of the Three Crosses."*

Visit Kizhi Island

Location Karelia, Russia
Website www.kizhi.karelia.ru   **Price** 🌓

The Karelian Republic, a fairy-tale land of pine and birch forest, marshes, and lakes in their tens of thousands, is a boundless wilderness. The area around the city of Petrozavodsk, in Karelia, is one of the most beautiful regions in the whole of Russia for hunting, fishing, hiking, and camping.

The most beautiful attraction in the region is the exquisite island of Kizhi on Lake Onega, an old pagan ritual site where twelfth-century Russian colonists settled, creating a parish of extraordinary wooden buildings that remain today. The Cathedral of the Transfiguration has twenty-two picturesque onion domes, and the building has wonderful decorations and gables to keep the rain from getting in. Also on the island is the nine-domed Church of the Intercession, full of icons; the fourteenth-century Church of the Resurrection of Lazarus, the oldest in Russia; and the Chapel of the Archangel Michael. Not a single nail or piece of metal was used in the construction of these buildings; instead, scribe-fitted horizontal logs and interlocking joinery keep the structures aloft.

In summer, students from nearby Petrozavodsk play the bells here, and young pale-skinned waifs dressed in traditional costume sing mournful folk songs about the sad forests. The island is a glorious idyll of long grasses, wildflowers, country lanes, and silence. If you can, stay at Sennaya Guba, where vacationing Russians flock. You will be taken care of, with a boat to take you to Kizhi, a wooden jetty to loll on, and very likely a wooden *banya* (sauna) on-site. **LB**

↩ *The domes of the Cathedral of the Transfiguration on Kizhi Island shimmer in the sun.*

Stay at Kempinski Moika 22

Location St. Petersburg, Russia
Website www.kempinski-st-petersburg.com   **Price** 💲💲

The one-time capital of Russia, founded in 1703 by Peter the Great, is like a living museum where white is a recurring theme. To live out those Dr. Zhivago fantasies, visit in winter when a dusting of snow covers the city's golden cupolas, whereas in summer, the sun shines all night during the "White Nights." Magical, full of history and charm, the Venice of the North's highlights include the Winter Palace, home to the Hermitage Museum's amazing three million pieces of art. Spoil yourself and book into the Kempinski Moika 22 overlooking the Hermitage. Located in a traditional St. Petersburg mansion, it dates back to 1853, during the reign of Czar Nicholas I.

> "At the Winter Palace, the former royal rooms . . . are as captivating as the art."

Clifford J. Levy, *New York Times*

Although the building's facade is unchanged, the interior has been updated and modernized. Cozy duplex rooms with a nautical theme are plush and romantic, especially thanks to the daily delivery of fresh roses: a nice touch on the windowsill against a backdrop of snowflakes. Another bonus is the daily English high tea, especially when it is well below freezing outside. The dedicated Tea Room blends England and Russia's finest traditions: The national ritual loved by the likes of Pushkin and Chekhov has been adapted with pastries and cakes, but also very English cucumber sandwiches, alongside the antique samovar bubbling away brewing zavarka tea. **RCA**

Take the Grand Express Train to St. Petersburg

Location Moscow–St. Petersburg, Russia
Website www.grandexpress.ru/en **Price** 🟢🟢

It might not be the same as a two-week Trans-Siberian extravaganza, but the Moscow to St. Petersburg overnight Grand Express offers the best of old and new Russia on wheels. The departure platform in the Russian capital is unchanged; from its name "Leningradskaya" to the austere atmosphere complete with James Bond–movie steam and attendants in sharp red uniforms and matching pillbox hats.

Stepping onboard Russia's first privately owned and operated luxury passenger train is a throwback to the time when travel was glamorous. The fourteen-car train is entirely decorated in red, with a very strong

---

"The journey on the Grand Express is nothing short of fantastic and ideal for a romantic evening."

James Logan, *Passport Magazine*

---

art-deco influence, from the deluxe cabins with their freshly laundered crisp sheets on the twin berths to the beautiful wood-paneled bar.

You are greeted with a hot cup of tea in a traditional tea glass with an intricately designed silver holder. Join other diners in the restaurant, reminiscent of a golden era movie theater, to nibble on tiger shrimp, assorted cold cuts, or caviar sandwiches. The train moves slowly throughout the night, and with the gently rocking steady motion, sleep comes easily. However, you would be forgiven for staying awake to take in the scenery. For miles, watch the countryside blanketed in snow, dark forests, and towns bathed in light. **RCA**

Visit the Cathedrals of the Kremlin

Location Moscow, Russia
Website www.moscow.info/kremlin/index.aspx **Price** 🟠

The first Kremlin was built at Borovinsky Hill during the eleventh and twelfth centuries. It went through a series of reconstructions, including one in 1485 that gave us the redbrick walls and towers that still stand today. At the heart of this mighty edifice is Cathedral Square, home to four cathedrals. Cool in summer, warm in the freeze of winter, the cathedrals are the most beautiful things in the Kremlin.

The oldest of the four is the fifteenth-century Cathedral of the Assumption. Its solemn simplicity and lightness come courtesy of Italian architect Aristotele Fioravanti, who was drafted in from Bologna in 1492, when the structure built by local architects came crashing down. He created a lightness and airiness that is quite distinct from the brooding, gloomy interiors of most orthodox churches. This is Russia's most important church: the place for coronations, burials, and inaugurations of czars.

The Cathedral of the Archangel Michael is the most Italianate of the four, built at the beginning of the sixteenth century by the Italian Aleviz Novyi—it is all gables, whorls, and pilasters. Until Peter the Great, this is where all of Russia's rulers were buried, including Ivan the Terrible. The Church of the Deposition of the Robe is bijou; tiny gilded cupolas grace its roof. Cozy, intimate, and musty, it was the domestic chapel for the czars. Finally, the fifteenth-century Cathedral of the Annunciation sparkles and glows. Here, Ivan the Terrible foresaw his own death when he saw a vision of a cross-shaped comet. Two days later, he died. **LB**

➡ *The dramatic interior of the Church of the Assumption in Cathedral Square, Moscow.*

Climb Mount Elbrus

Location Caucasus, Russia **Website** www.elbrus.org
Price 💲💲

The tallest mountian in Europe is not Mont Blanc, but rather the little-known Mount Elbrus, a brooding 18,519-foot (5,642-m) colossus set in the remote Caucasus Mountains in the extreme southwest corner of Russia. A twin-cone volcano that has lain dormant for 2,000 years, Elbrus has two peaks, the western being the higher by some 65 feet (20 m).

Reaching either of the summits can be strenuous but is certainly within the capabilities of a climber in reasonably good shape with moderate skills. However, it is crucial to acclimatize yourself properly to the high altitudes, and the specialist climbing tour companies that bring groups here require participants

> "The area is famous for its dramatic glaciers, which feed a handful of rivers in the summer."

Steve Connor, *Independent*

to complete a six-day or more training course, or to provide evidence of having previously acquired the equivalent skills or relevant experience elsewhere.

En route to base camp, winding mountain trails through stunning scenery present ample opportunity to interact with locals at the remote villages. This region is a colorful meeting place of cultures: Russian, Georgian, Azerbaijani, and Turkish. The real thrill, though, is in getting close to the wild. Eagles soar overhead, wild animals roam the forests, and trout swim the mountain streams. The terrain is truly awesome. The accommodation may be basic and the food challenging, but you are at one with nature. **RsP**

See Nalychevo Nature Park

Location Kamchatka, Russia **Website** www.park.kamchatka.ru
Price 💲

Getting back to nature is one thing; exploring the Nalychevo Nature Park in the depths of Siberia is quite another. Remote, silent, and far from anywhere, it's hard to put into words quite how isolated you feel in the far flung inhospitable Kamchatka peninsula in the Russian far east, renowned for its volcanoes (nearly 100 in Kamchatka), bears, and rivers full of salmon.

Nalychevo is the most accessible of Kamchatka's five nature parks. But these things are relative; the Kamchatka peninsula is still 9 hours ahead of Moscow, which is over 4,000 miles (6,400 km) away.

Kamchatka is sparsely populated and is widely recognized as having the world's fastest changing geology, where mountains have grown measurably higher and valleys wider than anywhere else in the course of a single lifetime. Nalychevo itself is dominated by three volcanoes: Koryaksky last erupted in 1956, Zhupanovsky in 1957, and Avacha in 1991. All this volcanic activity gives rise to the formation of tremendous geothermal and cold mineral springs, concentrated near the headwaters of the Nalycheva River. Blueberry bushes, birch trees, flowing rivers, and hot springs fill the landscape, while the valleys are surrounded by snow covered peaks. There are no fences in these parks, enabling the wildlife such as bears, wolves, and Arctic foxes to roam freely.

You can go hiking up one of the active volcanoes, bathe in the hot springs, or fish for salmon. In the winter you can ski or go dogsledding. Whatever the season, breathe in the pure still air, drink the naturally carbonated water, and relish the perfect silence. **HA**

➔ *The park combines stunning mountain scenery with vast expanses of tundra and coastal seascapes.*

Visit Jardin Majorelle

Location Marrakech, Morocco
Website www.jardinmajorelle.com **Price** $

Tucked away from the traffic noise, hawkers, beggars, and hot, dusty streets of Marrakech is the Jardin Majorelle, an oasis of calm in a city of chaos. These tranquil gardens, just outside the Medina walls, were designed by French expatriate artist Jacques Majorelle in 1924, during the colonial period when Morocco was a protectorate of France. Majorelle's watercolors still survive, but his garden was his real creative masterpiece. It was opened to the public in 1947 and has been welcoming visitors ever since. Since 1980 the garden was owned by designer Yves Saint-Laurent and his friend and patron, Pierre Bergé. Yves Saint-Laurent's ashes were scattered there after his death.

The garden's most characteristic feature is the special shade of cobalt blue that Majorelle used extensively to color the walls of the Museum of Islamic Art, housed in the artist's former home, as well as on flowerpots and other garden features. This brilliant color is now known as "bleu Majorelle."

A variety of birds have been spotted here, including falcons, turtledoves, robins, and storks. A variety of pathways and viewing areas leads you around a series of small pools, in which water lilies, lotus, papyrus, and other aquatic plants grow profusely. This is a welcome respite from the bustle of the city, with only the trickling of water to disturb the peace.

Be sure to pay a visit to the Museum of Islamic Art while you are here. It contains many treasures from the Islamic world, including ceramics, textiles, weapons, pottery and jewelry from Africa and Asia, as well as some paintings by Majorelle himself. **HA**

← *The vibrantly colored "bleu Majorelle" walls of the museum contrast with the garden's plants.*

Stay at Dar les Cigognes

Location Marrakech, Morocco
Website www.lescigognes.com **Price** $ $

For anyone who may be wondering, a "cigogne" is a stork. In the case of Dar les Cigognes, it is not just any old stork, but specifically those that sit on the walls of Marrakech's Royal Palace, which is just across the road.

A former merchant's home, located slap-bang in the center of Marrakech's famous Medina, Dar les Cigognes was lovingly restored by architect Charles Boccara and a team of local craftsmen. The traditional techniques are evident throughout the property, from intricate floor mosaics to elegantly carved wooden doors. Enter the building's courtyard to be greeted by fragrant citrus trees and a gently bubbling fountain; seek out the elegant dining room, library, and a

> *"Boccara . . . applied his Midas touch to this seventeenth-century former merchant's home.*
>
> **The Times**

reading/relaxation salon. Although these public areas lean toward classic Asian decor, Dar les Cigognes's eleven rooms are an entirely different matter: beautiful local touches blended with eyeball-popping hipness. The rooms also have enormous, funky beds, creatively carved baths, and luxurious cotton bathrobes.

The overall experience is soothing, luxurious, and attentive. Have your meals made to order and enjoy them at the rooftop café, looking out over the Atlas Mountains. Alternatively, take advantage of the great in-house spa, with its massage room, hammam, and whirlpool tub. The location is also a mere stone's throw from most of the Medina's main sights. **PS**

Unwind at Riad Farnatchi

Location Marrakech, Morocco
Website www.riadfarnatchi.com **Price** 💲💲

Riad Farnatchi was originally devised as the home of hotel entrepreneur Jonathan Wix, until he decided to transform it into a boutique hotel—an idea that proved highly successful.

Situated in one of the oldest areas of Marrakech's dusty Medina, the *riad* (house)—actually three *riads* combined—is designed around two courtyards and offers nine deluxe suites. Although the buildings date back as far as 400 years, the decor and amenities are thoroughly modern. Light and airy, each suite is stylishly decked out with every high-tech feature needed as well as elegant desks and traditional rugs and furnishings. Relax in a marble bath or book a daily

> *"A blissful union of traditional and modern. . . . Flowers tumble down the high walls."*

Sophie Lam, *Independent*

appointment at the in-house hammam, which has a superb array of tempting treatments to offer—from traditional Moroccan to the latest fads.

Even when full, the *riad* retains an air of quiet intimacy, an atmosphere engendered by the numerous cozy nooks around the courtyards and a large rooftop terrace with plenty of lounging spots. Romantic candlelit dinners are available (with a menu that changes every night), and the service is effortlessly good, with staff seemingly invisible until the exact moment you need them. In a city that is famed for its chic accommodation spots, Farnatchi works hard to stay well ahead of the pack. **PS**

Experience Caravanserai

Location Marrakech, Morocco
Website www.caravanserai.com **Price** 💲💲

Although Caravanserai ranks among Marrakech's top luxury accommodation hot spots, it is easy to mistake it from the outside for a traditional Arabic home. A fifteen-minute drive from the center of Marrakech, this 200-year-old building has been renovated precisely to fit in seamlessly with its surroundings, a tiny Arabic village. Inside is a rather different story.

Designed by local legend Charles Boccara (with his son, Mathieu), Caravanserai is an intimate wonderland of rustic appeal. Ancient techniques have been applied to re-create an authentic kasbah feel, complete with mud walls, old wooden beams, and use of a local material called *tadelakt*. The eleven suites and five standard rooms are arranged around a courtyard and large swimming pool. Two rooms have their own private pools, and most have their own terrace. The bathrooms are breathtaking.

Caravanserai's robe-clad staff seem to mysteriously appear just when you need them and disappear when you do not, and almost all requirements (within reason) are dealt with efficiently and obligingly.

Although not far from the center of the city—taxis and chauffeurs can be arranged—there is a particularly pleasant restaurant/bar on-site with a Moroccan and French menu, plus a serene designer garden and a hammam to coax you to stay. Terraces offer views across the River Tensift, the Atlas Mountains, and the ancient date grove known as the Palmeraie. Sitting there on a clear night, looking out at the dramatic nightscape with a fresh cup of mint tea by your side, is to feel like Moroccan royalty. **PS**

> *Caravanserai's central courtyard is dominated by its luxurious heated swimming pool.*

Stay at Adrere Amellal

Location Siwa Oasis, Egypt
Website www.adrereamellal.net   **Price** 💲💲💲

This extraordinary eco-lodge sits in the middle of the Saharan oasis at Siwa, eight long, dusty hours' drive from Cairo. Surrounded by shifting sand dunes and overlooking a shimmering salt lake, the lodge is built from salt rock and mud and is the brainchild of Egypt's most prominent environmentalist, Mounir Neamatalla.

This is an Egypt far from the tourist hordes. There's no electricity, but that doesn't mean forsaking twenty-first-century luxuries. Light is provided by oil lamps and candles, and coal braziers keep the chill of the desert night at bay. There is nothing more relaxing than resting in a bathroom and bedroom lit up solely by dozens of flickering beeswax candles, together

> *"A very special, luxurious sense of the primitive, surrounded by the magic ... of majestic mountains."*
>
> Geordie Greig, *Tatler*

with the blessed absence of telephones, e-mail, television, or even cell phone reception. Primitive pampering doesn't get much better than this.

The lodge's rooms are decorated in traditional Siwan style, strewn artfully with Berber carpets, doors made of palm trees, and beds fashioned from palm fronds. It also has a refreshingly cooling swimming pool, whose water is supplied by an ancient Roman spring. Lie back in the water and soak up the pool's endless horizons, surrounded by olive and palm groves and looking onto the stark and desolate, but beautiful, desert. Enjoy dinner under the inky sky, marveling at the constellations. **HA**

Experience Blue Hole

Location Sinai, Egypt
Website www.allsinai.info/sites/sites/blue_hole   **Price** 💧

A deep sapphire encircled by a brilliant topaz rim, this Red Sea jewel has garnered a reputation for being the world's most dangerous dive spot, so devastating are its charms. Along the coast from Dahab, past the mountain-cradled desert and sprawling Bedouin camps, you arrive at the cobalt shoal leading to the Blue Hole. Urchins spike the promontory like guardians of the waters, an otherworldly marine adventure considered to be the pearl of the Gulf of Aqaba—the Red Sea's most enchanting stretch.

Enter a world in which psychedelic shoals zigzag, manta rays meander, and ultraviolet jellyfish beckon like sirens of the deep. Coral reefs turn from yellow to red and violet for the foolhardy intent on testing their mettle in exploring the brutal, near-mythic arch, a deceptive rock formation toward the bottom of this submarine pothole. Lying at the bottom of the Blue Hole are the bodies of divers committed to the sea forever—there are thought to be almost a hundred of them—who recklessly pushed themselves too far, and became disorientated under the water.

Waiting up above, for those sensible divers who do not tempt fate with dangerous diving, are Bedouin children dressed in desert cotton. They call out to enchant divers into buying their brightly colored bracelets and trinkets or daring them to a game of sheshbesh—a game they are almost never beaten at.

Beyond the Blue Hole, star-spangled mountain nights or the enchanting hippie villages of Nuweiba and Tarabin beckon. The truly informed may find a native tracker who will lead them to the nearby Rasta Boogaloo—a mountain-hugged cove-cum-Bedouin camp that is accessible only by walking over rocks when the tide is out at night. **VG**

See the Nile by Felucca

Location Aswan to Luxor, Egypt   **Website** www.egypt.travel
Price

Voyage the thoroughfare of the pharaohs in a classic white-sailed felucca and you will journey from the southernmost tip of Egypt to the Valley of the Kings.

The ancient Egyptians believed the Nile to be a route from life into death and the afterlife. It became the most important trading route in North Africa and the lifeline of their civilization. Egypt's most important temples are based along this route. The mummies of the pharaohs, their wives, their concubines, and even the odd crocodile are all committed to the spectacular sites on the West Bank. Along the route you will be able to soak up the mysterious spirits and legends of the ancient Egyptians, taking in the overbearing

> *"When I read [Death on the Nile] I feel myself back on the steamer from Aswan to Wadi Halfa."*
>
> Agatha Christie, writer

Nubian rock temples of Abu Simbel and Kom Ombo, Egypt's most perfectly preserved temple at Edfu, beautiful and exotic peasant villages, and the largest religious site in the world, Karnak, which is the project of thirty of the world's most powerful rulers.

If you alight at the magnificent Valley of the Kings, you will discover proud sphinxes lining the causeway and the magisterial statue of Ramses II. Like the temples themselves, a journey along the Nile from Aswan to Luxor withstands the test of time. **VG**

← *A boat trip along the Nile remains a rite of passage fit for a king—or a pharaoh.*

Stay at Mandina Lodges

Location Makasutu, The Gambia
Website www.gambia.co.uk; www.makasutu.com **Price** $ $

Imagine a silence disturbed only by the rustle of monkeys hurling themselves through adjacent trees. Makasutu Culture Forest, an hour's drive from the busy coastal resorts of the Gambia, was founded in 1993 by Englishmen Lawrence Williams and James English. Their aim was to establish a cultural center to highlight how local people lived, prevent deforestation, encourage wildlife to return to the area, and create employment for villagers.

Tucked away inside the forest in an idyllic mangrove-lined tributary of the River Gambia is a luxury eco-resort that sleeps a maximum of sixteen. Guests reach Mandina Lodge by elevated walkways or

---

"Mandina Lodge, a gem of a luxury lodge tucked deep in the mangroves."

Kevin Rushby, *Guardian*

---

dug-out canoe. The accommodation is solar-powered with private roof terraces, beautiful views, and carved four-poster beds dressed in white linens. Bathrooms are roofless for bathing under the stars. There is an enormous pool and a relaxing bar. Dinner can be enjoyed alfresco or in your lodge, after a personal talk with the chef. The stillness, heavy with heat all year-round, lulls even the most stressed executive into total relaxation.

Guides will take guests to explore in the forest or on the river. Legend has it that Makasutu (holy forest) is haunted, but you are more likely to spot a baboon or monitor lizard than a supernatural being. **WG**

Bird-watch in the Gambia

Location The Gambia
Website visitthegambia.gm/bird-watching **Price** $

Even as the sun is sinking toward the horizon, the birds of the Gambia continue to sing. You will hear this melodic chorus from the moment you wake to well after the stars start shining in the dark African sky. The Gambia is a bird-watcher's paradise. A staggering 540 different species call this tiny country on the west coast of Africa home, probably because of the wide range of habitats found in such a small area: from the shoreline of the Atlantic Ocean, to the inland wetlands, to the dry African bush. The sheer number and variety of birdlife attracts ornithologists from all over the world. However, you do not have to be a serious bird-watcher to appreciate the stunning views.

What you see depends on where you look. Travel the western shoreline of the Atlantic Ocean and you can expect to see kingfishers, seabirds such as egrets and herons, and the curiously named white-faced whistling duck. Head inland and the birds change with the landscape. In the dry dust of the African bush, you will find raptor species, such as goshawks, buzzards, eagles, and vultures. You do not need any particular equipment to enjoy the birdlife, although a pair of binoculars will help you get a better view. It is also a good idea to get a guide who can direct you to the best vantage points and explain the difference between an African fish eagle and a pygmy sunbird.

You can also customize your own bird-watching experience. Paddle a canoe down the mangrove creeks to look for goliath herons, or take a leisurely walk around the wetlands and let the Egyptian plovers and African pygmy geese find you. Spend a few hours at the fishponds of the Gambia River, or an entire day at the Abuko Nature Reserve. You are guaranteed to find the inner bird lover in you. **JP**

Discover Brava

Location Brava, Cape Verde Islands
Website www.archipelagocapeverde.com **Price** 🌑

At the southwestern end of the Cape Verde Islands, about 400 miles (640 km) off the West African coast, lies Brava, the archipelago's "island of flowers." The mist-covered mountains rising from the arid, volcanic terrain that dominates the scenery conceal a hidden world. Up to 3,200 feet (976 m) high, these peaks are capable of trapping clouds, and thus create the peculiar humid and temperate microclimate of the country's smallest inhabited island.

Generally undisturbed by tourists because of its lack of outstanding beaches, Brava is the perfect antithesis of the rest of the archipelago and has retained its unspoiled charm. There is no airport, and the irregular

"This tiny island's wet climate produces lush green vegetation and swirling mists."

Janine Kelso, *Travel Weekly*

ferry service from neighboring Fogo makes careful planning imperative. Visitors can walk the ragged coastline, with its steep lava cliffs, or climb the mountains to gaze on deep, flower-filled valleys.

The island's main town is Vila Nova Sintra, at an altitude of 1,700 feet (520 m). It is a colorful town with markets, quaint colonial houses, ubiquitous gardens, and paths offering spectacular views. The true star of the island is the picturesque seaside village of Fajã d'Agua on the west coast, sheltered from the northeast wind by the mountains, with a stunning black-sand beach. Despite the volcanic-colored sand, no volcanic activity has ever been recorded. **DaH**

See the South Omo Valley

Location Near Jinka, Ethiopia
Website www.tour-to-ethiopia.com **Price** 🌑🌑

Deep in southern Ethiopia is a world largely untouched by modern society. In the South Omo Valley, tribal communities live much as they have done for hundreds of years, with mud huts for homes and goatskins for clothes. A trip here is hard going but unforgettable. This is a total escape from modern civilization as we know it.

The route does demand a four-by-four vehicle, however, to negotiate either the mud or the dust (depending on the time of year) on the bumpy dirt tracks. You will need at least ten days to explore this lush region, plus a driver/guide and a cook, which can all be arranged through socially responsible tour agencies in Addis Ababa or from home.

It is the people rather than the region that you will come here to see. With more than twenty tribes all adhering to ancient traditions and beliefs, the ethnographic diversity is amazing—including the women of the Mursi tribe with clay plates the size of saucers in their bottom lips, the Karo people renowned for their elaborate body scarification and decoration, and the Hamar tribe famous for their rites-of-passage ritual of "jumping the bulls" and their mesmerizing dances in the dark of night. The markets in the Omo Valley are as vibrant as the people, selling animal skins, beads of cowry shells, gourds of all shapes and sizes, sorghum, honey, straw, and wood—all essential items in everyday life here. Do not forget to try a bottle of *tej* while you are at the market—the local mead made with honey is quite an experience.

On the long road back to Addis, you can treat yourself to your first shower in days at the reviving hot springs in Wendo Genet, and wash away the dust—but not the memories—of the Omo Valley. **SWa**

Go Gorilla Tracking

Location Volcanoes National Park, Rwanda
Website www.rwandatourism.com/primate.htm **Price** $$

"No one who looks into a gorilla's eyes . . . can remain unchanged, for the gap between ape and human vanishes; we know that the gorilla still lives within us." So wrote Dr. George Schaller, the eminent field biologist, in 1963 on first realizing that mountain gorillas were gentle giants rather than the brutal beasts they were hitherto believed to be.

Once the domain of intrepid scientists like Schaller and Dian Fossey, the opportunity to spend time with these amazing primates is now open to all, provided you pay the $500 permit fee (which is channeled back into their conservation) and are prepared to trek for at least three hours through dense undergrowth and rain forest to find them with the help of expert trackers. Permits are not easy to obtain: Only thirty are issued daily. Gorillas move on every day, too, so the trek does not follow a simple path. Then, once you do find them, you are limited to just one hour in their company to ensure that they do not become too used to humans or catch our harmful germs and diseases.

That single hour, however, will be the most magical and mesmerizing of your life. When you come face-to-face with a silverback and his group of gorillas, you simply forget everything else. As with human families, you will see mothers nurturing their babies or chiding their children; toddlers frolicking and fighting or playing peekaboo; and frisky teenagers flirting with each other or smooching in silence. And the silverback saunters and swaggers around grunting protectively, communicating in a secret language with the trackers who know each individual gorilla by name. **SWa**

➡ *A pair of mountain gorillas cross a log through the thick forest of Rwanda's Volcanoes National Park.*

Stay at Shompole

Location Lake Natron, Kenya **Website** www.shompole.com
Price 💲💲💲

When Shompole opened in 2001, its coolly stylish interiors—free-flowing white concrete, rough-hewn figwood, smooth, round river stones, and plunge pools under thatch—sent shivers up the spines of regular safari goers. Yet the hotel, which clings to southern Kenya's Nguruman escarpment with views over the Rift Valley, is also here to benefit the wildlife and local Maasai people.

Since the conservancy was established, the number of lions on the previously overgrazed, overpoached land has increased tenfold, and elephants have come back down from the Loita Hills—exhilarating night drives also reveal glimpses of civets, bat-eared foxes, and aardwolves. Game drives are a big part of a stay here, as is watching flamingos on Lake Natron.

The community has also used its conservation fee to pay for rangers, teachers, nurses, and secondary school bursaries, and helped to build and run the six-bedroom lodge. This has evolved to include a two-suite annex with a long, thin lap pool (Little Shompole), an intimate, family house with lawns and fountains (Shompole House), and another private unit, 360, practically tumbling down the escarpment, with a dumbbell-shaped pool and a helipad for flying to Ol Donyo Lengai, an active volcano across the Tanzanian border. There is also a shop selling unique pieces of African jewelry and a modest spa, which offers treatments incorporating the muds of Lake Natron.

Even without leaving the lodge, guests can enjoy the astonishing sunsets over Shompole Mountain, and a feeling of utter peace. **LJ**

← *Architect Anthony Russell designed the smooth lines and flowing curves of Shompole.*

Relax at Ndali Lodge

Location Fort Portal, Uganda **Website** www.ndalilodge.com
Price 💲💲

Ndali Lodge sits right on the equator—a colonial-style mansion at the center of a farm. It stands on a narrow ridge 5,000 feet (1,524 m) above sea level, at the rim of an extinct volcano that has become a deep circular lake. It offers 360-degree views of the ancient volcanic landscape and the Rwenzori Mountains, known by explorers as the Mountains of the Moon.

The main lodge holds the reception area, sitting room, and restaurant. Guests stay in eight individual stone-built thatched cottages. Ndali feels luxurious, but in a very traditional way. Evenings are spent by candlelight, and all the lodge's water comes from the lake, pumped up by hydraulic technology invented in

> *"[Ndali Lodge] overlooks its own private crater lake and is an immensely relaxing place."*
>
> **Jack Barker,** *Independent*

the 1770s. The lodge has been owned by the same family since 1920 and is still staffed by local villagers. Ndali provides guides for walks to the Mahoma waterfall, around the crater, as well as a boat for discovering the birds, butterflies, and primates. There are many local walks you can take on your own, a swimming pool, and a sturdy jetty on the lake where guests can swim and lounge in the sun, spotting five different types of kingfishers.

Ndali is a perfect Ugandan base, situated between three national parks. It is just forty-five minutes to Kibale Forest National Park, home of the largest concentration of chimpanzees in Africa. **SH**

Unwind at Chole Mjini

Location Chole, Tanzania   **Website** www.africatravelresource.com   **Price** 😊😊

Chole Mjini's tree houses seem to meld into the canopy of the ancient baobab trees that provide them with shelter. Crafted from wood, ropes, and reeds, the rustic hideaways are open on three sides and are set amid verdant jungle, wild orchards, mangrove forests, and age-old Hindu ruins slowly being strangled by the roots of fig trees. The area teems with wildlife, and guests can see fruit bats dangling upside down in the tree branches that surround their rooms, as well as monkeys and a variety of exotic birdlife.

Even though six of the seven rooms are up in a tree, they house four-poster beds lined with fine Egyptian cotton and elegantly swathed in mosquito nets. There are also alfresco showers surrounded by bamboo. If sleeping in a tree bothers you, ask for the ground house suite, complete with sunken Persian bath.

This place is perfect for serious escapism. There is no electricity (although oil lanterns are left on overnight and reading flashlights are provided) on the tiny island of Chole. Which means there is no telephone, television, cars, e-mail, or air-conditioning. Chole is part of the Mafia archipelago and is situated some 60 miles (100 km) south of Tanzania. Scuba diving and snorkeling are big in these parts, with turtles, rays, dolphins, and ray sharks providing the underwater attractions.

At Chole Mjini, meals are usually of fresh fish with plenty of fruit and vegetables, and guests eat with the friendly lodge owners in a number of different locations, the best of which is among the ruins, lit by lanterns hanging from the trees.

A stay here means you are doing your bit for the community, too, because the owners donate $10 per visitor per night to a trust fund that pays toward the local hospital, school, and training programs. **JK**

⬆ *Chole Mjini has luxurious tree houses complete with four-poster beds and wonderful views.*

Stay at Greystoke Mahale

Location Lake Tanganyika, Tanzania **Website** www.greystoke-mahale.com **Price** ❸❸❸

Reaching Greystoke Mahale is an adventure. It is set on the remote eastern shores of vast Lake Tanganyika, and getting to the camp involves a four-hour flight on a small plane from Arusha, followed by a ninety-minute dhow trip on the lake. There are no roads within 60 miles (100 km) of this secluded sanctuary, and it is a two-hour boat ride to the nearest town. It is well off the tourist map, so if you are seeking solitude, Greystoke Mahale has plenty.

Accommodation consists of six *bandas* (traditional thatched huts, common in Central Africa). The beach-fronted *bandas* are stylishly designed, with open fronts, spacious decks, and interiors crafted from old dhow timber, giving the camp a look and feel of modest, rustic charm.

At night, gaze at the stars while enjoying a barefoot meal at the water's edge, sip cocktails on a dhow, or head to the bar, which is set picturesquely in the rocky headland. The dining area has four decks that face in every direction, affording fabulous views of the landscape. The hotel also has a library of rare books on the local wildlife.

Behind the lodges are the dense forests of the Mahale Mountains, home to Africa's last remaining wild chimpanzees, mankind's closest relative. Trek through the lush rain forest to spot the endangered primates as they swing noisily and energetically from tree to tree. The rain forest is dotted with waterfalls and giant verdant vines and populated by leopards, monkeys, porcupines, mongooses, butterflies, and birds. There are treasures, too, to be found beneath the lake's transparent water, where 250 species of tropical fish reside, making it ideal for swimming, snorkeling, and kayaking. With no cell phone reception or wireless Internet, this is the perfect hideaway. **JK**

⬆ *Part of Greystoke Mahale's charm lies in its rustic furniture and use of traditional textiles.*

Unwind at Kahawa Shamba

Location Kahawa Shamba, Tanzania
Website www.kahawashamba.co.tz   **Price** ◐

Thousands of trekkers flock to Kilimanjaro every year to try to conquer Africa's highest mountain, but not many of them stop long enough to take a breath and look around them at the lives and culture of the local tribes who live in the mountain's shadow.

Kahawa Shamba, which means "coffee farm," is a village where the Swahili people have resided for centuries, farming the land and hunting for game. The coffee farmers who live here struggle with poverty caused by falling prices and rising costs. Thanks to a community project, the local people now host tourists who want to stay at the village, cooking for and taking care of them while earning a salary. Through this program, the finances of the local people have been enriched, and guests are provided with a genuinely meaningful travel experience.

In the village, tourists sleep in traditional-style *chugga* huts, thatched from top to bottom with banana leaves. The accommodation is basic, but there is still luxury—in the warmth of the local people and in the beauty of the surrounding landscape of verdant valleys and gorges, skewered by tall banana trees and small coffee bushes.

If you consider yourself a coffee addict, you can learn more about the origin and journey of your favorite brew by visiting the small Fair Trade coffee farms, eating lunch with the farmers, and being allowed to pick coffee beans and see how they are pulped, roasted, and ground. A guide will explain the process of organic coffee farming and the standards that are expected from Fair Trade farmers. If you're feeling tired after the hard day's sightseeing, you can finish up with a cup of freshly brewed coffee. **JK**

Stay at Ngorongoro Crater Lodge

Location Serengeti, Tanzania
Website www.ngorongorocrater.com   **Price** ⊖⊖⊖

The word "spectacular" does not even begin to encapsulate the experience of staying at Ngorongoro Crater Lodge in northern Tanzania. Perched on the edge of a vast crater in the Serengeti, it feels as though it could be straddling the edge of the world.

The lodge is next to the largest unbroken volcanic caldera in the world, more than 4,970 miles (8,000 km) of pristine African wilderness, a paradise for the wild animals that roam its rich grassland. Most impressive of all is the thundering, dust-raising annual "great migration," when around two million wildebeest and zebra storm across the Serengeti in search of food.

> *"If you could spend one day in Africa, Ngorongoro Crater might be the place to do it."*
>
> Laura Riley, *Nature's Strongholds*

Ngorongoro Crater Lodge was inspired by the Maasai mud and stick *manyatta* (homestead), but with an injection of luxury. Your fireplace is stoked by a personal butler, who will also run rose petal–strewn baths (with a view) between twice-daily game drives, crater picnics, and cocktails. The three intimate, romantic, stilted camps all have stone-and-thatch suites and lavish interiors. This area is known as "Africa's Eden," and it needs to be seen to be believed—preferably from Ngorongoro Crater Lodge. **LP**

➡ *The lavish interiors of Ngorongoro Crater Lodge were inspired by Maasai simplicity.*

Enjoy Singita Faru Faru

Location Grumeti Reserves, Tanzania
Website www.singita.com **Price** ⊖⊖⊖

Animal lovers will be spellbound by Singita Faru Faru Lodge, in the heart of the sun-kissed Serengeti, not least because it is in a prime location to view the epic, annual "great migration" of more than a million wildebeest. The lodge is positioned on a rocky slope next to the Grumeti River and a watering hole, a region abundant with magnificent animal life all year-round.

The location—in a private concession on the western corridor of the Serengeti—is not the only thing Faru Faru Lodge has going for it. This hotel is utterly intimate and classically elegant; going on safari has never felt so exclusive. Faru Faru Lodge has just six open-style, air-conditioned tented suites, each with huge picture windows, an outdoor shower or bath, and a deck with a state-of-the-art telescope, from where visitors can enjoy spectacular sunsets and their own private game show. Not to mention the likely chance of seeing herds of elephant meander past while you wallow in the tub.

The colonial, 1940s East Africa–style lodge also comes with a Swahili-inspired "beach," two swimming pools, and a spa. There is a dining room and barbecue area where mouthwatering nouvelle-African cuisine is served, as sometimes exaggerated stories of wild adventures from the day are swapped.

When not on one of the twice-daily four-by-four safari drives, guests can relax in the lounge, although the game action outside is much more entertaining. The lodge can also arrange walking or horseback safaris for you to experience nature in the raw.

The word "Serengeti" comes from the Maasai word "Siringit," which means "endless plains" or "the place where the land stretches to forever." It seems to sum up this natural beauty just perfectly. **LP**

Discover Mnemba Island

Location Mnemba Island, Zanzibar
Website www.mnemba-island.com **Price** ⊖⊖⊖

When Bill Gates wants respite from the fast-paced business world, he disappears to exclusive Mnemba Island, just off the northeastern tip of Zanzibar. In the bathlike Indian Ocean, Mnemba—Arabic for "octopus head"—offers just ten romantic and understated beachside *bandas* (huts) with thatched palm roofs and wraparound verandas.

Apart from the sweet isolation, one of the biggest draws is the diving. Colorful ocean life flourishes on the protected coral reefs of the Mnemba Atoll; dolphins, whales, bright tropical fish, and giant turtles drift through the lagoons. Nature is omnipresent—guests awake to the song of red-eyed doves in the

> *"Of all the small islands to stay on, Mnemba is one of the most romantic . . . it has everything."*
>
> *Daily Telegraph*

forest, where suni antelope and white butterflies also abound, and sidestep ghost crabs on their walk past coconut palms to the main lodge.

The food is equally impressive, with fresh fruit and seafood brought to Mnemba daily. Meals are sumptuous, with candlelit feasts in the dining area, on your private veranda, or on the beach, where eating with the waves lapping at your feet is just sublime.

Tours can be arranged to give visitors a taste of the ancient "Spice Island" of Zanzibar, and guests can enjoy therapeutic massages and deep-sea fishing trips. Or you can just kick off your shoes, lie back, and savor the private sanctuary that is Mnemba. **LP**

Kayak at Mumbo Island

Location Lake Malawi, Malawi **Website** www.kayakafrica.co.za
Price ⊖

You have to kayak 6 miles (10 km) to reach Mumbo Island from Cape Maclear on the southern shore of Lake Malawi (although the less energetic can take Kayak Africa's boat) but then you have the place to yourself. You will find luxury tents with bathrooms, thatched roofs, and viewing decks, complete with hammocks overlooking the lake. The only other people to break the solitude are the staff who prepare your meals and serve at the bar.

It would be easy to lounge in hammocks all day, watching the sun twinkling on Lake Malawi and spotting the multicolored cichlid fish darting like electric flashes around small islets of granite boulders. If you feel some activity is called for, however, these are among the world's safest waters in which to learn to scuba dive, or you could snorkel from the beach or paddle around the shores of the island in a kayak. Do not be surprised if an otter or two join you for a swim.

For landlubbers, there are five easy nature trails that meander around this tiny paradise full of baobab trees and figs, leading to even more secluded coves and inlets. Spend some time ambling around the island looking for giant fish eagles, colorful kingfishers, or paradise flycatchers. If that all sounds too energetic, simply watch the birds as you chill and sway on your hammock, sipping a glass of wine.

Back in 1861, the renowned explorer David Livingstone named Lake Malawi the "lake of stars" for the way the sun sparkles on its waters. Today, there is no better place to appreciate this romantic epithet than on Mumbo Island. **SWa**

← *You can kayak from the beach at Mumbo Island and take advantage of Lake Malawi's clear waters.*

Stay at Ku Chawe Inn

Location Shire Lowlands, Malawi
Website www.malawi-travel.com **Price** 🍃

Set against the backdrop of the forests of the Zomba Plateau, with spectacular views of the Great Rift Valley and the Shire Lowlands, is Malawi's most upmarket hotel. The landscape is a veritable Garden of Eden. The slopes and ravines are covered with exotic trees, junglelike creepers, wildflowers, orchids, and lichen. Yet despite the beautiful scenery and Lake Chirwa with its white-sand beaches, Malawi is not known as a vacation destination and is unspoiled by tourism.

The Ku Chawe Inn is hidden away in lush vegetation at the end of a long, winding mountain path. Being tucked into this jungle idyll does not mean facilities are primitive. The forty spacious rooms all have their

---

"The beautiful Zomba plateau . . . unrivaled beauty, crystal-clear streams, and numerous species."

Friends of Malawi Association

---

own private bathrooms, telephones, and satellite televisions. Malawians have a very well-deserved reputation for warmth and friendliness, and the staff at Ku Chawe are helpful and attentive. It is wonderful to lunch on the large, shady outdoor veranda watching the resident baboons snacking in the gardens. This is a place to enjoy an evening drink and feast on the spectacular views before dining on delicious food, enjoyed, in cooler winter evenings, around a flickering fire. You could rise early and hire a mountain guide to take you above the clouds to the top of the plateau. Or simply gaze out over the endless views of the lake shimmering in the distance. **SWi**

Unwind at Azura

Location Benguerra Island, Mozambique
Website www.azura-retreats.com **Price** 🍃🍃🍃

Azura is not easy to get to: it is a two-hour flight from Johannesburg, followed by a breathtaking helicopter swoop over the myriad hues of the Indian Ocean, but it is worth the effort. Although the lodge itself is a honeymooners' idyll, the real draw is the pristine beauty of the island itself.

The retreat was created in 2007 by British couple Christopher and Stella Bettany, who saw their opportunity when Gabriel Cossa, a Mozambican who ran a backpackers' resort on the site, was told to upgrade or move out. Happily, Cossa is now the Bettanys' business partner, his son Zito has been to hotel school in Durban, and many of the original staff are still working here.

Local techniques and talents are on show in the construction and decoration of the fourteen wooden villas. Driftwood stools and timber floors conjure a mood of laid-back beach chic, whereas tasseled leather stools and Panton chairs add boutique funkiness. Guests can be as private or as sociable as they choose, with firelit dinners à deux on the beach or communal drinks at the Gecko Bar, stargazing in hammocks. The diving and fishing are both exceptional—you can expect unbleached corals, turtles, and sailfish—and humpback whales can be seen between July and October. There are magical excursions to Pansy Island, a sandbar sprinkled with the delicate skeletons of sea urchins at high tide, or a vast dune with the ocean on one side and freshwater pools full of crocodiles and wading birds on the other. Alternatively, just sit by the beach, musing on the moon and the tides. **LJ**

➔ *The shaggy jekka-thatch roofs are an example of local building techniques—and talents.*

Dive at Matemo Island

Location Matemo Island, Mozambique
Website www.matemoresort.com **Price** 🟢🟢

It may only be 5 miles (8 km) long and 1.8 miles (3 km) wide, but few places on Earth can match Matemo Island for fishing and diving. In the heart of the Quirimbas archipelago off the northern Mozambique coast, Matemo is all white-sand beaches dotted with coconut palms and thatched mud huts. In the deep waters lie the real treasures: kingfish, barracuda, queenfish, dog-tooth tuna, and sailfish, not to mention huge shoals of yellowfin tuna. The abundance of exotic fish is thanks to the fact that the waters are part of a marine sanctuary. This is good news for divers: unspoiled coral reefs and warm waters are alive with a kaleidoscope of marine life, including humpback

> "Ruins of large Portuguese plantations can still be seen on Quisiva and Matemo."

Malyn Newitt, *A History of Mozambique*

whales between August and October. Turtles can often be seen as well as, very occasionally, the much-endangered dugong. After a hard day's diving or fishing, take a walk to explore the island's verdant vegetation or take a water taxi to nearby Ibo Island, which has a rich history of piracy and ivory trading.

If you want to stay on Matemo Island, there are twenty-four air-conditioned, thatched chalets situated on the beach just a few short steps from the sea, and a restaurant serves locally caught seafood. **JK**

◁ *Matemo Island is a paradise for anyone who wants to dive, fish, or simply enjoy the beautiful beaches.*

Relax at Ibo Island Lodge

Location Ibo Island, Mozambique
Website www.iboisland.com   **Price** ⓢⓢ

For those who have had the pleasure of discovering this Indian Ocean gem, Ibo Island is impossible to forget. The small, forested island lies at the southern end of the beautiful Quirimbas archipelago, a string of thirty-two tropical islands stretching more than 125 miles (200 km) north to the Tanzanian border.

Ibo Island Lodge is housed in historic and stunning buildings that date back to colonial times. The walls are 3 feet (1 m) thick, and high ceilings promote an impression of elegant space. With just fourteen luxury rooms, each individually designed and with views of the waterfront, this is a wonderful retreat in which to escape the world. Antique and handcrafted furniture and the lodge's magnificent wooden doors and shutters evoke the buildings' origins.

Visitors can take a cruise on a dhow around the archipelago and go ashore to visit the historic old town, dating back to the 1600s, and now earmarked as a potential World Heritage site. It was chosen by the Portuguese in 1754 as their main clearinghouse for slaves and ivory, then left deserted for almost a century. It is a mysterious town to wander around, amid forts and ancient buildings, watching silversmiths melt coins to create delicate pieces of silver jewelry.

As well as enjoying the pool and private beach, guests can snorkel or go diving among some of the world's richest coral reefs, or go kayaking through mangroves, with the chance to see turtles, dolphins, and whales in the waters of the Quirimbas national park. Maybe this is the Mozambique that Bob Dylan sang about all those years ago. **AD**

← *Ibo Island Lodge is made up of three beautiful mansions, all of which are over 100 years old.*

Stay at Marlin Lodge

Location Benguerua Island, Mozambique
Website www.marlinlodge.co.za   **Price** ⓢⓢ

One of the coolest destinations in southern Africa, Marlin Lodge makes the perfect post-safari stop. Wood and reed-thatched chalets stretch along the sandy, white sands of tranquil Flamingo Bay, connected by walkways on stilts over the vegetation. The freshwater swimming pool is tucked away in a glade of coconut palms. The rooms have glorious sea views from the four-poster beds.

The island is part of a National Marine Park, home to many protected species. Look out for whales, whale sharks, dolphins, dugongs, and manta rays; out on the reef are turtles, stingrays, and moray eels. A tag-and-release program means fishing enthusiasts can still

> *"Guests come here mainly to pad along pristine sand and swim over unspoiled reefs."*
>
> Rhiannon Batten, *Independent*

hunt for marlin and other big-game fish. There is also catamaran sailing, windsurfing, and water skiing, as well as more laid-back cruising in a traditional dhow.

On land, guests can explore the island's grasslands, coastal dunes, freshwater lakes—which are inhabited by Nile crocodiles—and acacia woodland, keeping eyes peeled for colorful parrots.

The lodge charges guests a park fee, which goes into a fund used to benefit the natural environment and the local community, so you can enjoy the surroundings safe in the knowledge that you are doing your part to maintain Benguerua Island as a special slice of paradise for future generations. **AD**

Unwind at Quilalea

Location Quirimbas Archipelago, Mozambique
Website www.quilalea.com **Price** ⬢⬢⬢

From Prince Harry to Leonardo diCaprio, this diamond of the Indian Ocean seduces royalty and A-listers alike, with its awe-inspiring nature and undisturbed intimacy. There are no inhabitants on Quilalea, the pearl of the thirty-two islands dotting the Quirimbas archipelago, whose coastlines are so pristine that it feels as if the shore is untrodden by human feet.

Quilalea was the first member of the Quirimbas archipelago to be designated a protected nature sanctuary. No commercial fishing is allowed. Clear, azure waters, peerless diving in which mesmeric corals flirt with rainbow shoals, 2,000-year-old baobab trees, and mangroves supply the setting. Butterflies flutter

> *"The island of Quilalea is too small for an airstrip. It's too small for much of anything, in fact."*
>
> Douglas Rogers, *Travel+Leisure* magazine

by, turtles rest on the beach, and white-sailed dhows minnow past. In the past, Quilalea was the main rest stop for mariners and merchants. Today it is a rest stop for pleasure-seeking tourists (adults only—children are not allowed here).

On the island are just nine thatched, stone-clad villas, with panoramic views over the sea. Guests can explore nearby Ibo, an electricity-free town that time forgot—the mansions that once marked its riches left to crumble, the inhabitants forever welcoming—or have a desert island picnic on Sencar, rubbing shoulders with the Samango monkeys. Quilalea is a portal to another world, an overlooked world. **VG**

Explore Fish River Canyon

Location Fish River Canyon, Namibia
Website www.nwr.com.na; www.canyonnaturepark.com **Price** ⬢

At almost 100 miles (160 km) long, Fish River Canyon is one of the world's most impressive gorges and one of Namibia's national parks. It sweeps through desolate escarpments and steep cliffs, bringing a whole new meaning to the word "remote."

Namibia Wildlife Resorts runs a five-day hiking trail along 50 miles (80 km) of the canyon, but it is not for the fainthearted or the out of shape. Temperatures are gaspingly hot, the terrain underfoot rocky and hard going with a backpack on your back, and there are no quick escape routes or shortcuts should you change your mind. There is, however, a raw beauty in the landscape that somehow makes the hardship worthwhile. Steep ravines with deep orange and pink rocks constantly changing color in the sun, weird-looking, bulbous quiver trees (Namibia's national tree) perched on the edge of precipices, and panoramic views as far as the eye can see all add to a feeling of splendid isolation in its truest sense. The Fish River itself is perfect for skinny-dipping, its cool, clean waters an elixir for parched and exhausted trekkers. In the evening, cook a meal over the fire and watch the flames flickering to sleep as you curl up under the stars, literally miles from anyone and anywhere.

If all this sounds a bit too wild, try the Canyon Nature Park, just north of the national park conservation area where the Löwen and Fish rivers meet. Here, in landscapes equally as stunning and remote, you can opt for guided hikes lasting between two and five days on private trails, complete with food, tents, and even a vehicle to transport your bags. **SWa**

➡ *Fish River Canyon is the second-largest canyon in the world, beaten only by the Grand Canyon.*

Stay at Abu Camp

Location Okavango Delta, Botswana
Website www.abucamp.com   **Price** ⊘⊘⊘⊘

Abu Camp is a luxurious retreat offering three-night stays and elephant-back safaris. Guests arrive and depart together to appreciate, at the same pace, the diversity of flora and fauna found here in the open savannas and island sanctuaries.

Guests stay in custom-made tents set on raised decks adjacent to their own private, natural lagoon. All rooms in the camp are furnished with sleigh or four-poster beds and come complete with full baths and private bathrooms. Each tent has its own private deck, and a separate outdoor layered teak deck and viewing platform is built around matured sycamore and ebony trees that can double as a dining area, with fine wine and gourmet cuisine prepared by Abu Camp's experienced safari chefs. A newly built villa across the lagoon sleeps up to four people and comes with its own chef, guide, butler, and private pool.

Abu Camp is named after former resident celebrity elephant Abu. The camp's present herd of elephants take their human cargo, comfortably seated in large padded saddles, on excursions into the Okavango Delta's wilderness at a sedate pace, accompanied by experienced guides.

The camp's elephants grant unprecedented and unfettered access to resident herds of zebra, antelope, giraffe, and buffalo. Sunrise and sunset rides are offered daily, as well as extended daylong safaris that transplant you into the midst of the wildlife that calls the waters of the delta home, all the while providing a memorable insight into the complex social structures of the African elephant. **BS**

← *Abu Camp, on the western side of the Okavanga Delta, stretches over 500,000 acres (202,340 ha).*

Experience Jack's Camp

Location Kalahari Desert, Botswana
Website www.unchartedafrica.co.za   **Price** ⊘⊘⊘⊘

Jack's Camp stands on a vast saltpan on Botswana's Kalahari Desert. Ten five-star canvas tents, private bucket showers, flush toilets, and a plunge pool succeed in distracting you from the fact that you have journeyed to the edge of nothingness to sleep over the dried-up bed of an ancient lake.

Established in the 1960s, Jack's Camp is one of the true pioneers of southern Africa's contemporary safari-style retreats and one of the few accommodation options in this remote region of central Botswana. In the Makgadikgadi Saltpans, endless salt flats represent all that is left of what was once the largest inland lake in Africa; the camp's resident archaeologists and

> ## "The silence is so complete you can hear the blood circulating in your ears."
>
> **Proprietors, Jack's Camp**

geologists will lead you to almost forgotten sites and ancient fossil beds to see the remains of long-extinct hippos and giant ancestors of the modern zebra. Or explore it by yourself on a quad bike.

The arid landscape is transformed in March and April when summer rains swell the Okavango Delta, whose waters flow across the saltpans attracting thousands of wildebeest, zebra, and buffalo and vast numbers of aquatic birds such as pelicans and flamingos. A stay at Jack's Camp will almost guarantee sightings of the extremely rare brown hyena, and the camp's ever-present meerkats will delight even the most seasoned traveler with their presence. **BS**

Enjoy White Elephant Lodge

Location KwaZulu-Natal, South Africa
Website www.whiteelephantlodge.co.za **Price** 💲💲

For a touch of luxury with your safari, head to White Elephant Lodge in the idyllic Pongola Game Reserve, the first game reserve created in South Africa back in 1874. At the foot of the Lebombo Mountains in the steamy Maputuland plains, the tented camp overlooks the shimmering waters of Lake Jozin.

With a classic feel and all the comforts you could imagine, the luxurious safari-style canvas rooms have everything from fluffy bathrobes to fabulous views over the unspoiled savanna. Originally built in the 1920s, the lodge sleeps just sixteen guests and definitely has a colonial-era romance theme, from the mosquito-netted beds to the Victorian-style, claw-

---

"We want our visitors to feel as though they have arrived at an oasis where time has stood still."

Proprietors, White Elephant Lodge

---

footed bathtubs. For a surreal experience, take a bath out in the plain. Filled with scented bubbles and lit by candles, it is a unique way to experience nature.

Go for game drives, guided walks, and tracking, but you could also try tiger fishing, sunset cruises, and bird-watching. At night, the bush is aflutter. You can lie in bed and be rocked by Mother Nature's lullaby, or take a drive huddled under a warm blanket to see some extraordinary sights: hippos racing past, lionesses and cubs climbing up trees under cover of darkness, or elephants on moonlight patrol. The best time of day is twilight, when it becomes the ideal place to soak up the liberating panorama. **RCA**

Camp at Thanda Reserve

Location KwaZulu-Natal, South Africa
Website www.thanda.com **Price** 💲💲

Thanda's award-winning five-star safari in northern Zululand is an incomparable experience, despite tough competition in the region. There are more than 400 bird species, not to mention the "big five," to spot in its 14,825-acre (6,000-ha) private game reserve. Guests are invited on two four-by-four game drives a day, with optional guided nightly bush walks to get the best of the animal attractions. Trackers help visitors see the best of the surrounding natural world—whether that be lion, wild dog, buffalo, or giraffe.

In the evening, you can sit around the central lounge and discuss the day's events before retiring to your choice of accommodation: the luxury unfenced and nonelectric tented camp, based on a colonial design, or the main lodge. With four-poster beds and plump mattresses, you are guaranteed a good night's sleep. The lodge is divided into nine private villas with indoor and outdoor showers, plunge pools, and a thatched outdoor game-viewing deck.

One of the greatest things about Thanda is its connection with the community, and staff are happy to share cultural treasures of the region, not to mention the Zulu remedy to help digestion: buchu tea. There is also an exquisite spa wellness center with treatments such as African Queen and Zulu King.

Because of its location near the Indian Ocean, Thanda also offers "bush and beach" packages where you can enjoy a trip to Isimangaliso, formerly St. Lucia, for horseback riding along the beach, turtle-watching, whale-watching, and diving. Luxury fans, spa seekers, and true naturalists will not be disappointed. **LD**

➡ *Thanda brings five-star luxury to the safari-spa experience they offer guests.*

Ride the Rovos Railroad

Location South Africa   **Website** www.rovos.co.za
Price $ $ $ $

Taking a ride on a Rovos Rail train through South Africa is like returning to a bygone era of elegance and glamour. The carriages of its two trains have been restored to their former Edwardian splendor; in keeping with the old-fashioned style, there are no televisions or radios on board. Although the train is mostly hauled by diesel and electric, part of the journey is pulled by steam, normally on departure or arrival at Pretoria. Each train accommodates seventy-two passengers in thirty-six spacious suites, all of which are decked out with mahogany paneling and period furnishings. Beds are queen sized and the Royal Suites even have Victorian baths.

This is a train with a gourmet reputation; there is one sitting for dinner and the dress code is strictly black tie. Food is top-notch, with South Africa's finest game as a specialty, washed down with the country's best wines. It is all served up with style, using the finest china and the crispest linen.

Recline comfortably in an observation car while watching the ever-changing and vast landscape of southern Africa roll past your window. The train's most popular route runs from Cape Town to Pretoria, a 995-mile (1,600-km) journey that thunders through the lush grasslands of the Highveld, the stark emptiness of Great Karoo, and the mountains and winelands of the Cape. Other itineraries take in Namibia, Durban, Kruger Park, and Victoria Falls.

The train fare includes all food, drink, wine, and excursions, although you will have to cough up a little extra for some champagne. **JK**

◄ *The Rovos train takes in the best sights of South Africa while offering you the best in luxurious travel.*

Visit Shamwari
Eagles Crag Lodge

Location Eastern Cape, South Africa
Website www.shamwari.com **Price** 🗲🗲

Tucked away in a gorge on South Africa's malaria-free Eastern Cape is Eagles Crag Lodge, one of six lodges in the Shamwari Game Reserve. Each of the nine detached suites has its own plunge pool, deck, and foldaway glass walls that offer great vistas over the cliffs. Shamwari is the vision of one man, Adrian Gardiner, who in 1990 bought a small farm as a weekend retreat. The indigenous fauna and flora of the Eastern Cape had been eradicated by the early twentieth century because of farming, hunting, and drought: lions, buffalo, and rhinos no longer lived here. Gardiner made it his mission to buy more land, to reintroduce the decimated species, and to turn his property into a wildlife reserve. Now Shamwari is one of southern Africa's largest private game reserves.

Game drives take place morning and evening in small vehicles: each ranger takes a maximum of six passengers. Guests are also invited to take part in game walks to visit two big cat sanctuaries, which the reserve operates in partnership with the Born Free Foundation, a British charitable organization that is dedicated to conservation, preventing animal abuse, and keeping wildlife in its natural habitat.

After a busy and productive day, you can then retire for a few peaceful hours to Eagles Crag's dedicated spa. Afterward, head to the upstairs dining room, with the option of outdoor dining, a lounge with fireplace, a library, and a cocktail bar.

If, after all that, you find that you cannot bear to go home, then why not stay a little longer? Shamwari offers a six-week field guide training course, during which you will learn the skills needed to make this little patch of paradise your home forever. **PS**

Experience Samara
Private Game Reserve

Location Karoo, South Africa
Website www.samara.co.za **Price** 🗲🗲

South of Bloemfontain and southwest of Durban, Samara Private Game Reserve is one of the most exclusive safari experiences in the world. Situated in the Great Karoo, South Africa's arid and malaria-free heartland, the lodge has been a regular feature on the top hotel lists from the likes of *Condé Nast Traveler* and *Tatler*. These discerning magazines rave about the colonial-style lodge and the fantastic food and wine.

Karoo Lodge sleeps six, and the manor sleeps up to eight, so you will not feel crowded. There is a pool for cooling off, and staff are constantly on hand. Dining might be in the lodge or outside underneath the stars.

"The lodge is a stylish interpretation of the original Karoo farmhouse, complemented by gracious service."

Condé Nast Traveler

Wildlife-wise, this is a superlative experience. With none of the traffic or 5 A.M. starts that you would find in Kruger, guests are taken on four-by-four tours of the private reserve, which has rare mountain zebra, white rhino, armadillo, aardvark, kudu, eland, and black wildebeest. The stellar attraction is the cheetahs, however. One in particular steals the spotlight: Sibella. She nearly died at the hands of hunters, but has lived in Samara since 2003. She has had eighteen cubs in that time, thus contributing two percent of the wild cheetah population in South Africa. Visitors can walk in the park in clear sight of cheetahs for stunning photo opportunities with a ranger on hand. **LD**

Enjoy Blaauwbosch Private Game Reserve

Location Karoo, South Africa
Website www.blaauwbosch.co.za **Price** 💲💲

In the foothills of the Winterhoek mountain range on South Africa's Eastern Cape are nestled the five-star thatched chalets of Blaauwbosch. Husband and wife owners Craig and Gill Cullingworth firmly believe in luxury amid the lions: Their seven air-conditioned suites each have their own dressing rooms and bathrooms with freestanding tubs that allow you to gaze out over the bush as you soak. Crisp white linen gleams against the polished dark wood of the bedsteads; elegant black-and-white etchings of animals grace the sand-yellow walls. Spacious private decks give onto rolling mountain views.

There is also an exclusive lodge, Kaai's Camp, which is available for use during peak season. Sleeping a maximum of eight people, Kaai's Camp sits between two mountains and enjoys spectacular valley views. Bedrooms featuring the same bare-thatched ceilings as the chalets open onto an extensive veranda that flanks the house.

Whether you stay in chalets or camp, you will rise early for a game drive—lion, buffalo, elephant, leopard, rhino, cheetah, giraffe, zebra, and antelope may all be seen. Cheetah have been introduced to the reserve, and Blaauwbosch offers a "walk and stalk" excursion during which guests can follow a cheetah as it stalks its prey. Afternoons are relaxing times, but even if you intend to read or just to snooze on your deck, you may find yourself distracted by the abundant birdlife that comes to spy. During evening game drives, rangers stop high in the hills so that guests may enjoy the dramatic purple and orange sunsets of the Eastern Cape before returning for a dinner enhanced by fine South African wines. **PE**

Unwind at Grootbos

Location Western Cape, South Africa
Website www.grootbos.com **Price** 💲💲

There are more than a handful of nature reserves in the Western Cape but Grootbos is among the best of them. Only two hours down the coast from Cape Town, this is a family-run venture with a dedicated team of award-winning conservationists who together have rescued the area and restored its beauty.

This is a place for nature trails and running wild, for horseback riding on deserted beaches and picnicking among the flowers. Many tourists come to the sandy beach to see the 40-ton southern right whales, and watch spellbound as mothers, calves, and energetic bulls come to within 100 feet (30 m) of the shoreline.

> *"[The Cape Floral Kingdom is] the best example of conservation of biodiversity I have ever seen."*
>
> David Bellamy, botanist

Two lodges of twenty-seven suites nestle in the lush and colorful vegetation. There is the family-oriented Grootbos Garden or the newer Forest Lodge, with its fresh, contemporary design that will appeal to the style conscious. The private decks of the large suites place you amid the beauty of the vegetation while you enjoy all the comforts of a luxury hotel. Through large windows you can gaze out over a vast expanse of unspoiled fynbos heathland or the ever-changing seascape down toward the coast. In the tranquility of the outdoor restaurants, the talented young chef satisfies guests with a five-course dinner menu that would do justice to a gourmet restaurant. **SWi**

Experience Bushman's Kloof Wilderness Reserve

Location Western Cape, South Africa
Website www.bushmanskloof.co.za   **Price** ⊝⊝

There is something spiritual about swimming in the rock pools of Bushman's Kloof. Perhaps it comes from the knowledge that they are ancient aspects of this awe-inspiring landscape, or maybe it is because the water is so crystal clear you feel as though you are suspended by air. The reserve in the heart of the Cederberg Mountains, a three-hour drive from Cape Town, overflows with natural wonders. As well as the mystical pools, there are jagged rock formations, indigenous gardens, and mountainous terrain that provide sanctuary for a myriad of wildlife, including the endangered Cape Mountain zebra. Thanks to its seclusion and affinity to nature, Bushman's Kloof is somewhere that encourages reflection, but there is also much to explore.

Bushman's Kloof hosts daily visits to unique rock-art sites that it also guards and conserves. The mountain drawings were produced by the Bushman tribes as long as 120,000 years ago. Nature drives give opportunities to encounter the wildlife and ever-changing landscape, dramatically carpeted in colorful Cape wildflowers each spring. Drinks are served at scenic spots, and "bush breakfasts" are laid on next to cascading waterfalls. Other activities include fishing in the Biedouw River and indulging in spa treatments.

The individually designed rooms have bathrooms, terraces, and in some cases lounges and fireplaces. For the ultimate treat, there is Koro Lodge, a fine villa with a pool, chef, and guide. Meals make use of the retreat's organic garden and local produce. **LP**

← *Bushman's Kloof Reserve is an ecological oasis offering the ultimate wilderness experience.*

Unwind at Kurland Hotel

Location Western Cape, South Africa
Website www.kurland.co.za   **Price** ⊖⊖

"The elegant Cape Dutch architecture . . . complements the sumptuous interiors."

Independent

More than fifty years ago, Baron Peter Behr bought himself quite a large patch of paradise near Plettenberg Bay on South Africa's Garden Route. He named his estate Kurland after the Baltic province in which he was born. Two generations later, the baron's grandson and his wife have transformed their idyllic inheritance, which lies between the unspoiled beaches of Nature's Valley and the pristine forest of Tsitsikamma, into a boutique hotel.

The estate covers 1,730 acres (700 ha) but there are only twelve suites, each uniquely furnished with family heirlooms and tasteful objets d'art. A spa, a swimming pool, a veranda, and a library are available for those who wish to relax. For those more energetically inclined, there is a wide choice of activities on hand.

For starters, the place is famous for its polo: Kurland attracts professionals and enthusiasts from December to April each year. The season's highlight is the Kurland International match between South Africa and Australia, which the estate hosts each December. For those who do not know their chaps from their chukkas, there are plenty of other ways to work up an appetite for Kurland's candlelit dinner. Opportunities for canoeing, waterskiing, sailing, and surfing are nearby. Calmer pursuits include dolphin- and whale-watching—the Indian Bottlenose dolphin and the southern right whale both frequent these waters—or, on land, there are bird and elephant sanctuaries and a monkey reserve close by. Mountain biking and guided walks are available, or guests might take a stroll around Kurland's famous rose gardens. **PE**

⬑ *The Kurland Hotel combines traditional Cape Dutch style with English country charm.*

Rent Franschhoek Pass Villa

Location Western Cape, South Africa
Website www.franschhoekpassvilla.co.za **Price** 💲💲

Franschhoek Valley may not be at the top of many people's "To See" lists when they visit South Africa, but rest assured, once you have been there it will be well up on the list of places you will want to return to.

It is hard to put into words the sheer jaw-dropping beauty of the Franschhoek Valley. It is as if the best of New Zealand, the Alps, and the American West have been joined together to create one of the most idyllic spots in the world, never mind South Africa.

But there is a lot more to enjoy than just the view. Food and wine are the mainstays of the Franschhoek valley, with some of the oldest and finest vineyards to be found in such a notable winemaking country, vying with what are regarded as some of the best restaurants in South Africa.

Head for the Franschhoek Pass Villa, part of the acclaimed Franschhoek Valley Winery. Perched high on the cool slopes of the Franschhoek Pass, it offers breathtaking views from the privacy of your own luxury private villa, where you can walk or bicycle through the estate's vineyards and nature reserve, or simply kick back and take in the amazing scenery. This self-catering villa sleeps up to four people, and there are many restaurants nearby with mouthwatering menus so you don't have to self-cater the whole time. The villa and winery are both run by Nick Davies. He and his wife made their fortune in interior design and have decorated the villa beautifully.

Golf lovers will also be delighted by the location, and everyone is encouraged to play on what must be one of the most exclusive golf ranges in the world in the valley below. You could also pick up a fishing rod and look for dinner in your own trout-fishing dam before heading back home to Franschhoek. **RS**

Relax at Le Quartier Français

Location Western Cape, South Africa
Website www.lequartier.co.za **Price** 💲💲

Those in the know say this luxurious hidden country inn was the place to launch Franschhoek as the culinary capital of the Western Cape. In the very heart of the Cape Winelands, it has as much charm as the surroundings—once home to the French Huguenots.

The former farm laborers' cottages have been transformed into a seriously chic retreat with a nod to the French style. The rooms are arranged around herb and flower gardens, some with private pools and exclusive butler service. To really get away from it all, book into The Four Quarters, four sumptuous suites with a lounge, dressing room, and outdoor veranda, grouped around a central courtyard with its own pool.

"The serious business of fine dining . . . has been set apart and defined by The Tasting Room."

Proprietors, Le Quartier Français

The rooms might be fantastic, but the big draw here is the food. Michelin-starred fine dining restaurant The Tasting Room has been listed as one of the world's fifty best restaurants thanks to the inspired cuisine of chef Margot Janse. Using the very best Cape products and its finest wines, she offers an innovative Cape Provençal menu in this beautiful setting. Choose from a four-, six-, or eight-course dining experience; the eight-course extravaganza also provides a different wine to complement each course. For lighter, less complicated meals, you can always try the café-style iCi, which flows from the street-side terrace to an outdoor fireplace in the garden. **AD**

Explore Kirstenbosch Botanical Gardens

Location Cape Town, Western Cape, South Africa
Website www.sanbi.org/frames/kirstfram.htm   **Price** 🌓

Whether you are a full-fledged botanist or simply in need of a tranquil escape from the heat and bustle of Cape Town, the Kirstenbosch Botanical Gardens offer everything from breathtaking views to pastoral oases.

Considered one of the "Seven Magnificent Botanical Gardens of the World," the gardens sprawl effortlessly over the eastern slopes of Table Mountain. The beautiful lawns, softly trickling streams, and winding pathways were created in the early 1900s by a Cambridge botanist, Henry Harold Pearson. However, its origins date back to the 1660s, when its colonial status was confirmed by Jan van Riebeeck, who planted a wild almond hedge around the fledgling settlement that had been established there. Sections of the hedge can still be seen today among the rest of the relatively new 300 acres (121 ha).

There are a variety of themed areas and walks to choose from: The Fynbos Trail is a must if you want to meander through acres of South Africa's indigenous flora, and the magnificent Protea Flower Garden is at its colorful best in winter. One of the trails, up the Skeleton Gorge Ravine, is an easy and popular route for walkers and mountaineers, who pass through the gardens on their way to the summit of Table Mountain. The Dell, the oldest part of the garden, is a soothing place to stop and rest. Clear spring water flows out of Colonel Bird's Bath around stepping-stones to the small pond below, and ferns, impatiens, and gardenias fill the area under large yellowwood trees and provide dappled shade on hot Cape summer days. **SWi**

➔ *Tree ferns flourish in the verdant Kirstenbosch Botanical Gardens in Cape Town.*

Unwind at Beau Rivage

Location Belle Mare, Mauritius
Website www.naiaderesorts.com **Price** 💲💲

When twelve brand new thatched villas were opened in 2007 at the Beau Rivage resort on the east coast of Mauritius, it was not just another five-star exercise in self-improvement. The villas, replete with Chinese porcelain and Indian artworks that reflect the peculiar Mauritian mix of cultures, represent the quest for perfection and pure indulgence that is an ongoing challenge at the Beau Rivage resort.

Overlooking an offshore coral lagoon and the powdery-white sands of Belle Mare beach, Beau Rivage is one of the leading resorts in a country that prides itself on having some of the finest tropical hideaways anywhere. Rooms have plush interiors and plantation shutters on the windows; butler service and a 21,500-square-foot (2,000-sq-m) swimming pool ensure you will not be rubbing shoulders with other people unless you want to. For diving enthusiasts, nine dive sites up to 111 feet (34 m) in depth are just a ten-minute boat ride away. Nearly all water sports are complimentary, and there is a dedicated children's pool and club that ensures everyone, regardless of age, is pampered.

The east coast of Mauritius is the least developed region in the country. It offers guaranteed evening breezes through warm Mauritian summers, and can still give you that deserted tropical island atmosphere that is becoming increasingly hard to find elsewhere. The supreme comfort of the guest is what matters here. After all, not too many hotels have a "menu of pillows" to ensure your sleep is every bit as tranquil as your surroundings. **BS**

← *The treatment tents at the Beau Rivage spa are as exotic and exclusive in feel as the resort itself.*

Stay in a Tepee at One&Only

Location Belle Mare, Mauritius
Website www.oneandonlyresorts.com **Price** 💲💲

With a hand-sewn, bejeweled, canvas covering and a white and gold gauze interior, camping has never been this glamorous. This is no ordinary tent. Iconic British designer Alice Temperley has styled the tepee at the exclusive Indian Ocean resort with seriously stylish people in mind. Inside, there is an antique glass chandelier from Paris, a natural wood floor, gorgeous cushions and fabrics, and a chest full of champagne.

Guests can book the tepee for private dinners, celebrations, and even indulgent spa treatments. Or try a whole new experience—the Glampfire. Lounge on silk cushions, sipping champagne cocktails served by a butler, then have dinner at a low table set in the

> ## "One&Only is about delivering distinctive experiences fueled by imagination and style."
>
> Helen McCabe-Young, One&Only vice president

soft sand. Spend the rest of the evening watching fireworks, then dance on the sand into the early hours to the music of local musicians. Alternatively, loved-up couples can have the tepee to themselves, feasting on lobster and caviar, followed by spa treatments.

With restaurants headed by two Michelin-starred chefs—Alain Ducasse and Vineet Bhatia—taste buds are spoiled for choice. There is pampering on hand at the award-winning spa, and activities range from waterskiing, windsurfing, and sailing to tennis and golf. The temptation to lie back on a hammock strung between the palm trees or simply chill out in the decadent tepee is hard to resist. **AD**

Relax at Shanti Andana Maurice Spa

Location St. Felix, Mauritius
Website www.shantiananda.com   **Price** $

Shanti Ananda Maurice is the sister resort to the much lauded Ananda in the Himalayas, and it shares the same philosophy. The resort's holistic approach to well-being is evident at every turn—from the personalized spa program to the extensive yoga and meditation programs, practiced in dedicated pavilions and yoga rooms.

The setting is 35 acres (14 ha) of tropical gardens sporting spectacular views of the coral reef–sprinkled Indian Ocean. The coastal location is integral to the atmosphere and philosophy of Shanti Ananda Maurice; there are views of the turquoise waters at almost every corner, from the spa's Pebbles restaurant, to the junior ocean-view suites. Two of the room types—the luxury villas and luxury suite villas—come with their own swimming pools. The superlative presidential villa goes one step further, with a built-in whirlpool tub and steam room, as well as a pool and verdant landscape gardens.

The 50,000-square-foot (4,645-sq-m) spa makes liberal use of both ayurvedic and Western-style treatments. As well as the ayurvedic panchakarma treatment rooms, there is a couples' spa therapy suite, and there are multipurpose treatment rooms, scrub rooms, and hydrotherapy rooms. It is unusual to find a resort and spa that combines Eastern- and Western-style philosophy and relaxation so seamlessly. Guests begin their stay with a private consultation with a lifestyle assistant, who tailors the programs according to individual needs and wishes. **LC**

→ *The Shanti Ananda Maurice offers a pampering experience that treats mind, body, and spirit.*

Discover Denis Island

Location Denis Island, Seychelles **Website** www.denisisland.com **Price** ❺❺❺❺

Denis Island encapsulates every desert island dream rolled into one. A mere dot in the western Indian Ocean, it is the epitome of unpretentious simplicity. The lush island is named after a French explorer, Denis de Trobriant, who first sighted it in 1773. De Trobriant landed on the fertile island and found it to be a haven for a diversity of wildlife, as it remains today. Now visitors will find twenty-five Creole-influenced cottages nestled close to the shore, filled with huge beds and plump armchairs. They have chic, romantic bathrooms with alfresco showers, private verandas, and courtyards dotted between casuarina and coconut trees.

There is little need to do anything but while away sun-drenched days marooned on your very own silky slice of beach, pausing only to cool off in the small pool or stroll around the island's pathways to the old village, chapel, and lighthouse. There are no televisions, radios, or anything else to disturb your peace, except perhaps for the island's endearing inhabitants—some rather large turtles. Active guests can always venture into the turquoise waters and take advantage of the snorkeling and diving—turtles, sharks, and rays abound—and year-round game fishing. Common catches include sailfish, marlin, and tuna, and from September to November, whale sharks and manta rays can be sighted in the area.

Mealtimes are refreshingly casual, incorporating an array of fresh produce from the island's own very well-stocked farm, which includes chickens, pigs, cows, and quail, as well as native vanilla, herbs, and vegetables. Days revolve lazily around long, lavish breakfasts, lunches, and relaxed à la carte dinners, and the hardest decision you might face is whether to dine in the restaurant or on the beach, underneath a starry canopy. Hmm, now that is a tough one. **LP**

⬆ *Set in a secluded natural environment, Denis Island is a favorite among those looking for a romantic escape.*

Stay on Cousine Island

Location Cousine Island, Seychelles **Website** www.cousineisland.com **Price** ❸❸❸❸

Cousine Island may be tiny, but it is unique, spectacular, and enticingly hidden away. It is also, as an official nature reserve, ecologically important. Measuring only 62 acres (25 ha) in area and 2,625 feet (800 m) in width, the island has been dedicated to the preservation of the Seychelles natural environment since coming under private ownership in 2000. Its pedigree is impressive: the vegetation consists of ninety-five percent endemic plants and is home to more than five species of endemic land birds. The remaining five percent of vegetation is made up of indigenous fruit trees and plants, and hawksbill turtles come here to nest.

Amid this natural splendor, guests can stay in one of four luxury villas, which nestle 100 feet (30 m) from the pristine beach. Each villa aims to be 100 percent in keeping with its surroundings: Architecture is French colonial, materials are locally sourced where possible, and each villa comes with generous floor space, allowing for plenty of relaxation and tranquility. Guests

dine in a single, airy dining room, The Pavilion, overlooking the freshwater swimming pool and the ocean. Headed by South African chef Adriaan van Niekerk, the restaurant produces an array of dishes drawn from Creole and European influences and crafted from fresh, locally sourced ingredients.

The select feel of this island is enhanced by the fact that guests are encouraged to arrive by helicopter, guarding against the introduction of alien species: So far the island's delicate web of endemic bird and supporting flora remains intact. Tourists are also invited to take part in various conservation programs such as tree planting and turtle monitoring. For lazier days, there is always the lure of the spa (the Beach House Wellness Retreat), the beaches, and the simple, gentle lull of the Indian Ocean. **LC**

⬆ *Cousine Island's rare ecological importance attracts visitors with a strong interest in conservation.*

Enjoy Frégate Island Private

Location Frégate Island, Seychelles   **Website** www.fregate.com
Price

In years gone by, if you were a visitor to Frégate Island you were quite likely a privateer. These days, pirates are nowhere to be seen on this idyllic Indian Ocean island. From the tropical forests to the white-sand coves, the watchword of the island is privacy—and lots of it.

With no more than forty guests in residence at any one time, this tiny granite island is one of the area's most secluded and desirable destinations. There are sixteen expansive villas, all of which blend in with the surrounding landscape. Fourteen nestle atop the cliffs and afford spectacular views of the Indian Ocean; the remaining two lie in their own private tropical gardens. The interior decor combines colonial and Seychellois design influences and the furniture is reminiscent of artifacts gathered by Indian Ocean traders on their travels. All the villas have their own private swimming pool, whirlpool tub, and dining pavilion, plus sliding glass walls and French doors, which are often left open to place the visitor firmly within the tropical paradise. The paradise can be further explored with the resident ecologist, who leads regular hikes along the coast and into the jungle. The reef-protected lagoon offers safe diving, swimming, and snorkeling, and for experienced divers, boats are available to find dramatic dive sites.

The spectacular Rock Spa—reached through a canyon of waterfalls and freshwater pools—provides holistic treatments, and the Castaway Kids Club takes good care of the children while you work out in the gym, head off to Praslin Island for a round of golf, or just lie back and think about how those lucky pirates must have felt to wash up at a place like this. **SH**

➔ *The thatched-roof villas are built from locally sourced mahogany and teak and all have spectacular views.*

The breadth of experiences available to you in Asia is awe-inspiring. Stay in a temple in the Himalayan mountains or visit an ancient shrine in Cambodia. Alternatively, embrace everything the modern city has to offer by staying in a penthouse in Tokyo or visiting a luxury spa in Hong Kong. If these don't appeal, how about a beachfront lodge in Thailand?

← The Sarojin, Thailand

ASIA

Explore the Farasan Islands

Location Farasan Islands, Saudi Arabia **Website** www.sauditourism.com.sa **Price** ❶

The waters of the Red Sea are renowned for their great diversity of animal and plant life, but for a long time only those with ties to the Saudi royal family were allowed to admire the dazzling underwater world around its largest group of islands. Thanks to the kingdom's recent forays into the tourism market, the Farasan Islands—25 miles (40 km) off the southern Saudi Arabian port of Jizan—have become a more accessible divers' paradise that remains (at least for the time being) unaffected by human activity.

These eighty-four low-lying limestone islands and islets were created when sea levels rose after the last ice age, giving rise to vast areas of shallow water around them that have become home to expansive coral "gardens" full of marine life. The area is now a nature reserve. Farasan Kebir, the biggest island, is one of only three that are permanently inhabited, whereas the deserted islands making up the rest of the archipelago are ideal breeding grounds for sea turtles and birds. The islands are also home to Saudi Arabia's largest population of gazelles, and they are one of the last habitats for the endangered dugong.

The tourist infrastructure here is quite refreshingly unsophisticated. The three-star Farasan Hotel—the only guesthouse on the islands—has limited space as well as some inadequacies, but the staff's genuine excitement about having visitors from faraway places more than makes up for its foibles. When you wander along the empty beaches on the larger islands (where the only traces of life you will encounter are animal tracks and the occasional flock of flamingos curiously looking at you), or when you come face-to-face with dolphins, stingrays, and whale sharks in the warm waters surrounding the islands, you will feel as though you are truly in a different world. **DaH**

⬆ *For many years, only Saudi royalty and their guests were allowed to dive or swim around these islands.*

Stay at Al Bustan Palace Hotel

Location Muscat, Oman **Website** www.ichotelsgroup.com **Price** ⦵⦵

Imagine a hotel designed by an Arab prince. Then add lashings of gold and a load of jewels, and throw piles of rials at it. The result will not be far off the Al Bustan Palace Hotel. Complete with 250 rooms, the hotel sits against a dramatic mountain backdrop on 200 acres (80 ha) of private beach and lush, verdant gardens. It has recently been refurbished, and some of its worst excesses have been reined in, to be replaced by more elegant, stylish interiors.

However, the foyer of the hotel is anything but subdued; it is still as opulent as befits a property occasionally commandeered for use by none other than HM the Sultan of Oman himself. With bright blue and green mosaic tiles, and a vast lofty atrium, you could be forgiven for thinking you had accidentally stumbled into a mosque instead of an Arabic outpost of the Intercontinental chain. Huge glittering chandeliers hang like stalactites from the ceiling, and richly ornate Asian rugs are scattered over the marble

floor. The rooms are all equally luxurious, with rich colors and fabrics used in abundance to optimum effect. Bathrooms are wall-to-wall marble, with some baths big enough for a football team.

As you would expect from a hotel of this impressive size, there is a well-equipped fitness center with state-of-the-art body conditioning equipment, as well as both a sauna and steam room. However, given the searing temperatures of the typical Omani summer, these latter facilities might be somewhat redundant. Far better to break into a gentle sweat by taking a stroll along the beach, or through the beautifully manicured gardens, and enjoy the space and solitude of your surroundings. If you are looking to live out those Arabian Night fantasies, and you have got princely pockets to match, this is the place for you. **HA**

⬆ *Even more opulent inside than it apears from the outside, this hotel is luxury at its most extreme.*

Drive Through Wadi Adai

Location Muscat to Wadi Shab, Oman
Website www.gulfleisure.com/wadibashing.htm   **Price**

No trip to Oman would be complete without experiencing what is referred to locally as "wadi bashing." A wadi is a dried-up riverbed, and in the blistering heat of this Middle Eastern sultanate, where temperatures have been known to nudge 122°F (50°C), riverbeds are more often found cracked and parched than flowing with life-giving water.

One of the best drives is through Wadi Adai to the village of Mazara, set in an oasis of swaying date palms. This picturesque settlement is almost biblical in appearance, with locals wafting around in crisp white dishdasha and herds of goats skittishly leaping around. Press on through the foothills of the jagged Eastern Hajar mountains through dramatic stark landscapes. You will soon leave the paved road behind and hit the coastal off-road path, lurching across ancient dried-up seabeds and careering along dusty red mountain tracks toward Dihab. You will come upon a huge natural water hole, known as Bait Al Afreet, with clear, emerald water. Farther on, you reach Wadi Shab, which means "gorge between the cliffs." This wadi rarely dries up completely, which makes it the perfect spot for a cooling dip. Situated in a deep ravine, the wadi is a lush oasis of trees, date palms, and grass, and makes a welcome contrast to the rugged terrain.

Make sure you spend some time in the desert, too, to experience some dune bashing; this is how the modern-day Bedouins drive across the soft undulating sand. Ideal for thrill seekers, this involves some hair-raising steep climbs up the vertiginous dunes and stomach-lurching drops over the other side. **HA**

➲ *Drive with a local guide; it is easy to get lost in the various dunes and rocky moonscape of the wadis.*

Discover the Sultan Qaboos Grand Mosque

Location Muscat, Oman
Website www.omanet.om/english/Relegious/grandmosq.asp   **Price** ◖

In a blistering summer when the mercury can reach 122°F (50°C), where better to find a respite from the blazing sun than in the beautiful Sultan Qaboos Grand Mosque. Walk through the traditional Islamic gardens and enter the dazzling white marble courtyard through a series of symmetrical white stone archways. At midday, it is difficult to see at all because of the harsh glare of the sun reflecting off the marble, but enter into the cool sanctity of the mosque—ensuring you are modestly dressed—and your eyesight will soon adjust to the awe-inspiring spectacle within.

The mosque, which was completed in 2001, is the largest in the world outside Saudi Arabia, with room for up to 20,000 worshippers. The main prayer hall is square with a central dome rising to a heady height of 165 feet (50 m). The dome, main minaret, and four flanking minarets are the mosque's chief architectural features. Women have their own private *musalla* that can accommodate 750 worshippers.

The stunning 230-by-200-foot (70-by-60-m) prayer carpet is the largest single piece of carpet in the world. It was handwoven by 600 Iranian women, took four years to make, weighs over 21 tons and includes more than 28 colors (all vegetable dyes). The mosque also has some of the most stupendous crystal chandeliers you will ever see, dominated by the centerpiece, a truly awesome 600,000-crystal, 1,000-bulb creation by Austrian company Swarovski. It is second in size only to one in Abu Dhabi. Despite the grandeur of the Grand Mosque, and its impressive statistics, it is a place of great calm, peace, and tranquility. **HA**

> *"It must be one of the world's most serenely beautiful buildings … polished marble and smooth."*
>
> Martin Love, *Observer*

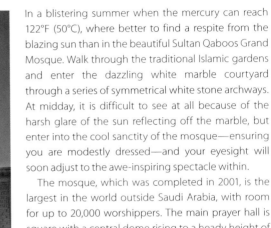

◹ *The Sultan Qaboos Grand Mosque allows up to 20,000 people to worship together.*

Unwind at Zighy Bay

Location Musandam Peninsula, Oman
Website www.sixsenses.com **Price** 💲💲💲

For centuries Zighy Bay has been hidden away in the far north of Oman in the Musandam peninsula. Now a resort of the same name has been built and guests have a choice of how they arrive: paraglide; take the winding mountainous drive; or take a scenic fifteen-minute speedboat ride over the water, zipping past traditional fishing dhows and schools of dolphins.

Zighy Bay sits on a bay of golden sand in a dramatic, rugged mountain setting overlooking the Arabian Gulf. The hotel is owned by the luxury Evanson Hideaway brand, and was built in keeping with traditional Omani style. A cluster of dung-colored cubes studded with palm trees does not make for the

---

"Four long, hazy, sunkissed days on Zighy Bay and I have to admit to being . . . utterly smitten."

Annabelle Thorpe, *Observer*

---

most aesthetically pleasing of properties, but it does blend in well with the stark beauty of the Hajar mountain range. All the villas have their own private plunge pools, outdoor showers, daybed areas, and terraces, and your own private Jeeves is only a phone call away. If you feel in need of further relaxation, make your way to the Six Senses spa.

It is at night, however, that the resort really comes into its own; then it is transformed by candlelit pathways, and dining tables on the beach are lit up by flaming torches. After dinner, take a stroll along the beach, gaze up at the inky starlit sky, and enjoy the perfect peace of what is still a hidden gem. **HA**

Relax at Al Maha

Location Dubai, United Arab Emirates
Website www.al-maha.com **Price** 💲💲

Dubai, a flittering, thriving metropolis risen from the sand, is the cosmopolitan hub of the Middle East. Unique and ever changing, it is a feat of modern architecture and cutting-edge design.

Just an hour's drive away from the hustle and bustle of "the city of gold" lies the desert resort of Al Maha. Driving into the desert conservation area feels how it must feel to change planets. After the frenetic chaos of Dubai, Al Maha is still and peaceful, inhabited by smiling camels ambling about. Despite being inspired by Bedouin tented camps, Al Maha is the ultimate in desert opulence.

The intense heat limits activities. Rise early for a spot of falconry or take a walk from your tent and keep an eye out for the oryx, the rare elegant desert antelopes that roam free. Riders should jump in the saddle on the noble-looking pure-blood horses in true Lawrence of Arabia fashion. If it all feels too much, a golf buggy will be available to take you back to your tent.

During the day it is simply too hot to do much aside from relax and take in the beautiful scenery. Rest in the air-conditioned comfort of the decadent suite, with its huge bed, glitzy bathroom, and two-person tub, or relax by your very own dipping pool with a view onto the golden sands. Read that novel you always intended to read, or indulge in the spa. At dusk, join the camel walk. A reward awaits after the trek: a champagne cocktail in the soft, silky dunes. The sand turns a bright orange in the dim light, and couples spread out, adopting their own dune from which to watch the sun disappear in a warm velvety breeze.

There is a pervading sense of isolation here, a feeling that you are really lost in the land of *One Thousand and One Nights*, albeit totally voluntarily. **RCA**

Experience the Burj Al Arab

Location Dubai, United Arab Emirates   **Website** www.burj-al-arab.com   **Price** ❸❸❸❸

"Dubai's most famous hotel is as extravagant and outrageous as you've been led to believe."

Time Out, Dubai

⬆ *The Burj Al Arab was built to resemble a full, billowing sail—the sail of an extremely exclusive yacht.*

➡ *There are simply not enough synonyms of the word "opulence" to do justice to this hotel.*

There are luxury hotels, and then there is the Burj Al Arab. Taking glitz, bling, glamor, call it what you will, to a whole new level, the iconic sail-shaped Dubai resort is a benchmark of no-holds-barred extravagance that others have tried and failed to emulate since the hotel opened in 1999. Soaring proudly to a height of 1,050 feet (321 m), the hotel is in its element at night when, dramatically and colorfully lit, it stands out on the coastline like a spectacular beacon.

All the suites (the word "room" does not exist here) are arranged over two floors and have a whirlpool tub, living and dining area, and dedicated butler, plus frivolous touches like extensive pillow and bath menus. Lavishly decorated, some suites have spiral staircases, private cocktail bars, dressing rooms, snooker tables . . . the list is endless. Excess is practically a dirty word and the sheer opulence is staggering. There is a helipad on the twenty-eighth floor, and the royal suites have a private elevator and cinema, a marble-and-gold staircase, and even a rotating four-poster canopy bed.

Tempting as it may sound, holing up in your suite would mean missing out on more fun elsewhere. The Assawan Spa and Health Club on the eighteenth floor boasts jaw-dropping views of the gulf, and the immaculate Majles Al Bahar private beach is fit for royalty. There are nine restaurants and bars, including the hotel's underwater restaurant, which contains a shark aquarium. If all that is not enough, guests can charter yachts or get the chance to brandish clubs at world-class golf courses.

A visit to the world's most palatial hotel is certainly eye opening, perhaps as a result of all the sparkly gold with which it is adorned. Just be sure to come with a stuffed wallet—and a head for heights. **LP**

Go on a Camel Safari

Location Dubai, United Arab Emirates
Website www.nettoursdubai.com/camel_trek.htm   **Price** 💲💲

Dubai is an ultra-modern vacation destination, with astonishingly opulent six-star hotels and entire new towns seemingly emerging out of the sea on an almost daily basis. However, if you want to get away from the tourists who come to the Emirates just for the air-conditioning, and experience the real Arabia, you need to get on the back of a camel.

Known locally as Allah's gift to the Bedouins, camels can go for weeks without food and water, plodding across the red sands in stately caravans. With their slipperlike feet, armchair saddles, and gently swaying gait, they really do make for a comfortable ride.

A camel safari into the Arabian Desert will take you into a mysterious wilderness, dotted with date palms and acacias and populated by unusual desert animals, such as the sand cat, desert hare, and dune gerbil. Sometimes the sleepy desert fox may put in an appearance, and the plentiful geckos will skitter around the feet of your unfazed and reliable mount. At the end of the day, you can enjoy a traditional Bedouin feast, prepared in front of you as you stretch out on a carpet beside your tent and watch the unforgettable desert sunset, lengthening the shadows of the dunes and shifting the sculpture of the red Arabian sand.

Many people say climbing to the top of a high mountain is the best way to clear your head, gain perspective, and find your own place in the world. But devotees of the desert claim that a wander through the beautiful wilderness of the dunes, where maps and charts and plans are of no real use, is the perfect way in which to discover yourself. **SWi**

➡ *The best way to discover the majesty and silence of the desert is atop a camel.*

Relax at Bab Al Shams

Location Dubai, United Arab Emirates
Website www.jumeirahbabalshams.com **Price** 😊😊😊

It is easy to imagine that you are luxuriously marooned in the desert at this wonderful Arabian fantasy resort, but the incredible Jumeirah Bab Al Shams is actually less than an hour's drive from Dubai. Built to resemble a traditional fortress, there is a real feel of desert adventure about the unique setting. All the rooms are traditionally styled with dark wood and soft rugs, balconies and terraces look out across the dunes, and suites have a separate Majlis-style lounge and large walk-in dressing room connected to the bathroom with separate rain shower.

A great escape for all ages: While the little ones are being entertained at the kids' club, adults can chill out

> *"Inspired by traditional Arabian forts . . . [a] mishmash of styles that fits together seamlessly."*
>
> Matthew Lee, *Daily Telegraph*

by the infinity pool with glorious views across the dunes or be pampered in the Satori Spa. There are also six restaurants and bars, offering international and Arabian cuisine; the rooftop bar is the place to go for cocktails and watch the sun dip below the sands.

Plan desert adventures with a range of Arabian-inspired activities, from horseback riding and camel treks to falconry displays. Or explore the desert and eat an early breakfast among the rippling sands.

There is only one good thing about leaving Bab Al Shams and that is getting the chance to go shopping for gold, leather, and spices at the bustling souk (marketplace) in Dubai on the way home. **AD**

Enjoy the Royal Mirage

Location Dubai, United Arab Emirates
Website www.oneandonlyresorts.com **Price** 😊😊😊😊

Along Dubai's Jumeirah golden strip, which runs alongside the Arabian Gulf, opulent hotels jostle for space. There is, however, one essential place to escape the city's eternal buzz: the divine hammam at the One and Only Royal Mirage.

The Moorish and Arabian design of the Royal Mirage is pristine. Sand-colored structures are dominated by arches and domes standing out against the azure sky. It is an oasis of lush green palm trees, fountains, secluded pools, gazebos, and exotic Arabian style throughout. In keeping with the spirit of the Orient, the spa has an impressive central towering dome of intricate design and mosaic tiling, and here you will find a beautiful and traditional hammam. The entire experience is extraordinary: ceremonial with a touch of the theatrical. The hammam aims to nurture beauty and well-being within its steamy, wet walls. There is a defined cleansing and bathing ritual. Dressed in a *pestemal*, a traditional soft cotton wrap, a hammam masseur or masseuse will take command and will cleanse, scrub, and pummel your skin until it gleams—and your mind is thoroughly relaxed. You will be led to the alcoves where the air is hot and heavy, a few shafts of light come through the dim light, and lanterns shine off the mosaics.

Continual running water, the gleam of pristine silver bowls, and the rich, heavy heat have an entrancing effect. Being taken care of in such detail is exhausting; spend a little more time relaxing and sipping cardamom tea, sweet with a marked touch of spice. What more could anyone need? **RCA**

➭ *Everything about the One and Only Royal Mirage is designed to relax the body and mind.*

Experience a Kibbutz

Location Near Eliat, Israel
Website www.kibbutz.org.il/eng/welcome.htm   **Price** ❶

Labor Zionism originated in late-nineteenth-century Imperial Russia, and with it the Kibbutz Movement came into being. The socialist leaders of the movement regarded physical labor in the fields of their ancient homeland of Israel as a means of redemption, as well as a vehicle to free themselves from the social constraints the Diaspora experienced at the time. One of the results of this movement was the establishment of the first kibbutz, at the southern end of the Sea of Galilee, in 1909. By the time the State of Israel was created in 1948, kibbutzim were thriving.

Today, farming is no longer the raison d'être of kibbutzim. Kibbutz Ketura, 31 miles (50 km) north of Eilat, is one of the few remaining Israeli collectives resisting private ownership. Founded in 1973, Ketura distinguishes itself because of its highly educated inhabitants and the resulting prominence of artistic and technological endeavors. The kibbutz's work opportunities range from accounting and algae farming to photography and painting, and, unlike other vacations, a stay at the Ketura will earn you money rather than cost a fortune.

Volunteers are housed in shared two-room apartments, and in addition to free accommodation and three meals a day they receive $65 per month. Staying for two to six months, the volunteers work mostly in the service sector, although some get agricultural work or look after the children of the kibbutz. No matter what you do, the experience of living in a kibbutz will be unlike anything you are likely to encounter in everyday life. **DaH**

← *There are a variety of different tasks that need to be undertaken on a kibbutz, such as picking nectarines.*

Relax at Isrotel Agamim

Location Eilat, Israel
Website www.isrotel.co.il   **Price** ❷❷

Near the shore of the Red Sea and the Eilat promenade, the Agamim—also known as "The Water Garden Hotel"—attracts young, laid-back guests who come here to soak up the relaxing atmosphere. Chilled-out tunes play by the pool, tropical cocktails are mixed at the bar, and hammocks are hung between the palm trees in the lush gardens.

This is a very popular hotel for romantic vacations. Lovesick couples can book to stay in one of the hotel's signature water rooms. The ground-floor rooms open directly onto a private stream that connects with the main lagoon pool. Guests can relax on the private deck or step into the stream under a stone archway.

"[Enjoy] tropical cocktails, cozy hammocks, and the freedom to do absolutely nothing."

Proprietors, Isrotel Agamim

There is no rush to get up early in the morning, with the option of a late breakfast served until noon, and room service is available directly through the swimming pool's On the Water bar. For those who want to venture beyond the hotel, there are jeep safaris into the mountains above Eilat, a wonderful chance to see the breathtaking desert landscape in panoramic detail. This area is teeming with history. South of Eilat is the arrival place of the Queen of Sheba, when she made her historic visit to King Solomon, and farther north, the caves around the Dead Sea are the where the famous Dead Sea Scrolls were discovered in the late 1940s by a young Bedouin shepherd. **AD**

Bathe in the Dead Sea

Location Israel/Jordan **Website** www.deadsea.co.il
Price ⬤

The Dead Sea is the lowest place on Earth—and it is fast disappearing because of the local thirst for water. The spiritual nature of the Dead Sea is mesmerizing, as is the privilege of floating in the world's largest natural spa. Biblical references hang heavily in the air, but visit the Dead Sea because it is a beautiful epic in itself, not simply because this is your last chance to see it.

The sea's function as a natural spa is linked to its microclimate, a combination of ozone-rich air, low humidity, high evaporation and atmospheric pressure, and healthy, ultraviolet filtered sunshine. The salty, mineral-rich waters and mud are claimed to help provide soft "Cleopatra skin." For those squeamish

> "A dip in the Dead Sea is a unique sensation. It is so buoyant . . . you can't even submerge your legs."

Jacqueline Head, *Daily Mail*

about swimming with fish, the Dead Sea is perfect: Between Jordan and the West Bank, the water contains nothing living but algae.

Slather off the mud and float away toward Jericho, Sodom, or Gomorrah, watching the sun set crimson over Jerusalem. The world's largest natural spa now also has a purpose-built spa, the Ishtar. If your body is your temple, let it be an epic temple. Designed with a passing nod to the Hanging Gardens of Babylon, the Ishtar is a pastiche of Babylonian splendor. **LGS**

➔ *The Dead Sea is so thick with salt and other minerals that people can lie on the surface without sinking.*

Stay at Feynan Lodge

Location Wadi Araba, Jordan
Website www.rscn.org.jo   **Price** $

Arriving at Feynan Lodge takes a six-hour hike or a two-and-a-half-hour bumpy ride in a four-wheel-drive vehicle but it is worth the effort. Deep in the remote, arid mountains of Wadi Araba, Feynan Lodge forms the western gateway of the Dana Biosphere Reserve. The Royal Society for the Conservation of Nature (RSCN) constructed this unique, solar-powered eco-lodge to provide a base and accommodation for tourists.

At dusk, the lodge is transformed into a shimmering desert mirage as candles are lit in rooms, on terraces, and around the dining area. It is like stepping back in time to a traditional caravansary. In keeping with the lodge's green credentials, the candles that light it are

> *"The Lodge represents a brave attempt to create a unique tourism experience in Jordan."*
>
> The Royal Society for the Conservation of Nature

made by local Bedouin women and the restaurant uses fresh local ingredients to make traditional Bedouin vegetarian dishes. The RSCN built the lodge to provide an alternative, sustainable source of income to local Bedouins suffering from the overgrazing of their land. It was built entirely with local materials, and its unique arabesque design incorporates traditional adobe building techniques.

Its wonderful isolation and stunning landscape make this the perfect location for walkers. The region also has fascinating archaeological treasures, including the remains of ancient Roman copper mines and the ruins of a Byzantine settlement. **AD**

Camp at Wadi Rum

Location Wadi Rum, Jordan
Website www.baitali.com; www.visitjordan.com   **Price** $$$

Wadi Rum is a wilderness of more than 270 square miles (700 sq km), and one of Jordan's star attractions. Boulders and cliffs, shaped by millennia of winds and sand, stand like cathedrals. Seminomadic tribes live and herd their goats here as they have for centuries. The dramatic beauty of the mountains (known as *jebels*) can be seen by camel, jeep, or on foot, and mountaineers can try their luck on cliffs that reach 5,740 feet (1,750 m).

Many of the tribespeople will offer adventurous travelers a bed for the night in their goat-hair tents. These desert camps provide a unique experience. The curl of smoke from a hookah pipe slowly perfumes the air as tribesmen entertain the guests with live music, stories, and strong Arabic coffee.

There are also permanent sites, including the luxurious Bait Ali, which has a swimming pool, luxury tents, and hot showers. Guides can also take you into the desert for a private camping experience under the stars, with candles, a barbecue, and a luxury bed, in an ancient riverbed bordered by sandstone mountains. Here, in the Valley of the Moon, legends abound from ancient and more recent history—tales of Lawrence of Arabia, who had his headquarters here during the Arab revolt of World War I, are a common topic.

As the campfire flickers, crags and wind-sculpted rocks are illuminated. Deep in the canyons and caves, rock canvases show ancient etchings from people of the desert dating back 4,000 years. The area inspired Lawrence's *Seven Pillars of Wisdom*, in which he called the scenery "vast, echoing, and God-like." **LD**

➡ *The camp provides a base for exploring the vast, eerie expanse of desert that is the Wadi Rum.*

Stay at Hotel Albergo

Location Beirut, Lebanon   **Website** www.albergobeirut.com
Price 💲💲💲

Located just outside the city, in the quiet, green area of Achrafiye, the traditional Christian quarter of Beirut, Hotel Albergo is a relaxed and tranquil place. A converted city mansion, it makes the ideal base from which to explore the many treasures of Lebanon's capital city.

The only true boutique hotel in Beirut, Albergo has thirty-three luxurious rooms and suites that are notable for their luxuriant individuality (being a Relais & Châteaux member, the quality is pretty much guaranteed). Themed along various lines, including Asian, colonial, Mediterranean, and European, the rooms boast antiques alongside local curios. Each suite has been separately designed with the absolute comfort of the guest in mind, with such touches as Frette sponges and Dead Sea bath salt adding to Tarfa Salam's exceptional touch as a designer. Lebanon's location has always seen the country draw influences from the Near East, Middle East, and Mediterranean Europe, and this is reflected in the decor of what is essentially a peaceful hotel, with a playful twist. The red velvet bar lifts the lobby to neo–Louis XIV elegance, making it a warming and cozy venue to sip an ice-packed drink or two.

The garden, swimming pool, and whirlpool tub have unparalleled views of the Lebanese mountains. Sit and enjoy the warm, dry air, borne on winds dancing in directly from the African plains.

Albergo also has two restaurants. The Rooftop Restaurant, as its name suggests, provides peerless views, whereas Al Dente is on the ground floor and offers fantastic Italian and Lebanese cuisine. If you feel like a stroll or night out, the clubs, bars, and restaurants of the historic city of Beirut lie literally at your feet. **PS**

Enjoy Beit Al-Mamlouka

Location Damascus, Syria   **Website** www.almamlouka.com
Price 💲💲

Damascus has become an increasingly fashionable destination for Western tourists. Unlike Beirut in the 1960s and present-day Tel Aviv, however, the allure of Syria's capital and largest city does not lie in the decadence of its nightlife or the presence of overpopulated beaches lined with dozens of bars. Instead, it draws people interested in culture and with a penchant for Middle Eastern romance.

Opened in 2005 and situated in a seventeenth-century house in the Christian quarter of Bab Touma—the city's oldest borough—Beit Al Mamlouka is Syria's first boutique hotel. It is inconspicuous from the outside, and only those in the know are able to tell that

---

"In Damascus, your best bet is to simply get lost in the truly ancient Old City."

Seth Sherwood, *New York Times*

---

behind the salmon-pink walls there is a dazzling and intimate eight-room establishment centered on a courtyard whose citrus trees and fountain complete the picture of traditional Arabic aestheticism.

Inside, the two single rooms, two doubles, and four suites all have their own character and are furnished with handmade local products. Everywhere in the hotel arched doorways and lavishly painted ceilings abound, whereas the stables of this formerly private home have been turned into a restaurant and bar. Stepping out of the hotel, Damascus's bustling alleyways and its vibrant, atmospheric, covered souk (marketplaces) are only a short walk away. **DaH**

Stay at Four Seasons Hotel

Location Damascus, Syria **Website** www.fourseasons.com
Price 💲💲

The world's oldest city has just one five-star hotel and this is it. Sitting outside the old city, the Four Seasons towers above the minarets and domed rooftops of nearby mosques. It is not all modern glitz, however; there are enough touches of traditional style to ensure even the most well-traveled guests get a sense of staying somewhere suitably exotic and with an ancient history. The suites and rooms have all mod cons, but are beautifully decorated with handwoven Syrian textiles and locally made, handcarved furniture.

The hotel has three different restaurants: Al Halabi features the best of the Aleppo cuisine of northern Syria; at Il Circo, savor traditional regional southern Italian dishes in a contemporary setting; and Safran offers alfresco dining with breathtaking views of the city from the terrace.

Pamper yourself with a relaxing or rejuvenating treatment in the elegant surroundings of the Balloran Spa. The hotel's signature massage is the wonderfully calm-inducing Zanobia massage, which was once the favorite of Palmyrian royalty. Heated poultices infused with aromatic oils are used to soothe tired muscles, nourish the skin, and induce relaxation. Alternatively, go for a swim in the outdoor pool, where attentive staff will be waiting to greet you with chilled towels and water spritzes when you reemerge.

Damascus is a living museum—the world's oldest, continually inhabited city. Its mosques, markets, and ruins—including the Roman city wall—entice visitors to imagine themselves in another era, yet the city manages to live to a modern beat with good shopping and acclaimed restaurants. Visit the souk and step back in time to an empire that once stretched all the way from the Atlantic coast to central Asia. **AD**

Relax at Mansouriya Hotel

Location Aleppo, Syria **Website** www.mansouriya.com
Price 💲💲💲💲

Located in the old part of a very ancient city, Aleppo's Mansouriya Hotel is straight out of *One Thousand and One Nights*. An extensively renovated sixteenth-century building, this tiny boutique hotel pays tribute to the different cultures that have shaped Aleppo, from Hittite and Greco-Roman to Ottoman.

The hotel's alleyway entrance is as inconspicuous as its interior is sumptuous. Unmarked, it is impossible to spot unless you already know where it is. Pass through a small hall and a second arched doorway to enter a stunning courtyard. Everything has been considered with painstaking attention to detail, such as the bathtubs carved from single pieces of marble.

> *"Aleppo stands alone … one of the great lost, thoroughly underrated cities in the world."*
>
> Tariq Elkashef, suite101.com

The hotel has two sitting rooms, the Iwan for balmy summer nights and the impressive, wood-paneled Kaha, complete with cozy sofas and a fountain. There is also a well-stocked and (highly adorned) library, a whirlpool tub, and a hammam.

Two of Aleppo's main attractions—the souks and the citadel—are just around the corner from the hotel. Visit one of the coffeehouses to observe fashionable young Aleppians at dusk, in one of the most enchanting and welcoming cities on the planet. The Mansouriya Hotel's friendly service, delicious food, and gentle care of its guests gives you the impression that your Syrian grandmother is looking after you. **DaH**

Explore Alaçati

Location Izmir, Turkey   **Website** www.tasotel.com
Price $

Alaçati, on Turkey's Aegean coast, is a historic Greek town, set just inland, filled with achingly tasteful boutique hotels and gourmet restaurants—it is also home to a small sandy bay, which has become a popular windsurfing center, complete with very high-end resorts. Just ten years ago none of this existed.

In 2001, Zeynep Ozis, a retired marketing executive, had the idea of turning one of the village's dilapidated old houses into an upmarket hotel. Such was the success of the Alaçati Tas Otel that it spawned a nation of imitators. Now there are thirty-six, and counting. Thankfully, strict planning laws ensure that each respects the architecture and character of the town.

> ## "Whitewashed walls, pale-blue window frames, antique furniture, and an enticing log fire."
>
> *The Times*

None of these pretenders, however, has managed to improve upon the Tas. The large rooms are charmingly decorated, outside are a peaceful walled garden and a secluded swimming pool, and the delicious food—most of it locally sourced—is served on a leafy terrace. The hotel is quiet and serene, yet it is just a few minutes' walk from the town center, with its lively bars and restaurants that come to life in the evenings, and a short ride from the sunbathing and water sports opportunities offered by the beach. **JF**

← *What makes these bustling streets different is the abundance of opportunities for people-watching.*

Walk the Lycian Way

Location Fethiye to Antalya, Turkey
Website www.lycianway.com **Price** ❶

Lycia is the ancient name for Turkey's Tekke peninsula, which juts into the Mediterranean on the south coast. Mountains rise steeply from tiny bays along the coast, creating beautiful views for walkers on their wooded slopes. The Lycian Way was established ten years ago. It is a 316-mile (509-km) marked path around the coast of Lycia, from Fethiye to Antalya. The route is easier at the start near Fethiye and becomes more difficult as it progresses, with some hefty ascents and descents.

Whether you tackle the whole route or just a small part, it is a spectacular way to spend a few days. You can expect to see the ruins of lost Lycian cities, quaint old houses in remote spots, and the forests, rocks, and blue Mediterranean Sea sparkling beyond. Highlights include the 7-mile (12-km) beach at Patara, views of mountains like Baba Dagi, and gasp-worthy vistas over the coast at Kas and Kalkan.

Along the way, some walkers stay at the lighthouse at Cape Gelidonia; others will tackle the 7,835-foot (2,388-m) Mount Olympos. There will doubtless be some manic splashing in deep cool canyons, jittery but memorable ridge walks, and the thrill of discovering tiny ancient churches far up in the hills. The trail is marked with red-and-white paint every 328 feet (100 m) to the standards of the European Grande Randonnée paths.

The best times to explore this beautiful trail are in the spring or fall. You can stay in one of the many simple pensions or small hotels along much of the trail, but in places it may be easier to stay in a village house or simply camp out in the wild. **SH**

← *When walking the Lycian Way, you will pass ancient ruins like these tombs carved into the mountainside.*

Camp at Huzur Vadisi

Location Lycia, Turkey
Website www.huzurvadisi.com **Price** ⑤⑤

While away a week or two in this Lycian oasis that translates to "peaceful valley." Set among fig and olive groves and based around a restored farmhouse, Huzur Vadisi promises a relaxing stay and holistic activities, such as yoga, in pine-forested mountains. Float away your worries in the natural stone swimming pool, rock yourself to sweet slumber in one of the many hammocks, or relax with an indulgent massage.

You will stay in traditional—albeit fully equipped—yurts. The relaxed, friendly vibe and groups (usually of about twenty) make it a perfect destination for solo travelers, and the array of interesting courses on offer means you are bound to make a new friend or two.

> *"Guests often comment on how visiting Huzur Vadisi is like being welcomed to someone's home."*
>
> responsibletravel.com

You will sample the vibrant village cooking in serene silence—save for the occasional shepherd's flute in the distance or the tinkling of goat bells from the surrounding hills. The mainly vegetarian menu draws on the spectrum of fresh local produce, including the nuts, cheese, and yogurts the region is famous for.

There are plenty of possible excursions to tempt you to leave for a day. Check out the bars and restaurants in laid-back Gocek, the local village, sail around the islands in a traditional wooden boat, or stop for a swim. Long, sandy beaches are within an hour's drive, as is Dalyan for those keen to visit the ancient ruins, mud baths, and hot sulfur springs. **JS**

Dive at Bodrum

Location Bodrum, Turkey
Website www.divingturkey.com/dive_bodrum.htm   **Price** 🌓

The ancient city of Bodrum in Turkey is one of the world's top dive locations thanks to the warm, clear waters of the Aegean Sea. They give reliable conditions and great visibility while avoiding any major problems caused by fierce tides or currents.

The safe bays in the area are perfect for learning to scuba dive or snorkel, yet the rugged volcanic islands offshore appeal to even the most experienced divers. The very diverse locations on these islands include hot springs, caverns, reefs, and spectacular drop-offs. There are even some modern wrecks to explore, and Bodrum offers great diving for those interested in archaeology. Artifacts from the ancient civilizations of

---

"Discover a rich variety of marine life in the crystal clear water surrounding the Bodrum peninsula."

motifdiving.com

---

the area can be seen on almost every dive. Visitors can spot shards of pottery even if the historic vessels themselves are out of bounds. Hundreds of these protected wrecks lie on the seabed, including the oldest-known shipwreck. This was a Bronze Age ship with a cargo of copper and glass ingots and various objects, such as ebony, amber, and elephant teeth.

The Institute of Nautical Archaeology has the largest underwater archaeology library, and Bodrum Museum of Underwater Archaeology houses the world's largest collection of artifacts from underwater excavations. This is housed in the striking fifteenth-century castle of St. Peter that dominates the waterfront. **SH**

Stay at Anatolian Houses

Location Cappadocia, Turkey
Website www.anatolianhouses.com.tr   **Price** 💲💲

If asked to come up with a list of romantic hotel settings, a cave probably would not rank too highly—not unless you had been to Cappadocia, that is. Here, the region's strange, almost lunar landscape is dotted by groups of giant stone pillars, known as "fairy chimneys." Today many are also home to swish, upmarket hotels of which the Anatolian Houses is probably the most swish and upmarket of all.

The complex of suites (no rooms, only suites), which weaves in and out of a group of undulating, Gaudi-esque chimneys, has been created in the traditional style with arched doorways and barrel-vaulted rooms, but to modern specifications. The hotel is well equipped with indoor and outdoor swimming pools, a spa and wellness center, a hammam (Turkish bath), a top-class restaurant, and an extensive wine cellar. Everything has been very tastefully done in a style that could perhaps best be described as designer Ottoman. The beds are draped in muslin, colorful kilims (flat-woven rugs) hang from the walls, and the furniture is a well-chosen mixture of antiques and modern designer pieces. Fourteen of the rooms have private hot tubs. In other words, everything the modern cave dweller could possibly wish for.

To get a better look at the area's unique landscape, which stretches for some 50 square miles (130 sq km), try a hot-air balloon tour, around twenty of which take to the skies every day from May to September. Passengers are often served "Cloud Nine," a mixture of champagne and cherry juice, a suitably bizarre drink for appreciating this alien but beautiful world. **JF**

➥ *The locals have been carving dwellings out of the soft volcanic rock at Cappadocia for centuries.*

Take a Balloon Ride over Cappadocia

Location Cappadocia, Turkey
Website www.cappadociaflights.com **Price** 🌕🌕

Hot-air ballooning is one of the greatest ways to travel: floating peacefully with the wind across a landscape. Over Cappadocia, it is truly sublime. This rugged region of central Turkey has some of the most stunning terrain in the world. Soft volcanic rocks have been eroded into strangely shaped pillars and stacks. There are hundreds of these "fairy chimneys" in natural colors ranging from dark pink to yellow, and ballooning is sometimes the only way to see them.

You are collected from your hotel and taken to the launch site just before sunrise. After the balloon is inflated, you climb into the basket. Takeoff is a gentle experience, like rising into the air on an invisible elevator. Then you fly over the valleys and rocks for about ninety minutes. After a gentle landing, passengers usually celebrate with a champagne breakfast.

Cappadocia is in the middle of a landmass with a great difference in night and day temperature. During the night, cold air accumulates in the valleys. Thanks to this reliable flow, which begins around sunrise, balloon pilots can fly almost every day of the year. Passengers can enjoy Cappadocia's great seasonal variety: In spring there is a carpet of miniature poppies, in summer a rush of fruit and flowers, and autumn is the time for grapes. Winter is often beautiful, with a covering of snow. Balloon experts often agree that Cappadocia is the best place in the world to fly. The predictable thermal conditions allow balloons to fly very close to the ground—you can even fly low enough to trees to pick ripe apricots. **SH**

→ *The steady currents of air in Cappadocia ensure that there is always good ballooning.*

See the Harem at the Topkapi Palace

Location Istanbul, Turkey **Website** www.topkapisarayi.gov.tr
Price $

"*[At] the main door of the Topkapi harem, the sense of enclosure and secrecy begins to grow.*"

Nick Trend, *Daily Telegraph*

Escape is not a concept that has always been associated with the imperial harem—harem means "forbidden" in Arabic. Built in the mid-sixteenth century, the harem at Topkapi Palace was the private living quarters of the female members of the Ottoman sultan's rather large family. Its 400-plus rooms provided lavish (and not so lavish) accommodation for the sultan's mother, the sultan's wives, and, most famously, the sultan's numerous concubines (which during the last days of the Ottoman Empire reputedly numbered in excess of 800).

The complex was strictly controlled by a unit of eunuchs, chosen because they would be unable to abuse their position. Contact with the outside world was via one carefully guarded exit, the Carriage Gate. Within, the harem was a hotbed of intrigue, where concubines vied for the sultan's favor, hoping to advance their, and more importantly their sons', fortunes. Indeed, many concubines rose to positions of great power, dominating the royal household, and in some instances saw their sons' rise to the position of sultan, whereupon they would ascend to the coveted rank of sultan's mother, or Valide Sultan.

Today you can tour many of the harem rooms that make up one of the most intriguing sections of the giant Topkapi Palace, the Ottoman Empire's seat of government until the mid-nineteenth century. Ironically, considering the intense history of the place, the harem quarters are today rather serene and quiet—the tour group crowds notwithstanding—and make a welcome escape from downtown Istanbul. **JF**

◪ *Added to and embellished over a four-century period, the palace has many examples of fine craftsmanship.*

Stay at A'jia Hotel

Location Istanbul, Turkey **Website** www.ajiahotel.com
Price 💲💲

This former pasha, a palatial summer mansion of the Ottoman elite, sits on the Asian banks of the Bosphorus and offers commanding views of life on the teeming river. An hour away from the center of the city, the A'jia—which means "Asia" in Japanese—offers the perfect refuge from busy Istanbul.

With only sixteen rooms, the hotel is one of a new breed of boutique hotels fast opening in the city. It has an original, dazzling white facade, but the interior is firmly twenty-first century, with cool contemporary decor and minimalist furnishings. A white-and-beige color palette dominates the rooms, which come complete with every modern convenience you could

> ## "The striking purity of the hotel's decoration completes the beauty of the Bosphorous."
>
> *Hayallere Visa* magazine

desire: LCD TVs, DVD players, and wireless Internet. There are king-size beds to snuggle up in, and equally impressive bathrooms, kitted out in creamy marble with vast bathtubs.

The bedrooms offer amazing views of the river and give the impression that you are floating above the Bosphorus. Watch an endless parade of cruise ships, ferries, tankers, and fishing boats glide past on the shipping lanes of the Bosphororus en route from the Marmaris to the Black Sea. Whenever you need to head back into the bustling throng of the city, take the hotel's private boat on a quick but utterly enchanting journey to the European side of Istanbul. **HA**

Relax at Ciragan Palace

Location Istanbul, Turkey **Website** www.kempinski.com
Price 💲💲💲💲

A legendary place straddling two diverse continents, Istanbul is a mythical city that is at once bewitching, exotic and intriguing. A true melting pot of culture and architecture, the city that was once Byzantium and Constantinople comes as an assault to the senses.

The historical sights are all grouped together in Old Istanbul or Eminönü, home to the impressive Topkapi Palace built by Sultan Mehmet II in 1459, the Hagia Sophia, the former Eastern Orthodox church converted to a mosque in 1453 often dubbed the "eighth wonder of the world," as well as the Grand Bazaar, the world's largest indoor market.

Escape the chaos and check into the Ciragan Palace. Once the residence of the last Ottoman Sultans, first built in wood in the sixteenth century, it was rebuilt in marble for Sultan Abdülaziz in 1857. Now a lavish five-star hotel with a guest list boasting Prince Charles, Elizabeth Hurley, Uma Thurman, and Giorgio Armani, it has all the trimmings any A-lister could desire: a gorgeous pool and a boat and helicopter service. To go overboard, book into the Sultan's suite overlooking the Bosphorus, which comes with private butler service, opulent chandeliers, period furniture, and art.

Take an extravagant voyage through Turkish cuisine at the palace's fancy Tugra restaurant. The Ottoman tasting menu ranges from the meze appetizers of spicy hummus and dolma (vine leaf wraps), to steamed shrimp and lamb *börek* pastries. For dessert, there are sticky sweet baklava and *tavuk gögsü*, a creamy dessert made with milk-white chicken-breast meat.

If you can tear yourself away, take a drive to Ortaköy, where the city's famous felines roam, and on to Bebek, a traditional village where luxurious mansions and summer residences sit quietly on the water. **RCA**

Relax at Rakhmanovskie Kluchi Hot Springs

Location Rakhmanovskie Kluchi, Kazakhstan
Website www.kazakhstan.orexca.com **Price** ⑤⑤

As far as escapes from modern life go, it is difficult to find a more remote place than rural Kazakhstan. The biggest landlocked country on the planet—as big as the whole of Western Europe—Kazakhstan has only 15 million inhabitants. However, with its wealth of natural resources, it has prospered since the collapse of the Soviet Union, and is (very slowly) gaining ground as a tourist destination, too.

In the Arasan River Valley in the eastern part of the country—close to the borders of Russia, Mongolia, and China—the waters of the Rakhmanovskie hot springs are said to contain curative radon, a byproduct of the disintegration of radioactive elements. According to legend, a peasant called Rakhmanov discovered the hot springs in the 1760s while chasing a deer he had wounded. The animal allegedly entered the hot waters and left them a short while later having fully recovered. Nowadays, the thermal waters are used to treat joint and back problems, as well as skin diseases. Built on the ruins of a Buddhist sanctuary, the spa of Rakhmanovskie Kluchi is surrounded by cedar forests and alpine meadows, with peaceful mountain passes offering great views over pristine lakes and summits that are up to 14,750 feet (4,500 m) high.

The felt yurts of Kazakh nomads are located on the banks of a mountain stream near the springs. For those who think that breathing the fresh air in one of the most remote corners of this world is not enough, it is possible to spend a few days with the nomads and share their everyday experiences: caring for the horses, milking the fillies, and preparing their traditional meat and dairy dishes—an existence that is far removed from the comforts of home. **DaH**

Explore Dal Lake by Boat

Location Dal Lake, Jammu and Kashmir, India
Website www.kashmir-tourism.net **Price** ⑤

Edged by spiky, snow-glazed Himalayan peaks, the only way to reach the houseboats on Dal Lake is to glide across the crystal waters on a shikara taxi. On this island of tranquility in a region that has seen a troubled past, visitors are now making a welcome return to Dal Lake after a long period of absence.

There are several permanently moored houseboats offering accommodation on the lake, but the Pahktoon Palace comes highly recommended. It sleeps up to eight people and has a large living room and separate dining room, both of which are heated by cozy wood-burning stoves. The interior of the Pahktoon is very

"The floating palaces of Kashmir [houseboats] are closely associated with the valley's traditions."

trekearth.com

ornate; the high ceilings, chandeliers, antique furniture, and intricately carved wood paneling would not look out of place in an English stately home.

Delicious Kashmiri curries are prepared by friendly hosts, who are happy to enlighten guests about the area's history. Sip your morning tea on deck and watch eagles dive for fish that dart among the underwater gardens. Rise early if you want to catch the floating morning market where locals sell okra, lotus flowers, and other produce grown on the lake's islands. **SB**

➔ *Catch the sun setting behind the Himalayan horizon across Dal Lake, one of Kashmir's most magical places.*

Visit the Golden Temple

Location Amritsar, Punjab, India   **Website** www.amritsar.com
Price $

At the end of a causeway in the middle of a man-made lake in the Punjabi city of Amritsar, the Harmandir Sahib (house of God), commonly referred to as the Golden Temple, is the most significant shrine of the Sikh religion. Designed with an entrance on each of its four sides echoing the tent of the Old Testament prophet Abraham, which also had four entrances to welcome travelers, the Golden Temple is a worldwide symbol of equality and tolerance, a serene place of worship whose doors are open to all men and women regardless of faith, race, or caste.

Construction on the site began in 1574 and was completed in 1604 under the reign of Guru Arjan Dev. The interior of the temple is replete with shrines honoring past gurus and is also home to three trees, known as Bers, that are symbolic of significant events in Sikh history. The exquisite gilding and intricate marble work on the temple's exteriors were initiated under Emperor Ranjit Singh and completed in 1830.

The Adi Granth, a collection of prayers and hymns representing the sacred texts of the Sikh religion, can be found inside the sanctuary inscribed on a jewel-studded raised platform. Surrounding the temple is the Pardakshna, a wide pathway that allows you to stroll around the temple and gaze up at its cusped arches and extravagant detailing. The temple's setting, its accessibility, and the profound sense of peace you feel when you approach the temple under the Darshani Deori arch at the beginning of the causeway will leave you in no doubt that this is one of the world's most monumental religious buildings. **BS**

← *The Golden Temple draws heavily upon the cultural and artistic traditions of both Islam and Hinduism.*

Stay at Basunti

Location Himachal Pradesh, India   **Website** www.basunti.com
Price $ $

If you are a keen angler, you may already know that the golden mahseer is India's most prized freshwater fish. What you may not know is that if you decide to spend a couple of nights at Basunti in the mountains of India's Himachal Pradesh, you are likely to catch these 26-pound (10-kg) beauties by the bucket load.

Angling in the man-made wetlands that pass by Basunti's doorstep is by no means the only pursuit afforded in this idyllic retreat. Located in the heart of a wildlife reserve and designed to leave the smallest possible ecological footprint, this boutique six-room retreat also has its own thatched Balinese-style yoga and meditation center. Bathed in tranquility and

> *" . . . a jewel, the kind of magical place that you might spend months looking for . . . and still never find."*
>
> *Sunday Telegraph*

seclusion, Basunti's two guesthouses both have shaded verandas and commanding views of the surrounding wetlands. The area is rich in birdlife, with almost 230 recorded species of bird and more than 50 species of waterfowl. Serious bird-watchers may wish to visit Ranser Island, one of the region's premier bird sanctuaries. In spring, when the waters are at their lowest before the monsoon, the gated temples of the ancient city of Bathu ki Larhi, representing the pinnacle of Hindu art and architecture, eerily reappear above the waterline. The traditional village of Khatiyar is just a thirty-minute walk away, and the area is a lovely mix of quaint rural villages and unspoiled woodlands. **BS**

Explore Shimla in the Foothills of the Himalayas

Location Shimla, Himachal Pradesh, India
Website www.shimlaindia.net   **Price** ◖

For untouched, rugged mountain scenery Himachal Pradesh is the Indian state to visit. Dominated by the mountains that rise steeply from the Punjabi plains, it is formed of several culturally distinct regions, isolated from each other by the mountain ridges.

Shimla is a wonderful place from which to contemplate the foothills of the Himalayas and the faded, melancholy grandeur of the Raj. These days, the town is popular as a honeymoon destination. There is a lot to enjoy, from the lively bazaars on narrow gullies that hug the steep ridges to the extraordinary Viceregal Lodge, a pleasant 3-mile (5-km) walk along pine-shaded roads, where the destiny of the subcontinent was once decided.

Wildflower Hall provides a genuine Himalayan experience without having to sacrifice all the comforts of home. Set in more than 20 acres (8 ha) of pine and cedar forests at an altitude of 8,250 feet (2,500 m), this five-star mountaintop retreat looks out over snowcapped peaks, verdant forests, and deep valleys. Activities at Wildflower Hall represent a departure from the usual choice of hotel pursuits and include archery, white-water rafting on the Sutlej River, horseback riding, and ice-skating. You can even take a day trip to Mount Everest on one of the hotel's two helicopters, or be deposited, with a minimum of fuss, in remote Himalayan valleys. Take in the sunset at the Hanuman Temple, at the highest point of the Shimla ridge. Monkeys appear from nowhere; they might try to divest you of anything not firmly attached to your being. **LB/BS**

➥ *The mountainous terrain can be quite hostile without the experience of a guide and his mule.*

Stay at Rambagh Palace

Location Rajasthan, India
Website www.tajhotels.com   **Price** ⊖⊖

Situated in the heart of Rajasthan's capital city Jaipur within 47 lush green acres (19 ha), the extravagant Rambagh Palace was built combining traditional Rajput and Mughal architectural styles. Graceful arches line the majestic building, and ornate turrets rise from either end. Inside, elaborate walkways surround a central courtyard, where guests and peacocks roam in the warm Indian sunshine. Perfectly manicured lawns, gently trickling fountains, and ornamental gardens complete the look.

The Rambagh was originally built in 1835, and in 1925 it was given its palatial overhaul, creating the regal masterpiece that locals named The "Jewel of

> *"Where in the world—but at the Rambagh—will you find a running fountain inside a suite?"*
>
> *Daily Telegraph*

Jaipur." In 1957, it was converted once again to become India's first palace hotel. The rooms were faithfully renovated to retain the glamour and to provide guests with an authentic royal retreat. High ceilings and four-poster beds add an air of grandeur to every room. The look is one of over-the-top opulence.

With a fitness center, golf course, and several bars and restaurants on-site, there is no need to leave your palatial surroundings, although it is worth exploring the picturesque streets of Jaipur. The romantic "Pink City" earned its nickname in 1853, when a state visit by the Prince of Wales prompted residents to celebrate his arrival by painting all the buildings pink. **JP**

Unwind at Neemrana Fort

Location Rajasthan, India
Website www.neemranahotels.com   **Price** ⊖

In 1464, before the rise of the Mughal empire, the Maharajah Devi Singh began construction of a fortified palace complex near the city of Alwar. The building first opened as a hotel in 1991, and today the Neemrana Fort is the oldest heritage resort in India and one of the architectural jewels of Rajasthan. It offers guests a rare opportunity to live in medieval splendor and to immerse themselves in the history and traditions of the old Rajputs.

Similar in scale to other monumental forts and palaces of Rajasthan, like Jodhpur's Umaid Bhawan Palace and Mehrangarh Fort, the Neemrana Fort's seventy rooms are individually decorated and themed, with most boasting private balconies. Although overwhelming in its scale, with ten overlapping layers of construction, there are some lovely architectural flourishes, such as the hanging garden that was recently laid along the southern ramparts and an eighteenth-century, eleven-story underground stepwell in the gardens near the palace wall, complete with Roman-style arches and a wraparound staircase. A mere 80 miles (130 km) from New Delhi, the Neemrana Fort Resort is one of the more accessible of India's palace hotels, as well as being the closest Rajasthan palace to the nation's capital.

The hotel is spread over four wings, and its rooms are all beautifully furnished in the traditional Indian style. Within its chiseled walls, there is a swimming pool and fully equipped health spa offering traditional treatments such as ayurvedic rejuvenation. Guided tours of the fort are available every day, but in the unlikely event that you feel the need to get out, camel safaris, trekking, and numerous day excursions can be easily arranged in the surrounding areas. **BS**

Relax at Samode Haveli

Location Rajasthan, India **Website** www.samode.com
Price 🟢🟢

This hidden gem is tucked away down the dusty backstreets of the old walled "Pink City" of frenetic Jaipur, and offers an oasis of calm in a manic hive of noise and activity. Built as a town house for the Samode royal family 150 years ago, this grand old house was converted into a heritage hotel in 1988. It has since been hailed by those in the know as one of the world's hippest hotels.

Surrounded by bougainvillea, this majestic property has a spectacular entrance, with an ornately tiled door, that is reached via an elephant ramp constructed for a wedding ceremony in the 1940s. The lavish decoration continues inside the hotel, which is awash with murals and frescoes. A labyrinth of narrow passages and dark staircases unexpectedly opens out onto endless charming courtyards. The prettiest of these is the central courtyard, studded with pomegranate trees, flowers, and ornamental pools, and frequented by playful monkeys.

Oozing with character, the hotel's twenty-two rooms are all differently shaped and have unique designs. For lovers of jewels, the suites even have floor-to-ceiling mirror mosaics. The huge outdoor pool is stunning, decorated with Moroccan tiles and surrounded by large comfy daybeds, complemented by a whirlpool tub and a wading pool for children. The dining hall is an elaborate affair, richly painted with flowers and dancing girls. If you prefer a more laid-back setting, staff can arrange private lunches or romantic candlelit meals for guests in the hotel's lush garden, alive with flowers and trees. **JK**

← *All the rooms are extremely plush, with old stone arches, Rajasthani antiques, and marble bathrooms.*

Ride Marwari in Rajasthan

Location Rajasthan, India
Website www.thetharmarwarisafari.com **Price** ⊖⊖

The children gather by the dusty road chattering excitedly. Village women walk alongside the paths balancing huge urns of water on their heads. The men bow their heads and press their palms together in greeting. This is a side of Rajasthan that you will not see in the crowded cities, or on the usual bus tours. This glimpse into everyday Indian life can be seen by horseback riding, quite literally, off the beaten track.

A hundred years ago, Rajputs relied on horses for transport. Even kings and noblemen preferred to travel by trusty steed, sparking the saying: "One cannot separate a Rajput from his horse." For centuries, a particular breed of horse, the Marwari, was the chosen mount of Rajput royalty. Fearless warhorses, found only in Rajasthan, they were also bred for their beauty. They became renowned for their grace and elegance, as well as their distinctive inwardly curved ears. To this day, the majestic Marwari is considered a treasured symbol of strength and wealth in Rajasthan. Trekking on horseback is, therefore, a most fitting way to travel through the region that is still referred to as "the land of kings."

Nothing can beat the romance of riding such beautiful horses, and it is a much more authentic way to experience the "real" Rajasthan, following the same ancient routes the maharajas themselves once rode. View ornate temples and marble castles. Stop in rural villages, untouched by tourism, and drink cups of sweet chai tea. Ride alongside lakes and rivers, and through forests of juniper and jacaranda. Forget the noise and congestion of the bustling cities—the only traffic jam you will need to worry about is a queue of goats being herded slowly home. It is a unique and rewarding way to experience India. **JP**

Enjoy Wilderness Camp

Location Rajasthan, India
Website www.rohetgarh.com **Price** ⊖

If you are looking for a remote place in India, the Thar desert is as good as it gets. The rolling sands of western Rajasthan are the ultimate backdrop for this luxury camp. Stunning sunrises and sunsets, as well as trekking across the endless dunes, are on offer here.

Wilderness is a seriously impressive tented camp, complete with comfortable beds and tiled bathrooms. Soft rugs underfoot, luxurious fabrics, and beautiful polished teak furniture make the Wilderness Camp a wonderful experience. Eat in the traditional thatch and plaster dining room, then soak up the magic of this desert wonderland. During the day guests can go camel and horseback trekking, visit remote tribes, or

"The elegant tents flutter in the breeze, providing an exotic contrast with the desert wilderness."

Gourmet Travel magazine

take a trip to spot wildlife. The camp is overseen by the Singh family, and they have ensured that special touches give a traditional Rajasthani feel to your stay, from the furnishings to the warm welcome by staff.

The ultimate romantic desert retreat, this is the perfect place to get away from it all with your other half. The candlelit lounge is the ideal location to end a day out on the sea of sand and enjoy a well-earned drink. Most of all, come here to soak up the sense of peace and quiet. The sounds of birdsong and gentle lilting of local voices as shepherds pass by is all you will hear. It also goes without saying that this far out in the desert, the stargazing is second to none. **AD**

Enjoy Taj Lake Palace

Location Rajasthan, India **Website** www.tajhotels.com **Price** ⑤⑤⑤

Taj Lake Palace, in the middle of Lake Pichola in Udaipur, is a gleaming homage to romance and indulgence. This 250-year-old "pleasure palace" of former Maharana Jagat Singh promises luxuries and comforts that, although matched by other hotels around the world, are enhanced by its location. The hotel is surrounded by a lake, which itself is surrounded by mountains, so although the bustling streets of Udaipur are just a two-minute boat ride away, stepping onto the 4-acre (1.6-ha) island transports you into a realm of peaceful contentment that is sure to bring a smile to your face.

Each of the eighty-three rooms is individually themed, with the large suites being especially grand. Particularly arresting is the honeymoon suite, with stained-glass windows dappling the interior with reds, greens, and yellows, and a love swing hanging from the ceiling. The smaller rooms, with the lake's water slapping against the walls just a few feet from the windows, give a sense of being on a luxury yacht bound for the open seas. All the rooms come with a personal twenty-four-hour butler.

The hotel also has a small sculpted garden, three fantastic restaurants, a bar, and a luxury spa, so it would be very easy never to leave the island. For the more adventurous, however, the old king's ceremonial barge floats off over the lake each evening offering food, drinks, and traditional music. Romantic boat rides are also available, replete with lace privacy veil, for those who care to drift over the water leaving all but themselves behind.

To make the Taj experience even more memorable, go in low season and book a basic room (called luxury rooms). Taj has a policy of upgrading guests if better rooms are vacant at the time of check-in. **JD**

⬆ *The white marble and mosaic building almost appears to float on the waters of Lake Pichola.*

Stay at Udai Bilas Palace

Location Rajasthan, India
Website www.udaibilaspalace.com   **Price** Ⓢ

Pretend you are a maharaja by spending a night or two in an opulent Indian palace. Majestically set on the banks of Lake Gaibsagar, this heritage hotel can be found way off the tourist trail in southern Rajasthan.

Built in the nineteenth century by Maharawal Udai Singhji, the Udai Bilas Palace has always been home to the Rajput family, the maharajas of Dungarpur, and to this day it remains a royal residence. Recently treated to a revamp, the hotel has retained many of its original features—the wallpaper may be fifty years old but it is still in tip-top condition. The miniature paintings, elaborate murals, and carved stones reveal the rich and colorful cultural heritage of the Rajput royal family. The bluish gray building is as grand as you would expect, festooned with sculptured stone pillars and marble-clad arches. At the building's heart are an attractive courtyard, a pool, and an intricately carved pavilion. The lake itself is magical and peaceful, attracting an abundance of birdlife, such as egrets, storks, and night herons, best enjoyed by taking a relaxing boat trip.

Every one of the palace's spacious guest rooms and suites has been decorated in an individual style, but all are kitted out with ornate balconies, mahogany furnishings, and delightful decorations. The grandest suite even has an impressive mirrored floor. An elegant banquet hall provides the dramatic setting for dinner, with lighting provided by crystal chandeliers. The center of the long marble table is inlaid with water, on which float candles and flowers.

If you loathe blood sports, this may not be the pad for you. The family members are respected hunters, and the stuffed trophies of the sport are proudly displayed on the walls of the dining room. **JK**

Enjoy Udaivilas

Location Rajasthan, India
Website www.oberoihotels.com   **Price** ⓈⓈⓈ

Inspired by the great palaces of the sixteenth and seventeenth centuries, Udaivilas is a vast assemblage of columns, tiered gardens, decorative arches, and alcoves that immerses its guests in a world of luxury.

This imposing Oberoi property is set against the stark backdrop of the Aravalli Hills and has views across Lake Pichola to Udaipur's famous Jagmandir and Jagniwas palaces. Nothing has been overlooked in this re-creation of the royal Rajasthan palaces of old. Open-air colonnades are set amid hand-carved columns, extensive hand-painted murals, and ornate cupolas finished in gold leaf, with fountains rising from ornamental pools of shimmering white marble.

> *"This may be one of Rajasthan's best examples of contemporary Indian architecture."*
>
> concierge.com

Many of the rooms have private walled courtyards and are furnished with inlaid chairs and tables in the classic Rajput style. Some rooms open onto a semiprivate moated swimming pool that affords views across the lake and back up to the hotel's own 20-acre (8-ha) wildlife conservatory, with its resident wild boars, peacocks, and Indian spotted deer. For the ultimate in indulgence, the Kohinoor Suite is a vast private world of courtyards and pools, and a breathtaking view over Udaipur's City Palace complex.

The hotel's Banyan Tree Spa offers treatments ranging from aromatherapy to ayurveda in rooms that are nothing short of royal in scale. **BS**

Discover Orcha

Location Madhya Pradesh, India
Website www.spiritualjourneys.net/Venues/orcha.htm **Price** 🌗

Tucked away off the main road leading to the bustling city of Jhansi, the appropriately named village of Orcha (hidden place) is made up of sixteenth- and seventeenth-century palaces and temples with elaborate ornamental spires. The Bundelas clan that ruled large parts of central India from the early 1500s until the mid-twentieth century chose this island in the picturesque Betwa River as the site for their capital. Nowadays, the palaces are populated only by macaques, but time has been kind to the buildings, which perfectly blend into the peaceful surroundings.

The village's centerpiece is the stunning Jehangir Mahal (palace), which was built in honor of the Mughal ruler Jehangir's visit to Orcha in the early seventeenth century. Standing in the empty, windowless rooms on the top floor of the palace, you have great views over the lush surrounding areas. You can see the locals washing their clothes in the gently cascading river, and bird-watchers will delight in getting a closer look at the many vultures circling in the sky. The Raj Mahal next door has some exquisite murals and is equally isolated from the main part of the village, which is situated on the right bank of the river. The temples in this part of Orcha are still used by the villagers and offer a glimpse into Hindu life outside northern India's overpopulated cities.

With its ancient buildings that complement and enhance the natural beauty of the area, Orcha is well worth a visit simply because of its visual appeal. However, throw in the fact that few tourists have as yet discovered this charming part of India and also that the village is the perfect antithesis to the chaos of the country's towns and cities, and you have a wonderful place in which to get away from it all. **DaH**

Visit Kanha National Park

Location Madhya Pradesh, India
Website www.kanhanationalpark.com **Price** 🌐

Located in the geographical center of India, the state of Madhya Pradesh is covered by dense forests that are home to 22 percent of the world's tiger population. The best place to spot the animals is Kanha National Park, where the lush bamboo and sal forests, open grasslands, and innumerable streams make for an area of stunning natural beauty—so much so that Rudyard Kipling was inspired to write his novel *The Jungle Book* after visiting the area.

Established in 1955, the wildlife reserve runs several conservation programs to protect its animals, and the number of tigers, bharasinghas (a near-extinct species of deer), gaurs (Indian bison), and leopards roaming

> *"At first sight [the park] looks almost like English parkland designed by Capability Brown."*
>
> Lynn Barber, *Observer*

the park has steadily increased over the years. The period between March and July is the best time to see Kanha's wildlife, because as the temperatures rise, the animals leave their hideaways in the woods to look for water. The local rangers track the tigers down every morning and generally know where to find them. Bird-watchers will also have a field day at Kanha, where the majestic peacocks are probably the pick of the bunch.

One of the largest parks in India and considered to be among the best maintained in the whole of Asia, Kanha provides a unique opportunity to see some of the planet's most fascinating—and sadly most threatened—animals in the wild. **DaH**

Discover the Ganges

Location Varanasi, Uttar Pradesh, India
Website www.varanasicity.com/ganges-ghats.html **Price** 🌓

The Ganges sustains life. Across the scorching northern plains of India, the river rises up from Gangotri, before twisting and turning for hundreds of miles to empty in the Bay of Bengal. It also sustains faith. It is a sacred river, and the most sacred place on it is the city of Shiva, otherwise known as Varanasi or Benares. Here, Hindu pilgrims come to bathe in the waters of the Ganges, a ritual that washes away sin. The city is also an auspicious place to die, because if you leave earth here, you will attain *moksha*—liberation from the endless cycle of birth and death.

The most intimate rituals of life and death take place here in public. On the ghats—stepped areas that lead down to the river—there are people doing their laundry, praying, practicing yoga, playing cricket, shaving, or just improving their karma by giving money to beggars. Alongside, water buffalo wallow in the shallows, and bodies are burned on funeral pyres. Devout pilgrims and sadhus are cheek by jowl with tourists and dollar-hungry locals; unfortunately, this means that this holiest of places is also popular with fake holy men and rip-off merchants. In the mazelike streets, touts stick to you like glue. To escape all of this, take a boat trip at dawn, before the river is bathed in light. As the boat slips downstream, the mantras from the loudspeakers will fade, lost in the breeze. The only sound will be the swishing of oars as candlelit offerings float by in the dark, like traveling stars. Soon the dawn will come, and the river will be bathed in a magical light. Pilgrims will appear to perform *puja* to the rising sun, and the cycle begins again. **LB**

➡ *The mighty River Ganges is a magical place: the hub of life, both practical and spiritual.*

Visit Chowmahalla Palace

Location Andhra Pradesh, India
Website www.chowmahalla.com **Price** ⊛

Chowmahalla Palace takes your breath away. In the heart of Hyderabad's old city, just a stone's throw from the ever-manic Laad bazaar full of glitzy bangle stores and sari shops, the palace is an oasis of serenity. Walk through the huge wooden gates obscuring the beauty of the grounds and you find another world. Once home to the ruling Nizams of Hyderabad, there are in fact four palaces here set in 12 acres (5 ha) of grounds dating back to the late eighteenth century: *Chow* means "four" and *mahalla* means "palaces."

The first thing that strikes visitors is the sweet aroma of frangipani, its white blossoms complementing the columns and archways of the northern courtyard, which in turn are mirrored in the still-water channels alongside. In these tranquil surroundings, the noise of traffic around the Charminar mosque is replaced by birdsong and the soothing sound of running water from the fountains. Walk slowly through the courtyard to savor every moment of peace, and then prepare to be amazed as you enter the grand Khilwat, or Durbar Hall. You need time to take in the grandeur of your surroundings. Here, in this stylish opulence, the Nizams held their religious ceremonies and banquets.

After extensive renovations, the palace opened to the public for the first time in 2005. Glimpses of the Nizam's grand lifestyle are provided in the museums and anterooms full of photographs and portraits. They include an exhibition on the life of the women of the palace—of whom princesses Durru Shehavar and Niloufer were deemed to be among the most beautiful of their generation. **SWa**

◁ *Belgian crystal chandeliers seem to fill the entire space between the high stucco ceiling and cool marble floor.*

Unwind at SwaSwara

Location Karnataka, India
Website www.swaswara.com **Price** ⊛⊛

Immersed in coconut groves and paddy fields overlooking the twin coves of Om Beach, SwaSwara invites you to rejuvenate your soul through yoga and meditation and to reconnect to the inner experience of the self. The approach to self-awareness determines everything here, from the daily rituals and preparation of meals to the design of SwaSwara's air-conditioned villas, built in the local Konkan style. Balconies have been created with the pursuit of yoga in mind, and study areas provide privacy for the exercising of the mind. For the more experienced practitioner, a ten-day "Panchakarma" course, applying ancient methods of relaxation, will realign your body, mind, and soul.

> *"Here is a place oozing peace and isolation . . . where you can really remember what you are about."*
>
> Tatler

SwaSwara is an environmentally progressive resort. A bio-gas converter turns composted organic matter into gas for cooking, and there is a rainwater treatment plant on-site. Meals are more like diets and are tailored to your individual needs and body type. Meat is avoided in favor of fresh seafood and vegetables sourced from surrounding farms. Time seems to run a little slower here amid the tranquility of the 30 acres (12 ha) and along the walking trails that take you past medicinal shrubs. Only the sound of the rolling waves of Om Beach and SwaSwara's resident long-tailed langurs, geckos, and kingfishers will accompany you on your journey of peaceful self-discovery. **BS**

Explore Hanuman Temple

Location Karnataka, India
Website www.hampi.in/sites/Anjaneya_Hill.htm   **Price ()**

The journey from the hot, sweaty center of Hampi, the medieval capital of the Hindu empire and a UNESCO World Heritage site, to the Hanuman temple on Anjaneya Hill is not easy. Start in the bazaar and wind your way to the river, beside sandstone caves carved with Hindu gods. Pay a boy to take you downstream in a coracle and fix your eyes to the horizon. There, a flash of white on top of a hill will show you your destination: Hampi's Hanuman temple. Of all the temples in the city, it is the one that you will remember.

When you reach the foot of the hill, having walked across fields and along a lane where children greet you with cries for pencils and rupees, you will see what you are in for. A man sells cones of peanuts and, up the hundreds of whitewashed steps that zigzag to the top of the site, monkeys scamper while sadhus, pilgrims, and tourists huff and puff their way up to the top in the burning sun. The journey takes about forty-five minutes—do not forget your water. At the top, the temple is garishly lit inside and smells of incense and bare feet. This is where the god and monkey general is said to have been born—the place has particular significance for followers of Rama.

From the top you can see everything in the area: the vast boulder-strewn plain, the elephant stables, the sunken palace gardens, flocks of white ibis flying across the landscape, and the ruins of the old stone bridge in the river. All the colors of the state spread out before you, and there is almost total peace and quiet, save for the fluttering of the orange flags and the light footsteps of the monkeys. **LD**

← *It is well worth the effort it takes to get to the small whitewashed temple to the monkey god Hanuman.*

Relax in Style at Shreya's

Location Bangalore, Karnataka, India
Website www.shreyasretreat.com   **Price** 💲💲

"For the first time in an Indian yoga school, I felt the potential of a merger with cosmic bliss."

Lucy Edge, writer

To stay at Shreya's, an idyllic yoga retreat on the outskirts of the bustling Indian city of Bangalore, is to set off on a journey of self-discovery. Surrounded by more than 25 acres (10 ha) of impeccably landscaped gardens, Shreya's not only offers one of the largest outdoor yoga pavilions in southern India but will also encourage you to get your hands dirty working in the extensive vegetable garden and rice paddy. You can be educated in the principles of sustainable agriculture or even learn to abandon your inhibitions and reconnect with the child within by playing games with the children of an adjacent village before relaxing in one of the strategically placed hammocks.

Shreya's offers an informal mix of canvas tents and stone and garden cottages, sprinkled around an 83-foot (25-m) oxygenated free-form swimming pool. All the accommodation has its own private veranda and is sufficiently remote to ensure absolute privacy. Gourmet vegetarian dining with ingredients from the organic garden is encouraged in the communal dining hall, or enjoyed outdoors on warm nights, and the menus are meticulously crafted to complement Shreya's wellness program and the individual's own body type and personal goals.

Massage treatments include Balinese oil-based therapies, which concentrate on muscle tissue, and traditional Thai techniques focusing on the practice of reflexology and the principles of acupressure. At Shreya's it is the inner journey that matters: the pursuit of tranquility, self-awareness, and an exposure to the layered philosophies of ancient India. **BS**

◤ *Shreya's is for those who like to practice yoga while ensconced in five-star luxury surroundings.*

De-stress at Soukya

Location Bangalore, Karnataka, India
Website www.soukya.com **Price** 🔾🔾

After the hectic buzz of Bangalore, being welcomed into Soukya's airy reception with a glass of tender coconut juice is like walking into a parallel universe—one full of flagstone pathways, green lawns, fragrant temple trees, and lots of space. It is just you, 24 guests, 116 staff, and 30 acres (12 ha) of peaceful gardens, water features, organic farmland, and orchards.

Soukya is a carefully crafted holistic healing center rather than a spa. The expert care on offer has attracted the rich and famous from all over the world because it gets results. Some guests want to de-stress, others to lose weight or recuperate after an illness or injury. An initial consultation explores where you are,

> "To many, this euphoric place might seem a little contrived, but the fact is that it works."

Society magazine

from health to relationships, social life to personality traits. After that, you get a personal program that includes a combination of ayurvedic treatments, homeopathic remedies, an organic, vegetarian diet, and a wide range of therapies—whatever your body needs to kick-start it into a better place. Modern, allopathic medicine comes into play, too.

The programs may include more than one hundred treatments and last a month or more, depending on the individual. Although many treatments are luxuriously relaxing, it is not all about pampering. You will like the rewards, though. Weight falls off, skin glows, and you leave a little wiser about yourself. **OM**

Ride the *Golden Chariot*

Location Bangalore, Karnataka, India
Website www.goldenchariot.com **Price** 🔾🔾

A new chapter in India's increasingly sophisticated tourism market pulled out of Yashwantpur railway station in Bangalore in March 2008. The *Golden Chariot* left on its maiden journey around a circuit that includes the great palace at Mysore and the sun-drenched beaches of Goa. This is luxurious, high-end tourism on a railway that is the rival of any of the great continental train journeys of the world.

The nineteen magenta-colored carriages of the *Golden Chariot* can accommodate up to eighty-eight passengers in sumptuous, air-conditioned chambers, complete with double-glazed windows, decorative wood panels on the walls, and carved reliefs on the ceiling reminiscent of the days of the maharajahs. Western-style breakfasts are served in two dining carriages, as well as fine local and continental cuisine. The menu includes traditional vegetarian dishes and local delicacies such as Neer Dose, a rice dish served with chutney and grated coconut. Meals are accompanied by a fine collection of wines and spirits. The impeccable furnishings of the lounge bar are modeled after the palace at Mysore. There is even a sauna and on-board masseur, with a gym coach and conference coach rounding out the amenities. The only requirement made of the passengers, whose average age is more than fifty years old, is to relax and enjoy the ride.

The journey is not a demanding one, with fewer stops than one might expect. The itinerary is a perfect blend of comfort and extraordinary experiences that will stay with you for a lifetime. Highlights include watching baby elephants washing themselves in the Kabini River in the grounds of the Kabini River Lodge, once the property of the maharaja of Mysore. **BS**

Unwind at Tranquil Resort

Location Kerala, India
Website www.tranquilresort.com **Price** 🔾🔾

A regular winner of Keralan Tourism's "Best Homestay Award," Tranquil Resort can be found within the boundaries of a privately owned 400-acre (160-ha) coffee and vanilla plantation amid the untainted landscapes of the Indian state of Kerala. With a mere eight rooms, including two extraordinary tree houses, the theme here is exclusivity. On your approach to the main house, you are excused for feeling as though you are entering a privileged, manicured world. Paths and verandas are swept anew twice a day in this retreat, which is in many ways a microcosm of the verdant Wayanad rain forest that surrounds it.

The main house is wrapped in endless, expansive verandas filled with wicker and cane furniture and overhead fans that echo the era of Kipling and Somerset Maugham. There is also a free-form swimming pool set among luxuriant gardens, which provides a perfect setting for a snooze in one of the poolside hammocks. The Tree Villa sprawls over 500 square feet (45 sq m) and is perched 40 feet (12 m) above the ground on four enormous tree trunks. It has 8-foot- (2.4-m-) wide verandas and is safe for children. The nearby Tree House is more than 1,000 square feet (90 sq m) in area and is one of the largest such structures in Kerala. Both have hot water and electricity; they are just a short walk from the main house and are reached via their own inclined walkways.

Guests here are encouraged to take a close-up look at the day-to-day operations and processes of a working coffee plantation, from planting through to harvesting. If you have the time, there is the option of a walk through the 40-acre (16-ha) vanilla plantation to witness the hand pollination of the vanilla pods and the curing process that gives the vanilla its flavor. **BS**

Relax at Kalari Kovilakom

Location Kerala, India
Website www.kalarikovilakom.com **Price** 🔾🔾

An unusual upmarket ashram in a former maharaja's palace, Kalari Kovilakom offers ayurveda programs in luxurious surroundings. While most people are mooching about on the beaches in the south of Kerala, you can enjoy being off the tourist trail, because this elegant retreat is set inland on the edge of Kollengode, a village in the foothills of the Annamalai mountains.

The minimum stay is two weeks: the time required for ayurveda treatments to have any real effect. Daily programs include gentle yoga and meditation, and you will be guided through a set of expertly devised treatments using this ancient Indian holistic system of health. You can also watch locals train in the martial art

> *"The environs . . . are very beautiful. The high mountains pour down cascades of a prodigous height."*
>
> Francis Buchanan, traveler (1762-1829)

of Kalaripayattu. Combining body movements with a strong spiritual focus, it is strangely relaxing, and the locals will teach you the technique if you like.

Some rooms are in the original palace, but most are in the interior-designed guest wing, beautifully painted in muted colors with four-poster beds, dark-wood furniture, and cool, tiled floors. Delicious meals are cooked according to ayurvedic principles and served on giant thali dishes at communal tables. Although you will be well looked after, this is not the place to come if you want to live the high life: Red meat and leather shoes are not allowed, and specially prepared beverages take the place of alcohol. **CSJ**

Stay at Coconut Lagoon

Location Kerala, India
Website www.cghearth.com **Price** 💲💲

The only way to reach Coconut Lagoon is by boat. It sounds like a bit of an adventure and it is—but a very worthwhile one, because you get a glimpse of Kerala's fabulous wildlife and rich tropical vegetation along the way. On reaching Coconut Lagoon, you quickly realize why the resort was thus named. Situated in an abandoned coconut plantation, it lives up to all the glorious resonances of its title.

Accommodation on the resort comes in the shape of traditional Keralan wooden houses known as *tharawads*. Some are traditionally built, others more modern, but all have been constructed to the highest standards by skilled local master craftsmen. The oldest of the residences dates back to the early 1700s, whereas several others are one hundred years old or more. The history of the villas aside, all the residences guarantee a luxurious and thoughtfully designed experience. Bathrooms open out onto private gardens; there are Western-style toilets and beautiful dark-wood furnishings, and a colonial style of decoration adds to the authentic Keralan experience. The grounds are also wonderfully natural. A cow, as opposed to a lawnmower, keeps the grass in check, and butterflies and birds dart freely around the gardens.

Many come to Coconut Lagoon for the ayurvedic treatments, which include physiotherapy, yoga, and a host of alternative therapies, although if you are feeling more active, a wealth of water sports is available, including speedboating, canoeing, and fishing. If you were taken by the scenery on the way in, why not take an hour-long sunset cruise, or rent the resort's traditional wood and straw *Kettuvallom* (houseboat)? Then you can see the mangroves, coconut trees, and paddy fields up close and personal. **PS**

Enjoy Marari Beach Resort

Location Kerala, India
Website www.cghearth.com **Price** 💲💲

Set in 25 acres (10 ha) of coconut palm groves, Marari Beach Resort boasts a 10-mile (16-km) expanse of coastline. The resort is surrounded by fishing villages that exist today just as they have for centuries—by bringing in the day's catch to make a living.

Marari's cottages are laid out with comfort and elegance in mind, and are resplendent with bamboo, dark woods, and wickerwork that root you firmly in rustic India. The vast bedrooms, each with a veranda, are fully air-conditioned, and the gorgeous bathrooms, part open air, have sloping roofs, ornamental stone rockeries, tropical palms, and part-sheltered showers. This being India, there is a spiritual aura surrounding

> *"A beach is a beach is a beach. Until you seek out its living heart, the culture that calls it home."*

Proprietors, Marari Beach Resort

Marari, the focus of which is the resort's stunning ayurvedic center, which runs beachside yoga classes to boost body, mind, and soul. Once energized, the resort bar, situated in a 200-year-old building, serves local cocktails: Try the Panchamrutam, a drink as psychedelic as the sunset views. Only the best local produce is on the menu in the restaurant, barbecued or cooked to order depending on the day's catch.

Marari is not just a pretty face: It is very eco-friendly, with an organic vegetable garden, solar panels, and a methane gas generator fueled by food waste. You do not often hear the words "luxurious" and "conscientious" in the same sentence—Marari insists on both. **PS**

Explore the Kerala Backwaters

Location Kerala, India
Website www.southernbackwaters.com; www.keralatourism.org   **Price** $

> *"A crystal clear river, which is filtered through the forest . . . is great for shaking off the heat."*

Poorna Shetty, *Guardian*

Located close to Kollom, Valiyavila is a Fair Trade and traditional homestay, far away from India's usual hustle and bustle. Arriving at the tranquil lakeside retreat is like stepping back in time. Twice a day ferries transport guests from Kollom to Panamukkam jetty; otherwise negotiate with a local who will row you serenely across the lake in a wooden canoe.

Surrounded by the Ashtamudi Lake on three sides, Valiyavila is the perfect place to relax and plan a tour of the Kerala backwaters. Shady palms, cooling watery breezes, and swinging hammocks adorn the mansion's verandas, and the six spacious guest rooms each have a private sundeck. Unwind to the sound of the swishing water and hear the inimitable language used by the fishermen to communicate with the many *Kettuvallom* houseboats cruising by.

The backwaters comprise 560 miles (900 km) of lakes, lagoons, canals, and estuaries, and the Southern Backwaters Company offers tours around Ashtamudi Lake and the Kallada River from Munroe Island. Mindful of the wildlife and environment, and in a style reminiscent of Venice, a local punter will expertly paddle the canoe around Kerala's tiny canals and waterways. View Keralan life at close quarters as you pass water-bound villages where locals cook and wash their clothes on the riverbanks; sail past luminous hibiscus flowers, water hyacinths, disused canoes sinking in the water, and cashew trees boasting enormous nuts. Back at Valiyavila, you can look forward to some delicious Keralan cuisine, a Kingfisher beer, and a stunning sunset. **SD**

⬉ *It is an altogether timeless and calming experience to explore the backwaters of Ashtamudi Lake.*

Enjoy Motty's Homestay

Location Kerala, India
Website www.mottys.uniquehomestays.com **Price** 💲💲

Escape into the depths of southern Indian culture by staying at the delightful home of Motty and Lali Mathew. Their traditional Keralan house is stuffed with intriguing artifacts from the subcontinent: from a Victorian washstand to old framed prints, from ancient walking sticks to displays of antique crockery.

Motty's Homestay boutique guesthouse is in Alleppey, a peaceful town known as "the gateway to the Kerala backwaters." You can walk from the house to the local canals, shops, and temples. Accommodation is basic but comfortable. Guests can stay in the Mathews' home or in one of four fisherman's cottages on the edge of Marari beach, where the palm-fringed

> *"It is like discovering the home of a long-lost uncle in the heart of the Kerala backwaters."*

Ellison Roberts travel website

sands are littered with fishing boats. Rooms in the main house have private facilities; those in the beach houses have open-air bathrooms.

The cuisine of Kerala is one of the highlights of the area, and the food at Motty's is often highly praised. Guests can even learn how to cook the traditional recipes of southern India. Lali uses only homegrown produce and local ingredients, including the latest catches from the fishermen. You may eat with the family in the candlelit dining room and try traditional rice breads, spicy curries, pickles, and baked bananas. Most guests are so impressed that Lali is compiling a book of recipes that you can take home. **SH**

Experience Kodaikanal

Location Tamil Nadu, India
Website www.kodaikanal.com **Price** 💷

In the south of Tamil Nadu, the town of Kodaikanal offers a welcome respite from the sweltering heat. Located in the Western Ghats mountain range, which stretches from Mumbai all the way down to India's southernmost tip, Kodaikanal is the country's only hill station set up by U.S. missionaries. At 6,900 feet (2,100 m), the temperature—which is not subject to great seasonal variations because of the town's near-equatorial setting—rarely exceeds 68°F (20°C) and hardly ever drops below 46°F (8°C).

Established in the 1840s, the hill station has always been popular with visitors, initially with expatriates who wanted to escape the hot weather of the lowlands and, since the twentieth century, also with affluent Indians. At the periphery of the town center with its more than fifty hotels is the star-shaped, man-made Kodaikanal Lake. Often considered to be the town's landmark, it is beautifully set in the evergreen rolling landscape, and boating is very popular with the many newlyweds who spend their honeymoon in the area. At the southeast end of the lake, the botanical garden Bryant Park is worth a visit before starting on the nearby Coaker's Walk, which offers splendid views of the surrounding peaks and valleys. A couple of miles uphill from Kodaikanal, Kurinji Andava Temple and its surrounding lands are well known as the home of an endemic plant called kurinji shrub. Its color is a mix of purple and blue, although you will have to be very lucky to see it bloom because it flowers only once every twelve years.

Known locally as the "princess of hill stations," Kodaikanal is a scenic retreat that quite literally offers a breath of fresh air after a stay in the more congested and bustling cities on India's plains. **SD**

Discover Mahabalipuram

Location Tamil Nadu, India   **Website** www.mahabalipuram.co.in
Price 🎫

Famous for its shore temple, Mahabalipuram was the seaport of the Pallava kings of Kanchipuram, who were at the height of their artistic and political power from the fifth to the eighth century C.E. The beautiful and romantic temple, home to various shrines carved from solid rock and ravaged by wind, salt, sun, and time, was built around the middle of the seventh century.

The wonderful sculptures show scenes of everyday life: women milking buffalos; officious city dignitaries; young girls posing; as well as animals and deities from the Hindu *Panchatantra* stories. Such images are unusual in the state, where other carvings depict divinities, not normal folk. The joy of Mahabalipuram is that the art of stone carving is still very much alive; sculptors and their workshops line the street, chiseling from dawn to dusk. A local sculpture museum contains more than 3,000 works by local artists, some in wood, metal, and brass, as well as granite.

The town is popular with day-trippers from Chennai, but tranquility descends after dusk, when the casual beachside restaurants serve delicious seafood. Along the great expanse of beach, fishermen bring in their catch in the afternoons, and vendors sell chillums and other stone pieces. The shoreline has receded somewhat since the tsunami of 2004, revealing more remains, such as a granite lion. During the tsunami, the waters went back so far that they revealed another temple under the ocean. Those on the beach caught a brief glimpse of its beauty before water covered it again. After the tsunami, a diving expedition confirmed the ruins' existence. **LB**

➡ *The shrines were hidden in the sand until excavated by the British about 200 years ago.*

Enjoy River House

Location Balapitiya, Sri Lanka
Website www.taruvillas.com   **Price** ⊖⊖

On the southwest coast of Sri Lanka, the fabulous River House sits half a mile up a narrow road, on the outskirts of Bentota. Turn a corner and the house comes into view in all its glory, nestling at the top of a grassy hillside, shaded by palm trees, looking down to the Madhu Ganga River. Set in 7 acres (3 ha) of lush private gardens, this is a serious retreat from the outside world. A haven of style and tranquility, the house is the creation of Nayantha Fonseka, a fashion designer who has turned his talented hand to architecture. Sri Lankan woods such as kitul and jak fruit have been used throughout the accommodation, and carefully chosen antiques blend in with hand-carved reproduction pieces of furniture.

Guests may take it easy on a rattan sofa sitting on an open veranda, surrounded by tapestries, drapes, and luxurious carpets. The five sumptuous suites are named after Sri Lankan astrological signs: Kanya and Singhe have massive beds that are almost as big as some budget hotel rooms; Tulu and Danu are adjoining and perfect for a family group; whereas Makara sits close to the river, just a short distance from the main house. Each suite has a private garden or terrace, with indoor or outdoor plunge tub or pool.

Stay in the enclosed grounds or five minutes away at the private beach house. Take a dip in the infinity pool, head to the private beach, or take out the motorboat. Then come back to the villa to eat in the restaurant or garden, with a choice of mouthwatering dishes. The service is attentive yet discreet, ensuring the ultimate in cocooned privacy. **AD**

"It is unique in its concept and design and is one of the most beautiful properties in Sri Lanka."

indiatravelite.com

↖ *The River House borders the peaceful Madhu estuary, a haven for bird enthusiasts and fishermen.*

Stay at the Mudhouse

Location Near Anamaduwa, Sri Lanka
Website www.themudhouse.lk   **Price** 💲💲

The area near the town of Anamaduwa is just a couple of hours north of Colombo, in the western part of Sri Lanka. It is home not only to the imposing Paramakanda Rock Temple, but also to an isolated forest retreat at the sanctuary's foot. Consisting of individually designed huts that are scattered across 60 acres (24 ha) of rain forest, the peacefulness of the Mudhouse befits its remote but beautiful location.

Built from natural materials only, the huts combine modern aesthetics with traditional craftsmanship, and their design ranges from regular Sri Lankan village houses to tree houses. They all come with indoor bathrooms, outdoor showers, a dining area, and an

> *"[There is] a secluded romantic hut on stilts . . . with a curtained four-poster bed and views of the lake."*
>
> *Guardian*

area for meditation and yoga. However, this being an eco retreat there is no electricity, meaning that candles and lanterns are used at night, further contributing to the Mudhouse's poetic charm.

Part of the retreat is also an organic farm that provides most of the fruits and vegetables for the dishes served at the Mudhouse. Guests can help pick the fruit, and other activities include bicycle and boat tours, bird-watching at the local bird sanctuary, and trips to the ancient cities of Anradhapura, Yapahuwa, and Pandurasnuwara. The Mudhouse truly is a hidden gem that distinguishes itself by blending in effortlessly with the area's own natural beauty. **DaH**

Unwind at Paradise Farm

Location Kithulgala, Sri Lanka
Website www.paradisesrilanka.com   **Price** 💲💲

Sri Lanka's tea country has become prime territory for visitors, who pour into the area to enjoy its serenity and to see exactly where the country's fantastic tea is grown. Set in the heart of this tourist region, Paradise Farm stands out. An independent, organic, green-tea farm that gives all its profits back to its workers, the organization is small scale and community focused.

The villa, Paradise Farm itself, is an idyllic retreat with nothing but forest around it. It is popular with artists, writers, and anyone who wants some peace and quiet away from the hectic *tuk-tuks* and potholed roads. There are two double bedrooms in the main villa and two bungalows behind it for guests. The accommodation is not five-star luxury, but it provides a complete back-to-nature retreat. Staying here enables the Worldview International Foundation to train local people in sustainable agriculture and helps to give back to the local community. The owners keep a low profile on-site, allowing guests to do exactly what they wish. Traditional Sri Lankan curries arrive from the kitchen at lunchtime and at dusk, and breakfast is fresh fruit from the forest and delicious pancakes.

From the open-fronted villa's infinity pool, you can look out over the rain forest and see birds soaring high above the ground. Sitting in the swinging cane chair over the pool, you can immerse yourself in a book or just relax among the cushions. On a good day you will be able to take in views of Sri Pada (also known as Adam's Peak), one of Sri Lanka's holy mountains, as well as blue-hazed hillsides and lush plantations. Buffalo graze, monkeys play, and, at night, fireflies drift in the air. Paths from the villa lead you down into the jungle, via spice gardens growing cinnamon, and guides can take you tracking leopards here, too. **LD**

Relax at Helga's Folly

Location Kandy, Sri Lanka
Website www.helgasfolly.com **Price** ⦵

The Stereophonics were so enamored of Helga's Folly that they wrote a song about the place after spending an unforgettable night here. It is situated atop a hill just outside the frenetic city of Kandy, which is teeming with antiques, jewelry, and trinket-rich shops. However, it is an ideal pad to escape from it all, which might explain its reputation as a celebrity haunt.

Dimly lit by wax-dripping candles and soft lamps, the place has a louche and decadent feel to it. Think nineteenth-century opium den meets Moulin Rouge. Guests can lounge about the many communal rooms, stuffed full of cozy sofas, puffed-up cushions, antique furniture, vases, and dark velvety drapes. The vibrantly colored walls are adorned with pictures of legendary Hollywood movie stars, paintings, drawings, and photographs of the family of owner Helga, a wildly eccentric woman who sports big sunglasses and crazy hats. The sprawling building is musty and dusty, but this adds to the charm. The decor of the bedrooms continues in the same vein, with four-poster beds swathed in black lace and gold sheets.

Outside, the hotel is set in thick unruly jungle, a lush tangle of green. There is a swimming pool surrounded by fairy statues, a paradise for children who love to explore. A sign reads: "Please ensure your windows and doors are firmly closed before leaving your room. The management cannot accept responsibility for the monkeys." The cheeky creatures lurk in the trees and appear in force at breakfast time, so eat outside at your peril. Whatever you make of this eccentric boutique pad, you will be sure never to forget a stay here. **JK**

⬅ *The decor at Helga's Folly is a mix of bohemian and traditional, which makes it stand out.*

Enjoy Tree Tops Lodge

Location Moneragala District, Sri Lanka
Website www.treetopsjunglelodge.com **Price** ⦵

Tree Tops Jungle Lodge is set within the Sri Lankan Weliara forest, situated between the Yala National Park and the Arahat Kanda Mountains. It is the perfect place to watch and listen to wildlife, in particular some of the jungle's 161 bird species and its wild elephants. Experiences such as sighting an elephant mother and child are truly magical.

The accommodation is pretty basic. Visitors stay in simple huts built from a combination of clay, cow dung, and wood in the local fashion, and they wash in a freshwater well. Guests can go to sleep listening to the murmur of the jungle, after taking a moonlit trek under the stars, and wake up to the chatter of birds.

"An awesome viewpoint into jungle life … the atmosphere is charged with the noise of the wild."

ecohotelsoftheworld.com

Tree Tops is not just a place for animal and plant lovers; staff will also take guests to see some of the nearby Buddhist rock temples that are otherwise off the beaten track for tourists. The vegetarian food is cooked on a wood fire, and the soups and curries are prepared by cooks who know the secrets of ayurvedic plant medicine, often using herbs and spices that grow in the jungle. Wildlife sightings vary according to the time of year and whether it is the rainy or dry season. However, there is always the option to kick back and relax in a hammock and admire the stunning views, as far away from twenty-first-century urban living as it is possible to imagine. **CK**

Experience Baros

Location Baros, Maldives   **Website** www.baros.com
Price 💲💲

This could be the very definition of paradise: tiny hummocks of sandy islands bathed endlessly in golden sun, encircled by turquoise lagoons, soft white shores, and some gently swaying palm trees for good measure. It's a perpetual photo opportunity that will make your vacation pictures look amazing.

From the air, the Maldives are like smudges. They peek out above the water, often by no more than three or four feet (around 1 m), and are inhabited only by the luxury accommodation and spas that cater for the sanctuary-seeker. After touching down at Male airport, the only way to get to your remote and exclusive destination is by private sea-plane or boat. Only 25 minutes after skimming over the still waters, maybe taking in a school of playful dolphins or an occasional flying fish, you'll be marooned in paradise on your very own Robinson Crusoe island.

Baros is one of the most secluded and unspoiled islands in the Northern Atoll. You can snooze all day on your private deck, join the scuba-lovers to explore the crystalline waters, or be pampered to perfection in the Aquum Spa. Or you could book a sunset cruise, a day's deep-sea fishing, or dine on the moonlit sands for a spot of beach-based star-gazing.

First you must find your own portion of Baros bliss by walking barefoot to a private strip of beach. Stretch out on your own portion of powdery sand or indulge in a bit of underwater exploring. You might have a memorable close encounter with a balletic stingray or a darting shoal of tropical fish. And don't forget the Maldivian mantra: no news, no shoes. **SWi**

⬅ *With the amazing sunsets and the unspoiled views, Baros is the epitome of a true escape.*

Stay at Hotel Dhonakulhi

Location Haa Alifu Atoll, Maldives
Website www.island-hideaway.com **Price** ⑤⑤⑤

A thousand Robinson Crusoe islands and lagoons with varying depths and infinite shades of sparkling blue: This is the sublime setting for the Hotel Dhonakulhi, which has bagged the best spot in the whole of the Maldives—the previously uninhabited virgin atoll of Haa Alifu. The resort is surrounded by lush vegetation, and the luxurious villas have the Indian Ocean lapping at their terraces. Graced with private beaches, and some with their own pools, too, the huts have open-air bathrooms that highlight the general feeling of back-to-nature luxury. Visitors may be marooned on an island paradise, but there are first-class restaurants, a rejuvenating spa, and a variety of state-of-the-art media equipment, just in case you need to contact home.

You do not have to be an avid snorkeler to visit the Maldives. Although you could spend a day or two with the dive school, a wade through the aquarium-clear waters will give you just as good a glimpse of the fish in the coral reefs. That is before you stretch out under a coconut tree or relax with a massage in your private open-air treatment room overlooking the ocean.

Dhonakulhi stands out from its Maldivian rivals thanks to its utterly unspoiled setting. Some 95 percent of the island remains undeveloped, so visitors are completely surrounded by the sheer natural beauty of the Maldives. Even the marina, the only one in the entire archipelago, is formed from a channel in the reef, splitting it in two, and thereby making a natural harbor. If you sail over in your private yacht, you will have no trouble docking—otherwise, you can take the speedboat like the rest of us. **SWi**

◄ *Designed to provide the ultimate in seclusion, the airy hut-like residences have their own spacious plots.*

Relax at Dhoni Mighili

Location Ari Atoll, Maldives
Website www.scottdunn.com **Price** ⑤⑤⑤⑤

The island of Dhoni Mighili, in the Ari atoll southwest of Malé, is something special. It is the only Maldivian island that you can book outright, and it provides a unique luxury experience pairing a secluded island hideaway with boat accommodation. Reached by seaplane, the island itself has just six beach bungalows situated 30 feet (9 m) from the turquoise sea, four of which have private plunge pools. To make your stay even more special, each comes with a Maldivian butler who will be at your beck and call 24/7. They are able to arrange anything you might need, whether that's personalized diving lessons, the perfect martini, or a unique and secluded spot for a marriage proposal.

"The Maldives really do deserve their reputation as the pearls of the Indian Ocean."

Maldives Review website

In this decadent paradise of palm trees, coral-sand beaches, and clear warm sea, you are encouraged to spend the day lazing on your private *dhoni*, a 65-foot (20-m) Maldivian sailboat. As night falls, your butler will organize dinner beneath the stars. You can spend the night in the thatched bungalow or on board the *dhoni* with the hush of the sea lulling you to sleep.

Cruise during the day to unvisited sandbars for a swim, or visit undersea treasure troves to marvel at the reef's brightly colored sea life. There is a chance of spotting gray reef sharks, manta rays, and even enormous whale sharks around the exotic coral. For the lucky few, Dhoni Mighili is paradise found. **LD**

Enjoy Huvafen Fushi Underwater Spa

Location North Malé Atoll, Maldives
Website www.huvafenfushi.com   **Price** ❺❺❺❺

Set in translucent turquoise seas covering an area of the Indian Ocean the size of Portugal, the otherworldly Maldives are likely to sink in 150 years' time, as global warming continues to make the sea levels rise. Get there while you still can, and when you do, stay at Huvafen Fushi, a sexy and serene resort for dreamers.

Whichever of its forty-three stylish, contemporary, uncluttered water bungalows you choose, you will be guaranteed immaculate luxury. Some bungalows have glass floors so you can watch marine life as you sip a cooling cocktail; others boast giant whirlpool tubs in the bathroom, with only a sheet of glass

---

"The butler feeds the manta rays at sunset, which is a major hit with the children."

Harper's Bazaar

---

between you and expansive private views of the lagoon. Outside, skinny-dip from your deck, sprawl on your daybed, and cool off in your plunge pool.

The spa, built on stilts above the ocean, has underwater treatment rooms, where you can commune with the tropical fish while you have your head massaged. A range of inventive "rituals" using wraps, scrubs, facials, and massages is available; there is private yoga and meditation, and even a resident "wellness mentor." Swim at night in the infinity pool, when it is lit up by colored fiber-optic lights, then dip into the Lonu Veyo, a Malaysian saltwater pool in which it is extremely relaxing to float. **CSJ**

Stay at One&Only Reethi Rah

Location North Malé Atoll, Maldives
Website www.oneandonlyresorts.com   **Price** ❺❺❺

Arriving at One&Only Reethi Rah on a sleek, 55-foot (16-m) yacht, one doubts that there could be anywhere else quite so stunning on the planet. A sparkling lagoon encircles the softest white sand imaginable, and spacious luxury villas are dotted around the beach or hover in the water.

Everything at the resort amounts to one little word: wow! It is a remarkable place to stay, and it is not unusual to bump into glamorous celebrities sipping a cocktail at the Rah Bar. Villas come with mysterious black infinity pools on large decks with cool daybeds. Inside there are plasma televisions, enormous beds, and bathrooms with sunken tubs fit for kings and queens, underneath soaring triple-height ceilings.

There is little to do, which suits most blissed-out visitors down to the ground. Time in the inviting waters is spent swimming, snorkeling, and diving; time above it fishing, enjoying Zen-like spa treatments, and soaking up the sun's rays in one of many secluded spots. In the evenings, a well-dressed clientele savors delectable dishes in the main restaurant, the Japanese tapas fusion restaurant, and the Middle Eastern beach restaurant, described by One&Only as exuding "shipwreck chic." Golf carts and bicycles provide modes of transportation around the island—which is large by Maldivian standards—making discovering its twelve gorgeous beaches that little bit easier.

In case you are wondering what the name means, Reethi Rah is translated as "pretty island"—a serious underestimation if ever there was one. **LP**

➡ *There has been not one iota of skimping in the design of the shamelessly glitzy resort at Reethi Rah.*

Trek to Gokyo Ri

Location Solu Khumbu, Nepal   **Website** www.nepaltrailblazer.com
Price 💲💲💲

The summit of Mount Everest must surely be the ultimate escape. The training and risks involved in climbing it are too much for most mortals, so try a twelve-day trek to Gokyo Ri instead and marvel at the sunset reflecting on the world's highest mountain. Here, in the Solu Khumbu region of Nepal, you will encounter the charming Sherpa people, renowned for their climbing skills, and stunning mountain landscapes in the heart of the Himalayas.

The trek itself does not demand technical climbing skills. However, with the summit of Gokyo Ri at 17,500 feet (5,350 m), take your time ascending to avoid altitude sickness. Hire porters to carry your kit and a guide to lead the way, or book the trip through an agency, leaving you free to enjoy the hike without fear of getting lost or exhausted. In the evenings, experience the warm Nepali hospitality in teahouses or lodges—although they are far from luxurious, you can relax in front of the stove and dig in to a hearty meal of *dhal bhat*, the traditional fare of vegetables and rice, washed down with reviving Khukri rum.

The mountain village of Gokyo is on the shores of the glistening Dudh Pokhari, and a two-hour hike above this lake takes you to Gokyo Ri. Here you will see four summits higher than 26,000 feet (8,000 m): Everest, Cho Oyu, Lhotse, and Makalu, sparkling like enormous diamonds in the sky. You will soon forget your shortness of breath and the cold gnawing at your fingertips as you watch the sun casting shades of brilliant gold, turning fiery red and finally baby pink, on the snows of the highest peak in the world. **SWa**

⬅ *From Gokyo Ri, your vantage point reveals an amazing landscape of peaks, high passes, and glaciers.*

Stay at Amankora

Location Paro, Bhutan **Website** www.amanresorts.com
Price 💲💲💲💲

If trekking in the Himalayas conjures up images of trudging behind Ghurkas and freezing in tented accommodation, then think again. There is another way, thanks to Aman Resorts, which recently opened Amankora, the first luxury hotel and the first foreign venture of its kind in Bhutan.

The resort sits in a quite spectacular setting in the shadow of Jamalhari, Bhutan's highest peak, which overlooks a picturesque village surrounded by thick pine forests. The retreat consists of five separate luxury hideaways. The largest and most impressive lodge successfully combines the rustic with the contemporary, and the twenty-four bedrooms are in six rammed-

---

> *"A cluster of austere buildings whose . . . exteriors belie interiors of epic scale and opulence."*

Mike Carter, *Observer*

---

earth houses that mirror the shape of a ruined seventeenth-century fort on the hill above. However, there is no getting away from the biggest attraction: those stunning mountain views, which can be best admired from the living room.

The Paro Valley is the starting point for many of Bhutan's treks, which take in spectacular landscapes of soaring mountains, deep valleys, terraced rice paddies, fields of millet, and little hamlets dotting a thickly forested backdrop. It is likely that after a hard day's trekking your aching muscles will be in need of some soothing; luckily, all of the Amankora lodges have spas that offer a variety of relaxing treatments. **HA**

Relax at Uma Paro

Location Paro, Bhutan **Website** www.uma.como.bz
Price 💲💲

High in the Himalayan mountain kingdom of Bhutan, Uma Paro is a study in spiritual stillness. The luxury boutique hotel blends the best of Bhutan's exquisite traditions with modern elements to create a retreat as stunning as the scenery. Drawing on the serenity of yoga and meditation practices, a stay here is transcendent.

The hotel consists of a central lodge and nine villas, set in 38 acres (15 ha) of wooded hillsides. Rooms overlook the pine forests and peaks rising in the distance, and the two-bed villas are a highlight, with outdoor hot stone bath tubs and open-air courtyards with fire pits in the center. The rooms are all sleek and modern with brightly colored, hand-painted Bhutanese wall designs and views to die for.

The Buddhist kingdom places much emphasis on yoga and meditation, and with the cool, fresh, unpolluted air here in the mountains, *pranayama* (yogic breathing) has never felt so good. Staff are on hand twenty-four hours a day to make your stay as relaxing as possible. The Shambala spa offers treatments to soothe the soul, with an emphasis again on the spiritual and physical nature of the treatments. Stone bath therapies are just one of many to slow your pulse and help you relax. The Bukhari restaurant serves up Bhutanese-inspired delicacies from yak burgers to chai-infused hot chocolate and local noodle soup.

Bhutan is not the easiest country to visit, and it is to the hotel's credit that it starts the soothing process even before you visit, by helping you to organize all the necessary entry permits, visas, and flights. It is less a hotel stay and more a spiritual experience. **LD**

→ *The luxurious setting of Uma Paro means it is the finest place to unwind at the end of a Bhutan hike.*

Visit the Gardens of Suzhou

Location Suzhou, Jiangsu, China
Website www.chinavista.com/suzhou/tour/garden.html   **Price** $

Suzhou is a historic gem, filled with canals, bridges, and its famous gardens. The center of silk production in China, Suzhou was for centuries a popular residence for scholars, officials, and merchants. Eager to fill their leisure hours with beauty, they built private gardens in which to escape from the hurly-burly of city life.

There were once 200 private gardens in the city, each designed as a harmonious combination of the elements. Rocks, ponds, trees, and pavilions were meticulously placed so that the view was perfect, wherever one sat. Fewer than half the gardens survive today, but the largest of Suzhou's gardens open to the public, the Humble Administrator's Garden, dates from

---

*"A very great and noble city. . . .
It has 1,600 stone bridges under
which a galley may pass."*

Marco Polo, explorer, on Suzhou

---

the Ming dynasty. It radiates with bamboo and bonsai, clear, chattering streams, carefully molded rock pools, and pavilions with upturned roofs. More than half of the garden is filled with water, and intricately latticed walkways allow erstwhile scholars to admire the landscapes even in rain and snow. Also worth visiting are the artfully designed Lingering Garden, the long walkway of which is adorned with calligraphy, and the Blue Wave Pavilion, an eleventh-century retreat featuring glorious, mature trees. **PE**

◄ *The Garden of the Master of Nets blends vertical
with horizontal, water with land, and yin with yang.*

See Mount Huangshan

Location Mount Huangshan, Anhui, China
Website www.huangshantour.com   **Price** ❶

The seventy-two peaks of Mount Huangshan, or Yellow Mountain, have been a tourist attraction for more than a millennium. Painters and poets across the ages have flocked here for inspiration from the granite crags and oddly shaped pine trees.

Anyone with a good level of fitness should avoid the crushing cable car line—Huangshan is a top domestic tourist haunt—and instead walk to the summit via the well-marked paths. The Eastern Steps provide a steep, short, 5-mile (8-km) route. The Western Steps are twice as long, and equally arduous, but reward hikers with outstanding views. On either route, though, you will find yourself almost alone

"Huangshan [is] known as 'the loveliest mountain of China.'"

UNESCO World Heritage Committee

except for the tough, wiry porters who haul supplies to the mountaintop hotels and restaurants. Away from the preferred package tour routes at the top, it is easy to find solitude. On a clear day, the scenery is spectacular. But it is not for the sunshine that travelers have swarmed here over the centuries; it is for the clouds. In misty weather, there seems at first to be no view at all. Then, the air currents send the brume gently billowing away. Magically, from behind the flurrying alabaster curtain, peaks of rough-hewn rock appear. For a few moments, they seem to hover mystically above a soft sea of white. Then the clouds shift once more, and the heavenly vision vanishes. **PE**

Enjoy Fuchun

Location Shanghai, China
Website www.fuchunresort.com   **Price** ❸❸

Surrounded by the surreally beautiful Hangzhou Mountains, mist-swathed lakes, and a working tea plantation, the peacefulness of the Fuchun resort belies its proximity to the bustling modern cities of Hangzhou and Shanghai. This exclusive lakeside hideaway, the first of its kind in China, offers a quiet and luxurious take on rustic rural living. All seventy lakeside and garden rooms and the twelve villas with private pools offer Zen-inspired living quarters. Decked out in soothing neutrals and dark teak furniture, the rooms provide a welcome respite from the heat and humidity of the day.

The resort was originally inspired by a 700-year-old Yuan dynasty painting of the local landscape, and it has successfully captured the dreamlike feel of the art. Total relaxation and revitalization is the philosophy of the resort, where peace and serenity reign supreme. Take time out in the spa for a soothing treatment, such as the Hangzhou-spun silk cocoon package, which is inspired by local traditions, or a jasmine and pearl scrub by the Balinese therapists to buff your body into baby-smooth perfection. Alternatively take a dip in the cool black swimming pool or soak in one of the three outdoor granite whirlpool tubs, and savor the silence and the solitude.

You can indulge your inner hippie with a yoga or tai chi class, both of which are held on the picture-perfect waterside verandas. Golfing enthusiasts will be in seventh heaven because there is an eighteen-hole course within the hotel's grounds, as well as two tennis courts where you can perfect your serve. When hunger strikes, the award-winning T8 restaurant serves up excellent East meets West cuisine, whereas the Asian Corner offers a selection of local specialties. **HA**

Join in Tai Chi at Dawn

Location Shanghai, China
Website www.chenqiang.net   **Price** ❶

Do not stay up too late in the ritzy bars and high-rise restaurants of Shanghai, because you will need to wake up early if you are to enjoy one of the city's more fascinating sights: its residents practicing tai chi at dawn. There is no specific location. Just wander the streets and lanes of the former French Concession and you will see them in groups. Sometimes four or five elderly neighbors slowly undulate their limbs to music played from a tinny old tape recorder.

Head to any one of the city's green spaces and you will find hundreds of people exercising. By the rose beds in Fuxing Park, an old man, totally bald, is wrapped in solitary concentration as he twists his

> *"Tai chi does not mean oriental wisdom or something exotic. It is the wisdom of your own senses. "*
>
> Chungliang Al Huang, tai chi master

hand above his head. Others exercise in groups—and it is not just tai chi. A gathering of about fifty people stands in formation and practices aerobics to loud, tape recorder tones. Women with fancy hairdos dance with fans, while a few feet away a young man is coached by an elder in sword-fighting techniques. Doddering old men walk with birds in cages, which they hang from the trees' branches before sitting on benches and slowly sipping green tea from jam jars.

It is certainly a sociable scene, and one that somehow transcends the modern rush of Shanghai. The traditions still remain in this slick, supercharged city. You just have to get up early enough to see them. **PE**

Stay at Sanya Nanshan

Location Hainan, China
Website www.treehousesofhawaii.com/nanshan.html   **Price** ❾❾

The island of Hainan is the southernmost of China's provinces and the world's second-largest oceanic island. Bathed in the warm waters of the South China Sea, with a mountainous interior, mild climate, and miles of white-sand beaches, the Chinese refer to it as the "Oriental Hawaii." If you walk back from the beach near the southern city of Sanya on Yalong Bay and gaze up into the forest canopy, you will discover that the hinterland along Hainan's southern shoreline is an excellent place to build a tree house.

Four tree houses, to be precise, all safely ensconced high in the canopies of a small cluster of carefully selected tamarind trees, known for their dense, durable wood and more than capable of keeping aloft your average tree house. The tree houses at Sanya Nanshan are integrated into their living hosts to the point of being camouflaged, and they are linked to one another by rope and plank walkways high above the forest floor. The tree houses do have electricity but a brief walk is required if you need to have a shower. By their very nature they are not spacious, but they are very neat, and all have spectacular views of the ocean beyond. Big Beach in the Sky can sleep up to six people over two levels, or Beach Club Treehouse sleeps two and is just a minute's walk from the beach.

The nearby Sanya Nanshan Buddhist Cultural Theme Park is the largest Buddhist temple built since the establishment of the People's Republic of China in 1959 and is a must-see when in the region. Covering 66 acres (27 ha), it has unrivaled representations of late Tang dynasty (618–907) architecture and also contains the beautiful Golden Jade Kwan-yin statue, a national treasure which is encrusted with more than 221 pounds (100 kg) of gold, silver, and jade. **BS**

Explore Sun Moon Lake

Location Sun Moon Lake, Central Taiwan, China
Website www.sunmoonlake.gov.tw/sun.aspx?Lang=EN   **Price** 🌗

Located at an altitude of 2,500 feet (760 m), the emerald and often misty waters of central Taiwan's Sun Moon Lake epitomize Far Eastern serenity and natural beauty. Surrounded by mountains, and consisting of two parts that are crescent-shaped and circular respectively (hence giving the lake its name), Taiwan's largest inland body of water has emerged as one of the island's most popular tourist destinations.

The area is populated by the Thao people, Taiwan's smallest aboriginal tribe, who consider Lalu, the island that divides the two sections of the lake, the home of their ancestral spirits. For just over twenty years a so-called "matchmaker pavilion" that hosted group weddings was situated on the island, but this government institution (along with most other parts of the island) vanished in the lake during the big earthquake of 1999, leaving only a quaint islet behind.

Meanwhile, the scenic shoreline road is interspersed with twentieth-century yet traditional-style temples and parks like the Peacock Garden, where two hundred of the majestic birds roam the grounds. Ita Thao—the local tribe's main settlement—on the other hand, gives a glimpse into Thao culture, with exhibitions and performances providing a stimulating insight into their customs. But a visit to Sun Moon Lake is mostly about the tranquil scenery that is reminiscent of Far Eastern landscape paintings, with Taiwan's tropical location guaranteeing good weather all year-round. The fact that swimming in the lake is prohibited contributes to the region's peacefulness, and renting a rowboat is the perfect way to enjoy some solitude on the water and to appreciate the stunning forests of the surrounding mountains. **DaH**

Visit Big Buddha and Po Lin Monastery

Location Lantau Island, Hong Kong, China
Website www.discoverhongkong.com; www.plm.org.hk   **Price** 🌗

Forget the commercial side of Hong Kong for a minute. Visit Lantau Island by ferry and you will see the grand seated statue of the Big Buddha, the world's largest outdoor bronze Buddha, and the most peaceful place to spend an afternoon in the city.

The Buddha is part of Po Lin Monastery, which has been on this mountainous site since 1906. The bus drops you at the bottom of the steps; with the bronze Buddha smiling down on you, it is up to you whether to climb the steps to the top next to the fluttering multicolored flags, browse the trinket stalls, or visit the museum. Inside the monastery are two of the

"Three things cannot be long hidden: the sun, the moon, and the truth."

Buddha

Buddha's relics, which magically appear to change color according to who looks at them. Just looking at the Buddha, you will feel him radiating inner peace—and that is no casual accident. It is all in the design: As he sits in the Lotus pose, his features are wide and calm, signifying serenity. His raised right hand removes all fear, and his left hand on his thigh is placed in the "wish-fulfilling" posture. Take a moment to let it sink in, soaking up his tranquil features and air of peace, before heading back to the hyperactive city. **LD**

➲ *Big Buddha symbolizes the harmonious relationship between man and nature, and people and religion.*

Unwind at Jia

Location Causeway Bay, Hong Kong, China
Website www.jiahongkong.com **Price** $\$$$\$$

"The interior focuses on spatial clarity, comfort, and style, with ultra-modern amenities."

Proprietors, Jia

Jia means "home" in Mandarin, and this Philippe Starck–designed boutique hotel, the first in Asia, certainly offers a welcome respite from the buzzing hustle and bustle of Hong Kong. Situated in the Causeway Bay area of the city, Jia has been styled using nature as its central theme, creating an ultra-chic yet supremely comfortable environment.

With fifty-four rooms in a twenty-five-story former office block, this hotel may look unremarkable from the outside, but once inside, you find yourself in a contemporary oasis: all white walls, teak floors, and tasteful objets d'art. If you are really pushing the boat out, book into one of the one-bedroom suites or two-bedroom penthouses, which offer breathtaking views over the city and outstanding furnishings. If you want to catch some sun, head to the sundeck on the second floor, where you can relax quietly with a complimentary glass of wine at cocktail hour.

Although Hong Kong offers a huge diversity of eating opportunities, from swanky restaurants to stalls in the street, rooms at the Jia come kitted out with well-equipped kitchenettes, so you need not leave your room if you do not want to. That would be a pity, though, because there is so much to see in the local vicinity. Across the road is a traditional Chinese medicine shop that sells birds' nests and more, whereas next door is Jardine's Bazaar with its lovely afternoon vegetable and flower market and its heaving night market. The famous Sogo department store and Causeway Bay subway are just a street away, and Victoria Park is a short stroll to the east. **HA**

◥ *The penthouse living area is simply designed, filled with clean lines, warm lighting, and cozy couches.*

Walk the MacLehose Trail

Location New Territories, Hong Kong, China
Website www.oxfamtrailwalker.org.hk/en/home.html **Price** ◑

Those who think that Hong Kong is one big concrete sprawl should think again. Some 40 percent of the territory is protected as country park. The 60-mile (96-km) MacLehose Trail cuts across some of the best parts, traversing the New Territories' lush, snake-infested jungles, immaculate white beaches, turquoise waters, and soaring mountain peaks, including Hong Kong's highest, Tai Mo Shan (Big Hat Mountain), which climbs to more than 3,000 feet (915 m).

Named for a former Hong Kong governor, Crawford Murray MacLehose, who was fond of hiking, the trail was opened in 1979, and two years later the Gurkhas inaugurated the first Trailwalker event—a race that covers the trail's entire length—as a training exercise. In 1986, the race opened to the public and since then almost 50,000 people have taken part, raising funds for international charity Oxfam. The fastest-ever team completed the distance in just under twelve hours.

Meet any of the competitors in the week after the race and they will be sure to tell you about their knees. Those with bad joints, beware: the trail specializes in ups and downs, and there are an awful lot of concrete steps. You do not have to walk the entire distance all at once, however, or in fact more just than a little bit if you want. The route is divided into ten stages, from Pak Tam Chung, on the east coast of the New Territories in Sai Kung Country Park, to Tuen Mun in the west. Most of the sections are around 6 miles (9 km) long, so you can hike just one or two of them, stopping for a dip in the ocean on the way. And, this being Hong Kong, they are all easily accessible from the road, so when you finish, you can hop in a taxi or on a bus and go directly to the nearest noodle restaurant for a much-deserved refuel. **PE**

Stay at Langham Place

Location Mong Kok, Hong Kong, China
Website www.hongkong.langhamplacehotels.com/en **Price** ◉◉

One of the most exciting things about Hong Kong is its bustle. Set in the middle of Mong Kok, a good distance from any other five-star hotels, Langham Place is technically out on a limb. Yet that is what makes it so special. Just one block away from the humid markets where you can buy anything from durian to goldfish and Nike sneakers, the hotel is the calm in the eye of the storm.

Langham Place was built with the local people in mind; sure, you can see them in clear focus from your hotel window as they hang their laundry out and go about their daily business in the nearby tenements, but just by being in this area, the hotel is giving back

> *"[Langham Place] is a refreshingly elegant and luxurious hotel in the bustling heart of Mong Kok."*
>
> luxurytravel.com

to the local economy. All across the hotel, local art sets the scene, and the stand-out feature, the Chuan spa, is Chinese, too. This offers a sauna, steam room, plenty of Chinese treatments including reflexology, and a rooftop pool, open to all guests.

Service is impeccable, and rooms are wonderfully technologically advanced, from the pillows to the iHome MP3 players. The stand-out room is the Chuan Spa Suite, where breathtaking views of Hong Kong harbor greet you alongside trays of Chinese sweets, herbal teas, soothing music, and an exceptional spa suite. Switch off in your own private steam room, or watch the water overflow in your infinity bath. **LD**

Explore Mai Po Wetlands

Location Mai Po, Hong Kong, China
Website www.wwf.org.hk/eng/maipo **Price** Ⓢ

The sky suddenly darkens as a cloud gathers overhead. It is not a storm brewing over the Mai Po wetlands; rather it is a huge flock of birds filling the winter sky. Every year up to 60,000 waterbirds, such as gulls, herons, egrets, and black-faced spoonbills, descend on the marshy wetlands during their annual southerly migration. They travel along the East Asian–Australasian Flyway, which starts in the Arctic Circle and extends through Southeast Asia and on to Australia and New Zealand. Mai Po is a handy midway point—a tropical stopover where the birds can rest and refuel before completing their grueling journey.

More than 350 species of domestic and migratory birds throng to the natural reserve in the northwest corner of Hong Kong, which was designated a Wetland of International Importance in 1995. They flock to the traditional shrimp-breeding ponds, known as *gei wai*, and roost in the trees in their thousands. In spring the weather warms, the winter birds start to make their way back home, and the wetlands enter a new phase of life. The trees bud and blossom; the *gei wai* fill with juicy shrimp, and the shorebirds gorge hungrily before continuing their long flight home. Brightly colored damselflies and dragonflies complete their metamorphosis and begin to emerge from the freshwater ponds.

Summer brings the breeding season. It is at this time that the resident birds shed their dull winter coats and transform into the colorful plumage that they will use to entice mates. In the evening, the night air is filled with the soothing chirrup of the insects and the croaky sound of frogs. You may even see snakes slithering along the paths. In autumn, the annual bird migration begins, and the cycle starts all over again. **JP**

Relax at the Peninsula

Location Kowloon, Hong Kong, China
Website www.peninsula.com **Price** ⓈⓈⓈ

A stay at Hong Kong's grand old lady begins at the airport when you are swiftly whisked to the hotel by a chauffeur-driven Rolls-Royce, part of the Peninsula's famous fleet. Or if you are feeling really flash (and flush), you can arrive by helicopter, because the hotel has two rooftop helipads for its super-rich guests.

Opened in 1928, the Pen is the city's oldest hotel. Like the buzzing metropolis of Hong Kong, the hotel's opulent and palatial lobby is a hive of frenzied activity, shimmering with sophistication, but once you step into the elevator to your room, silence and calm prevail.

Right in the heart of Hong Kong's entertainment district, the Peninsula offers dramatic views of Victoria

> *"The service is beyond attentive—it makes you say 'wow' every time."*
>
> concierge.com

Harbour. Choose a top-floor suite to drink in the city's glittering skyline. Rooms are plush, and the devil is in the detail; guests can operate the temperature, curtains, humidity, lights, and television from a bedside panel. Marble bathrooms have mood lighting, and the decor fuses European style with Asian touches; it is all old-world elegance combined with richly colored fabrics, Western furniture, and Asian art, lamps, and porcelain.

On the rooftop is Felix, one of Hong Kong's hippest restaurants, and a Roman-themed pool, festooned with columns, friezes, and statues. If you have not got the cash to splash at this fine hotel, then dress up smart and pay a visit for afternoon tea. **JK**

Camp at Three Camel Lodge

Location Gobi Desert, Mongolia
Website www.threecamellodge.com **Price** 🌏

Nomadic souls can rest their weary heads at this luxury wilderness camp in Mongolia's rugged Gobi Desert. Sitting in the shadows of the beautiful Gobi-Altai Mountains in Gurvansaikhan National Park, Three Camel Lodge blends perfectly with the stunning natural beauty of the surrounding desert.

Sheltered by a 54-million-year-old volcanic outcrop and laid out across the Gobi's floor are the forty-five felt *gers* (nomadic tents) and a striking main lodge. Like the homes of the nomadic herders that inspired them, the handmade gers are rustic, roomy, and comfortable, with wood-burning stoves, hand-painted wooden beds, and indigenous furniture. Each one can accommodate up to four guests and has twenty-four-hour electricity from solar panels. The main lodge has been crafted by local artisans, without using a single nail, in the style of Mongolian Buddhist architecture.

This is a serious eco-retreat; solar and wind power are harnessed to provide evening light and constant hot water, and animal dung fuels the stoves. The remote location in the wild heart of the desert is the perfect place to see ancient stone carvings of wild sheep, ibex, and antelope around the volcanic outcrop. There is also the chance to meet modern-day nomads who pass through the lodge to tend their livestock. Go hiking in the foothills of the Gobi-Altai Mountains, camel trekking through sand dunes, horseback riding in mountain valleys, and digging for dinosaur fossils at the legendary Flaming Cliffs. When the sun sets, simply sit back to watch the spectacular night sky cover the desert. **AD**

↗ *At night take in the views across the desert from the wooden porch and stone terraces of the endless steppe.*

"This is top hospitality in one of the world's most inhospitable regions, the Gobi."

Independent

Discover Lake Khövsgöl

Location Khankh, Mongolia
Website www.mongoliatourism.gov.mn **Price** 🛈

One of the most beautiful and accessible areas of Mongolia, Lake Khövsgöl is surrounded by forest-clad hills and flower-filled meadows. Overlooked by the dramatic Khoridol Saridag Mountains, the crystal-clear waters form the country's largest and deepest lake, and it holds 2 percent of the world's fresh water. Khövsgöl is also one of the most pristine lakes, with water so clean it can be drunk without treatment.

Come here to fish for Siberian grayling or learn how nomad families tend their reindeer herds. Take the ferry between Khatgal and Khankh to explore the reaches of the Khövsgöl National Park, which is bigger than California's Yellowstone Park. The park is home to a variety of wildlife, from ibex and elks to wolves, brown bears, and moose. It is also a stopping-off point for migrating birds from Siberia, which means there is serious bird-watching to be done. For the full-on experience, sleep in a cozy yurt, lined with felt to insulate against the cold and heated with a traditional wood-burning stove.

In an arid land where so many lakes are salty, it is no surprise to learn that Khövsgöl is considered sacred in this Buddhist country. There are few roads in the region, and locals travel on horseback. In winter, when temperatures plummet and the lake freezes over, horse-drawn sleds cross the ice, piled with goods for trading on the Siberian border. The highlight of the season is the Ice Festival, a midwinter celebration held on the frozen lake. Watch nomadic strongmen pit their wits against each other in ice sumo and tug-of-war competitions, then see sled and skating races. **AD**

➡ *One of the world's seventeen ancient lakes, Khövsgöl is more than two million years old.*

Explore Kamakura

Location Kanagawa, Japan
Website www.asahi-net.or.jp/~qm9t-kndu   **Price** ◑

This sleepy town might be just 31 miles (50 km) from Tokyo, but it feels like a world away. There are no high-rise buildings reaching dizzyingly up into the sky or neon-lit karaoke bars here. Kamakura was the capital of Japan during the shogunate from 1185 to 1333, when it was the fourth-largest city in the world. Steeped in history, it is the antithesis of the modern capital. Day-trippers from Tokyo flock here to enjoy the cooling sea breezes while they visit the Buddhist temples and Shinto shrines. Surrounded to the north, east, and west by mountains and to the south by the waters of Sagami Bay, Kamakura is a natural fortress. The setting is as dramatic today as it was in its heyday all those centuries ago. The landmark is the monumental bronze Buddha, which looks out over the city.

During the thirteenth century, Kamakura was also the cradle of Nichiren Buddhism. Nichiren was not local; he was born in Awa Province, but came to the political center of the country to teach, and the town has been associated with him ever since.

To see Kamakura at its best, follow the three-hour walk from the Tokeiji, up through the forest to the Kotokuin. Go to the Zeniarai Benten shrine to see the money-washing ceremony, which purifies offerings, and stop at temples along the way. The only sound you will hear is the song of nightingales as you pass blooming purple irises and bountiful plum trees.

The city is not all about ancient history. The beach is a big attraction, as well as the *senbei*—crisp rice cakes grilled and sold fresh along the main shopping street. Try one for a taste of the real Japan. **AD**

◀ *The bamboo forest by the Hokoku-ji Temple is famed for its beauty and Zen-like serenity.*

Unwind at Hoshinoya

Location Nagano, Japan
Website www.hoshinoya.com   **Price** ◔◔

The ritual of bathing has never been more sublime than at the new, stylish Hoshinoya resort. This is no traditional *onsen* (hot spring); Hoshinoya sits firmly in the twenty-first century. Green geothermal energy supplies the underfloor heating, and the surroundings are seriously contemporary. Dark wood and stone floors replace the familiar tatami mats. As well as open-air baths, a maze of low-ceilinged indoor baths leads to a meditation bath lit by underwater spotlights. Soothing music works well with the heat and sulfurous vapors to give a memorable bathing experience.

Outside, lush terraces and waterfalls are a feast for the senses, surrounded by Karuizawa's thick forest of

> *"The most essential elements of an onsen ryokan are its location and quality of onsen water."*

Hiroshi Ebisawa, architect and designer

Japanese maple, which turns glorious shades of gold and crimson in the autumn. Near Nagano, in central Honshu, the resort's cottages are arranged around a small river. No two rooms are the same, although each one has a private bathtub that looks out over the river and luxuriously fills with onsen water at the touch of a button. Walls are the soothing color of green tea, and bedrooms have majestic cathedral ceilings.

Away from the onsen, there are guided eco-tours of the forest and stargazing evenings. Curl up in the library with a good book or join other guests for gentle morning stretching exercises at the Chaya wooden tea house pavilion. Hoshinoya is hot spring heaven. **AD**

Stay in Myoren-ji Temple

Location Kyoto, Japan
Website www.pref.kyoto.jp/visitkyoto/en   **Price** 🅢

Although many people who have never been to Japan associate it with *Lost in Translation*–style luxury hotels, those in the know and in search of isolation head for one of the country's many *shukubos*. These are Japanese temples or shrines that provide accommodation for all, even for those who are not spiritually inclined but who would nonetheless like to experience traditional, religious Far Eastern life. Customarily places of worship, these days the *shukubos* welcome people of all denominations, and visitors are able to learn about the Zen Buddhist practice of *zaza* (an exercise aimed at calming both the body and the mind in order to gain insight into the essence of existence).

The thirteenth-century Myoren-ji temple in the former imperial capital of Kyoto is a remarkable sanctuary belonging to the Nichiren Buddhist sect, and it offers basic accommodation in a picturesque setting. Situated in a quiet area and within easy walking distance of Kyoto's city center, the temple's accommodation for visitors consists of rooms with sliding (and often intricately painted) *shoji* partitions and traditional tatami mats. The bathroom has to be shared with fellow travelers and the resident monks, and the only bathing facilities are at the public bathhouse outside the premises. Fundamentally, however, the experience of staying at this temple is not about luxurious indulgence. The stunning rock garden in front of one of the eight smaller temples and the peaceful surroundings more than offset the inconveniences of its limitations.

The elaborate architecture of the old buildings combined with the hands-on introduction to time-honored Japanese traditions make for an experience that is truly worthy of the term "escape." **DaH**

Visit Fushumi Inari Shrine

Location Kyoto, Japan
Website www.japan-guide.com   **Price** 🅟🅟

The beautiful maple tree–lined woodland trails up Mount Inari in southern Kyoto have been a Japanese pilgrimage destination for the last 1,300 years. Driving a line straight through this natural beauty, however, and somehow managing to create something even more impressive, is the winding pathway of man-made, bright red torii gates that leads from the base of the mountain up to the Fushimi Inari shrine at the top. The 2.5-mile (4-km) passageway passes serene ponds, small waterfalls, beautiful cemeteries, and numerous areas dedicated to private worship. Free to walk around, and open every day at all hours, the walk will take you about two hours, and ends with the same

> *"Wander through the tunnels of torii in the woods . . . it is a magical experience as daylight fades."*
>
> sacred-destinations.com

spectacular view over the entire city of Kyoto, whether you see it in broad daylight or glittering neon at night.

Each season provides the walk with a different backdrop, mesmerizing in its own way. Summer offers a luscious, verdant forest setting, with the torii gates providing much-needed shade, whereas winter offers a snow-covered backdrop, the torii ensuring the steps of the path are clear and safe. Whether it is the bright red on green in the summer, or the more dramatic red on white in the winter, the effect is captivating. **CW**

→ *Individual torii gates are common in Japan, but at Fushimi more than 10,000 line the way up Mount Inari.*

Unwind at Leyana Spa

Location Bangkok, Thailand
Website www.leyanaspa.com   **Price** ⊖

Amid the mayhem and chaos of Bangkok lies a haven of peace and tranquility, a lush green garden where the Leyana Spa offers original healing treatments that are the perfect antidote to the madness of the Thai capital. Four- and five-star hotels have long dominated the Bangkok spa scene, striving to outdo each other in trendy treatments and exotic preparations, yet too often forgetting the original purpose of a spa: to heal the body and refresh the spirit.

Kae, the young proprietor of Leyana Spa, believes in the healing powers of the touch of a good masseuse, a calm atmosphere, and freshly prepared scrubs and aromatic oils. She offers this in thirteen treatment

> *"All things here must not only be beautiful but super clean because that is what I would like."*

Proprietor, Leyana Spa

rooms (six of them doubles to accommodate couples), with whirlpool tubs and large, petal-filled white baths. Come early and sit in the Zen-like garden before your treatment while a therapist bathes your feet in warm water thick with soft rose petals. Sit back amid the greenery and count the delightful ceramic figures of cartoonlike Thai children peeking from behind the palm trees. Choose the ingredients for your treatments—honey and oatmeal, fresh coconut, juicy lemon, Thai tamarind—or discuss the benefits of an herbal steam bath versus a floral milk bath. Free from the day-to-day stresses at last, you will have the best spa treatment in Bangkok—healing and relaxing. **MN**

Relax at the Eugenia

Location Bangkok, Thailand
Website www.theeugenia.com   **Price** ⊖⊖

Tucked away in the heart of downtown Bangkok sits the old-world beauty that is the Eugenia. The late-nineteenth-century, family-owned colonial house is more like a private home than a hotel, charmingly furnished with tasteful antiques and a garage full of vintage sedans and limousines.

Stepping through the door is a bit like taking a trip back in time, but the contemporary touches bring the hotel up to date. The twelve high-ceilinged suites have been lovingly put together with furniture collected from British and French colonial Myanmar, as well as India and Indo-China. Even the bathtubs have a glamorous boudoir feel, made of hand-beaten copper. The crisp white bed linen and soft feather pillows come all the way from Belgium.

Understated elegance is the key here. Guests can sip afternoon tea or a cocktail under swaying palm trees by the courtyard pool, or take a trip around the city in one of the chauffeur-driven Mercedes-Benzes or Jaguars. There is fine dining on offer at the D. B. Bradley dining room, named after a Christian missionary who was a pioneer in the introduction of Western medicine to Siam in 1835. The room is adorned with painted gold wallpaper and delicate china, but the menu has a more contemporary feel and serves truffles and quail eggs as well as crab miso soup and pad thai. The Zheng He lounge is named in honor of the great Chinese voyager Admiral Zheng He; it serves breakfast and an evening tapas menu.

Find a quiet corner during the day in the library to curl up with a good book, or browse the selection of art and design books on the shelves. It is a far cry from Bangkok's high-rise five-star hotels with their hundreds of rooms and full-on bling. **AD**

Stay at Shangri-La Hotel

Location Bangkok, Thailand
Website www.shangrila.com **Price** ⊗⊗

In a noisy, humid, and polluted city like Bangkok, a good hotel is absolutely essential, and they do not come much better than the Shangri-La. Its location on the banks of the Chao Phraya River and its relaxing waterside dining terrace mean that cooling breezes counteract the heat of the day. With club rooms of quiet elegance, discreet service, and the famous Chi Spa, the Shangri-La deserves its reputation.

Old Bangkok was built on the river that once was its lifeline. The Shangri-La is right at its center, convenient for private trips on longboats or on the express boat that stops at the Grand Palace, nearby Wat Po, the Temple of Dawn, and Chinatown. Forget the crowds

---

"Your hotel's Tibetan spa massage was a truly exceptional experience —the finest I have ever had."

Jeremy Irons, actor

---

and relax on a riverboat as you enjoy Bangkok from the water, cooled by the breeze as you journey upriver.

Afternoon tea followed by a Chi treatment in the spa before dinner is just perfect. Treatments comprise a blend of Asian techniques, including energizing massage for yang stimulation, and relaxing massage for yin. The essential in the Chi treatment is the Tibetan brass bowl that, when struck, fills the room with waves of sound and has an unbelievable effect. Many people speak of having an out-of-body experience, of being transported to Shangri-La, a legendary land where no one grows old. The Shangri-La Hotel cannot guarantee agelessness, but it certainly offers a peaceful stay. **MN**

Cruise the River of Kings

Location Chao Phraya, Thailand
Website www.manohracruises.com **Price** ⊗⊗

Taking a voyage up the Chao Phraya River, Bangkok's lifeline, is a rare and exceptional insight into life in Thailand. The voyage on board a luxuriously converted one-hundred-year-old teak rice barge, the grand *Manohra Song*, is without a doubt the right way to see the River of Kings. The lavishly refurbished, four-cabin, floating hotel is all about classic elegance. The air-conditioned staterooms are decked out in Thai silks with crisp white linens and ethereal white drapes.

On the shore, industrial buildings stand shoulder to shoulder with glittering temples and rickety wooden shacks. The river is busy: Children take running jumps into the murky brown waters for some cool relief as enormous barges heave past, towed by minuscule boats. The journey aboard *Manohra Song* includes several stops. The first is Wat Arun, also known as the Temple of Dawn, with a central Khmer-style tower soaring over four others representing the thirty-three heavens. Later the boat moors up at Wat Nivat, a temple modeled on an English neo-gothic cathedral, where young saffron-robed monks live. Then there is Bang Pa Na, one of the king's summer palaces.

At 4 P.M. a civilized English afternoon tea is served with delicate smoked-salmon finger sandwiches, tiny chocolate fancies, and scones with cream. Surreal but wonderful in these exotic surroundings. Later, delicious classic Thai specialties are served on deck. Traditional Thai soup in a coconut shell is followed by a parade of dishes: everything from fragrant green curry to king prawns with asparagus. In true Thai custom, dessert is deliciously rich and sweet.

The boat's slow rhythmic sway, the gentle breeze, and the mellow pace are mesmerizing, and the sights even more so. It is a truly bewitching experience. **RCA**

Unwind at Chiva-Som

Location Pranburi, Thailand   **Website** www.chivasom.com
Price ❸❸❸

Chiva-Som is a very exclusive hideaway and has a clientele of royalty, celebrities, and VIPs. Located between the world-class beach resorts of Hua Hin and Pranburi in Thailand, Chiva-Som is the crème de la crème of spa resorts. Its policy of no cell phones and no laptops is an inspired one. Anyone who has hankered after total peace and had it disturbed by someone wheeling and dealing on the telephone will understand the thinking.

Nestled on the white-sand beach of the Gulf of Siam are luxurious ocean-fronting rooms and suites with swimming pools; elegant Thai-style pavilions face onto green manicured lawns and lakes reflecting clear, blue skies. The master chefs produce inventive gourmet menus on-site using fresh produce from their own organic garden. (Does herb-encrusted snow fish on a bed of fennel with saffron sauce followed by chocolate cake strike your fancy?)

Guests of the resort can indulge in luxurious massages and beauty treatments, learn to dance, or enjoy aqua aerobics, water sports (including sea kayaking), pilates, yoga, tai chi, and Thai boxing. Try the exclusive Watsu treatment, a passive technique derived from Zen shiatsu and performed in a special warm-water pool in which a sequence of gentle rhythmic movements stretch and manipulate the body, taking relaxation to the next level. If you can tear yourself away from the tranquility of the spa, go shopping in nearby Hua Hin for exquisite Thai silks and carvings, or have something run up by a tailor for the "new" you at a price you will not believe. **MN**

◀ *The name Chiva-Som means "haven of life" —a perfect name for a perfect place.*

Stay at the Sarojin

Location Khao Lak, Thailand
Website www.sarojin.com   **Price** 💲💲

There is a sense of timelessness surrounding the Sarojin. Its centerpiece, an ancient fig tree, is huge and dominating, towering impressively over a lagoon on one side and the ocean on the other. The fig gazes benevolently upon its reflection in the peaceful lotus pond—another symbol of eternity and nature.

In total, the Sarojin comprises 10 acres (4 ha) of grounds, including a private white-sand beach. The fifty-six residences are blessed with a variety of personalized touches: private gardens, sundecks, two-person baths, and outdoor waterfall showers, plus plunge pools and spa pools. The style is contemporary Asian, and the seven separate two-story buildings are designed to blend seamlessly into the surrounding landscape. The one-bed garden residences have Thai lounges and a private terrace, whereas fourteen pool residences add a plunge pool and a sun garden. The luxurious Sarojin suites, on the upper floor, have an air-conditioned pavilion and outdoor circular relaxation pools. Such luxury is only the beginning, though. The Pathways spa is integrated with the natural surroundings and lulled by the sounds of the Andaman Sea.

Overlooking a deserted coconut grove and the sea, there is a range of activities on offer, from snorkeling, scuba diving, and lagoon fishing to sea-cave canoeing in Phang Nga Bay, renowned for its dramatic limestone islands. You can also visit hot springs, trek on an elephant, or just watch the wildlife. A private charter on the luxury boat *Lady Sarojin* or a Thai cooking class and lunch by the waterfall are particularly magical ways of enjoying the Sarojin and its environs. **PS**

> *"The open air suites are protected by dunes yet close enough to hear waves washing over the coral."*
>
> Condé Nast Traveler

⬉ *Dining on the beach with your own personal chef is just one of the perks of staying at the Sarojin.*

Enjoy Veranda Resort

Location Phetchaburi, Thailand
Website www.verandaresortandspa.com   **Price** ⊖⊖

The Thai town of Hua Hin lies 124 miles (200 km) south of Bangkok and is the country's oldest beach resort. It first became popular in the 1920s when King Rama VII built a palace there, and members of the Thai royal family still take vacations in Hua Hin. Unsurprisingly, over the years, Hua Hin has acquired a glamorous air as visitors have been drawn to its white-sand beaches, upmarket hotels, and winding streets that are crammed with bars and restaurants, some of which stretch out along jetties into the sea. The town's night market is vast, and you can spend hours wandering through stalls that sell everything from jewelry to cashmere suits and silk dressing gowns; it is a great place to find a bargain and it is always advisable to arrive with an empty suitcase.

The trendy Veranda Resort and Spa lies outside Hua Hin, so you can get away from the town's bustle and relax. Its stunning modern, minimalist architecture houses thirteen pool villa suites and eighty-four rooms. They offer spectacular views out to sea over the Gulf of Thailand, outdoor bathtubs, and whirlpool tubs. Water is a big element at the Veranda: There is a spa where you can take in one of the beauty or massage treatments to really wind down; rooms look out to a central courtyard water feature that is soothingly candlelit at night; and there is an infinity swimming pool with water curtains, surrounded by decking and an artificial beach where you can relax and eat alfresco. As you might expect from a resort like this, the food is superb; the seafood fusion dishes and inventive blend of savory and sour using fresh pineapple and coconut are particularly good. If you are looking for a hip hotel away from the crowds, the Veranda offers the chance to relax in style. **CK**

Relax at Baan Taling Ngam

Location Koh Samui, Thailand
Website www.baan-taling-ngam.com   **Price** ⊖⊖

The signature infinity pool at Koh Samui's Baan Taling Ngam Resort & Spa offers unrivaled views of the waters of the Gulf of Thailand and Ang Thong National Marine Park. Sip a cocktail at the swim-up bar and look across the azure sea to limestone islands and jungle-covered hillsides along the southwest coast.

Set in a coconut plantation perched on the side of a hill, rooms at the resort are furnished in traditional Thai style with vaulted ceilings, teak furniture, rich batik silks, and polished hardwood floors. Terraces look out far across the bay, and the gardens are a riot of color, bursting with tropical, scented blooms. Cliff villas, high on the hillside, have the most dramatic views.

> *"The views are stunning—small islands disappear over the horizon into flat, calm seas."*
>
> Caroline Wingfield, *Independent*

Sit at low tables to eat Thai cuisine at Baan Chantra restaurant while musicians play classical Thai music, or have a private dinner in the romantic setting of the covered *sala* next to the infinity pool or on the beach surrounded by flaming torches. After a day on the private white-sand beach or at one of the seven pools, retreat to the spa for a traditional massage, then relax in the herbal steam room or soak in a petal-filled bath.

Beyond the beach, go diving in the marine park, or try windsurfing and kayaking. Or head inland to explore the jungle interior with waterfalls, craggy cliffs, and elephant treks. It is difficult to stay away for long when such tranquility awaits at the resort. **AD**

Recharge at Kamalaya

Location Koh Samui, Thailand **Website** www.kamalaya.com
Price ⊖⊖

"The idea behind Kamalaya is that by the time you leave, you'll be happy, healthy, and relaxed."

Tiffany Darke, *The Times*

On the tropical island of Koh Samui in the Gulf of Thailand, Kamalaya is a wellness sanctuary and holistic spa. Its name is an amalgamation of *kamal*, meaning "lotus," and *alaya*, an ancient symbol for the growth and unfolding of the human spirit. Everything at Kamalaya is aimed at nurturing the spirit: from the food, to the environment, to the many health programs on offer, such as qigong, tai chi, meditation, yoga, Tibetan singing bowls therapy, and spirit dance. This is a place geared toward finding inner peace.

Guests can relax on a white-sand beach or by a swimming pool set among flowering lotus ponds and waterfalls, or try out the warm and cool plunge pools. The center is elegantly designed with large open spaces that offer breathtaking views and allow guests to feel at one with the surrounding nature. Drawing on holistic medicine and complementary therapies from Eastern and Western traditions, there is a wealth of treatments aimed at detoxification, losing weight, or rejuvenating the tired body and mind. Visitors can choose from Indian head massage, Chi Nei Tsang Taoist abdominal massage, and the traditional Chinese medicinal practices of acupuncture, moxibustion, and cupping. The food is a fusion of Eastern and Western cuisine, and guests can also try out a range of herbal elixirs and medicinal teas.

Whether you are simply taking in the view or exploring the benefits of yoga, the sense of serenity and community spirit at Kamalaya provides an escape, and may perhaps help you hold on to a feeling of peace even when you have left Kamalaya behind. **CK**

↖ *The spa is set on a hilltop among granite rocks and trees with spectacular views out to sea and mountains.*

Discover Tongsai Bay

Location Koh Samui, Thailand   **Website** www.tongsaibay.co.th
Price ⑤⑤⑤⑤

Outdoor life is what the Tongsai Bay is all about. The beautifully designed rooms have as much space outside on the open-air terrace as they have inside, which means cooling sea breezes and jaw-dropping ocean views are never far away. The huge teak Grand Villas nestle into the hillside to the right of the bay. Soak in the petal-strewn outdoor bathtub while watching the sunset and sleep under the stars in the gazebo draped with white curtains. Each of the Pool Villas has a private 50-foot (15-m) plunge pool, surrounded by palm-fringed gardens—the perfect place for a cooling dip after soaking up the sun.

Still run by the Hoontrakuls, The Tongsai Bay is the only five-star, family-run resort on the island, with service that is genuinely warm and welcoming. Find a quiet spot to relax on the stretch of beach shelving into the azure sea, or chill by one of the two pools. There is sailing, canoeing, windsurfing, and snorkeling to experience and a chance to meet some of the family at the twice-weekly cocktail party. If you can pull yourself away from the resort, go to nearby Wat Phra Yai to see the mighty Big Buddha statue glittering in the sun. Return in the evening to sample authentic Thai cuisine in chef Chom's à la carte restaurant, or else have an intimate dinner in the Butler's Restaurant, which seats a maximum of twenty guests on the hillside overlooking the crescent-shaped pool.

The place to ease away the stresses of modern life is the Prana Spa, a haven of relaxation on the beachfront, offering soothing treatments and revitalizing massages —plus wonderful open-air floral baths, of course. **AD**

◁ *Overlooking a secluded white-sand beach, the resort sits on the exclusive northeast corner of the coast.*

Stay at the Sanctuary

Location Koh Phangan, Thailand
Website www.thesanctuarythailand.com **Price** $

It takes two speedboats to get to the Sanctuary on Haad Tien beach, but the secluded location merely adds to the allure. With daily yoga, meditation, tai chi, and shamanic journeys, as well as a phenomenal seafood and vegetarian restaurant by the sea, this holistic hideaway feeds body and soul.

Visitors come from around the globe to take part in the on-site fasting and cleansing programs. Led by Moon, a fasting devotee who looks far younger than his years, participants can be spotted popping herbal tablets on schedule, emerging from their daily colonics, and, finally, returning to real food with the restaurant's colorful raw menu. There is also massage

> *"The Sanctuary has grown from a single hut into a full-fledged retreat ... overlooking the beach."*
>
> *Time* magazine (Asia)

within stumbling distance from the shore, and the Sanctuary spa, where you can get scrubbed down with pineapple before you get to work on your tan.

By night the restaurant has an L.A. feel, with a collection of flip-flops by the entrance, twinkling lights strung above hammocks, and a constant soundtrack that never gets boring. The fire circus likes to come out and play after dinner, and every Friday night you can dance until dawn at the beach's renowned parties, a far tamer and more pleasant alternative to the legendary full-moon parties on nearby Haad Rin. A few Westerners came to work here and never left. They look like the happiest people in the world. **JS**

Relax at Amanpuri

Location Phuket, Thailand
Website www.amanpuri.com **Price** $ $ $

At Amanpuri, an austere sanctuary set off a dirt path, hidden walkways, sliding doors, and clever camouflage effects create instant Zen—a perpetual sense of infinity extending from the slate-gray pools peeping out onto the Andaman up to the ocean-view rooms reaching up into the sky. It is the ultimate hideout in which to recuperate from the strains of everyday life, because the sounds of the sea, birds, and leaves act like a salve to the soul, and the slatted *sala* affords glimpses of the trees beneath your feet. Posited high on the jungle knoll, you are king, disturbed by nothing but the silent service laying out refreshments or scuttling geckos come to nose around.

Back at ground zero, the sense of space and consideration continues. Amanpuri lays claim to the only private beach on the island of Phuket: an arcing, golden crescent of coastline flanked by the slate-gray boulders that set the tone for the design.

Amanpuri's restaurant ranks among the best on the island. Like the resort itself, it offers a textbook example in subtlety, well-being, and flair. The Italian menu is crafted from the pearls of the southern hemisphere; its views extend over the inky sea by night. If private beaches, hidden salas, and treetop contemplation are not enough, then Amanpuri's adjoining private residences offer total seclusion and multiple spaces, from swimming pools to games rooms and a variety of bedrooms in which to sleep. Personal staff are ready to minister to your every need. Amanpuri means "place of peace," and the resort certainly lives up to its name. **VG**

➔ *A haven of exclusivity, the flagship Aman residence sets a precedent in discretion and design aplomb.*

Stay at the Nam Hai

Location Quang Nam, Vietnam
Website www.ghmhotels.com **Price** 💲💲💲

Professional traveler Bill Bryson once wrote that as tourists we expend vast quantities of time and money in a largely futile attempt to re-create the comforts we already have at home. Bill's travels have clearly never allowed him the pleasure of a stay at the Nam Hai.

The resort is a showcase of pure luxury, with one hundred stunning designer villas set in perfect symmetry around manicured lawns and infinity pools that glide seamlessly into the unspoiled white sands of Ha My beach and the aqua-blue waters of the South China Sea, creating an air of peace and tranquility. Inside the opulent villas, there is an abundance of space and light: Split-level platforms contain king-size beds adorned with a mountain of soft cushions; bathrooms boast lengthy, eggshell-lacquered baths opening out onto private gardens for optional alfresco showering; daybeds and giant sofas are located on the terrace for afternoon napping. The forty pool villas have private temperature-controlled swimming pools and the added indulgence of a personal butler.

The five-star quality extends to the two restaurants, which feature an appetizing fusion of traditional Vietnamese fare, international cuisine, and fresh seafood. Rejuvenation can be sought at the eight peaceful spa villas surrounding a lotus pond, where a variety of exquisite treatments will almost certainly bring about an enormous sense of well-being—if not, there is always the comfort of the bar to iron out any last remaining vestiges of stress. Should you begin to suffer from relaxation fatigue, the ancient port city of Hoi An is a mere fifteen-minute car ride away. An intoxicating mix of tailor's shops, markets, riverside cafés, art galleries, and historic buildings, the city is a must-see if you wish to reach inside the real Vietnam. **SG**

Enjoy Résidence Phou Vao

Location Luang Prabang, Laos
Website www.residencephouvao.com **Price** 💲💲

La Résidence Phou Vao sits on top of a hill blanketed in frangipani and palms, and has breathtaking views over Mount Phou Si, Luang Prabang's sacred mountain, and the golden dome of the Vat Chamsi stupa.

The hotel is a sprawling French colonial mansion, with bleached white walls, burnt sienna–tiled roofs, and spacious shuttered verandas—a serious temple to Asian chic. Narrow footpaths wind past crumbling Buddhist stupas and tropical gardens to the spa—local-style pavilions set around a lily pond. Massages and facial treatments use traditional Lao remedies to nurture the body and soul. Relax in the herbal steam room, or float in the infinity pool overlooking the

> *"The ancient city of Luang Prabang, in Laos, is one of the most magical in the world."*
>
> *Evening Standard*

valley. More adventurous guests can rent a bicycle to explore Luang Prabang, the ancient capital and home to the Golden Buddha, or take a cooking class with the hotel chef, who serves French cuisine and traditional Lao dishes in the poolside restaurant.

Rooms are in a traditional style with rich cottons and rosewood furniture. Private terraces look out across the forest canopy to distant mountains dotted with pagodas. There is no noise, apart from the occasional chanting of monks drifting up from the valley. **AD**

➡ *It can be difficult to pull yourself away to explore the World Heritage town nestled in the valley below.*

Unwind at Six Senses Hideaway Ninh Van Bay

Location Khanh Hoa, Vietnam **Website** www.sixsenses.com
Price 💲💲💲

Accessible only by water, the Six Senses Hideaway at Ninh Van Bay is utterly secluded and dazzlingly beautiful. Velvety white sand glistens below towering verdant mountains, and the sea is mesmerizing with its multiple shades of blue.

All the villas at the resort were designed according to Vietnamese architectural traditions and offer the utmost in luxury, with their own gardens, handcrafted wooden bathtubs, wine cellars, and walk-in closets. The Water Villas are easily the most romantic and are accessed by wooden teak boats. Each one has a private teak deck and faces the unparalleled sunsets—perfect for honeymooners. The Spa Suite Villas are for those who want to be pampered; they have their own steam rooms and in-villa spa treatment facilities.

The world-class Six Senses Spa blends into the environment and nestles beside a gentle waterfall to allow the soothing sound of the water and the aroma of essential oils to infuse the air. Expert therapists melt troubles away with traditional Vietnamese and holistic treatments. Such pampering works up an appetite, and thankfully the dining options are impressive. The restaurants are intimate and romantic, but you can also enjoy private barbecues at your villa or on the beach, dinner on the jetty or in the intimate wine cave. By day there are lots of castaway beaches and coves to explore, water sports, and scuba diving. The coastal city of Nha Trang is twenty minutes away by boat. For the ultimate in elusive beach escapes, Six Senses Hideaway Ninh Van Bay is hard to beat. **LP**

⮕ *There is a range of lavish villas on the beachfront, where pools have been crafted over rock formations.*

Relax at Whale Island Resort

Location Khanh Hoa, Vietnam
Website www.iledelabaleine.com   **Price** Ⓢ

North of Nha Trang, Vietnam's largest seaside resort, tiny Whale Island lies in Van Phong Bay amid the warm waters of the South China Sea. The island is circled by a protective archipelago, and diving is its main attraction. From January to October each year, experienced divers can swim among tropical fish and coral gardens, through labyrinths and caves. They will find sting rays, manta rays, and moray eels, sea horses, clown fish, and giant Spanish dancers. There are dives for beginners, too, and qualified instructors ready to guide novices.

The months between April and July are particularly spectacular around Whale Island. Whales and whale sharks come to Van Phong Bay to feed on the abundant krill and plankton, and, toward the end of March and beginning of April, the locals hold religious ceremonies to welcome these creatures to their waters.

For those who like to keep their head above water, Whale Island also offers catamarans, windsurfing, and canoes. On land, meanwhile, the island features accommodation in twenty-three bamboo bungalows. They are simple thatched constructions—think fan and shower room rather than air-conditioning and whirlpool tub—but simplicity is the joy of this place. Step out of your door and your toes will sink into the island's white sands. Bamboo loungers surrounded by trees and flowers beckon indolent afternoons. The restaurant's menu depends on what the fishermen bring in during the morning: One evening you may be served swordfish and barracuda, another tuna, crab, grouper, and shrimp. The menu is new each day—and the ingredients are sensationally fresh. Robinson Crusoe fans, should look no farther. On Whale Island your desert island dreams could come true. **PE**

Unwind at Evason Ana Mandara Villas Dalat

Location Lam Dong, Vietnam
Website www.sixsenses.com   **Price** ⓈⓈ

Evason Ana Mandara Villas Dalat is a sophisticated getaway with a heavenly spa, hidden among woodland in the rural highlands of south central Vietnam. Dalat abounds with vivid green landscape and a plethora of colorful flowers, and has a year-round pleasant climate, giving rise to its affectionate nickname of "the city of eternal spring." It is a strikingly beautiful, seemingly magical land of tumbling waterfalls, pine-scented forests, and lakes such as the majestic Xuan Huong. When mist descends during the rainy season (April to October), the city and forests are swallowed up in it, as if a strange spell has been cast.

> *"Striking views . . . abound from all areas of the gently sloping hillside property."*
>
> vietnamstay.com

Guests are housed in French colonial villas that were built in the 1920s and 1930s. They are well located to explore the city of Dalat, with its European-inspired architecture, palaces, and flower park. There is much to awaken the senses inside the retreat, too, not least the Six Senses spa. Treatments include traditional Vietnamese massage and therapies incorporating fresh rose petals and Vietnamese green tea.

Romantics will enjoy a visit to Than Tho lake, where a *Romeo and Juliet*–type story is said to have taken place. A woman, who wrongly believed her lover had died, drowned herself in the lake, and the surrounding pine trees are said to have sighed in grief ever since. **LP**

Explore the Mekong by Boat

Location Mekong River, Vietnam
Website www.cruisemekong.com **Price** ⊖⊖

As the sun slowly sinks into the horizon, the entire sky is ablaze with red and orange. The waters of the Mekong River seem to be on fire as the tour boat slowly cruises toward the sunset.

The Mekong River is a huge 2,980 miles (4,800 km) long. Beginning on the Tibetan Plateau, it is fed by myriad lakes and waterways as it stretches through China, Myanmar, Laos, Thailand, Cambodia, and Vietnam before emptying into the South China Sea. Cruising down the river is a unique and picturesque journey. By day you will glide through wide waterways, past wetlands and thick tropical forest. In the evening, nothing beats sitting up on deck with a glass of wine, watching the magnificent sunset. The entire sky burns bright orange, the warm hues lighting up the water. The sun blazes so brightly you almost expect to hear a sizzling noise as it dips below the watery horizon.

The delta is one of the most densely populated places in the world. It gives a fascinating glimpse into the everyday lives of the Vietnamese people who reside and work along its banks. You will see floating schools, markets, and houses, all designed to cope with the annual floods. They may seem like an inconvenience, but the floods that occur every rainy season are actually a vital natural process. They bring millions of fish south to spawn and replace soil worn away through natural erosion. The locals have adapted their lives around the river. Traders chatter noisily at the floating markets, enticing you to buy fresh fish, fruit, and exotic tropical flowers. **JP**

⊡ *The locals paddle their wooden boats through the muddy brown waters as tourists watch the sunset.*

"This river has seen the rise and fall of empires and battles between foes of different races and cultures."

mekongboat.com

Hide Away at Amanpulo

Location Pamalican Island, Philippines
Website www.amanresorts.com   **Price** ⑨⑨⑨

Escape the world in style on this private island in the Philippines where powder-white sands meet crystal-clear seas and tropical palms sway across bright turquoise skies. Amanpulo means "peaceful island," which could not be a more fitting description. It is part of an archipelago of more than 7,000 tropical islands dotted along the coast southwest of Manila. Fly in on the resort's own nineteen-seater twin-engine plane to the island's airstrip for an unforgettable arrival.

The beach, hillside, and treetop casitas are modeled on authentic *bahay kubo* dwellings, a centuries-old style of family home with steep pitched roofs on timber frames. Hillside casitas offer magical sea views, whereas beach casitas have private overgrown paths leading to the beach. They are all discreetly nestled among the sand-floored tropical foliage, and guests have their own buggy for island exploration. Inside, subtle interiors are warm and sun-dappled, in shades of caramel and bamboo. Bathrooms have raised Cebu marble bathtubs and honey-brown wooden floors.

Laze on the beach, swing in a hammock under a coconut palm, or lie back in one of the open-air *salas* and enjoy a relaxing holistic body treatment. There is a 100-foot (30-m) pool to cool off in, or head out to sea and dive the coral reef, only 1,000 feet (300 m) from the shore. Choose from a European and Asian menu in the restaurant, which spills out onto a terrace that has views to Manamoc Island across the channel. After dinner, take in the star-studded night sky from the terrace of the bar where a telescope looks heavenward and staff offer a guide to the stars for beginners. **AD**

← *What could be more romantic than a dinner served to you on the beach as you listen to the waves breaking?*

Visit El Nido Lagen

Location Palawan, Philippines
Website www.elnidoresorts.com   **Price** ⑨⑨

The setting for El Nido Lagen Island Resort is surely the definition of seclusion. It overlooks a cove fringed by a white-sand beach and is surrounded by limestone cliffs and rain forest. Part of a marine reserve of more than 600 islands off the most northern tip of Palawan, El Nido is ideal for castaways with a taste for eco-chic. Some cottages are built on stilts over the water; others overlook the 10 acres (4 ha) of tropical grounds. All have verandas, and inside furnishings are crafted from wood from traditional Filipino houses.

This resort is paradise for snorkelers and divers, with its crystal-clear water and reefs teeming with tropical fish. Take a kayak out to get a closer look at limestone

> *"[El Nido] is among the conservation minded places on a mission to protect the local environment."*
>
> *Travel+Leisure* magazine

caves and lagoons; try rock climbing or a hike through the rain forest to see monkeys. The Lagen trail is one of the best sites for bird-watching, to spot flocks of hornbills taking off early in the morning. Guests may also take a boat trip to explore the tiny islands, deserted beaches, and cliffs in the area.

In the evening, an open-air buffet restaurant serves delicious fresh local seafood. After dinner, you can escape to the nearby lagoon where the soaring limestone cliffs provide the perfect acoustics for concerts. A string quartet and tenor appear on a floating platform in the water, under the spotlight of a full moon. A slice of heaven right here on earth. **AD**

Relax at Datai

Location Langkawi, Malaysia
Website www.ghmhotels.com **Price**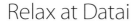

Beautifully cocooned in Langkawi's ancient tropical rain forest, Datai is a true hideaway heaven. Set on the island's less-developed northern coast, the complex fronts onto a sumptuously sandy beach facing the Andaman Sea. Blending comfortably into its verdant jungle setting, the well-designed resort features open-air walkways, pavilions, and hutlike villas on stilts, leaving the lush surroundings intact and alive with wildlife. Chattering monkeys and giant flying squirrels leap from tree to tree while geckos and lizards laze in sun-splashed spots. A resident conservationist leads nature walks through rough tracks in the surrounding virgin rain forest to point out birds and bats.

"Datai bay has the island's best beaches—white sands and jungle-clad cliffs."

Andrew Catchpole, *Guardian*

Although this is real back-to-nature stuff, a stay at the opulent Datai is a lavish affair. Expect Bose sound systems, Molton Brown products, and staff who remember every guest's name. For top Thai food in an open-air setting, head to the Pavilion, a stilted restaurant raised up in the rain forest canopy. Fancy a dose of pampering? Amble along to the open-air spa where signature treatments range from warm stone massage to an aromatherapy foot polish. The resort's golf course is gloriously set amid the rain forest, flanked by the Andaman Sea and the Mat Cincan mountain range. Active types can rent a bicycle—a great way to explore the mainly traffic-free island. **JK**

Unwind at Pangkor Laut

Location Pangkor, Malaysia
Website www.pangkorlautresort.com **Price**

Situated off the west coast of Peninsular Malaysia, the resort at Pangkor Laut was opened by Luciano Pavarotti in 1994, who is said to have fallen in love with the island, exclaiming, "How beautiful God has made this paradise." Pangkor Laut's beauty is much more than skin deep, however, and there is substance here alongside style, with an excellent standard of service and top-of-the-range facilities. The accommodation is luxurious, with the most opulent being the Pavarotti Suite. This elegant two-bedroom suite has an open-roofed bathroom and a large balcony overlooking the sea, which affords some of the island's best views from its position high in the rain forest.

Delicious local dishes are served in the elegantly contemporary Fisherman's Cove restaurant, which employs homegrown ingredients, including herbs from the spa village garden, in its fresh seafood dishes. But, for something really special, shun the restaurant in favor of the luxury of private dining, offered either in your own villa or in a romantic setting under the stars on the beach at Emerald Bay.

The languorous pace of life at Pangkor Laut continues in the spa village, where a complete range of treatments inspired by the region's abundance of natural resources and renowned history of healing is on offer. The traditional Malay massage, consisting of long, kneading strokes performed with a unique oil made from local ingredients, including cinnamon and citronella, is a deeply relaxing treat, but the pinnacle of indulgence has to be the ultimate spa experience that takes place in the Belian Spa Pavilion, with its own outdoor whirlpool tub, yoga pavilion, nap gazebo, steam room, and private treatment area—this is one pampering session that is not to be missed. **HO**

Explore Perhentian Islands

Location Perhentian Islands, Malaysia
Website www.perhentian.com.my **Price** $

The Perhentian Islands off the east coast of Malaysia are about as near to perfect as a beach retreat can get. There are two islands to choose between. Perhentian Besar is the largest; it is more appropriate for families and those looking for some tranquility. Perhentian Kecil is more often chosen by price-conscious backpackers. Both islands offer several palm-fringed beaches that arc their way past jungle-covered inlands, each of which has a choice of accommodation.

Although most visitors come here to while away a few days under the palm trees, there are a few other things to do. Snorkeling and diving are the major activities, and competition between diving schools

> *"The Perhentian Islands are such a nice place to be. . . . No roads, no mass-market tourism—bliss."*
>
> Jack Barker, *Independent*

makes Perhentian one of the world's cheapest places for a dive. Green turtles and black-tipped reef sharks can often be found around the reefs, and myriad other aquatic species, such as clams, eels, sea snakes, and cuttlefish, are a common sight. Jungle treks can also be arranged with guides, and sea kayaks can be rented if you fancy exploring the water on your own.

Inevitably the islands have, in some places, lost their untouched quality, with Long Beach on Perhentian Kecil being particularly built up. Many other beaches contain just a single resort, and some are completely free of man-made intrusions. During peak season, February to October, it can get quite busy. **JD**

Recharge at the Aryani

Location Terengganu, Malaysia
Website www.thearyani.com **Price** $

Inspired by an ancient sultan's palace, the Aryani was built in the style of a traditional fortress and draws on classical Malay architecture throughout. Situated on the east coast of Malaysia, which has one of the longest coastlines in the country and offers white-sand beaches, marine parks, and top-class snorkeling and diving, the Aryani sits at the edge of the warm South China Sea, in the fishing village of Kuala Terengganu.

This is a gorgeous hideaway where it is easy to relax and instantly feel at one with nature. Succumb to an incredible massage or float away under the relaxing ministrations of one of the facialists. If you are a bit of a spa princess who likes her treatments in pristine white surroundings, you might be better off elsewhere. Set amid coconut fronds, banana trees, and tropical flowers, and reconstructed from original timber to provide an authentic sense of an old Malay building, the Aryani's Heritage Spa is a wooden hut on stilts. The tiny gaps in the wooden walls allow fresh flower-scented air to flow inside, and the lack of cold, tiled treatment rooms gives the exquisite sense of being pampered inside a luxurious tree house. There is no need for oxygen facials here, because the fresh ocean breeze and exotic scents wafting through the windows do the job naturally.

Surrender to a floor cushion and be massaged, scrubbed, and invigorated with herbs, spices, fruits, and flowers. Then soak in the outdoor tub with fragrant jasmine, tropical magnolia blooms, and rose petals while the waves crash on the shore beyond shady frangipani leaves. Afterward, sip a chilled lemongrass tea, the Aryani's signature drink, at the Pulau Beach Club. The Aryani's rich and royal ambience soon has guests feeling every bit the sultan or sultana. **SD**

Trek Through Gunung Leuser National Park

Location Sumatra, Indonesia
Website www.geocities.com/rainforest/4466/leuser1.htm   **Price**

Gunung Leuser National Park in Sumatra—the largest island belonging entirely to Indonesia—consists of several different nature reserves covering a 62-mile (100-km) stretch of the volcanic Bukit Barisan mountain range. Named after its highest peak, 11,100-foot (3,381-m) Gunung Leuser, the park comprises many steep areas that are inaccessible to humans and hence constitute a refuge for threatened animals such as the Sumatran orangutan, the smaller and rarer of the two species of orangutan. Estimates put their number at 5,000, and at the Orangutan Rehabilitation Center in Bukit Lawang—the park's main access point—visitors can get a closer look at these great apes.

The region also distinguishes itself as the only place where orangutans, crocodiles, rhinoceroses, elephants, and tigers all share the same habitat. The great differences in altitude mean the park also boasts an eclectic mix of plant species, exemplified by the various types of forest that cover the terrain, ranging from rain forest in the lowlands to beech and swamp forests as well as subalpine forest higher up the mountains.

In order to explore this vast expanse, it is best to go on an organized trekking tour. These tours can last from a few hours to two weeks, with accommodation provided in tents that are pitched in caves, or in basic bungalows by the river. Given the park's extraordinary biodiversity—with more than 700 animal species—an extended stay is advisable to fully appreciate the contrast between this unspoiled natural habitat and the man-made world we know as home. **DaH**

→ *One of the three national parks within the Tropical Rainforest of Heritage of Sumatra World Heritage site.*

Stay at Amanjiwo

Location Java, Indonesia **Website** www.amanresorts.com
Price ❸❸❸❸

The world's largest Buddhist sanctuary, the eighth-century Borobudur temple stands opposite a breathtaking circular limestone monolith; the Menoreh Hills rise behind, and volcanos smoke gently in the distance. A deep sense of serenity pervades throughout. This is Amanjiwo; perhaps the world's most spiritual escape.

Do not be surprised to see fellow guests meditating in quiet spots or discussing the meaning of life. Amanjiwo, set in the verdant countryside of central Java, provokes serious contemplation thanks to its awe-inspiring setting amid ancient monuments. A box of watercolors is even provided in each suite for those who feel moved to capture their resplendent surroundings on canvas. However, there is no monklike abstinence here. Guests stay in one of thirty-four domed suites with beds surrounded by majestic pillars and hand-carved furniture. Many have private pools and all have views of sacred mountains, hills, or the Borobudur temple. Then there is the colonnaded pool club, with a 130-foot (40-m) infinity pool stretching into paddy fields, serene dining room and bar, and the spa area, where guests can sample the royal treat of Mandi Lulur, a traditional Javanese preparation of a princess on the eve of her wedding.

It is the less tangible things at Amanjiwo that leave a lasting impression, such as being showered with rose petals by local sarong-clad girls upon arrival and exploring Dagi Hill on the back of a Sumatran elephant. Guests return home from Amanjiwo feeling, quite literally, blessed. **LP**

> *"Amanjiwo's architecture renders it the perfect complement to Borobudur's timeworn grandeur."*
>
> *Daily Telegraph*

↖ *Amanjiwo has a grand temple-like appearance with soaring stone columns and a mystical aura.*

Relax at Waka Gangga

Location Bali, Indonesia **Website** www.wakagangga.com
Price 💲💲

Perched on rolling rice terraces overlooking the Indian Ocean, Waka Gangga's blend of elegance, luxury, and seclusion is as magical as it is seductive. These ten exclusive natural bungalows and six private villas are built from local materials, and the resort's eco-credentials are solid enough to have earned it an environmental tourism award. On one side are the slick rice fields and on the other a black-sand beach slips into the sea, although swimming in the sea in trickier weather is discouraged due to some often harsh undercurrents. Horses from the local stables can take you the short journey down the sand toward the famous rock-cleaved Tanah Lot temple, one of South Bali's most sacred places.

Waka Gangga is purely about relaxation. The rooms, shorn of some of the ultra-slick modern gadgets you might find elsewhere, almost demand that you forget your worries and learn how to relax. Unpainted woods, local fabrics, alang-alang grass roofs, and stone villas with their dressed slate and copious flowers all flow harmoniously with the surrounding area. Despite the rustic nature of the resort, basic amenities such as air-conditioning are provided, and all rooms have deluxe king-size beds, open fireplaces, large sofas, sunken bathtubs, garden showers, and an outside sundeck. The resort's shared areas are also comprehensive, and include an art gallery, library, and spa and yoga area—all perfect ways to help you unwind even further. Cocktails are served at sunset in the bar before you dive into the delightful Balinese food served in the restaurant, which comes with a camera-grabbing ocean view thanks to its cliff-edge location. That spectacular vista is a reminder as to why Bali's nickname is, deservedly, "island of the gods." **PS**

De-stress at Alila Ubud

Location Bali, Indonesia **Website** www.alilahotels.com/Ubud
Price 💲💲

Ten minutes from the Balinese cultural capital Ubud lies an oasis of sheer beauty that cannot fail to alleviate stress. The real world seems light years away when you alight at the tranquil and secluded hill resort of Alila Ubud, a place designed specifically to complement its gorgeous surroundings as well as to emulate a traditional Balinese hill village.

With fifty-six rooms and eight villas, a stay here is about waving the wider world good-bye and entering an idealistic inner state of peace and tranquility. There are lots of ways to de-stress, starting with the rooms themselves. Those on the ground floor boast their own garden terraces, plus invigorating and refreshing

> *"The emerald infinity pool … has been called one of the most beautiful pools in the world."*
>
> *Daily Telegraph*

open-air showers and bathrooms that let you commune as closely with nature as you like. The views from the wraparound private balconies of the rooms above are nothing short of stunning.

Massages, needless to say, are magnificent at Spa Alila, and the resort's library and 24-hour, in-room dining service help promote the relaxed vibe. Tours of the mountain village of Kintamani and the nearby rice terraces at Tegalalang are available; the volcanic surroundings provide not only a sense of eternal majesty but are also a reminder of the harsh forces that created this place millions of years ago. All in all, Alila Ubud is the perfect place to be at one with yourself. **PS**

Stay at Gajah Mina

Location Bali, Indonesia
Website www.gajahminaresort.com   **Price** $

This simple little hideaway stands in a lonely spot on the picturesque southwest coast of the island, among rice paddy fields and local temples, miles from tourist resorts. There are only nine Mediterranean-style villas forming an intimate boutique beach hotel. They stand in a garden of fragrant flowers and enormous butterflies, overlooking Gajah Mina's private black-sand beach and jagged volcanic rocks, riddled with caves and ancient stone carvings. Guests explore grassy cliff tops, rice paddies, coconut groves, and empty sandy beaches that stretch for 19 miles (30 km). Energetic visitors take mountain bike trails through cocoa plantations to a nearby volcano; others surf the powerful, pounding waves.

Back at your villa, it is peaceful and private within individual walled gardens with terraces looking out across the rugged coast and rice fields. Inside the bungalows you will find the same simple atmosphere —natural materials like volcanic stone, coconut wood, and teak, a few Indonesian antiques, a big, comfortable bed, a bit of stained glass, and a lounge chair under your private veranda to slump in and stare at the waves. You can slump still further under the influence of a traditional Balinese massage in a thatched pavilion alongside the palm-fringed swimming pool or with a yoga session among the bird songs and fragrant flowers. Food is another relaxed highlight at Gajah Mina. The restaurant menu, with lots of organic vegetables and fresh seafood, is a unique blend of local Balinese cuisine and the owner's French influence. Specialties include banana flower curry or mahi mahi fish in green pepper sauce. And that is it. Gajah Mina is just a quiet and beautiful spot—a place to be romantic and a place to relax. **SH**

Experience Tembok Bali

Location Bali, Indonesia
Website www.spavillage.com/tembokbali   **Price** $ $

Set among a striking landscape of soaring peaks, black volcanic beaches, and the twinkling sapphire Indian Ocean, Spa Villa Resort Tembok Bali is a mecca for spa aficionados. Balinese spas are not only about hedonistic pampering but are also infused with a heritage of ancient healing remedies. Visiting a spa is about cleansing the mind and soul as well as the body, and that is exactly what the Spa Villa Resort, in the unspoiled north of the island, is all about.

The resort provides each visitor with a tailored program, which begins upon arrival. Guests are welcomed with a foot massage and are invited to select a "discovery path": balance, creativity, or vigor.

> *"Tembok Bali's only neighbors are small fishing settlements and the odd roadside shop."*
>
> *Independent*

Everything from wood carving and basket weaving to guided meditation and scuba diving can be incorporated into a program.

Despite the focus on spirituality, life's simple pleasures are not denied. Guests may enjoy cocktails beside the large infinity pool, and a spectacle of seafood and organic seasonal fare is served daily in the Wantilan restaurant. The suites and villas both provide flawlessly luxurious accommodation. There are also many activities offered, such as a sunset cruise on a traditional Balinese boat to admire the towering Gunung Agung mountain. Above all, the resort delights in celebrating ancient Balinese culture, and is all the better for it. **LP**

Relax at Panchoran Retreat

Location Bali, Indonesia
Website www.lindagarland.com   **Price** 🟢🟢

What do you do when you have a beautiful home in an idyllic location and you feel inclined to share your good fortune with others? Well, in Linda Garland's case, you turn your home into an incredible hotel. Garland's unique and peaceful 25-acre (10-ha) haven, Panchoran Retreat, located along a river gorge close to Bali's cultural capital of Ubud, was transformed in 2003 from her own private hideaway into a blissful ecological sanctuary for worldwide visitors.

Panchoran—meaning "water spring" in Balinese—blends in effortlessly with its surroundings. Throughout the Main House, Waterfall House, and River House, the style is shabby-chic. The large thatched villas embody effortless cool, with lots of scented flowers, Javanese carvings, hammocks, open-air showers, and beds draped in mosquito nets. Waterfall House has a natural spring-fed pool and outdoor whirlpool tub. It overlooks the waterfalls, which provide a perpetual soothing soundtrack. River House is larger and has a pool and a generous deck overlooking rice fields and a bamboo forest.

Delicious Indonesian meals are whipped up using ingredients from the estate's organic garden, and a masseuse trained in traditional Balinese techniques is at hand to help ease away any nagging stress. The estate seems to cast a spell over artists and romantics seeking absolute solitude. Only a short walk through the Monkey Forest from the bohemian town of Ubud with its ancient temples, hip cafés, and thriving cultural scene, the retreat offers a different kind of magic just waiting to be discovered. **LP**

> ⬀ *Panchoran was built and decorated using recycled ironwood, bamboo, and other natural materials.*

"I wanted to promote the use of bamboo as an alternative to wood in decoration and architecture."

Linda Garland, designer, Panchoran Retreat

Enjoy Villa Balquisse

Location Bali, Indonesia
Website www.balquisse.com **Price** ⊝⊝

Step through the carved stone doorway into Villa Balquisse and you will find glorious Indian fabric draped across an old Moroccan sofa and old metal lamps hanging from wooden roof beams. An antique Indonesian carved wooden elephant stares out across the worn stone floor. Welcome to one of Bali's most glamorous boutique hotels.

The hotel and its restored Balinese villas are set in tropical gardens between a mangrove swamp and a coconut grove in the popular village of Jimbaran. The beach is a few hundred yards away. The owner is a Moroccan-born interior designer, hence the stunning eclectic atmosphere. Among the traditional Balinese

> *"Chairs and tables stretch down toward the water attracting visitors eager to dine under the stars."*

Jo Adetunji, *Guardian*

architecture there are chandeliers, French baroque chairs, enamel standalone baths, and Arabic screens.

The villas have private pools, and guests in the main hotel have an emerald swimming pool surrounded by bamboo, palms, and bougainvillea. Dinner is a fine mix of local ingredients with culinary inspiration from India, Indonesia, South-East Asia, the Middle East, and Europe. Enjoy a Moroccan couscous by candlelight, followed by a wonderful five spice crème brûlée. The open-air, thatched spa is as unique as the hotel, and traditional Balinese massages are a specialty. Many glossy magazines have published photographs taken at Villa Balquisse—but it is even better in real life. **SH**

Cruise Lesser Sunda

Location Lombok Strait, Indonesia
Website www.lomboksailing.com **Price** ⊝⊝⊝

Traveling on a boat that blends in with the stunning scenery is the best way to enjoy the turquoise waters surrounding Indonesia's Lesser Sunda islands. A few hours' sail west of Bali in the Lombok Strait—the biogeographical boundary between the Indo-Malayan animal kingdom and its distinctively different Australasian counterpart—the small island of Gili Trawangan is home to an 82-foot (25-m) hand-built wooden vessel whose elegance is reminiscent of the ships used by European explorers in centuries gone by. Staffed with four crew members and a captain, the *Bulan Purnama* has a maximum capacity of nine passengers and ensures high standards of comfort. A lack of air-conditioning and hot showers prevents it from being classified as a luxury boat, but its nostalgic flair and the spectacular tropical surroundings make for an unforgettable and relaxing experience that is far removed from the daily grind.

The company that owns the boat can recommend several itineraries, but passengers are welcome to plan their own route according to the length of their cruise. However, one place that should not be missed is the 55,700-acre (22,540-ha) nature reserve Moyo Island Hunting Park on the island of the same name just north of Sumbawa. Covering most of the island, the park teems with wildlife such as deer, wild cattle, and numerous species of bird. The local marine park's coral reefs are popular with divers and snorkelers. Farther east, the World Heritage site of Komodo National Park is worth a visit, too. It is home to the world's largest lizard, the Komodo dragon: a 10-foot (3-m) carnivorous animal that looks like a relic from prehistoric times. A cruise on the *Bulan Purnama* is an experience that is unlike anything you will find back home. **DaH**

Stay at the Oberoi

Location Lombok, Indonesia
Website www.oberoilombok.com **Price** $$$$

The hotel is encircled by thick jungle, stands on a remote peninsula miles from any settlement, and is on a small, poor, and undeveloped island. But when guests step into the Oberoi's open-air reception area, immaculate uniformed staff descend from all directions —just as they would at the Ritz in Piccadilly, London.

Half the accommodations are villas surrounded by high stone walls, each with an individual gatehouse. Inside this personal perimeter, there is a pool, patio, thatched dining pavilion, fishponds, and lush gardens. The villa itself is a thatched stone bungalow with a giant canopied bed overlooking the sea and has a marvelous marble bathroom with private garden.

> *"A self-contained temple of pleasure complete with swimming pool and ornamental ponds."*
>
> Richard Madden, *Daily Telegraph*

Evening passes amid a spectacular amphitheater of bars and gourmet restaurants around a series of pools leading down to the beach. Everyone waits for the sun to set behind a distant volcano on Bali. By day, local craftsmen squat by the reception hall carving wonderful mahogany animals. Later local musicians play simple Indonesian music accompanied by a chorus of frogs and insects. The sea is calm, clear, and warm. Hotel boats will whisk you away for fishing, snorkeling, diving, or sightseeing trips to reefs and islands. Guests who opt for a sunset cruise will arrive at the jetty to find four staff members—one to steer the boat and three to mix the cocktails. **SH**

Unwind at Amanwana

Location Moyo Island, Indonesia
Website www.amanresorts.com **Price** $$$

Most of us have never heard of the island of Moyo, probably because it is one of the world's few remaining, totally unspoiled paradise islands—and it deserves protecting all the more so for it. A 135-square-mile (350-sq-km) drop in the ocean off the coast of Sumbawa, to the east of Bali, Moyo is remote, wild, and definitely not somewhere you are likely to bump into neighbors.

Reached by motor boat, turboprop floatplane, or even helicopter, Amanwana is set in one of Moyo's secluded coves and caressed by the bath-like waters of the Flores Sea. Twenty luxury tents—either jungle or ocean-front—provide stylish accommodation while macaque monkeys swing in the surrounding trees and sea eagles soar above in the aquamarine sky. Although covered in canvas, you can banish all thoughts of the boy-scout school of camping. These tents have solid wall foundations, king-size beds draped romantically in netting, large bathrooms, and elegant, polished wood interiors. Delicious Asian meals are served in an open-air pavilion with a soaring bamboo roof, and Borneo body scrubs take place beneath shady tamarind trees at the Jungle Cove spa.

There is plenty to do on the castaway island: Observe turtles mingling with pygmy seahorses on a scuba trip and wild boar foraging the land deeper into the nature reserve. The more adventurous guests can book the Komodo expedition, which combines time at the resort with a boat trip that takes you to two nearby islands inhabited by Komodo dragons.

How to round off a day in paradise? At Amanwana, which aptly means "peaceful forest," a campfire dinner on the beach with a dazzling sunset as a backdrop provides the perfect epilogue. **LP**

See Kelimutu Mountain

Location Flores, Indonesia
Website www.bali-travel-online.com   **Price** ❶

The island of Flores, east of Java and part of Indonesia's Lesser Sunda islands, has many claims to fame. For one, it is the home of indigenous giant rats and dwarf elephants. For another, archaeologists recently unearthed the remains of "real-life hobbits," a race of people that only averaged a height of 3 feet (1 m) and a possible predecessor of the pygmy.

Kelimutu Mountain is one of the best places in the world to watch the sun rise. Three volcanic crater lakes sit at its peak, and, because of the unusual geochemical conditions, the water in the lakes changes color. At the far west, the Lake of Old People has blue water; next to it, the Lake of Young Men and Maidens has green water, and sitting beside that is the red water of the Bewitched or Enchanted Lake on the southeast side of the volcano. Over time, the water changes color due to the fluctuating acidity levels—what was green one day might be black, coffee-colored, or bright blue on another day. Streaks of mineral deposits leak into the lake and provide yet more colors, confirming the theory that things on Flores do not operate according to the usual rules.

Visitors have to get up in the very early hours of the morning to drive up the mountain and walk the final steps to the top, but it is worth it. Watching the sun rise over an ethereal scene in the barren volcanic moonscape, with the painted pools of water behind, is an extraordinary experience. Some people have called the lakes "god's paint pots"; others say that they should be on the list of the Wonders of the World. You can certainly sit for hours and enjoy the view. **LD**

⬅ *The different colors of the lakes at the top of Kelimutu are a source of intrigue for geologists and tourists alike.*

Discover Nihiwatu

Location Sumba, Indonesia
Website www.nihiwatu.com   **Price** ❸❸

Sumba was once regarded by foreign traders as an island of fierce warriors where head-hunting expeditions were common. After battles with enemies and between clans, heads were considered to be trophies and were displayed on "skull trees" in the villages. Although this particular gory practice has—thankfully—died out, much of the small eastern Indonesian island's fascinating culture remains and the Sumbanese people still cherish their traditional way of life and tribal unity.

At Nihiwatu resort, which has been applauded for its dedication to helping local communities, visitors get an insight into the islanders' history from the Stone

> *"The resort is famous among surfers for the fat left-hander that breaks off its beach."*

Condé Nast Traveler

Age sites and villages that have remained unchanged for centuries. Nihiwatu is an exclusive tropical retreat where guests enjoy simple luxury unknown to the ancient Sumbanese. There are just seven spacious air-conditioned bungalows and three two-bedroom villas with thatched roofs, built by Indonesian craftsman using local materials. The style is contemporary, with glass walls and doors magnifying the stunning views.

In addition to exploring the island, visitors can indulge in more contemporary pleasures like surfing, diving, and game fishing. A rustic open living area and clifftop bar complete the laid-back island vibe. There is also a pool, jungle spa, and water sports center. **LP**

Whether it's a visit to the earthly paradises of Bora Bora or the Cook Islands, a journey through the mesmerizing Australian outback, or a stay at a luxurious mountain lodge in New Zealand, Oceania offers a range of seductive destinations. Why not enjoy the best of both worlds by relaxing on a quiet beach one week and exploring inland jungles the next?

OCEANIA

← Le Taha'a, French Polynesia

Ride the *Indian Pacific* Train

Location Perth to Sydney, Australia
Website www.trainways.com.au **Price** $$

Packs of wild kangaroos, never-ending stark desert plains, and mountains swirling in blue mists—these are all just part of the view when you grab a seat on the world's last remaining transcontinental train journey. Chugging along from coast to coast, the *Indian Pacific* takes sixty-five hours—that is three days and three nights—to travel a distance of 2,702 miles (4,352 km), making it one of the world's longest train rides. After leaving Sydney's Central Station, the train rattles through the suburbs before winding its way up through the dramatic Blue Mountains, so-called because of the eerie blue mist that rises up from the eucalyptus trees. There is a short stop at the outback town of Broken Hill, a small and remote mining town home to numerous artists who love the inspiring landscape. Further along, the train passes through the stark, desert-like Nullarbor Plain, where the train bolts through the longest straight stretch of track: a cool 297 miles (478 km).

There is plenty of wildlife to spot along the way, such as wild camels, emus, kangaroos, wombats, and parrots. Keep an eye out for the Australian wedge-tailed eagle, with a wingspan of 6.5 feet (2 m), as it is the train's striking emblem. Accommodations are comfortable and divided into two classes: sleeper cabins or airline-style seats.

Although 65 hours is a long time to travel from one side of Australia to the other when you can fly from Sydney to Perth in five hours, if you take the *Indian Pacific* you can do your bit for global warming and treat yourself to a once-in-a-lifetime scenic feast. **JK**

← *The* Indian Pacific *passes a historic viaduct on its journey across the vast continent of Australia.*

Snorkel in Ningaloo

Location Ningaloo Marine Park, Western Australia, Australia
Website www.environment.gov.au **Price** $

If you are an enthusiastic snorkeler, you should head directly to Ningaloo Marine Park on the coast of Western Australia. Here you can swim with the largest fish in the world—the whale shark. This giant of the sea measures in at up to 40 feet (12 m) and can weigh 14 tons, yet has a pleasing tendency toward not eating the divers. It is a filter feeder whose diet consists of plankton and krill.

The Ningaloo Reef—most of which remains pristine thanks to low levels of pollution—is one of only two places on Earth where whale sharks regularly congregate, and they are here from March until June. The reef is also home to humpback whales and manta

> *"Ningaloo Reef . . . is at the heart of the region's outstanding natural heritage significance."*
>
> UNESCO World Heritage Committee

rays, and hawksbill, green, and loggerhead turtles all breed in the area. Ningaloo Reef is about 200 miles (322 km) long. The marine park that was created in 1987 to protect it covers 600 acres (243 ha). In all, there are 500 species of fish and more than 200 species of coral at Ningaloo—and the reef's marine life is remarkably accessible to visitors. Close to the shore, it encircles shallow lagoons that are suitable for family snorkeling and less confident swimmers. Here you can see vividly colored clown fish, tiger fish, and sea anemones. For those who do not want to get their feet wet, there are also whale-watching trips, glass-bottomed boat tours, and scenic flights. **LD**

Enjoy the Kimberley Region

Location Kimberley Region, Western Australia, Australia
Website www.elquestrohomestead.com.au   **Price ◑**

Western Australia's rugged Kimberley region boasts some of the most spectacularly remote and rugged landscapes in the world. The area, roughly the size of California and three times larger than the United Kingdom, contains breathtaking natural attractions such as Purnululu, (a World Heritage site), the flowing Mitchell Falls, and the fabulous 410-mile (660-km) Gibb River Road.

El Questro Wilderness Park occupies one million acres (404,685 ha) of the Kimberley expanse, set across the top of the Chamberlain Gorge above a river that is home to fish, turtles, and crocodiles. Surrounded by lush tropical gardens that cascade down to a pool and tennis court, the homestead offers seven individually themed guest rooms, all of which were given a contemporary makeover by Sydney interior architect Pike Withers in 2007. Rustic Australian artifacts nestle next to Zanotta sofas, modern Italian ottomans, and woven cane chairs. The Chamberlain Suite is simply to die for, with a bathtub on the outdoor balcony and panoramic views from a wraparound veranda.

Yet the real highlight of El Questro is the dizzying range of excursions. You can boat on the Chamberlain Gorge, relax at nearby thermal pools (Zebedee Springs), horseback ride, or take a scenic helicopter flight through the Kimberley's canyons and gorges. Many trips are included in the room fee, although adventurers can book many more. In the mood for a gourmet picnic at Mirimiri Falls or a heli-fishing tour? El Questro will organize it in a heartbeat. When you are back from admiring the Kimberley terrain, the homestead's chef will titillate you with delicious food. You can even dine beneath the palms that grace the clifftop ledge—just do not feed the crocs below. **PS**

Explore Purnululu

Location Purnululu National Park, Western Australia, Australia
Website www.westernaustralia.com   **Price ◉**

The World Heritage-listed Purnululu National Park (also known as Bungle Bungle) is often considered to be Australia's equivalent of the Grand Canyon. Situated between the Western Australian towns of Kununurra and Halls Creek, the 593,000-acre (240,000 ha) expanse is characterized by a multitude of beehive-shaped karst mountains that rise up to 1,000 feet (300 m). The flat land that is home to these eroded sandstone peaks is located at another 1,000 feet above sea level. The plains are covered by woodland and grass, whereas the western area is distinguished by steep rocks. The rugged territory became a national park in 1987, when it was unknown to most foreign travelers.

"[Bungle Bungle] is not only totally unique . . . it's also breathtakingly weird and completely inexplicable."

Mark Moxon, travel writer

Two camp sites provide basic accommodation in the park: Kurrajong Campground is 4 miles (7 km) north of the visitor center, and Walardi Campground is 7.5 miles (12 km) to its south. The park possesses a number of captivating stone formations including the Echidna Chasm, Piccaninny, Frog Hole, and Cathedral Gorges. Still relatively inaccessible and largely unknown outside Australia, this extraordinary scenery provides the perfect setting for those in need of a break from their own hectic surroundings. **DaH**

➡ *The beehive-like domes of Purnululu, with their distinctive stripes, are an unusual sight.*

Enjoy Bamurru Plains

Location Bamurru Plains, Northern Territory, Australia
Website www.bamurruplains.com   **Price** ⊖⊖⊖

Within the boundaries of Swim Creek Station, not far from the western edge of Kakadu National Park, is the exquisitely isolated retreat of Bamurru Plains. Just a twenty-five minute flight from the Northern Territory capital of Darwin, Bamurru Plains offers guests the ultimate Australian outback experience.

Bungalows of timber and corrugated iron are a mix of undiluted rustic charm and unpretentious luxury, raised above the red earth on timber platforms high enough to deter the herds of buffalo that amble past at dusk. Nights relaxing on your private balcony are accompanied by the sounds of barking owls, raptors, black flying foxes, frogs, and cicadas. From December

> *"Bamurru Plains has taken the quintessential safari experience and made it Australian."*
>
> *The Australian*

to March, the annual monsoon rolls in from the Timor Sea and brings with it egrets, blue-winged kookaburras, geese, and an abundance of bird life, all of which can be seen from the comfort of your own personal airboat or on organized safaris.

Mouthwatering meals are prepared by your own five-star chef. They will likely include Bamurru staples such as oysters, barramundi, and buffalo fillets. Each of Bamurru's nine bungalows is sufficiently isolated from the next to ensure a private sense of discovery. **BS**

⊟ *The outback experience offered here is markedly different to those of drier, rockier regions.*

Ride the Kuranda Scenic Railway

Location Cairns to Kuranda, Queensland, Australia
Website www.kurandascenicrailway.com.au **Price** 💲

Conceived in 1882 and built nine years later, the Kuranda Scenic Railway was originally intended to connect Cairns and Kuranda in northern Queensland, and so help local tin miners deprived of food and essential supplies.

The thick jungle and steep rocks, up to 1,000 feet (300 m) high, were the main barriers to construction. Workers, mainly Irish and Italian, had to build fifteen tunnels and dozens of bridges in order to complete the 47 miles (75 km) of rail tracks. Many workers lost their lives achieving this dangerous engineering feat, but today's visitors have a far more leisurely experience

> *"The historic Kuranda Scenic Railway climbs the mountain past waterfalls and ravines."*
>
> Jay Canning, *Daily Telegraph*

of the journey, enjoying dramatic views of Cairns and the Stoney Creek Falls as the train makes its way along the track to Kuranda.

The village of Kuranda occupies an area of rain forest that has been inhabited by indigenous people for more than 10,000 years. These days Kuranda is most famous for its picturesque train station (built in 1915) and the Skyrail Rainforest Cableway, which provides splendid aerial views of the World Heritage-listed tropical rain forest and the spectacular Barron Falls. Various packages are available to allow tourists to discover some of the world's oldest rain forest in the comfort of a train or gondola. **DaH**

Stay at Dunk Island

Location Dunk Island, Queensland, Australia
Website www.dunk-island.com **Price** 💲💲

The Bandjin and Djiru people who have lived on this island for thousands of years call it "Coonaglebah"—isle of peace and plenty. Renamed Dunk Island by Captain Cook, it lies off the northern Queensland coast by the Great Barrier Reef and is Australia's most beautiful resort island complete with perfect, white-sand beaches, tropical gardens, and virgin rain forests.

The resort is just a forty-minute flight from Cairns, but devotees approach it by ferry from Mission Beach. On the journey, they trail their hands in the water, watching out for dolphins, sea turtles, dugongs, and migrating whales. Dunk is designated a national park for its outstanding natural attractions, which include Mount Kootaloo, standing at 889 feet (271 m) high. From the look-out point at the top, you can see the turquoise sea studded with dark islands, with coral reefs strung around them like necklaces. Up here in the rain forest, you will see the Ulysses butterfly, also called the Blue Mountain Butterfly, a beautiful iridescent blue creature with a wingspan of 5.5 inches (14 cm), a key draw for nature lovers.

The resort is run by Voyages, with all the modern conveniences you could wish for; boats to take you snorkeling or diving on the Great Barrier Reef, tennis courts, visits to the artists' colony, or sailing trips. The Spa of Peace and Plenty offers Elemis treatments near a water lily pond, where you can watch dragonflies hum as your cares are soothed away. The service is first class—no wonder so many honeymooners choose the resort as an idyllic island getaway. **LD**

➜ *Beachfront properties don't come much more heavenly than this resort at Dunk Island.*

Stay at Qualia

Location Whitsunday Islands, Queensland, Australia
Website www.qualia.com.au **Price** ⊖⊖⊖

Qualia is the epitome of Australian laid-back style. The retreat harmoniously makes use of local timber and stone and takes pride of place on the Great Barrier Reef. Guests stay in private hideaways, either Leeward Pavilions or Windward Pavilions, dotted among the native eucalyptus with picture-postcard views from spacious wooden decks and infinity plunge pools.

The word "qualia" derives from Latin and refers to a collection of sensory experiences, thus it was deemed by the resort's creators to "fit the essence" of their handiwork. And the senses come alive at Qualia— sight is stimulated by panoramic views of turquoise waters and the lush green Queensland coastline, while the sound of the sea rushing over the pebble shore and the scent of eucalyptus leaves permeates the air.

Visitors can take a closer look at the extraordinary underwater life to be found here on a snorkeling or scuba trip. They can also savor an array of taste sensations rustled up daily; for example, gourmet treats overlooking the Coral Sea at Long Pavilion or informal Australian fare waterside at Pebble Beach.

The world-class spa at the resort is also very much a part of the sensory experience. Guests can be pummeled into blissful submission, or indulge in Roman baths and an invigorating Swiss shower, or make use of the steam room and an open-air yoga and meditation pavilion. The overwhelming sense is one of peace and harmony, enhanced no doubt by the adults-only rule. For those willing and able to splash out a bit of extra money, chartering a private yacht or a helicopter trip is the icing on the cake. **LP**

← *The views from the infinity pool are wonderful. You will feel as though you are in a different world.*

Enjoy Paradise Bay

Location Whitsunday Islands, Queensland, Australia
Website www.paradisebay.com.au **Price** ⊖⊖⊖

Zipping across the calm waters of the Coral Sea to the aptly named Paradise Bay, the lush green mountain peaks rise dramatically from the azure depths and incredible white-sand beaches resemble scenes that most people only experience in their dreams. Perched on the edge of South Long Island, on Australia's Queensland coast, is Paradise Bay Island Eco Escape, the most exclusive, sustainable resort on all seventy-four islands of the Whitsunday Island chain.

Hosting only sixteen guests at any one time, the owners of this eco-tourism development are keen to provide all the luxury trimmings of an island retreat, while at the same time considering the environmental

> *"This utopia sits in sublime isolation on the northernmost tip of Hamilton Island."*
>
> *Condé Nast Traveler*

cost. Built using locally sourced materials, the resort uses 100 percent alternative energy and everything that can be, is recycled. Waterside guest bungalows are simple but elegantly decorated; each has a king-size bed, bathroom, and solar lighting.

Guests are free to roam the dense bushlands of the surrounding national park, take a trip on the resort's own yacht which sails daily to nearby deserted bays and coves, or go snorkeling in the warm waters of the Great Barrier Reef which is just in front of the resort. Dinner is served outdoors beneath the stars along with fine wines and the company of kindred spirits happy to abandon the hustle of everyday life. **LM**

Experience Hayman Island

Location Whitsunday Islands, Queensland, Australia
Website www.hayman.com.au   **Price** $$$$$

As your boat cruises toward Hayman, the Great Barrier Reef's most feted island retreat, you witness the stark natural beauty of this captivating archipelago rising out from the deep blue sea. Here, every care and whim is catered to by the ever-ready, unobtrusive service. There are eight restaurants, including convivial weekly sittings at the chef's table where guests are joined by expert food and wine specialists. Meals of a more intimate nature can be savored via a candlelit supper from your balcony or veranda, or a gourmet hamper on a secluded beach.

Total pampering and relaxation is on offer at Spa Chakra, with luxury treatments carried out in idyllic settings. Meditation and dedicated wet treatment rooms sit alongside a restorative itinerary of health and fitness regimes. Afterward, relax in the serenity of your room, suite, villa, or penthouse.

Natural fauna can be found in the Retreat Wing, which is set within delightful tropical gardens. Other enclaves offer access to Hayman's dreamily iconic swimming pool, ash-blond sandy beaches, cerulean lagoon, or a bird's-eye view from high across the Coral Sea and islands, each with their own soothing, beautifully considered, classic designs.

The reason most visitors travel to Hayman is to experience its gateway to one of the greatest natural wonders of the world: the mesmerizing Great Barrier Reef. Sea kayaking, sailing, whale watching, and game fishing are also on the menu. In fact, the options are endless: golf, tennis, and trips to the purest beach in the world, Whitehaven, are all available, too. **VG**

➔ *Hayman offers a lush, tropical island paradise at the end of the world, with activities to fit every mood.*

Stay at Seabreeze House

Location Town of 1770, Queensland, Australia
Website www.seabreeze1770.com **Price** 🌑🌑🌑🌑

The explorer Captain James Cook first stepped ashore here as a lieutenant on May 23, 1770. It was his second landing in Australia, and today the Town of 1770 represents the birthplace of the state of Queensland. The great English navigator would almost certainly recognize this unspoiled mix of rivers, reefs, and lagoons even today, thanks in no small part to the careful development of the region with ecologically sensitive hideaways such as Seabreeze House.

Set within 1,600 acres (647 ha) of pristine nature reserve, Seabreeze House is part of a handful of beach houses at Agnes Waters, just minutes from Bustard Bay where Cook and his small landing party first came

---

"Nature lovers will enjoy walking the Red Rock trail . . . to view loggerhead turtles."

Proprietors, Seabreeze House

---

ashore. A gated compound surrounds this carefully designed home, which blends seamlessly into the surrounding flora. Bedrooms have king-size beds draped in Egyptian cotton sheets and massive sunken baths. A glorious 40-foot (12-m) lap pool looks out over the azure waters of the Coral Sea and the lagoons and reefs of the Great Barrier Reef.

Don't miss the chance to swim in the Fitzroy Reef lagoon, rated one of the top snorkeling sites in the world. Just an eighty-minute boat ride from 1770, it boasts 2,500 species of marine life. Or you could spend the night on the lagoon's calm waters aboard Seabreeze's very own 75-foot (23-m) superyacht. **BS**

Visit Fraser Island

Location Fraser Island, Queensland, Australia
Website www.fraserisland.net **Price** 🌑

Some 78 miles (126 km) long, and 9 miles (15 km) wide, Fraser Island, the largest sand island in the world, is an ecological paradise of wild horses, where multitudes of dingoes howl by night, and countless humpbacks pass by from August to October, making the 5,000-mile (8,050-km) round trip from Antarctica. There is so much sand here; one beach is 75 miles (120 km) long. It is not for swimming though—these waters are pulled about by currents and owned by the menacing tiger sharks, even the shallows. If you go up to India Head, you can see them gliding around in the surf.

The usual mode of transport for the visitor is simply to hop in a four-by-four vehicle and drive over the hard-packed sand; if you see a plane descending to land on the beach, it is up to you to give way. In the interior, as well as hushed, virgin rain forest, the island has deep-green, pristine lakes of pure water—more than one hundred of them—some surrounded by sand dunes. The Aboriginal name for Fraser is *K'Gari*, which means "beautiful woman," and a myth maintains that the spirit who created the island was so awed by its beauty that she stayed there alone, inviting the wildlife to help stave off her loneliness.

The waters of these beautiful lakes are exceptionally cleansing. The beach sand of Lake McKenzie is nearly pure silica, and it is possible to wash hair, teeth, jewelry, and exfoliate one's skin. Watch out for the dingoes, though; they will eat anything that is not nailed down once the darkness descends. These are some of the last remaining pure dingoes in Eastern Australia, so whatever you do, do not feed them. **LB**

➔ *The wonderful long beaches of Fraser Island stretch for miles, with barely a tourist to be seen.*

Enjoy Old Leura Dairy

Location Blue Mountains, New South Wales, Australia
Website www.oldleuradairy.com   **Price** 💲💲

The Old Leura Dairy is a collection of lovingly restored, typical bush structures that has grown into one of Australia's most eclectic and unique escapes. The grounds and associated buildings that were once a working dairy farm have been given an invigorating new lease on life. What was once a modest 1920s weatherboard building is now the Workers Cottage, a three-bedroom home with typically irreverent Australian flourishes, such as walls made from fence palings and furniture fashioned from old lining boards. The Milking Shed is a Dali-esque building with crooked walls and angled floors, as well as clever internal uses of wrought iron and tin. The owners have also maintained the shed's hayloft and original barn doors that can still be melodramatically flung open should the mood be right.

A recent addition is the eco-friendly, solar-powered Straw Bale House, with its thick walls packed with straw to provide insulation throughout Leura's bone-tingling winter months. Inside you will find recycled timbers from an old jetty on Sydney's Parramatta River, and the doors and windows were sequestered from the city's famous old Queen Victoria Hospital.

Paddock grass has been transformed into an extensive native garden, and drought-resistant shrubs have been planted throughout to stabilize the soil and attract native birds. Instead of succumbing to the wrecking ball, this dairy farm and some fine examples of Australia's pioneer heritage have been preserved, set within the boundaries of the majestic, World Heritage-listed Blue Mountains. **BS**

◀ *The Old Leura Dairy is the culmination of eight years of painstaking and loving restoration.*

Explore Barrington Tops

Location Barrington Tops, New South Wales, Australia
Website www.barringtons.com.au   **Price** 💲

A two-and-a-half-hour drive north of Sydney, the rolling subtropical forest of the World Heritage area of Barrington Tops is an easily accessible region of unadulterated natural wilderness. Benefiting from a climate that supports both southern Australian and tropical flora and fauna, this plateau connecting two extinct volcanic peaks within the Mount Royal Range is home to more than fifty uncommon plant and animal species.

Often shrouded in mist, the peaks rise up to just over 5,000 feet (1,500 m) and offer splendid views of the lush meadows and endless forests. The Antarctic beech forests that thrive above 3,000 feet (900 m)

> *"Barrington Tops is a world of streams, waterfalls, forests, and soaring cliffs."*
>
> visitnsw.com

are a reminder of the Triassic southern hemisphere supercontinent Gondwana, and the granite boulders scattered across the park are thought to considerably predate Australia's separation from that landmass 167 million years ago. The ubiquitous rivers—fed by mist as well as melting snow and large quantities of rain—often turn into spectacular waterfalls.

Although it is possible to find accommodation in the forest itself, another option is to stay in nearby towns such as Gloucester and Dungog. European settlers arrived in the area in the early 1800s, and local history museums offer a fascinating insight into the challenges faced by those pioneers. **DaH**

Stay at Tower Lodge

Location Hunter Valley, New South Wales, Australia
Website www.towerlodge.com.au **Price** ⊛⊛⊛

Set in the heart of Hunter Valley within the grounds of Tower Estate winery, Tower Lodge is an exclusive haven of unrivaled comfort and intimacy. The impeccable rooms complement the gastronomic delights of Roberts Restaurant, one of the valley's most iconic eateries. The meals are accompanied by an extensive award-winning wine list and are served in the historic ambience of an early settler's slab cottage.

From a distance, the lodge has the appearance of a classic European manor house, characterized by rendered external walls and a formidable facade, all dominated by a square bell tower and set around a delightful cloistered courtyard. All the rooms are filled

> *"Should you want to venture out for a spot of wine tourism, there's no shortage of wineries."*

John Stimpfig, *Observer*

to overflowing with antiques and furniture crafted from recycled local timbers. A number of the rooms have a fountain, whereas others have a private courtyard or plunge pool. Throughout the lodge there are tiny eccentricities that are typical of the attention to detail brought to every corner of this grand hideaway, such as the 300-year-old Rajasthani bed and Louis VXI writing desk that are yours if you book the opulent Chairman's Suite.

Memorable events in this popular region include jazz and opera festivals, hot-air ballooning, walking the convict trail, wine-tasting excursions, and visiting historic towns such as Wollombi and Morpeth. **BS**

Relax at St. Killians

Location Hunter Valley, New South Wales, Australia
Website www.stkillians.com.au **Price** ⊛⊛

Built in 1879 to be the religious focus of the then-tiny farming community of Brookfield in the Hunter Valley north of Sydney, the sandstock church of St. Killians has been lovingly transformed into a romantic getaway with a mix of old world charm and contemporary luxury.

At St. Killians you can do as much or as little as you like. Beneath its aging cedar cathedral ceilings, there are two cozy lounge areas where St. Killians's masseurs can provide a private massage in front of one of two open fireplaces. Or, should you choose to venture outside, you can picnic down by the nearby Williams River, go bargain hunting in the local antique shops, or indulge in an afternoon of wine tasting in some of the eighty-plus wineries for which the region is famous.

There are two bedrooms, one in the choir loft and one in the old vestry, which has superb views from the comfort of its antique, queen-size brass bed. A gourmet kitchen allows you the choice of cooking for yourself and dining alfresco in the sun-drenched courtyard, or you can call on the expertise of St. Killians's chef, who will happily prepare breakfast, lunch, or dinner using the freshest of locally sourced ingredients. Prawn and salmon cakes with saffron dressing, Mediterranean lamb tagine, lime and almond friands, and toasted banana bread bagels give you an idea of some of the cuisine provided by the European-trained chef Stephen Kennedy.

At St. Killians, elaborate Persian rugs are spread over polished timber floorboards, and white internal walls combine with dark cedar ceilings and stained-glass windows to provide a visual feast of elegance and spaciousness. This is a relaxing setting guaranteed to slow pulse rates and recalibrate the soul. **BS**

Enjoy Eagle View Escape

Location Lake Lyell, New South Wales, Australia
Website www.eagleview.com.au **Price** 💲💲

If an underground passageway to your room appeals to your sense of the dramatic, then the spa suites of Eagle View Escape are waiting for you. Overlooking Lake Lyell, a man-made lake created by the damming of the Coxs River and stocked with enough bass and rainbow trout to tempt even the most jaded of anglers, Eagle View Escape is a romantic, couples-only resort for those looking for complete privacy.

Five "wilderness cabins" come with corrugated iron bathrooms and outdoor verandas complete with sunken tubs overlooking untouched native bush land. Picnic baskets are available, leaving you free to walk the impressive network of bush trails, where you are

> *"Our Wilderness Cabins have private verandas looking out through trees towards Lake Lyell."*
>
> **Proprietors, Eagle View Escape**

almost guaranteed to meet some of the other residents, including wombats, kangaroos, echidnas, and wallabies. Lake Lyell's sprinkling of sand beaches makes swimming its pristine waters a delight, and its five boat ramps allow for easy access to this meandering lake's many inlets and hidden coves.

The 110 acres (45 ha) that comprise Eagle View Escape will provide you with panoramic views of the Australian bush and a true sense of isolation. The resort is only a half-hour drive from the towns and antique-filled hamlets of the World Heritage-listed Blue Mountains, and a short drive from the splendor of the subterranean world of the Jenolan caves. **BS**

Walk Mrs. Macquarie's Road

Location Sydney, New South Wales, Australia
Website www.discoversydney.com.au/parks/mmc.html **Price** 🚹

Much of the great beauty of Sydney is in its harbor, and walking to the top of Mrs. Macquarie's Road is one of the loveliest ways to appreciate the city's character.

More than 150 years ago, the wife of the first governor of Australia, Mrs. Macquarie, liked to sit in this particular spot. From her vantage point, directly east of the Opera House, on the eastern edge of the Royal Botanic Gardens, she enjoyed unrivaled views of the natural harbor. Today, you look west from here to Harbor Bridge and Circular Quay—the iconic heart of Sydney—where the First Fleet arrived in 1788. On a clear day, you can spy the Blue Mountains in the far distance. Looking north and east you can see Kirribilli House, Pinchgut Island, and the navy dockyards at Wooloomooloo. Watch the green and cream ferries chug past and the people of Sydney go about their business: workers on their cell phones, joggers going for a run, tourists taking photographs, and romantic couples posing for wedding shots (countless Japanese and Korean couples marry in the gardens).

This spot is in the heart of the city, yet you can still find a patch of grass to drink your coffee and shoot the breeze with a friend under a blue sky. The Royal Botanic Gardens next door are a wonderland of Australian native and European trees, bathed in sunlight and shade by turn, and home to more than a million specimens. There are wild creatures here, too: shrieking parakeets, enormous bats hanging upside down in the trees, ibises and cockatoos, melodious mynah birds, and ducks. This is where the first Europeans tried their hand—albeit fruitlessly—at agriculture. Since then, a couple of hundred years of composting have made this a paradise of tropical foliage: the green heart of the city. **LB**

Walk From Bondi to Bronte

Location Sydney, New South Wales, Australia
Website www.bondivillage.com **Price ()**

"Bondi beach is iconic ... a crescent of golden sand lapped by an ocean the perfect shade of blue."

Peter Moore, *Guardian*

World-famous Bondi Beach, where Australia's first surf club was founded in 1906, was conceived as a kind of Coney Island for Sydney when surfing was a new sport. These days, Bondi is a rag-tag mix of boutique cafés, restaurants, hotels, burger joints, juice bars, and cheap clothing stores. The walk from Bondi Beach to Bronte Beach is a rite of passage, a simple, free-of-charge pleasure for new visitors and locals alike, and it is the best way to imbibe the windswept spirit of the relaxed eastern beach suburbs.

Set out from North Bondi and walk the length of the beach, past the bustling surf club, baking tourists, and lifeguards until you reach the south end of the beach and the rockpool, where you will find a stunning, glass-fronted bar that hangs over the rocks. Ascend to the coastal walk there and tread the path that hugs the cliffs toward Bronte Beach. You will pass jogging moms with strollers, bronzed hunks bench pressing, and, if the time of year is right, you might spot breaching humpback whales. The area also hosts the Sculpture by the Sea exhibition, and you might witness an informal wedding (many Australians like to get married outdoors when possible). The route takes you through Tamarama, a thin wedge of yellow sand book-ended by cliffs, and also goes through the most romantic graveyard in the world, its Celtic crosses and Victorian headstones blasted by salty sea air and sun. When you arrive in Bronte, where a perfectly sized beach awaits, backed by a nature reserve and a lawn where people grill burgers on the public barbecues, you may wonder why you do not live here. **LB**

↖ *The beach was opened to the public in 1882; its name is an Aboriginal word for "water breaking over rocks."*

Stay at the Shangri-La

Location Sydney, New South Wales, Australia
Website www.shangri-la.com   **Price** $$

Sydney's five-star Shangri-La Hotel rises up from the fringes of the city's business district and casts a long shadow across the blue waters of Sydney Cove. It is as though the phrase "location, location, location" was coined by the real estate industry and applied specifically to this Sydney landmark, where everything you could possibly want to see in the city is only an invigorating stroll away.

The hotel rooms provide jaw-dropping panoramas that take in all the iconic images of this vibrant city. Look down on Sydney Harbor Bridge, the Sydney Opera House, Botanical Gardens, the former harbor island prison of Fort Denison, and the comings and goings of the city's fleet of ferries at Circular Quay. Enjoy views of the tree-lined suburbs of North Sydney all the way to the Pacific Ocean beyond.

The Shangri-La is the largest hotel in a sassy city where size still matters. Its 563 rooms and suites are some of the largest in Sydney, and the hotel towers above the city streets, topping out at the thirty-sixth floor where guests can enjoy bird's-eye views of the city courtesy of the massive floor-to-ceiling windows. Here you may dine in the award-winning and aptly named Altitude Restaurant, followed by a cocktail in the Manhattan-inspired Blu Horizon Bar, which was awarded Sydney's best hotel bar by *Forbes Magazine*. A mouth-watering selection of pastries and breads is available daily, fresh from the hotel's own bakery. Hart's Pub, a traditional Australian pub restored to reflect its colonial heritage and housed in an original private residence, is open day and night for pizzas, light snacks, ales, and wines, after which you can return to your room and gaze at the array of lights laid out across the city beneath you. **BS**

Enjoy Paperbark Camp

Location Jervis Bay, New South Wales, Australia
Website www.paperbarkcamp.com.au   **Price** $$

For owners Irena and Jeremy Hutchings, the vision to bring sustainable safari-style camping to Australia started in Africa. On their return, they happened upon pristine Jervis Bay and set up camp in a protected bush wetland. The rest, as they say, is history.

With twelve "tents" floating on timber platforms underneath a canopy of spotted gums and peeling paperbark trees, Paperbark Camp is the perfect foil for those who like roughing it, without actually roughing it. Wafts of eucalyptus and pine tickle your senses at every turn, and eco-tourism is taken very seriously.

Paperbark is near one of the world's best beaches (Hyams), and you can rent a canoe for paddling along

> *"Ideal for those who love being close to nature, but equally appreciate the finer things in life."*
>
> *Travelling in Australia* magazine

Currambene Creek, or a bicycle for forays into the eucalyptus forest, woodland, or nearby town of Jervis Bay. Locals come from miles around for gourmet treetop dining at the Gunyah restaurant. Aboriginal for "meeting place," the Gunyah doubles as the camp's nerve center—a place to chill with a book by day and chat by the fire at night. The eclectic menu might include kangaroo kebabs with lemon and myrtle yogurt, salmon baked in paperbark, and kaffir lime and ginger sorbet with lychees and rum. Pesky possums have been known to poke their noses into unzipped tents and, come morning, you will wake to a dawn chorus that is second to none. **TM**

Stay on Kangaroo Island

Location Kangaroo Island, South Australia, Australia
Website www.southernoceanlodge.com.au **Price** 💲💲💲

There is nothing between wild, untouched Kangaroo Island and Antarctica. As soon as you arrive, you inhale the fresh smell of eucalyptus and a sense of remoteness. This is Australia's answer to the Galapagos.

The island has twenty-one conservation and national parks and a panoply of different plants and animal species. The beaches are rugged and banked by dunes and sheer cliffs. Some are dominated by wild colonies of sea lions or tiny penguins; others are overlooked by granite outcrops sculpted by the wind and saltwater into extraordinary shapes; many are pounded by vicious waves. It is a place of endless bush broken by the occasional paddock or the path of a bush fire, creeping with kangaroos, wallabies, possums, echidnas, and koalas. At night, kangaroos and wallabies shoot across the road with no warning; trying to drive is like playing bumper cars.

The locals are unhurried; no one on the island has personal space issues—there are only 3,000 residents on this 1,737-square mile (4,500-sq km) island. It is unlikely that Aborigines were here: When Flinders circumnavigated in 1802, he realized there were no bush burn-offs and that the kangaroos were not perturbed by human presence. So they clubbed some, had a feast, and named the place Kangaroo Island.

Southern Ocean Lodge is a low-rise palace that snakes down the cliffs at lonely Hanson Bay, in a remote southerly corner of the island. Its public spaces are so vast that they give the sensation of being in a very cool airport terminal. It is a marvelous place to stay when exploring the wildness of the island. **LB**

← *Perched on rugged cliffs, Southern Ocean Lodge has a beautiful view out to the sea.*

Hike Around Bay of Fires

Location Bay of Fires, Tasmania, Australia
Website www.bayoffires.com.au   **Price** ⑤⑤

The Bay of Fires is an untamed landscape. Along parts of its coastline, stretching some 20 miles (32 km) from Binalong Bay to Eddystone Point, there are more extraordinary white-sand beaches than houses.

The four-day, fully guided Bay of Fires walk serves up some of Tasmania's best attributes: fine local foods, cool-climate wines, and breathtaking landscapes. With a maximum of ten walkers and at least two guides on every tour, guests are guaranteed individual attention. Besides eating, drinking, and walking (a maximum of about 8 miles [13 km] is walked on any one day), time is also allowed for guests to relax, snorkel in the beautiful Tasman Sea, and kayak on Ansons River.

> *"From far away to up close, the sea offers up a myriad of delight, both intricate and wild."*

Anthology Travelers' Collection website

The walk begins at Boulder Point where secluded beaches and rocky headlands dress the landscape. At the end of day one, a standing camp melds into one of the dunes and yet is so close to the water you could just about fish from your bed. Typically the sleeping "tents" have canvas roofs but they also have timber floors. Two nights are spent at the Bay of Fires Lodge—something of a benchmark for stylish and sustainable accommodation. Sitting low among the sand dunes, the lodge has a light carbon footprint. Rainwater is collected and used on-site; solar panels provide power for all lighting. This helps not only the house, but also the guests to blend into the environment. **GC**

Relax at Islington Hotel

Location Hobart, Tasmania, Australia
Website www.islingtonhotel.com   **Price** ⑤⑤

A basic audit of the Islington Hotel may prove disturbing to accountants, because each of the hotel's rooms has something near the value of a Lamborghini attached to its refurbishment. It will doubtless pay off. It is not too hard to imagine guests spending the better part of a week here soaking up the numerous features and the personable service.

The Islington Hotel opened in January 2006 in an 1847 Regency-style mansion that was once home to the Tasmanian premier Sir James Milne Wilson. The transformation from private home to eleven-room luxury hotel has been helped in no small part by an eclectic collection of antiques: Louis XV chairs, a Biedermeier table, Chinese cabinets, and Austrian beds in the Grand House Room. There are also works by Picasso, Brett Whiteley, and Ju Ming, fabrics from Jim Thompson, and a well-stocked library.

Although king-size beds, private bathrooms, back-lit marble panels, wonderfully deep baths, and heated granite floors are standard in all of the rooms, each one has its own character. Indeed, the owners have helped meld an extraordinary bespoke hotel. The Islington has a striking conservatory. It opens out onto a terrace where there is a reflecting pond and, beyond that, formal gardens. There are views to forested Mount Wellington from the rear of the property. Guests are offered complimentary drinks and canapés on the terrace at sunset. In the mornings, sumptuous breakfasts using fresh Tasmanian produce are prepared in the stylish and visible kitchen, which has a French farmhouse theme. The Islington chef will even prepare bespoke dinners on request. Allow some time to choose an accompanying wine though, because the hotel's cellar runs to 1,000 bottles. **GC**

Unwind at Cradle Mountain Lodge

Location Cradle Mountain, Tasmania, Australia
Website www.cradlemountainlodge.com.au   **Price** 🅢🅢

With an alpine spa retreat and comfortable cabins on the edge of a World Heritage location, living the green life at Cradle Mountain Lodge has never been so luxurious. It is certainly no hardship to be at one with nature at this eco-certified wilderness retreat on the Australian island state of Tasmania, surrounded by misty, mirror lakes and craggy peaks.

Some of the cozy cabins have a hot tub out on the deck and a wood-burning fire in the lounge to keep evening mountain chills at bay. If you can pull yourself away from the views, there is even more inspiring scenery on offer from the Waldheim spa. Treatment rooms have floor-to-ceiling windows to let the outside in, and the adjoining Sanctuary relaxation area has an open-air hot tub with panoramic views of the forest.

In keeping with the lodge's green credentials, the menu features the best of local produce, and helpful staff offer recommendations on Australian wines from the extensive cellar. A delight for food and wine lovers is the annual three-day "Tastings at the Top" gourmet extravaganza, a showcase for boutique winemakers, growers, and handmade cheese makers.

The site attracts hikers of all abilities. Take a picnic and follow self-guided walking trails to find a peaceful spot to enjoy the solitude of Cradle Mountain and Dove Lake. Go canoeing on the lake or rent mountain bikes to get off the beaten track. Local guides offer tours to get a closer look at native animals such as wallabies, possums, and maybe even a Tasmanian Devil. Or look out over the forest to spot them while enjoying a relaxing massage in the spa. **AD**

↗ *The secluded but luxurious cabins are tucked away in the fairy tale setting of an ancient forest.*

"The cradle in question is more literally a crater, spectacularly fenced with rocky peaks."

Daily Telegraph

Enjoy Meadowbank Estate

Location Meadowbank, Tasmania, Australia
Website www.meadowbankwines.com.au **Price** ⊖

Meadowbank Estate is way more than a vineyard. It has an award-winning restaurant, a cellar-door food and wine shop, an art gallery, and a concert program—all just a fifteen-minute drive from Hobart's waterfront.

The location is sensational. The restaurant's massive windows look out over the vineyards of the Coal River Valley and the estuaries of Barilla Bay. There is an appreciation of history here, too: For example, the restaurant's timber pillars were once used as ballast for Tasmanian ships. The restaurant's concept is small-dish and local—think smoked eel with potato pancakes, Dunalley oysters, and kingfish seviche—with wines, all available by the glass, to match. A large proportion

> "The hilltop view over the vineyards and some 11,000 fine-wool merinos soothes the soul."
>
> John Bell, *Daily Telegraph*

of the produce used by the kitchen is sourced in the vicinity of the Coal River Valley, and the menu changes almost daily. The cellar-door shop, meanwhile, offers free tastings of up to six of Meadowbank's standard wines. The art gallery holds exhibitions of local artists' work, and Meadowbank hosts regular concerts of, for example, Tasmanian chamber music and Tasmanian jazz guitarists—Tasmania itself is a distinct theme.

It is the wine that started it all, though. The first vines were planted here in 1974. The idea was to create a few bottles for personal enjoyment, but the results exceeded expectation, and the vineyards grew. Now Meadowbank produces an enviable range. **PE**

Discover Wineglass Bay

Location Freycinet National Park, Tasmania, Australia
Website www.wineglassbay.com **Price** ◖◗

Wineglass Bay is perhaps Tasmania's most curvaceous figure. This natural beauty's prized feature is a stretch of white sand that replicates the shape of a wine glass rim. Wonderfully, however, there is not a hint of exploitation here, not a building or even a sniff of commercial enterprise about the mile-long beach.

Wineglass Bay is on Tasmania's east coast, on a peninsula known as Freycinet National Park. Dutchman Abel Tasman may have been the first European in these parts, but it was the French in the early nineteenth century who named the peninsula. An imposing granite range, known as the Hazards, watches over the park. It is a bodyguard of sorts because it has made road building fortuitously problematic. There is no vehicular access to Wineglass.

At the beginning of the trail there is no clue to a beach. Rather, a cleverly honed trail is sculpted through the pervasive granite and forest. The trail rises steeply to a saddle wedged between some of the Hazard's highest peaks. Indigenous green rosellas, fan-tailed cuckoos, and wallabies are often encountered on this part of the journey. The first views of the bay come from the lookout in the saddle. From this elevated position, a mile or so away, the waves lap at the curve of sand as though on a quest to reach into the nearby forest. The eucalyptus gives off a bluish hue and contrast with the shimmering turquoise water. In short, the view is a pinup for beaches the world over, but many visitors, satisfied with the view, return to their cars from the lookout. How could you come this far and not put footprints in the sand? **GC**

→ *The sand appears white enough to suggest somebody has taken to manicuring it regularly.*

Relax at Eagles Nest

Location Bay of Islands, North Island, New Zealand
Website www.eaglesnest.co.nz **Price** ⊖⊖⊖

Located within strolling distance of the historic town of Russell on New Zealand's Bay of Islands, Eagles Nest can be found perched on the edge of a private peninsula. Surrounded by a largely secluded 75-acre (30-ha) estate, this luxury resort has only five self-contained villas to rent—but they are all exclusive.

The resort has been designed in resolutely contemporary style, although the owners have ensured all gardens and lodgings blend seamlessly into the natural environment. Each villa is uniquely appointed, with a mix of modern and antique furnishings, original local artwork, and all the modern conveniences you will ever need. The villas vary in size: The smallest sleeps two, the largest eight, but all have generous dimensions and are filled with oodles of natural light. Although Eyrie and Eagle Spirit rooms have their own 60-foot (18-m) infinity pools, First Light Temple offers a more romantic ambience that is perfect for a honeymoon vacation. The two-story Sacred Space serves as the resort's showpiece, with three suites, a living area, and private cinema, plus butlers and personal trainers on request. Gleaming chrome and marble bathrooms featuring glass-encased showers and heated floor tiles are just some of the attention-grabbing details within the villas.

Accommodation aside, the scenery is breathtaking. The Bay of Islands is world renowned and contains more than 144 islands to explore. With everything from big-game fishing, sailing, diving, mountain biking, hiking, and helicopter flights on offer, there is little chance of getting bored. Eagles Nest has it all. **PS**

→ *The design is simple—glass walls, expansive decks, private pools—but the effect is nothing short of majestic.*

Stay at Mollies

Location Auckland, North Island, New Zealand
Website www.mollies.co.nz **Price** 💲💲💲

Mollies is an impressive building that was built in the 1870s. It has been fully renovated recently by Frances Wilson, a singing teacher, and opera set designer Stephen Fitzgerald. The pair are justifiably proud of their masterful restoration of what is now the city center's best five-star boutique hotel.

There are thirteen luxury suites and apartments within this outstanding building. The upstairs suites have elegant balconies whereas downstairs the rooms open onto a beautifully maintained garden. Dotted with antiques and contemporary touches, the rooms are large by Auckland standards, and even the smaller studio rooms include private bathrooms and their own view of the courtyard's garden. Guests can dine among the sea of flowers in the conservatory, or simply at leisure in their own suites. The cunningly named restaurant, the Dining Room, is renowned throughout New Zealand for its gourmet cuisine and, of course, a range of excellent local wines. Mollies has won several awards, and the Dining Room itself was recently named one of the top Auckland restaurants, such is the quality of the fare.

To burn it all off, the hotel's East Day Spa offers a range of ayurvedic treatments including facials, massage, and many holistic treatments. The level of service at this St. Mary's Bay gem is second to none, and the library, although on the bijou side, is impeccably stocked. The sense of relaxation when you close the door of your suite is enhanced by the knowledge that attentive staff are only a call away, a reassurance that resonates throughout your stay. **PS**

← *The atmosphere of grandeur is partly due to the fact that it was once the home of Auckland's first mayor.*

Unwind at Puka Park

Location Coromandel, North Island, New Zealand
Website www.pukapark.co.nz **Price** 💲💲

Guests at Puka Park are shown to their rooms via a creaking wooden pathway through the misty rain forest. There you will find a luxurious tree house with living plants incorporated into its structure. In the morning, step out onto your wooden balcony and gaze out through the foliage. It is quite a spectacle: the long, empty, sandy beach and the Pacific surf curving away toward more trees and hills to the north. Puka Park sits on a steep green mountainside above Pauanui Beach on the wild and beautiful Coromandel Peninsula. It is only a two-hour drive from Auckland, but secluded in its 25 acres (10 ha) of lush and verdant bush, the city seems like a world away.

"Amid New Zealand's beautiful native bush, you will find an idyllic and very special hideaway."

escapenewzealand.com

The resort has an award-winning restaurant—eat in by the open fire or out on the deck overlooking the ocean. Guests collapse into incredibly soft sofas in the cocktail bar enjoying views through every window. Some sit and gaze out from their private balconies among the trees, hypnotized by the panoramas. Others are inspired to visit Puka's gym, pool, or spa. Daring guests can try the purpose-built, high-ropes course through the tree tops, including the "sky plunge"—a 755-foot (230-m) rope ride across the valley. There are boat trips to nearby islands and walking trails up the 1,310 foot (400-m) Pauanui Mountain for more spectacular views. **SH**

Enjoy Hot Water Beach

Location Coromandel, North Island, New Zealand
Website http://mercurybay.co.nz/index.php **Price** ◐

Digging yourself into a big hole is not usually recommended—unless you are on Hot Water Beach located on the east coast of Coromandel Peninsula.

New Zealand is crisscrossed by fault lines. Centuries of shifting tectonic plates and volcanic activity have created a geothermal wonderland of steaming mineral lakes and bubbling mud pools. Hot Water Beach is a picturesque sweep of flat golden sands. It is fringed on one side by scarlet-flowered Pohutukawa trees and on the other by frothy aquamarine seas.

The entire Coromandel coastline is stunning. What sets this beach apart is the fact that it sits over a superheated underground lake. Two conveniently placed natural fissures allow rivers of boiling water to bubble upward through the cracks. When they reach the cooling waters of the Pacific Ocean, you can actually see plumes of steam rising from the water, except for the two hours either side of low tide when these volcanic vents empty onto the golden sands of Hot Water Beach. During these times, if you burrow just beneath the sand, you will hit a spring of water rich in salt, calcium, and magnesium. Dig deeper and the water rushes to fill the sandy pit, so you can literally carve out your own private spa pool. Although now drastically cooled, the mineral water still reaches temperatures up to 147°F (64°C). Add some cooling seawater if necessary, and sit back and enjoy a muscle-relaxing soak. Always keep an eye on the incoming tide, because Hot Water Beach has strong currents and rip tides that can cause problems.

The springs bubble up throughout the year. For a unique experience, visit the beach at nighttime. Dig out your hot pool, then lie back and watch the shooting stars as they streak across the dark night sky. **JP**

Relax at Polynesian Spa

Location Rotorua, North Island, New Zealand
Website www.polynesianspa.co.nz **Price** ◓

According to Maori legend, the high priest Ngatoroirangi felt cold as he prayed on the summit of Mount Tongariro. The gods in the mythical Maori homeland of Hawaiki responded by sending jets of fire deep underground. More recent scientific research counters that Rotorua's frenzy of geothermal activity is caused by shifting tectonic plates.

The bubbling mud, scalding geysers, and lurid mineral pools have kept Rotorua high on the tourist agenda for more than a hundred years, and the Polynesian Spa has transformed these natural assets into an oasis of relaxation. It has no fewer than twenty-six hot mineral pools, many of which overlook Lake

"The steam rising off the water creates a dreamy state and is the perfect prep for a . . . mud wrap."

Ranch & Coast magazine

Rotorua. The Priest Spa pools—named for Father Mahoney who hiked 50 miles (80 km) from Tauranga in 1878 to bathe in a hand-dug pool and thus alleviate his arthritis—feature slightly acidic water, which is famous for soothing tired muscles, aches and pains, arthritis, and rheumatism.

The other pools are slightly alkaline. Among them are the deluxe Lake Spa, where you can laze in warm waters beside two waterfalls; a family spa; an adults-only spa; and private spas for those who want to bathe with just their nearest and dearest. Treatments include the use of New Zealand manuka honey, New Zealand kiwis, and Rotorua thermal mud, of course. **PE**

Unwind at Huka Lodge

Location Taupo, North Island, New Zealand
Website www.hukalodge.com **Price** 🖒🖒

The low-rise, postwar building looks innocuous from a distance. A big family summerhouse, perhaps, nestled in the woods near a river? The sleepy-looking lodge between the trees is actually one of the world's finest luxury hotels. Huka has won numerous global awards and accommodated many famous guests, but one is definitely worth a mention: H.R.H. Queen Elizabeth II has chosen to stay here five times.

Not surprising then that the hotel is exquisitely designed, equipped, and decorated. Food, service and attention to detail are superb. A stay here is fantastically expensive, too. All twenty rooms open out toward the river just a few yards away. Many guests sleep with the huge glass doors open, listening to the Waikato River, New Zealand's longest, rushing through the rain forest toward the Huka Falls nearby (*huka* is a Maori word meaning "falling water").

The relaxed hunting lodge theme includes touches such as antelope heads above roaring fireplaces, tartan rugs, leather sofas, and timber paneling. Dine fabulously in the formal dining room or at a private table by the river, watching ducks waddle across the lawns under overhanging ferns.

Huka's position in the middle of New Zealand's North Island is close to Lake Taupo, whose clear blue waters are surrounded by forested mountains. Guests are offered private trips to Taupo or the erupting White Island off-shore volcano—both by helicopter, of course. Only in New Zealand would guests at this category of hotel be offered a 150-foot (45-m) bungee jump above the Waikato or a hair-raising jet-boat ride under the Huka Falls. Nobody seems to be letting on as to whether Her Majesty decided to try any of these activities—but one suspects not. **SH**

Stay at Treetops Lodge

Location Bay Of Plenty, North Island, New Zealand
Website www.treetops.co.nz **Price** 🖒🖒🖒

Treetops Lodge and Wilderness Experience is in one of the most unspoiled natural landscapes on Earth. Set within 2,500 acres (1,012 ha) of private wilderness and surrounded by 800-year-old trees that make up the local native virgin forest, this eco-lodge sits within a carefully managed game and wildlife habitat where fly fishermen make the most of the wild trout in the seven spring-streams.

The lifelong dream of owner John Sax, the lodge took eight careful years to build. It is located in the Maori heartland and trout fishing capital of the world, Rotorua, and the ecology-inspired architectural style was derived from the country's pioneering past.

> *"Treetops was . . . a place of calm, beauty, and intimate connection with a sublime landscape."'*

Victoria Homewood, *Daily Telegraph*

Fine cuisine is an integral part of Treetops, with flavorful and healthy dishes created by talented chefs using the finest game and local produce. Dining is complemented by premium New Zealand wines. Among the wilderness experiences at Treetops are on-site trout fishing, four lakes, and more than 44 miles (70 km) of adventure trails. Other activities include photography safaris, helicopter tours, luxury treks to spectacular waterfalls, and a four-wheel-drive experience. You can, of course, choose to lay back and give in to the sedative sounds of nature all around you. You may even hear the distant voices of fishermen on the breeze, discussing the "ones that got away." **PS**

Visit Karamea

Location Karamea, South Island, New Zealand
Website www.karameainfo.co.nz   **Price** ❶

Karamea is where the road runs out. After this, there is just bush. It is for the bush that most people come, because Karamea sits at the end of the Heaphy Track, which runs for 50 picturesque miles (80 km) through the Kahurangi National Park and along the white-sand beaches of the coast.

If preferred, you could skip the hiking and drive here. Even the road up to Karamea is glorious. A verdant canopy of green reigns facing a long beach often strewn with driftwood, where the waves shimmer silver. For lodging, try the Last Resort or the Karamea Village Hotel, where the landlord will serve you a whitebait patty and a pint of local beer.

> *"Karamea serves as the beginning (or the end) of the famed Heaphy Track—a gorgeous, rugged trail."*
> viewpoints.com

Karamea is a tiny, sleepy little place, but there is plenty to keep the active crowd occupied, such as kayaking and bird-watching in the estuaries that are home to pied stilts, black swans, oyster catchers, and blue herons. Even if you do not want to hike very far, walk at least a little of the wonderful Heaphy Track. At the Karamea end, groves of princely nikau palms soar overhead before the path leads onto a coastline replete with flashing spuming waters, weaving bays, and boulder-strewn beaches. **PE**

← *Although the landscape can vary around Karamea, you will always find unspoiled stretches of beach.*

Enjoy Hidden Valley Lodge

Location Lake Poerua, South Island, New Zealand
Website www.hiddenvalleylodge.co.nz   **Price** ⊖

In 1923 a small wooden lodge was built at the back of New Zealand's Grey Valley. In 1953 it was relocated a few miles from Lake Poerua, where it served a small Catholic community for the next forty-three years. In 1996 the small church was put up for tender, purchased by its present owners, and now sits nestled in a small grove of native New Zealand ferns overlooking the trout-filled waters of Lake Poerua.

After an extensive internal renovation using native timbers and ensuring the preservation of its original detailing, such as its many stained-glass windows, Hidden Valley Lodge can now accommodate up to seven guests. Visitors enjoy perfect isolation by the

---

"There are wild red deer in the bush and mountains around the lodge along with chamois on the tops."

Proprietors, Hidden Valley Lodge

---

shores of Lake Poerua. One side of the lake is under private ownership, and the other is managed by the Department of Conservation.

Anglers come here for the bounty of brown trout that inhabits the lake and surrounding streams. You can also take to the water on one of the lodge's kayaks, a popular activity affording the chance to view some of the area's abundant birdlife, including wild geese, keas, swans, and the elusive white heron. Hidden Valley Lodge provides an excellent base for exploring the rugged beauty of New Zealand's west coast. The drive from Christchurch will take you along precipitous gorges and beneath towering snow-clad peaks. **BS**

Stay at Wilderness Lodge

Location Arthur's Pass, South Island, New Zealand
Website www.wildernesslodge.co.nz   **Price** ⊖

The snowcapped peaks of the Southern Alps soar majestically across the horizon. At their base, the Waimakariri River winds like a silvery ribbon. Such views make the Wilderness Lodge at Arthur's Pass the ultimate eco-retreat.

Built in 1996, the elegant timber and corrugated iron building was designed to complement and blend into the natural forest clearing. The twenty Mountain View rooms are modestly decorated. Extravagant decor is an unnecessary distraction when you have such a spectacular landscape on your doorstep. The four Alpine Lodges provide more luxurious accommodation. Nestled within a beech forest, all the rooms have gas fires and spa baths that look out over the mountains. With no television or Internet, the real attractions lie outside. The lodge is set in a 6,000-acre (2,400-ha) nature reserve and is also a working sheep farm. Owners Ann and Gerry are passionate conservationists, who also own the original Wilderness Lodge further south at Lake Moeraki.

The lodge is nirvana for hikers, with a myriad of surrounding tracks to explore. Take in the fresh air and unspoiled forest, and keep an eye out for the native bellbirds and keas. Guests can choose from any number of other excursions, from canoeing on nearby Lake Pearson to discovering the Southern Cross during a night sky stargazing trip.

Alternatively you can explore the nearby Arthur's Pass National Park. From trout fishing in the crystal-clear lakes to mountaintop picnics among the alpine flowers, such is the unique and diverse landscape of New Zealand that you can be relaxing on a beach in the morning, trekking through a rain forest in the afternoon, and scaling an ice cave the next day. **JP**

Discover Vatulele Island

Location Vatulele Island, Fiji
Website www.sixsenses.com   **Price** $$$

Newly arrived guests emerge tentatively from their private thatched Fijian house or *bure* (pronounced "boo-ray") hidden in the beachside jungle. Shaking off their jet lag, they decide to test Vatulele Island Resort's internal communications. If they want anything—and that means anything—they simply have to raise a flag on their personal flagpole on the white-sand beach. A uniformed, barefoot waiter will promptly appear scurrying across the sand to take the order. With anything from chilled French champagne to fresh local seafood snacks available, flags are soon whizzing up and down the poles.

There is acclaimed diving and snorkeling along the reef, but it is the laid-back hours that characterize this resort. Egos dissolve in the easy warmth as barefoot bankers and off-duty celebrities foresake candlelit dining in their villas and choose to eat communally in the central open-sided *bure*. There is a cooperative, sustainable aura across the small island. The architecture is locally inspired, the kitchen uses seafood caught offshore and fresh produce from its own organic garden, and, unlike other luxury resorts, Vatulele staff do not call guests "Sir" or "Madam." Everyone is addressed by their first name.

Smiling villagers assemble to sing a welcome to guests at the airstrip, where tiny planes land on a path cut into the vegetation after a spectacular twenty-five-minute flight from Fiji airport. Cynical visitors who ask whether villagers are paid to deliver this welcome are always met with puzzled expressions. "We do it to welcome you to our island," they explain. **SH**

← *The combination of top-end luxury and beachcomber's informality makes Vatulele a top destination.*

Canoe at Kosrae Island

Location Kosrae Island, Micronesia
Website www.kosraevillage.com   **Price** $

Kosrae Island is one of Micronesia's least-developed islands. Lying southeast of Guam, it is the most easterly of the Caroline islands and has an impressive seagoing history—when you take to the waters here, know that you are doing it in the shadow of many, many others.

For a start, the island is supposed to have been settled in the first millennium by the seafaring people from the Marshall Islands of Vanuatu. These were the area's first and bravest explorers. Skip forward several hundred years, and the island was regularly visited by whaling parties, traders, and pirates. The infamous nineteenth-century pirate of the South Seas, Bully Hayes, supposedly left buried treasure on the island.

> "Dive for a coral-monitoring project, learn to weave . . . and dine on coconut-smoked wahoo."
>
> *National Geographic*

Naturally, a great way to explore is by boat. There are numerous diving and snorkeling trips to take out to the reefs, but the real delight is the Utwe-Walung Marine Park in the very south of the island. This protected area of mangrove channels offers a unique look at the forests and the ecosystem as you travel around them by traditional canoe. You can see the ancient stone ruins in the rain forest from the water, reach isolated beaches, and even come upon the site of Bully Hayes's famous shipwreck. Slow paddling takes you to parts of the island that are unreachable by foot and out to areas where you can snorkel in clear water and see the healthy coral beneath. **LD**

Unwind at
Etu Moana

Location Aitutaki, Cook Islands
Website www.etumoana.com **Price** 🔆🔆

As you enter Aitutaki's rustic airport, you may have a sneaking suspicion that you have stumbled across paradise. Untouched by the modern world, this simple structure is filled with melodic local music and the heady aroma of handmade leis. A short ride away is Etu Moana: a boutique resort on one of the largest atolls in the Cook Islands.

With just eight villas, this exclusive hideaway is tucked away in a perfect location framed by a long, white, sugary beach and the warm crystal waters of a Pacific lagoon. Each of the Polynesian-style villas has an authentic thatched roof and exposed timbers, and

---

"Etu Moana does great foliage. In fact, the gardens are drop-dead gorgeous."

Yvonne van Dongen, *Listener* magazine

---

is filled with teak furniture and fresh linens. There is also a private garden and a spacious shaded veranda decorated with luxurious outdoor furnishings. The owners and staff at Etu Moana are delightful—nothing is too much trouble. Delicious breakfasts are served by a private pool surrounded by volcanic rocks and colorful gardens and there is also an honesty bar. The resort is also just a short stroll away from some of the island's best restaurants, which serve delicious eclectic local cuisine in candlelit settings. Choose whether to relax in your own romantic abode or to discover island life and explore the diverse culture above and below the waters of this charming paradise. **JH**

Relax at Bora Bora
Lagoon Resort and Spa

Location Motu Toopua, Bora Bora
Website www.boraboralagoon.com **Price** 🔆🔆🔆

Adam and Eve would feel at home in this small enclave of paradise where the air is heavy with the rich scent of hibiscus and the pristine beaches are fringed with palms. Bora Bora Lagoon Resort and Spa is set on the secluded island of Motu Toopua, a fragment of an ancient volcano on a shimmering turquoise lagoon.

The tiny island has no roads, no villages, and no nightlife, so visitors have no choice but to plunge headfirst into a world of laid-back luxury. The resort's accommodation can be found in Polynesian-style bungalows, thatched with pandanus leaves and decked out with polished wood interiors. There are forty-four over-water stilted bungalows, each one of which has a glass-topped coffee table from where guests can watch or feed the sea life.

Discover further serenity in the resort's beachfront spa, ringed by exotic basins, waterfalls, and lilies. Bathe in coconut milk and fresh flowers before receiving a massage in one of the treatment rooms, dramatically positioned in wooden cabins in the canopy of two large Banyan trees. Therapists use Polynesian products that incorporate local plants, flowers, and fruits, renowned for their benefits to the skin and hair. Honeymooners can choose to have treatments side by side in double massage rooms, followed by an exotic rain shower. If you tire of gazing dreamily into each other's eyes, the resort has a good, freshwater swimming pool, deep enough to practice scuba diving. Other activities include snorkeling, kayaking, shark-feeding excursions, and sunset cruises. **JK**

➡ *This view of the extinct volcanic peaks of Bora Bora must surely be one of the finest our planet has to offer.*

Relax at Le Taha'a

Location Taha'a, French Polynesia   **Website** www.letahaa.com
Price ❸❸❸

Hot honeymoon destinations do not come any more exclusive than this. The ultimate hideaway, Le Taha'a Private Island & Spa is tucked away in the sparkling waters of French Polynesia. The flower-shaped island is located 143 miles (230 km) west of Tahiti and sits on its own coral atoll. Spread out at the foot of soft mountains, where farmers grow watermelons, vanilla, and copra, the resort is surrounded by tiny *motu*, or islets, with sandy beaches.

There are twelve cool and spacious beach villas, all with private pools, which are decorated in traditional Polynesian style and have wooden floors and thatched roofs. Or for something really special, stay in one of the over-water suites. Spend your day snorkeling in the coral gardens, relaxing on the white-sand beach, taking in the sweeping views of the lagoon and Bora Bora, or being pampered in the magnificent Manea Spa. Nestled in the shade of coconut groves between the meandering waters of a small lake and the lagoon, the spa has been built from natural materials to ensure that it merges perfectly with the environment. Try a Polynesian massage or treatment using pure natural oils and essences.

Whatever you do, it is impossible to escape the rich aroma of vanilla lingering in the air, the scent of traditional Tahitian life. This might only be a tiny island in the middle of the Pacific but there is no shortage of excellent cuisine. Indulge in an exquisite meal at Ohiri, the fine-dining restaurant hidden away among the trees in the middle of the island and watch Tahitian dancers perform while you eat. Bliss. **AD**

➔ *The beach villas have their own private pool and tropical gardens, and are surrounded by rock walls.*

Fly into Space with Virgin Galactic

Location Space **Website** www.virgingalactic.com **Price** ⓢⓢⓢⓢ

> *"[We make] the 'Final Frontier' a reality for tens of thousands of pioneering space tourists."*

Will Whitehorn, Virgin Galactic President

↑ *This shows White Knight and Spaceship One, the space vessel and its "mother ship" transport.*

→ *A view like this is difficult to put into words. Imagine staring out at it from your passenger window.*

Imagine careering through that most enigmatic, mystifying terrain, the black space that is seen every night yet touched by so few. Imagine undertaking a journey past the stars on virgin odysseys said to leave an indelible mark. Imagine the ultimate escape, where so few people have gone before. This is a Kubrick-esque fantasy where budding astronauts will have the chance to venture into extra-terrestrial climes.

In a world where so little remains unexplored, Richard Branson's flagship spacecrafts are at the head of the new, commercial space race. Disembarking from the New Mexico spaceport close to Roswell, designed by the chief architect of otherworldly genius, Philippe Starck, your companions will comprise a two-man crew at the helm and five fellow space adventurers. Experience the sensation of weightlessness in this gravity- and belief-defying adventure as you are propelled over the sky, past the stars, and out into space. This trip will take up only two and a half hours of your life, but those hours will change you forever.

After three days' training, in which every care is taken to prepare you for an experience for which nothing can fundamentally prepare you, you will follow in the path of previous space-buccaneers and adventurers as the sky morphs from blue to mauve to indigo to black. Eerie, startling silence engulfs as Mother Earth is left behind you, as you ascend gently and smoothly into the galaxy.

It is a privilege that has been reserved for a very few—and at $200,000 it will remain so—representing the future, the past, and all the mysteries of human existence. Forthcoming expeditions include a plan to fly through the Aurora Borealis. Who knows? Maybe, one day, we will all have our chance to fly through the stars and experience the ultimate escape. **VG**

General Index

Index of Destinations

Contributors

(AD) Angela Dewar is a travel writer and photographer who travels extensively. She is a specialist on India and the Far East, contributing to travel guides and consumer and trade magazines in the U.K. and U.S.

(AM) Andy Moss is a travel writer based in the U.K.

(BS) Barry Stone is a travel writer based in Sydney, Australia. A compulsive traveler, he has co-authored books on geography, history, and architecture. Stories of his wanderings have appeared in some of Australia's leading newspapers, including Sydney's *Sun-Herald* and *The Canberra Times*.

(CD) Christabelle Dilks chose Argentina as her place of escape twenty years after leaving dramatically during the Falklands War. In 1982, she was living with her family on the edge of the Pampas, and was in love with an Argentine man. In 2002, she returned to fall in love all over again, this time with the wild landscapes and wonderful people. Argentina remains her place of dreams.

(CK) Carol King is a freelance writer based in London, England and a small town in Sicily, Italy. She has lived in Madrid, Spain and Buenos Aires, Argentina, and her appetite for travel has seen her track gorillas in Uganda, climb Adam's Peak in Sri Lanka, visit salt mines in Poland, and puff cigars in Cuba.

(CM) Chris Moss lived in Argentina for 10 years. He is the author of *Patagonia: A Cultural History*, published in 2008.

(CFM) Caroline Mills has been a magazine editor for twelve years and a freelance writer for two years. She specializes in travel throughout Europe, particularly lesser-known places and gardens. She has written for many U.K. publications, including *French Magazine*, *The Times*, *Practical Motorhome*, *France Magazine*, and *Great British Food* and is currently working on another travel book.

(CR) Claire Rigby is a British writer and editor who has lived in many countries, including Hong Kong, Kuwait, Brazil, and the U.S. She is currently based in Argentina, where she is editor of *Time Out*'s *Buenos Aires for Visitors* magazine.

(CSJ) Caroline Sylger-Jones is a spa and retreat specialist and the author of *Body & Soul Escapes* and *Body & Soul escapes: Britain and Ireland*. She writes regular reviews and features for newspapers and magazines, which include *The National* in the UAE, and the *Daily Telegraph*, *The Times*, *Guardian*, *Condé Nast Traveler*, *Wanderlust*, *Red*, and *Psychologies* in the U.K. Based in Devon, she's at her happiest when walking the southwest coastal path. *www.carolinesylgerjones.co.uk*

(CW) Chrissy Williams is half-English, half-Italian, and has traveled extensively worldwide. She has written for a variety of British travel publications and organizations, including *Italian Magazine*, *Red Guide Florida*, *Weddings and Honeymoons*, and the Portuguese Chamber of Commerce.

(DA) David Atkinson is a travel writer based in Chester, England. He writes for U.K. newspapers the *Observer*, *Sunday Telegraph*, and *Daily Express*. He is the author of *Bolivia: The Bradt Travel Guide* and his Bolivia feature for *Wanderlust* magazine was named Latin America Travel Association (LATA) Article of the Year in 2008. *www.atkinsondavid.co.uk*

(DaH) David Hutter was born in Germany and briefly lived in both England and France during his teens. After finishing high school he moved to Italy for a lackluster and ultimately futile attempt at studying economics. Two years later, he moved to England to study creative writing and religious studies at Middlesex University. Having travelled extensively in Europe, the Middle East, Asia, and Australasia, he now works as a freelance writer and editor and is based in London.

(DN) Daniel Neilson is a freelance journalist and guidebook editor. He has contributed words and pictures to *Four Four Two*, *CNN Traveler*, and *The Wire* among many others, and has edited five guides for *Time Out*.

(EP) Eleanor Parkman has written about her travel experiences for U.K. newspaper the *Observer* among other publications. She met her husband while living in Turin, and they now live in London with their two daughters.

(GC) Greg Clarke is an Australian writer who contributes regularly to magazines in Australia and Asia. He once lived in London's East End, which proved handy while he was at the *Sunday Times*. When he's not traveling or writing, his daughters take him on trips in search of the fairies that live around their house.

(GMD) Giles MacDonogh A former Paris resident, Giles MacDonogh wrote about luxurious destinations for the *Financial Times* for fifteen years. He is also an authority on food and drink, and is Chairman of the juries for Germany and Austria at the World Wine Awards. MacDonogh has written for many publications, including *The Times*, *Guardian*, *Spectator*, *New Statesman*, and, more recently, *Standpoint*. He received a Glenfiddich Special Award in 1988 and is the author of thirteen books, many of them about Germany.

(HA) Helen Arnold is a travel and food and drink journalist with over 17 years' experience. She has contributed to a wide range of newspapers and magazines, including the *Observer*, *High Life*, *Scotland on Sunday*, *Travel Weekly*, *Woman & Home*, *Family Circle*, *Harpers Wine & Spirits*, *Zest*, and *Eve*. She has also written for corporate clients, including the Orient Express Group, Easy Jet, and Thomas Cook. First bitten by the travel bug after a year-long, around-the-world trip in 1992, she has lived in Oman in the Middle East and has since settled in London, where she lives with her husband and children.

(HO) Helen Ochyra is a freelance travel writer. She has lived in California and is now based in north London. She currently contributes to many publications, including the *Guardian*, *Observer*, and *Time Out*.

(IA) Ismay Atkins is a travel writer and editor based in the wild western reaches of Cornwall, England. She writes about travel for a range of publications, including the *Independent*, *Rough Guide*, and *Time Out*, and regularly edits books for *Time Out* guides. Thanks to a long-standing fascination with Latin America, Ismay has lived in Havana, rural Mexico, and Buenos Aires.

(JA) Jane Archer is a freelance travel journalist and one of the U.K.'s leading cruise writers. She has a weekly column on the *Telegraph* online and has contributed to the *Daily Telegraph*, *House and Garden*, and *Condé Nast Traveler*, among a host of other titles.

(JC) Joe Cawley is an award-winning travel writer based in Tenerife, Canary Islands. He has written for many publications, including the *Sunday Times*, *New York Post*, and *Condé Nast Traveler*. His first book, *More Ketchup than Salsa*, was voted Best Travel Narrative 2007 by the British Guild of Travel Writers.

(JD) James Durston has written for numerous publications, which include *Travel Weekly*, the *Independent*, and the *Express*. He spent his formative years in East Africa, one developmental year in Japan, and has spent the last two years trying not to fall in love with India. It hasn't worked, so he currently lives in the middle of Mumbai, India.

(JED) Judy Darley is a U.K. travel writer who has contributed extensively to *Portugal Magazine*, *Greece Magazine*, and *The Italian Magazine*. Before becoming a freelance writer, she was the Features Editor for *Spanish Homes Magazine*. She recently completed her first novel.

(JDA) Jess Darby is a former BBC Magazines journalist (writing for *Eve* and *Vegetarian Good Food*) turned freelance feature writer. She spent her formative years in places as diverse as Ibiza, Zimbabwe, and Ireland before settling in southwest London, England with the three men in her life and Digby the dog.

(JF) Joe Fullman has been a travel writer for over ten years, during which time he has written for many of the major international guidebook publishers, including Rough Guides, Lonely Planet, A.A., and Cadogan. He is the author of guides to Costa Rica, Belize, London, England, Paris, Berlin, Venice, and Las Vegas, and has also contributed to guides to Italy, Turkey, Central America, and the Caribbean. He is currently based in London, England.

(JH) Jane Hannon had her first short story published in the 2007 travel anthology *More Sand in My Bra* and has also written for *Psychologies* magazine. A freelance writer based in Essex, she's had 24 jobs, explored 34 countries, and has lived and worked in New York and Australia.

(JK) Janine Kelso is based in London, England, and has written for *Travel Weekly* and numerous women's magazines. She has a special passion for Latin America after spending nine months traveling there. Her other specialist areas include the Caribbean and Poland. While at university, she spent two summers living and working in the United States, in New York, Colorado, and Maryland. Her trips often include an extreme sports element, such as rock climbing, surfing, skiing, or skydiving.

(JP) Jacqui Paterson is a travel and features journalist, with 15 years' experience writing for newspapers and magazines in New Zealand, Australia, and the United Kingdom. Her travels have included parachuting onto a beach in northern Queensland, bungy jumping over the Zambesi River in Zambia, and swimming among the icebergs in the Arctic Circle.

(JS) Jessica Stone grew up a Cuban American in Miami before studying journalism in New York. She has contributed to a variety of international publications, including the *New York Times*, *The Times*, *Guardian*, and *Men's Health*. *Ripelondon.com* is a website that chronicles her dining and dating journeys in her adoptive home in London, England.

(JW) James Williams is a U.K., London-based travel journalist specializing in Greece, and writes for a host of U.K. magazines. His travels have taken him everywhere across the world, from far-flung tropical islands to hidden corners of Athens, Greece.

(KF) Kathryn Farmer worked in legal publishing for fifteen years and, following a career break when her children were very young, now works as a freelance writer and has written for many U.K. publications.

(LB) Lydia Bell currently lives in London, England and was the deputy travel editor of *Harper's Bazaar*. She has lived in (or spent months hanging out in) Scotland, Spain, Greece, India, and Australia.

(LC) Lucia Cockcroft traveled around Spain for Rough Guides and is the Spanish writer for *Luxury Travel Magazine*. She recently contributed to *Body & Soul*, and also writes for *EasyJet Inflight* and *Overseas Living Magazine*.

(LD) Laura Dixon writes about style, travel, and trends for fashion magazines and travel publications. She reviews boutique hotels for l-escape.com, and has been featured in *Sunday Times Travel Magazine*, *Sunday Express*, *Business Life*, and many more. She is a member of the British Guild of Travel Writers.

(LGS) Lisa Gerard-Sharp is an award-winning journalist and travel writer who has lived in Paris, Brussels, Rome, and Tuscany. Although currently based in London, England, she spends much of her time traveling and researching features for *Vogue*,

for whom she is correspondent, as well as contributing to national newspapers and magazines in the U.K. and abroad.

(LJ) Lisa Johnson was an arts writer at *The Bulletin* in Brussels, Belgium for three years before switching to travel to continue using her languages (French, German, and Spanish). Now based in London, England, she has written for a number of publications including *Condé Nast Traveler*, *House and Garden*, *Red*, *Evening Standard*, *Guardian*, *Spectator*, and the *Daily Mail*.

(LM) Linda McCormick is the senior writer and editor for news website *Environmental Graffiti* and content editor of *EcoTravelLogue.com*. She has traveled extensively, having put down roots for a while in Australia, but now lives in London, England; although she continually threatens to move to Barcelona, Spain.

(LP) Lisa Pollen is an experienced U.K. London-based journalist, specializing in the luxury travel and celebrity market. Formerly the Features Editor at *Star* and *OK!* (Hot Stars), she contributes to publications including the *Daily Express*, *Now*, *Closer*, *She*, and various in-flight magazines.

(ML) Martin Li has a passion for exploring the adventure and culture of the world's great mountain regions. He is the author of *Inca Trails*, the story of a journey across the Andes tracing the rise and fall of the Inca empire, and *Adventure Guide to Scotland*.

(MN) Mari Nicholson is an award-winning travel writer based in the Isle of Wight. Published by major outlets including *Guardian*, *The Times*, *BBC History*, *Wanderlust*, and the major inflight magazines, she is the feature

writer for east Asia on the online travel magazine of *www.suite101.com*.

(NB) Nick Bruno is an Anglo-Italian journalist who divides his time between Scotland and Italy, writing and taking photographs for various publications. His latest book, *Naples and Amalfi Coast*, is published by Footprint.

(NS) Nicola Smith is a freelance journalist based in Cornwall, England. She has written travel features for a number of different titles, including *The Times*, New Zealand's *World*, *Coast*, and *Cornwall Today*.

(OM) Olivia Mackinder is a travel and lifestyle writer, for print, online, and television. An N.L.P. Practitioner, she is also now in the process of setting up her own retreat center in the U.K.

(PE) Polly Evans is a London-based award-winning travel journalist who writes for publications that include the *Independent on Sunday*, *Wanderlust*, *Condé Nast Traveler*, and *Food and Wine*. She has also written five travel books, including *It's Not About the Tapas* and *Mad Dogs and an Englishwoman*.

(PS) Paul Sullivan is a Berlin-based writer/photographer specializing in travel and music. His articles have appeared in many publications, including the *Independent*, *Observer Music Monthly*, *Fly Europe*, *National Geographic Music*, BBC magazines, and others. His previous travel books include *A Hedonist's Guide To Berlin, Marrakech & Prague*, *Time Out Italy*, and *Cool Camping France* and *Cool Camping Europe*.

(RB) Rory Brogan is a U.K. journalist who has traveled extensively in South America.

(RCA) Rowena Carr-Allinson has been published in everything from the *Toronto Star* to London's *Metro*, *Elle*, *Harper's Bazaar*, *OK!*, and many more. She has traveled from Buenos Aires to Bangkok via Maui and Moscow, and can't decide if home is in France or the U.K. *www.carrallinson.com*

(RS) Richard Siddle is an award-winning U.K. business journalist. A former editor of *Travel Weekly*, he currently travels the world as editor of *Harpers Wine & Spirits* magazine.

(RsP) Roger St. Pierre has visited 125 countries and counting during his long and illustrious career as a travel writer and broadcaster. He is the author of 33 published books including a number of bestselling travel guides, as well as works on cycling and music.

(SB) Sam Baldwin specializes in Japan, adventure, and winter sports writing, especially off-the-beaten-path locations. He is the editor of *SnowSphere.com* and has also contributed to the *Guardian*, the *Scotsman*, and Footprint books, and is also a columnist for several ski and snowboard magazines.

(SD) Sally Dowling is a freelance travel writer based in the U.K. She is a regular contributor to *Take a Break* magazine and associated titles and was the winner of the 2006 Visit U.S.A. Media Travel Award. She specializes in finding memorable hotels and unique resorts. *www.sallydowling.co.uk*

(SG) Si Gray began his writing career as editor for Itchy U.K. city guides. He has visited over fifty countries, compiling his observations on the popular food and travel blog featured on *jamieoliver.com*, which is being published in extended form.

(SH) Simon Heptinstall is a U.K. author, journalist, and broadcaster who visited 23 countries in his first year as a travel writer and once even held the world record for the most countries visited in one day (12). His ultimate escape, however, remains his quiet family house on the edge of a village in rural Wiltshire, England.

(SM) Shona Main, a Shetlander, started out as Pop Editor of *Jackie* and pursued lackluster careers in law and politics before settling back into journalism. She splits her time between Scotland and Italy, and her latest book is the *Footprint Guide to Venice and the Veneto*.

(SoH) Solange Hando is a professional travel writer. She has won a number of awards and contributes to a broad range of publications worldwide. She is a member of the British Guild of Travel Writers and Travel Writers U.K.

(SP) Sudi Pigott is passionately committed to good food and travels widely in pursuit of new gastronomic experiences. Sudi writes on food, restaurants, and travel for a wide range of international publications, including *TIME* magazine, *FT How to Spend It*, *High Life*, *Centurion*, *Delicious*, and *The Good Food Guide*.

(SWa) Sue Watt is a freelance travel writer based in London. She mainly specializes in Africa, inspired by her belated gap year traveling across the continent. Sue contributes regularly to *Travel Africa Magazine* and is also published in British publications such as the *Guardian*, and *Italy Magazine*.

(SWi) Stephanie Wilson made the most of her long vacations as a teacher to travel extensively in Europe and Turkey, before giving up the profession to focus on travel writing.

(TL) Tim Locke's writing spans many subjects, from national parks, walks, and numerous regions of Britain; rail travel in Europe; and guides to New England and Thailand. He is also a consultant in sustainable travel and an editor of the *Good Pub Guide*. He lives in Lewes in southeast England.

(TM) Teresa Machan sees life as one big adventure where she can go pearl-diving in Panama or get tips from a gondolier in Venice. She has been published in more than 20 worldwide travel publications, including national newspapers, guidebooks, and magazines. Lucky enough to have lived in Hong Kong, she returns regularly to Asia while continuing her globe-trotting.

(TW) Tina Walsh is a freelance journalist specializing in travel and lifestyle. She has written for the *Guardian*, *Sunday Times*, and *Daily Mail*, among many others, and is a contributor to the Dorling Kindersley *Eyewitness Guide* series.

(VG) Victoria Gill is an author, broadcaster, and journalist for U.K. Channel Five, *Mr. and Mrs. Smith*, and the *Sunday Times*, among others. A bonafide globetrotter living in Highgate, London, she is the author of *Cityspots Fez*, published in 2009.

(WG) Wendy Gomersall spent ten years on staff at the *Daily Mail*, and went freelance in 2000. She is now a freelance travel writer, writing for many newspapers, magazines and websites, including the *Mail on Sunday*, *TravelMail.co.uk*, *ABTA magazine*, and the *Scotsman* magazine. She has also written for the *Daily Mail*, *Zest*, the *Guardian*, and many other local newspapers and international magazines.

2 Johnny Stockshooter / Photolibrary.com 20 Little Good Harbour 22 Pep Roig / Alamy 24 Inn on the Lake 25 Stefan Wackerhagen 26 AlaskaStock / Photolibrary.com 27 Buddy Mays / Alamy 29 Clayoquot Wilderness Resort 30 Poets Cove 31 Mowgli Frere / Frere Images 32 All Canada Photos / Alamy 34 Fairmont Chateau 36 Baker Creek Chalets 38 AndrC Kedl 39 AndrC Kedl 41 All Canada Photos / Photoshot 45 John Shaw / Photoshot 47 Michael S. Lewis/Corbis 48 Sundance 51 The Point 54 Wave Hill Gardens 55 Gramercy Park Hotel 56 Waldorf-Astoria and Waldorf Towers 58 Della Huff / Alamy 60 East Brother Light Station 62 Calistoga Ranch 63 Spa Vitale 64 Philip Lee Harvey / Getty 68 Radius Images / Photolibrary.com 71 All Canada Photos / Photoshot 73 Cody Duncan / Alamy 75 Mii Amo 76 Mowgli Frere / Frere Images 77 Ml Sinibaldi / Photolibrary.com 80 The Setai 85 Rod McLean / Alamy 86 Kevin Spreekmeester / Photolibrary.com 88 David Muench/Corbis 89 Peter French / Photolibrary.com 90 nik wheeler / Alamy 92 Esperanza Resort 93 Las Ventanas Al Paraiso 94 Blaine Harrington III / Alamy 96 One&Only Palmilla 98 Cuixmala 102 Hemis / Alamy 103 M. Timothy O'Keefe / Alamy 104 Esencia 107 La Lancha 108 Nitun Reserve 111 Blancaneaux 112 Stephen Frink Collection / Alamy 115 Mowgli Frere / Frere Images 116 Christabelle Dilks 118 Bob Stefko / Getty 122 IML Image Group Ltd / Alamy 125 Musha Cay 126 Parrot Cay 128 Danita Delimont / Alamy 130 Alex Bartel / Photoshot 133 Rolf Nussbaumer / Alamy 134 The Caves 137 Biras Creek 138 Jean-Marc Lecerf (Ocean Images) / Photoshot 140 Rodger Klein / Photolibrary.com 143 La Samanna 144 Tom Bean/Corbis 147 Tim Larsen-Collinge / Photoshot 148 Rock Cottage 150 Jade Mountain 153 Jean-Marc Lecerf (Ocean Images) / Photoshot 154 Charlie Knight / Alamy 156 Palm Island 157 L'Anse aux Epines 161 Pies Specifics / Alamy 162 Jose Enrique Molina / Photolibrary.com 164 Arco Digital Images / Tips 165 Rosemary Calvert / Photolibrary.com 167 Andoni Canela / Photolibrary.com 169 Vidler Vidler / Photolibrary.com 170 Hotel Monasterio 173 Jason Rothe / Alamy 176 Image Brokers / Photoshot 178 De Agostini / Photoshot 179 Worldwide Picture Library / Alamy 180 Interfoto / Alamy 185 Villas de Trancoso 186 Fasano Hotel 188 Robert Harding Picture Library Ltd / Alamy 190 Frédéric Soreau / Photononstop / Tips 193 Ponta dos Ganchos 194 Frédéric Soreau / Photononstop / Tips 197 Sunset / Tips 198 Elqui Domos 200 Secret Ranchito 201 Hemis / Photoshot 203 Cephas Picture Library / Alamy 205 Christabelle Dilks 207 Martin Harvey / Photoshot 209 Javier Etcheverry / Alamy 210 Eduardo Longoni/Corbis 212 Christabelle Dilks 214 Estancia El Colibrí 219 Faena Hotel 221 Christabelle Dilks 223 Christabelle Dilks 225 Christabelle Dilks 227 Ismay Atkins 229 David Tipling / Photoshot 230 Castello di Vicarello 233 blickwinkel / Alamy 235 StockPile Collection / Alamy 236 Gregory Gerault / Photolibrary.com 238 Danita Delimont / Alamy 240 Blue Lagoon 243 Chad Ehlers / Tips 244 Hotel Kakslauttanen 246 Snow Castle 248 Finland Tourist Board 250 Arctic-Images/Corbis 251 Hans Strand/Corbis 252 Nordic Light Hotel 255 Yasuragi 256 Frank Chmura / Alamy 261 OJPhotos / Alamy 262 Park Hotel Kenmare 264 Temple County retreat 267 John Warburton-Lee Photography / Alamy 268 Ard Nahoo 269 O fabulous 271 Belle Isle Castle 272 Radius Images / Alamy 275 Derek Croucher / Alamy 276 Rua Reidh Lighthouse 278 Paul Glendell / Alamy 281 Alistair Petrie / Alamy 285 Hebridean Princess 286 The Witchery 289 james jagger / Alamy 291 Steve Peake, St. Curig's Church 292 Eco Retreat 295 Mint Photography / Alamy 296 Les Gibbon / Alamy 299 Roger Coulam / Alamy 303 Le Manoir 304 Oxford Picture Library / Alamy 307 The Victoria 311 james kerr / Alamy 313 Ellen Rooney / Photolibrary.com 314 Terry Williams / Getty 316 Alamy 319 SenSpa 322 Royal Crescent Hotel 325 Lundy Island Tourism 328 ImagesEurope / Alamy 331 Marc Hill / Alamy 332 way out west photography / Alamy 334 Arco Digital Images / Tips 338 Liz Garnett / Alamy 341 Island of Rugen 342 Carsten Koall/Stringer / Getty 345 68images 68images / Photolibrary.com 348 Bildagentur RM / Tips 351 Martin Rugner / Photolibrary.com 353 imagebroker / Alamy 356 Camille Moirenc / Photononstop / Tips 358 Yann Guichaoua / Tips 359 Arco Digital Images / Tips 361 Steve Vidler / Photolibrary.com 365 S.Nicolas / Photolibrary.com 367 TTL Images / Alamy 368 Bateau Simpatico 371 Roy Rainford / Photolibrary.com 375 Picture Contact / Alamy 376 Tristan Deschamps / Tips 379 Hemis / Photoshot 380 Robert Harding Picture Library Ltd / Alamy 383 Yann Guichaoua / Tips 384 A. Demotes / Tips 387 Jupiter Images / Agence Images / Alamy 389 Les Fermes de Marie 392 Marion Bull / Alamy 397 Emmanuel Lattes / Alamy 399 Papilio / Alamy 400 Abbaye de Sainte Croix 402 tbkmedia.de / Alamy 405 Hemis / Photolibrary.com 406 Le Couvent des Minimes Spa 408 Horse and Ventures 412 Arco Digital Images / Tips 417 Piotr & Irena Kolasa / Alamy 419 Dumrath Dumrath / Photolibrary.com 421 imagebroker / Alamy 422 Liebes Rot-Fluh Hotel 425 Corbis / Photolibrary.com 426 Bella Tola 427 The Lodge 428 Riffelalp Resort 431 Lisa Pollen 433 Daniele Comoglio / Alamy 434 CuboImages srl / Alamy 437 Brian Lawrence / Photolibrary.com 438 L'Albereta 441 Vigilius 442 Roy Rainford / Photolibrary.com 444 Bauer Palladio 446 David Noton Photography / Alamy 449 Mark Bolton / Photolibrary.com 453 Silwen Randebrock / Photolibrary.com 457 Arco Digital Images / Tips 459 The Travel Library Limited / Photolibrary.com 460 Todi Castle 463 La Posta

Vecchia **465** Sue Watt **467** Sextantio Albergo Diffuso **468** Vito Arcomano / Alamy **471** Regina Isabella **475** Villa Rufolo **476** La Masseria San Domenico **479** Bruno Morandi / Photolibrary.com **480** JTB Photo Communications / Photoshot **484** Juan Carlos Munoz / Photolibrary.com **486** ROBIN SMITH / Photolibrary.com **488** Gonzalo Azumendi / Photolibrary.com **490** Westend61 / Photoshot **491** Hostal Sa Rascassa **492** Gavin Hellier / Photolibrary.com **497** The Travel Library Limited / Photolibrary.com **498** Visual&Written SL / Alamy **503** Parador de Ubeda **504** Image Brokers / Photoshot **507** Ignasi Rovira / Photolibrary.com **509** Hemis / Photoshot **511** Imagesource / Photolibrary.com **514** Hoopoe Yurt Hotel **516** Jesus Sierra / Photolibrary.com **518** Parador de Granada **521** Canabi Hugo / Photolibrary.com **524** Abama **527** David Robertson / Alamy **531** Michael Howard / Photoshot **532** John Ferro Sims / Alamy **535** Mark Edward Smith / Tips **537** Michael Krabs / Photolibrary.com **541** Ruth Tomlinson / Photolibrary.com **543** Cephas Picture Library / Alamy **544** Reid's Palace **546** MIXA Co. Ltd. / Photolibrary.com **549** terry harris just greece photo library / Alamy **550** Jon Arnold Images / Photolibrary.com **553** Raga Raga / Photolibrary.com **555** Matthew Smith / Alamy **556** Max Stuart / Alamy **557** Elixir Spa **559** Photononstop / Tips **560** Terry Harris Just Greece photo library / Alamy **562** R Matina / Photolibrary.com **564** Elounda Peninsula **566** Andrea Matone / Alamy **571** Jon Sparks / Alamy **572** Johnny Greig Travel Photography / Alamy **573** Pucic Palace **574** Villa Dubrovnik **576** Croatian National Tourist Board **578** Cubolmages srl / Alamy **581** Wilmar Photography / Alamy **583** Richard Nebesky / Photolibrary.com **586** blickwinkel / Alamy **589** Jan Wlodarczyk / Alamy **591** Padaste Manor **592** Ellen Rooney / Photolibrary.com **595** Aflo Co. Ltd. / Alamy **596** Wolfgang Kaehler / Alamy **599** Wolfgang Kaehler / Alamy **601** Wolfgang Kaehler / Alamy **602** Shompole **605** Maison M.K. **607** Amanjena **608** Ethel Davies / Photolibrary.com **611** Caravanserai **612** john angerson / Alamy **616** Alan Keohane **619** TTL Images / Alamy **621** Sylvain Grandadam / Photolibrary.com **623** Egyptian Tourist Authority, Gardel Bertrand/hemis.fr **624** Body Philippe / Photolibrary.com **629** Andrew Plumptre / Photolibrary.com **631** Pepeira Tom / Photolibrary.com **632** Shompole **634** J Marshall - Tribaleye Images / Alamy **635** Greystoke Mahal **637** Craig Lovell / Eagle Visions Photography / Alamy **638** Chumbe Island Coral Park **640** Selous Project **642** Demelza Cloke / Alamy **645** Azura **646** Reinhard Dirscherl / Photolibrary.com **648** JL Photography / Alamy **651** Nigel Dennis / Photolibrary.com **653** www.namibweb.com, the online guide to Namibia and Elena Travel Services **655** John Warburton-Lee / Photolibrary.com **656** Abu Camp **658** Photononstop / Tips **660** Steve Vidler / Photolibrary.com **665** Earth Lodge **669** Ariadne Van Zandbergen / Alamy **671** Thanda Reserve **672** Rovos Rail **676** Bushman's Kloof Wilderness Reserve & Retreat **678** Kurland Hotel **681** Robert Cundy / Photolibrary.com **685** Le Prince Maurice **686** Trevor Neal / Alamy **689** Shanti Andana Maurice Spa **691** Labriz Aquum Spa **693** Sunset / Tips **694** Denis Island **695** Cousine Island **697** Frégate Island Private **698** The Sarojin **700** Farasan Islands Tourism **701** FotoLibra **703** Paul Thuysbaert / Photolibrary.com **704** Widmann Widmann / Photolibrary.com **706** Amanda Hall / Photolibrary.com **707** Martin Kreuzer / Photolibrary.com **709** isifa Image Service s.r.o. / Alamy **711** Hemis / Photoshot **714** Hanan Isachar/Corbis **717** Hanan Isachar / Photolibrary.com **719** Jon Arnold Images Ltd / Alamy **722** Images&Stories / Alamy **724** Robert Harding Picture Library Ltd / Alamy **727** Anatolian Houses **729** Andrea Pistolesi / Tips **732** Renato Valterza / Photolibrary.com **735** Dennis Cox / Alamy **736** Michele Falzone / Photolibrary.com **739** Indiapicture / Alamy **740** Luciano Mortula / Alamy **743** Image100 / Photolibrary.com **747** Brand X Pictures / Photolibrary.com **750** Samode Haveli **755** John Henry Claude Wilson / Photolibrary.com **756** Fort Chanwa **757** Mark Hannaford / Photolibrary.com **761** John Henry Claude Wilson / Photolibrary.com **762** Dave Pattison / Alamy **767** Ben Pipe / Alamy **768** Noah Seelam/Stringer / Getty **770** Kathleen Watmough / Aliki image library / Alamy **772** Shreya's **776** Sally Dowling **779** Richard Ashworth / Photolibrary.com **780** Douglas Peebles Photography / Alamy **783** Amangalla **784** Angela Dewar **786** Helga's Folly **788** Eye Ubiquitous / Photoshot **790** Hotel Dhonakulhi **793** One&Only **794** Horizon International Images Limited / Alamy **797** Look Die Bildagentur der Fotografen GmbH / Alamy **798** Royal Geographical Society / Alamy **801** Uma Paro **802** Tony Waltham / Photolibrary.com **807** Red Capital Club **808** Susan Seubert / Photolibrary.com **813** Adina Tovy / Photolibrary.com **814** Jia **817** Camel Lodge **819** Bruno Morandi / Photolibrary.com **821** Zao Onsen **822** Demetrio Carrasco / Photolibrary.com **825** JTB Photo / Photolibrary.com **826** Kuba Noto / Alamy **829** Boe Oote / Photolibrary.com **830** Hiiragiya Ryokan **833** Four Seasons Tented Camp **835** Orient Express **837** Sukhothai **840** Chiva Som **842** The Sarojin **844** Kamalaya **846** Tongsai Bay **849** Amanpuri **853** Rob Henderson / Photolibrary.com **855** Résidence Phou Vao **857** Six Senses Resorts & Spas **859** Jtb Photo / Photolibrary.com **860** Amanpulo **864** Giles Robberts / Alamy **867** Robert Francis / Photolibrary.com **869** David W. Hamilton / Tips **871** Tony Waltham / Photolibrary.com **872** Amanjiwo **875** Lisa Pollen **878** Michael Freeman/Corbis **880** Le Taha'a **882** Indian Pacific **885** FotoLibra **887** Bamurru Plains **888** Roberto Rinaldi / Photolibrary.com **891** Daintree Ecolodge and Spa **893** Iconsinternational.Com / Alamy **894** Qualia **897** aeropix / Alamy **899** Jochen Knobloch / Photolibrary.com **903** Yann Guichaoua / Tips **904** Old Leura Dairy **908** David Messent / Photolibrary.com **910** William Robinson / Alamy **912** Poltalloch Station **914** Southern Ocean Lodge **917** Cradle Mountain Lodge **919** Alistair Scott / Alamy **921** Eagles Nest **924** Mollies **928** Jim Harding / Photolibrary.com **931** TranzAlpine Train **934** Vatulele Island **937** Bora Bora Lagoon Resort **939** Le Taha'a **940** Virgin Galactic **941** Virgin Galactic

Acknowledgments

Quintessence would like to thank the following picture libraries, and in particular the individuals named:

Tim Kantoch/Photolibrary.com

Tim Harris/Photoshot

Katja Rowedder and Charles Montgomery/Tips

Maria Kuzmin/Alamy

Gwyn Headley and Yvonne Seele/FotoLibra

John Moelwyn-Hughes/Corbis

Hayley Newman/Getty

Quintessence would also like to thank the following individuals for their assistance in producing this book:

Helena Baser

Robert Dimery

Rebecca Gee

Lucinda Hawksley

David Hutter

Fiona Plowman